The Developmental Psychology of

Jean Piaget

The Developmental Psychology

of

Jean Piaget

JOHN H. FLAVELL

University of Minnesota

With a Foreword by Jean Piaget

D. VAN NOSTRAND COMPANY
New York Cincinnati Toronto London Melbourne

D. Van Nostrand Company Regional Offices:
New York, Cincinnati

D. Van Nostrand Company International Offices:
London, Toronto, Melbourne

Copyright © 1963 by LITTON EDUCATIONAL PUBLISHING, INC.

Library of Congress Catalog Card Number 63-2423

ISBN: 0-278-22416-8

Published by D. Van Nostrand Company
450 West 33rd Street, New York, N.Y. 10001

10   9   8   7   6   5

To

Ellie,

Beth,

and

Jimmy

Foreword

IT IS BOTH A GREAT PLEASURE and a great honor to have been asked to write a foreword to the fine book you are about to read. A great pleasure, because it *is* a fine book, and hence there is no reluctance about praising its virtues and expressing my deepest appreciation to its author. But it is also a great honor, because this book seeks to present an integration of my own thought and work, and its appearance is an indication of esteem and confidence which I find deeply gratifying.

The goal which Professor Flavell has successfully achieved was a very difficult one and required a great deal of work, not only because I have written too much in the course of tackling too many different problems (moreover, only a portion of my books and very few of my articles have appeared in English) but above all because I am not an easy author; hence it must have required an immense effort at comprehension and intellectual empathy to have produced the clear and straightforward presentation that is found here. The principal source of difficulty, as Professor Flavell well knows, is the following. Naturalist and biologist by training, interested in epistemological problems, without ever having undertaken formal study (nor passed any examinations) in psychology, my most central concern has always been to determine the contributions of the person's activities and the limiting aspects of the object in the process of acquiring knowledge. Fundamentally, it was the wish to resolve this problem using the experimental method that brought me into the field of developmental psychology. But it follows logically, since this point of view is not often held by psychologists in general—and even less by child psychologists—that those who read my work often find themselves confused. Thus a tremendous effort both in focusing and in reinterpreting had to be made to achieve a rendition of my work which is at once clear, well integrated, and fundamentally psychological in nature. Professor Flavell is certainly to be congratulated for having surmounted these difficulties in such an outstanding manner.

Professor Flavell has therefore done a most useful job and his book will certainly meet with the success it deserves. Its organization is a very well chosen one. Part One is given over to a presentation of the theoretical hypotheses. It was well to begin with these since the experiments, taken

up in Part Two, were inspired by them. Finally, there is the critique
(Part Three). It seems clear that Professor Flavell is more interested in
the experiments than in the theory, which sometimes gives me the impression—perhaps not of having been misunderstood, but, if you will—
of having been understood on certain issues more from without than
from within. But since the great majority of readers are not likely to be
primarily oriented toward the theory either, the emphasis he has chosen
is probably the most useful one.

Likewise, I am highly pleased that Professor Flavell concluded his
book with a critical section because it may lead the reader to take his
positive comments about the system much more seriously than if he had
blindly and uncritically gone along with me on all points.

On the other hand, although I have read these criticisms with much
interest, it is difficult for me to find them all convincing. More specifically, I find it impossible at the present time to decide whether this
highly significant critique is well-founded or not, because the psychology
of operational structures is still only in its infancy and a final decision
would have to hinge on a substantial body of research data yet to be
gathered. When Professor Flavell argues that I have expended too much
energy spinning an intricate theoretical spider web which does not catch
enough of reality in it, I am reminded of my collaborators at the Center
for Genetic Epistemology who are currently weaving considerable im-
provements into the web and I have the distinct impression that it is
already catching more than flies. Likewise, he says that I do not clearly
show how classes and relations synthesize into numbers; but this problem
has been dealt with a number of times by Grize, Papert, Gréco, Inhelder,
and myself (volumes XI, XIII, XV and XVII of *Etudes d'Epistémologie
Génétique*) and both new formulations and new experimental results
alike have already shown that the initial hypothesis was not such a wild
venture after all. Professor Flavell also thinks, both that I have multiplied
intellectual structures beyond necessity, and that the group structures in
particular make neither as early nor as clear-cut and well-marked an en-
trance into cognitive life as I had indicated (owing to a lack of sufficient
study of the identity and associativity properties of the group). But here
again the research is far from being completed and its course so far does
not support his criticism. And in any case it is apparent, from the current state of research evidence, that the formal operations which appear
at twelve to fifteen years really do show novel structure; they are not
called "formal" simply because of their late appearance.

In short, as regards the entire first set of criticisms—the general trend
of which is that, in Professor Flavell's opinion, there is too wide a gap
between the facts I describe and the theories I invoke—it could be argued
that the differences between us stem from the fact that his approach is
perhaps too exclusively psychological and insufficiently epistemological

while the converse is true for me. The solution is then to be sought in the field of interdisciplinary endeavor, and it is precisely because of this that our Center for Genetic Epistemology is designed to provide an opportunity for psychologists, logicians, and mathematicians to collaborate in the furtherance of such research.

As to the criticisms usually directed toward me regarding the qualitative method which we use in our intellectual development studies and regarding the role of language in the interpretation of data—criticisms on which Professor Flavell takes a comprehensive and moderate position —it must again be said that our research is far from completed and that all sorts of controls, both statistical and nonverbal, are currently in progress. It is important to understand clearly that in order to explore intellectual development in its creative spontaneity, without distorting it by *a priori* assumptions drawn from our experience with adult thought, it has been necessary to proceed in two phases: first, to unearth what is original and easily overlooked in the child's successive stages of evolution, and to do this with methods, including verbal ones,[1] which are as free and flexible as possible; then, in a second phase, varied controls and more refined analyses become feasible. Indeed, we are currently trying the latter: for example, Dr. B. Inhelder has made use of the longitudinal method and more recently, with Dr. J. Bruner, has been trying to train logical operations by various means. The results of this study ought to prove extremely instructive.

The picture of our work which Professor Flavell provides extends only up to about 1960 and thus it cannot be considered the final word. But for the period of its coverage it is excellent, and our sympathetic spokesman and commentator—by his intellectual honesty, good will, and immense labor—has certainly earned our deepest gratitude.

Geneva   JEAN PIAGET
November 1962

---

[1] For some time now I have had doubts about the verbal methods used in the research described in my first books. But the excellent book by M. Laurendeau and A. Pinard, *La pensée causale* (Paris: Presses Universitaires de France, 1962)—which Professor Flavell has probably not yet read—both supports the generality of my early results and makes a trenchant methodological criticism of my early critics. This interesting statistical study could make an important contribution to the points of discussion raised by Professor Flavell in Part 3.

Preface

THE MAJOR PURPOSE of the book is simply to speak clearly for Piaget to anyone who has reasons to listen to what he has to say and who has some background and sophistication in psychology or related disciplines. Who might such a reader be? He certainly might be a psychologist—budding or full-fledged, by vocation or by avocation, with child-developmental interests but also with other interests. He might also be a student of education, psychiatry, philosophy, sociology, and perhaps other fields; Piaget has done and said things which have implications well beyond the boundaries of psychology proper. The book has a secondary aim, important but nonetheless secondary: to evaluate Piaget's work, both methodologically and in view of related work done by others. The first ten chapters serve the primary objective, while the last two, and particularly the last one, attempt to fulfill the secondary aim.

Like the objects of Piaget's theory, this book began life as something quite other than what it eventually became. In 1955 I set out to write a graduate text on theories of child development. All was smooth sailing at first, and I judged that the whole project would be completed within a year. The theories I planned to write about appeared for the most part to be in just the kind of state which would make my task a quick and easy one. That is, their authors—or someone else—had already given a reasonably clear, detailed, and integrated account of them in some one or several publications each. All I had to do was to read these publications carefully and distill what I had read into a one-chapter summary of each theory, with perhaps a little restructuring and change of emphasis here and there.

One very important theory of child development—Piaget's—turned out to be in a state so utterly recalcitrant to this plan that the plan itself finally unraveled. As I began to learn more about Piaget's work, certain conclusions—initially resisted—eventually seemed inescapable. First, Piaget's work obviously had to be an important segment of the proposed text if it was to be a text on developmental theories. Second, it became all too clear that it would take me several years to read enough Piaget to feel at all confident about constructing an accurate and properly balanced summary of his theory. More than that, I began to worry about what function even the best of one- or two-chapter summaries could serve in the particular case of Piaget's system. Might not such a summary have to be so compressed and elliptical that it could do little more than tease and frustrate any reader who had a really serious commitment to understand Piaget? He might read my summary, want more detail on most if not all points, and then have no recourse but to delve into the same dismaying expanse of scattered primary literature from which the summary was pieced together in the first place. So it was that the first plan was finally discarded for a second, of which the present volume is the outcome: write a book-length exposition of Piaget's work alone, something which might serve at once as a guide to the multivolume original literature and as a backstop for any future digests of a briefer sort, e.g., as part of a text like the one which never got written!

Many minds, hands, and circumstances helped to make this book a reality, and I feel grateful to them all. I owe a special debt of thanks to Dr. Heinz Werner and others of his staff who were at Clark University during my graduate years; without their formative and enduring influences I might conceivably have written a book, but it almost certainly would not have been a book on Piaget. I feel likewise indebted to the late Dr. David Rapaport, whose incisive commentary on an early version of the manuscript profoundly influenced all subsequent writing. Also deserving of thanks for invaluable assistance in various forms are Drs. Jean Piaget, Bärbel Inhelder, Joachim F. Wohlwill, Peter H. Wolff, David Elkind, Edith Meyer Taylor, Crane Brinton, and David C. McClelland, the Psychology Editor for D. Van Nostrand Co., Inc. In addition, I should like to thank as a group the numberless faculty, graduate students, and others, both at the University of Rochester and elsewhere, who have helped to shape my thinking about Piaget over the past six years; collectively, they have played at least as important a ghost writer role as those singled out by name.

I am grateful to Social Science Research Council for a grant-in-aid which permitted me to work full time on the manuscript during the summer of 1961. Likewise, the University of Rochester has been most helpful in providing the needed time, intellectual atmosphere, and secretarial and library facilities over the years. I feel particularly indebted to Mrs. Marcia Macklin, who did all the typing. Surely the most competent secretary anyone ever had, she would without apparent effort read my wretched handwriting and mentally correct errors of substance as well as of spelling and punctuation, all the while typing at supersonic speed a manuscript which would later require almost no proofreading. This book is studded with quoted extracts from the works of Piaget and others, and I am most grateful to the individuals and publishing houses concerned for granting the necessary permissions. Thus, I wish to express my thanks to Dr. Jerome S. Bruner of Harvard University, Dr. Betsy W. Estes of the

University of Kentucky, Dr. Alberta E. Siegal of Pennsylvania State University, Dr. Hans Aebli of the University of Saarland, and most especially, to Professors Jean Piaget and Bärbel Inhelder of the University of Geneva. Similarly, I am indebted to International Universities Press, Humanities Press, Basic Books, and W. W. Norton of New York and to The Journal Press of Provincetown; to Routledge and Kegan Paul, Tavistock Publications, and the British Psychological Society of London; to Presses Universitaires de France and Librairie Armand Colin of Paris; and to Delachaux et Niestlé of Neuchâtel and the Institut des Sciences de l'Education, University of Geneva.

Finally, I owe more than can be repaid to my wife, Ellie, who for years submitted cheerfully to the regimen of a morose husband when the book was going badly, and an absent one when it was going well.

Rochester   JOHN H. FLAVELL
December 1962

Contents

xv

Part Three: Critique

Introduction

JEAN PIAGET—best known as developmental psychologist but also philosopher, logician, and educator—is one of the most remarkable figures in contemporary behavioral science. For more than forty years he and his associates have been constructing, in bits and pieces across an enormous bibliography, a broad and highly original theory of intellectual and perceptual development.[1] Like Freudian theory, with which one is tempted to compare it in certain respects, Piaget's theoretical system is a detailed and complicated one, not renderable in a few mathematical or verbal statements. Unlike Freudian theory, however, the system in its totality has not been widely assimilated by others. The major purpose of this book is to present an integrated overview of Piaget's achievements, an overview sufficiently detailed to do justice to the complexity of his theory and the variety of his experimental contributions. This introductory chapter is intended to explain why a book on Piaget is desirable— or at least why it was written—and to summarize the plan or organization which the book will follow. In order to put these matters in context and to set the stage for a detailed description of Piaget's system, it may be useful to examine briefly the man himself—the chronology of his life and achievements.

THE MAN AND HIS WORK

Jean Piaget was born on August 9, 1896, in Neuchâtel, Switzerland. From his own account he was always a studious child and, as is clear from his childhood achievements, a decidedly precocious one (1952d). He was early addicted to scientific studies, especially biological, and relates successive interests in mechanics, birds, fossils, and sea shells between the ages of seven and ten. As a portent of scholarly productivity to come, he published his first scientific paper at the age of ten—a one-page note on a partly albino sparrow he had observed in a public park. Shortly

---

[1] Throughout this book "Piaget" will refer to both the man and his many able collaborators, of whom the most eminent is Bärbel Inhelder.

1

after, he contrived to serve after school hours as a volunteer laboratory assistant to the director of the local natural history museum, a malacologist or specialist in mollusks. During the four years he worked with the director, and in the ensuing years until 1930, he published about twenty-five papers on mollusks and related zoological matters, of which about twenty were in print before he reached the age of twenty-one. In his autobiography (1952d) Piaget tells of some humorous situations which resulted from his precocious productivity—for example, being offered (on the basis of his publications) the position of curator of the mollusk collection in the Geneva museum while still in secondary school! He pursued his formal higher education at the University of Neuchâtel, where he received his baccalaureate degree in 1915 and, following a dissertation on the mollusks of Valais, his doctorate in the natural sciences in 1918.

Throughout his adolescent and postadolescent years, Piaget read extensively in the fields of philosophy, religion, biology, sociology, and psychology, writing copious notes on a variety of problems. Some of the ideas developed during this period were prophetic of theoretical concepts fully elaborated only much later. First, from reading Bergson and others he became imbued with the idea that biology could be profitably brought to bear upon the epistemological problem, the problem of knowledge. But he felt that something else was needed to tie the two together and that philosophical analysis could not fulfill this role. In subsequent years, developmental psychology came to serve as the mediator, and a series of works on genetic epistemology was the final outcome (e.g., 1950b).

Second, he came to believe that external actions as well as thought processes admit of logical organization, that logic stems from a sort of spontaneous organization of acts. In his later work this notion seems to have been expressed in two related forms: first, that logical structures can be used to describe the organization of concrete, motor acts as well as that of symbolic, interiorized "thought" in the conventional sense (1954a); second, that all thought is essentially interiorized action, and it therefore follows that the organization of overt action and of inner thinking can be characterized in the same general way, can be placed on the same general continuum (1949b).

Finally, in this early, "prepsychology" period Piaget began formulating tentative views about totalities—Gestalt-like structures-of-the-whole—and about the possible kinds of equilibria which could characterize such structures. In any structure consisting of parts and of a whole containing these parts, he believed, there are only three possible forms of equilibrium: predominance of the parts with consequent deformations of the whole, predominance of the whole with consequent deformation of the parts, and reciprocal preservation of both whole and parts. Of these three, only the last is a good and stable equilibrium, the others deviating to a greater or lesser degree from this optimum. Piaget asserts (1952d) that even at that time he believed the third, stable form of equilibrium would characterize the organization of intelligence at its higher levels, and that the inferior forms would describe the structure of perception. It is interesting to note that, although almost all his writings from the early 1920's reflect his preoccupation with problems of equilibrium, a really definitive statement on cognitive development as an equilibration process was not published until some forty-three years after these adolescent musings (1957c).

Upon receiving his doctorate in 1918, Piaget left Neuchâtel in search of training and experience in psychology. During the next year or two he wandered from place to place, not finding any problems in which he could really get involved. His activities included academic and practicum work at the laboratories of Wreschner and Lipps, at Bleuler's psychiatric clinic, and at the Sorbonne. While studying at the latter, he was offered the opportunity to work in Binet's laboratory at a Paris grade school. Dr. Simon, who was in charge of the laboratory, suggested that Piaget might try to standardize Burt's reasoning tests on Parisian children. Although Piaget undertook this project without enthusiasm, his interest grew when he began the actual testing. He found himself becoming increasingly fascinated, not with the psychometric and normative aspects of the test data, but with the processes by which the child achieved his answers— especially his *incorrect* answers. By adapting psychiatric examining procedures he had acquired at Bleuler's clinic and in practicum courses at the Sorbonne, he was soon using the "clinical method" which was later to become a kind of Piagetian trademark.

During the next two years Piaget continued to do research on the child's responses to the Burt test questions and to other stimulus situations. He published the results of these first psychological experiments in a series of four articles (Piaget, 1921a, 1921b, 1922; Piaget and Rossello, 1921). One of the four was accepted for publication by Claparède at Geneva, editor of the *Archives de Psychologie* (1921a). Claparède, evidently impressed by this one sample of Piaget's work, offered him the job of Director of Studies at the Institut J. J. Rousseau in Geneva. In this position he was to have ample research time and an almost completely free hand in developing his own program of child study. Piaget accepted the job on trial in 1921 and shortly after embarked on a series of studies which was to make him world-famous before he was thirty years old.

Piaget's studies of the child's language, causal reasoning, "theories" about everyday phenomena, moral judgment, etc., which were conducted in the period 1921-1925 are still his best-known experiments. They are described in his first five books (1926, 1928b, 1929c, 1930a, 1932) [2] and in a less-known series of important articles (Piaget, 1923, 1924a, 1925a, 1927b, 1929b, 1931b; Krafft and Piaget, 1926; Margairaz and Piaget, 1925). In his autobiography (1952d) Piaget offers some interesting comments on this early, highly controversial work. It is clear that these studies were planned and conducted primarily with a view to providing data for the systematic and comprehensive epistemology which, since his youth, had been one of Piaget's chief aims. That is, only for the naive reader were the famous five books simply interesting studies of child development. It is likewise clear that Piaget regarded them at the time as tentative and sketchy first drafts to be followed by a later more careful and comprehensive work. He was greatly surprised at the widespread attention they received and apparently a little dismayed that preliminary ideas should be treated by others as final statements of position. Finally, whatever shortcomings others have found in these studies, Piaget himself was in retrospect impressed by two essential ones. First of all, only an incomplete picture of cognitive structure and its development can be gained by the study of verbally expressed thought alone, that is, by questions put to the child in the absence of concrete manipulanda towards which the child's responses can be directed. Yet the 1921-1923 work was almost wholly of this type. It was only later that Piaget became clearly aware, through the study of infants and the restudy of school-age children, of the necessity of distinguishing between logic-in-action, logic applied to concrete givens, and—the kind of behavior with which most of the early work dealt—logic applied to purely symbolic, verbal statements.[3] The second shortcoming, related to the first, was one of which Piaget was fully aware in the early 1920's but could not remedy until later. In accord with his concern about part-whole relations mentioned earlier, he strove in vain to find structures-of-the-whole which would adequately describe logical operations. To be sure, the distinction between reversible and irreversible thought had already been made (e.g., 1924b, 1928b). However, the embedding of the reversibility concept into structures, such as the groupings of middle childhood, which could satisfactorily characterize the organization of operations only came later.

Two other developments of importance occurred during Piaget's early incumbency at Geneva. First, he read the work of the Gestalt psychologists with great interest but reacted to it with mixed feelings (1952d). He was gratified to learn that others had succeeded in formu-

[2] For books available in English translation, such as these five, the date cited always refers to the translated volume, not to the original French publication.

[3] Although Piaget does not mention this in his autobiography, early writings show that the distinction between concrete operations, bearing on sense data, and formal operations, or "operations to the second power" performed on the results of concrete operations, was already dimly sensed (1922, 1924b).

lating a coherent theory concerning part-whole relationships, a theory which could be experimentally fruitful. However, he early became convinced that the Gestalt doctrine of nonadditivity of parts within a whole (whole not equal to the sum of the parts), while correctly describing the structure of perception, did not apply to the equilibrium states which logical operations tend to achieve. To be sure, the *specific* nature of such equilibrium states and of the algebraic structures describing operations-in-equilibrium was not yet elaborated. At this time Piaget felt sure only that the Gestalt structures were not descriptive of logical operations; in later articles, he was to treat the relation of Gestalt theory to his own system more fully (1937a, 1954d, 1955a, 1955e).

A second and probably less important trend during the early 1920's was what Anthony has called Piaget's "flirtation" with psychoanalytic theory (Anthony, 1957). It is clear that Piaget read Freud (and Bleuler and Jung as well) and was particularly interested in the psychoanalytic conception of cognitive as opposed to affective functioning. Thus, there is an early attempt to relate the structure of unconscious adult thought, conscious adult thought, and the conscious thought of the child (1923). Similarly, he relied somewhat on Freudian theory in interpreting certain childhood myths in connection with his studies of artificialism (1929c). However, as his own studies proliferated and his own theory began to assume form and direction, references to psychoanalytic theory tended to drop out. Only rarely in later years did Piaget discuss psychoanalytic concepts in the context of his own work; and when he did, his treatment was more critical than sympathetic (e.g., 1951a). While it is certainly true that others have attempted to bring the two systems together (Anthony, 1956a, 1956b, 1957; Odier, 1956; Wolff, 1960), all the evidence suggests that Piaget himself has neither been profoundly influenced by Freud nor has tried to wed the two theories in any systematic way.

In 1923 Piaget was given a part-time appointment at the University of Neuchâtel and until 1929 divided his activities between Neuchâtel and Geneva. This four-year period was a busy one for him; he had a heavy teaching load in addition to his research work. The latter consisted principally of two lines of investigation. First, he did some preliminary work on the child's reaction to changes in the shape of substances like clay, transformations which left weight and volume invariant. These investigations were important both because they led to more thorough studies of number and quantity later (Piaget, 1952b; Piaget and Inhelder, 1941) and because they were the first experiments with school-age, verbal subjects in which the shift to less exclusively verbal tasks becomes apparent.

But by far the most important new development in Piaget's research during this period was a series of studies of intellectual development in infancy. With his wife's assistance (Valentine Châtenay, a former student at the Institut J. J. Rousseau), he spent a great deal of time carefully observing both spontaneous and elicited behavior in his own infants. This work was reported in most complete form in three books (1951a, 1952c, 1954a) and one article (1927a) but is also summarized in many other places (e.g., 1937a, 1950a, 1957a). These investigations of infant behavior did more than simply provide Piaget with needed data on the early foundations of cognitive development. They also clarified his thinking on such fundamental problems as the specific nature of cognitive adaptation, and the relation between cognitive organization in the initial (presymbolic) sensory-motor period and in the subsequent periods of symbolic thought.

During the 1925-1929 period Piaget also concluded his work in the field of malacology. Although he never again did experimental studies in this area, a number of conceptions based on this work survived as integral parts of his psychological theories, most notably in his views on organism-environment relationships, both biological and psychological (1952c).

In 1929 Piaget returned to full-time status at the University of Geneva, becoming assistant director and later (in 1932) codirector of Institut J. J. Rousseau. During the 1929-1939 interval, Piaget became involved in two time-consuming administrative enterprises. First, the Institut, hitherto a private organization, became affiliated with the University of Geneva and Piaget was the prime mover in the reorganization which followed. Second, he became director of the Bureau International d'Education, a newly formed intergovernmental organization which has since become jointly affiliated with and sponsored by the International Office of Education and UNESCO. Although the job was time-consuming, it gave Piaget an opportunity to work towards a translation of developmental findings into educational practices. To this end Piaget and his co-workers have in the subsequent decades written extensively on the application of his theory to pedagogic methods (e.g., Piaget, 1951b, 1956; Aebli, 1951; Szeminska, 1935). In the postwar years, Piaget has remained active in educational affairs, both with the Swiss government and with UNESCO.

The period 1929-1939 saw a number of significant scientific activities. The teaching of a course on the history of scientific thought gave Piaget an excuse to pursue, more intensively than before, serious reading in the history of mathematics, physics, and biology. Although he had already done some writing in the area of genetic epistemology (1924a, 1925b, 1929a), the later three-volume work on this subject (1950b) seems largely to have been the fruit of his extensive reading and reflection during this period.

Another major achievement was the resumption, on a larger scale and with the help of Szeminska, Inhelder, and many other able assistants, of his earlier, preliminary studies of number and quantity concepts. Portions of this work were first described in several articles and monographs in the middle to late 1930's (Piaget, 1937c; Piaget and Szeminska, 1939; Inhelder, 1936; Szeminska, 1935). In 1941 a fuller account was presented in two books (Piaget, 1952b; Piaget and Inhelder, 1941). This work was important for two reasons. It constituted a systematic redirection of attention towards the intellectual constructions of early through middle childhood after an interlude of several years of studying infant development. This renewed attack was to be more concerted and long-lasting than the famous work of the early 1920's directed towards the same subject population. A wide variety of important areas of cognitive functioning were eventually studied: first, number and quantity; later, movement, velocity, time, space, measurement, probability, and logic. These studies are among the most interesting and ingenious that Piaget has made.

This series of studies of middle childhood was also important because it provided, as the earlier series did not, the sought-for insights into the structural properties of thought. The first structural model to come out of this work was the *grouping* (1937b, 1937c, 1937d).[4] A grouping is a hybrid logico-algebraic structure, possessing properties of both mathematical groups and lattices, which Piaget uses to describe cognitive structure in the 7-11-year-old. To be sure, there had been premonitions of this kind of model-building prior to this. Thus, Piaget had earlier described a *group of spatial displacements* in infancy (1954a) and had even earlier spoken of *reversibility* (a group property) as a major characteristic of cognition in the school years (1928b). The theoretical enterprise begun in 1937, however, was to be far more comprehensive and ambitious. In 1942 Piaget published a systematic and detailed description of the eight groupings which concrete operations form (1942a), and this was only the beginning. In 1949 there followed a more rigorous treatment of the same groupings plus a discourse on the structures which the sixteen binary "interpropositional" operations assume (1949a). Finally, three years later, Piaget wrote a thinner but even more difficult book on the structure of ternary interpropositional operations (1952a). It is difficult to overemphasize the importance of this shift towards logico-algebraic models for the form and content of Piaget's writings in the last twenty years. Unlike the earlier work, experimental data since 1937 or so are systematically interpreted in terms of these structural models and these models serve to unify and permit comparisons among diverse findings in a way not possible in the earlier work. Also, it is fair to state that the search for structures became more than just this for Piaget. Evidently he also became interested in working out the myriad implicative possibilities of such structures for its own sake, as a logician would. At any rate, it is quite clear that he wanted to interest logicians as well as psychologists in his work, both in terms of its contributions to logic and in terms of its psychological implications (1949a, 1952a).

[4] In French: *groupeme*

From 1940 on, Piaget has been engaged in a variety of activities. To begin with those of an administrative nature, he assumed the directorship of the Psychology Laboratory at Geneva in 1940. He continued to edit the *Archives de Psychologie* with Rey and Lambercier and became first president of the newly formed Swiss Society of Psychology, assuming in 1942 joint editorship of its journal, the *Revue Suisse de Psychologie.* He managed to give a lecture series in Paris in 1942 during the German occupation and delivered a briefer series after the war in Manchester, England. These lectures were subsequently published in English and constitute the principal summaries of Piaget's system in that language by Piaget himself (1950a, 1957a). He received honorary degrees at various universities, including Harvard (at the 1936 tricentennial), Brussels, and the Sorbonne. Finally, as was mentioned, he remained active in the International Office of Education and, after it was organized, UNESCO.

As to scholarly activities, these fall into three major classes. Most of the studies of space, time, probability, movement, etc., were reported in a series of books (Piaget, 1946a, 1946b; Piaget and Inhelder, 1951, 1956, 1959; Piaget, Inhelder, and Szeminska, 1960). Two other volumes in the same vein are of particular importance. First, Inhelder published a book describing the use of the quantity tasks (conservation of mass, weight, and volume) as diagnostic instruments for testing intellectual ability in mental defectives (Inhelder, 1944). Later, with Piaget, she did a very interesting series of studies concerning adolescent thought (Inhelder and Piaget, 1958). This book, besides constituting the only major study of adolescent reasoning by the Piaget group, also contains a thorough theoretical analysis of concrete operations, formal operations, and the relations between the two.

The second major project by Piaget and his collaborators is a series of perception experiments begun in the early 1940's and still in progress. These perception studies, reported in some forty articles, are more rigorous as regards methodology and reporting of quantitative data than are the studies of intellectual development. Put differently, these experiments would appear to the reader much more like conventional perception experiments than his intelligence studies would look like conventional studies of intellectual development. Again, quite unlike his theories of intellectual development, the perceptual theory which has emerged from these experiments is intended to be rigorously predictive of perceptual response, given known conditions of the perceptual field (e.g., Piaget, 1955-1956a; Piaget, Albertini, and Rossi, 1944-1945; Piaget, Vinh-Bang, and Matalon, 1958). Although the perception work has been to some extent an autonomous body of research in its own right in relation to the larger corpus of intellectual studies, the autonomy is far from complete. Piaget has continually tried to specify how perceptual structures compare with intellectual structures and to profit from the study of one in the study of the other (Piaget, 1951c, 1954b, 1955a, 1955e; Piaget and Morf, 1958a, 1958b).

The third major endeavor, like the second, is still very much in progress: a systematic theoretical and experimental attack on problems of genetic epistemology. In 1950 Piaget published a comprehensive three-volume work on this topic, focusing particular attention on the implications of developmental findings for epistemological problems in the fields of mathematics, physics, biology, psychology, and sociology (1950b). In 1955, aided by a grant from the Rockefeller Foundation, Piaget established at Geneva the Centre International d'Epistémologie Génétique. The Centre operates in the following way (Beth, Mays, and Piaget, 1957, pp. 1-11). Each year three distinguished scholars with epistemological interests are invited to come to Geneva for an academic year to collaborate with Geneva psychologists on certain delimited problems of a genetic epistemological nature. An attempt is made to pose problems which admit of experimental as well as theoretical study. At the end of the year, findings and conclusions are presented at a symposium composed of these scholars plus eight or nine others invited in from outside to participate in critical discussion and to help formulate plans for the next year. The results of a given year's work are then published in a series of monographs (the one cited above, for example, is the first of four for the year 1955-1956).

At the time of this writing, Piaget's scientific energies are principally directed towards the continuing perception studies and the work of the Centre International d'Epistémologie Génétique.[5] His return to the study of genetic epistemology was a long-overdue labor of love. As Piaget is fond of remarking (1950b, Vol. 1; 1952d), he had originally planned to spend only a few years studying children and then devote the remainder of his career to epistemological problems. It is difficult to predict what he would have accomplished if this carefully laid plan had actually been carried out. One thing is clear, however: this book would not have been written.

THIS BOOK

Why write a book summarizing Piaget's system? For three reasons. First, his work appears to be of sufficient scope and stature to deserve recognition and understanding by a wide community of scholars interested in the ontogenesis of intelligence and perception. Second, there is every reason to believe that Piaget's system has not, over the years, received anything like its due in this recognition and understanding. And finally, there is evidence of a burgeoning interest in the system, something of a contemporary Piaget revival.

[5] For other recent research, see the first section of Chapter 11.

As to the first, little need be said. Piaget's work does in fact constitute a very substantial portion of the available theory and experimentation in the area of cognitive development, and anyone seriously interested in this area simply cannot afford to be ignorant of it.

As to the second point, there is good evidence for a definite, although irregular, pattern of underassimilation of the system, especially in the English-speaking professional world. The pattern appears to be this. There is ample enough citation and discussion of Piaget's early studies on language and thought, moral judgment, etc.—the work reported in his first five books (1926, 1928b, 1929c, 1930a, 1932). But the bulk of Piaget's contributions came later, and most of this bulk has not yet become part of the living literature. Indices of low assimilation are everywhere apparent. One index is latency of translation. To take two examples: Piaget's basic work on infancy was published in French in 1937 and translated into English in 1952 (Piaget, 1952c); his studies of the child's measurement operations first appeared in 1948 and remained untranslated until 1960 (Piaget, Inhelder, and Szeminska, 1960). Another index is citation by secondary sources in the child-development field. A 1295-page manual of child psychology (Carmichael, 1954) refers only to Piaget's first five books. Jersild's child psychology text cites only three of these five (1954), and his book on adolescence cites no Piaget work at all (1957). And two source books on cognition (Vinacke, 1952; Johnson, 1955) also follow the pattern of referring exclusively to the early studies.

As for the rising surge of interest in the system, there is again an abundance of clues. For instance, the pace of translation has become brisker. There were no Piaget books translated into English between 1933 and 1949, but there have been nine or more since 1950, with several others said to be on the way. Similarly, the number of Piaget-relevant experiments by workers outside the Geneva circle has definitely accelerated (see Chapter 11).

This is surely a happy combination of circumstances from the standpoint of someone having in mind the writing of a book on Piaget: here is a body of work of indisputable import in which there is currently a lively and growing interest, and at the same time one which has not generally been either well or widely understood. But it must also appear to be a rather puzzling combination. In particular, one might ask why there is such an apparent discrepancy between the volume and significance of Piaget's output and the relatively meager extent to which it has been taken up by the rest of the field. This is an important question to consider here, because the aim and organization of the book partly hinge on the answer.

Consider what is in store for anyone who sets out to master Piaget's system. He will soon discover that the pertinent theory and experiments are distributed across more than twenty-five books and a hundred and fifty articles (and some of the latter are nearly book length). He will also discover that most of the available publications which summarize more than limited portions of the system are too brief on the one hand, and either too elementary or too difficult on the other, to be of more than limited help to anyone who has not already read the original sources. When, reluctantly, he decides he must plough through the primary literature, he will be confronted with still more difficulties. Very few of the articles are available in English translation; many of the books are, but by no means all. Ph.D. language examinations notwithstanding, this is likely to be a problem. Furthermore, most of Piaget's writings are very difficult to read and understand, in French or in English. For one thing, there are many new and unfamiliar theoretical concepts, and they intertwine with one another in complicated ways to make the total theoretical structure. In addition, much of the theoretical content requires some sophistication in mathematics, logic, and epistemology. It is not easy to assess the extent to which this characteristic of Piaget's writings constitutes an obstacle, either intellectual or emotional, for the average behavioral scientist. Even with the requisite background, he may be repelled by a system which so liberally mixes mathematics and philosophy with developmental psychology. And there are still other hurdles, difficult to convey without having already described the system (they are discussed in Chapter 12, however).

It is small wonder, then, that Piaget's work has been underassimilated. And the fact and causes of this underassimilation help to dictate the way in which this book was conceived and written. Thus, its primary aim is to communicate and inform, not to criticize and evaluate. Accordingly, eleven of its twelve chapters are primarily expository, and only one principally critical-evaluative. The majority of the expository chapters deal with theory rather than experiments, because we think it is Piaget's theory, rather than his experiments, which people find especially difficult to grasp.

Hence, the organization of the book is as follows. There are three parts. The first attempts an integrated and detailed summary of Piaget's theory, and consists of Chapters 1-7. The second part, comprising Chapters 8-11, is devoted to experiments: Piaget's own in Chapters 8-10, and Piaget's plus other relevant studies in Chapter 11. Part III consists of one long chapter which tries to evaluate the system, both theory and experiments. Piaget's system does not of course neatly divide itself into theory and experiments for the convenience of his Boswell. For this reason, Part I necessarily makes considerable reference to experimental work. In fact, in the case of sensory-motor and early conceptual development, it seemed to make sense to include almost all the experimental material in the first section. Similarly, the experimental chapters are far from devoid of theoretical discussion. The result of such overlapping is naturally a good deal of repetition—of both concepts and experimental findings. But if the writer's own past (and continuing) difficulties in trying to understand Piaget are any basis for judgment, a certain measure of redundancy may be a blessing for the reader.

Part One

THE THEORY

CHAPTER ONE

The Nature of the System

A NUMBER of facts about Piaget's work lie not so much in the system as about and around it. Information of this kind, of which only a part can be termed *metatheory* in the strict sense, is primarily orientative: it helps to place the system in the context of other systems, both similar and different. This chapter offers such peripheral and perspective-giving information.

First and most basic will be a discussion of Piaget's scientific aims: precisely what he has attempted to study and what he has not attempted to study. A description of Piaget's methodology—or methodologies—follows this. Since some of his experimental methods have come under critical attack, it will be especially important to describe these with some care. The third and final section is more difficult to define. It will include what might be called a "personality profile" of Piaget's theoretical writings—a description of idiosyncrasies of the system, of characteristics of the work and its written presentation which make it uniquely a Piaget production.

In discussing these things—scientific aims, methodologies, and idiosyncrasies of the system—a lot of important theoretical and experimental content will be sketched much too briefly and superficially for complete understanding; most of this content will, however, be taken up again in detail in subsequent chapters. This chapter means to convey a preliminary and global image of the system, rather than a detailed mapping.

SCIENTIFIC AIMS

It is possible to give a rough definition of Piaget's principal scientific concerns in a single sentence: he is primarily interested in the theoretical and experimental investigation of the qualitative development of intellectual structures. The pertinent words and phrases of this definition need examination and qualification.

Intelligence

A persistent and overriding interest in the area of *intelligence* is a salient feature distinguishing Piaget's work from that of most child psychologists. To be sure, he has been and is interested in other areas, most notably perception, but also moral attitudes and other value systems (Piaget, 1932, 1934c; Inhelder and Piaget, 1958) and even motivation (1952c). As for perception, much of its value as an object of study for Piaget lies in the fact that it can be compared and contrasted with intelligence. Values and attitudes are seen as cognitive systems imbued in the later stages of development with the same formal organization as more unambiguously intellectual achievements (1954c). As Chapter 2 will show, motivation is treated almost exclusively in terms of motivation to intellectual adaptation. Moreover, the motives seen as most important are thought to be intrinsic to intellectual functioning itself and can at least approximately be conveyed by such terms as *exploratory drive, drive to mastery,* etc.; conventional bodily needs as motivators, the perennial favorites of learning theory, are given short shrift in Piaget's system. Finally, his interests in education, logic, and epistemology are almost exclusively intelligence-oriented.

Development

Piaget is also and just as fundamentally a *developmental* psychologist in the great tradition of Hall, Stern, Baldwin, the Bühlers, Binet, Werner, and the rest. He firmly believes that the study of ontogenetic change is a valuable undertaking in its own right. Even more, he is convinced that adult human behavior cannot be fully understood without a developmental perspective and deplores what he sees to be an unfortunate contemporary hiatus between child psychologists and those who study only adults (1957b, pp. 18-19). The addition of the genetic dimension, as he calls it, does more than simply give historical status to adult cognition; it makes possible, he believes, at least tentative solutions to age-old epistemological problems, especially those concerned with the ontogenetic precursors of certain important classes of cognitions.

We need to make clear precisely what Piaget's developmental approach —the study of the genetic dimension—does and does not involve. It does involve the careful description and theoretical analysis of successive ontogenetic states in a given culture. Thus behavior *change* from less to more advanced functioning is the primary datum. Further, it involves painstaking comparisons among these successive states; the dominant characteristics of a given state are described in terms of states preceding and states following. It is characteristically not concerned with any systematic exploration of other independent variables which may temporally accelerate or retard the appearance of the behavior studied. In this almost exclusive preoccupation with age changes *per se*, Piaget is poles apart from many contemporary child psychologists (see Chapters 11 and 12).

Structure, Function and Content

A third important feature of Piaget's system is a particular bent towards studying the *structure* of developing intelligence, as opposed to its *function* and *content*. Piaget has made distinctions among these three, and especially between the first two, in a number of places (1928a, 1931a, 1931c, 1952c).

In speaking of *content*, he refers to raw, uninterpreted behavioral data themselves. Thus, when one of Piaget's subjects asserts that one object sinks because it is heavy and another sinks because it is light (1930a), or behaves as though time were a function of the distance an object traveled but not of its velocity (1946a), we witness behavioral content. So also are the substantive, external aspects of earlier sensory-motor behavior, such as the child's capacity to make detours, to estimate distances visually, etc. (1954a).

By *function*, on the other hand, Piaget refers to those broad characteristics of intelligent activity which hold true for all ages and which virtually define the very essence of intelligent behavior. As will be seen in Chapter 2, intelligent activity is always an active, organized process of assimilating the new to the old and of accommodating the old to the new. Intellectual content will vary enormously from age to age in ontogenetic development, yet the general functional properties of the adaptational process remain the same.

Interposed between function and content, Piaget postulates the existence of cognitive structures. Structure, like content and unlike function, does indeed change with age, and these developmental changes constitute the major object of study for Piaget. What are structures in Piaget's system? They are the organizational properties of intelligence, organizations created through functioning and inferable from the behavioral contents whose nature they determine. As such, Piaget speaks of them as mediators interposed between the invariant functions on the one hand and the variegated behavioral contents on the other (1928a).

In the above example of objects sinking in water for two opposed reasons, certain structural properties can be said to mediate or be responsible for this content. First, the child is *phenomenistic* in the sense that his cognitive structure is so organized that the surface appearances of things are overattended to; his thought is dominated by the environmental properties which strike him first and most vividly—in this case the lightness or heaviness of the object. Second, he fails to relate in a logical way successive cognitive impressions; thus, heaviness and lightness are successively invoked as explanatory principles with no thought to the contradiction involved, as though the need to reconcile opposing impressions were not a characteristic of his cognitive structure. These are structural properties in the sense that they determine precisely what will and will not result when a given cognizing organism attempts to adapt to a given set of external events. To use a simple and somewhat imprecise capsule definition, *function* is concerned with the manner in which any organism makes cognitive progress; *content* refers to the external behavior which tells us that functioning has occurred; and *structure* refers to the inferred organizational properties which explain why this content rather than some other content has emerged.

The different structural characteristics posited for the various developmental levels are in large part the subject matter of the following chapters and are not specified here. Suffice it to say that Piaget's career can be divided into two rough eras with respect to the way structures are described. During the first twenty years or so, structures were defined primarily in verbal, intuitional terms. The structural properties of behavior towards sinking objects, in the example given above, were described in such terms, e.g., expressions like *phenomenistic, lack of need to reconcile opposing impressions,* etc. There are a large number of concepts of this type, especially in the earlier work: *egocentrism, syncretism, juxtaposition, reversibility, predicative thinking, realism, animism, artificialism, dynamism, precausality, transductive reasoning.* Beginning with the introduction of the *group of displacements* in the early 1930's (1954a) and of the *grouping* a few years later (1937b, 1942a), structural characteristics tend more and more to be framed in terms of logical algebra and equilibrium theory. This tendency to substitute mathematical for verbal terminology is not to be taken as a rejection of earlier interpretations in favor of new and different ones. Rather, it is an attempt to discover (or even invent, whenever necessary) mathematical structures which express the essence of these verbally given organizational properties. For example, and to anticipate a bit, a child of eight who possesses the grouping structure will, by implication from the structure, show reversibility of thought, a relative lack of egocentrism, a capacity for synthesizing rather than simply juxtaposing data, and a number of other characteristics.

Finally, it should be said that Piaget's concern with structure as opposed to content and function is by no means absolute. It can hardly be said that he has ignored function and content. As regards function, one of the distinguishing characteristics of his theory has been an attempt to isolate the abstract properties of intelligence-in-action which hold for all sentient organisms. These properties—*organization* and the two components of *adaptation* mentioned above, *assimilation* and *accommodation*—

are called *functional invariants* (1952c, p. 4). As Chapter 2 shows, an examination of these functional invariants is crucial in any discussion of structural change. Similarly, the content of developmental acquisitions is taken to be important otherwise than simply as evidence for structural properties. To take one example, Piaget has made suggestions for the teaching of elementary mathematics on the basis of content aspects of the development of number in children (1956). And the content aspects of Piaget's studies tend in themselves to be interesting to the average reader; they would scarcely be less than interesting to Piaget himself.

Qualitative Stages

The fourth and final key word in the definition of Piaget's aims is *qualitative*. He is interested in the qualitative characteristics of development. His concern with structure versus content betrays this, since structural changes are in their essence qualitative in nature. In Piaget's system, the panorama of changing structures in the course of development is conceptually partitioned into *stages* whose qualitative similarities and differences serve as conceptual landmarks in trying to grasp the process. Piaget and Inhelder have tried to specify some of the criterial aspects of the stage concept (Piaget, 1955d; Tanner and Inhelder, 1956).

THE REALITY OF STAGES

In order to posit a succession of developmental stages for a given behavior domain, they argue, the behavioral changes in the domain must first of all be susceptible of such a breakdown. That is, if behavior simply becomes better and better in a completely continuous way with no readily discernible qualitative changes in the process, if earlier behavior patterns do not naturally seem to segregate themselves in a qualitative sense from later clusters, any abstraction of "stages" becomes meaningless and arbitrary. Although there are some discriminable differences between earlier and later perceptual structures, Piaget feels that these are not sufficient to warrant a stage-by-stage analysis of perceptual development, and he does not offer one. For intellectual structure, on the other hand, it is suggested that such an analysis is both justified and fruitful; intellectual development does show sufficient qualitative heterogeneity, enough *"coupures naturelles bien nettes"* (1955d, p. 33) to permit such analysis.

INVARIANT SEQUENCE OF STAGES

Granted that a developmental series is amenable to stage description, the stages abstracted must possess certain properties. First, they must emerge in development in an unchanging and constant order or sequence; a stage *A* must, by this criterion, appear in every child before stage *B* occurs. If the behaviors which define the two stages do not occur in a constant ontogenetic sequence, it is erroneous to speak of them as *stages*. Although sequence is taken as invariant, the age at which a given stage appears may of course vary considerably (1928a). Put otherwise, the series of stages form an ordinal but not an interval scale. Thus, Piaget readily admits that all manner of variables may affect the chronological age at which a given stage of functioning is dominant in a given child: intelligence, previous experience, the culture in which the child lives, etc. For this reason, he cautions against an overliteral identification of *stage* with *age* and asserts that his own findings give rough estimates at best of the mean ages at which various stages are achieved in the cultural milieu from which his subjects were drawn. Furthermore, as a corollary to the foregoing, of course not all individuals need achieve the final stages of development. In this connection, for example, Inhelder has demonstrated arrested developments in mentally deficient subjects (Inhelder, 1944). Piaget has also for a long time freely conceded that not all "normal" adults, even within one culture, end up at a common genetic level; adults will show adult thought only in those content areas in which they have been socialized (1928a). In other words, as will be shown in the discussion of *décalages* below, a given individual need not be able to function at the same structural level for all tasks.

HIERARCHICAL RELATIONS BETWEEN SUCCESSIVE STAGES

A second essential characteristic of true stages is that the structures defining earlier stages become integrated or incorporated into those of the stages following. For instance, the stage of formal operations—the final stage in Piaget's developmental system—involves cognitive activities which are performed *upon* the concrete operations elaborated in the stage just preceding. Concrete operations must precede formal operations in the temporal series, logically as well as psychologically, since the constitution of the former is absolutely necessary to the activation of the latter.

INTEGRATED CHARACTER OF STAGES

A third and most crucial criterion is that the structural properties which define a given stage must form an integrated whole. Piaget refers to this kind of totality as a *structure d'ensemble*. That is, once structural properties reach an equilibrium state (see below), they characteristically show a high degree of interdependence, as though they formed part processes within a strong total system. Or better, the existence of the equilibrium condition implies this interdependence (1957c). This unified and organized character of structures makes it possible to define the totality which they form, e.g., a *grouping*, a *group of four transformations*, etc., and then to interpret a broad and diverse range of seemingly unrelated behaviors in terms of this underlying structural whole. As

Piaget's biography has shown, his lifelong professional goal has been to find those structural wholes, of great abstraction and generality, which correctly identify the essence of organized intelligence at its various levels.

PREPARATION AND ACHIEVEMENT PERIODS

A stage is further characterized as containing an initial period of preparation and a final period of achievement. In the preparation period, the structures which define the stage are in process of formation and organization. Because of this, behavior in the initial substage of any stage tends to lack tight organization and stability in so far as it is directed towards those cognitive problems whose solution requires *that* stage's intellectual structures (behavior is of course not disorganized and unstable when confined to tasks solvable by earlier structures). When confronted with problems appropriate to the stage-in-process, the child's cognitive activities are likely to reflect a mélange of organized but inappropriate earlier structures and the halting and sporadic use of as yet incompletely organized new structures. The preparatory phase, with its flux and instability, gradually gives way to a later period in which the structures in question form a tightly knit, organized, and stable whole. It is only in this phase of achievement, of stable equilibrium, that the structures defining the stage exist as the *structures d'ensemble* described above. Thus, the developmental process is decidedly not homogeneous at all points from the standpoint of cognitive organization. Relatively speaking, some periods in an individual's development are much more stable and coherent than others as regards structural properties. However, periods of lesser stability tend to be followed eventually by periods of greater stability. As will be seen, the concept of intellectual development as a movement from structural disequilibrium to structural equilibrium, repeating itself at ever higher levels of functioning, is a central concept for Piaget.

HORIZONTAL AND VERTICAL DÉCALAGES

Another important aspect of stage development is embodied in Piaget's concept of *décalage* (1941, 1955d)—a Piagetian concept easier to illustrate than to define precisely. In its most general meaning, a décalage (literally, unwedging or uncoupling) refers to the fact that one frequently sees similar cognitive developments occurring at different ages across the ontogenetic span.[1] There are various recurrent patterns in development, and a good theory ought to make due note of them. Piaget distinguishes two general classes of such recurrences: *horizontal décalages* and *vertical décalages*.

[1] In one translated work, *décalage* is rendered *temporal displacement* (1954a). This catches some of the meaning; formative patterns repeat or "displace" themselves in ontogenetic time.

Horizontal décalage refers to a repetition which takes place within a single period in development. It involves a single general level of functioning, e.g., the level at which the child can symbolize or represent internally the events he tries to cope with, as opposed to an earlier level at which he was capable only of overt action with respect to them (sensory-motor level). The repetition which takes place on the level in question is of the following kind. A cognitive structure, characteristic of that level, can first be successfully applied to task X but not to task Y; a year or so later—and here is the recurrence—the same organization of operations can now be extended to Y as well as to X. Moreover, the developmental process whereby Y comes to be mastered (i.e., whereby the structure can successfully be applied to it) is essentially the same as that which characterized the mastery of X.

But an example is better: the recognition by a child (see Chapter 9 below) that the total *mass* or *quantity of matter* of an object remains the same when the shape of the object changes implies a certain cognitive structure. The recognition that the *weight* also remains unchanged implies the same structure. Furthermore, the general level of functioning is the same in the two cases; in both cases the child has to perform symbolic, internal operations as opposed to mere overt actions. It so happens, however, that invariance of *mass* is typically achieved by children a year or two earlier than invariance of *weight* (Piaget and Inhelder, 1941). Moreover, the developmental sequence of acquisitions leading to correct performance is about the same in both cases, although of course occurring at different ages. This is an example of a horizontal décalage. Other examples exist. An infant can take account of spatial changes of position which are directly visible earlier than invisible changes, changes which can only be inferred from other displacements (1954a). What the child has conquered with respect to visible displacements has to be reconquered when he deals with invisible displacements. Again, the organization is similar in both instances (a network of coherent spatial relationships in which stable, enduring objects are displaced) but is temporarily asynchronous in its application to content.

Vertical décalage refers to the case where the repetition occurs at a distinctly different level of functioning, rather than within the same level. There is a formal similarity between the structures at the two levels, on the one hand, and a similarity or identity in the contents to which the structures are applied, on the other. The crucial difference concerns the level of functioning; different kinds of operations are involved in the two cases. For example, with the development of object constancy, the infant comes to recognize a given object—*behave* towards it in a constant fashion—despite changes in the perspective from which it is seen. It is not until much later that the same child can internally *represent* the system of possible perspectives, as opposed to *acting* appropriately within any one perspective. For example, it is only in middle childhood that a child, while sitting at position *A*, can predict (i.e., represent to himself) what perceptual image of a visual display another person will have sitting at position *B* (Piaget and Inhelder, 1956). The cognitive *structures* in the two cases do possess certain formal similarities (coordination of perspectives) and in both cases the *content* operated upon is essentially the same (objects seen from different vantage points). The two performances, however, occur on radically different *planes* of activity: sensory-motor versus symbolic-representational.

Here is another example. Late in the sensory-motor period, the child gradually develops a precise behavioral map of his immediate surroundings. He can quickly and efficiently go from *A* to *B* to *C* and back to *A*; he can make detours when obstacles block his path, etc. (1954a). In other words, his motor movements definitely possess a strong structure, a tight organization as regards spatial relationships. It will be several years later, however, before he can represent the terrain and its relationships *symbolically*, in contradistinction to direct motor *action* with respect to it. He will for a long time be incapable of drawing a simple map of his immediate environment, or even of correctly filling in objects on a map constructed by others (Piaget, Inhelder, and Szeminska, 1960). Yet, in the two cases there are clear similarities in the reality *content* and in the formal cognitive *organization* (as opposed to the kinds of *operations* so organized).

Both concepts, horizontal and vertical décalage, are felt to be useful in pointing up important aspects of intellectual development. The concept of horizontal décalage represents the fact that, whereas it may be useful to think of an individual as being generally characterized by a given cognitive structure, he will not necessarily be able to perform within that structure for all tasks. Task contents do differ in the extent to which they resist and inhibit the application of cognitive structures. This is a fact which a stage theory must reckon with, however much it may lend a certain equivocality to statements like "Individual *A* is in stage *X*." In brief, the existence of horizontal décalages seems to point up a certain *heterogeneity* where only *homogeneity* might have been suspected.

The implication of vertical décalages, on the other hand, seems to be quite the opposite. In effect, vertical décalages express a hidden *uniformity* within the apparent *differences* between one stage and another. There seems to be little in common between the spatial perambulations of the toddler and a map-making project in which a fifth-grader participates. Yet there are structural similarities buried in the obvious differences, and it is this recurrence which defines a vertical décalage.

There are still a few components of Piaget's views on developmental stages which it is important to grasp in order not to misunderstand his position. In the first place, he does not consider the delineation of developmental stages to be an end in itself. On the contrary, the classification of stages is a means to the end of understanding the developmental process in rather the same way that zoological and botanical classification is a first step in the analysis and understanding of biological phenomena (1955d, pp. 56-57). He also recognizes that, since the positing of stages is a process of abstracting highlights—within some frame of reference, from a panorama of gradual change—different theorists will naturally differ somewhat in the stages they posit.

Further, Piaget takes for granted the fact that considerable continuity lies behind or beneath the sequence of stages elaborated by the developmental theorist. Thus, he admits that between the behavioral configuration defining one stage and that defining the next stage one can usually discern a number of intermediary, transitional steps. The *degree* of continuity—the *number* of such intermediary steps—varies considerably with the content studied, the frame of reference of the experimenter, etc., and is not in itself a problem of primary importance for the developmental psychologist (Piaget, 1957c, pp. 91-95). Actually, Piaget and his associates (Piaget, 1955-1956b; Gréco, 1956-1957) now tie the continuity-discontinuity question both to the distinction between structure and function and to the theory of equilibrium (Chapter 7). Thus cognitive structures, i.e. the equilibrium states which development yields, are essentially discontinuous and qualitatively distinct, one from another. However, each one arises from a developmental equilibration process which is continuous, more or less all of a piece, throughout ontogenesis.

Finally, it is clear that a theory stressing qualitative changes in the developmental process—a theory built on stages and stage differences— will inevitably tend to understate across-stage similarities. More accurately, Piaget's theory somewhat underplays differences among children who fall within the same stage and underplays similarities among children who fall within different stages. This is probably an inevitable consequence of the abstraction process whereby stages are conceptually isolated: two stages are defined in large part by their differences. But Piaget does not subscribe to the view that adult and child are completely different entities with no commonalities between them (1931c). What he does subscribe to is the belief that there are important differences in addition to the obvious similarities and that a developmental theory must above all deal with these.

METHODOLOGY

Piaget's methods of collecting and organizing experimental data on development vary considerably with the content studied. His methodology in the perception work is radically different from the approaches he uses in studying intellectual development. There is even considerable variation within each of these areas; this is especially true of the intelligence studies, to which we first turn.

METHODOLOGY IN INTELLIGENCE STUDIES

Variations in Experimental Method

In some reported work on intellectual development, Piaget and his co-workers have simply made careful observations of ongoing behavior without any experimenter intervention at all. For example, a good portion of Piaget's first book (1926) is devoted to reporting careful observations of children's spontaneous language behavior. Similarly, much of the behavior reported in Piaget's three books on development in infancy and early childhood (1951a, 1952c, 1954a) was not elicited in any way by the experimenter. Most of his studies, however, have involved one or another form of experimenter intervention. In some cases, this intervention has consisted of the mere interpolation of some kind of stimulus at a given point in a spontaneous action sequence.

In most cases, however, his studies do have the formal properties of experiments proper, in the sense that the behavior studied is elicited from the start by some stimulus provided by the experimenter. The great majority of Piaget's studies of intellectual development fall into this broad class. Within this class of experiments proper, there are various subvarieties which may be distinguished in terms of the importance of verbal stimuli and responses in the test situation.

VERBAL BEHAVIOR CONCERNING REMOTE EVENTS

In much of Piaget's early work, both the stimuli produced by the experimenter and the responses which they elicited in the child were entirely verbal. Furthermore, the content of the interchange between child and experimenter concerned events and objects nowhere present in the test situation. The following is a sample of this kind of study; the child's code name and age in years and months is given at the beginning of the behavior protocol:

METR (5:9): "Where does the dream come from?—I think you sleep so well that you dream.—Does it come from us or from outside?—From outside.— What do we dream with?—I don't know.—With the hands? . . . With nothing?—Yes, with nothing.—When you are in bed and you dream, where is the dream?—In my bed, under the blanket. I don't really know. If it was in my stomach (!) the bones would be in the way and I shouldn't see it.—Is the dream there when you sleep?—Yes, it is in the bed beside me." We tried suggestion: "Is the dream in your head?—It is I that am in the dream: it isn't in my head (!). When you dream, you don't now you are in the bed. You know you are walking. You are in the dream. You are in bed, but you don't know you are.—Can two people have the same dream?—There are never two dreams (alike).—Where do dreams come from?—I don't know. They happen.—Where?—In the room and then afterward they come up to the children. They come by themselves.—You see the dream when you are in the room, but if I were in the room, too, should I see it?—No, grownups (les Messieurs) don't ever dream.—Can two people ever have the same dream?—No, never.—When the dream is in the room, is it near you?—Yes, there! (pointing to 30 cms. in front of his eyes)" (1929c, pp. 97-98).

VERBAL BEHAVIOR CONCERNING IMMEDIATE EVENTS

A second subclass of experiments similarly makes use of verbal interview but with the important difference that the questions and answers pertain to some concrete event which the child is witnessing. The child's only recorded responses are still verbal, but they concern immediate rather than remote events. For example, in one study Piaget deflated a punctured rubber ball, directing the jet of air towards the child's cheek. Then, he asked questions about where the air came from, where it went to after the deflation, etc. Here is a sample protocol:

> RE (8½): "What is happening?—There is air. Because there is a hole, then it comes out.—Where does the air come from?—They put it in.—Who? —The man. The man who took the ball and put air into it." The ball is deflated and allowed to fill itself again: "It is coming back.—How?—By the hole.—But where from?—It is going in.—Is it the air of the room that is going in, or the air that I took away?—The air that you took away" (1930a, pp. 16-17).

In a more recent study, the experimenter gave the child a ball of clay (*A*) and asked the child to make another of the same size and shape (*B*). After the child did this, the experimenter changed the shape of either *B* or *A*, or else cut it into several pieces, and then asked questions designed to discover whether or not the child still believed *A* and *B* to be of equal mass, weight, and volume:

> PIE (7;1): "You see these two little balls here. Is there just as much dough in this one as in this one?—Yes.—Now watch (the experimenter changes one of them into the shape of a sausage).—The sausage has more dough.—And if I roll it up into a ball again?—Then I think there will be the same amount." The clay is rolled into a ball once more and the other ball is molded into the shape of a disc: "There's still as much dough? (in the disc) —There is more dough in the ball" (Piaget and Inhelder, 1941, p. 11).[2]

MIXED VERBAL AND NONVERBAL BEHAVIOR

A third methodological subvariety is like the one just described except that the responses which form the data are now both verbal and motor. That is, the child has to do something to solve the problem; in

---

[2] Wherever, as here, quotations come from untranslated French works, the translation is my own.

addition, however, he is also constrained to say something about what he has done. In one experiment the investigator placed six counters or tokens on the table in a straight line with equal spaces between them. The child's task was to pick out of a box the same number of counters. Here is a sample protocol:

> JON (4;5): "Take the same number as there are there (6 counters).—(He put 7 counters close together, and then made the correct correspondence.)— Are they the same?—Yes.—(His row was then spread out.)—Are they the same?—No.—Has one of us got more?—Me.—Make it so you have the same number as I have.—(He closed his up.)—Are they the same?—Yes.—Why?— Because I pushed mine together" (1952b, p. 79).

It would be roughly correct to state that Piaget's methods of studying cognitive development almost always include some verbal, interviewlike component wherever questioning is feasible. Piaget has tended, however, in the post-1930 work to favor experiments which are not wholly verbal and divorced from immediate manipulanda; in other words, he has leaned towards studies of the second and third subclasses.

NONVERBAL BEHAVIOR

Finally, in his studies of infant development no verbal interchange of any kind was possible, of course, and these experiments fall into a fourth methodological subgroup:

> At 1;6 Jacqueline is sitting on a green rug and playing with a potato which interests her very much (it is a new object for her). She says "po-terre" and amuses herself by putting it into an empty box and taking it out again. . . . I then take the potato and put it in the box while Jacqueline watches. Then I place the box under the rug and turn it upside down thus leaving the object hidden by the rug without letting the child see my maneuver, and I bring out the empty box. I say to Jacqueline, who has not stopped looking at the rug and who has realized that I was doing something under it: "Give Papa the potato." She searches for the object in the box, looks at me, again looks at the box minutely, looks at the rug, etc., but it does not occur to her to raise the rug in order to find the potato underneath (1954a, p. 68).

Characteristics Common to All Methodological Variations

There are certain characteristics common to Piaget's approach in all studies which go beyond mere observation of ongoing behavior. First, there is the presentation of some kind of task to which the child makes some kind of response. Not all children, even within a single age group, will be given exactly the same task, nor will a given task be administered in exactly the same way to all children to whom it is presented. As soon as the child makes his response, the experimenter will then ask him a question, pose a variation of the problem, or in some way set up a new stimulus situation. This new stimulus situation is in part a response to the child's response. That is, the experimenter selects some question or some task which he hopes, in the light of his experience and theoretical frame of reference, will clarify what lies beneath the child's response, will provide additional insight into the child's cognitive structure. The process then continues in the same way, each successive response by the child being a partial determinant of the experimenter's next move. Because of the dependent relationship between the child's behavior and the experimenter's behavior, no two children will ever receive exactly the same experimental treament; typically, experimental treatment will vary a great deal across subjects in any one investigation.

The protocols quoted above convey the flavor of this kind of experimental method and are more or less typical of those encountered in Piaget's writings. Piaget refers to his experimental technique as *the clinical method* and rightly calls attention to its similarity to psychiatric procedures (1929c). The approach does have much in common with diagnostic and therapeutic interviews, with projective testing, and with the kind of informal exploration often used in pilot research throughout the behavioral sciences. The crux of it is to explore a diversity of child behaviors in a stimulus-response-stimulus-response sequence; in the course of this rapid sequence the experimenter uses all the insight and ability at his command to understand what the child says or does and to adapt his own behavior in terms of this understanding.

Rationale

It is clear that Piaget's method is not the only one which might reasonably be used in trying to study child behavior, and it is fair to ask why he has repeatedly selected this one. The answer is that Piaget feels that only through such a method can one get to the heart of the child's cognitive structure and describe it as it really is. One simply must adopt a technique, whatever its hazards and difficulties, which permits the child to move on his own intellectually, to display the cognitive orientation which is natural to him at that period in his development. Thus, a Piaget experiment usually originates in careful and extensive observation of children's spontaneous behavior. The experimental tasks which will later be used in a systematic study are designed in terms of hunches or intuitions which emerge from these observations. The hope is that in this way the problems posed will really be relevant to the child's ongoing intellectual functioning and will permit pertinent, interpretable behavior to emerge. Once the task is presented to the child, one is likewise committed to try to follow the child's thought wherever it seems to be going, and this precludes a standard, unvarying interview. Piaget freely admits the usefulness of more standardized, "testlike" procedures for a number of psychometric purposes (1929c, p. 3). However, if one's primary concern is simply to describe and explain the variety of intellectual structures which children at different levels possess rather than to construct rigorous developmental scales for diagnostic purposes, he believes the clinical method to be the method of choice.

Dangers and Difficulties

The use of this method is beset with dangers and difficulties, as Piaget is quick to recognize (1928a, 1929c). Even for the highly skilled interviewer there are ever present temptations to lead and suggest, dangers of missing the significance of important behaviors, and other pitfalls of all kinds. Similarly, in evaluating the resultant behavior protocols, one should try neither to overestimate nor to underestimate the child's intellectual level through incautious interpretation of what the child has said and done. Further, it is necessary to weed out the common and recurrent from the idiosyncratic and occasional; in short, one must identify those structural characteristics which many children of the same age possess and which can thereby define a meaningful stage or level. Finally, and above all, the skill and ingenuity of the examiner must in part compensate for the inherent deficiencies in the clinical method itself. In an early book Piaget expresses this point of view quite clearly:

> Moreover, it is our opinion that in child psychology as in pathological psychology, at least a year of daily practice is necessary before passing beyond the inevitable fumbling stage of the beginner. It is so hard not to talk too much when questioning a child, especially for a pedagogue! It is so hard not to be suggestive! And above all, it is so hard to find the middle course between systematization due to preconceived ideas and incoherence due to the absence of any directing hypothesis! The good experimenter must, in fact, unite two often incompatible qualities; he must know how to observe, that is to say, to let the child talk freely, without ever checking or side-tracking his utterance, and at the same time he must constantly be alert for something definitive; at every moment he must have some working hypothesis, some theory, true or false, which he is seeking to check. When students begin they either suggest to the child all they hope to find, or they suggest nothing at all, because they are not on the look-out for anything, in which case, to be sure, they will never find anything.
> In short, it is no simple task, and the material it yields needs subjecting to the strictest criticism. The psychologist must in fact make up for the uncertainties in the method of interrogation by sharpening the subtleties of his interpretation. . . . The essence of the critical method is . . . to separate the wheat from the tares and to keep every answer in its mental context. For the context may be one of reflection or of spontaneous belief, of play or of prattle, of effort and interest, or of fatigue (1929c, pp. 8-10).

In summary, Piaget believes that one has to recognize and learn to live with the hazards which his methodology inevitably presents, because other techniques, whatever the gains in simplicity and objectivity, are simply not adequate to the scientific task he has set for himself.

Analysis and Presentation of Data

The philosophy which guides Piaget's choice of method is also responsible for the manner in which he analyzes and presents his experimental findings. In almost all studies primary data in the form of behavior protocols are presented in the text. These are preceded, followed, and accompanied by a good deal of interpretation and explanation by the author. There are variations in the way protocols and commentary are set forth in print, depending on the nature of the study and, in part at least, on the period in Piaget's career in which the study was done. The most typical format, perhaps, is the one found in most of Piaget's post-1940 books on number, quantity, space, and the rest. Here Piaget begins his account of each experiment or set of experiments by posing the experimental question at hand and the theoretical background from which it emerged. Next, the experimental techniques are described in some detail; if for certain children the general procedure varied from that used for the majority, the variation is also described. Following this, Piaget generally summarizes the findings he is about to present in detail. In the summary one is told that so and so many developmental stages were found with respect to the task presented (usually three or four, perhaps further divided into substages) and that these stages consist of such and such general characteristics. Then the stages and substages are described in further detail, one at a time and in sequence, along with a number of verbatim protocols adduced to support and illustrate Piaget's analysis. Following this, or in a concluding chapter or section, Piaget presents an extended discussion of these findings, their theoretical meaning, their relationship to other studies, and so forth.

The number of children tested at each age level may be given in the report. Often it is not, although there is usually good reason to suppose that the sample was of reasonable size. Again, the identifying information as to tested intelligence, socioeconomic background and so on usually found in published reports in the field of child psychology is almost always absent. The conventional statistical treatment of results—number of children performing this or that way as a function of this or that procedure, etc.—is usually meager or missing entirely.

Rationale

Piaget's preference for a quasi-anecdotal rather than quantitative-statistical presentation of data is really a preference and not due to ignorance of quantitative methods. One has only to glance at one of his logic books to be convinced that lack of mathematical sophistication can hardly be invoked in Piaget's case. Since his primary interest is that of identifying successive cognitive structures in ontogenetic development by techniques which inevitably differ from child to child, he simply sees no need to give what he believes would be an illusory aura of objectivity and precision. In this connection he has stated:

> The object of these studies, initially, was not to establish a scale of development and to obtain precise determinations of age as regards stages. It was a question of trying to understand the intellectual mechanism used in the solution of problems and of determining the mechanism of reasoning. For that we used a method which is not standardized, a clinical method, a method of free conversation with the child. . . . That is why, personally, I am always very suspicious of statistics on our results. Not that I dislike statistics; I worked on biometrics enthusiastically when I was a zoologist, but to make statistical tables on children when each was questioned differently appears to me very much open to criticism as regards the results of the dispersion (Tanner and Inhelder, 1956, p. 89).

None of the foregoing should imply that Piaget is given to hasty, poorly thought-out conclusions on the basis of a few cursory and unsystematic experiences with a handful of children. The impression is, on the contrary, that he works very hard at testing children, formulating and checking hypotheses, testing more children, rethinking and revising theoretical concepts, and so on. In one article, for example, he almost complains of the fact that the manifest contents of his early books seem meager to him in proportion to the time, effort, and mountainous accumulation of data involved behind the scenes (1928a). Nonetheless, it is true that the reader of Piaget's writings has to take more on faith—faith in Piaget's experimental skill, theoretical ingenuity, and intellectual honesty—than would be the case for the bulk of child psychology publications. Whether, as Piaget would probably argue, this condition is really indigenous to the kind of problems he studies and hence unavoidable is open to question (see Chapter 12).

METHODOLOGY IN PERCEPTION STUDIES

Differences Between Perception and Intelligence Experiments

Piaget's studies of perceptual phenomena are different from the intelligence investigations in a number of ways. In a typical publication in this area, Piaget and associates give detailed information as to subjects, apparatus, method, and results. The latter are conventionally organized into tables and figures which give quantitative expression to the data. Moreover, these studies typically involve a very systematic exploration of dependent variables as a function of several independent variables; in most of these experiments, age is one independent variable just as in the intelligence studies, but here it is only one among several. For example, in one of a number of investigations involving the Müller-Lyer illusion (Piaget and Albertini, 1950-1952), the experimenters measured the size of the illusion as a function of both age and a whole complex of other variables concerning the size and form of the illusion figure. This kind of multivariate design is simply never found in the studies of intellectual development. Finally, Piaget's theory of perceptual functioning is itself essentially quantitative (Piaget, Albertini and Rossi, 1944-1945; Piaget, 1955-1956a; Piaget, Vinh-Bang and Matalon, 1958); the theory of intellectual development is in part mathematical, but it is not quantitative. As a consequence, the numerical data in the perception experiments are often fed directly into theoretical equations, a thing unheard of in the intelligence work.

Similarities Between Perception and Intelligence Experiments

There are also similarities between the perception and intelligence studies, although these are less obvious than the differences. The perception experiments do in various subtle ways still bear the Piagetian stamp. In the first place, Piaget and his co-workers make frequent use of a variation of the psychophysical method of constant stimuli which they call the *clinical concentric method* (Lambercier, 1946a). In this method as in the traditional constant-stimuli procedure, thresholds are determined by presenting a series of stimuli of different values and requiring the subject to judge each of these stimuli with respect to some standard stimulus (greater than, less than, or equal to the standard). Unlike the traditional method, however, the experimenter does not decide beforehand upon some fixed set of variable stimuli which he then presents in some predetermined random order to all subjects. Rather, he tends to determine the threshold by a kind of bracketing process in which stimuli of considerably greater magnitude than the standard are ordinarily first alternated with those of obviously lesser magnitude and the threshold is then determined by moving in towards the center from these extremes (hence the expression "concentric").

Its psychophysical characteristics notwithstanding, this technique is similar to the clinical method used throughout the intelligence studies in a number of ways. The experimenter tries to "follow" the child in deciding which stimuli to present in the course of the testing period just as in the intelligence experiments. He must exercise careful clinical judgment in a variety of situations. For example, he may attempt to reduce the number of variable stimuli presented if the juvenile subject seems to show fatigue or distractibility. He may purposefully include easy discriminations if the subject seems to feel he is performing inadequately. Finally, the experimenter, while obviously not presenting the stimuli randomly, tries to avoid a fixed and unvarying bracketing sequence, e.g., presenting stimulus values in a predictable sequence like 12-6-11-7-10-8, etc. In effect, Piaget and his associates have tried to adapt a traditional psychophysical procedure to meet what they believe to be the special problems involved in using children as subjects in perceptual experiments. They feel that the clinical concentric method retains much of the precision of the parent method while eliminating features which would be undesirable in testing children.

There are a few other similarities between the perception and intelligence work which are somewhat less obvious. For one thing, there is the familiar Piagetian tendency to present and discuss experiments in great detail and at considerable length, although perhaps not to the same extent as in the intelligence studies. For example, one of the perception publications is 204 pages long (Lambercier, 1946a); a number of others exceed 100 pages. More important, Piaget and his associates deliberately codify their perception data in a symbolism which purports to make possible direct comparisons between perceptual and intellectual be-havior (Piaget, Lambercier, Boesch and Albertini, 1942-1943). As has been mentioned, Piaget had early been interested in describing the equilibrium condition of perceptual structures against the standard of intellectual equilibrium.

Despite these similarities in experimental method, written presentation and symbolism, a naive reader of Piaget's writings is likely to be more impressed with differences between the perception and intelligence volumes than with points of congruence. It is therefore all the more important to recognize the fact that Piaget considers the perception work as integral part of his total endeavor: to describe and analyze the development of adaptational structures, cognitive structures in the broad sense of the term, and the various equilibrium systems which they form (1957c).

IDIOSYNCRASIES OF THE SYSTEM

There are certain components of the form and content of Piaget's writings which are neither theoretical concepts nor experimental data nor methodology nor scientific aims. Yet these components taken to-gether definitely set the system apart from other systems as surely as does the content of theory and experimentation. They do not form a coherent and integrated set of attributes or features; some refer to writing style, some to book organization, some to experimental content, and so on. The writer has been unable to find a more apt and appropriate rubric than "idiosyncrasies of the system" for this heterogenous collection.

Although it is admittedly possible to grasp much of the essence of Piaget's work without examining or even identifying these idiosyncrasies, there is good reason to do so nonetheless. It is these features which in large part connote the flavor as opposed to the substance of Piaget's writings. An awareness of them permits one better to immerse oneself in the system, to see and explore problems as Piaget sees and explores them. Piaget the scientific worker and writer is a decided individualist, a nonconformist, and a grasp of the idiosyncracies of his system puts this individuality in bold relief. A book on Piaget's system ought to encompass the whole system; the subtraction of theory, experiments, methods, and aims from the total Piagetian output leaves the important, if hard to categorize, remainder to which we now turn.

Holism

As the recapitulation of his professional career has shown, the relation of the part to the whole has been a matter of profound interest to Piaget since his youth. In his writings he emphasizes again and again the conviction that intellectual operations never exist in isolation from a governing totality, an organization whose laws of composition it is crucial to discover. In his later writings especially, he has tried to describe as precisely as possible the equilibrium characteristics of the different structural wholes one actually encounters across the span of ontogenetic development. One gets the impression that each new study, each reanalysis of development, reinforces the holistic credo for Piaget: adaptive behavior, whether in early infancy or in adulthood, can be meaningfully interpreted only in terms of its organization as a total system, whether the system consist of simple sensory-motor schemes, perceptual organizations, or combinatorial logical systems of great complexity and mobility (1957c).

Mathematics, Logic, Physics, and Biology

Piaget tends to saturate his work, at one level or another, with mathematics and logic, physics, and biology.

MATHEMATICS AND LOGIC

Mathematics is involved in both the structure of the theory and in the content of the experimental work. The theory of intellectual development makes use of logico-algebraic systems—*groups, lattices,* and *groupings*—in its treatment of intellectual structure. Similarly, the perception theory is definitely a quantitative affair, involving equations with variables and constants which take their values from experimental data. It seems to be true that Piaget strives always to give mathematical-logical expression to theoretical constructs whenever the latter lend themselves to such treatment. Moreover, he tries to select the kind of expression most appropriate to the behavior formalized: qualitative and nonnumerical algebra for conceptual structures; quantitative equations for certain aspects of perceptual functioning.

Mathematics and logic also permeate the experimental work itself, this time as content studied. Piaget and his co-workers have done developmental studies of number concepts (Piaget, 1952b), of probability (Piaget and Inhelder, 1951), of topological, projective, and Euclidean spatial relationships (Piaget and Inhelder, 1956), and of a variety of measurement operations (Piaget, Inhelder, and Szeminska, 1960). And of course logical reasoning appears directly or indirectly as content studied in almost all experiments.

PHYSICS

Physics, like mathematics, enters the system both as a contribution to theory and as content studied. The concept of systems in equilibrium, which pervades theoretical analyses in both the perception and intelligence studies, derives primarily from the fields of thermodynamics and mechanics. Physics as content studied is frequently encountered from the earliest experiments. Thus, Piaget's fourth book (1930a) has the phrase "physical causality" in the title and describes children's explanations of a host of phenomena from elementary physics. Later works treat of mass, weight, and volume concepts (Piaget and Inhelder, 1941), temporal duration and temporal succession (Piaget, 1946a), relations among velocity, time, and distance (Piaget, 1946b), and again, a wide range of phenomena of the elementary physics text variety (Inhelder and Piaget, 1958). One paper is even entitled *The Child and Modern Physics* (1957d).

Taking logico-mathematical and physical phenomena together, one can scarcely fail to be impressed with the extent to which Piaget has been preoccupied with developmental responses to the grand and fundamental categories of human experience—space, time, motion, and the rest (e.g., 1952c, p. 9). It is as if a Kantian philosopher had turned developmental psychologist and set out to study the *anlagen* of epistemological fundaments; indeed, considering Piaget's abiding interest in epistemological problems, the analogy is not an unapt one (although Piaget is epistemologically a Kantian in certain respects only).

BIOLOGY

Biology is a third important thread in the system. Unlike those of mathematics and physics, biological concepts enter primarily at the theoretical end. To be sure, there are a few experiments whose content could be construed as biological, e.g., Piaget's studies of the concept of age (1946a) and the concept of life (1929c). The contribution of biology to basic theory, however, has been more substantial. Piaget's concept of functional invariants, to be described in Chapter 2, is founded squarely on a primarily biological model of organism-environment interchange (1952c). In discussing the problem of selecting an adequate formulation of intellectual functioning, Piaget shows how various conceptions of biological adaptation have their parallels in conceptions of intellectual adaptation: Lamarckism with associationism, vitalism with intellectualism, etc. It is also clear that the particular interpretation of cognitive adaptation which Piaget himself favors is a direct outcome of his earlier biological studies of mollusks. He was impressed with how these lower organisms, while accommodating to the environment, also actively assimilate it in accord with structural givens. An image of an active organism which both selects and incorporates stimuli in a manner determined by its structure, while at the same time adapting its structure to the stimuli, emerged from these early studies as a ready-made model for cognitive development. In Piaget's view, cognitive development must have its roots firmly planted in biological growth, and basic principles valid for the former are to be found only among those which are true of the latter.

Description and Explanation vs. Prediction

There are attributes of a different sort which also characterize the system. First of all, Piaget is oriented more towards description and explanation of developmental change than to making predictive statements about the outcomes of developmental experiments.[3] The system is obviously descriptive in the sense that it has over the years provided a wealth of detailed information on the changing characteristics of cognition in the course of ontogenetic development. Less obviously, it also purports to explain the changes it describes. This is especially apparent in a theoretical article which proposes the concept of equilibrium, not only to describe the developmental process in a generalized, abstract way, but also to explain it (1957c). However, the stylistic device of explicitly stating a set of experimental hypotheses in formal terms and then presenting the data as confirming or disconfirming them is much rarer in Piaget's publications than in the field at large. Logically, it could perhaps be argued that predictions, except of the grossest and most superfluous kind, have no meaningful place in studies which typically manipulate only one independent variable—chronological age. Needless to say, Piaget recognizes with the rest of us that age is a vehicle for causes rather than a cause in itself; nonetheless, the "real" causes are not systematically varied at the experimental level in Piaget's studies (although attempts are made to identify them theoretically) and hence few predictive statements are made. Piaget's general "hypothesis" is simply that cognitive development is a coherent process of successive equilibrations of cognitive

---

[3] This much is less true for the percepton studies, involving as they do quantitative equations from which specific predictions can be and are made.

structures, each structure and its concomitant equilibrium state deriving logically and inevitably from the preceding one (1957c). Much of what constitutes his theory is concerned in one way or another with the details of this hypothesis, and it would not be unfair to say that most experiments appear to be set up to demonstrate its validity, rather than to "test" it in any rigorously predictive sense.

"Loose" vs. "Tight" Concepts

As the theory (and again the intelligence theory is specifically referred to) is essentially descriptive-explanatory rather than predictive, so also could it be characterized as "loose" rather than "tight" in its specification of concept meanings. Theoretical concepts tend to be broad and global, difficult to tie unequivocally both to specific behaviors and to each other. For example, constructs like *schema, reversibility, assimilation, preconcept,* and the like do in general come to connote a great deal to the careful reader, but tend nonetheless to be denotatively imprecise. The expression *come to connote* is used advisedly because Piaget often defines his concepts bit by bit across a single volume (or even across several volumes) and understanding tends to come in installments. In later writings, to be sure, there is more of a tendency towards formal or quasi-formal definitions as concepts are introduced (e.g., 1957c); even here, however, the problem of firmly anchoring concepts in behavior remains. Again, whether concepts in this complex area could be really precise is arguable; the point made here is simply that imprecision of terms does tend to characterize Piaget's system, although this obviously does not render it unique among psychological systems.

Ratio of Discussion to Data

Another characteristic, alluded to earlier, which more definitely tends to mark off a work as Piaget's is a high ratio of discussion, analysis, and interpretation to data. This trait is equally prominent in both perception and intelligence writings. Much more than is the case among psychologists writing in most American publications, Piaget is given to painstaking and leisurely analyses of all conceivable facets of the experimental data at hand, the minutiae as well as the global aspects. What would be articles for many writers become monograph length when Piaget writes them; what would be monographs become substantial books.

Why such lengthy and discursive writing? In the first place, the data are interpreted within a theory which is inherently space-consuming to present, both *qua* theory and in its specific relation to the data at hand. Secondly, Piaget sees his many studies as aspects of one common endeavor; thus, experimental findings in one area are typically related to those in other areas, and this also takes space. Finally, Piaget is more prone than most psychologists to relate his findings to traditional philosophical issues, again adding pages to the text.

Symmetry

Piaget's writings seem to have a penchant for symmetry and neatness of classification. For example, he posits exactly eight major groupings of concrete operations, which, as in a factorial design, are further subclassified as to class versus relation, additive versus multiplicative, and in terms of a third dichotomy which is difficult to label in any simple way (1942a). Similarly, adolescents are said to make use of the sixteen binary operations of propositional logic and also possess eight operational schemas (Inhelder and Piaget, 1958). Stages of development in any given area are very apt to be either three or four in number, each with two substages. The table of functional invariants and categories of reason in the first book on infancy is likewise neat and symmetrical (1952c, p. 9). There are enough other examples of this sort to suggest that Piaget strives to attain as orderly and symmetrical a classification of phenomena as the data will tolerate; Anthony apparently has this tendency in mind in referring to Piaget's "classificatory zeal" (Anthony, 1957, p. 260).

Closely related to this aspect of Piaget's conceptual style is a tendency toward posing two antithetical positions, approaches, etc., and then showing how they can be resolved, Hegelian fashion, into a third—again a kind of symmetry. Thus, the psychological construction of number, at once cardinal and ordinal, results from a synthesis of a system of class inclusions (cardination) and a system of asymmetrical relations (ordination) (1952b). Analogously, the concept of a unit of measurement results from a synthesis of partition and displacement (Piaget, Inhelder, and Szeminska, 1960). A third reconciliation of differences is shown in Piaget's conception of intellectual adaptation as a coordination of two seemingly antithetical functions: assimilation and accommodation.

Logical-Analytical Approach

Two additional stylistic features, related to the above and to each other, are a propensity for what might be called a logical, analytical approach to the interpretation of experimental findings on the one hand, and on the other, a tendency to view data in the context of traditional philosophical issues. The first of these is rather hard to describe except by specific example. In general terms, what is meant here is a kind of faith or belief in the power of careful reasoning to decide among possible interpretations. It has something of the character of a Thomistic or

Socratic argument: the various possible interpretations are set out in series and all but one are rejected on the basis of logical argument. In the example cited earlier of the pairs of cognitive-biological positions on the adaptation problem (Lamarckism-associationism, vitalism-intellectualism, etc.), Piaget analyzes each pair of positions one by one and then proceeds to muster closely reasoned arguments against all but one of them. Although, of course, this kind of analysis ought to be and is essentially present in some form in psychological publications everywhere, it is likely to strike the reader as especially prominent and ubiquitous in Piaget's writings.

Data Viewed in Philosophical Context

Piaget has always regarded developmental data as having an important bearing on philosophical, especially epistemological, problems. His first venture into child study was motivated by epistemological interests, for instance. It is therefore not surprising that his writings show a continual moving back and forth between experimental findings and philosophical problems. Thus, discussion of the adaptation problem proceeds within the context of traditional positions on the relation between cognizer and world cognized (1952c). Similarly, Piaget is impelled to proceed from experimental studies of logico-arithmetic operations in children to consider the philosophical status of logico-arithmetic systems (e.g., 1957b). Do such systems, as the positivists would have it, simply constitute a kind of formal language or general syntax which is transmitted to each child by his culture? If so—and here the return to the empirical data—why do we see definite stages in its acquisition? This kind of rumination is very common in Piaget's writings. Again, he moves from developmental studies of number concepts to a formulation of the nature of numbers which is intended to compete with those of Russell and Poincaré (Piaget, 1952b). Finally, the creation of the Centre International d'Epistémologie Génétique was of course intended as a fillip to further liaison between developmental psychology and epistemology. It is an understatement to say that philosophical issues no longer tend to dominate the thinking of psychologists, although this was perhaps once true; the fact that they do permeate Piaget's thinking, and to a very great extent, vividly sets his system apart from others on the contemporary scene.

Relative Isolation from Other Work

A final distinguishing characteristic is a tendency to present his work in isolation from other related research and theory. This tendency is only a tendency, to be sure, and it would be erroneous to state it as an absolute. However, one is bound to be struck by the relative infrequency with which references to potentially related work appear in any randomly chosen Piaget volume. To a certain extent this may be justified by the originality, the offbeat character of his work; there simply may *be* only a few really relevant studies to cite in some instances. This is scarcely an explanation for many apparent omissions, however, and it is fair to conclude that a tendency to think, produce, and write in relative insulation from the mainstream does exist in Piaget. Again, however, the qualifier "relative" must be taken seriously.

These, then, are some of the more obvious "diagnostic signs" which, if found in combination, predict a Piaget volume at a high level of probability. Neither the identification of them nor the quasi-clinical manner in which the identification is couched should imply value judgments of any kind. They exist, and they help to convey the unique flavor of Piaget's system. They can of course be evaluated, as can the more substantive aspects of the system, but they should be evaluated soberly and on their own separate merits.

CHAPTER TWO

Basic Properties of Cognitive Functioning

IN CHAPTER 1 a distinction was made between the functional and
structural aspects of intelligence. It was said that most of Piaget's work
concerns the details of *structural* change, that is, the kind of intellectual
organizations encountered in the course of development and the relations
among these organizations.

However, Piaget has also described in considerable detail a general
conception about the nature of intellectual *functioning*. He has tried to
uncover the basic and irreducible properties of cognitive adaptation
which hold true at all developmental levels. These invariant and fundamental properties are to be found in the functional rather than structural aspects of intelligence; the functional characteristics form the
intellectual core—in Piaget's words, the *ipse intellectus*—which makes
possible the emergence of cognitive structures from organism-environment interactions (1952c, p. 2). Piaget's general conception of functioning
and related matters constitutes the subject matter of this chapter.

BIOLOGY AND INTELLIGENCE

Every theory of intelligence, Piaget argues, ought to begin with some
basic conception of its subject matter. What sort of thing is this intelligence we study? What relationship, if any, does it bear to other processes
not ordinarily called by that name? In Piaget's view these are related
questions. The search for the defining and fundamental characteristics
of intelligence must begin by a search for even more fundamental
processes from which intelligence derives and to which, in its essentials,
it remains similar. For Piaget, the key to *ipse intellectus* lies in a careful
examination of these "even more fundamental processes." What are they?

They are biological in nature. For Piaget, the one-time biologist,
intelligence can be meaningfully considered only as an extension of
certain fundamental biological characteristics, fundamental in the sense
that they obtain wherever life obtains. (It is indicative of Piaget's biological orientation toward matters intellectual that he sometimes refers

41

to cognitive development as "mental embryology," e.g., 1947, p. 143.) Intellectual functioning is a special form of biological activity and, as such, possesses important attributes in common with the parent activities from which it derives. In other words, intelligence bears a biological imprint, and this imprint defines its essential characteristics. But to say that intelligence is founded upon a biological substrate can imply two quite different things (1952c, pp. 1-3). Let us examine each of these in turn.

Specific Heredity

Intelligence is first of all allied to biology in the sense that inherited biological structures condition what we may directly perceive. For example, our nervous and sensory system is such that only certain wavelengths give rise to color sensations, and we are unable to perceive space in more than three dimensions. Our perceptions constitute only a selected segment within a totality of conceivable perceptions. There can be no doubt that these biological limitations influence the construction of our most fundamental concepts. In this sense, there is certainly an intimate relation between basic physiological and anatomical fundaments and intelligence.

However, this relation is not the most important kind of liaison between biology and cognition. As a matter of fact, it is characteristic of intelligence that it will eventually transcend the limitations imposed upon it by these structural properties, this *specific heredity,* as Piaget calls it (*ibid.,* p. 2). We come to be able to *cognize* wavelengths which we never *see.* We *hypothesize* spatial dimensions we can never *experience* directly. In short, the neurological and sensory structures which constitute our species-specific inheritance can be said to impede or facilitate intellectual functioning, but they can hardly be said to *account for* functioning itself. For this we must look to a second kind of connection between biology and intelligence.

General Heredity

This second kind of relation is more subtle and elusive than the first. Most simply, it is this. We inherit as biological *anlagen* not only structural limitations but also something else, which, as we have seen, permits these limitations to be overcome. That is, our biological endowment consists not only of inborn structures which can be thought of as obstacles to intellectual progress, but it also consists of that which makes intellectual progress possible at all, that something which lies behind intellectual achievement. Two questions immediately arise. First, what is the nature of this something? And second, what is its relation to biological processes at large?

The positive, constructive something which we inherit, Piaget argues, is a *mode of intellectual functioning*. We do not inherit cognitive structures as such; these come into being only in the course of development. What we do inherit is a *modus operandi*, a specific manner in which we transact business with the environment. There are two important general characteristics of this mode of functioning. First, it generates cognitive structures. Structures come into being in the course of intellectual functioning; it is through functioning, and only through functioning, that cognitive structures get formed. Second, and this is a most important point, the mode of functioning which Piaget says constitutes our biological heritage remains essentially constant throughout life. That is, the fundamental properties of intellectual functioning are always and everywhere the same, despite the wide varieties of cognitive structures which this functioning creates. It is because of this constancy of functioning in the face of changing structures that its fundamental properties, soon to be described, are referred to as *functional invariants*.

Let us review what has been said so far. The really important biological endowment, so far as intelligence is concerned, is a set of functional characteristics rather than a set of inborn structural limitations. These functional characteristics are at the very heart and soul of intelligence because they constitute unvarying common elements amid a panorama of structural changes and because it is precisely through functioning that the succession of structures get constituted. The sought-for *ipse intellectus* is to be found in intellectual functioning itself, nowhere else.

But it remains to be shown in what sense intellectual functioning can be considered a biological endowment. In order to do this, it is necessary to take a preliminary look at the fundamental characteristics of intellectual functioning, those defining attributes which were said to be invariant over the whole developmental span. There are two principal ones. The first is *organization;* the second is *adaptation* and comprises two intimately related but conceptually distinct subproperties: *assimilation* and *accommodation*. The nature of these functional invariants is the subject of the next section. The important thing which needs to be understood in advance of their definitions is this. *These invariant characteristics, which define the essence of intellectual functioning and hence the essence of intelligence, are also the very characteristics which hold for biological functioning in general.* All living matter adapts to its environment and possesses organizational properties which make the adaptation possible. Intellectual functioning is only a special case, a special extension of biological functioning at large; and its fundamental and invariant properties are the same as those found in biological activity. This is the second and more important sense in which it could be said that a biological substrate underlies intelligence. In addition to a *specific heredity* of inborn and limiting anatomical *structures,* we have a *general heredity,* of a functional kind, upon which all positive cognitive acquisitions are built *(ibid.,* p. 2). By virtue of the fact that we are living organisms, we begin life with certain irreducible properties held in common by all organisms, and these fundaments are a set of peculiarly functional characteristics. It is these characteristics which supply the continuity between biology in general and intelligence in particular. And it is these which, despite their lowly origins, make possible the most sublime of intellectual accomplishments. Piaget sums it up in this way:

> Now, this second type of hereditary psychological reality is of primary importance for the development of intelligence. If there truly in fact exists a functional nucleus of the intellectual organization which comes from biological organization in its most general aspect, it is apparent that this invariant will orient the whole of the successive structures which the mind will then work out in its contact with reality. It will thus play the role that philosophers assigned to the *a priori;* that is to say, it will impose on the structures certain necessary and irreducible conditions *(ibid.,* pp. 2-3).

And again the continuity with biological functioning:

> In fact there exist, in mental development, elements which are variable and others which are invariant. . . . Just as the main functions of the living being are identical in all organisms but correspond to organs which are very different in different groups, so also between the child and the adult a continuous creation of varied structures may be observed although the main functions of thought remain constant *(ibid.,* p. 4).

THE FUNCTIONAL INVARIANTS

Of the two basic invariants of functioning, *organization* and *adaptation,* the latter is subdivided into two interrelated components, *assimilation* and *accommodation.* These invariants provide the crucial link between biology and intelligence because they hold equally for both. This isomorphism permits us to see intelligence in its proper context, as an interesting and highly developed extension of more primitive activities whose most general characteristics—the functional invariants—it shares. Let us then begin our analysis of the functional invariants by first seeing how they characterize an elementary biological process; their application to intelligence will follow later. There are two advantages to doing this. First, basic physiological events are more palpable for most of us than psychological processes are, and a preliminary understanding of these concepts may be facilitated if they are first demonstrated in their biological context. Indeed, Piaget himself introduces them in this way *(ibid.,* pp. 5-6). Second, the isomorphism between biology and intelligence as regards these invariants needs to be documented, not simply asserted. An illustrative biological example would help to serve that need.

A Biological Example

A very fundamental—probably the most fundamental—function of living matter is that of incorporating into its structure nutrition-providing elements from the outside. The organism sustains itself and grows by means of such transactions with its milieu. The invariant attributes of this kind of functioning are the following.

First of all, the process is one of *adaptation* to the environment. Adaptation is said to occur whenever a given organism-environment interchange has the effect of modifying the organism in such a way that further interchanges, favorable to its preservation, are enhanced (*ibid.,* p. 5). Not everything that an organism does is adaptive in this sense, of course, but the incorporation of nutritive substances ordinarily is. Now this particular form of adaptation (and all adaptations generally) involves two conceptually distinguishable components.

First, the organism must and will transform the substances it takes in in order to incorporate their food values into its system. An initial transformation occurs when the substance is ingested by chewing. Thus, hard and sharply contoured objects become pulpy and formless. Still more drastic changes occur as the substance is slowly digested, and eventually it will lose its original identity entirely by becoming part of the structure of the organism. The process of changing elements in the milieu in such a way that they can become incorporated into the structure of the organism is called *assimilation,* i.e., the elements are assimilated to the system. The manner in which the incorporation is carried out and the structures into which elements are incorporated are extremely variable. But the process itself, *qua* process, always obtains whenever and wherever adaptation takes place. In this sense Piaget speaks of assimilation as a functional invariant.

In the process of assimilating foodstuffs to itself, the organism is also doing something else. It is also adjusting itself to them. This it does in a variety of ways and at all stages in the adaptation process. The mouth (or whatever corresponds to it in a given species) must open or the substance cannot enter the system at all. The object must be chewed if its structure demands chewing. And finally, the digestive processes must adapt themselves to the object's specific chemical and physical properties or no digestion can take place. Just as objects must be adjusted to the peculiar structure of the organism in any adaptational process, so also must the organism adjust itself to the idiosyncratic demands of the object. The first aspect of adaptation has been called *assimilation.* The second aspect, the adjustment to the object, Piaget labels *accommodation* —i.e., the organism must accommodate its functioning to the specific contours of the object it is trying to assimilate. As was the case for assimilation, the details of the accommodatory process are highly variable. What is invariant is its existence, as a process, in all adaptation.

Although assimilation and accommodation are distinguished conceptually, they are obviously indissociable in the concrete reality of any adaptationa'. act. As will become clear when intellectual adaptation is discussed, .very assimilation of an object to the organism simultaneously involves an accommodation of the organism to the object; conversely, every ϲ ϲommodation is at the same time an assimilatory modification of the object accommodated to. Taken together, they make up the constant attributes of even the most elementary adaptational act.

Adaptation, through its twin components assimilation and accommodation, expresses the dynamic, outer aspect of biological functioning. But an adaptive act always presupposes an underlying *organization,* and this is the second major functional invariant *(ibid.,* p. 5). Actions are coordinated affairs, governed by laws of totality—this is Piaget's now familiar holism again. The assimilation of foodstuffs to the organism and the simultaneous accommodation of the organism to these nutritive substances are organized activities carried out by an organized being. Adaptive, directed behavior cannot proceed from a chaotic and completely undifferentiated source. There are subordinating structures and subordinated structures, and so on. Once again, the specific nature of the organization which lies behind an adaptive act will vary, but organization of some kind there must be.

It is Piaget's position, as we have said, that intellectual functioning can be characterized in terms of the same invariants that hold for more elementary biological processes.[1] Let us begin with *organization.*

Cognitive Organization

Cognition, like digestion, is an organized affair. Every act of intelligence presumes some kind of intellectual structure, some sort of organization, within which it proceeds. The apprehension of reality always involves multiple interrelationships among cognitive actions and among the concepts and meanings which these actions express.

As to the nature of this organization, its specific characteristics, like those of biological organizations, differ markedly from stage to stage in

[1] Our treatment of the functional invariants of cognition will contain some deliberate (although minor) deviations from Piaget's own presentation for the sake of clarity and consistency. Piaget initially uses the expressions *regulative function, implicative function,* and *explicative function* when referring to the intellectual counterparts of the biological invariants organization, assimilation, and accommodation, respectively *(ibid.,* p. 9). However, since the former terms tend to drop out of usage in his subsequent discussions of intellectual functioning, it seems superfluous to define and discuss them here. We also refrain from systematic presentation of the *categories of reason (ibid.,* p. 9) under the same rationale.

development. Though structural change is what Piaget studies, there are stage-independent properties which the very fact of organization always implies. All intellectual organizations can be conceived of as *totalities,* systems of *relationships* among elements, to use Piaget's terms (*ibid.,* p. 10). An act of intelligence, be it a crude motor movement in infancy or a complex and abstract judgment in adulthood, is always related to a system or totality of such acts of which it is a part.

The relation of part to whole need not be simply static and configurational, as the proverbial trees are to the forest. Acts are also organized directionally in terms of means to ends, or *values* to *ideals* in Piaget's phraseology (*ibid.,* pp. 10-11). Moreover, the finalism which may characterize individual sets of actions—an infant bangs his rattle (means) in order to hear a noise (end)—also holds, in the large, for cognitive development itself. As will be shown in Chapter 7, the ontogenetic development of structures can be thought of as a process of successive approximations to a kind of ideal equilibrium, an end state never completely achieved. Development itself, then, constitutes a totality with a goal or ideal subordinating means.

Cognitive Adaptation: Assimilation and Accommodation

Intellectual functioning, in its dynamic aspect, is also characterized by the invariant processes of *assimilation* and *accommodation*. An act of intelligence in which assimilation and accommodation are in balance or equilibrium constitutes an intellectual *adaptation.*[2] Adaptation and organization are two sides of the same coin, since adaptation presupposes an underlying coherence, on the one hand, and organizations are created through adaptations, on the other. In Piaget's words:

> . . . Organization is inseparable from adaptation: They are two complementary processes of a single mechanism, the first being the internal aspect of the cycle of which adaptation constitutes the external aspect. . . . The "accord of thought with things" and the "accord of thought with itself"

[2] This restriction of the meaning of the term is likely to puzzle the reader, since adaptation is supposed to be an invariant of all intellectual functioning. Although the matter will become clearer in the course of subsequent reading in this chapter, a few things may be said at this point. Organization, assimilation, and accommodation are truly invariant; every instance of cognitive functioning presupposes these three characteristics. However, the *relationships between* assimilation and accommodation are quite variable, both across development and within any developmental period. In the most narrow meaning Piaget ever gives it, adaptation refers to those organism-environment exchanges in which assimilation and accommodation are in equilibrium, neither one predominating (1951a, 1952c). This implies that some intelligent actions are more truly adaptations than others. Except when specific arguments are made which hinge on these distinctions, e.g., Piaget's analysis of imitation and play (1951a), the term tends to become denotatively broader than this and even appears to be synonymous with intellectual functioning itself at times. Taken in its broadest meaning, then, adaptation is certainly a functional invariant.

express this dual functional invariant of adaptation and organization. These two aspects of thought are indissociable: It is by adapting to things that thought organizes itself and it is by organizing itself that it structures things (1952c, pp. 7-8).

What is the nature of cognitive as opposed to physiological assimilation and accommodation? Assimilation here refers to the fact that every cognitive encounter with an environmental object necessarily involves some kind of cognitive structuring (or restructuring) of that object in accord with the nature of the organism's existing intellectual organization. As Piaget says: "Assimilation is hence the very functioning of the system of which organization is the structural aspect" (*ibid.*, p. 410). Every act of intelligence, however rudimentary and concrete, presupposes an interpretation of something in external reality, that is, an assimilation of that something to some kind of meaning system in the subject's cognitive organization. To use a happy phrase of Kelly's (1955), to adapt intellectually to reality is to *construe* that reality, and to construe it in terms of some enduring *construct* within oneself. Piaget's epistemological position is essentially the same on this point, requiring only the substitution of *assimilate* for *construe* and *structure* or *organization* for *construct*. And it is Piaget's argument that intellectual assimilation is not different in principle from a more primary biological assimilation: in both cases the essential process is that of bending a reality event to the templet of one's ongoing structure.

If intellectual adaptation is always and essentially an assimilatory act, it is no less an accommodatory one. In even the most elemental cognition there has to be some coming to grips with the special properties of the thing apprehended. Reality can never be infinitely malleable, even for the most autistic of cognizers, and certainly no intellectual development can occur unless the organism in some sense adjusts his intellectual receptors to the shapes reality presents him. The essence of accommodation is precisely this process of adapting oneself to the variegated requirements or demands which the world of objects imposes upon one. And once again, Piaget underscores the essential continuity between biological accommodation, on the one hand, and cognitive accommodation, on the other: a receptive and accommodating mouth and digestive system are not really different in principle from a receptive and accommodating cognitive system.

However necessary it may be to describe assimilation and accommodation separately and sequentially, they should be thought of as simultaneous and indissociable as they operate in a living cognition. Adaptation is a unitary event, and assimilation and accommodation are merely abstractions from this unitary reality. As in the case of food ingestion, the cognitive incorporation of reality always implies both an assimilation *to* structure and an accommodation *of* structure. To assimilate an event it is necessary at the same time to accommodate to it and vice versa. As subsequent pages will make clear, the balance between the two invariants can and does vary, both from stage to stage and within a given stage. Some cognitive acts show a relative preponderance of the assimilative component; others seem heavily weighted towards accommodation. However, "pure" assimilation and "pure" accommodation nowhere obtain in cognitive life; intellectual acts always presuppose each in some measure:

> . . . From the beginning assimilation and accommodation are indissociable from each other. Accommodation of mental structures to reality implies the existence of assimilatory schemata[3] apart from which any structure would be impossible. Inversely, the formation of schemata through assimilation entails the utilization of external realities to which the former must accommodate, however crudely . . . (1954a, pp. 352-353).

> Assimilation can never be pure because by incorporating new elements into its earlier schemata the intelligence constantly modifies the latter in order to adjust them to new elements. Conversely, things are never known by themselves, since this work of accommodation is only possible as a function of the inverse process of assimilation (1952c, pp. 6-7).

Having endowed the organism with these twin mechanisms of intellectual adaptation, two problems remain. First, how does the action of assimilation and accommodation permit the organism to make cognitive progress as opposed to remaining fixated at the level of familiar and habitual cognitions? That is, how is the organism able to do something other than repeat past accommodations and assimilate the results of these accommodations to the same old system of meanings? Secondly, assuming that cognitive progress or cognitive development can somehow result from assimilatory and accommodatory operations, what prevents it from occurring all at once and of a piece? That is, why is intellectual development the slow and gradual process we know it to be? To indulge in metaphor, we need to know both what makes the cognitive engine progress at all and what limits its velocity and acceleration, assuming the possibility of movement.

Cognitive progress, in Piaget's system, is possible for several reasons. First of all, accommodatory acts are continually being extended to new and different features of the surround. To the extent that a newly accommodated-to feature can fit somewhere in the existing meaning structure, it will be assimilated to that structure. Once assimilated, however, it tends to change the structure in some degree and, through this change, make possible further accommodatory extensions. Also, as discussion of schemas will show, assimilatory structures are not static and unchanging, even in the absence of environmental stimulation. Systems of meanings

---

[3] The plural of *schème* is sometimes rendered *schemas* and sometimes *schemata* in translations of Piaget's works; usage varies. We use *schemas* in this book except when quotations (such as the above) demand *schemata*. The meaning and significance of the schema concept itself is taken up in the next section of this chapter.

are constantly becoming reorganized internally and integrated with other systems. This continuous process of internal renovation is itself, in Piaget's system, a very potent source of cognitive progress (1952c, p. 414). Thus, both kinds of changes—reorganizations of purely endogenous origin and reorganizations induced more or less directly by new accommodatory attempts—make possible a progressive intellectual penetration into the nature of things. Once again the twin invariants innervate each other in reciprocal fashion: changes in assimilatory structure direct new accommodations, and new accommodatory attempts stimulate structural reorganizations.

If cognitive progress is insured under this interpretation of the invariants, it is certainly well established empirically that this progress is typically slow and gradual. It is not immediately clear why this should be so. What prevents the organism from mastering, in one fell swoop, all that is cognizable in a given terrain? The answer is that the organism can assimilate only those things which past assimilations have prepared it to assimilate. There must already be a system of meanings, an existing organization, sufficiently advanced that it can be modified to admit the candidates for assimilation which accommodation places before it. There can never be a radical rupture between the new and the old; events whose interpretation requires a complete extension or reorganization of the existing structure simply cannot be accommodated to and thence assimilated. As Piaget states (1954a, pp. 352-354), assimilation is by its very nature conservative, in the sense that its primary function is to make the unfamiliar familiar, to reduce the new to the old. A new assimilatory structure must always be some variate of the last one acquired, and it is this which insures both the gradualness and continuity of intellectual development.

In summary, the functional characteristics of the assimilatory and accommodatory mechanisms are such that the possibility of cognitive change is insured, but the magnitude of any given change is always limited. The organism adapts repeatedly, and each adaptation necessarily paves the way for its successor. Structures are not infinitely modifiable, however, and not everything which is potentially assimilable can in fact be assimilated by organism A at point X in his development. On the contrary, the subject can incorporate only those components of reality which its ongoing structure can assimilate without drastic change.

A Concrete Example

Piaget's concepts tend to become more meaningful when examined in behavioral context. Let us consider a sample of cognitive activity and see how it would be described in the terms we have been discussing. An infant comes in contact for the first time with a ring suspended from a string. He makes a series of exploratory accommodations: he looks at it, touches it, causes it to swing back and forth, grasps it, and so on. These accommodatory acts of course do not take place *in vacuo;* through past interactions with various other objects the child already possesses assimilatory structures (schemas) which set in motion and direct those accommodations. Piaget would say here that the ring is assimilated to concepts of touching, moving, seeing, etc., concepts which are already part of the child's cognitive organization. The child's actions with respect to the ring are at once accommodations of these concepts or structures to the reality contours of the ring and assimilations of this new object to these concepts.

But the infant does more than simply repeat behaviors acquired earlier. The structures which are defined by grasping, seeing, touching, etc. are themselves modified in a number of ways as they accommodate themselves to the ring and assimilate it. The varieties of structural modification constitute the subject of the following section on the schema concept, but we may anticipate two of them here. First, the structures are *generalized* to assimilate the new object. In ordinary language, the child learns that rings *too* may be sucked, pulled at, visually scanned, etc.; his cognitive structures are modified in the sense of being extended to fit one more object. Second, they are changed in so far as the structure of the new object necessitates some *variation* in the way one sucks it, pulls at it, scans it, etc. In other words, cognitive structures are not only *generalized* to the new object but are also *differentiated* as a consequence of its idiosyncratic structural demands. Thus, the child learns that one sucks ringlike objects a little differently from other objects sucked in the past, and that ringlike objects look and feel somewhat different from objects seen and touched in the past. The important consequence of the structural changes wrought by this generalization and differentiation is, of course, the fact that this change makes possible new and different accommodations to future objects encountered. These new accommodations engender further changes in intellectual organization, and so the cycle repeats itself.

The example of the child and the ring can also serve to illustrate the limitations to which structural change is subject in a single organism-reality transaction. In the first place, there are a number of potentially cognizable features of the ring which we may be sure the infant will not accommodate to and will not assimilate. There is nothing in the infant's present structural repertoire which will permit him to accommodate to the ring as an exemplar of the abstract class of circles, for example. Similarly, he cannot apprehend the ring as an object which can be rolled like a hoop, as an object which can be worn as a bracelet, and so forth. In Piaget's terms, the organism cannot accommodate itself to those object potentialities which it is unable to assimilate to something in its present system of meanings. The hiatus between the new and the old cannot be too great. This fact, that new structures must arise almost imperceptibly from the foundations provided by present ones, is what always insures the gradualness of cognitive development.

THE CONCEPT OF SCHEMA

We have said that assimilatory and accommodatory functioning always presupposes some sort of quasi-enduring organization or structural system within the organism. Objects are always assimilated *to* something. Although the differing properties of cognitive structures at various ontogenetic levels constitute the subject matter of subsequent chapters, the over-all character—the stage-free properties—of structures in general can be discussed here. Piaget makes extensive use of a cerain structural concept which, although more specific than the noncommittal term *structure* itself, is nonetheless transdevelopmental, not bound to any particular stage. The concept in question is the one Piaget would invariably insert in sentences of the following type: "The infant assimilated the nipple to the _____ of sucking." In Piaget's system the missing term could only be *schema*.

Basic Properties

The notion of *schema* needs careful examination in any explication of Piaget's system. First, it occupies a very prominent place in Piaget's account of cognitive development, especially cognitive development in infancy.[4] Second, a thorough explanation of what schemas are and how they function sheds further light on the functional invariants of organization and adaptation to which they are so closely related in the theory.

What is a schema? As we have seen to be the case for other theoretical concepts, Piaget does not give a careful and exhaustive definition of the term in any single place; rather, its full meaning is developed in successive fragments of definition spanning several volumes (1951a, 1952c, 1954a, 1958a). It is, despite its vagueness, a rich and subtle notion, full of shifting nuances and most thoroughly bound up with Piaget's whole conception of cognitive development. A preliminary and somewhat inadequate rendering may be the following. A *schema* is a cognitive struc-

---

[4] Although the concept of schema is definitely stage-free and is invoked by Piaget at all age levels, it is used most frequently and elaborated most extensively in connection with the sensory-motor period of infancy, probably because Piaget has available more specific and delimited structural concepts (*groupings*, etc.) to describe postinfancy developments. Nonetheless, schemas of one kind or another do continue to be introduced in connection with these later periods, often in textual contiguity with the more specific structural concepts. The most important of these postinfancy schemas, perhaps, are the *operational schemas* of adolescence (Inhelder and Piaget, 1958).

ture which has reference to a class of similar action sequences, these sequences of necessity being strong, bounded totalities in which the constituent behavioral elements are tightly interrelated. In actuality, it is easier to get at least a global image of what schemas are and how they operate than this rather forbidding definition might suggest. A word of caution, however. Just as the concepts of organization, assimilation and accommodation become enriched when schema is explained, so also will a really adequate grasp of the latter probably have to await a detailed description of infantile development, the period in which schemas figure so prominently.

The first and most obvious thing to be said about schemas is that they are labeled by the behavior sequences to which they refer. Thus, in discussing sensory-motor development, Piaget speaks of the *schema of sucking*, the *schema of prehension*, the *schema of sight*, and so on (1952c). Similarly, there is in middle childhood a *schema of intuitive qualitative correspondence* which refers to a strategy by which the child tries to assess whether or not two sets of elements are numerically equivalent (1952b, p. 88). And, as mentioned in footnote 4, adolescents possess a number of *operational schemas* also defined, ultimately, in terms of observable behavior in the face of certain tasks.

But if schemas are named by their referent action sequences, it is not completely accurate to say that they *are* these sequences and nothing more. To be sure, Piaget would certainly say that an infant who performs an organized sequence of grasping behaviors is in fact applying a grasping schema to reality, and that the behavior itself does constitute the schema (1952c, pp. 405-407; 1957c, pp. 46, 74). However, and the point is a rather subtle one, to say that a grasping sequence forms a schema is to imply more than the simple fact that the infant shows organized grasping behavior. It implies that assimilatory functioning has generated a specific cognitive *structure,* an organized *disposition* to grasp objects on repeated occasions. It implies that there has been a change in over-all cognitive organization such that a new behavioral totality has become part of the child's intellectual repertoire. Finally, it implies that a psychological "organ" has been created, *functionally* (but not, of course, *structurally*) equivalent to a physiological digestive organ in that it constitutes an instrument for incorporating reality "aliments" (1952c, pp. 13, 359). In brief, a schema is the organized overt behavior content which names it, but with important structural connotations not indigenous to the concrete content itself.[5]

There are certain characteristics that a behavior sequence must pos-

[5] The cognitive-structure connotations of the concept of schema become more apparent in the postinfancy periods. There, where so much of intelligent behavior is internalized and symbolic, Piaget's use of the term more unequivocally implies a plan of action, a strategy, or literally, a *scheme*. Note, for example, the *schema of intuitive qualitative correspondence* alluded to above.

sess in order to be conceptualized in schematic terms. To be sure, it is clear that schemas subsume behavior sequences of widely differing magnitude and complexity: compare the brief and simple sucking sequence of the neonate with the complex problem-solving strategies of a bright adult. Schemas come in all sizes and shapes. However, they all possess one general characteristic in common: the constituent behavior sequence is an organized totality. Thus, an action sequence, if it is to constitute a schema, must have a certain cohesiveness and must maintain its identity as a quasi-stable, repeatable unit. It must possess component actions which are tightly interconnected and governed by a core meaning. However elementary the schema, it is a schema precisely by virtue of the fact that the behavior components which it sets into motion form a strong whole, a recurrent and identifiable figure against a background of less tightly organized behaviors. Piaget states:

> As far as "totality" is concerned, we have already emphasized that every schema of assimilation constitutes a true totality, that is to say, an ensemble of sensorimotor elements mutually dependent or unable to function without each other. It is due to the fact that schemata present this kind of structure that mental assimilation is possible and any object whatever can be incorporated or serve as aliment to a given schema (1952c, p. 244).

One sees this "ensemble of sensorimotor elements mutually dependent or unable to function without each other" in any behavior series governed by a schema. For example, an elementary schema of prehension or grasping consists of interconnected reaching, finger-curling, and retracting subsequences which together make up an identifiable and repeatable unit. At certain phases of infant development, this particular schema, as a unit, tends to run itself off whenever an object is placed near the child. In Piaget's terms, all reachable objects become "aliments" which nourish this schema.

Another characteristic of schemas is hinted at by the phrase "class of similar action sequences" in our initial definition. A schema is a kind of concept, category, or underlying strategy which subsumes a whole collection of distinct but similar action sequences. For example, it is clear that no two grasping sequences are ever going to be exactly alike; a grasping schema—a "concept" of grasping—is nonetheless said to be operative when any such sequence is seen to emerge. Schemas therefore refer to *classes* of total acts, acts which are distinct from one another and yet share common features. Although the terms *schema* and *concept* are not completely interchangeable, Piaget has recognized a certain similarity between them: "The schema, as it appeared to us, constitutes a sort of sensorimotor concept, or more broadly, the motor equivalent of a system of relations and classes" (*ibid.,* p. 385).

The earlier discussion of functional invariants suggests two more important general properties of schemas. A schema, being a cognitive structure, is a more or less fluid form or plastic organization to which actions and objects are assimilated during cognitive functioning. As Piaget expresses it, schemas are "mobile frames" successively applied to various contents (*ibid.*, pp. 385-386). The fact that schemas accommodate to things (adapt and change their structure to fit reality) while assimilating them attests to their dynamic, supple quality. In short, they are the very antithesis of congealed molds into which reality is poured.

Again schemas, being structures, are both created and modified by intellectual functioning. They may be envisaged as the structural precipitates of a recurrent assimilatory activity. Not all the connotations of the term *precipitate* hold, however; schemas, unlike chemical precipitates, are far from being static and inert residues. The fact that schemas are created by functioning and are highly mobile and plastic is repeatedly stressed by Piaget:

> From the psychological point of view, the assimilatory activity . . . is consequently the primary fact. Now this activity, precisely to the extent that it leads to repetition, engenders an elementary schema . . . (*ibid.*, p. 389).

> In effect, the schemata have always seemed to us to be not autonomous entities but the products of a continuous activity which is immanent in them and of which they constitute the sequential moments of crystallization (*ibid.*, p. 388).

Operation and Development of Schemas

We have so far described schemas from a more or less static, attributive standpoint: what schemas are and what characteristics describe them. It remains to describe them in their dynamic aspect: how they function and change with development, how they relate to one another, and so forth.

One of the most important single characteristics of an assimilatory schema is its tendency toward repeated application. In fact, only behavior patterns which recur again and again in the course of cognitive functioning are conceptualized in terms of schemas. It is fundamental to Piaget's conception of development that organized behavior totalities are in evidence from birth onward (organization is a functional invariant, as we have seen) and that these totalities are set into motion again and again. Piaget speaks of *reproductive* or *functional assimilation* in referring to this ubiquitous tendency towards repetition (1951a, 1952c, 1954a). This concept of reproductive assimilation—the almost repetition-compulsion character of assimilation—will be shown to have important bearing on Piaget's conception of intellectual motivation (later in this chapter) and on a construct called the *circular reaction* (in Chapter 3). For the moment, suffice it to say it is indigenous to schemas that, once constituted, they apply themselves again and again to assimilable aspects of the environment.

In the course of this repeated exercise, individual schemas are of course transformed in several important ways (1952c, pp. 33-36); functioning not only creates structures but, as we have seen, changes them continually. First of all, schemas are forever extending their field of application so as to assimilate new and different objects. Piaget speaks of *generalizing assimilation* to indicate this important characteristic of assimilatory activity. In discussing reflex schemas in early infancy, he states:

> This need for repetition is only one aspect of a more general process which we can qualify as assimilation. The tendency of the reflex being to reproduce itself, it incorporates into itself every object capable of fulfilling the function of excitant. Two distinct phenomena must be mentioned here. . . . The first is what we may call "generalizing assimilation," that is to say, the incorporation of increasingly varied objects into the reflex schema. . . . Thus, according to chance contacts, the child, from the first two weeks of life, sucks his fingers, the fingers extended to him, his pillow, quilt, bed clothes, etc.; consequently he assimilates these objects to the activity of the reflex. . . . the newborn child at once incorporates into the global schema of sucking a number of increasingly varied objects, whence the generalizing aspect of this process of assimilation (*ibid.*, pp. 33-34).

Discrimination is the complement of generalization, as students of learning have long known, and the second important kind of change which schemas are said to undergo is that of internal differentiation. In a rudimentary way, the infant gradually discriminates objects which are to be sucked from those which are not to be sucked, or, at least, not to be sucked when one is very hungry. An elementary "recognition" of certain objects is the consequence of this differentiation within an initially undifferentiated schema, and Piaget speaks here of *recognitory assimilation:*

> This search and this selectivity seem to us to imply the beginning of differentiation in the global schema of sucking, and consequently a beginning of recognition, a completely practical and motor recognition, needless to say, but sufficient to be called recognitory assimilation (*ibid.*, p. 36).

> More precisely, repetition of the reflex leads to a general and generalizing assimilation of objects to its activity, but, due to the varieties which gradually enter this activity (sucking for its own sake, to stave off hunger, to eat, etc.), the schema of assimilation becomes differentiated and, in the most important differentiated cases, assimilation becomes recognitory (*ibid.*, p. 37).

Thus we see the three basic functional and developmental characteristics of all assimilatory schemas: repetition, generalization, and differentiation-recognition. These three are naturally contemporaneous in the stream of intellectual functioning, as Piaget points out. The following summary, although stated in connection with neonatal reflex schemas, holds true for the operation of schemas at any developmental level:

> In conclusion, assimilation . . . appears in three forms: cumulative repetition, generalization of the activity with incorporation of new objects to it, and finally, motor recognition. But in the last analysis, these three

forms are but one: The reflex must be conceived as an organized totality whose nature it is to preserve itself by functioning and consequently to function sooner or later for its own sake (repetition) while incorporating into itself objects propitious to this functioning (generalized assimilation) and discerning situations necessary to certain special modes of its activity (motor recognition) (*ibid.*, pp. 37-38).

We have so far seen how cognitive development proceeds through the vicissitudes of a single schema. Repetition consolidates and stabilizes it, as well as providing the necessary condition for change. Generalization enlarges it by extending its domain of application. And differentiation has the consequence of dividing the originally global schema into several new schemas, each with a sharper, more discriminating focus on reality. But it is characteristic of schemas not only to undergo individual changes of this kind but also to form ever more complex and interlocking relationships with other schemas. Two schemas may undergo separate developments up to a point, e.g., generalization to new objects, differentiation, etc., and then unite to form a single, supraordinate schema. The principal uniting relationship between two hitherto separate schemas is called *reciprocal assimilation,* that is, each schema assimilates the other:

> Organization exists within each schema of assimilation since . . . each one constitutes a real whole, bestowing on each element a meaning relating to this totality. But there is above all total organization; that is to say, coordination among the various schemata of assimilation. Now, as we have seen, this coordination is not formed differently from the single schemata, except only that each one comprises the other, in a reciprocal assimilation. . . . In short, the conjunction of two cycles or of two schemata is to be conceived as a new totality, self-enclosed (*ibid.*, pp. 142-143).

A concrete illustration of the coalescence of originally separate and independent structures can be seen in Piaget's account of the development of visual schemas:

> Thus it may be said that, independently of any coordination between vision and other schemata (prehension, touch, etc.), the visual schemata are organized among themselves and constitute more or less well-coordinated totalities. But the essential thing for this immediate question is the coordination of the visual schemata, no longer among themselves, but with the other schemata. Observation shows that very early, perhaps from the very beginnings of orientation in looking, coordinations exist between vision and hearing. . . . Subsequently the relationships between vision and sucking appear . . . then between vision and prehension, touch, kinesthetic impressions, etc. These intersensorial coordinations, this organization of heterogeneous schemata will give the visual images increasingly rich meanings and make visual assimilation no longer an end in itself but an instrument at the service of vaster assimilations. When the child seven or eight months old looks at unknown objects for the first time before swinging, rubbing, throwing and catching them, etc., he no longer tries to look for the sake of looking (pure visual assimilation in which the object is a simple aliment for looking), nor even for the sake of seeing (generalizing or recognitory

visual assimilation in which the object is incorporated without adding anything to the already elaborated visual schemata), but he looks in order to act, that is to say, in order to assimilate the new object to the schemata of weighing, friction, falling, etc. There is therefore no longer only organization inside the visual schemata but between those and all the others. It is this progressive organization which endows the visual images with their meanings and solidifies them in inserting them in a total universe (*ibid.*, pp. 75-76).

ASSIMILATION-ACCOMMODATION RELATIONSHIPS

Assimilation and accommodation constitute the most fundamental ingredients of intellectual functioning. Both functions are present in every intellectual act, of whatever type and developmental level. However, while their co-occurrence may be said to be strictly invariant, this is not the case for the relationship between them. On the contrary, it will be shown that this relationship changes drastically, both within and between developmental stages. Because the functional invariants themselves make up the core of intelligence in Piaget's system, alterations in the relationship between them must necessarily have important consequences for the kind of intellectual functioning which takes place. For this reason an analysis of the vicissitudes of this relationship is as necessary to an account of Piaget's theory as was the basic description of the invariants themselves.

The first evolution of this kind occurs during the period of sensory-motor development in infancy and carries with it momentous changes in the relationship between cognizer and cognized. The basic characteristics of this evolution are then repeated again, in vertical décalage (see Chapter 1), in the course of subsequent, postinfantile ontogenesis—and again with similar alterations in the organism-environment relationship. Finally, beginning early in the sensory-motor period but becoming increasingly important just subsequent to it, one sees changes of an essentially nondevelopmental kind, that is, momentary, short-lived variations in the assimilation-accommodation relationship within a given stage.

Developmental Changes in Infancy: The Basic Paradigm

The fundamental transformation in the assimilation-accommodation relationship which occurs during the first two years of life can be broadly stated as follows: development proceeds from an initial state of profound egocentrism, in which assimilation and accommodation are undifferentiated from each other and yet mutually antagonistic or opposed in their functioning, to a final state of objectivity and equilibrium in which the two functions are relatively separate and distinct, on the one hand, and coordinated and complementary, on the other (1954a, Conclusion). Let us now examine the constituent terms of this "law of evolution," as Piaget refers to it (*ibid.*, p. 352).

The young infant begins life with certain elementary schemas which, in accord with the schema development we have already described, soon begin to stabilize, differentiate, and generalize through repeated applications to the surround (1952c). For example, the newborn tends to assimilate objects placed in his mouth to a slowly forming sucking schema, making the necessary crude accommodatory adjustments to object structure as he does so. Now, according to Piaget, it is characteristic of this early period that assimilation and accommodation are both undifferentiated one from the other and yet—paradoxically—antagonistic or opposed to each other in their action (1952c, pp. 19, 364; 1954a, pp. 350-354).

Early assimilation and accommodation are undifferentiated in that an object and the activity to which the object is assimilated constitute for the young infant a single, indivisible experience. Thus, the act of assimilating an object to a schema (the sensory-motor equivalent of making sense out of the object) is hopelessly confused with and undifferentiated from the accommodatory adjustments intrinsic to this act. It is not that the infant fails to take account of objects, i.e., accommodate his movements to their specific contours. This he does, and these clumsy accommodations produce changes in the assimilatory schemas. Rather, the infant has no way of distinguishing his acts from the reality events which these acts produce or the reality objects upon which they bear. In short, agent and object, ego and outside world are inextricably linked together in every infantile action, and the distinction between assimilation of objects to the self and accommodation of the self to objects simply does not exist. Piaget describes this pervasive undifferentiation as follows:

> In its beginnings, assimilation is essentially the utilization of the external environment by the subject to nourish his hereditary or acquired schemata. It goes without saying that schemata such as those of sucking, sight, prehension, etc., constantly need to be accommodated to things, and that the necessities of this accommodation often thwart the assimilatory effort. But this accommodation remains so undifferentiated from the assimilatory processes that it does not give rise to any special active behavior pattern but merely consists in an adjustment of the pattern to the details of the things assimilated. Hence it is natural that at this developmental level the external world does not seem formed by permanent objects, that neither space nor time is yet organized in groups and objective series, and that causality is not spatialized or located in things. In other words, at first the universe consists in mobile and plastic perceptual images centered about personal activity. But it is self-evident that to the extent that this activity is undifferentiated from the things it constantly assimilates to itself it remains unaware of its own subjectivity; the external world therefore begins by being confused with the sensations of a self unaware of itself, before the two factors become detached from one another and are organized correlatively (1954a, p. 351).

The opposition between assimilation and accommodation stems from this very undifferentiatedness. Since the infant cannot distinguish his actions from their environmental consequences, the necessity to make new and difficult accommodations in order to assimilate novel objects to already established schemas can only be experienced as frustrating. There is a fundamental antagonism, in this developmental period, between assimilation to the familiar, which is essentially "conservative," and accommodation to the novel, which is inherently "progressive." It is in the nature of assimilatory schemas, as we have seen, to apply and reapply themselves to any reality "aliments" which have the capacity to nourish and sustain them. A new, exploratory accommodation, instead of constituting a welcome foray into the unknown which will result in a differentiation of existing schemas, is at first experienced simply as a troublesome obstacle to habitual assimilation and is performed, as it were, only under duress:

> In their initial directions, assimilation and accommodation are obviously opposed to one another, since assimilation is conservative and tends to subordinate the environment to the organism as it is, whereas accommodation is the source of changes and bends the organism to the successive constraints of the environment (*ibid.*, p. 352).

This initial state of undifferentiation and antagonism between the functional invariants essentially defines what is perhaps the most widely known (although perhaps also the most widely misunderstood) of Piagetian concepts: *egocentrism*. The concept of egocentrism is a most important one in Piaget's thinking and has been from the very earliest writings (e.g., 1926). It denotes a cognitive state in which the cognizer sees the world from a single point of view only—his own—but without knowledge of the existence of viewpoints or perspectives and, *a fortiori*, without awareness that he is the prisoner of his own. Thus Piaget's egocentrism is by definition an egocentrism of which the subject cannot be aware; it might be said that the egocentric subject is a kind of solipsist aware of neither self nor solipsism (1927a, 1954a). To quote Piaget again:

> Through an apparently paradoxical mechanism whose parallel we have described à propos of the egocentrism of thought of the older child, it is precisely when the subject is most self-centered that he knows himself the least, and it is to the extent that he discovers himself that he places himself in the universe and constructs it by virtue of that fact. In other words, egocentrism signifies the absence of both self-perception and objectivity, whereas acquiring possession of the object as such is on a par with the acquisition of self-perception (1954a, p. xii).

If assimilation and accommodation are undifferentiated and opposed in the radical egocentrism of the neonate, one of the most important fruits of sensory-motor development is their growing articulation and complementation. With a gradual separation between self and world, fine-grained accommodations to the nuances of things come to be experienced as interesting pursuits in and of themselves, pursuits now distinguished from the assimilations that these new discoveries make possible. The network of assimilatory schemas is now so rich and complex that it can with relative effortlessness extend itself to encompass and interpret the reality products which accommodation presents to it; reflexively, this very richness and complexity of schemas provides a guiding framework of meanings which can explicitly direct accommodatory exploration further and further into the unknown. If the invariants may be momentarily reified for the sake of exposition, one might say that schemas not only interpret better what accommodation presents, they also tell it what to look for on the next sortie. In summary, assimilation and accommodation are now at once articulated and in a state of complementary balance or relative equilibrium, one with the other:

> To the extent that new accommodations multiply because of the demands of the environment on the one hand and of the coordinations between schemata on the other, accommodation is differentiated from assimilation, and by virtue of that very fact becomes complementary to it. It is differentiated, because, in addition to the accommodation necessary for the usual circumstances, the subject becomes interested in novelty and pursues it for its own sake. The more the schemata are differentiated, the smaller the gap between the new and the familiar becomes, so that novelty, instead of constituting an annoyance avoided by the subject, becomes a problem and invites searching. Thereafter and to the same extent, assimilation and accommodation enter into relations of mutual dependence. On the one hand, the reciprocal assimilation of the schemata and the multiple accommodations which stem from them favor their differentiation and consequently their accommodation; on the other hand, the accommodation to novelties is extended sooner or later into assimilation, because, interest in the new being simultaneously the function of resemblances and of differences in relation to the familiar, it is a matter of conserving new acquisitions and of reconciling them with the old ones (*ibid.*, pp. 353-354).

Consequences of the Changing Assimilation-Accommodation Relationship During Sensory-Motor Development

With increasing differentiation and equilibration of the two functions during the sensory-motor period comes a development of great significance for intelligence: there is simultaneously a centrifugal process of gradual objectification of external reality and a centripetal process of burgeoning self-awareness—the self comes to be seen as an object among objects. Initially, as we have said, the infant knows neither self nor world as distinct and differentiated entities; he experiences only a mélange of feelings and perceptions concomitant with what an adult observer would label as contacts between his actions and outside objects. Cognition really begins at the boundary between self and object and with development invades both self and object from this initial "zone of undifferentiation" (*ibid.*, p. 356). Knowledge of self and knowledge of objects are thus the dual resultants of the successive differentiation and equilibration of the invariant functions which characterize sensory-motor development. Piaget describes this highly significant consequence in the following way:

> Thus it may be seen that intellectual activity begins with confusion of experience and of awareness of the self, by virtue of the chaotic undifferentiation of accommodation and assimilation. In other words, knowledge of the external world begins with an immediate utilization of things, whereas knowledge of self is stopped by this purely practical and utilitarian contact. Hence there is simply interaction between the most superficial zone of external reality and the wholly corporal periphery of the self. On the contrary, gradually as the differentiation and coordination of assimilation and accommodation occur, experimental and accommodative activity penetrates to the interior of things, while assimilatory activity becomes enriched and organized. Hence there is a progressive formation of relationships between zones that are increasingly deep and removed from reality and the increasingly intimate operations of personal activity. Intelligence thus begins neither with knowledge of the self nor of things as such but with knowledge of their interaction, and it is by orienting itself simultaneously toward the two poles of that interaction that intelligence organizes the world by organizing itself.
>
> A diagram will make the thing comprehensible. Let the organism be represented by a small circle inscribed in a large circle which corresponds to the surrounding universe. The meeting between the organism and the environment takes place at point A and at all analogous points, which are simultaneously the most external to the organism and to the environment itself.

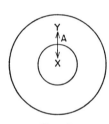

FIG. 1

In other words, the first knowledge of the universe or of himself that the subject can acquire is knowledge relating to the most immediate appearance of things or to the most external and material aspect of his being. From the point of view of consciousness, this primitive relation between subject and object is a relation of undifferentiation, corresponding to the protoplasmic consciousness of the first weeks of life when no distinction is made between the self and the non-self. From the point of view of behavior this relation constitutes the morphologic-reflex organization, in so far as it is a necessary condition of primitive consciousness. But from this point of junction and undifferentiation A, knowledge proceeds along two complementary roads. By virtue of the very fact that all knowledge is simultaneously accommodation to the object and assimilation to the subject, the progress of intelligence works in the dual direction of externalization and internalization, and its two poles will be the acquisition of physical experience (→ Y) and the acquisition of consciousness of the intellectual operation itself (→ X) (*ibid.*, pp. 354-356).

The centrifugal process, that of objectification and solidification of things in the milieu, merits particular attention for the relation it bears to developmental changes in assimilatory schemas. Once more, the details, especially the empirical details, of this objectification must be reserved for Chapter 3. In brief, Piaget's position is that the objectification of sensory-motor reality is a consequence of the increasingly rich network of interrelated assimilatory schemas which the child constructs during this period (1952c, pp. 413-415). In early infancy, as we have seen, external objects are cognitively indissociated from the few simple action schemas (sucking, grasping, etc.) through which the baby comes in contact with them. There are no objects as such, only undifferentiated object-action amalgams. Objectification of reality—the population of the external milieu with things recognized as independent of a self which cognizes them—can come about only when objects come to be inserted into a whole network of intercoordinated schemas. For the adult, the object *chair* may be said to have status as an independent entity with discriminated properties as a function of the network of interconnected concepts or classes in which it can be inserted: "wooden," "four-legged," "to-sit-on," etc. So it is with the infant. The rattle gradually emerges as a thing distinct from his action only when he can insert it in multiple sensory-motor schemas, e.g., when he can apprehend it as something which can be visually fixated (schema 1), in order to grasp (schema 2), in order to shake and listen to the sound (schemas 3 and 4), and so forth. As Piaget puts it:

> It is coordination itself, that is to say, the multiple assimilation constructing an increasing number of relationships between the compounds "action × object" which explains the objectification (*ibid.*, p. 415).

In summary, the constant working of assimilation and accommodation gives rise during sensory-motor development to an increasingly elaborate and complex schematic organization. In turn, the elaborate network of interrelated schemas so constituted makes it possible to see objects as things-out-there, independent of one's activity.

Developmental Changes after Infancy

It has been asserted that the fundamental change in the assimilation-accommodation relationship during infant development is one from undifferentiation and antagonism to differentiation and balance or equilibrium. The important cognitive consequences of this development have been shown to include a gradual change from an initial and profound egocentrism in which subject and object are indissociable to an articulation and objectification of outside reality and a parallel differentiation and objectification of the subject himself. The discussion of the concept of vertical décalage in the preceding chapter may have led the reader to anticipate that the ontogenetic scheme just described repeats itself again in post-infantile developmental periods.

Consider first the case for the general paradigm: evolution from an assimilation-accommodation undifferentiation and antagonism to differentiation and equilibrium. As Chapter 1 also stated, the concept of equilibrium is of central importance in Piaget's recent thinking about development; a major portion of Chapter 7 will be devoted to this crucial topic. What is important for present purposes is that Piaget sees the whole of ontogenetic development as a series of differing equilibrium states, or perhaps as a succession of phases or nodes in a grand equilibration process (1955e, 1957c, 1957f). The immediate and concrete significance of this rather complicated thesis for the assimilation-accommodation problem is as follows. Whereas we have said that assimilation and accommodation are in relative equilibrium or balance with respect to the two-year-old's overt, *sensory-motor* acts, this is not at all the case for his *symbolic* or *representational* manipulations of the world. Quite the contrary, the toddler's first attempts at conceptual or symbolic rapport with reality bear all the earmarks of relative disequilibrium, of relative undifferentiation and antagonism between assimilation and accommodation, seen in the neonate's first traffic with the sensory-motor world (1954a, Conclusion).

The fact that, through vertical décalage, the undifferentiation and opposition now concern symbolic-representational rather than sensory-motor cognitions does not mean the consequences are any less drastic. The preschool child shows every bit of the egocentrism which this undifferentiation and antagonism ordinarily imply. In fact, Piaget first introduced the concept of egocentrism, not in connection with sensory-motor intelligence, but to describe the character of the child's conceptual thought in the preschool and early school years (e.g., 1923, 1926). As we shall see, the egocentric preschooler, analogous to the egocentric three-month-old, is unaware of the fact that his representations of reality are in various ways distorted as a consequence of his failure to see things from points of view other than his own. As with the infant, his representational accommodations to reality are both confused with and antagonistic to one-perspective assimilations by which he is forced to interpret it. Since it is always a subject-object undifferentiation relative to a differentiation and equilibrium yet to be achieved, egocentrism of course reappears in attenuated form at genetic levels beyond those of neonate and preschooler. As Piaget points out, the subject in middle childhood and early adolescence can also be considered egocentric and in relative assimilation-accommodation disequilibrium with respect to certain more abstract symbolic manipulations which he tries to perform (Inhelder and Piaget, 1958, ch. 18).

Just as egocentrism reappears in its various forms in post-infantile development, so also do its opposite terms get repeatedly reconstituted at ever higher levels: objectification of external reality and undistorted knowledge of self. As in sensory-motor development, this dual progression forms an indissoluble whole: it is by conceptualizing the self as a distinct and separate center which perceives reality from a particular viewpoint that it becomes possible to correct egocentric distortions about reality; it is by penetrating deeper into the fabric of reality that self-knowledge becomes possible. Thus, with the various developmental levels of symbolic construction as well as with elemental sensory-motor behavior, cognition always begins on the margins of both self and milieu and works its way simultaneously into the inner regions of each.

Nondevelopmental Changes

The subject of the preceding pages has been *developmental* changes in the assimilation-accommodation relationship: namely, an ontogenetic movement towards differentiation and equilibrium between the invariant functions, first during infancy for sensory-motor cognitions and later, through vertical décalage, for cognitions of a conceptual-symbolic nature. In each case the ideal norm towards which intelligence moves is, to repeat, one or another form of equilibrium between the twin invariants. Although the concept of equilibrium will be shown to mean much more than this in Piaget's system, so far as assimilation and accommodation are concerned it connotes a kind of balance, a functional state in which potentially slavish and naively realistic (in the epistemological sense) accommodations to reality are effectively held in check by an assimilatory process which can organize and direct accommodations, and in which assimilation is kept from being riotously autistic by a sufficiency of continuing accommodatory adjustments to the real world. In short, intelligent functioning, when equilibrium obtains, is made up of a balanced recipe of about equal parts of assimilation and accommodation. Through this fine balance, a both realistic (accommodation) and meaningful (assimilation) rapport between subject and object is secured.

However, there are two important kinds of cognition which do not manifest this delicate balance between the functions. The first of these is *play* in the broad sense, including all forms of dream and dreamlike activity as well as the various kinds of play and make-believe. The second is termed *imitation* and includes all copying or imitative behavior, either in overt behavior or internally. Piaget has devoted a separate book (1951a) to the complexities of play and imitation, much of which will be taken up later. For the matter at hand, play and imitation are significant primarily as cognitive activities in which assimilation and accommodation are decidedly not in balance. In play the primary object is to mold reality to the whim of the cognizer, in other words, to assimilate reality to various schemas with little concern for precise accommodation to that reality. Thus, as Piaget puts it (*ibid.*, p. 87), in play there is "primacy of assimilation over accommodation." In imitation, on the other hand, it is accommodation which reigns supreme. All energy is focused on taking exact account of the structural niceties of the reality one is imitating and in precisely dovetailing one's schematic repertoire to these details. In other words, as in play the primary concern is to adapt reality to the self (assimilation), in imitation the paramount object is to adapt the self to reality (accommodation). When referring to the case in which neither function dominates the other—that is, the case of equilibrium or balance—Piaget uses variously the terms *adapted intelligence, intelligent adaptation, adaptation,* or simply *intelligence* (*ibid.*). The distinction between the three can best be expressed by concrete example:

> . . . Intelligence tends towards permanent equilibrium between assimilation and accommodation. For instance, in order to draw an objective towards him by means of a stick, the child must assimilate both stick and objective to the schema of prehension and that of movement through contact, and he must also accommodate these schemas to the objects, their length, distance, etc., in accordance with the causal order hand-stick-objective. Imitation, on the contrary, is the continuation of accommodation . . . to which it subordinates assimilation. For instance, imitation will reproduce the motion made by the stick in reaching the objective, the movement of the hand thus being determined by those of the stick and the objective (which is by definition accommodation), without the hand actually affecting the objects (which would be assimilation). There is, however, a third possibility, that of assimilation *per se*. Let us assume, for instance, that the stick does not reach its objective and that the child consoles himself by hitting something else, or that he suddenly becomes interested in moving the stick for its own sake, or that when he has no stick he takes a piece of paper and applies the schema of the stick to it for fun. In such cases there is a kind of free assimilation, without accommodation to spatial conditions or to the significance of the objects. This is simply play, in which reality is subordinated to assimilation whch is distorting, since there is no accommodation. Intelligent adaptation, imitation and play are thus the three possibilities, and they result according as there is stable equilibrium between assimilation and accommodation or primacy of one of these two tendencies over the other (*ibid.*, pp. 85-86).

It remains to be shown in what sense the alterations in assimilation-accommodation relationship indigenous to play and imitation can be considered nondevelopmental in contrast to the developmental changes described earlier. It is certainly not the case that play and imitation themselves are nondevelopmental phenomena; on the contrary, from their indistinct beginnings in the sensory-motor period, both play and imitation are said to undergo a whole series of important genetic changes (*ibid.*). Rather, it is that within any given developmental stage (except possibly early sensory-motor development) cognition may show *either* a relative balance between assimilation and accommodation, and hence some kind of adapted intelligence, *or* an imbalance in one direction or the other, and hence play or imitation in any of their myriad forms. In other words, within any developmental period one sees momentary, essentially agenetic fluctuations in the assimilation-accommodation recipe —now play, now imitation, now intelligent adaptation. Thus, one might think of the relationship between the functions as changing simultaneously along two dimensions. There are the "horizontal" genetic changes from undifferentiation and antagonism towards equilibrium and mutual complementation; these are cyclic developments, and recur at ever higher genetic levels. Then there are the "vertical" nondevelopmental shifts in assimilation-accommodation balance which are moment-to-moment affairs superimposed on the developmental changes.

THE ASSIMILATION-ACCOMMODATION MODEL AS A THEORY OF INTELLIGENCE

The content of this chapter so far constitutes the germ of a theory about the fundamental properties of intelligence. Intelligence is said to originate within a biological substrate, a substrate beyond which it soon extends. At its core are the invariant attributes of organization and adaptation, the latter including the two interacting functions, assimilation and accommodation. Through the continued operation of these last, structural units called *schemas* are born, develop, and eventually form interlocking systems or networks. We have seen that changes in the assimilation-accommodation relationship occur both within and between stages of development and that these alterations are crucial in determining the nature of cognition.

In keeping with his sensitivity to the historical-philosophical context of matters psychological (see Chapter 1), Piaget has from the beginning attempted to view his theory of intelligence within the framework of other existing interpretations (1921a, 1931c, 1937a, 1952c). In the process of doing this—and again in accord with his theoretical predilections— he implicitly gives us a preliminary vista of his basic epistemological position, his conception of the mind-reality relationship.[6]

There are at least three good expository reasons for taking a brief look at Piaget's attempts to relate his theory of intelligence to other theories, and for doing so at this time. First, like all compare-and-contrast methods, it gives us a sharper outline of the contours of the system as a whole, just at the point where we are ready to delve into the details of cognitive development. Second, it serves to round out our understanding of the theoretical content presented in this and the preceding chapter, for, in comparing Piaget's conception with others, it will be necessary to touch again upon the structure-function distinction, the character of the functional invariants, the nature of the schema, and so on. And finally, it will bring to light certain new content implied but not stated in what

[6] A fuller discussion of Piaget's many-faceted epistemological thinking is reserved for Chapter 7.

has already been covered, for example, Piaget's views on the role of experience in intellectual development.

There are four interpretations of intelligence with which Piaget compares his own position: *associationism, intellectualism, Gestalt theory,* and the *theory of groping* (1952c, Conclusions).[7] Of these four, the first and third are somewhat more illuminating with respect to Piaget's own theory and will therefore be examined in slightly greater detail than the other two.

Associationism

The first interpretation of intellectual development Piaget considers in relation to his own is the empirical one in which cognitive development consists of associations impressed upon a passive but receptive organism through its contacts with external reality. The empiricism Piaget discusses here is of the extreme and stark variety: reality is taken as ready-made and "really out there," and this reality imposes itself upon a docile subject in the form of associative complexes which get established within a classical conditioning paradigm of the simplest type. As Piaget is quick to admit (*ibid.,* p. 362), few contemporary theories (e.g., of learning) are quite as extreme as this, and his critique, or course, applies only where the shoe fits.

In analyzing the associationistic position, Piaget begins with those of its tenets which are consonant with his own theory. Thus, his observations lead him to accept as beyond question the crucial importance of experience in development, both intellectual and perceptual (1955e, p. 21). From the very first day of life (and presumably *in utero* also, although Piaget is not explicit about this), development is very much a function of the externals with which the child comes in contact. It would be ridiculous to assert otherwise.

But if experience *per se* is indispensable to mental development, it does not necessarily follow that the empirical, associationistic conception of *how* experience operates in development is the correct one. As Piaget states it:

> In short, at every level, experience is necessary to the development of intelligence. That is the fundamental fact on which the empirical hypotheses are based and which they have the merit of calling to attention. On this question our analyses of the origin of the child's intelligence confirm that

[7] Each of the above titles refers to the *psychological* (theory of intelligence) counterpart of a *biological* and/or *epistemological* position; e.g., the Gestalt interpretation of intelligence is said to be, philosophically, a Kantian, aprioristic one. By labeling the psychological counterpart alone, one avoids such monstrous but strictly speaking more precise titles as *aprioristic-Gestaltism, mutationistic-pragmatic-groping theory,* etc. Piaget has changed this categorization of fundamental approaches in a later, more systematic epistemological work (1950b).

point of view. But there is more in empiricism than just an affirmation of the role of experience: Empiricism is primarily a certain conception of experience and its action. On the one hand, it tends to consider experience as imposing itself without the subject's having to organize it, that is to say, as impressing itself directly on the organism without activity of the subject being necessary to constitute it. On the other hand, and as a result, empiricism regards experience as existing by itself and either owing its value to a system of external ready-made "things" and of given relations between those things (metaphysical empiricism), or consisting in a system of self-sufficient habits and associations (phenomenalism) (1952c, p. 362).

It is this interpretation of the role of experience with which Piaget disagrees. He emphatically rejects the notion that the subject is in simple and direct contact with the "real" external world, either at the beginning of development or at any time thereafter.[8] Rather, it is his epistemological position that the subject-object relationship is a subtle and complex affair which itself shows important developmental changes.

In the first place, the facts suggest that the importance of experience, the extent to which the subject comes to firm grips with reality patterns and profits by the encounter, increases with development. The young infant in his egocentrism cannot differentiate the simple accommodations which he makes to things from the assimilation to schemas within which they proceed. The subject's activity and the reality on which it operates are fused together, and this undifferentiation blocks any genuine apprehension of a world independent of the self. But with the gradual differentiation of assimilation and accommodation which ontogenesis brings, the infant comes to establish relationships between things-out-there, to experiment with properties of objects, in short, to profit from experience in the true sense. As Piaget says in one early article:

> We on the other hand have held that contact with experience is something subtle and higher towards which we strive, but which at first is all the more difficult of attainment in that previous subjective and egocentric connections interpose themselves between things and the mind (1931a, p. 137).

Experience is therefore not a simple and indivisible entity, homogeneous at every point in development in its insistent pressure upon the subject. But what can this fact mean, Piaget argues, but that it is the nature of the subject's activity which will determine how and to what extent experiences undergone will be used to modify future behavior?

It is precisely that central conclusion which the developmental changes in the nature of experiential contacts force upon Piaget: the apprehension of reality is ever and always as much an assimilatory construction *by* the subject as it is an accommodation *of* the subject. This is the episte-

---

[8] As Rapaport has correctly observed, the *Ding an sich* is as ultimately unknowable for Piaget as it was for Kant (Rapaport, 1951, p. 184). This is not to say, as the following sentences make clear, that the subject does not with development penetrate more deeply into the structure of things than he did in the beginning.

mological restatement of the notion that the twin invariants assimilation and accommodation are indissociably involved in all contacts with reality. In the beginning of sensory-motor development the essential role of assimilation is obvious. As Piaget puts it: "Things are only aliments for reflex use" (1952c, p. 365). But it is scarcely less obvious when the two functions become differentiated and active experimental accommodations dominate cognitive life. Here again, we have seen that it is by virtue of the network of reciprocally related assimilatory schemas that the child finds it possible to begin to objectify reality, i.e., to explore its relationships, trace out its attributes, etc.:

> It is, in effect, to the extent that the subject is active that experience is objectified. Objectivity does not therefore mean independence in relation to the assimilatory activity of intelligence, but simply dissociation from the self and from egocentric subjectivity. The objectivity of experience is an achievement of accommodation and assimilation combined, that is to say, of the intellectual activity of the subject, and not a primary datum imposed on him from without. The role of assimilation is consequently far from diminishing in importance in the course of the evolution of sensorimotor intelligence, by virtue of the fact that accommodation is progressively differentiated. On the contrary, to the extent that accommodation is established as centrifugal activity of the schemata, assimilation fills its role of coordination and unification with growing vigor. The ever-increasing complementary character of these two functions allows us to conclude that experience, far from freeing itself from intellectual activity, only progresses inasmuch as it is organized and animated by intelligence itself (*ibid.*, pp. 367-368).

> In other words, knowledge could not be a copy, since it is always a putting into relationship of object and subject, an incorporation of the object to the schemata which are due to activity itself and which simply accommodate themselves to it while making it comprehensible to the subject. To put it still differently, the object only exists, with regard to knowledge, in its relations with the subject and, if the mind always advanced more toward the conquest of things, this is because it organizes experience more and more actively, instead of mimicking, from without, a ready-made reality. The object is not a "known quantity" but the result of a construction (*ibid.*, p. 375).

Finally, there is a third and related objection to the associationistic interpretation. Even in the earliest stages of sensory-motor development, externals are not cognized as simple entities or *and-sum* associations between entities; even the most primitive contacts with reality entail organized totalities. An accommodation to an object, even at the neonatal reflex level, always presupposes an assimilation to an organized schema which has set the accommodation in motion. A simple habit is only retained for future exercise to the extent that its component acts derive from and have significance within some schema. In short, any association between act x and reality object y is retained, as an association, only if the xy compound has meaning for the organism, e.g., is assimilated to some schematic whole which gives it its significance.

In summary, associationism is beyond reproach in its emphasis upon the crucial importance of experience in cognitive ontogenesis. Piaget's theory in no way negates this. In contrast to pure empiricism, however, Piaget asserts that experience is a subtle and complicated affair, the role of which varies with development, and that contact with things always involves the apprehension of a complex of events within a meaning system which organizes them.[9] Together, these assertions imply the fundamental thesis of Piaget's epistemology: the cognizing organism is at all levels a very, very active agent who always meets the environment well over halfway, who actually *constructs* his world by assimilating it to schemas while accommodating these schemas to its constraints. In Piaget's view, things could not be otherwise. A really subtle and penetrating accommodation to reality—*really* being "realistic" about reality—is simply not possible without an assimilatory framework which, to substantiate assimilation once more, tells the organism where to look and how to organize what it finds. A cognitive world unorganized by the subject (were such a thing possible) would simply be an unorganized world, a chaos of unrelated accommodations.

Intellectualism

Stated most simply, intellectualism interprets intelligence as a kind of faculty or irreducible intellectual center of force which is simply brought to bear upon more and more complex reality data as development proceeds. Its biological counterpart is vitalism which postulates an entelechy or vital force which directs biological growth and development.

Piaget's position differs from intellectualism in two principle ways. First, and perhaps most important, the invariant and irreducible quality which intellectualism identifies with the whole of intelligence Piaget admits only for its functional aspects. The functions are indeed invariant and permanent but—and this is the crux of the disagreement—these constant functions in no way imply constant structures. As we have already seen, a substantial portion of the subject matter of Piaget's developmental psychology is the study of ontogenetic changes in cognitive structure. There is simply no place in the intellectualistic doctrine for such changes:

> But it is apparent that one could not draw from this permanence of functioning the proof of the existence of an identity of structures. The fact that the working of reflexes, of circular reactions, mobile schemata, etc., is identical to that of the logical operations does not prove at all that concepts are sensorimotor schemata nor that the latter are reflex schemata. It is therefore necessary, beside the functions, to make allowance for the structures and admit that the most varied organs can correspond to the same function. The psychological problem of intelligence is just that of the formation of those

[9] For a more recent statement of his views on the cognition-experience relationship and related matters, see Piaget, 1959b, 1959c, 1960b.

structures or organs and the solution of this problem is in no way preju-
diced by the fact that one acknowledges a permanence of the functioning.
This permanence does not at all presuppose the existence of a ready-made
"faculty" transcending genetic causality (1952c, p. 373).

The second important object of criticism is a characteristic which intellectualism shares with associationism: a tendency towards epistemological realism in which the function of intelligence is to catch hold of
a ready-made reality, a reality which the act of cognition itself does not
substantially transform. This view, of course, necessarily conflicts with
an assimilation-accommodation position which posits a radical interdependence between subject and object in all cognitive acts. An intellectualistic or vitalistic realism is as distasteful to Piaget as an associationistic
one.

Gestalt Theory

There is one famous psychological theory which is neither associationistic nor vitalistic. This is the Gestalt theory of form, which Piaget believes to be the psychological counterpart of Kantian apriorism.[10] Piaget
summarizes the Gestalt position and his reason for thinking it aprioristic
as follows:

> Finally, in the psychological field, a solution of the same kind took the
> place of associationist empiricism and intellectual vitalism. It consists in
> explaining every invention of intelligence by a renewed and endogenous
> structuring of the perceptual field or of the system of concepts and rela-
> tionships. The structures which thus succeed each other always constitute
> totalities; that is to say, they cannot be reduced to associations or combina-
> tions of empirical origin. Moreover, the Gestalt theory to which we allude,
> appeals to no faculty or vital force or organization. As these "forms" spring
> neither from the things themselves nor from a formative faculty, they are
> conceived as having their root in the nervous system or, in a general way, in
> the preformed structure of the organism. In this regard we can consider such
> a solution *"a priori."* Doubtless, in most cases, the Gestalt psychologists do
> not clarify the origin of the structures and confine themselves to saying that
> they are necessarily imposed on the subject in a given situation. This doc-
> trine is reminiscent of a sort of Platonism of perception. But, as Gestalt
> psychology always returns to the psycho-physiological constitution of the
> subject himself when it is a question of explaining this necessity for forms,
> such an interpretation certainly consists in a biological apriority or a variety
> of preformation (1952c, p. 377).

It is obvious that Piaget would find important components of such a
position highly congenial to his thinking. Both theories reject as un-

[10] At least one Gestaltist has explicitly denied Piaget's allegation that Gestalt psychology is fundamentally aprioristic or nativistic in its epistemology, and his arguments
appear to have some force (Koffka, 1928, p. 150). Whether one agrees with Koffka or
with Piaget, there is no doubt but that certain of the finer points of Piaget's own position—our primary interest here—are nowhere better delineated than when he attempts
to describe the system is opposition to Gestalt apriorism (1952c, pp. 376-395; 1955).

parsimonious the attribution of any special faculty or force to intelligence; therefore they unite in their opposition to the intellectualistic hypothesis. Also, they agree that cognitive activities and the realities upon which they bear are structured totalities from the outset and not, as classical associationism would have it, isolated elements or associative syntheses of such elements. Both theories (see Introduction) are holistic to the core. A third point of agreement, closely related to the second, was added in a later publication: under both interpretations intelligence and perception are seen as systems in progressive equilibration and Piaget acknowledges his and our debt to Gestalt theory for pioneer work in this connection (1955a, p. 72).

But if Piaget finds much to agree with in the Gestaltist interpretation of intelligence, he makes it clear that there are important points of disagreement also. One of these is a difference of opinion about the specific composition of intellectual structures rather than about fundamental epistemology *per se* (*ibid.*) and can have little meaning for the reader until Piaget's beliefs about structures-in-equilibrium have been described. Other and more basic differences between the systems (1952c, pp. 381-395) seem to have as a common core one major difference: the Piagetian schema is conceived to be a more dynamic and modifiable structural unit than is the Gestalt.

In the first place, Gestalten are basically ahistorical in so far as experience is concerned, whereas schemas are always conceptualized as the end products of a complex and continuous experiential history. A Gestalt reorganization is the necessary expression of a certain level of neural and sensory maturation, given such and such conditions of the perceptual field; it is not thought of as the product of past interactions with an environment.

A Piagetian schema, on the other hand, is always the product of the differentiation, generalization, and integration of earlier schemas, these transformations being in part a product of successive, repeated attempts at accommodation to the milieu. In Piaget's theory, there is always complete continuity between any given schema and earlier ones, and even the dramatic insight experiences to which the Gestaltists point so fondly can be shown not to arise in a historical vacuum. In a word, schemas are dynamic in the genetic sense; Gestalts are not:

> The schema is therefore a Gestalt which has a history. But how does it happen that the theory of form came to dispute this role of past experience? From the fact that one refuses to consider the schemata of behavior as being the simple product of external pressures (like a sum of passive associations) it clearly does not necessarily follow that their structure is imposed by virtue of preestablished laws, independent of their history. It is enough to acknowledge an interaction of form and content, the structures thus being transformed gradually as they adapt themselves to increasingly varied conditions (*ibid.*, p. 384).

The dynamic, center-of-activity character of the schema contrasts with Gestalten in other closely related ways. Thus, schemas are mobile and elastic structures which are continually modifying themselves as they generalize to fit new reality data. Gestalt forms, on the contrary, are not thought of as generalizing structures, structures which incessantly change their make-up as a consequence of a generalizing assimilatory activity inherent in them. This is a subtle difference, a difference in connotation, and it amounts again to saying that schemas have a built-in activity in a sense in which Gestalten do not. Gestalt forms, unlike schemas, are thought to be static automata which mindlessly click in and click out as the field conditions and maturational state of the organism dictate. Either perceptual reorganization of the field takes place or it does not, neither contingency really being under the active control of the subject himself. Although it would be quite incorrect to say that Piaget is not a determinist, one could speak loosely and say that Gestalt reorganizations are for him too predetermined, too inevitable, given such and such field-organism conditions, to square with the amount of autonomous activity he posits for cognizing organisms:

> This correlative generalization and differentiation reveal, it seems to us, that a "form" is not a rigid entity to which perception leads as though under the influence of predetermination, but a plastic organization, just as frames adapt themselves to their contents and so depend partially on them. This means that "forms," far from existing before their activity, are rather comparable to concepts or systems of relationships whose gradual elaboration works when they are generalized (*ibid.*, p. 387).

Finally, and once more a function of the dynamic character of the schema, in Piaget's system better forms do not replace poorer forms by a more or less inevitable and endogenous march towards good Gestalten. Rather, schemas more adequate to reality adaptation replace less adequate ones through corrective contacts with reality itself. Schemas grope their way to "good form" by repeated trial-and-error contacts with things. Groping is not an "extraintelligent activity," as Piaget believes it is within Gestalt theory (*ibid.*, p. 391), but is embodied in intelligent functioning from the outset. Schemas arise from successive-approximation-type experiences with things and get modified in the direction of better adaptation the same way. The implication of all this, as Piaget points out, is that the forms which intelligence attains are never "good" in some aprioristic, absolute sense, but only relative to those which precede and follow and relative to the environmental data which they attempt to organize. In this sense, it could be said that a "good" Piagetian schema is a less pretentious construct than a Gestalt good form: it is relative, not absolute; it is one structure for organizing experience among many possible, and not a kind of Platonic ideal towards which all other structures inevitably tend.

It is probably accurate to state that, despite these criticisms, Piaget basically feels a closer affinity to Gestalt theory than to either association-ism or intellectualism. A simple tally of number of agreements and dis-agreements in his critique would not show this, of course, because it cannot weight the separate entries for relative importance. However, one is left with the definite impression that Gestalt theory would not have to be transformed root and branch to accord with Piaget's own concep-tion of intelligence, as associationism quite likely would. The following passage conveys the tenor of this attitude and sums up the critique itself:

> Our critique of the theory of form must therefore consist in retaining all that is positive which it opposes to associationism—that is to say, all the activity it discovers in the mind—but in rejecting everything in it which is only restored empiricism—that is to say, its static apriority. In short, to criticize Gestalt psychology is not to reject it but to make it more mobile and consequently to replace its apriority with a genetic relativity (*ibid.*, p. 380).

The Theory of Groping

The conception of intelligence to which this inelegant title refers is described as follows:

> According to a famous hypothesis due to Jennings and taken up by Thorn-dike, an active method of adaptation to new circumstances exists—the method of groping: on the one hand, a succession of "trials" admitting, in principle, of "errors" as well as of fortuitious success, on the other hand a progressive selection operating after the event according to the success or failure of these same trials. The theory of "trials and errors" thus combines the *a priori* idea, according to which the solutions emanate from the subject's activity and the empirical idea according to which adoption of the right solution is definitely due to the pressure of the external environment. But, instead of acknowledging, as we shall do . . . an indissoluble relation between subject and object, the hypothesis of trials and errors makes distinction between two terms: the production of trials which are due to the subject since they are fortuitious in relation to the object, and their selection, due to the object alone. Apriority and empiricism are here juxtaposed, in a way, and not out-stripped. Such is the dual inspiration of the pragmatic system in epistemology and the mutational system in biology. Intellectual or vital activity remains independent in origin from the external environment, but the value of its products is determined by their success in the midst of the same environment (*ibid.*, p. 395).

It has already been shown that Piaget strongly emphasizes the role of corrective experience in the construction and transformation of schemas. The child clearly does grope in his contacts with reality; every assimila-tion of reality to schemas is at the same time a process of successive approximations to the structure of things—that is, a series of accommo-dations. Piaget is very much in sympathy with the theory of groping on this point.

However, to the extent that the burden of intellectual development is placed upon unsystematic and undirected gropings, gropings which stem autistically from within and are "fortuitious in relation to the object," Piaget cannot accept the theory. To the extent that all trials and errors are thought to imply at least a modicum of direction in relation to reality—some assimilatory schema whose form derives from past accommodations to reality—then the groping hypothesis does not differ substantially from Piaget's own. As was the case for the role of experience, it is the conception of groping which is in dispute; the existence of it is undeniable.

Piaget does not deny that the child may show a mélange of seemingly random accommodations, one of which is accidentally successful in "solving" a reality problem ordinarily thought to be beyond the child's capabilities. Such acquisitions are usually more apparent than real, for the child tends not to retain the solution he has stumbled upon. For example, a young infant may in the course of exploratory behavior succeed in lifting the cover off a box and in this way obtain its contents; if he is young enough, he will in all likelihood not be able to repeat the performance (nor even give the appearance of trying to repeat it) until several months later. But the real question is whether the exploratory behavior, which led to fortuitous success in this case, was itself really undirected in any other sense but in relation to this particular solution. Probably not. Rather, the infant's behavior could be shown to stem from lower-level schemas, such as grasping, pulling, pushing, etc., schemas which developed in the crucible of earlier subject-object interactions and could not therefore be called undirected in relation to reality. The nub of Piaget's argument here is that groping can vary along a directed-undirected continuum, but that a completely undirected groping, a "pure" groping, is precluded by the very nature of intellectual functioning:

> But there are two ways of interpreting groping. Either one asserts that groping activity is directed, from the outset, by a comprehension related to the external situation and then groping is never pure, the role of chance becomes secondary, and this solution is identified with that of assimilation (groping being reduced to a progressive accommodation of the assimilatory schemata); or else one states that there exists a pure groping, that is to say, taking place by chance and with selection, after the event, of favorable steps. Now, it is in this second sense that groping was at first interpreted and it is this second interpretation that we are unable to accept (*ibid.*, p. 397).

> Thereafter every external datum is perceived as function of the sensorimotor schemata and it is this incessant assimilation which confers on all things meanings permitting implications of every degree. Through that very fact it can be understood why all groping is always directed, however little: Groping proceeds necessarily by accommodation of earlier schemata and the latter become assimilated or tend to assimilate to themselves the objects **on** which the former operates (*ibid.*, p. 407).

The Assimilation Accommodation Interpretation

The basic elements of Piaget's theory of intelligence, as it relates to other theories, can be summarized briefly as follows. Piaget accepts, with empiricism, experience as a *sine qua non* but submits that it is a subtle and complex thing, the utilization of which depends very much upon the subject's structural and functional makeup and, in consequence, upon his developmental level. There is also, as intellectualism has it, an intellectual core which persists throughout development. But this core is, on the one hand, not hypostatized as a special force or faculty and, on the other hand, comprises the functional invariants of intelligence rather than the variable structures. With Gestalt theory, Piaget emphasizes the importance of organized totalities within the subject, intellectual forms which rescue the organism from being the passive receptacle for a ready-made reality. The Piagetian schema, however, is a more dynamic and mobile structure than the Gestalt form, neither ahistorical nor a pre-formed ideal towards which development is drawn. And finally, it accepts with the theory of groping the interpretation that acts originating in the subject either drop out, get established as is, or get established with corrections, as a function of their success in coping with objects. However, such gropings with after-the-fact selection by reality are never initiated in complete independence from the milieu; all present cognitive behavior is constructed on a base of past accommodatory experiences with the outside world and has some reality-oriented aim.

Thus, the theory is a kind of mixture—or as Piaget would surely prefer, synthesis—of several epistemological positions. For instance, it retains elements of apriorism, especially in its emphasis on the constructive activity of the subject and in its belief that the object is unknowable independent of this activity; yet it rejects aprioristic staticity and absolutism in favor of a developmental succession of cognitive forms, all of which emerge from a matrix of experience and none of which can be considered absolute or ideal. In the same way, it selectively includes and excludes portions of associationism, intellectualism, and the theory of groping. The residue of all this is a specific, firmly held theoretical frame of reference which shapes and colors Piaget's developmental investigations to a substantial degree. In fact, it could be argued that it is next to impossible to see what Piaget is really driving at in some of his studies without knowing something about the epistemological context within which the studies were conceived.

MOTIVATION AND ACTION

A précis of Piaget's theory of intellectual functioning would hardly be complete without at least a brief summary of his views on motivation and action as they relate to cognitive development. Piaget's conception of the motivational substrate of intelligence and of motivational-affective behavior in general is central to all that has been said so far about his theory of cognition; and only the exigencies of clear exposition cause it to be relegated to a separate section. The same is equally true of his views on action—for action,' in the special sense Piaget uses this general term, is the core ingredient of intellectual functioning, the very stuff of which it is made.

Motivation

As was stated in Chapter 1, Piaget focuses on problems of cognitive development *per se;* "dynamic" matters—motives, affects, and personal-social development in general—have not occupied a prominent place in his thinking or experimentation (Tanner and Inhelder, 1956, p. 180). What has been written on this topic can be categorized under two headings. First, Piaget has in various places (e.g., 1927a, 1935a, 1937a, 1951a, 1952c, 1959b) made assertions as to what motivates cognitive behavior in general, i.e., the principal motives or needs satisfied when the organism makes intellectual adaptations to reality. Second, he has on several occasions ventured into speculations about the relationships between cognition and affects, interests, and the like, and about the development of affective systems in general (Piaget, 1929b, 1932, 1951a, 1951b, 1953-1954a, 1954c, 1955d, 1955-1956b; Inhelder and Piaget, 1958).[11]

INTELLECTUAL MOTIVATION

The problem in question here is the following. What prompts the subject—infant, child, or adult—to engage in cognitive activities vis-à-vis the environment? Perhaps the most common answer among psychologists at large is that these actions are motivated by primary drives—hunger, thirst, sex, etc.—or by secondary needs derived from these. Piaget does not deny the role of bodily needs and their derivatives but maintains that the fundamental motive governing intellectual endeavor, the really necessary and sufficient one, is of a different sort entirely. His position is simply that there is an intrinsic need for cognitive organs or structures, once generated by functioning, to perpetuate themselves by more functioning. Schemas are structures, and one of their important, built-in properties is that of repeated assimilation of anything assimilable in the environment. It is in the very nature of assimilation that it creates schemas which, once created, maintain themselves by assimilatory functioning. In Piaget's expressive phraseology, the organism simply has to

---

[11] Inhelder, Piaget's principal disciple and co-worker, has been perhaps somewhat more interested than he in relating the theory to personal-social development in general (e.g., Inhelder, 1956; Noelting, 1956).

"nourish" his cognitive schemas by repeatedly incorporating reality "aliments" to them, incorporating the environmetal "nutriments" which sustain them. As Piaget repeatedly states,[12] assimilation is the dominant component of intelligence. And the principal attribute of assimilation is *repetition*—the intrinsic tendency to reach out into the environment again and again and incorporate what it can.

For Piaget, then, the need to cognize is not fundamentally an extrinsic motive, separate from intellectual activity and pushing it, as it were, from behind. The need is an intrinsic, almost defining property of assimilatory activity itself; it is indigenous to this activity from the outset. Both biological and psychological organs are created through functioning and, once created, must continue functioning. The need to function cannot be separated from the functioning itself. Several brief passages from Piaget's writings may serve to convey the flavor of this interpretation:

> In other words, the child does not only suck in order to eat but also to elude hunger, to prolong the excitation of the meal, etc., and lastly, he sucks for the sake of sucking. It is in this sense that the object incorporated into the sucking schema is actually assimilated to the activity of this schema. The object sucked is to be conceived, not as nourishment for the organism in general, but, so to speak, as aliment for the very activity of sucking, according to its various forms (1952c, p. 35).

> To explain these successive generalizations by the simple action of associations would explain nothing at all, because the problem is precisely to know why these associations are formed and not others among the infinity of combinations possible. In reality, each of these new associations is due to a generalizing assimilation: it is because the cord is assimilated to the totality of seizable objects that it is pulled the first time; it is because the result of this act is assimilated to an ensemble of visual schemata, auditory schemata, etc., that the act is repeated; it is because the new doll hanging there is assimilated to rattles-to-be-shaken-by-cord that the cord is pulled again (1937a, pp. 177-178).

> It is necessary, if one wants to speak of an instinctive tendency [to imitate], to have recourse only to a still more general need, the need to reproduce interesting results or experiences. The tendency to imitate thus has its source in the mechanism of assimilation itself (1935a, p. 2).

> It is the possibility of reproduction which interests the child, i.e., the interest is not external to the action but immanent in it, and is identical with recognitive and reproductive assimilation (1951a, pp. 81-82).

> . . . In the young child the principal needs are of a functional category. The functioning of the organs engenders, through its very existence, a psychic need *sui generis* . . . the principal motive power of intellectual

---

[12] It is indicative of the importance Piaget attributes to assimilation that one chapter section in the basic volume on sensory-motor development is entitled "Assimilation: Basic Fact of Psychic Life" (1952c, p. 42).

activity thus becoming the need to incorporate things into the subject's schemata (1952c, pp. 45-46).

It is clear that Piaget's motivational theory is basically akin to conceptions of learning and personality which stress the importance of curosity or exploratory drives, activity and sensory needs, etc., in opposition to an exclusive preoccupation with primary drive reinforcement (e.g., Berlyne, 1960b; Murphy, 1947; Maslow, 1954; Harlow, 1953; White, 1959). Moreover, it appears to be a direct and logical outgrowth from his epistemological position. The cognizing organism is neither pulled from without by external stimuli which, in poultice fashion, draw or "elicit" reactions from him, nor is he primarily pushed from within by imperious bodily needs of which cognition is a mere instrumentality (as in early Freudian theory). Rather, the "need" to cognize is contained in and almost synonmous with intellectual activity itself, an assimilatory activity whose essential nature it is to function.

COGNITION AND AFFECT

The fact that intellectual activity requires no impetus to function beyond that with which it is intrinsically provided does not of course mean that Piaget believes cognition is the sum total of human activity or, for that matter, that all cognition is of the cold, "pure reason" variety. Although problems of emotionality, values, personality development, and the like have not been topics of primary professional concern to him, he neither denies their importance nor wishes to negate them as objects of study. In keeping with his lifelong emphasis on intelligence, however, when he does discuss matters of this kind he naturally tends to view them in a cognitive setting. For example, he sees cognitive and personal-emotional reactions as interdependent in functioning—essentially two sides of the same coin:

> As for the affective innovations found at the same age [adolescence] . . . as usual, we find that they are parallel to intellectual transformations, since affectivity can be considered as the energetic force of behavior whereas its structure defines cognitive functions. (This does not mean either that affectivity is determined by intellect or the contrary, but that both are indissociably united in the functioning of the personality) (Inhelder and Piaget, 1958, pp. 347-348).

> Affective life, like intellectual life, is a continual adaptation, and the two are not only parallel but interdependent, since feelings express the interest and value given to actions of which intelligence provides the structure. Since affective life is adaptation, it also implies continual assimilation of present situations to earlier ones—assimilation which gives rise to affective schemas or relatively stable modes of feeling and reacting—and continual accommodation of these schemas to the present situation (1951a, pp. 205-206).

Moreover, cognitions with primary affective, interpersonal content function like those of a more purely intellectual sort:

It must be pointed out first of all that this generalized application of initial affective schemas raises no particular problems with regard to the mechanism of assimilation which is necessarily involved. It is the same as that of sensory-motor or intuitive assimilation. Actions related to others are like other actions. They tend to be reproduced (reproductive assimilation), and to discover new ones (generalizing assimilation), whether it be the case of an affection, an aggressive tendency, or any other. It is the same assimilation, because personal schemas, like all others, are both intellectual and affective. We do not love without seeking to understand, and we do not even hate without a subtle use of judgment. Thus when we speak of "affective schemas" it must be understood that what is meant is merely the affective aspect of schemas which are also intellectual (*ibid.,* p. 207).

A number of years ago Piaget gave what was perhaps his most detailed treatment of the relation between affect (in the broad sense of the term) and cognition in a series of lectures in Paris. The published summary of these lectures (1953-1954a) contains most of the essentials of his views on the problem. Thus, affect and cognition can be separated for discussion purposes but are indissociable in real life; both (like assimilation and accommodation) are necessarily involved in all human adaptation. The affective-motivational aspect provides the *énergétique* of behavior while the cognitive aspect provides the structure (affect cannot of itself create structures, although it does influence the selection of the reality content upon which the structures operate). Alongside the development of intellectual structures from birth through adolescence are found parallel forms of affective organization, i.e., parallel structures which bear primarily on persons rather than on objects. For example, the preschool child tends generally to apprehend objects in terms of their immediately salient characteristics in the here and now, without attempts to relate this momentary impression to a stable cognitive framework built up from past contacts with objects. His values, his wishes, his fears, etc., are likewise transitory and shifting, dependent more upon the present field than upon a persisting and time-binding organization. In the same way, isomorphic to the logico-arithmetic organizations which emerge in the period of concrete operations (7-11 years) are highly structured systems of values, concepts of justice and obligation, interpersonal relations founded on reciprocity and individual autonomy, and so on.

It is unnecessary to pursue here the details of Piaget's conception of affective development beyond what has been said above, since it is to a certain extent an excursion from the main axis of his work. Probably the most important general contribution this aspect of the theory makes is to underscore the need to see the realm of the affective-personal-social in its cognitive context. In Piaget's view, it is no accident that the child of, say, ten years is beginning to develop a hierarchy of values and well-ordered systems of beliefs about rules and laws, mutual obligations among peers, and the like (1932); he has developed cognitive structures which make these things possible—possible at ten and not possible at four. What can happen in what might loosely be called "extracognitive adaptation" is at any age very much dependent upon the nature of the cognitive organization so far developed, and therefore the study of the latter is of prime importance for students of personality and social psychology: this seems to be the really important message of Piaget's writings in this area (see Chapter 12).

Action

There is one more fundamental characteristic of intelligence (and also perception) which Piaget has stressed in a number of publications: cognition is at all genetic levels a matter of real *actions* performed by the subject (Piaget, 1949b, 1950a, 1950b, Vol. 1, 1954c, 1954e, 1955d, 1957b, 1957c; Piaget and Inhelder, 1956; Inhelder and Piaget, 1958). There is more meaning in this trite-sounding statement than may appear. This conception and its associated implications insinuate themselves into a wide variety of content areas in Piaget's writings and influence his theoretical analysis of many and diverse problems. Both conception and implications need brief examination to complete our survey of the general theory.

According to Piaget, actions performed by the subject constitute the substance or raw material of all intellectual and perceptual adaptation. In infancy, the actions in question are relatively overt, sensory-motor ones: the infant grasps and sucks objects, makes visual searches, etc. With development, intelligent actions become progressively internalized[13] and covert. At first, as subsequent chapters will illustrate, the internalization is fragmentary and overliteral; the child seems to do little more than replicate in his head simple concrete action sequences he has just performed or is about to perform. As internalization proceeds, cognitive actions become more and more schematic and abstract, broader in range, more what Piaget calls *reversible,* and organized into systems which are structurally isomorphic to logico-algebraic systems (e.g., groups and lattices). Thus, the overt, slow-paced *actions* of the neonate eventually get transformed into lightning-quick, highly organized systems of internal *operations.* However, despite the enormous differences between simple sensory-motor adjustments and the abstract operations which characterize mature, logical thought, the latter are as truly actions as are the former:

> Operations are nothing but interiorized actions whose efferent impulses do not develop into external movements (1954c, p. 141).

> In effect, an operation is psychologically an action which has been internalized and has become reversible through its coordination with other

[13] Piaget's term: *intériorisée.*

internalized actions within a structured whole, this whole obeying certain laws of totality (1957b, p. 35).

There are several nontrivial implications of this emphasis on cognition-as-action. First, it influences Piaget's theoretical interpretation of a number of psychological phenomena. For instance, an image is said to be an internalized or "deferred" *imitation* and hence rooted in motor activity (Piaget, 1951a; Piaget and Inhelder, 1956). That is, an image is the consequence of an internalized action, namely, a covert but active accommodation or "tracing out" by the subject of the object or event imagined. This interpretation plays an important role in Piaget's account of early symbolic thought. Similarly, Piaget's mathematical model of visual perception puts heavy emphasis on a kind of visual "sampling" of the stimulus, that is, again a quasi-motor *activity* as opposed to passive sensations (e.g., Piaget, Vinh-Bang, and Matalon, 1958). It is safe to say that whenever any form of cognitive behavior can be construed with an emphasis on concrete actions (especially motor actions), Piaget so construes it (e.g., Inhelder and Piaget, 1958, p. 246, footnote 1).

Second, the concept of intelligence-as-action provides the connecting link or bridge between the successive developmental forms of intelligence.[14] It is the common element which runs through all intelligent forms, the early and the late, and therefore provides the across-stage continuity in which Piaget believes. New and more complex forms of intellectual organization are seen as actions which have been abstracted from earlier, simpler organizations and then changed in some way, e.g., have become increasingly internalized and mobile, become further equilibrated in relation to reality and other actions, and so on: "In short, no structure is ever radically new; each one is simply a generalization of this or that action drawn from the preceding structure" (1957c, p. 114). Hence, Piaget's theory permits him to see adult logical operations as sensory-motor actions which have undergone a succession of transformations, rather than as a different species of behavior entirely. Both involve actions as the common denominator: overt (and therefore slow-moving, concrete, etc.) actions in the case of the simple schemas; internalized (and thereby mobile, abstract, etc.) actions in the case of the operations.

A final implication concerns certain of Piaget's beliefs about education (Piaget, 1951b, 1956; Aebli, 1951).[15] His argument runs as follows. In

[14] And parenthetically, it provides the rationale for carefully studying crude and habitlike sensory-motor actions as true if rudimentary forms of intelligence (as opposed to dismissing them as simply "early motor behavior" or something of the sort). Since actions are the bricks of all intellectual edifices, it is especially important to investigate their earliest organizations.

[15] There is still another problem in which the concept of intelligence-as-action figures prominently, but it concerns aspects of Piaget's system which we have not yet considered, namely, genetic epistemology and equilibrium theory. The gist of it is this. According to Piaget, the logical character of adult thought does not come about simply

trying to teach a child some general principle or rule, one should so far as is feasible parallel the developmental process of internalization of actions. That is, the child should first work with the principle in the most concrete and action-oriented context possible; he should be allowed to manipulate objects himself and "see" the principle operate in his own actions. Then, it should become progressively more internalized and schematic by reducing perceptual and motor supports, e.g., moving from objects to symbols of objects, from motor action to speech, etc. Piaget's theoretical emphasis on the action (and active) character of intelligence thus provides the rationale for certain specific recommendations about the teaching process.

Piaget's conception of the role of action in cognitive functioning is reminiscent of the "motor theories of thought" of Jacobson, Washburn, Dunlap, and others (Humphrey, 1951). This being the case, one might have predicted that Piaget would be interested in studying implicit speech movements in thinking (as Jacobson and others have done) or at least in making speculations in this area. His thinking took a different turn, however. He became particularly interested in the neural correlates of intellectual structures, and in one article in particular (1949b) he made some guesses about brain mechanisms underlying the various structures which intellectual actions form in their progressive internalization. Thus, implicit motor responses seem to have been essentially by-passed as an object of study in favor of action systems in the brain.

---

as a consequence of learning experiences vis-à-vis the physical, social, or linguistic milieu. Rather, the logical forms of thought—and here lies the importance of the action concept—constitute the end product of the internalization and coordination of cognitive actions. This coordination begins prior to language acquisition; one actually sees a kind of "logic-of-action" in sensory-motor behavior. Its ultimate form, however, is the lattice and group character of adult structures-in-equilibrium (e.g. 1955d, pp. 97-99; 1957b, section 2).

CHAPTER THREE

The Sensory-Motor Period: General Development

THE purpose of this and the following three chapters is to provide a description of intellectual development from birth to maturity. This chapter is devoted to the general and fundamental characteristics of the first major epoch: the sensory-motor period of infancy. Chapter 4 begins by analyzing certain more specialized sensory-motor evolutions—the development of imitation, play, objects, etc.—and concludes with a description of preoperational thought. Chapter 5 takes up the construction of concrete operations in middle childhood. And finally, Chapter 6 is (in part) given over to a description of adolescent formal operations.

The four chapters are not on a par with regard to the type of coverage accorded their respective developmental periods. Piaget has done a good deal less experimental work with infants than with the other age groups. Thus, while it makes sense to try to survey both theory and research on infancy within a chapter and a half, it is manifestly impossible to do this for the later periods. For this reason, Chapters 5, 6, and the latter portion of Chapter 4 describe primarily the general-system characteristics of thought structures—the more theoretical aspects of child and adolescent thought—and experimental evidence is brought in only occasionally and incidentally for purposes of illustration. The main body of experimental evidence on these periods is taken up later in Part II.

A SUMMARY OF DEVELOPMENTAL PERIODS

As an orientation for this chapter and the three which follow, it may be helpful to outline briefly Piaget's taxonomy of developmental periods, summarizing in a sentence or two the important aspects of each. In accord with Piaget's recently stated preferences (1955d, p. 36, footnote 1), the term *period* is used to designate the major developmental epochs and *stage* the smaller subdivisions within these; also used, where necessary, are the terms *subperiod* and *substage*.[1]

The period of sensory-motor intelligence (0-2 years). During this important first period, the infant moves from a neonatal, reflex level of complete self-world undifferentiation to a relatively coherent organization of sensory-motor actions vis-à-vis his immediate environment. The organization is an entirely "practical" one, however, in the sense that it involves simple perceptual and motor adjustments to things rather than symbolic manipulations of them. There are six major stages in this period, with substages here and there within these.

The period of preparation for and organization of concrete operations (2-11). This period commences with the first crude symbolizations late in the sensory-motor period and concludes with the beginnings of formal thought in early adolescence. There are two important subperiods. The first, that of *preoperational representations* (2-7), is the referent of the term *preparation for* in the title above. It is that period in early childhood in which the individual makes his first relatively unorganized and fumbling attempts to come to grips with the new and strange world of symbols. Piaget sometimes distinguishes three stages in this first subperiod: (1) beginnings of representational thought (2-4); (2) simple representations or intuitions ($4-5\frac{1}{2}$); (3) articulated representations or intuitions ($5\frac{1}{2}-7$). The labor of this preparatory era comes to fruition in the next subperiod, that of *concrete operations* (7-11). Here, the child's conceptual organization of the surrounding environment slowly takes on stability and coherence by virtue of the formation of a series of cognitive structures called *groupings*. In this subperiod particularly the child first begins to "look" rational and well-organized in his adaptations; he appears to have a fairly stable and orderly conceptual framework which he systematically brings to bear on the world of objects around him.

The period of formal operations (11-15). During this period a new and final reorganization takes place, with new structures isomorphic to the *groups* and *lattices* of logical algebra. In brief, the adolescent can deal effectively not only with the reality before him (as does the child in the preceding subperiod) but also the world of pure possibility, the world of abstract, propositional statements, the world of "as if." This kind of cognition, for which Piaget finds considerable evidence in his adolescent

---

[1] Although Piaget is quite consistent from article to article in his description of cognitive behavior changes across ontogenesis, he is less consistent in maintaining a fixed and constant classification of periods and stages within which these changes take place. For example, the subperiod of preoperational thought (2-7 years) may be given three component stages in one publication and two in the next. Even the names of the stages sometimes change slightly from one paper to another. This informality may reflect Piaget's view that stages are to be conceived more as abstractions which aid developmental analysis than as concrete immutables actually engraved in ontogenesis. In any event, the classification presented here is a kind of average or typical one, different in minor ways from some versions the reader may encounter.

subjects, is adult thought in the sense that these are the structures within which adults operate when they are at their cognitive best, i.e., when they are thinking logically and abstractly.

THE SENSORY-MOTOR PERIOD: GENERAL DEVELOPMENT

Source material on sensory-motor development is scattered through a number of Piaget's books and articles. The primary source is a three-volume series, originally published in French between 1935 and 1945 but based on empirical observations collected several years earlier. The first volume of the series (1952c) is the principal repository of theory and observation concerning the fundamental, "in general" characteristics of sensory-motor development; the contents of the present chapter are drawn almost entirely from this work. The second volume (1954a) is devoted to the infant's intellectual grasp of space, time, causality, and objects. The third (1951a) describes the early development of imitation and play as well as conceptual evolution in the early postinfantile years. These two books make up the principal sources for Chapter 4, especially the first section of that chapter. And finally, there are numerous other publications dating from the 1920's which are in one way or another concerned with sensory-motor development (e.g., Piaget, 1925a, 1927a, 1937a, 1941, 1942b, 1950a; Piaget and Inhelder, 1956); as a general rule, such sources contribute little not found in the three basic works described above.

The data which form the empirical basis for Piaget's analysis of sensory-motor development consist almost exclusively of systematic, careful, and minute observations of his own three children—Jacqueline, Lucienne, and Laurent—during their infancy and early childhood (roughly, thirty years ago). Many of these observations stud the text of his writings, each systematically labeled with an identifying number, the name of the child, and his or her age at the time the observation was made (e.g., 0;3 (20) means "three months and twenty days old").

Since these observations constitute the experimental basis for his theory of sensory-motor development, a few words should be said about them. In some of the observations, Piaget himself is literally an observer only, albeit a very sharp-eyed one, who simply records without intervention whatever the infant is doing. In many of them, however, he adopts the role of father-experimenter, e.g., posing some simple problems for the child, modifying some environmental condition relevant to the infant's ongoing activity, and so forth. Very commonly, the experimentation is done with some definite end in mind: occasionally just to see what would happen if he did such and such; more often to settle some point of interpretation, to confirm some earlier finding, etc. In this latter connection, there are occasions when Piaget holds an interpretation in cautious abeyance, only to settle the point by observations made later; in such cases one finds advantages in the method of longitudinal observation, a three-subject sample notwithstanding.

Piaget discriminates six major stages in the over-all developmental sequence of the sensory-motor period (1952c). In stage 1 (0-1 month) the child shows little besides the reflexes with which he is provided at birth. In stage 2 (1-4 months) the various reflex activities begin to undergo their separate modifications with experience and to intercoordinate in complex ways, one with another. In stage 3 (4-8 months) the infant begins to perform actions oriented more definitely towards objects and events outside and beyond his own body. In his attempts to reproduce again and again environmental effects first achieved by chance actions, the baby shows a kind of precursor of intentionality or goal-directedness. In stage 4 (8-12 months) there is definite intentionality, as manifested by the first means-ends or instrumental action sequences. Whereas in this stage the child is content to invoke only familiar or habitual behavior patterns as means in new situations, in the next (stage 5: 12-18 months), he experiments to find new means and seems for the first time to pursue novelty for its own sake. And finally, in stage 6, the last stage (18 months and on), the child begins to make internal, symbolic representations of sensory-motor problems, inventing solutions by implicit rather than explicit trial-and-error behavior. With the advent of these first and elementary representations, the child has essentially passed beyond the sensory-motor period into that of preoperational thought.

Before taking up these six stages in detail, several qualifications and explanations need to be made. The qualifications are in some instances already familiar. First, each stage is defined by the most advanced behaviors which are found within it; there is no question but that the persistence of developmentally prior behaviors is the rule, not the exception. In many cases, of course, the earlier form is integrated directly into its successor, but it is also true that the earlier forms may simply persist as is; e.g., the child of two may still show early sucking behaviors when one gives him a bottle, despite his obvious capacity for bigger and better adaptations:

> In a general way, the fact should be emphasized that the behavior patterns characteristic of the different stages do not succeed each other in a linear way (those of a given stage disappearing at the time when those of the following one take form) but in the manner of the layers of a pyramid (upright or upside down), the new behavior patterns simply being added to the old ones to complete, correct or combine with them (*ibid.*, p. 329).

Second, a glance at the observation protocols in the books on infancy is enough to convince anyone that the age intervals assigned to the stages are at best very rough averages; for instance, Lucienne might first show stage-5 behavior a month or more before one or the other of her siblings, or the converse. And related to this, it is clear that a stage can hardly be anything other than a kind of still-film abstraction plucked from a cinematic continuity. All these are qualifications which Piaget himself repeatedly makes (*ibid.*), and it is well to underscore them, even repetitiously, to be sure of avoiding any misunderstanding.

The domain of sensory-motor behavior is an especially apt one for a brief explanation concerning expositional problems, problems with which the reader is entitled to be aware. In summarizing Piaget's writings generally, it is impossible to avoid reorganizations, changes of emphasis, and other deviations from the original; the reasons for this concern Piaget's idiosyncrasies of expression and emphasis, the period in which the work was done and written, its intended audience, etc. In the specific case of the sensory-motor period, there are two topics to which Piaget devotes considerable space but which the present summary finds it expedient to underplay. One of these topics embraces his extended theoretical discussions of the complex vicissitudes of the invariant functions of organization, assimilation, and accommodation in explaining the behavior seen at each stage. The other is the repeated comparisons between his own theoretical explanation of infant development, cast in terms of these invariant functions, and alternative explanations which he feels associationism, Gestalt theory, and other theoretical positions would offer for the same phenomena. Both these topics have in a general way already been discussed in Chapter 2.

Stage 1: The Use of Reflexes (0-1 Month)

As is obvious to everyone who has ever observed a neonate, the behavioral repertoire which the infant possesses is most limited. He shows little other than a few uncoordinated, reflexlike activities: sucking, tongue movements, swallowing, crying, gross bodily activity, and the like. The stage is primarily characterized by the absence of genuine intelligent behavior, even of the most elementary sensory-motor sort, and for this reason Piaget is fairly brief in his discussion of it. Nonetheless, he does consider this period to be an extremely important one, since it is the crucible from which sensory-motor intelligence will subsequently emerge. This is true in two distinct senses.

First, as his discussion of the following stage makes abundantly clear, the simple reflexes with which the neonate is endowed soon undergo definite modifications as a consequence of environmental contact; in so doing, they imperceptibly become acquired adaptations instead of mere reflexes—"wired-in" responses of purely endogenous determination. Thus birth reflexes are truly the building blocks of the sensory-motor edifice; intelligence begins with them and is constituted as a function of their adaptation to the environment.

Second, and particularly important within Piaget's theoretical conception, the reflex behavior of the first month or so already possesses the faint beginnings of the invariants of functioning—the organization, assimilation, and accommodation which will persist as functional constants throughout development.

As to accommodation, there are two senses in which it could be said to be present, at least in embryonic form. First and most obvious, Piaget believes that the sucking reflex, to take only one example, "needs" objects on which to sustain its functioning. This is not to say that the reflex makes immediate and striking alterations in its structure, i.e., accommodations, as a function of experience with the various objects sucked. Rather, the objects perform the simple but basic function of providing grist for the activity itself, a functional sustenance which consolidates and strengthens the reflex. But in addition, Piaget sees evidence suggesting that there also are subtle and limited, but nonetheless genuine, accommodatory modifications in the reflex almost from the first hours of life. For example, Laurent shows minimal but definite progress in distinguishing and localizing the nipple as opposed to the surrounding skin areas. It is not so much that the sucking pattern itself—the actual *form* of the response—gets modified, but rather that the environmental conditions which trigger it off or the instrumental activities leading up to it undergo slight variation (*ibid.*, pp. 30-31).

One also sees faint precursors of the functional (or reproductive), generalizing, and recognitory assimilation activities described in Chapter 2. As to the first, Piaget cites observations suggesting that sucking activity seems to maintain itself by a kind of feedback-like autoexcitation: the very exercise of the sucking schema seems to induce further sucking and therefore to strengthen and consolidate the schema. There is also behavior which prefigures generalizing and recognitory assimilation: for the first, an ever-growing number of objects come to be included in the schema's field of application, come to be subsumed within the sensory-motor category of "something to suck"; for the second, the infant gradually comes to "recognize," in the most primitive possible sense of the term, that some objects are "suckable and nourishing" (breast, bottle, etc.) and others "suckable and nonnourishing" (fingers, blanket, etc.)—thus, for instance, the infant becomes more abrupt and definite in his rejection of the latter when hungry.

If the above constitute the upper limits of genuine accomplishment in the first stage, the shortcomings need also to be emphasized. The sucking-reflex schema is an almost completely empty and autistic one; it simply functions again and again as a rigid totality, "knowing" nothing of the objects it assimilates. Similarly, its accommodations form an undifferentiated whole with this assimilation; the former result in no pronounced changes in the schema which would in turn be reflected in the next subsequent assimilation. The infant therefore exists in a state of utter and complete egocentrism, an egocentrism in all essentials unaffected by the organism's aperiodic and only minimally profitable contacts with a shadowy outer reality. In sum, stage 1 is more a preamble than a first act; it is important more for what it presages than for what it produces directly.

Stage 2: The First Acquired Adaptations and the Primary Circular Reaction (1-4 Months)

This stage can be said to begin when neonatal reflexes start to change and alter their form as a function of experience. It is the period in which the first simple habits, the most elementary of sensory-motor acquisitions, really come into existence:

> In the use of the reflex, as we have seen, there is only fixation of the mechanism as such, and it is in this respect that accommodation of a hereditary schema, while presupposing experience and contact with the environment, forms only one entity with assimilation, that is to say, with the functional use of this schema. At a given moment, on the other hand, the child's activity retains something external to itself, that is to say, it is transformed into a function of experience; in this respect there is acquired accommodation. For instance, when the child systematically sucks his thumb, no longer due to chance contacts but through coordination between hand and mouth, this may be called acquired accommodation. Neither the reflexes of the mouth nor of the hand can be provided such coordination by heredity (there is no instinct to suck the thumb!) and experience alone explains its formation (*ibid.,* p. 48).

These early acquisitions, despite their obvious developmental superiority over birth reflexes, are still very primitive affairs; in particular, they lack the intentional and environment-oriented character of actions which come later:

> In general it may be said that the behavior patterns studied . . . consist in searchings which prolong reflex activity and which are as yet devoid of intention but which lead to new results of which the mere discovery is fortuitous and whose conservation is due to a mechanism adapted from combined sensorimotor assimilation and accommodation. These behavior patterns prolong those of the first stage in that the needs connected with the reflex (sucking, looking, listening, crying, grasping, etc.) are still their only motive power without there yet being needs connected with derived and deferred aims (grasping in order to throw, in order to swing to and fro, etc.). But, contrary to purely reflex searching, the searching peculiar to the present stage is displayed in gropings which lead to new results. Contrary to the subsequent stage, these results are not pursued intentionally (*ibid.,* pp. 137-138).

Two aspects of Piaget's lengthy and detailed exposition of this stage are of particular interest and importance. First, there is his over-all conceptual analysis of the stage-2 behavior. This entails a description of the operation and interplay of the functional invariants and an elaboration of the concept of *circular reaction*. The second aspect includes the more empirical material on development within individual behavior domains: specifically, those of sucking, vision, hearing, vocalization, prehension, and the various intercoordinations among these.

FUNCTIONAL INVARIANTS AND THE PRIMARY CIRCULAR REACTION

As the first of the two quotations above indicates, the behavior of this stage shows a slight but definite movement towards differentiation between assimilation and accommodation. In the reflex stage we said the two functions were essentially indistinguishable. A reflex schema is always activated *en bloc* as a rigid totality. If it can without alteration assimilate and accommodate to an object, it does so. But if the properties of the object necessitate some new accommodatory adjustments (which, once made, would naturally alter the schema in future assimilations) no adaptation is possible. In the present stage, on the other hand, the adaptation sequence is slightly more advanced (*ibid.*, pp. 138-139). As before, there is automatic and "autistic" application of schemas to whatever reality is at hand. If the structure of the reality resists being assimilated in the usual way, however, the infant is for the first time able to modify his accommodatory movements a little. This modification induces a slight change in the structure of the schema in question which in turn causes future assimilations and accommodations to be a little different from the initial ones. In this sense one can say that there is a beginning distinction between assimilation and accommodation; the infant ends up making accommodations which are not, so to speak, "intended" when the assimilatory schema began its operation, accommodations which constitute a slight departure from the initial schema.

This breaking apart of assimilation and accommodation, so minimal in stage 2, becomes much more pronounced in subsequent stages. In these later stages, the two functions work in tandem as complementary activities: assimilation provides the initial direction and organization, and accommodation modifies future assimilations (through the mediation of schema changes) in accord with the structural demands of the reality accommodated to. For stage 2, this differentiation and complementation is barely perceptible and, as with stage 1, there are decided limitations to the adaptations which can take place. The infant is still profoundly egocentric, much more invested in the act of applying schemas than in exploring and comprehending the external realities upon which these schemas operate. All that is really new here—and of course it is a most important novelty—is that the child's schemas begin to undergo definite alterations as a function of experience. Like stage 1, stage 2 is perhaps more important for what it portends than for what it actually achieves.

Piaget introduces the concept of *circular reaction*[2] to grasp the essence of stage-2 adaptations and to relate them to the accomplishments of later stages. The term refers to a series of repetitions of a sensory-motor response (or to *one* of these repetitions). The initial response in the series is always one which is new to the child in the sense that its specific results were not anticipated—not "intended" before the response was made. The important component of the reaction—the one from which the term circular derives—lies in what happens after this new, initial response has been made. Owing to reproductive or functional assimilation, indigenous to intelligent activity, the infant tends to repeat this new, chance adaptation again and again. And through a series of such repetitions, the new response becomes strengthened and consolidated into a new and firmly established schema. Thus the sequence consists, first, of stumbling upon a new experience as a consequence of some act, and second, of trying to recapture the experience by reenacting the original movements again and again in a kind of rhythmic[3] cycle. The importance of the circular reaction lies in the fact that it is the sensory-motor device par excellence for making new adaptations, and of course new adaptations are the heart and soul of intellectual development at any stage.

Piaget describes three types of circular reaction: *primary, secondary,* and *tertiary.* The differences between these three concern both what the initial response accomplishes and the nature of its repetitions. Primary circular reactions are found in stage 2—indeed, almost define it (1952c, p. 49); secondary and tertiary circular reactions make their appearance in stages 3 and 5, respectively. Although the distinction will become clearer when stage 3 is discussed, primary circular reactions differ from secondary ones in that they are more centered on and around the infant's own body than directed outward towards the manipulation of surrounding objects. The distinction is not a hard and fast one, to be sure, and it is best intuited when one compares concrete instances of the two. Piaget presents numerous examples of the primary circular reaction; perhaps one will suffice as an illustration:

> *Observation 53.*—From 0;2 (3) Laurent evidences a circular reaction which will become more definite and will constitute the beginning of systematic grasping; he scratches and tries to grasp, lets go, scratches and grasps again, etc. On 0;2 (3) and 0;2 (6) this can only be observed during the feeding. Laurent gently scratches his mother's bare shoulder. But beginning 0;2 (7) the behavior becomes marked in the cradle itself. Laurent scratches the sheet

---

[2] Piaget borrowed this concept from J. M. Baldwin (Baldwin, 1925, ch. 9) who had used it in trying to account for the selection and retention of infant habits within a quasi-Darwinian theoretical orientation. Although Piaget does not substantially alter the basic meaning which Baldwin originally gave to the term, he has made much broader and systematic theoretical use of it.

[3] Piaget distinguishes the *rhythm* characteristic of sensory-motor circular reactions from the higher-level system properties of *regulation* (perception and preoperational thought) and *grouping* (concrete operations) (1942b).

which is folded over the blankets, then grasps it and holds it a moment, then lets it go, scratches it again and recommences without interruption. At 0;2 (11) this play lasts a quarter of an hour at a time, several times during the day. At 0;2 (12) he scratches and grasps my fist which I placed against the back of his right hand. He even succeeds in discriminating my bent middle finger and grasping it separately, holding it a few moments. At 0;2 (14) and 0;2 (16) I note how definitely the spontaneous grasping of the sheet reveals the characteristics of circular reaction—groping at first, then regular rhythmical activity (scratching, grasping, holding and letting go), and finally progressive loss of interest (*ibid.,* pp. 91-92).

DEVELOPMENTS IN SPECIFIC BEHAVIORAL DOMAINS

Piaget attempts to trace, through observational examples, both the separate and interrelated developments of the various classes of behavior found in stage 2—sucking, vision, etc. Although for Piaget himself these data are doubtless of primary importance for the support they lend to his general theory, they are certainly of considerable interest in their own right as extremely acute observations of early development.

Acquired Sucking Habits. There are three classes of behaviors connected with sucking which can be distinguished during this period. First, there is establishment of the circular reactions of protrusion and movement of the tongue and of thumb and finger sucking. Tongue and other mouth movements begin as direct concomitants of the sucking reflex itself but gradually undergo complex developments independent of it:

Observation 14.—During the second half of the second month, that is to say, after having learned to suck his thumb, Laurent continues to play with his tongue and to suck, but intermittently. On the other hand, his skill increases. Thus, at 0;1 (20) I notice he grimaces while placing his tongue between gums and lips and in bulging his lips, as well as making a clapping sound when quickly closing his mouth after these exercises (*ibid.,* p. 50).

Piaget also traces the gradual development of the ability to bring the hand to the mouth and suck. This is the first of the numerous intercoordinations between schemas found in the sensory-motor period. In the beginning the child momentarily sucks the hand (if it accidentally touches the mouth or if an adult puts it there) and then loses it. Subsequently, the child becomes able to retain it for longer and longer periods, once placed in the mouth, and even shows hand and arm movements which appear to be genuine if unsuccessful attempts to bring the hand toward the mouth by his own deliberate effort. And finally, by the third or fourth month, the hand-mouth coordination tends to be well established: the hand moves more or less unerringly towards a mouth already open to receive it.

A second category of development seen in this stage entails associations between sucking and various postural and position cues. Although difficult to establish definite early origins here (*ibid.,* p. 57), it is clear that the infant does gradually begin to show anticipatory sucking movements when placed in the customary nursing position:

> Before the meal the child is only inclined to suck his fingers in the crib when he is not crying or is not too sleepy; but, as soon as he is in position to eat (in his mother's arms or on the bed, etc.) his hands lose interest, leave his mouth, and it becomes obvious that the child no longer seeks anything but the breast, that is to say, contact with food. . . . During the second month coordination between position and seeking the breast had made considerable progress. Thus at the end of the month Laurent only tries to nurse when he is in his mother's arms and no longer when on the dressing table (*ibid.,* p. 58).

And finally, to be distinguished from the above and appearing somewhat later in time, the child shows anticipatory sucking in the presence of visual cues alone:

> *Observation 27.*—Jacqueline, at 0;4 (27) and the days following, opens her mouth as soon as she is shown the bottle. She only began mixed feeding at 0;4 (12). At 0;7 (13) I note that she opens her mouth differently according to whether she is offered a bottle or a spoon.
> Lucienne at 0;3 (12) stops crying when she sees her mother unfastening her dress for the meal.
> Laurent, too, between 0;3 (15) and 0;4 reacts to visual signals. When, after being dressed as usual just before the meal, he is put in my arms in position for nursing, he looks at me and then searches all around, looks at me again, etc.—but he does not attempt to nurse. When I place him in his mother's arms without his touching the breast, he looks at her and immediately opens his mouth wide, cries, moves about, in short reacts in a completely significant way. It is therefore sight and no longer only the position which henceforth is the signal (*ibid.,* p. 60).

Vision. There are three general substages in the development of visual schemas. First, there is passive, reflexive response to visual stimulation; however, when the stimulus source moves, the infant makes little or no attempt to follow it. Next, emerging imperceptibly from reflex "seeing" there is circular-reaction "looking." That is, the child makes more and more active accommodatory attempts to look at stationary objects and then follow them when they move. Third, overlapping with the above in stage 2 but also extending beyond this stage, there are numerous and complex intercoordinations between active looking and other schemas— hearing, touching, grasping, etc. These intercoordinations will be discussed later (that between vision and sucking has already been mentioned).

As to the circular reaction of looking, Piaget finds its development a particularly appropriate one to illustrate the three varieties of assimilation. First of all, functional or reproductive assimilation: the child looks incessantly, more and more with each passing day, the objects he sees constituting aliments which feed and sustain the schema. It is also clear that visual assimilation quickly becomes generalized—more and more different objects fall within the pale of the looking schema. In the beginning, as we said, looking is passive and undirected. Later, however, the child systematically tries to look at and follow first one object and then another and another. New objects are not only stared at but even stared at in preference to familiar ones to which the child has already become adapted. And finally, there is recognitory assimilation. In this connection Piaget makes the interesting hypothesis that the infant smile, eventually to become a predominantly social response, is at first a simple (pleasureful) reaction to familiar objects, the sensory-motor equivalent of recognizing an object (*ibid.,* pp. 71-72).

Just as in the reflex stage, the infant does not yet perceive objects *qua* objects when he performs visual primary circular reactions. As we have said already, the construction of a cognitive world of stable, external objects requires the assimilation of things not to one schema but to a network of intercoordinated schemas:

> It is not enough that a sensorial image be recognized when it reappears for it to constitute by itself an external object. Any subjective state can be recognized without being attributed to the action of objects independent of the ego. The newborn child who nurses recognizes the nipple by the combination of sucking and swallowing reflexes without making the nipple a thing. So also a month-old child can recognize certain visual images without, however, really exteriorizing them. What is the next condition necessary for the solidification of such images? It seems to us essential that the visual schemata be coordinated with other schemata of assimilation such as those of prehension, hearing, or sucking. They must, in other words, be organized in a universe. It is their insertion in a totality which is to confer upon them an incipient objectivity (*ibid.,* pp. 74-75).

Vocalization and Hearing. Early vocalizations also show a gradual transformation from reflex to acquired circular reaction. Piaget here describes this transformation in the case of daughter Jacqueline:

> *Observaton 40.*—Jacqueline, until the middle of the second month, has only used her voice for daily wails and certain more violent cries of desire and anger when hunger became persistent. Around 0;1 (14) it seems as though crying stops simply expressing hunger or physical discomfort (especially intestinal pains) to become slightly differentiated. The cries cease, for example, when the child is taken out of the crib and resume more vigorously when he is set down for a moment before the meal. Or again, real cries of rage may be observed if the feeding is interrupted. It seems evident, in these two examples, that crying is connected with behavior patterns of expectation and disappointment which imply acquired adaptation. This differentiation of mental states concomitant with phonation is soon accompanied by a differentiation in the sounds emitted by the child. Sometimes crying is imperious and enraged, sometimes plaintive and gentle. It is then that the first "circular reactions" related to phonation may definitely be observed. Sometimes, for instance, the wail which precedes or prolongs the crying is kept up for its own sake because it is an interesting sound: 0;1 (22).

Sometimes the cry of rage ends in a sharp cry which distracts the child from his pain and is followed by a sort of short trill: 0;2 (2) (*ibid.*, p. 78).

Similarly, the first few months of life witness a gradual differentiation of reactions to external sounds. At first, the child will at most interrupt his own activity and look attentive in response to certain sounds. Subsequently, he will more or less consistently indicate pleasure at some sounds and displeasure at others (recognitory assimilation) and, in general, show genuine interest in an ever-broader range of noises (generalizing assimilation).

There are also the expected beginning coordinations between sight and hearing and between hearing and vocalization. Piaget argues that these coordinations are not so much simple associations as they are *reciprocal assimilations* of one schema by another (see Chapter 2). Take the case of sight and hearing as an example. It might be concluded that when the infant turns his head in response to a sound he is trying to see the object which produced the sound. However, Piaget doubts that this is the case during the first months of life and suggests instead that the activation of one schema (hearing) simply excites others (vision, in this case). As Piaget puts it, whereas the infant appears to be trying to see *what* he hears, he is in reality only trying to look *while* he hears (*ibid.*, p. 86). And conversely, he believes that the arousal of the looking schema sensitizes the child to listen. What takes place, then, is not a simple association between sight and sound but a reciprocal assimilation of each schema by the other. That is, the child tries to assimilate aural activity to the schema of looking and visual images to the schema of hearing; in Piaget's phrasing, the child tries to listen to the object seen and look at the sound which the object produces (*ibid.*, p. 87).

The same is true for vocalization and hearing, and even more obviously so. The infant certainly assimilates his own sounds to the schema of hearing; the sounds he makes stimulate listening activity and are in part controlled by the latter. And the reverse is also true. Young infants show a kind of primitive imitation or contagion phenomenon wherein external sounds tend to stimulate vocalization, especially if the sound and vocalization in question are similar. Thus, as with vision and hearing, the child assimilates sounds heard to his own vocalization schemas as well as assimilating vocalization to hearing.

Prehension. The domain showing the most complicated evolution during stage 2 is undoubtedly that of grasping behavior or prehension. The concept of reciprocal assimilation just described assumes particular importance here; Piaget uses it to lend organization and conceptual clarity to this difficult and entangled area. There are five substages in the development of prehension. The earlier ones primarily involve manual activity *per se;* the later ones relate to the coordinations between this activity and the schemas of sucking and vision.

Although it is our general intention to defer both positive and negative evaluations of Piaget's writings until later chapters, it is difficult to resist a few comments about his description of prehension development at this point. Careful reading of this material gives one the impression that one is seeing Piaget at his best in the things which he does uniquely well. The empirical observations seem especially keen and creative here—creative in the sense that he has looked for and found subtle phenomena which most would not have looked for and therefore would not have found. Part and parcel of knowing what to look for and how to find it is his theoretical framework which, for prehension perhaps more than for some other areas, seems especially apt and helpful. Imprecise as the concept of assimilation may appear when considered in the abstract, it turns out to be surprisingly useful in ordering and making conceptual sense out of what is otherwise a bewildering array of discrete observations. This said, now to the details.

The first substage is that of impulsive reflex activity and therefore belongs to stage 1. Specifically, the newborn shows a reflex closing of the hand when the palm is stimulated. About these early, automatic responses Piaget says:

> In effect when the child closes his hand around the object which touched his palm, he reveals a certain interest. Laurent, at 0;0 (12) stops crying when I put my finger in his hand and recommences shortly afterward. The grasping reflex is thus comparable to sight or hearing during the first two weeks and not at all comparable to reflexes such as sneezing, yawning, etc., which do not attract the subject's attention in any way. True, things remain thus for a long time and prehension does not from the outset lend itself to systematic use as does sucking. But we may ask ourselves whether the impulsive movements of arms, hands, and fingers, which are almost continuous during the first weeks (waving the arms, slowly opening and closing the hands, moving the fingers, etc.) do not constitute a sort of functional use of these reflexes (*ibid.*, pp. 89-90).

The second substage is that of primary circular reactions involving prehension alone (as opposed to its intercoordinations with other schemas). Also present in this substage are the hand-mouth coordinations described earlier (finger-sucking, etc.), and a unilateral rather than reciprocal assimilation of hand and finger movements to vision, i.e., looking with interest at his own hand actions.

As to the primary circular reactions, these follow the usual rule of gradual and progressive elaboration of the reflex. The child begins with an undifferentiated and automatic reflex grasping, which bit by bit becomes more systematic and frequently performed, becomes more generalized and differentiated as a function of experience with objects grasped—in short, becomes a true circular reaction (see Observation 53, pp. 93-94). Also classified as special cases of primary circular reactions are the various actions of touching and grasping parts of the infant's body, especially the face, frequently observed in the first few months.

Whereas hand movements definitely come under the control of the sucking schema during this substage, e.g., the child brings the hand to the mouth in order to suck it, keeps it there while sucking, and so forth, no such control of hand movements is yet exercised by visual schemas. To be sure, the child does follow with interest the movements of his hand, and in this sense it can certainly be said that manual schemas are assimilated to visual ones. But the corresponding assimilation of visual images to manual and prehension schemas is not yet achieved; the child does not in this substage attempt to grasp what he sees (i.e., manipulate his visual images manually); in fact, he does not yet even succeed in keeping his hands in the visual field in order to continue looking at them. Thus the eye-hand relation lags behind the mouth-hand relation. Although there is no ready logical explanation for this *décalage* (*ibid.*, p. 99), it is found to persist into the third substage as well.

During this third substage there are two important new achievements. First, a reciprocal assimilation develops between the schemas of prehension and sucking. Not only does the child bring to his mouth that which he grasps, he also grasps anything placed in his mouth. This coordination between schemas of course brings the infant one intellectual step closer to the world of objects (*ibid.*, p. 101). Through the auspices of the primary circular reactions of grasping, the child gains a tactile-motor recognition of various objects. This recognition is, however, only the germ of a concept of objects as objects—things-out-there as distinct from one's actions. But a most important increment of objectivity is gained as soon as the child can insert the objects into *two* schemas at once—in this substage, those of prehension and sucking (*ibid.*, p. 101).

Second, progress is made with respect to coordinations between prehension and vision, but without as yet there being a definite reciprocal assimilation between the two. The child does not yet grasp objects as a consequence of having seen them, but he does do two things which indicate a distinct advance over the previous substage. First, simply looking at the hand often seems to have the effect of augmenting the hand's activity; this is a kind of primitive visual control of manual behavior. Second, the infant develops the capacity to keep his hand in view, once it has (by chance, not intentionally) entered the visual field. The following is an example of this.

Observation 70.—Jacqueline, at 0;4 (1) looks attentively at her right hand which she seems to maintain within the visual field. At 0;4 (8) she sometimes looks at the objects which she carries to her mouth and holds them before her eyes, forgetting to suck them. But there does not yet exist prehension directed by sight nor coordinated adduction of objects in the visual field. It is when the hand passes at random before her eyes that it is immobilized by the glance (*ibid.*, p. 103).

This beginning control of manual activity by vision, however rudimentary in the present substage, is important because it will soon lead to genuine visually guided prehension. In order for the latter to occur, the infant must learn that visual images can be transformed by his own motor activity. Once this has been acquired, the assimilation as between schemas is truly reciprocal rather than unidirectional:

> The child discovers that in moving his hand in a certain way (more slowly, etc.) he conserves this interesting image for his sight. Just as he assimilates to his glance the movement of his hands, so also he assimilates to his manual activity the corresponding visual image. He moves with his hands the image he contemplates just as he looks with his eyes at the movement he produces. Whereas until now only tactile objects served as aliments for the manual schemata, visual images now become material for exercises of the hands. It is in this sense that they may be called "assimilated" to the sensorimotor activity of the arms and hands (*ibid.*, pp. 107-108).

In the fourth substage, there is further progress in the vision-prehension relationship, but once again with a definite limitation. The infant is now for the first time capable of deliberately grasping an object which the eye sees. But this can take place if and only if the object and the hand which grasps are perceived in a common visual field:

> *Observation 79.*—Lucienne, at 0;4 (15) looks at a rattle with desire, but without extending her hand. I place the rattle near her right hand. As soon as Lucienne sees rattle and hand together, she moves her hand closer to the rattle and finally grasps it. A moment later she is engaged in looking at her hand. I then put the rattle aside; Lucienne looks at it, then directs her eyes to her hand, then to the rattle again, after which she slowly moves her hand toward the rattle. As soon as she touches it, there is an attempt to grasp it and finally, success.—After this I remove the rattle. Lucienne then looks at her hand. I put the rattle aside. She looks alternately at her hand and at the rattle, then moves her hand. The latter happens to leave the visual field. Lucienne then grasps a coverlet which moves toward her mouth. After this her hand goes away haphazardly. As soon as it reappears in the visual field, Lucienne stares at it and then immediately looks at the rattle which has remained motionless. She then looks alternately at hand and rattle after which her hand approaches and grasps it (*ibid.*, p. 111).

Why should the child have to see both hand and object in order for visually directed prehension to occur? It is here that an understanding of the preceding substage turns out to be helpful:

> Actually, once the visual schemata and the sensorimotor schemata of the hand have been mutually assimilated during the third stage (the eye looks at the hand just as the hand reproduces those of its movements which the eye sees), this kind of coordination is applied sooner or later to the very act of grasping. Looking at the hand which grasps an object, the child tries, with the hand, to maintain the spectacle which the eye contemplates as well

as continuing, with his eye, to look at what his hand is doing. Once this double schema has been constituted, it is self-evident that the child will try to grasp an object while he looks at the same time at his hand when he is not yet capable of this behavior when he does not see his hand (*ibid.*, p. 115).

In the fifth and final substage, the reciprocal assimilation of prehension and vision is complete and unqualified. The child both tries to look at whatever he happens to grasp and—a tribulation to mothers for many months to come—tries to grasp whatever he sees. It is interesting that the two assimilations appear to emerge at about the same time:

> *Observation 84.*—At 0;6 (3)—that is to say, three days after the beginning of the fourth stage—Jacqueline, at the outset, grasped pencils, fingers, neckties, watches, etc., which I present to her at a distance of about 10 cm. from her eyes, regardless of whether or not her hands are visible.
> *Observation 85.*—The same day Jacqueline brings before her eyes the objects I put into her hand outside the visual field (pencils, etc.). This reaction is new and did not appear on the previous days (*ibid.*, p. 116).

It scarcely needs mentioning that the coordination between prehension and vision, even more than that between prehension and sucking, is a crucial move toward the sensory-motor objectification of the universe (*ibid.*, p. 121). Unlike sucking behavior, ultimately destined for a relatively minor role as an instrument of cognition (whether or not one espouses psychoanalytic theory), vision will grow in importance as a vehicle for forming liaisons with reality. The coordination between vision and grasping, therefore, is a critical one which will, as no other, eventually extricate the child from the stifling egocentrism of early infancy.

Stage 3: The Secondary Circular Reaction and Procedures for Making Interesting Sights Last (4-8 Months)

The achievements of this stage can be conveniently classified according as they relate to reproductive, recognitory, and generalizing assimilation. First, the *secondary circular reaction* itself will be seen to be a new and higher form of reproductive or functional assimilation, since it concerns the consolidation by repetition of certain motor habits leading to effects in the surrounding milieu which are of interest to the child. Second, recognitory assimilation also assumes a new and most interesting form: the child shows a "motor recognition" of familiar objects by performing abbreviated and reduced versions of the action schemas habitually made to these objects. Third, the generalization of secondary circular reactions gives rise to a peculiar class of behaviors which Piaget calls simply "procedures for making interesting sights last." Having discussed and solidified by repetition the secondary circular reaction of, say, shaking a rattle to hear the noise, the infant may make shaking movements in an attempt to maintain any interesting sound he has heard.

Finally, the accomplishments of this stage, taken as a whole, constitute the first definite steps towards *intentionality* or goal-orientation which, from this stage on, will become an increasingly characteristic property of sensory-motor adaptations.

REPRODUCTIVE ASSIMILATION: THE SECONDARY CIRCULAR REACTION

With the advent of the vision-prehension coordinations at the end of stage 2, the infant begins to show a new behavior pattern which Piaget terms the *secondary circular reaction*. These patterns are similar to the primary circular reactions in that, under the aegis of reproductive assimilation, they consist of the repetition of chance adaptations, that is, adaptations definitely not anticipated by the infant before they occur. But there is one all-important difference. Most simply stated, it is that the stage-2 infant is concerned primarily with his own bodily activities *per se*—sucking for the sake of sucking, grasping for the sake of grasping, etc.—the effects of these activities on the external environment being of relatively little interest. The child of the third stage, on the other hand, is much more interested in the environmental consequences of his acts, the secondary circular reaction consisting precisely in attempts to maintain, through repetition, an interesting change in the milieu adventitiously produced by his own action. Thus, the stage-2 infant simply grasps, touches, looks, listens, etc.; the stage-3 infant swings, strikes, rubs, and shakes objects with intense interest in the sights and sounds which these actions elicit in the objects. Of course, the distinction between primary and secondary reactions is at times difficult to ascertain, especially at the beginning of stage 3; like all developmental distinctions, it becomes clearer the greater the age difference between the infants serving as prototypes. In a general way, it can be said that the primary circular reaction is more *autocentric*, centered on its own functioning, and the secondary circular reaction more *allocentric*, more oriented outward beyond the confines of the self.

It is not difficult to see how the development of visually guided manual activity, the crowning achievement of stage 2, permits the gradual transition from primary to secondary reactions. This activity, above all others, makes possible the genuine alterations in the environment essential to the secondary circular reaction. It is inevitable that, in the course of his everyday primary manual reactions of grasping, striking, pulling, etc., the child should eventually notice that the rattle he grasps makes a rattling sound, the hanging doll he strikes swings to and fro, and so on. Reproductive assimilation then insures that the infant will try to conserve the new acquisition by repeating the grasping and striking acts again and again. This is exactly how the primary schemas themselves were first constructed. Thus it is that secondary circular reactions spawn from a context of primary ones, and thus it is that the first real exploration of the outside world begins.

Piaget gives numerous examples of secondary circular reactions he has observed in his own children. There are a number of different classes of secondary reactions, most involving manual activity (pulling, striking, swinging, rubbing, etc.) but some involving gross bodily movements, especially kicking with the feet and violent shaking of the body. The following observation illustrates the gradual evolution of a manual secondary reaction:

> *Observation 104.*—A final noteworthy example is the behavior pattern consisting in rubbing objects against hard surfaces such as the wicker of the bassinet. Lucienne, from 0;5 (12), and Jacqueline a little later, about 0;7 (20), used the toys they held in their hands to rub the surfaces of the bassinet. Laurent discovered this at 0;4 (6) in circumstances which it is worthwhile to analyze.
>
> At 0;3 (29) Laurent grasps a paper knife which he sees for the first time; he looks at it a moment and then swings it while holding it in his right hand. During these movements the object happens to rub against the wicker of the bassinet: Laurent then waves his arm vigorously and obviously tries to reproduce the sound he has heard, but without understanding the necessity of contact between the paper knife and the wicker and, consequently, without achieving this contact otherwise than by chance.
>
> At 0;4 (3) same reactions, but Laurent looks at the object at the time when it happens to rub against the wicker of the bassinet. The same still occurs at 0;4 (5) but there is slight progress toward systematization.
>
> Finally, at 0;4 (6) the movement becomes intentional: as soon as the child has the object in his hand he rubs it with regularity against the wicker of the bassinet. He does the same, subsequently, with his dolls and rattles (see Obs. 102), etc. (*ibid.*, pp. 168-169).

As an example of a nonmanual schema:

> *Observation 95.*—Lucienne, at 0;4 (27) is lying in her bassinet. I hang a doll over her feet which immediately sets in motion the schema of shakes (see the foregoing observations). But her feet reach the doll right away and give it a violent movement which Lucienne surveys with delight. Afterward she looks at her motionless foot for a second, then recommences. There is no visual control of the foot, for the movements are the same when Lucienne only looks at the doll or when I place the doll over her head. On the other hand, the tactile control of the foot is apparent: after the first shakes, Lucienne makes slow foot movements as though to grasp and explore. For instance, when she tries to kick the doll and misses her aim, she begins again very slowly until she succeeds (without seeing her feet). In the same way I cover Lucienne's face or distract her attention for a moment in another direction: she nevertheless continues to hit the doll and control its movements (*ibid.*, p. 159).

Two more things need to be said about the secondary reaction before turning to derived phenomena associated with recognitory and generalizing assimilation. First of all, this new-found interest in external events gives rise to the first sensory-motor analogues of classes and relations. As to classes, the rattle is seen as an instance of things "to shake-and-hear-noise," the doll "to-push-and-see-move," etc. Similarly, there are the dim precursors of relations, even quasiquantitative relations, between the intensity of the child's act and the intensity of its result:

> *Observation 106.*—In the evening of 0;3 (13) Laurent by chance strikes the chain while sucking his fingers (Obs. 98): he grasps it and slowly displaces it while looking at the rattles. He then begins to swing it very gently which produces a slight movement of the hanging rattles and an as yet faint sound inside them. Laurent then definitely increases by degrees his own movements: he shakes the chain more and more vigorously and laughs uproariously at the result obtained.—On seeing the child's expression it is impossible not to deem this gradation intentional.
> At 0;4 (21) as well, when he strikes with his hand the toys hanging from his bassinet hood (Obs. 103) he visibly gradates his movements as function of the result: at first he strikes gently and then continues more and more strongly, etc. (*ibid.*, p. 185).

A second point worth making is the extraordinary importance of secondary circular reactions for intelligent activity, not merely at this stage but throughout life. Piaget asserts that adults, when confronted with a piece of apparatus about which they know nothing, in effect resort to secondary circular reactions: they push this and pull that, repeating only those acts the unforeseen consequences of which turn out to be interesting in some sense. However, there are two differences between infant and adult in this connection. First, for the stage-3 infant, the secondary reactions constitute the zenith of his capabilities—certainly not the case for most adults! And second, the reactions of the adult are more purely and deliberately exploratory and experimental. He is from the outset systematically trying to make new adaptations; this is not yet the case for the infant of this stage, as we shall see when we discuss the problem of intentionality.

RECOGNITORY ASSIMILATION: MOTOR RECOGNITION

Among the more fascinating of Piaget's observations in stage 3 are those involving what he calls *motor recognition:*

> The facts hitherto studied constitute essentially phenomena of reproductive assimilation: through repetition rediscovering a fortuitous result. Before seeing how this behavior is extended into generalizing assimilation and thus gives rise to "procedures to make interesting sights last," let us once more emphasize a group of facts, which no longer constitute circular reactions in themselves but which are derived from secondary reactions, in the capacity of recognitory assimilations. What happens, in effect, is that the child, confronted by objects or sights which habitually set in motion his secondary circular reactions, limits himself to outlining the customary movements instead of actually performing them. Everything takes place as though the child were satisfied to recognize these objects or sights and to make a note of this

recognition, but could not recognize them except by working, rather than thinking, the schema helpful to recognition. Now this schema is none other than that of the secondary circular reaction corresponding to the object in question (*ibid.*, pp. 185-186).

The following is a sample of these observations:

> At 0;6 (12) Lucienne perceives from a distance two celluloid parrots attached to a chandelier and which she had sometimes had in her bassinet. As soon as she sees them, she definitely but briefly shakes her legs without trying to act upon them from a distance. This can only be a matter of motor recognition. So too, at 0;6 (19) it suffices that she catches sight of her dolls from a distance for her to outline the movement of swinging them with her hand.
>
> From 0;7 (27) certain too familiar situations no longer set in motion secondary circular reactions, but simply outlines of schemata. Thus when seeing a doll which she actually swung many times, Lucienne limits herself to opening and closing her hands or shaking her legs, but very briefly and without real effort (*ibid.*, pp. 186-187).

If these observations are correctly interpreted, they appear to be the forerunners of pure contemplative recognition, uncontaminated by anticipation. Thus, unlike the case of the infant who purses his lips when he sees the bottle, the recognition behavior here seems not to be a simple anticipation of an action the child hopes soon to perform—Lucienne is apparently not interested in actually swinging the doll at the moment. Rather, the infant appears to be indicating, in the only way possible at his level, that he knows the meaning of the event in question. In this connection it is interesting to speculate as to the relevance of these observations for Osgood's theory of meaning, in which meaning responses are said to be reduced and implicit fractions of the full-blown, overt responses made originally to the sign-object (Osgood, Suci, and Tannenbaum, 1957).

GENERALIZING ASSIMILATION: PROCEDURES FOR MAKING INTERESTING SIGHTS LAST

Piaget's contention is that the older the infant, the more actively he seeks to accommodate to the novel features of new and unfamiliar objects. For example, it will be demonstrated that the child in the fifth stage of sensory-motor development reacts to new situations with a decidedly active and versatile program of experimentation. He modifies usual schemas in all sorts of ways, intently taking note of how the novel stimulus responds to his various actions. Younger infants, on the other hand, tend to ride roughshod over the novel features of unfamiliar objects by simply assimilating them to habitual schemas, i.e., in so far as possible treating them as though they had all the properties of the nearest equivalent familiar object. As Piaget puts it: "It is a remarkable thing that the younger the child, the less novelties seem new to him" (*ibid.*, p. 196).

Now the behavior of the stage-3 infant falls towards the latter end of the continuum; in the face of new situations he pretty much contents himself with applying the usual schemas:

> At 0;4 (8) I place a large rubber monkey in front of Laurent; the mobile limbs and tail as well as its expressive head constitute an absolutely new entity for him. Laurent reveals, in effect, lively astonishment and even a certain fright. But he at once calms down and applies to the monkey some of the schemata which he uses to swing hanging objects; he shakes himself, strikes with his hands, etc., gradating his effort according to the result obtained. . . . At 0;6 (7) I offer him various new objects to see if he will resume his attempts at spatial exploration which seemed to appear in connection with the last object. This does not occur; the child utilizes the new object as aliment for his habitual schemata. So it is that a penguin with long feet and a wagging head is only looked at briefly: at first Laurent strikes it, then rubs it against the side of the bassinet, etc., without paying attention to the end by which he grasped it. Several knick-knacks receive the same treatment: he grasps them with one hand and strikes them with the other (*ibid.*, pp. 197-198).

This behavior is clearly generalization, in the sense that new events get incorporated into old schemas, but it is generalization without real discrimination, without much differentiation of schemas as a function of precise accommodation to new features.

There is also in stage 3 a form of generalization without differentiation more exotic than the one shown in the examples above. On occasion, the novel stimulus does not consist of a new object which the child manipulates directly but in an event which he witnesses from a distance. What happens here? The child proceeds to exercise one or more of his secondary circular reactions, in what looks like an attempt to preserve the spectacle through action at a distance. This behavior differs from the motor recognition reaction described earlier in that, here, the child appears to be making a full-scale, active attempt to reconstitute the event, rather than simply take cognizance of it by reduced movements. Such procedures are of course irrational only from the standpoint of an observer familiar with the causal texture of the environment; for the infant they simply constitute an altogether natural generalization from previous secondary circular reaction experiences. Here are some examples:

> At 0;7 (7) he [Laurent] looks at a tin box placed on a cushion in front of him, too remote to be grasped. I drum on it for a moment in a rhythm which makes him laugh and then present my hand (at a distance of 2 cm. from his, in front of him). He looks at it, but only for a moment, then turns toward the box; then he shakes his arm while staring at the box (then he draws himself up, strikes his coverlets, shakes his head, etc.; that is to say, he uses all the "procedures" at his disposition). He obviously waits for the phenomenon to recur. Same reaction at 0;7 (12), at 0;7 (13), 0;7 (22), 0;7 (29) and 0;8 (1) in a variety of circumstances (see Obs. 115).

It therefore seems apparent that the movement of shaking the arm, at first inserted in a circular schema of the whole, has been removed from its context to be used, more and more frequently, as a "procedure" to make any interesting spectacle last (*ibid.*, p. 201).

Observation 118.—Let us finally mention the manner in which Laurent has come to utilize his head movements as "procedures" charged with efficacity. From 0;3 Laurent is able to imitate a lateral displacement of the head. Now, as early as 0;3 (23) I find him moving his head in this way when confronted by a hanging rattle, as though to give it a real movement (see Vol. II, Obs. 88).

At 0;3 (29) he shakes his head when I stop swinging a paper knife. The following weeks he reacts in the same way as soon as I interrupt a movement he has observed.

At 0;7 (1) he does it to incite me to continue to snap my middle finger against my thumb. At 0;7 (5) same reaction in the presence of a newspaper which I unfolded and which remains motionless. At 0;7 (7) he shakes his head the same as he shakes his arms or draws himself up when he sees a tin box on which I have drummed.

Until toward 0;8 he thus continues to use this schema to make any interesting sight whatever last, whether it is visually perceived movement, regardless of the direction of this movement, or even a sound (humming, etc.) (*ibid.*, p. 205).

THE PROBLEM OF INTENTIONALITY

The various accomplishments of stage 3 have import for Piaget in relation to a problem other than those already discussed: the stage is a transitional one in the development of intentional cognition. For Piaget, intentionality—the deliberate pursuit of a goal by means of instrumental behaviors subordinated to this goal—is one of the hallmarks of intelligence (taken in a narrow rather than broad sense). The sensory-motor period shows a remarkable evolution from nonintentional habits to experimental and exploratory activity which is obviously intentional or goal-oriented. For Piaget there are two problems in connection with this evolution. First, whereas the presence or absence of intentionality is not difficult to sense intuitively when one compares infants of widely differing ages, e.g., the neonate and the fifteen-month-old, the behavior of children at intermediate ages poses problems. Criteria are needed, serviceable guidelines which will tell us whether one behavior is more intentional, or at least more clearly intentional, than another. And second, it is necessary to examine the intermediate stages carefully to see how the infant gets from nonintentionality to intentionality. For the present, this means a reexamination of stage 3 from a new point of view.

Piaget suggests several interrelated criteria to help establish the intentionality status of a behavior sequence. First of all, to what extent does the act have an outward, object-centered orientation? The sheer exercise for-exercise-sake character of the neonatal reflexes and the early primary circular reactions certainly puts them on the low end of the scale. Only when behavior becomes concerned with objects and their interrelationships can there be the genuine distinction between means and ends which intentionality presupposes. And in this same vein, intentionality can be said to obtrude more and more definitely as an increasing number of intermediary acts serving as means are inserted prior to the goal act. This is a particularly important criterion for Piaget:

> Since then we see only one method of distinguishing intentional adaptation from the simple circular reactions peculiar to sensori-motor habit: this is to invoke the number of intermediaries coming between the stimulus of the act and its result. When a 2-month-old baby sucks his thumb this cannot be called an intentional act because the coordination of the hand and of sucking is simple and direct. It therefore suffices for the child to maintain, by circular reaction, the favorable movements which satisfy his need, in order that this behavior become habitual. On the other hand, when an 8-month-old child sets aside an obstacle in order to attain an objective, it is possible to call this intention, because the need set in motion by the stimulus of the act (by the object to be grasped) is only satisfied after a more or less lengthy series of intermediary acts (the obstacles to be set aside) (ibid., pp. 147-148).

And finally, an intentional act is one which is more a deliberate adaptation to a new situation than a simple and myopic repetition of habitual schemas. Taking all three criteria together: a behavior sequence is the more definitely intentional the more it is directed outward towards objects, the more intervening instrumental acts or "means" involved, and the more obviously it is a forward-looking adaptation to the new rather than a backward-looking repetition of the old.

Stage 3 shows behavior which could be called semi-intentional by these criteria. First, it shares with the more definitely intentional behaviors of later stages the property of being oriented towards externals. It will be recalled that secondary circular reactions are defined as acts designed to maintain an interesting sensory event just produced—produced either by the child's act ("pure" secondary reactions) or by someone else (the "procedures for making interesting sights last"). Also, it is certainly more defensible to think of these acts as genuine means for producing a sensory-event goal than was the case for the more autocentric primary reactions.

The intentionality of stage 3 must be qualified, however, by certain definite limitations (ibid., pp. 180-183). The most important of these concerns the manner in which the intentionality comes about. In later stages the infant begins a behavior sequence with a goal to be attained and then looks for appropriate means to attain it. In these stages, intentionality is present at the outset and the sequence as a whole is more a new adaptation (since the means are not immediately given but have to be discovered) than an automatic repetition. In the secondary circular reaction, on the other hand, the interesting sensory event becomes a goal only *after* the means have been put into effect. Stated differently, the intentional aspects are *post hoc;* not present originally, they enter in only after the goal has been discovered, i.e., in the repetition rather than in the original act. And since secondary reactions, like primary ones, are fundamentally repetition-oriented rather than centered on new adaptations, this constitutes a second limitation on their intentionality. What Piaget sees in stage 3, then, is a highly interesting transitional form in the evolution from nonintentionality to intentionality. The latter, emerging at stage 3 only after the fact in the repetition of an active sequence, will eventually move backwards in the sequence so as to orient new actions from the outset. The first clear-cut examples of intention in this purer form occur in the stage we are about to discuss.

Stage 4: The Coordination of Secondary Schemas and Their Application to New Situations (8-12 Months)

Toward the end of the first year, the infant shows a series of new intellectual accomplishments. The secondary circular reactions developed in stage 3 begin to coordinate with each other to form new behavior totalities, totalities which are now unquestionably intentional. Certain advances are now made in the infant's use of signs or signals to anticipate coming events. Finally, there is a subtle but important difference in his reactions to new and completely unfamiliar objects.

NEW ADAPTATIONS THROUGH COORDINATION OF FAMILIAR SCHEMAS

It was shown that the secondary circular reactions of stage 3, deriving by generalization from the primary reactions, consist of repeated attempts to reproduce environmental events which have unexpectedly resulted from something the child has done. From the standpoint of stage 4, these reactions are limited in two ways. First, as we have seen, the secondary reactions at most entail a semblance of means-end differentiation and a quasi-intentionality only after the end has been attained, i.e., in the first repetition of the action. And second, the various secondary reactions which develop exist as separate response sequences. In stage 4, on the other hand, two or more independent schemas become intercoordinated within a new totality, one serving as instrument and another as goal. Moreover, and by virtue of this coordination, the goal is established from the outset, the means being called into play precisely in order to get to the goal.

Aside from the usual transitional and intermediate forms, there are two principal kinds of stage-4 intercoordinations. The most clear-cut is the behavior sequence of setting aside an obstacle in order to reach some desired object. This pattern of intercoordination shows a complex but fairly definite development. At first, the child ignores the objective if obstacles intervene or, at best, inaugurates irrelevant habitual schemas in a kind of magical attempt to secure it. Later, at least in the case of one of Piaget's children, the infant strikes at the offending obstacle, and from this schema of striking the successful "means" technique of pushing the object aside gradually develops. At stage 4, a part of the goal object must be visible behind the obstacle in order for the child to perform the act; in subsequent stages this restriction disappears. Here are excerpts from Laurent's development:

> Until 0;7 (13) Laurent has never really succeeded in setting aside the obstacle. . . . For instance at 0;6 (0) I present Laurent with a matchbox, extending my hand laterally to make an obstacle to his prehension. Laurent tries to pass over my hand, or to the side, but he does not attempt to displace it. As each time I prevent his passage, he ends by storming at the box while waving his hand, shaking himself, wagging his head from side to side, in short, by substituting magic-phenomenalistic "procedures" for prehension rendered impossible. . . . Finally, at 0;7 (13) Laurent reacts quite differently almost from the beginning of the experiment. I present a box of matches above my hand, but behind it, so that he cannot reach it without setting the obstacle aside. But Laurent, after trying to take no notice of it, suddenly tries to hit my hand as though to remove or lower it; I let him do it to me and he grasps the box.—I recommence to bar his passage, but using as a screen a sufficiently supple cushion to keep the impress of the child's gestures. Laurent tries to reach the box, and, bothered by the obstacle, he at once strikes it, definitely lowering it until the way is clear (*ibid.*, p. 217).

> *Observation 123.*—From 0;7 (28) the transitional schema of "pushing the obstacle away" is slightly differentiated in Laurent: instead of simply hitting the things which intercede between his hand and the objective, he has applied himself to pushing them away or even to displacing them.
> For example at 0;7 (28) I present to him a little bell 5 cm. behind the corner of a cushion. Laurent then strikes the cushion, as previously, but then depresses it with one hand while he grasps the objective with the other. Same reaction with my hand.
> At 0;7 (29) he immediately depresses the cushion with his left hand in order to reach the box with his right. He does the same at 0;8 (1): when my hand intervenes as the obstacle I definitely feel that he depresses it and pushes harder and harder to overcome my resistance (*ibid.*, pp. 218-219).

The second schema is in a way the opposite of the one just described. Instead of removing objects which interfere with achieving the goal, the infant tries to use objects as instruments in attaining the goal:

> *Observation 127.* If Jacqueline, at 0;8 (8) has shown herself capable of removing a hand which forms an obstacle to her desires, she has not delayed in making herself capable of the inverse behavior pattern: using the other person's hand as an intermediate in order to produce a coveted result. Thus at 0;8 (13) Jacqueline looks at her mother who is swinging a flounce of material with her hand. When this spectacle is over, Jacqueline, instead of imitating this movement, which she will do shortly thereafter, begins by

searching for her mother's hand, places it in front of the flounce and pushes it to make it resume its activity. . . . At 0;10 (30) Jacqueline grasps my hand, places it against a swinging doll which she was not able to set going herself, and exerts pressure on my index finger to make me do the necessary (same reaction three times in succession) (*ibid.*, p. 223).

The coordinations among schemas which define stage 4 are, in Piaget's view, the first unequivocally intentional behaviors. Prior to this stage, there is no way to distinguish intention from the act which is supposed to express it. But here, for the first time, there is a genuine differentiation. The infant tries to perform some desired action and finds that obstacles intrude. He then promotes the goal action to a future rather than present end and searches for an immediate act which will make this future end possible. Although Piaget makes no assumptions whatsoever about consciousness here, one could communicate the situation by saying the "wish" for the goal now exists apart from and prior to the consummatory, goal response, and it is this fact which permits us to attribute genuine intentionality:

> Perhaps the objection will be raised that the intersensorial coordinations peculiar to some of the primary circular reactions seem very early to make us witness seriations of the same kind. When the child grasps an object in order to suck it, look at it, etc., he seems to differentiate the means from the ends and, consequently, set a goal in advance. But, for want of an obstacle capable of attracting the child's attention, nothing warrants attributing these distinctions to the subject's consciousness. Grasping in order to suck constitutes a single act in which the means and the end are one, and this single act is formed by immediate reciprocal assimilation between the schemata present. It is therefore the observer, and not the subject, who makes divisions in the case of such schemata. It is only when the child seeks to put things in themselves into relationship that the differentiation of means from ends appears—in other words, the acquisition of consciousness characterizing intention and arising when external obstacles are produced (*ibid.*, 226-227).

There are other implications of this new behavior pattern. The secondary schemas are now more mobile and generic, in that they have been pried loose from their original contexts to intercombine in a variety of new adaptations. Once freely mobile, they make possible a new flexibility and versatility of cognitive functioning. And, as in stage 3, there are several interesting functional analogies with the class and relational logic of the older child and adult. Thus, the subordination of means to ends is reminiscent of the subordination of premiss to conclusion in logical reasoning. And there is the analogue of classification: the infant sees the obstacle as inhibiting and undesirable, and the goal object as facilitating and desirable. Most interesting of all perhaps are the primitive prototypes of spatial-temporal relations. The obstacle is perceived as being "in front of" the goal, one must remove it "before" trying to set in motion the goal schema, and so on.

THE USE OF SIGNS TO ANTICIPATE EVENTS

Stage 4, like all other sensory-motor stages, has its own characteristic advances towards an objectification of reality. For example, the coordinations among secondary schemas just described involve for the first time the establishment of relationships between two objects—the obstacle or instrument and the goal object—instead of simple and undifferentiated connections between an object and an action. This growing objectivity is also evidenced by the stage-4 infant's reactions to signs or signals.

In stage 2 only those signals are responded to which serve to announce some incipient action by the child. For instance, the infant hears a sound and this induces him to try to see the sound source; that is, the signal heralds an action of his rather than some outside event which occurs independent of his actions. While progress is definitely made here during stage 3, it is in stage 4 that one begins to see really clear examples of the anticipation of events independent of action. Of the several examples Piaget gives (ibid., pp. 249-250) perhaps the most informative are the following. An adult starts to get up from his chair and the child anticipates the impending departure by crying. Again, the infant sees the mother put her hat on, and since this has been followed by the mother leaving in the past, the child also cries. Thus it is that anticipatory reactions to signs evolve like other sensory-motor patterns: objects are first undissociated from the infant's own behavior and are only gradually cognized independent of this behavior. From what has been said earlier, it will come as no surprise that Piaget does not find it necessary to infer complicated symbolic or imaginal processes as mediators of sign behavior during this early period:

> When Jacqueline expects to see a person where a door is opening, or fruit juice in a spoon coming out of a certain receptacle, it is not necessary, in order that there be understanding of these signs and consequently prevision, that she picture these objects to herself in their absence. It is enough that the sign set in motion a certain attitude of expectation and a certain schema of recognition of persons or of food (ibid., p. 252).

EXPLORATION OF NEW OBJECTS

We have so far described how the stage-4 child reacts to familiar stimuli. There remains the question of his reactions to new and strange objects. It has been shown that the infant in stage 3 tends to respond to novelties by running through his repertoire of secondary circular reactions, trying each in turn. This is also true of the stage-4 child, but with a subtle difference in orientation:

> Like the "generalization of secondary schemata" the present behavior patterns consist, in effect, of applying acquired schemata to new objects or phenomena. Just as, at 4 to 6 months, the child strikes, shakes, rubs, etc., the

unfamiliar object which is offered to him, so also, at 8 to 10 months, he displaces it, swings it, shakes it, etc. The exploration of which we now speak therefore prolongs without adding anything to the generalization of the schemata to such a degree that all the transitions are exhibited between the two behavior patterns and it is impossible to draw a definite boundary between them. Nevertheless they do not seem to us to be identical because, however delicate the evaluation of such characteristics may be, their orientation is different. At the beginning of the third stage, in effect, the new object does not interest the child at all as a novelty. Its novelty only arrests his curiosity fleetingly and the object immediately serves as aliment to habitual schemata. Interest is consequently not centered on the object as such but on its utilization. On the other hand, when the 8-month-old child examines a cigarette case or a hanging necktie everything transpires as though such objects presented a problem to his mind, as though he were trying to "understand." Not only does he look at such objects for a much longer time than the 4- to 5-month-old child before proceeding to acts, but furthermore, he engages in an ensemble of exploratory movements relating to the object and not to himself. He feels, explores the surface, the edges, turns over and slowly displaces, etc., and the last behavior patterns are very significant of a new attitude. The unfamiliar obviously represents to the child an external reality, to which he must adapt himself and no longer a substance which is pliable at will or a simple aliment for the activity itself. Finally comes the application of habitual schemata to this reality. But in trying out each of his schemata in turn, the child at this stage gives more the impression of making an experiment than of generalizing his behavior patterns: he tries to "understand" (*ibid.*, pp. 258-259).

These reactions are obviously not radically discontinuous with those seen earlier. What difference there is can perhaps be expressed this way. The younger child is somewhat more concerned with what the object permits him to do, the older somewhat more oriented towards those characteristics of the object which do the permitting. A brief example of stage-4 exploratory behavior will suffice:

> *Observation 136.*—At 0;8 (16) Jacqueline grasps an unfamiliar cigarette case which I present to her. At first she examines it very attentively, turns it over, then holds it in both hands while making the sound *apff* (a kind of hiss which she usually makes in the presence of people). After that she rubs it against the wicker of her bassinet (habitual movement of her right hand, Obs. 104), then draws herself up while looking at it (Obs. 115), then swings it above her and finally puts it into her mouth (*ibid.*, p. 253).

Stage 5: The Tertiary Circular Reaction and the Discovery of New Means by Active Experimentation (12-18 Months)

If for the moment we consider stages 3 and 4 to be a single unified period, it is clear that two distinct but related developments have occurred. First, the infant evolves a method (the secondary circular reaction) for conserving new acquisitions and transforming them into new schemas. These new secondary schemas are, as we have said, distinguished by the fact that they involve an elementary cognition of external events and objects and therefore amount to primitive explorations of the environment. Second, once these secondary schemas are established it becomes possible to combine one with another in a means-ends relationship and, by so doing, to inaugurate new behavior totalities which are intentional and goal-directed from the outset.

The principal achievement of stage 5 is to replicate this dual development on a higher level. The *tertiary circular reaction* gradually emerges out of the secondary one as a more advanced and effective way of exploring the properties of new objects. And once the *modus operandi* of the tertiary reaction is evolved, it becomes possible for the child to discover new "means schemas" to use in goal-directed action sequences. The tertiary circular reaction is then the stage-5 counterpart of the stage-3 secondary reaction, and the achievement just described—Piaget refers to it as "discovery of new means through active experimentation"—is the analogue of the stage-4 means-end coordination.

THE TERTIARY CIRCULAR REACTION

As was the case for the distinction between primary and secondary circular reactions, the difference between secondary and tertiary reactions is elusive and hard to put in precise terms. Both reactions begin in about the same way: the infant stumbles upon some new datum in the marvelous and unpredictable world about him—most usually, a familiar action results in an unexpected but intriguing consequence when it is applied to a new object. And in both secondary and tertiary reactions there is a second phase of repetition, of repeated encounters with the novel phenomenon.

But there is an all-important difference in the character of these repetitions. In the secondary reaction, the infant seems at most to sense a dim connection between his behavior and its result and strives simply to reproduce the latter by activating the behavior schema again and again in a mechanical and stereotyped—one is tempted to say "mindless"—way. In the tertiary reaction, on the other hand, there is again repetition, but it is repetition with variation. The infant gives the impression —and here is the real significance of the tertiary reaction for intellectual development—of really exploring the object's potentialities, of really varying the act in order to see how this variation affects the object, of really subordinating his actions to an object seen as a thing apart, something "out there." Piaget summarizes the distinctive features of this new species of adaptation this way:

> Tertiary circular reaction is quite different: if it also arises by way of differentiation, from the secondary circular schemata, this differentiation is no longer imposed by the environment but is, so to speak, accepted and even desired in itself. In effect, not succeeding in assimilating certain objects

or situations to the schemata hitherto examined, the child manifests an unexpected behavior pattern: he tries, through a sort of experimentation, to find out in which respect the object or the event is new. In other words, he will not only submit to but even provoke new results instead of being satisfied merely to reproduce them once they have been revealed fortuitously. The child discovers in this way that which has been called in scientific language the "experiment in order to see." But, of course, the new result, though sought after for its own sake, demands to be reproduced and the initial experiment is immediately accompanied by circular reaction. But, there too, a difference contrasts these "tertiary" reactions to the "secondary" reactions. When the child repeats the movements which led him to the interesting result, he no longer repeats them just as they are but gradates and varies them, in such a way as to discover fluctuations in the result. The "experiment in order to see," consequently, from the very beginning, has the tendency to extend to the conquest of the external environment (*ibid.*, pp. 266-267).

The essence of the tertiary circular reaction is its pursuit of the novel, those features of an object which are not, or at least not quite, assimilable to the usual schemas. This tendency to pursue novelties in "experiments in order to see" has at least two important implications. First of all, it implies a very considerable differentiation between assimilation and accommodation. From a barely recognizable hiatus in stage 2, the two invariant functions have now attained an advanced state of distinctness and complementation. Genuine exploration of a new object requires that the accommodatory function break away from the original assimilatory act in order to place itself in the service of the object's structure and, by doing this, modify the schema for the next encounter. This is precisely what we see in stage 5. And related to this, the pursuit of the novel means a shift away from an autocentric action orientation towards an allocentric object orientation. The tertiary reaction child, as will be shown in detail later, is in an advanced stage as concerns development of the object concept. He clearly and obviously distinguishes act from object and strenuously bends his efforts towards accommodating the former to the latter. For this reason Piaget refers to stage 5 as "primarily the stage of elaboration of the 'object' " (*ibid.*, p. 264).

It goes without saying that the passage from secondary to tertiary reaction is a completely continuous, virtually imperceptible one with all manner of transitional forms. The responses to new objects which occur in stage 4 are examples. Moreover, even clear-cut tertiary reactions generally arise within a context of secondary ones. The child usually begins a given sequence by making near-exact repetitions of the secondary-reaction genre and then proceeds to the tertiary-reaction variations. The following are some examples of tertiary circular reactions; those of Laurent illustrate the transition from earlier forms:

> *Observation 141.*—This first example will make us understand the transition between secondary and "tertiary" reactions: that of the well-known behavior pattern by means of which the child explores distant space and

constructs his representation of movement, the behavior pattern of letting go or throwing objects in order subsequently to pick them up.

One recalls (Obs. 140) how, at 0;10 (2) Laurent discovered in "exploring" a case of soap, the possibility of throwing this object and letting it fall. Now, what interested him at first was not the objective phenomenon of the fall—that is to say, the object's trajectory—but the very act of letting go. He therefore limited himself, at the beginning, merely to reproducing the result observed fortuitously, which still constitutes a "secondary" reaction, "derived," it is true, but of typical structure.

On the other hand, at 0;10 (10) the reaction changes and becomes "tertiary." That day Laurent manipulates a small piece of bread (without any alimentary interest: he has never eaten any and has no thought of tasting it) and lets it go continually. He even breaks off fragments which he lets drop. Now, in contradistinction to what has happened on the preceding days, he pays no attention to the act of letting go whereas he watches with great interest the body in motion; in particular, he looks at it for a long time when it has fallen, and picks it up when he can.

At 0;10 (11) Laurent is lying on his back but nevertheless resumes his experiments of the day before. He grasps in succession a celluloid swan, a box, etc., stretches out his arm and lets them fall. He distinctly varies the positions of the fall. Sometimes he stretches out his arm vertically, sometimes he holds it obliquely, in front of or behind his eyes, etc. When the object falls in a new position (for example on his pillow), he lets it fall two or three times more on the same place, as though to study the spatial relation; then he modifies the situation. At a certain moment the swan falls near his mouth: now, he does not suck it (even though this object habitually serves this purpose), but drops it three times more while merely making the gesture of opening his mouth (*ibid.,* pp. 268-269).

Observation 146.—At 1;2 (8) Jacqueline holds in her hands an object which is new to her; a round, flat box which she turns all over, shakes, rubs against the bassinet, etc. She lets it go and tries to pick it up. But she only succeeds in touching it with her index finger, without grasping it. She nevertheless makes an attempt and presses on the edge. The box then tilts up and falls again. Jacqueline, very much interested in this fortuitous result, immediately applies herself to studying it. . . . Hitherto it is only a question of an attempt at assimilation analogous to that of Observations 136 to 137, and of the fortuitous discovery of a new result, but this discovery, instead of giving rise to a simple circular reaction, is at once extended to "experiments in order to see."

In effect, Jacqueline immediately rests the box on the ground and pushes it as far as possible (it is noteworthy that care is taken to push the box far away in order to reproduce the same conditions as in the first attempt, as though this were a necessary condition for obtaining the result). Afterward Jacqueline puts her finger on the box and presses it. But as she places her finger on the center of the box she simply displaces it and makes it slide instead of tilting it up. She amuses herself with this game and keeps it up (resumes it after intervals, etc.) for several minutes. Then, changing the point of contact, she finally again places her finger on the edge of the box, which tilts it up. She repeats this many times, varying the conditions, but keeping track of her discovery: now she only presses on the edge! (*ibid.,* p. 272).

DISCOVERY OF NEW MEANS THROUGH ACTIVE EXPERIMENTATION

These behavior patterns are similar to the means-ends sequences of stage 4 with one exception. The stage-4 child is able to inaugurate a successful means-ends series only if the instrumental or means response is already in his repertoire. What is new is the *coordination* of two schemas, not the separate schemas themselves. In stage 5, on the other hand, the child manages to solve problems which demand new and unfamiliar means. Through the method of tertiary circular reaction—that is, through an active process of trial-and-error exploration—he eventually succeeds in finding effective instrumental techniques which are truly new to him. Thus, unlike stage 4, both the coordination between means and ends and the means themselves are new. It goes without saying that the systematic discovery of new means requires a vigorous experimental orientation on the child's part, and for this reason clear-cut examples of these patterns are seldom seen prior to the tertiary circular reaction stage.

Piaget describes a variety of new means-ends sequences which come into existence in stage 5. An object out of reach rests upon a support of some sort (e.g., a blanket) and the infant draws the object to him by pulling the support. Analogously, he learns that an object with an attached string can be secured by pulling the string alone. Again, he invents the means by which an object can be brought towards him through judicious manipulations of a stick. There are also schemas of a quite different sort. The infant discovers that it is necessary to tilt long objects in order to draw them through the bars of his playpen. He learns to put objects only into containers large enough to receive them, how to make a watch chain or other slender and flexible objects pass through a narrow opening, and so on. The first pattern, that of pulling a support, will suffice as an example. The quotation which follows is of side interest as a sample of Piaget the experimenter-observer who varies experimental conditions, attempts to rule out alternative hypotheses, etc.:

> With regard to the "behavior pattern of the support," numerous experiments repeated between 0;7 (29) and 0;10 (16) reveal that Laurent, until the latter date, has remained incapable of utilizing it systematically. . . . At 0;10 (16) on the other hand, Laurent discovers the true relations between the support and the objective and consequently the possibility of utilizing the first to draw the second to him. Here are the child's reactions:
>
> (1) I place my watch on a big red cushion (of a uniform color and without a fringe) and place the cushion directly in front of the child. Laurent tries to reach the watch directly and not succeeding, he grabs the cushion which he draws toward him as before. But then, instead of letting go of the support at once, as he has hitherto done, in order to try again to grasp the objective, he recommences with obvious interest, to move the cushion while looking at the watch. Everything takes place as though he noticed for the first time the relationship for its own sake and studied it as such. He thus easily succeeds in grasping the watch.

(2) I then immediately attempt the following counterproof. I put two colored cushions in front of the child, of identical form and dimensions. The first is placed as before, directly in front of the child. The second is placed behind, at an angle of 45°, that is to say, so that a corner of the cushion is opposite the child. This corner is placed on the first cushion but I manage to flatten the two cushions at this place, where one is partially superposed on the other, so that the second does not protrude and is not too visible. Finally I place my watch at the other extreme end of the second cushion.

Laurent, as soon as he sees the watch, stretches out his hands, then grasps the first cushion which he pulls toward him by degrees. Then, observing that the watch does not move (he does not stop looking at it), he examines the place where the one cushion is superposed on the other (this is still the case despite the slight displacement of the first one), and he goes straight to the second one. He grasps it by the corner, pulls it toward him over the first cushion, and takes the watch (*ibid.*, pp. 282-283).

In commenting on this and other observations, Piaget effectively epit-omizes the means-ends pattern of stage 5 and its relation to that of stage 4 (familiar means, etc.) and to the stage-5 tertiary reaction itself:

The first examples show us at once in what the behavior pattern which we call "discovery of new means through active experimentation" consists. The whole situation is exactly the same as with respect to Observations 120 to 130, that is to say, the "application of familiar means to new circumstances": the child tries to attain a goal but obstacles (distance, etc.) prevent him. The situation is therefore "new" and the problem is to discover appropriate means. But, reversely from the behavior patterns mentioned (Obs. 120-130), no familiar method presents itself to the child any more. It is therefore a question of innovating. It is then that a behavior pattern intervenes which is analogous to that of the tertiary circular reactions, that is to say, an "experiment in order to see": the child gropes. The only difference is that, now, the groping is oriented as a function of the goal itself, that is to say, of the problem presented (of the need anterior to the act) instead of taking place simply "in order to see" (*ibid.*, p. 288).

Stage 6: Invention of New Means through Mental Combinations (18 Months on)

Piaget distinguishes three forms of intentional or goal-directed behav-ior in the sensory-motor period. The first is that involving the coordina-tion of familiar schemas seen in stage 4. The second, just described in the discussion of stage 5, entails the discovery of new means through experimentation rather than the simple application of habitual, already formed schemas. The third and most advanced form is that which defines stage 6: the invention of new means through internal, mental coordina-tions.

This important new pattern can be summarized as follows. The child wishes to achieve some end and finds no habitual schema which can serve as means. Thus the beginning of the sequence is identical to that of the stage-5 pattern: no available means exists, one must be discovered. However, instead of fumbling for a solution by an extended series of overt and visible sensory-motor explorations, as in stage 5, the child "invents" one through a covert process which amounts to *internal* experimentation, an *inner* exploration of ways and means. Unlike any previous stage, the acquisition of something genuinely new can now take place covertly—prior to action, instead of through, and only through, a series of actually performed assimilations and accommodations. Before analyzing the stage-6 reaction in more detail, let us consider a few of the examples of it Piaget has observed in his children:

> *Observation 181.*—At 1;6 (23) for the first time Lucienne plays with a doll carriage whose handle comes to the height of her face. She rolls it over the carpet by pushing it. When she comes against a wall, she pulls, walking backward. But as this position is not convenient for her, she pauses and without hesitation, goes to the other side to push the carriage again. She therefore found the procedure in one attempt, apparently through analogy to other situations but without training, apprenticeship, or chance.
>
> In the same kind of inventions, that is to say, in the realm of kinematic representations, the following fact should be cited. At 1;10 (27) Lucienne tries to kneel before a stool but, by leaning against it, pushes it further away. She then raises herself up, takes it and places it against a sofa. When it is firmly set there she leans against it and kneels without difficulty.
>
> *Observation 181 repeated.*—In the same way Jacqueline, at 1;8 (9) arrives at a closed door—with a blade of grass in each hand. She stretches out her right hand toward the knob but sees that she cannot turn it without letting go of the grass. She puts the grass on the floor, opens the door, picks up the grass again and enters. But when she wants to leave the room things become complicated. She puts the grass on the floor and grasps the doorknob. But then she perceives that in pulling the door toward her she will simultaneously chase away the grass which she placed between the door and the threshold. She therefore picks it up in order to put it outside the door's zone of movement (*ibid.,* pp. 338-339).

Another observation, although lengthy, is cited as an especially graphic illustration of the process of sensory-motor invention:

> *Observation 180.*—Another mental invention, derived from a mental combination and not only from a sensorimotor appresticeship was that which permitted Lucienne to rediscover an object inside a matchbox. At 1;4 (0), that is to say, right after the preceding experiment, I play at hiding the chain in the same box used in Observation 179. I begin by opening the box as wide as possible, and putting the chain into its cover (where Lucienne herself put it, but deeper). Lucienne, who has already practiced filling and emptying her pail and various receptacles, then grasps the box and turns it over without hesitation. No invention is involved of course (it is the simple application of a schema, acquired through groping) but knowledge of this behavior pattern of Lucienne is useful for understanding what follows.
>
> Then I put the chain inside an empty matchbox (where the matches belong), then close the box leaving an opening of 10 mm. Lucienne begins by turning the whole thing over, then tries to grasp the chain through the

opening. Not succeeding, she simply puts her index finger into the slit and so succeeds in getting out a small fragment of the chain; she then pulls it until she has completely solved the problem.

Here begins the experiment which we want to emphasize. I put the chain back into the box and reduce the opening to 3 mm. It is understood that Lucienne is not aware of the functioning of the opening and closing of the matchbox and has not seen me prepare the experiment. She only possesses the two preceding schemata: turning the box over in order to empty it of its contents, and sliding her finger into the slit to make the chain come out. It is of course this last procedure that she tries first: she puts her finger inside and gropes to reach the chain, but fails completely. A pause follows during which Lucienne manifests a very curious reaction bearing witness not only to the fact that she tries to think out the situation and to represent to herself through mental combination the operations to be performed, but also to the role played by imitation in the genesis of representations. Lucienne mimics the widening of the slip.

She looks at the slit with great attention; then, several times in succession, she opens and shuts her mouth, at first slightly, then wider and wider! Apparently Lucienne understands the existence of a cavity subjacent to the slit and wishes to enlarge that cavity. The attempt at representation which she thus furnishes is expressed plastically, that is to say, due to inability to think out the situation in words or clear visual images she uses a simple motor indication as "signifier" or symbol. Now, as the motor reaction which presents itself for filling this role is none other than imitation, that is to say, representation by acts, which, doubtless earlier than any mental image, makes it possible not only to divide into parts the spectacles seen but also to evoke and reproduce them at will. Lucienne, by opening her mouth thus expresses, or even reflects her desire to enlarge the opening of the box. This schema of imitation, with which she is familiar, constitutes for her the means of thinking out the situation. There is doubtless added to it an element of magic-phenomenalistic causality or efficacy. Just as she often uses imitation to act upon persons and make them reproduce their interesting movements, so also it is probable that the act of opening her mouth in front of the slit to be enlarged implies some underlying idea of efficacy.

Soon after this phase of plastic reflection, Lucienne unhesitatingly puts her finger in the slit and, instead of trying as before to reach the chain, she pulls so as to enlarge the opening. She succeeds and grasps the chain (ibid., pp. 337-338).

Piaget finds it useful to discuss the stage-6 pattern in terms of the dual processes of *representation* and *invention*. The first refers to the fact that the various schemas whose interrelations make up the pattern are internally represented by the child before being acted out in reality. The second concerns the interrelating of these representations.

As regards representation, it is Piaget's contention that the development of sign behavior described for earlier stages has taken an extremely significant turn in stage 6. The child now is able to represent events not present in the perceptual field by means of what Piaget calls *symbolic images*. The most transparent illustration of a symbolic image is contained in the observation cited above. According to Piaget, Lucienne makes a primitive, but nonetheless genuine, symbolic representation of the potential (but not yet performed) schema of widening the opening in the matchbox. This representation assumes the form of opening and closing her mouth. What Piaget is asserting is that, prior to language— the symbolic system par excellence through which the child is eventually socialized—there is good evidence that the infant has at his disposal certain motoric or imagistic symbolic devices which permit him some limited internal manipulation of reality. In fact, although lack of space has prevented a really extended discussion of it in this book, the several stages prior to stage 6 evidence still more primitive forms of sign behavior from which the present symbolic image has evolved (*ibid.*, pp. 185-196; 247-252; 327-328; 355-356). The problem of preverbal representation will crop up again in Chapter 4 when the development of imitation and play are considered.

The nature of invention in stage 6 can be stated simply: it consists of internally combining into a new totality, through the now familiar process of reciprocal assimilation, the representations of the various schemas involved in the act to be performed:

> The novelty of the case of invention consists, on the contrary, in that henceforth the schemata entering into action remain in a state of latent activity and combine with each other before (and not after) their external and material application. This is why invention seems to come from the void. The act which suddenly arises results from a previous reciprocal assimilation instead of manifesting its vicissitudes before everyone (*ibid.*, p. 347).

> In short, invention through sensorimotor deduction is nothing other than a spontaneous reorganization of earlier schemata which are accommodated by themselves to the new situation, through reciprocal assimilation. Until the present time, that is to say, including empirical groping, the earlier schemata only functioned due to real use, that is to say, by actual application to a concretely perceived datum. . . . On the contrary, in preventive deduction, the schemata function internally by themselves, without requiring a series of external acts to aliment them continually from without (*ibid.*, pp. 347-348).

With the advent of the capacity to represent actions rather than simply to perform them, the sensory-motor period draws to a close and the child is ready for an analogous but even more extended and tortuous apprenticeship in the use of symbols. The end of the sensory-motor period is thus synchronous with the beginning of the preoperational period. This does not, of course, mean that the child no longer continues to develop in the sensory-motor sphere. But it does mean that henceforth the most advanced *intellectual* adaptations of which a given child is capable will take place in a conceptual-symbolic rather than purely sensory-motor arena. And intellectual adaptations, after all, are what Piaget is concerned with.

CHAPTER FOUR

Special Sensory-Motor Evolutions and the Subperiod of Preoperational Thought

CHAPTER 3 described the over-all, general characteristics of sensory-motor development—the genesis of the basic adaptational forms from birth through late infancy. The first major section of this chapter takes up more specialized intellectual achievements of the same period: in particular, the sensory-motor construction of imitation, play, objects, space, causality, and time. The remainder of the chapter is devoted to a general-theoretical description of intellectual adaptations found in the so-called subperiod of preoperational thought.

THE SENSORY-MOTOR PERIOD: SPECIAL DEVELOPMENTS

The six special developments we are about to consider are not to be conceived as something detached from and outside the developmental mainstream described in Chapter 3. Rather, each special evolution is a particular aspect of the general evolution, or better, *is* that general evolution considered from a particular point of view. The development of imitation, for instance, concerns those sensory-motor activities which lean in the direction of a relative assimilation-accommodation imbalance in favor of accommodation, and the converse is true for the development of play (see Chapter 2). The genesis of objects, space, causality, and time also pertains to the same familiar sensory-motor forms—primary, secondary, and tertiary reactions, coordination of familiar means, and all the rest, but from the standpoint of the construction of these specific categories of experience.

When one examines the separate developments, it becomes clear that achievements in any one are completely intertwined with and dependent upon achievements in the remaining five and in the general development itself. To highlight this sense of interdependency, Piaget describes each special development in the framework of the six stages of general development presented in Chapter 3, e.g., the stage 4 of the development of space is approximately the same age interval as stage 4 of sensory-motor development-in-general. It would be unnecessarily space-consuming to detail, stage by stage, precisely how each achievement is a necessary function of all the others; the reader can probably deduce the connections himself anyhow, once the separate developments have been presented. Perhaps a single example here will serve for the whole class.

It will be recalled that stage 6 (18 months and older) is the period in which the child forms his first crude representations of reality and combines these internally to deduce problem solutions prior to experimentation. These achievements result in (and in part result from) the ability to imitate models not present in the immediate perceptual field, to engage in pretense play (pretending to go to sleep, play with a toy, etc.), to imagine correctly the location of an object whose itinerary he has inferred but not seen directly, to locate both self and objects in a common, all-encompassing space, to infer objective causes where only effects are seen and vice versa, and to reconstruct memories of past events.

Imitation

It was stated in Chapter 2 that sensory-motor development as a whole can be described in terms of a progression from an original assimilation-accommodation mélange to a state of differentiation and complementarity. Since imitation and play respectively represent specialized accommodatory and assimilatory activities, their genesis can be characterized in the same terms. That is, both imitation and play arise almost imperceptibly as separate functions from initial adaptational patterns in which neither can be clearly identified. And when they do emerge as really distinct subvarieties of intelligent action in stage 6, they proceed to interact and complement each other (1951a, pp. 102-103). For example, the stage-6 child who pretends to go to sleep is not only indulging in play, i.e., freely assimilating the immediate reality to a play (or *ludic,* as Piaget calls it) schema, he is also very clearly imitating past going-to-sleep actions.

An important consequence of the undifferentiation-to-differentiation hypothesis with respect to play and imitation is that Piaget will search the early sensory-motor period for *precursors* of these two activities, that is, behaviors which—not yet really imitation or play—are their functional predecessors, their extrapolations backward in the developmental sequence. This backward-extrapolation strategy is one which Piaget often uses in an attempt to find coherent explanations for developmental phenomena. As we have seen already (Chapter 3), stages 1-3 can be considered extrapolations of this kind with respect to intentional (intelligent, in the narrow sense) adaptations. Now to the specifics of imitation development.

STAGE 1

As usual, this stage is largely one of behavioral ciphers. At most, there are shaky and admittedly equivocal examples of the infant being stimulated to cry by hearing the crying of other infants. The most daring speculation here is that the child assimilates the crying of others to his own crying, and thus hearing it activates the schema in typical reproductive assimilation fashion.

STAGE 2

Here the reproductive assimilation interpretation becomes more clearly justified. As the infant develops and intercoordinates primary circular reactions, one sees isolated and sporadic instances where the child inaugurates, or at least intensifies, some habitual behavior pattern upon perceiving another person enact the pattern. For example:

> At 0;2 (17) he [Laurent] imitated me as soon as I uttered sounds identical with his own (such as *arr*), or even when it was merely my intonation which recalled his. He again imitated me even when he had not been crooning himself immediately before. He began by smiling, then made an effort with his mouth open (remaining silent for a moment) and only then produced a sound. Such a behaviour clearly indicates the existence of a definite attempt at imitation (1951a, p. 9).

Piaget considers the behavior of this stage preimitative rather than truly imitative, however. In gist, the child treats the action of the model as one of his *own* actions, simply assimilating it to a primary schema as though it were a repetition he himself had just made. The child never attempts to imitate a sound, a movement, etc., which is new to him at this stage. On the contrary, the "imitation" only takes place if the model has first imitated the child.

STAGE 3

In this stage there is definite progress. The child is frequently seen to make deliberate and systematic imitations of sounds and movements made by others:

> At 0;4 (23), without any previous practice, I showed L. my hand which I was slowly opening and closing. She seemed to be imitating me. All the time my suggestion lasted she kept up a similar movement and either stopped or did something else as soon as I stopped.
> There was the same reaction when I repeated the experiment at 0;4 (26). But was this response of L. merely due to an attempt at prehension? To test this, I then showed her some other object. She again opened and closed her hand, but only twice, then immediately tried to seize the object and suck it. I resumed the experiment with my hand, and she clearly imitated it, her gesture being quite different from the one she made on seeing the toy.
> At 0;5 (6) I resumed my observation, with my arm raised in front of her.

She alternately opened and closed her hand, without even bringing her arm nearer. She was therefore not attempting to grasp it. When, however, in order to check this I put a carrot in the same place, there was an immediate attempt at prehension. There was thus no doubt that in the first case she had been imitating (*ibid.*, p. 23).

There are nonetheless decided limitations to stage-3 imitation. In the first place, the child can still in general imitate only responses already in his repertory; there is only the slightest hint of accommodations to new responses. And secondly, there is the interesting limitation that the child can imitate only those of his responses which are visually or auditorily perceptible to him. Both these restricting conditions are present in the following observation:

> At 0;6 (1) I waved goodbye, then put out my tongue, then opened my mouth and put my thumb into it. There was no reaction, since the first parts of her face which she could not see. Same reactions at 0;6 (22), 0;6 (25), movement did not correspond to a known schema, and the others involved etc. (*ibid.*, p. 28).

STAGE 4

Both the growing flexibility and mobility of schemas and the growing coordination among visual, auditory, tactile, and kinesthetic modes permit the stage-4 baby to overcome the two limitations noted above, at least in part. The child first of all begins to imitate new models. Thus, there begins to be a perceptible opposition between the past—what he can do already—and the future—the sights and sounds he can accommodate to and thereby imitate. Imitation is now beginning to detach itself from adaptations-in-general to become a specialized tool of acquisition (*ibid.*, p. 50).

The infant also starts to imitate actions of others which correspond to actions of his own which he cannot see or hear. For example, he can imitate movements of sticking out his tongue, opening and closing the mouth, etc. A curious and instructive variation on this pattern is that in which the child imitates by making movements structurally analogous rather than identical with those of the model:

> OBS. 29. From 0;10 to 0;11 (0) the action of opening and closing the eyes produced no reaction in the case of L. At 0;11 (5), however, when I opened and closed my eyes, she first opened and closed her hands, very slowly and systematically. Then, equally slowly, she opened and closed her mouth, saying *tata* (*ibid.*, p. 39).

STAGE 5

In accord with the over-all strategy of experimentation and exploration we have seen to be characteristic of this stage, the child's imitative behavior becomes more deliberate and active and, above all, more precisely accommodated to the model. Although the difference is one of degree rather than kind, the stage-5 infant goes about his imitations with more subtlety and finesse:

> OBS. 42. At 1;1 (23) L. carefully watched me swinging my watch which I held by the end of the chain. As soon as I put it down, she imitated me, but held the chain at a point close to the watch. When her hand was too near the watch to allow it to swing properly, she put it down in front of her and then picked up the chain again, taking care to increase the distance (*ibid.*, p. 54).

STAGE 6

With the onset of primitive representations there is a corresponding advance in imitation. This advance takes three forms. First, the child is able immediately, without the empirical groping of stage 5, to imitate complex new models. Second, he begins to imitate the actions of objects as well as those of persons. An example of this is Lucienne's imitation, by mouth movements, of the opening and closing of a matchbox (see Chapter 3). Similarly, Laurent at 1;0 (11) imitated the sound and vibratory movements of a rattling window (1951a, p. 66).

The new pattern of the greatest ultimate significance, however, is that which Piaget calls *deferred imitation:* the child reproduces an absent model through memory. Piaget gives a number of interesting examples of deferred imitation but the following is surely the most amusing one:

> OBS. 52. At 1;4 (3) J. had a visit from a little boy of 1;6, whom she used to see from time to time, and who, in the course of the afternoon got into a terrible temper. He screamed as he tried to get out of a play-pen and pushed it backwards, stamping his feet. J. stood watching him in amazement, never having witnessed such a scene before. The next day, she herself screamed in her play-pen and tried to move it, stamping her foot lightly several times in succession. The imitation of the whole scene was most striking. Had it been immediate, it would naturally not have involved representation, but coming as it did after an interval of more than twelve hours, it must have involved some representative or pre-representative element (*ibid.*, p. 63).

Play

As with imitation, the origins of play are much more difficult to discriminate with confidence than are its various developed forms in the later stages. Once again, the assimilation-for-assimilation's-sake character, which Piaget believes to be the essence of play, only gradually emerges as a *modus operandi* distinct and separate from an undifferentiated general adaptation.

STAGE 1

Even less can be said here than of stage-1 imitation. The neonate shows at most a kind of functional equivalent of play when it indulges in "empty," accommodation-free sucking movements (without breast or bottle present).

STAGE 2

Once more, little is seen that is unequivocally play rather than straight adaptation. What one does see are primary circular reactions which are pursued with sober concentration in their apprenticeship but, once mastered, often appear to be pursued for the sheer pleasure of doing so.

> OBS. 59. It will be remembered that T. [Laurent], at 0;2 (21), adopted the habit of throwing his head back to look at familiar things from this new position. . . . At 0:2 (23 or 24) he seemed to repeat this movement with ever-increasing enjoyment and ever-decreasing interest in the external result: he brought his head back to the upright position and then threw it back again time after time, laughing loudly. In other words, the circular reaction ceased to be "serious" or instructive, if such expressions can be applied to a baby of less than three months, and became a game (*ibid.*, p. 91).

STAGE 3

The distinction between freely assimilative play and the serious business of adaptation becomes a little easier to see in this stage:

> OBS. 60. One need only re-read obs. 94-104 of the volume N.I. [1952c] to find all the examples needed of the transition from assimilation proper to secondary reactions, to the pure assimilation which characterises play properly so called. For example, in obs. 94, L. discovered the possibility of making objects hanging from the top of her cot swing. At first, between 0;3 (6) and 0;3 (16), she studied the phenomenon without smiling, or smiling only a little, but with an appearance of intense interest, as though she was studying it. Subsequently, however, from about 0;4 she never indulged in this activity, which lasted up to about 0;8 and even beyond, without a show of great joy and power. In other words assimilation was no longer accompanied by accommodation and therefore was no longer an effort at comprehension: there was merely assimilation to the activity itself, i.e., use of the phenomenon for the pleasure of the activity, and that is play (1951a, pp. 91-92).

STAGE 4

With the advent of means-ends behavior we are in possession of a better criterion for the play-adaptation distinction: the child abandons the end in favor of playing with the means itself.

> OBS. 61. At 0;7 (13), after learning to remove an obstacle to gain his objective, T. began to enjoy this kind of exercise. When several times in succession I put my hand or a piece of cardboard between him and the toy he desired, he reached the stage of momentarily forgetting the toy and pushed aside the obstacle, bursting into laughter. What had been intelligent adaptation had thus become play, through transfer of interest to the action itself, regardless of its aim (*ibid.*, p. 92).

There is also another play pattern which will later evolve into something more significant in stage 6; Piaget calls this *ritualization*. An example is the following. The child encounters some of the usual stimuli associated with going to sleep (e.g., pillow, blanket, etc.) and momentarily goes through the ritual of sleeping: he lies down, sucks his thumb, and so on.

STAGE 5

By stage 5 the differentiation between play and adaptation is well advanced. The child often turns a new adaptation into a play ritual almost as soon as it is discovered:

> Obs. 63. At 0;10 (3) J. put her nose close to her mother's cheek and then pressed it against it, which forced her to breathe much more loudly. This phenomenon at once interested her, but instead of merely repeating it or varying it so as to investigate it, she quickly complicated it for the fun of it: she drew back an inch or two, screwed up her nose, sniffed and breathed out alternately very hard (as if she were blowing her nose), then again thrust her nose against her mother's cheek, laughing heartily. These actions were repeated at least once a day for more than a month, as a ritual (*ibid.*, p. 94).

STAGE 6

The emergence of symbolization in stage 6 has as profound an effect on play as it did on imitation. Specifically, the child now becomes capable of true pretense or make-believe. In stage 4, the child indulges in simple rituals when confronted with stimuli adequate to the schemas in question; for example, the sight of the pillow triggers the usual schemas associated with it. In stage 6, on the other hand, the stimuli no longer need be adequate in this sense. The child can playfully reenact the schema by treating inadequate stimuli *as if* they were adequate, i.e., by treating them as symbols of something else. The following example makes the distinction clear:

> Obs. 64 (a). In the case of J., who has been our main example in the preceding observations, the true ludic symbol, with every appearance of awareness of "make-believe" first appeared at 1;3 (12) in the following circumstances. She saw a cloth whose fringed edges vaguely recalled those of her pillow; she seized it, held a fold of it in her right hand, sucked the thumb of the same hand and lay down on her side, laughing hard. She kept her eyes open, but blinked from time to time as if she were alluding to closed eyes. Finally, laughing more and more, she cried "Néné" (Nono). The same cloth started the same game on the following days. At 1;3 (13) she treated the collar of her mother's coat in the same way. At 1;3 (30) it was the tail of her rubber donkey which represented the pillow! And from 1;5 onwards she made her animals, a bear and a plush dog also do "nono."
>
> Similarly, at 1;6 (28) she said "avon" (*savon* = soap), rubbing her hands together and pretending to wash them (without any water).
>
> At 1;8 (15) and the following days she pretended she was eating various things, e.g., a piece of paper, saying "Very nice" (*ibid.*, p. 96).

Piaget's treatment of play, imitation, and related phenomena does not end with stage 6 of the sensory-motor period. For example, stage-6 accomplishments in the realms of play and imitation will later be shown to be crucial in the transition from sensory-motor to conceptual adaptation. And there are other things most of which, unfortunately, we shall not have space to cover in any detail in this volume. There is his account of the ultimate fate of play and imitation in later development; included here are his general explanation of play and his developmental-structural classification of games. And perhaps of most general interest, there is a critique of Freudian dream theory and his own highly provocative analysis of dream activity and unconscious or "secondary" symbolism.

The Object Concept

The four developments to be considered next involve looking at infant behavior from a position a shade different from the one from which general development, imitation, and play were examined (1954a, p. xxi). In the latter three, the emphasis is somewhat more upon the adaptive quality of the child's behavior itself, whether or not it is object-centered and exploratory, whether or not perceptually absent models can be imitated, etc. With the former, on the other hand, the orientation has more to do with how the infant interprets the world about him—what working conception of objects he seems to have, how he construes those connections between events which we call "causal," and so forth. The difference between the two approaches is not absolute: for example, in both cases Piaget considers careful observation of behavior the ultimate arbiter. But it is nonetheless a real difference, as will become apparent when we examine the four developments.

The first of these is the genesis of the object concept. In order to understand the details of this evolution, it is necessary from the outset to grasp Piaget's over-all position on what this development is moving towards, what conception of objects will constitute the criterion for "having" a developmentally mature object concept. For Piaget, a mature conception of objects most of all demands that an object be seen as an entity in its own right which exists and moves in a space common both to it and to the subject who observes it. Moreover, and very important, the continued existence of the object must be construed as separate from and independent of the activity which the subject intermittently applies to it. Thus, for the individual with this kind of object concept, the object is still believed to exist and live its own life even when he is no longer acting upon it, that is, looking at it, listening to it, manipulating it, etc. And finally, a necessary consequence of an independence and permanence imputed to external objects is the recognition that the self is also one object among others, which, like the others, has its own space-filling properties and its own movements in the common spatial field.

Piaget's analysis of object development is thus predicated on three guiding principles. The first is that the above are the appropriate criteria in terms of which this development can be interpreted. Second, from the point of view of these criteria, the young infant definitely does not apprehend objects as adults do, does not yet possess the object concept. And finally, the acquisition of this concept is by no means an all-or-nothing affair. There are distinguishable steps in its construction—stages in which the child has this aspect of it but not some other. In other words, there is a genuine *development* of the object concept.

STAGES 1 AND 2

If the young infant does not conceive of objects as adults do, what are they to him? Piaget believes that they are primarily sensations—images or pictures which, in his egocentricity, he cannot distinguish from the act of assimilating them. The infant "may consider the picture which he contemplates as the extension, if not the product, of his effort to see" (*ibid.,* p. 8). What he experiences are his own actions (but of course with no conception of the "he" which acts) and he is very, very far from considering the evanescent sensations which accompany these actions as indicating permanent and solid bodies which exist indifferently within and without his perceptual field. At most, Piaget feels, the infant in stages 1 and 2 tries to prolong or recapture the pleasing image by continuing to look, to listen, or to grasp.

Piaget believes that this interpretation of the infant's cognition of objects finds support in the behavior observed in these two stages. The characteristic response to the disappearance of an interesting object is a simple continuation of the accommodatory movements last made to it. For instance, the child continues to stare at the place where the object was last seen:

> OBS. 2. In the realm of sight, Jacqueline, as early as 0;2 (27) follows her mother with her eyes, and when her mother leaves the visual field, continues to look in the same direction until the picture reappears.
> Same observation with Laurent at 0;2 (1). I look at him through the hood of his bassinet and from time to time I appear at a more or less constant point; Laurent then watches that point when I am out of his sight and obviously expects to see me reappear (*ibid.,* p. 9).

STAGE 3

Stage 3 is a complex one from the standpoint of object development. The essential accomplishment is that the infant begins to extrapolate beyond the immediate perception in his attempts to maintain or recapture sensory-motor relations with objects. The essential limitation to this accomplishment is that what he seeks to maintain or recapture are still undifferentiated action-object experiences rather than objects *per se*. There are five principal behavior forms in which both the accomplishment and the limitation of this stage can be distinguished.

First, with growing ability to accommodate to rapid movements in the visual field, the infant begins to anticipate the future positions of moving objects by extrapolating from the seen trajectory. When, for example, an object drops to the floor the infant now leans over to look for it there instead of simply staring at the place from which it was released. Analogously, the child will make crude searching movements with his hands (outside the visual field) when he loses an object he was grasping. In both cases, however, the child gives up immediately if the vanished object does not come readily to hand or eye; the object still seems more an extension of the action encompassing it than a separate, enduring entity. For example, Jacqueline reaches for an object in front of her but immediately abandons the search as soon as Piaget covers the object with his hand, in general behaving as if the object no longer existed (*ibid.*, pp. 21-22).

A third behavior pattern which indicates definite progress is what Piaget calls the *deferred circular reaction*: the child begins an activity involving an object, abandons it for a short while to do something else, and then relocates the original object without error or hesitation. Once again, however, Piaget believes that it is the *action* rather than the *object* which has acquired an incipient permanence. A fourth and very interesting response pattern is that of anticipating a whole object on the basis of seeing only a part. Piaget cites a number of rich observations here (*ibid.*, pp. 28-32), some of which illustrate a curious sequence: nonreaction when a certain portion of the object shows, positive reaction when more shows, nonreaction again when less shows, and so on. To the question of whether these reactions indicate a concept of permanent and substantial objects, Piaget replies in the negative:

> Everything occurs as though the child believed that the object is alternately made and unmade. . . . When the child sees a part of the object emerge from the screen and he assumes the existence of the totality of that object, he does not yet consider this totality as being formed "behind" the screen; he simply admits that it is in the process of being formed at the moment of leaving the screen (*ibid.*, p. 31).

The fifth and final class of behaviors involves something which the child can do and also something else—very important in terms of later stages—which he cannot do. He can and does free his *perception* by removing obstacles, e.g., a blanket resting on his face. But, despite this advance and the considerable manual skill acquired by this age, he seems unable to free an *object* in the sense of looking for it behind a screen:

Obs. 28. At 0;7 (28) Jacqueline tries to grasp a celluloid duck on top of her quilt. She almost catches it, shakes herself, and the duck slides down beside her. It falls very close to her hand but behind a fold in the sheet. Jacqueline's eyes have followed the movement, she has even followed it with her outstretched hand. But as soon as the duck has disappeared—nothing more! It does not occur to her to search behind the fold of the sheet, which would be very easy to do (she twists it mechanically without searching at all). . . . I then take the duck from its hiding-place and place it near her hand three times. All three times she tries to grasp it, but when she is about to touch it I replace it very obviously under the sheet. Jacqueline immediately withdraws her hand and gives up. The second and third times I make her grasp the duck through the sheet and she shakes it for a brief moment but it does not occur to her to raise the cloth (*ibid.*, pp. 36-37).

STAGE 4

Stage 4 is easy to summarize from the standpoint of object development: the child begins to search actively for hidden objects, but with a highly interesting restriction on the searching pattern. First comes a transitional substage between stages 3 and 4 when the child searches behind a screen only if he was already in the process of reaching for the object at the moment it was hidden. Then the pattern becomes generalized; he regularly removes screens to attain objects without this limitation (providing, of course, that the actions of hiding the object were clearly visible to him the moment before). As to the "highly interesting restriction," Piaget summarizes it as follows:

The chief interest of this stage is that the active search for the vanished object is not immediately general, but is governed by a restrictive condition: the child looks for and conceives of the object only in a special position, the first place in which it was hidden and found. It is this peculiarity which enables us to contrast the present stage with the succeeding stages and which should be emphasized now.

The procedure is as follows, at least in the most characteristic period of the stage. Suppose an object is hidden at point A: the child searches for it and finds it. Next the object is placed in B and is covered before the child's eyes; although the child has continued to watch the object and has seen it disappear in B, he nevertheless immediately tries to find it in A! We shall call this the typical reaction of the fourth stage. Toward the end of the stage a reaction appears which we shall consider residual. It is as follows: the child follows with his eyes the object in B, searches for it in this second place, and if he does not find it immediately (because the object is buried too deeply, etc.) he returns to A (*ibid.*, pp. 49-50).

Here are two samples of the pattern:

Obs. 40. At 0;10 (18) Jacqueline is seated on a mattress without anything to disturb or distract her (no coverlets, etc.). I take her parrot from her hands and hide it twice in succession under the mattress, on her left, in A. Both times Jacqueline looks for the object immediately and grabs it. Then I take it from her hands and move it very slowly before her eyes to the corresponding place on her right, under the mattress, in B. Jacqueline watches this.

movement very attentively, but at the moment when the parrot disappears in B she turns to her left and looks where it was before, in A.

During the next four attempts I hide the parrot in B every time without having first placed it in A. Every time Jacqueline watches me attentively. Nevertheless each time she immediately tries to rediscover the object in A; she turns the mattress over and examines it conscientiously. During the last two attempts, however, the search tapers off (*ibid.*, p. 51).

OBS. 52. Let us cite an observation made not on our children but on an older cousin who suggested to us all the foregoing studies. Gérard, at 13 months, knows how to walk, and is playing ball in a large room. He throws the ball, or rather lets it drop in front of him and, either on his feet or on all fours, hurries to pick it up. At a given moment the ball rolls under an armchair. Gérard sees it and, not without some difficulty, takes it out in order to resume the game. Then the ball rolls under a sofa at the other end of the room. Gérard has seen it pass under the fringe of the sofa; he bends down to recover it. But as the sofa is deeper than the armchair and the fringe does prevent a clear view, Gérard gives up after a moment; he gets up, crosses the room, goes right under the armchair and carefully explores the place where the ball was before (*ibid.*, p. 59).

What is the meaning of these examples for object development? Once again we let Piaget speak for himself:

It is possible that . . . the object is still not the same to the child as it is to us: a substantial body, individualized and displaced in space without depending on the action context in which it is inserted. Thus the object is, perhaps, to the child, only a particularly striking aspect of the total picture in which it is contained; at least it would not manifest so many "moments of freedom" as do our images. Hence there would not be one chain, one doll, one watch, one ball, etc., individualized, permanent, and independent of the child's activity, that is, of the special positions in which that activity takes place or has taken place, but there would still exist only images such as "ball-under-the-arm-chair," "doll-attached-to-the-hammock," "watch-under-a-cushion," "papa-at-his-window," etc. Certainly the same object reappearing in different practical positions or contexts is recognized, identified, and endowed with permanence as such. In this sense it is relatively independent. But, without being truly conceived as having several copies, the object may manifest itself to the child as assuming a limited number of distinct forms of a nature intermediate between unity and plurality, and in this sense it remains a part of its context (*ibid.*, pp. 62-63).

STAGE 5

At this stage the child overcomes the dependence upon past searching habits and learns to search only at the place where the object was last seen. However, when the object's journey to its hiding place is not directly *perceptible* to the child (although, for an older subject, easily *inferable*), the child fails to find it. The following example illustrates both the progress and the limitations inherent in the stage-5 pattern. If one moves a small object behind screen A, then behind B, then behind C (and leaves it there), the child at this stage—unlike the child at stage 4—

goes immediately to C to find the object. However, if one transports the same small object *in one's closed hand* behind screen A and leaves it there, the child will search assiduously in the hand, look perplexed when he fails to find the object, but will not think of looking behind A. There is a kind of *décalage* here. Just as the stage-4 child has difficulty in managing *visible* displacements, the stage-5 child fails to cope with *invisible* displacements, i.e., displacements which must be inferred or imagined (*ibid.*, p. 77).

STAGE 6

It is obviously no accident that the sensory- motor mastery of invisible displacements comes in stage 6, the stage in which the child first becomes capable of representational and symbolic adaptations. The following observation illustrates this achievement:

> OBS. 64. I. At 1;7 (20) Jacqueline watches me when I put a coin in my hand, then put my hand under a coverlet. I withdraw my hand closed; Jacqueline opens it, then searches under the coverlet until she finds the object. I take back the coin at once, put it in my hand and then slip my closed hand under a cushion situated at the other side (on her left and no longer on her right); Jacqueline immediately searches for the object under the cushion. I repeat the experiment by hiding the coin under a jacket; Jacqueline finds it without hesitation.
>
> II. I complicate the test as follows: I place the coin in my hand, then my hand under the cushion. I bring it forth closed and immediately hide it under the coverlet. Finally I withdraw it and hold it out, closed, to Jacqueline. Jacqueline then pushes my hand aside without opening it (she guesses that there is nothing in it, which is new), she looks under the cushion, then directly under the coverlet where she finds the object.
>
> During a second series (cushion and jacket) she behaves in the same way.
>
> I then try a series of three displacements: I put the coin in my hand and move my closed hand sequentially from A to B and from B to C; Jacqueline sets my hand aside, then searches in A, in B and finally in C (*ibid.*, p. 79).

Piaget feels that behavior of this kind strongly presumes an object concept which is developmentally mature in terms of the criteria stated earlier. Quite independent of his own actions with regard to it, the child now imagines a series of possible loci for an object conceived as substantial and permanently existing in the common space. The object is now definitely seen as a thing apart, subject to its own laws of displacement just as the child himself—another object—is subject to them. As to the latter, Piaget's section on the development of the spatial field cites evidence that the stage-6 child does in fact see himself as an object which occupies a segment of space, an object which from time to time changes its spatial position relative to other objects, and so on (*ibid.*, pp. 206-208). It is of course true, and later chapters will document it, that the child will eventually learn much more about the invariant and variant properties of objects than the mere fact of their substantiality and existence independent of self. But the cognition of this "mere fact" is an important acquisition in its own right, and the one upon which all others must necessarily build.

Space

Not surprisingly, the evolution of the child's grasp of space parallels very closely that of objects. In the beginning the infant's space seems really to be a collection of separate "spaces," each entirely centered on his own activity. At the term of sensory-motor development, on the other hand, the child apprehends a single, objective space within which all objects, including the perceiver, are contained and interrelated. Just as with object development, the development of space is primarily one of progressive externalization and desubjectification.

THE ALGEBRA OF GROUPS

Throughout his discussion of space development Piaget constantly refers to what in logical algebra are called *groups*. The group concept is very important for Piaget. It appears at all developmental levels as a reference point for analyzing the structure of cognitions, in childhood and adolescence as well as in the development of space in infancy. Before examining the latter, then, it is necessary to digress a bit and describe what a group is.

A group is an abstract structure or system which possesses certain definite properties. A system is said to be a group if it consists of a specified set of *elements* (arbitrary) and a specified *operation* performed on these elements (also arbitrary) and the following hold true:

Composition. The product which results from combining any element with any other by means of the defined operation is itself an element in the system. Thus, if we let A and B represent any two group elements and let 'o' represent the operation, then for any $A \circ B = C$, C is itself a group element.

Associativity. $(A \circ B) \circ C = A \circ (B \circ C)$.[1] That is, combining C with the result of combining B with A yields the same result as combining with A the result of combining C with B. And of course the associativity also holds for more complex combinations: thus, $(A \circ B) \circ (C \circ D) = (A \circ B \circ C) \circ D = A \circ (B \circ C) \circ D$, etc.

Identity. The set of elements contains one and only one element, called the *identity element,* which combined with any other group element leaves that element unchanged. If we arbitrarily call the identity element X, then $A \circ X = A$, $B \circ X = B$, etc.

---

[1] If it is also true that $A \circ B \circ C = C \circ B \circ A$, $B \circ C \circ A$, etc., for any group elements (commutativity), the group is said to be *Abelian*; if commutativity does not hold, it is said to be *non-Abelian*. Most of the spatial groups Piaget describes in connection with sensory-motor development appear to be non-Abelian.

Reversibility. For each and every group element there is one and only one element, called an *inverse,* which when combined with that element yields the identity element. If we represent inverse elements by the prime sign (e.g., A'), then $A \circ A' = X, B \circ B' = X$, etc.

There are a number of familiar examples of groups. For instance, the set of positive and negative integers (as elements) under the operation of addition form a group. Taking the four requisites of a group in sequence, any integer added to any other yields an integer; it is true that $2 + (3 + 4) = (2 + 3) + 4$; there is one and only one identity element—zero —so that $0 + 2 = 2, 0 + 3 = 3$, etc.; and there is one and only one inverse for each element, e.g., $2 + (-2) = 0, 3 + (-3) = 0$, etc. A nonarithmetic example would be the rotations of a rigid bar attached at one end to a fixed center (as the hand of a clock is). Here, the rotary movements are the elements and the addition of the rotary movements is the operation. The addition of any two rotations amounts to a rotation; the sum of two rotations added to a third is equal to one rotation added to the sum of the two others, thus $(A + B) + C = A + (B + C)$; the 360° rotation (or the 0° rotation to which it is equivalent) serves as the identity element $(A + 360° = A)$; and for each and every turn in a given direction, there is an equal and opposite inverse turn which annuls it (yields the identity rotation). Not all sets of elements and constituent operation form groups, however. For instance, the set of positive integers from 1 to 10 under addition violates all but the associativity condition. Thus, $9 + 10 = 19$ (19 not a defined element of the set); there is no identity element (0 not in the set) and no inverses (negative integers not in the set).

PIAGET'S USE OF THE GROUP CONCEPT

How does Piaget make use of the concept of group structure in his analysis of intellectual development? This question cannot be given anything like a complete answer until the cognitive organizations of middle childhood and adolescence and the notion of systems-in-equilibrium are examined in detail (Chapters 5, 6, and 7). A few things can be said at this point, however.

In the first place, Piaget believes that certain group properties—in particular, the *reversibility* property—hold very generally for adaptations of otherwise widely differing form and complexity (1954a, p. 101). For instance, all circular reactions can in a sense be said to possess at least the reversibility characteristic: the child performs an action (A), then returns to the (identity) starting point by an inverse action (A'), then repeats the direct action A again, etc. One sees this rhythmic and cyclic direct-inverse-direct character in, for example, the primary circular reaction of scratching an object, withdrawing the hand, scratching again, withdrawing the hand, etc. And much later, we shall see that the 8-year-old shows a parallel use of direct and inverse operations in his cognitive manipulations of reality, now however on a symbolic rather than sensory-motor plane. Although not discussed by Piaget in this way, the group structure is reminiscent of the functional invariants (assimilation, accommodation, and organization) in that it provides a kind of constant organizational standard against which or in terms of which cognition at all stages is analyzed.

As for the specific problem of spatial organization, Piaget finds it useful to analyze the successive steps by describing the *kind* of spatial group predominant at each level. Each of the three types of spatial groups discriminated—*practical, subjective,* and *objective*—naturally has reference to the dimension in which object development was cast: namely, the extent to which, in cognition, self and actions are dissociated from the externals with which they interact. In a sense, a brief description of these three almost summarizes the sensory-motor development of space.

The *practical group* refers to an organization of sensory-motor actions with respect to objects in space which, when viewed by the observer, does possess some or all the characteristics of a mathematical group. However, and hence the term *practical,* the infant himself is aware of neither action nor object as separate domains and therefore cannot perceive these grouplike regularities, either among objects themselves or between action and objects. For instance, for the observer the 3-month-old infant exhibits group characteristics when he looks at *A*, then successively at *B, C, D,* etc., then inverts the latter movements to return again to *A*. But the young infant cannot yet perceive himself act and hence cannot in any sense recognize the organization inherent in his acts, let alone recognize the grouplike regularities indigenous to objects displacing themselves through space.

In the *objective group,* on the other hand, objects in space are seen as related to each other directly, independent of the subject in so far as the subject himself is one more object in the spatial matrix. Freed from the egocentric illusion, the child is able to take account of the movements of objects from one spatial position to another and be cognizant of the fact that an object which moves from *A* to *B* can be returned from *B* to *A*, that one can get to *C* either stepwise by the route *AB* then *BC* or by going directly—nonstop—from *A* to *C* (associativity) and so forth through all the group properties. In short, there is now an organized space, distinct from the subject but including him, which consists of an orderly and coherent array of positions and potential displacements between positions.

The *subjective group* is intermediate between these two. Unlike the case with the practical group, the child can perceive his own acts with respect to objects in space (arm and hand movements mainly). But unlike the case with the objective group, the actions which he perceives are still not dissociated from the objects upon which they bear. He does not yet apprehend the interrelations among objects *per se*; what are "grouped" are the action-object amalgams. Most simply, the subjective group can be described as a practical group in which the subject is in part aware of the role of his own actions in the various outcomes (*ibid.*, pp. 121, 150).

STAGES 1 AND 2

These are the stages[2] in which pure practical groups hold sway. The child does perform reversible actions—losing and finding a sensory image, etc.—but with no separation between sensation and stimulus and hence no awareness at all of the role of his own action. Piaget makes the interesting additional point about stages 1 and 2 that what the child apprehends (with the primitive meaning of "apprehend" understood) is not a single, unitary space but a collection of unrelated spaces organized around the major sensory-motor spheres of activity. Thus, there is a buccal space, a visual space, an auditory space, a tactile space, and so on, rather than a common spatial container in which all are included. Only when these various activity spheres have been coordinated does a unitary space even become possible for the child.

STAGE 3

With the growing coordination between schemas, especially between vision and prehension, come two acquisitions which transform practical groups into subjective groups. First, the child begins actively to manipulate objects via the secondary circular reaction; in doing this, he is for the first time in a position to notice the spatial relations which unite perceived objects to each other. Second, he begins to perceive himself acting on things; or more accurately, he perceives his hands and arms interacting with objects. But the basic limitation of the subjective group is very much with him: the organization which he perceives is an organization of undifferentiated action × object and not that of an objective space containing self and other objects.

The concrete details of stage-3 spatial acquisitions are complex and difficult to summarize (to some degree, and unfortunately for presentation purposes, this tends to be true for the whole of Piaget's treatment of early space development). They mainly cluster around accomplishments relating to the visual search for rapidly moving objects, the visual rediscovery of objects after having looked away for a period of time, the manual rotation of objects (e.g., finding the "business end" of a bottle

---

[2] In his book on space (Piaget and Inhelder, 1956, ch. 1) Piaget describes another approach to the sensory-motor evolution of space perception, complementary and parallel to the one described here (1954a). In that approach, which we do not have space to describe in this book, the emphasis is upon the type of geometric relations—topological, projective, and euclidean—the child copes with at the various stages.

presented in positions other than the usual one), the space-development aspects of ordinary secondary circular reactions, and the perception of depth (the distinction between front and back, near and far, etc.).

As regards the last Piaget makes the interesting hypothesis, based on his behavioral observations, that near space (within grasping distance especially) is cognized quite differently than far space by the stage-3 child. While near space gradually becomes inserted in subjective groups relating to depth, far space is still the flat picture-screen of the first two stages. The following passage vividly expresses Piaget's views on both the early development of depth and infantile space perception in general:

> How, then, can we form an image of this space of the third stage? To resume our comparison, distant space remains analogous to the sky in immediate perception, whereas near space is comparable to our perception of the terrestrial environment in which planes of depth are regulated by the action. But here the sky must be envisaged as closely enveloping the subject and receding very gradually. Before the prehension of visual objects the child is in the center of a sort of moving and colored sphere, whose images imprison him without his having any hold on them other than by making them reappear by movements of head and eyes. Then when he begins to grasp what he sees the sphere expands little by little and the objects grasped are regulated in depth in relation to the body itself; distant space merely appears then as a kind of neutral zone in which prehension is not yet ventured, while near space is the realm of objects to be grasped. Doubtless it is only toward the end of this stage—after the establishment of planes of depth makes it possible to adjust objects in near space in relation to prehension—that distant space really appears distant, that is, a background in which relative distances remain undiscernible (*ibid.*, pp. 145-146).

STAGE 4

This is a stage of transition from subjective to objective spatial groups. There are a number of important acquisitions which can be briefly summarized, all of which indicate progress towards the construction of objective, dissociated-from-self spatial relations among objects. First, the child forms one very simple objective group: deliberately hiding and finding an object behind some kind of screen (e.g., a rug). Here, for the first time, the child forms a truly objective relationship between two entities in space (object and screen). Second, the child shows evidence of a budding constancy of size and shape; at least the child does things which look as though he were "studying" these constancies:

> OBS. 86. Lucienne, at 0;10 (7) and the days following, slowly brings her face close to objects she holds (rattles, dolls, etc.) until her nose is pressed against them. Then she moves away from them, looking at them very attentively, and begins over and over again (*ibid.*, p. 156).

A third and related achievement relevant to space is the discovery of perspectives or changes in shape resulting from different positions of the head. Although admittedly a difficult distinction, Piaget feels that these behaviors are no longer the simple attempt, seen in earlier stages, to "cause" an environmental change by one's actions; the child really seems to investigate the phenomenon in a tertiary-reaction, exploratory fashion:

> Obs. 91. At 0;11 (23) Jacqueline is in her baby swing and perceives her foot through one of the two openings for the use of the legs. She looks at it with great interest and visible astonishment, then stops looking to lean over the edge and discover her foot from the outside, Afterward she returns to the opening and looks at the same foot from this perspective. She alternates thus five or six times between the two points of view (*ibid.*, p. 160).

A fourth advance consists of further acquisitions in the manual rotation of objects, a behavior pattern begun in the preceding stage. The child now definitely treats objects as three-dimensional, solid entities which have an invisible but very real and permanently existing reverse side. The child in this stage also begins spontaneously to impart movement to objects in order to study their successive trajectories. Just as he hides objects to find them again, so also he displaces them from place to place with no other apparent motive than to watch and study their movements. Correlatively, he accurately takes account of object movements imparted by others, and in a way which suggests that the distinction between his own action and the objective trajectory of the outside entity is quite advanced:

> But the pertinent experiment is one that can be made by displacing objects in a straight line behind the child (cf. Obs. 74). For instance, at 0;9 (12) Laurent is in the garden, seated in a cárriage and unable to see behind it because of the half-raised hood; nevertheless when someone walks quietly from left to right or vice versa behind his carriage, he follows the movement on his left with his eyes to the point where he no longer sees anything, then turns abruptly to the right to rediscover the moving object (*ibid.*, pp. 167-168).

And finally, the distinction between near and not-so-near space begins to be abolished; in particular, the latter ceases to be a single, undifferentiated plane and becomes arranged into regions of differential depth:

> At 0;11 (7) Jacqueline is seated on a sofa. I make an object disappear under the sofa; she bends over to see it. This action shows that for her the vanished object is located on a plane deeper than that of the edge of the sofa, the latter plane itself belonging to distant space (inaccessible to prehension) (*ibid.*, p. 172).

STAGE 5

The objective groups which appear sporadically and in simplified form in stage 4 become both complicated and almost ubiquitous in stage 5. It could be said that the stage-4 child masters relations between self and object and only begins to discover the subtle interrelations among objects themselves. In stage 5, the child not only more actively pursues these last but also begins to place himself—his whole body, not just hands and arms—into the spatial nexus. The developmental advances of stage 5, like those of stages 3 and 4, appear in a variety of different behavioral patterns.

First, there is the heightened study of visual displacements of all kinds which comes from the tertiary-reaction strategy of exploration so characteristic of this stage: the child moves objects from *A* to *B* and then back to *A*, slides them up and down inclines, and in general investigates the position-filling and displacement properties of objects. The critical feature of all these patterns is that it seems to be not the child's *action* itself but the *objects* themselves which are studied—how they behave and relate to each other in space. Similarly indicating an interest in the spatial relations among objects are such new behaviors as: stacking a series of objects on top of each other; putting objects into containers and then removing them; rotating and reversing objects, no longer simply in relation to the self and its perspective, but in relation to other objects; and finally, organizing his own perambulations through space into grouplike structures. An example of this last is the following:

> OBS. 117. From 1;2 (15) Laurent has known how to construct, by walking, true groups of displacements. Here are two examples.
> The first is related to a gate which attracted him every day during his walk in the garden. To reach gate P, he was obliged either to follow two paths, AB and BP, together describing a right angle at point B, or to follow the rectilinear trajectory AP by going directly through the grass. At the beginning of his daily outings, when Laurent arrived at A he looked from afar at gate P, but thought he had to follow the trajectory ABP in order to reach it. Moreover he returned by the same path, extending line BA to reach another gate at the opposite end of the garden. After a few days he began the return trip by following line PA, whence the group AB, BP, and PA. Next he followed the same itinerary in the opposite direction, AP, PB, and BA. Thus it may be seen that an actual group is constituted by the child's own displacements (*ibid.*, p. 197).

STAGE 6

The child in stage 6 does two things still inaccessible to the infant of stage 5. First, he is able to keep a running tab on his own movements in space, internally representing his own previous displacements relative to those of other bodies. And second, as we know from object development, he is able to represent the invisible displacements of external objects. An example of the first is the child who has walked away from and out of sight of his house and, when asked where his house is, immediately turns around and points in the right direction (*ibid.*, p. 207). The best examples of the second achievement are those involving detour behavior:

Obs. 123. At 1;6 (8) Jacqueline throws a ball under a sofa. But instead of bending down at once and searching for it on the floor she looks at the place, realizes that the ball must have crossed under the sofa, and sets out to go behind it. But there is a table at her right and the sofa is backed against a bed on the left; therefore she begins by turning her back on the place where the ball disappeared, goes around the table, and finally arrives behind the sofa at the right place. Thus she has closed the circle by an itinerary different from that of the object and has thereby elaborated a group through representation of the invisible displacement of the ball and of the detour to be made in order to find it again *(ibid.,* p. 205).

Causality

Just as with the other special developments, an understanding of the development of causality is furthered by first having some general notion as to where the infant begins and what he is developing towards. As to the former, Piaget finds it useful to define two kinds of precausality— like assimilation and accommodation, logically distinguishable but virtually indissociable in early cognitive functioning (1925a, p. 33; 1927a, p. 108; 1954a, p. 228). The first, *efficacy* (sometimes referred to as *dynamism*), refers to a dim sense that the inchoate feelings of effort, longing, etc., which saturate one's actions are somehow responsible for external happenings. Efficacy is therefore a causality of action-at-a-distance (since presence or absence of spatial connection between self as cause and event as effect is irrelevant to it) in which the cause is vaguely sensed as inhering in one's action without, however, the subject being sufficiently advanced to see self and actions as a separate causal agent in the universe. The second, *phenomenalism,* refers to the feeling that temporal (but not necessarily spatial) contiguity between any two events means that one caused the other. It leads to a kind of causal anarchy in which, as Piaget puts it, *"n'importe quoi produit n'importe quoi"* (1925a, p. 33).

Piaget's hypothesis is that the early stages of sensory-motor development are characterized by a causality best described as an undifferentiated mixture of efficacy and phenomenalism. As a knowledge of the evolution of space and objects would predict, this early causality knows nothing at all of objects as causal centers acting upon each other through spatial contact. With development, on the other hand, causality becomes both spatialized and objectified, and efficacy and phenomenalism, originally undifferentiated, break apart to undergo separate fates (1954a, pp. 288-289). Efficacy eventually becomes *psychological causality,* by which Piaget means the sense—now in a self aware of its thoughts and wishes—of causing one's own actions through volition, of willing to perform such and such action before performing it. And phenomenalism becomes *physical causality,* the causal action one object exercises on another through spatial contact.

STAGES 1 AND 2

Once again, Piaget feels that he can at best make an educated guess about this period by working backwards from what comes later. His guess, as already indicated, is that the infant faintly experiences that, with the temporal co-occurrence (this is the phenomenalistic aspect) of some result with some complex of action-tension-need, etc., the latter is somehow charged with efficacy. This hypothesis is in a way a more cautious and toned-down version of the psychoanalytic "feelings of omnipotence" conception. As would be anticipated, Piaget rejects out of hand any notion that, for instance, the infant regards the moving rattle seen as the objective cause of the sound heard, the bottle the causal source of the gustatory impression of eating, and so on. Causality according to the adult interpretation simply demands too much ancillary development in the domains of object, space, time, and so on, to be possible at this stage.

STAGE 3

In this stage causality is still predominantly an undifferentiated efficacy-phenomenalism. But with the development of visually guided prehension and the secondary circular reactions, the infant begins to see himself act and therefore can begin to form an incipient distinction between act and external result:

> It is at this precise moment of development that the initial causality begins to be differentiated and to take on the form which will characterize it during the third stage. The nature of causality will not yet change, and the union of efficacy and phenomenalism will always define it in each of its aspects. But the difference will doubtless be that because with prehension and the handling of objects the child's behavior becomes more systematic and consequently more intentional . . . he will better dissociate the purpose or the desire preceding the result from the action and the result itself. Hitherto cause and effect were, so to speak, condensed into a single mass centered around the effect perceived; the feeling of efficacy was merely one with the result of the act (the action being too global to be analyzed in two phases: the search and its result). Henceforth, on the contrary, as a result of the greater complexity of acts and consequently of their greater purposefulness, cause reveals a tendency to be internalized and effect to be externalized (*ibid.*, pp. 230-231).

There are three types of causal situations in which both the progress and limitations of stage 3 are evident. The first comprises actions of the subject which do not result in external, objective effects. In this stage the child first studies the various movements of his hands, the only apparent motive being an interest in his ability to dominate them. However tempted one might be to impute a genuine psychological causality and consciousness of self here, Piaget feels that on the basis of our general knowledge of the stage-3 child, it would be a mistake to do so.

The second kind of causal situation is the one in which the child's act does produce an external result, i.e., the everyday secondary circular reaction. Again it might be supposed that, when the child performs the secondary circular reaction of repeatedly pulling a string to shake a rattle attached to it, he clearly recognizes the successive, spatially connected links in the series (hand must pull string, string must in turn pull rattle, etc.) as causal necessities. But we have seen (Chapter 3) that the child tends eventually to use the efficacious action in a quasi-magical way to reproduce any interesting phenomenon and especially phenomena which are spatially distant and beyond direct, objectively causal contact. Rather than an objective and spatialized causality, it seems that there is simply a dim sense of power inherent in the action and its concomitant sensations, wishes, etc. (efficacy) which is activated whenever this feeling-action complex co-occurs in time with some interesting external event (phenomenalism).

A third paradigm is the one in which the child witnesses happenings which really do occur independently of his action, e.g., the experimenter's hand A is the objective cause of some effect B which interests the child. The question here is how to decide whether or not the child in this stage really conceives of A as a causal center acting to produce B. Piaget reasons as follows. If the child did so conceive A, he would wherever possible try to act directly on A to induce A to repeat the causal action, e.g., try to push the hand in the causal direction. But the infant does not yet respond this way; instead, he either goes through his repertoire of magical gestures in the empty air or at most fruitlessly strikes or shakes the hand:

> The child's whole behavior seems to indicate that at the time the interesting sight is interrupted he has recourse to a single causal agent only—his own activity. Sometimes he tries to reproduce the observed effect B directly by himself, and he always goes about it by procedures depending on efficacy and phenomenalism. Sometimes he tries to act on hand A; but he behaves toward it not as though it were a real motive power to be released but as though it remained subordinate to his own activity, the activity of another person being similarly conceived as depending on his own (*ibid.*, p. 247).

STAGE 4

Causality based on efficacy-phenomenalism, like most primitive patterns, is not easily surrendered by the child as development proceeds. Piaget describes a number of florid examples of it in stage 6 (*ibid.*, pp. 301-304) and, needless to say, it is found in stage 4 in abundance.[3] Alongside these tenacious immature forms, however, patterns begin to spring up which indicate a causality at least in part objectified and spatialized.

[3] The concept of *décalage* leads one to expect to see primitive causality also reappear on the conceptual level in the early postinfantile years, and this is in fact the case (1930a; 1954a, pp. 376-379).

This is seen most clearly in the various means-ends sequences so characteristic of stage 4. The child now pushes aside the experimenter's hand when, for instance, it is holding onto some object the child wants for himself. Even more instructive is the behavior the child shows when he wants the adult to continue some causal action the latter has been performing. In stage 3, it will be recalled, the child makes no direct, objectively effective attempts to induce the causal agent to continue. Here, on the other hand, the child really regards the agent as an external causal center and behaves accordingly.

> At 0;8 (19) Jacqueline watches me as I alternately spread my index finger and thumb apart and bring them together again. When I pause she lightly pushes either the finger or the thumb to make me continue. Her movement is brisk and rapid; it is simply a starting impulse and not a continuous pressure.
> Finally, and most important, as we have already noted . . . at 0;10 (30) Jacqueline takes my hand, places it against a singing doll which she is unable to activate herself, and exerts pressure on my index finger to make me do what is necessary. This last observation reveals to what extent, to Jacqueline, my hand has become an independent source of action by contact (ibid., p. 260).

There is, however, one factor which tends to restrict the extent to which causality is objectified and spatialized in stage 4. That is the fact that the child appears to regard external sources as truly causal only where his own action intervenes in some way, e.g., he pushes the adult's hand. It remains for stage 5 to produce a causality which has overcome this final obstacle.

STAGE 5

The two chief characteristics of stage-5 intelligence—*tertiary circular reaction and invention of new means through active experimentation*—both contribute to the objectification and spatialization of causality. The diligent explorations of the immediate universe which make up the tertiary reactions incessantly confront the subject with a system of causes independent of himself. This is seen clearly in cases where the child places an object in such a position as to set itself into motion. For example, he now puts a ball on a slight incline and sits back waiting for it to roll (ibid., p. 273). Similarly, people as well as objects are seen as causal centers completely independent of the child's action:

> Obs. 152. At 1;0 (3) Jacqueline is before me and I blow into her hair. When she wants the game to continue she does not try to act through efficacious gestures nor even, as formerly, to push my arms or lips; she merely places herself in position, head tilted, sure that I will do the rest by myself. At 1;0 (6) same reaction when I murmur something in her ear; she puts her ear against my mouth when she wishes me to repeat my gesture (ibid., p. 275).

In the same way, the stage-5 means-ends behaviors teach the child the necessity of spatial contact between successive terms in a causal series. For example, one sees this growing spatialization of causality when the child gradually learns that, in order to make an object move by using a stick, the stick must touch the object—a by no means obvious fact of life for an organism whose previous causal strategies have been thoroughly imbued with efficacy and phenomenalism. There is also a gradual evolution in connection with the analogous behaviors of pulling one object to get another resting on it or tied to it by a string; in the beginning, the child does not hesitate to repeat the successful maneuver even when the experimenter very obviously removes the second object from the support or unties the string attached to it!

A natural consequence of the foregoing achievements is that the child begins to see himself as an object which has to submit to causal action, one more object subject to the forces which act on all objects. He now conceives himself not only as a cause but as the recipient of causes:

> So also at 1;3 (10) Jacqueline, in her playpen, discovers the possibility of letting herself fall down in a sitting position; she holds the bar and lowers herself gently to within a few centimeters of the floor, then lets go of her support. Before this she has not released the bar until she was suitably placed, but from now on she lets herself go, foreseeing the trajectory her movement of falling will follow independently of any activity on her part.
>
> Let us again note that at 1;3 (12) she knows how to step backward when her dress catches on a nail and try to detach herself instead of simply pulling to overcome the resistance; her attitude reveals awareness of the relations of dependency existing between her movements and external objects (*ibid.*, p. 291).

STAGE 6

The capacity for representation characteristic of this stage makes possible two new achievements in the realm of causality: the child can through representation infer a cause, given only its effect, and foresee an effect, given its cause. An example of each follows below:

> At 1;1 (4) Laurent is seated in his carriage and I am on a chair beside him. While reading and without seeming to pay any attention to him, I put my foot under the carriage and move it slowly. Without hesitation Laurent leans over the edge and looks for the cause in the direction of the wheels. As soon as he perceives the position of my foot he is satisfied and smiles (*ibid.*, p. 296).

> Obs. 160. At 1;4 (12) Jacqueline has just been wrested from a game she wants to continue and placed in her playpen from which she wants to get out. She calls, but in vain. Then she clearly expresses a certain need, although the events of the last ten minutes prove that she no longer experiences it. No sooner has she left the playpen than she indicates the game she wishes to resume!
>
> Thus we see how Jacqueline, knowing that a mere appeal would not free her from her confinement, has imagined a more efficacious means, foreseeing

more or less clearly the sequence of actions that would result from it (*ibid.*, p. 297).

Time

Piaget devotes relatively few pages to this special development, probably for the very good reason that here evidence is exceptionally hard to come by. The only strategy which he feels can make possible even a minimum of understanding is to draw heavily upon parallel concepts regarding the development of causality, objects, and especially space (*ibid.*, p. 321). Usually willing to risk a fair amount of ambiguity and shaky conjecture in most areas which he studies, he seems ready to tolerate even more here in an effort to gain some rudimentary understanding of how temporal phenomena are cognized in infancy.

STAGES 1 AND 2

The time of the young infant is most probably a practical time, formally similar to the practical space described earlier. The child's actions are for the observer arranged in temporal series (e.g., he brings hand to mouth before sucking, hears the sound before turning to look at the source, etc.), but there is no reason to suspect that the infant himself has any impression of before and after, now and later, etc. As Piaget puts it, a sequence of perceptions does not necessarily imply a perception of sequence (*ibid.*, p. 325). What does the child experience in the temporal domain? Piaget guesses that it is a vague feeling of duration immanent in his own actions, a feeling intermixed with other, similarly vague sensations of effort, need, and the like.

STAGE 3

In analogy to the development of space and causality, the infant in this period is for the first time in position to see his own actions and to seriate these with the environmental effects they cause. In this way the practical series gives way to the subjective series: in the context of his secondary circular reactions (e.g., pulling a chain to activate an object) the child probably has some elementary consciousness of a before and an after in the action-result sequence. A related development is the beginning capacity to keep track of an event in the very immediate past:

> OBS. 170. At 0;8 (7) Laurent sees his mother enter the room and watches her until she seats herself behind him. Then he resumes playing but turns around several times in succession to look at her again. However there is no sound or noise to remind him of her presence (*ibid.*, p. 332).

The limitation of the subjective series is the same one which holds for all stage-3 behavior. The seriation of events is apprehended by the child only if his own action intervenes in the sequence. Temporally successive events in which the subject plays no part are not yet cognized serially (*ibid.,* p. 334).

STAGE 4

This stage witnesses the transition from the subjective to the objective temporal series. There is certainly an advance in the objectification of temporal sequences when the infant first relates one object as means (occurs first in time) to another as end (occurs second in time). But perhaps the most clear-cut instance is the case, already discussed in our presentation of object development, where the child searches behind a screen to find an object he has seen the experimenter hide there. Piaget believes that it is in this behavior pattern that the child for the first time reveals a capacity for retaining a series of events in which his action did not directly intervene, for really recalling an event rather than a past action.

STAGE 5

The seriation of events independent of one's own actions, still a fragile and occasional thing in stage 4, becomes well-developed in stage 5. Again, the improvement in coping with perceived displacements of objects (hide object under *A*, then move it under *B*, etc.) bears witness to the increasing ability to seriate events *per se.* It is also shown in the child's growing capacity to retain events in memory for longer and longer periods of time:

> At 1;3 (12) she [Jacqueline] plays with an eyeglass case at the moment when I am putting a book on the other side of the bars of the playpen in which she is seated. As she wants to reach the book she puts behind her the case which is in her way. For at least five minutes she tries unsuccessfully to pass the book through the bars. Each time the book slides out of her hands. Then, tired, she searches unhesitatingly for the case which she no longer sees; turning halfway around she extends her hand behind her back until she touches it (*ibid.,* p. 343).

STAGE 6

With the increasing ability to evoke representationally events outside of immediate perception, the recall of ever more remote past happenings is naturally given an important assist:

> So also, at 1;7 (27) Jacqueline, on the terrace of a mountain chalet, locates the people I name, taking into account their recent displacements. "Where is Mother?" She points to the chalet. "Where is Grandpa?" She points down to the plain where her grandfather went two days before. "Where is the boy?" She points to the chalet. "Where is Vivianne?" She points to the woods where Vivianne went for a walk. And so on (*ibid.,* pp. 346-347).

Piaget believes that the child is now starting to apprehend time as a generalized medium, like space, in which self and objects can be located relative to each other. It goes without saying that the development of time cognition is far from complete at this period, but at least personal duration has become placed in relation to that of external things, and the way is paved for an orderly arrangement of temporal happenings in terms of outside referents.

Conclusion

In this and Chapter 3 we have described, in a synopsis from which much interesting detail has been necessarily excluded, the general and special evolutions which take place in the sensory-motor period. In the course of these developments the infant undergoes a truly remarkable metamorphosis from a neonatal stage, where all seems chaos, to a state in which he is able to manage the multifarious aspects of his immediate environment with considerable skill and orderliness. To be sure, the skill and orderliness which one sees are very much limited to nonsymbolic and mute overt actions. It will be many years before he will achieve a parallel degree of coherence in adaptations which are more and more divorced from sensory-motor performance, that is, in adaptations which require him to think and talk about reality rather than to act upon it directly. Thus, there has to be a long and tortuous *redevelopment,* as it were, of space, of causality, of time, and all the rest on this new symbolic plane. It is in fact redevelopments of this kind to which most of Piaget's scientific career has been devoted, for the obvious reason that they are more accessible to study than their counterparts in infancy.

Before proceeding to the developmental events of postinfancy, it may be useful to try to extract the elements of the six sensory-motor stages which can be conceived as common to both the general evolution and the six special ones. There is the ever present menace of oversimplification and an illusory sense of neatness and closure in all summaries of this kind, especially in a summary of summaries, but they are useful in forming a generalized picture of things. Stages 1 and 2 constitute the period in which the infant is locked up in his own egocentrism. He is confined to surveying what must be an orderless array of stimulation without really being able to act on things and thereby observe, in even the most limited way, how these actions cobehave with the things they contact.

In stage 3 he begins to move out into the unknown medium which surrounds him, thanks primarily to the growing, all-important ability to direct his hand movements. In doing so, he begins to be able to perceive simple liaisons between the two realms of self and outside world. To be sure, this perception is still very egocentric in that the child apprehends the two only as an undifferentiated whole; nonetheless, this movement outward is fraught with cognitive possibilities which the infant will gradually exploit. Stage 4 is a transitional period of decisive progress in substituting object-object relations for subject-object ones. The child begins to see things relate to other things, still in the context of his own action, of course, but increasingly independent of it. With the growing hiatus between original intention and final, objective goal, the gap between self and world widens and the action-object compounds begin to break apart.

Stage 5 is really the culmination, so far as sensory-motor development in the strict sense is concerned. Objects are now really detached and independent entities which can be imitated, inserted in play schemas, and related spatially, temporally, and causally. The self also begins to be treated like other objects, as something with its own texture and resistance, its own locomotion relative to fixed object positions in space, and so on. Finally, the child of stage 6 crowns these achievements with added finesse and skill and enriches them through the powerful tool of a burgeoning symbolization. And, in doing all these things, the child has passed into a new era in which this symbolic capacity, much more than overt actions, becomes the important instrument of cognition.

PREOPERATIONAL THOUGHT

The subperiod of preoperational thought includes roughly the developmental era which is bounded at one end by stage 6 of sensory-motor development (1½-2 years) and at the other end by the beginning construction of concrete operations (6-7 years). Its upper portion (5-7 years) constitutes an age group which Piaget has studied very thoroughly indeed—at least as thoroughly as any other between birth and maturity. Its lower end (2-4 years), on the contrary, is the least investigated period in the entire developmental span, as Piaget himself admits (1955d, p. 38).

To cite the articles and books which describe one or more aspects of preoperational thought would be to list more than half of Piaget's extensive bibliography. Material can be found (especially as regards the much studied upper end of the subperiod) in the many "content" books on language, reasoning, space, time, chance, number, and the like (1926, 1928b, 1929c, 1930a, 1932, 1946a, 1946b, 1952b, etc.). And of course Piaget's two summary books (1950a, 1957a) give a brief treatment. Important aspects are also mentioned in a variety of journal articles, of which the following are only a sample: 1923, 1937b, 1941, 1942b, 1951d, 1954e, 1957c, 1957-1958, 1959d; Krafft and Piaget, 1926; Inhelder, 1955. Finally, two sources in particular can be singled out as especially useful in providing detailed information: one of Piaget's earliest articles (1924b) and the book on play, dreams, and imitation (1951a).

The Transition to Preoperational Thought

During the preoperational subperiod the child is transformed from an organism whose most intelligent functions are sensory-motor, overt acts to one whose upper-limit cognitions are inner, symbolic manipulations of reality. Piaget's own account of this transformation is complicated and at times difficult to follow (1951a, 1954e); the present description is a more schematic and, it is hoped, simplifying one.[4] There are two principal questions around which the explanation revolves. First, precisely what is representation as opposed to sensory-motor action and what are its important differentiating characteristics? And second, how or by what means does the sensory-motor infant become a manipulator of representations?

THE NATURE OF REPRESENTATION

According to Piaget, the paramount requirement for representation is what he calls the ability to differentiate *signifiers* from *significates* and thereby to become capable of evoking the one to call forth or refer to the other. The generalized capacity to perform this differentiation and thus be able to make the act of reference Piaget designates as the *symbolic function* (1951a, p. 69; 1954e, p. 53). Although he recognizes that the sensory-motor infant does in fact show a kind of reference behavior, e.g., treating a perceptual cue as a sign that some event is soon to follow, he maintains that the infant is not capable of the genuine signifier-significate distinction which defines possession of the symbolic function. The young infant cannot himself evoke, internally, a signifier (a word, an image, etc.) which symbolizes a perceptually absent event (the significate) of which the signifier is not in some sense a concrete part, i.e., from which the signifier is clearly differentiated. In other words, there are certainly reference-giving cues in infancy (Piaget refers to them as *indices* and *signals*) but they are the functional predecessors of the true signifier rather than being identical with it (1950a, p. 124).

It goes without saying that representational intelligence, through its possession of the symbolic function, will differ in profound ways from sensory-motor intelligence (1941, pp. 230-233; 1950a, pp. 120-121; 1951a, pp. 238-239; 1954a, pp. 359-361). First, sensory-motor intelligence is capable only of linking, one by one, the successive actions or perceptual states with which it gets involved. Piaget likens it to a slow-motion film which represents one static frame after another but can give no simultaneous and all-encompassing purview of all the frames. Representational

---

[4] The best single source for the reader interested in the subtleties of Piaget's position not adequately covered here is the book on play, dreams, and imitation (1951a), especially pp. 66-78; 97-104; 213-214; 273-284.

thought, on the other hand, through its symbolic capacity has the potential for simultaneously grasping, in a single, internal epitome, a whole sweep of separate events. It is a much faster and more mobile device which can recall the past, represent the present, and anticipate the future in one temporally brief, organized act.

Second, sensory-motor intelligence, being an intelligence of action, is limited to the pursuit of concrete goals of action rather than to the quest for knowledge or truth as such. Representational thought by its very nature can (not that it always will) reflect on the organization of its acts as they bear on things rather than simply register empirical success or failure. It has indigenous to it the wherewithal to be *action-contemplative* rather than simply *active*.

Third, by its very potential to get outside the immediate present, representational thought can eventually extend its scope well beyond actual, concrete acts of the subject and actual, concrete objects in the environment. The ultimate in this freedom from concrete reality is the symbolic manipulation (as in scientific and mathematical thought) of entities which are not even picturable, let alone tangible.

And finally, since it is confined to actions *in* reality rather than to representations *of* reality, sensory-motor cognition is inevitably a private event, an individual, nonshared affair. Conceptual intelligence, on the other hand, can and eventually does become socialized through the medium of a system of codified symbols which the whole culture can share. In summary, then, the possession and use of the symbolic function, the ability to differentiate signifiers from significates and the act of reference between them, makes for a cognitive form with potentialities far beyond anything available to sensory-motor intelligence. The next problem concerns the route by which the infant passes into this new cognitive form.

THE DEVELOPMENT OF THE SYMBOLIC FUNCTION

Piaget contends that the child acquires the symbolic function through specialized developments in assimilation and, especially, accommodation (1951a). We have already seen that an important developmental product of the general accommodation function is imitation, i.e., the active, accommodatory replication by the subject of some external event serving as model. Now the central point of Piaget's argument is that accommodation-as-imitation is the function which supplies the infant with his first signifiers, signifiers capable of internally representing for him the absent significate. What happens, he believes, is that with the growth and refinement of the capacity to imitate the child is eventually able to make internal imitations as well as external, visible ones. He is able to evoke in thought, as opposed to actually carrying out in reality, imitations made in the past. This internal imitation takes the form of an image, broadly defined, and this image constitutes the first signifier (the significate being here the action, object, or word of which the image is a reduced and schematic replicate).[5]

Once the capacity to evoke image-signifiers is established, the child can of course use them as anticipative outlines of future actions. Originally, accommodation could be considered a relatively passive process of fitting subject to object; in Piaget's words, a simple, run-of-the-mill accommodation is a kind of photographic negative of the object accommodated to (*ibid.*, p. 84). The evoked imitative image, on the other hand, is more a photographic positive which serves as an anticipative draft, outline, or schema (in the everyday, plan-of-action sense of this term) which can direct future action; past accommodations are evoked in the present as internal images which, in turn, are the anticipative mediators of actions not yet performed.

As evidence for his conception of the accommodation-imitation origin of the image-signifier he cites transitional cases in which the child appears to symbolize a possible but not yet performed act by imitating it in a reduced but not completely covert and internalized way. The most clear-cut case is that of Lucienne, cited earlier (pp. 119-120): the child imitates the potential widening of a matchbox opening by opening her mouth. When, in the course of development, these reduced imitations go farther underground in the form of internal and schematized images, the true signifier is born.

The role of assimilation in the development of the symbolic function is less complicated to describe. Assimilation supplies the significate to which the signifier (derived from imitation) refers (*ibid.*, p. 102). In other words, the subject provides meaning for his signifiers by assimilating them to the events (more accurately, the schemas subtending the events) which the signifiers denote. Thus, just as with sensory-motor intelligence, representation results from a differentiated partnership between assimilation and accommodation. However, Piaget calls attention to the fact that the operation of these invariants becomes considerably more complicated where representations are involved. Not only does the child assimilate and accommodate to objects in the present perceptual field as did the sensory-motor infant, but at the same time he has to carry out an additional set of assimilations and accommodations: he has

---

[5] Although we shall not pursue Piaget's conception of images as such, it is worth emphasizing that the theory discussed here is as much a specific theory of what images are and whence they derive as it is an attempted explanation of how the child acquires representational abilities in general. For Piaget an image, far from being a passive engram of its external referent, is an active accommodation to the referent which differs from sensory-motor accommodation only in that it is internalized. His later, experimental work on imagery is briefly described in the first section of Chapter 11.

to assimilate the present data to the nonpresent significate and also accommodate to the latter through the medium of the evoked imitative image. Piaget sums up this complicated state of affairs as follows:

> The fundamental difference between sensory-motor equilibrium and representative equilibrium is that, in the former, assimilation and accommodation are always in the present, whereas in the latter, earlier assimilations and accommodations interfere with those of the present. It is true that the sensory-motor schema itself is the past acting on the present, but the action is not localised in the past in the same way as, for instance, an evoked memory as distinct from a habit. What characterises representation, on the other hand, is that earlier accommodations persist in the present as "signifiers," and earlier assimilations as "signified." Thus the mental image, the continuation of earlier accommodations, intervenes as symboliser in both ludic and conceptual activity, thanks to which (and of course to the verbal, collective signs which accompany it in individual thought), present data can be assimilated to non-perceived, merely evoked objects, *i.e.*, objects that have taken on meanings provided by earlier assimilations. On the representative plane, accommodations are therefore two-fold: present (simple accommodations), and past (representative imitations and images), and the same is true of assimilations, which are present (incorporation of data in adequate schemas) and past (connections established between these schemas and others whose meanings are merely evoked, and not provoked by present perception) (*ibid.*, p. 241).

Piaget draws at least two important consequences from what has been said so far about the evolution of symbolic behavior. First of all, much of the extreme and long-enduring hardship the child encounters in trying to cognize the world symbolically results from the complications in the assimilation-accommodation functioning just described (*ibid.*, pp. 241-242). Not only must the child as of old equilibrate assimilations and accommodations connected with the present field, he must also try to balance those related to the evoked, symbolic schemas, both *per se* and in relation to the former set of assimilations and accommodations. One of the many expressions of this difficulty in balancing the functions is the tendency of young children to vacillate incessantly between play, imitation, and adapted intelligence (*ibid.*, p. 283). Such vacillations, in Piaget's theory, are symptomatic of perturbations in the assimilation-accommodation equilibrium (see Chapter 2).

The second consequence is of greater general significance and consists of several related implications. But first, a terminological distinction. Piaget discriminates between two general kinds of signifiers (1950a, p. 124; 1951a, p. 68; 1954e, p. 52). There are *signs* whose meanings are socially shared and which are arbitrary in the sense that they bear no systematic resemblance to their significates. Words are the commonest signs, but there are also others (e.g., mathematical and scientific symbols). *Symbols,* on the other hand, are more or less private, noncoded signifiers which usually do bear some physical similarity to their referents. Piaget includes here dream symbols, the image-signifiers the young child evokes in symbolic play and deferred imitation, the concepts which he struggles to form in early preoperational adapted thought, and the first linguistic signs he acquires from the social surround.

Piaget makes two important points. First, he asserts very strongly that representational thought does not begin with and result from the incorporation of verbal signs from the social environment (1954e, pp. 52-54). Rather, the first signifiers are the private, nonverbal symbols which emerge towards the end of sensory-motor development and whose evolution we have described in terms of the internalization of imitation in the form of image-signifiers. The very first signifiers are not linguistic signs but things like the piece of cloth which Jacqueline used to represent a pillow in pretended going-to-sleep actions, the piece of paper she playfully treated as a food symbol, and so on (see p. 128). It is not the acquisition of language which gives rise to the symbolic function. Quite the contrary, the symbolic function is a very general and basic acquisition which makes possible the acquisition of both private symbols and social signs. Piaget of course admits, in fact, stresses, the enormous role which a codified and socially shared linguistic system plays in the development of conceptual thinking. Language is the vehicle par excellence of symbolization, without which thought could never become really socialized and thereby logical. But thought is nonetheless far from being a purely verbal affair, neither in its fully formed state nor, above all, in its developmental origins. In essence, what happens is that language, first acquired through the auspices of a symbolic function which has arisen earlier, will reflexively lend tremendous assistance to the subsequent development of the latter (1954e, p. 54).

The first signifiers, then, have the properties of private symbols rather than of social signs, and the second major point centers on this fact. The first words the child acquires function at most as semisigns, signs which are thoroughly impregnated with private-symbol characteristics (1951a, pp. 215-221). These semisigns refer much more to idiosyncratic and everchanging schemas of action than to fixed and stable classes of objective realities. Just as the piece of cloth signifies a past schema of going-to-sleep-on-pillow, so may an early word like "mommy" signify (among other things, depending upon the context), not a class of objects, but simply that the child wants something (*ibid.*, p. 217). The fact of the matter is that for a long time the child finds verbal signs as such both difficult to grasp and generally unsuitable for the representational expression of the entities with which he is preoccupied (1950a, p. 127). He responds to this state of affairs both by continuing to rely heavily on nonverbal symbols and by assimilating words to his symbolic orientation, i.e., treating the word as just another private symbol.

The Nature of Preoperational Thought

Preoperational thought can scarcely be called "good" thought, relative to the conceptual forms into which it eventually evolves. Most simply, it is not "good" thought for the excellent reason that it is an initial sortie into a new and unfamiliar terrain, a terrain quite different from the one upon which sensory-motor intelligence operated. But it remains to be seen in precisely what ways it falls short of later achievements, exactly what sorts of "not-good" characteristics it presents. The principal ones appear to be the following.

EGOCENTRISM

The preoperational child is egocentric with respect to representations, just as the neonate was egocentric with respect to sensory-motor actions (1954a, Conclusion). Piaget once characterized the preoperational child's thought as midway between socialized adult thought and the completely autistic and egocentric thought of the Freudian unconscious (1923). Pre-operational egocentrism is a very general characteristic with numerous sequelae. First and foremost, the child repeatedly demonstrates a relative inability to take the role of the other person, that is, to see his own viewpoint as one of many possible and to try to coordinate it with these others. This is clearly seen in the area of language and communication, where he appears to make little real effort to adapt his speech to the needs of the listener (1926). It is seen even more graphically when the child is given the task of simultaneously *looking* at a visual display from a given position A and *representing* what the appearance of the display would be from some different position B (e.g., from behind the display). The most common response to this task in early childhood is the simple egocentric representation of the child's own perspective (Piaget and Inhelder, 1956, ch. 8).

There are two other difficulties which derive directly from the child's egocentrism (1924b; 1928b, chs. 4 and 5). First, the child—lacking other-role orientation—feels neither the compunction to justify his reasonings to others nor to look for possible contradictions in his logic. And causally related to this, he finds it exceedingly difficult to treat his own thought processes as an object of thought. He is, for example, unable to reconstruct a chain of reasonings which he has just passed through; he thinks but he cannot think about his own thinking. One of Piaget's firmest beliefs, repeated over and over in scores of publications (e.g., 1950a, ch. 6), is that thought becomes aware of itself, able to justify itself, and in general able to adhere to logical-social norms of noncontradiction, coherence etc., and that all these things and more can emerge only from repeated interpersonal interactions (and especially those involving arguments and disagreements) in which the child is actually forced again and again to take cognizance of the role of the other. It is social interaction which gives the ultimate *coup de grâce* to childish egocentrism. But this is a development the preoperational child has yet to undergo.

CENTRATION AND DECENTRATION

One of the most pronounced characteristics of preoperational thought is its tendency to *center*, as Piaget says, attention on a single, striking feature of the object of its reasoning to the neglect of other important aspects, and by so doing, to distort the reasoning. The child is unable to *decenter*, i.e., to take into account features which could balance and compensate for the distorting, biasing effects of the single centration (e.g., 1924b, 1950a, 1957-1958). Like the young sensory-motor infant in the field of direct action, the preoperational child is confined to the surface of the phenomena he tries to think about, assimilating only those super-ficial features which clamor loudest for his attention. For example, while admitting that two identical and thin containers (*A* and *A'*) contain identical quantities of liquid, he will tend to deny this equivalence of quantity after the contents of *A'* have been poured (before his eyes) into a short, broad container *B*, i.e., he will assert that contents $A \gtreqless$ contents *B* (1952b, ch. 1). In this situation he will center solely on the width of *B* and say it contains more liquid "because it is wide," or else he will center on the height of the column of liquid in *A* and say that *A* con-tains more "because it is tall." What he characteristically fails to do is decenter by considering both width and height simultaneously, and thus reason that the thinness of *A* is compensated by the height of the column, the lack of height in *B* by the width of the column, etc.

STATES AND TRANSFORMATIONS

Characteristics very closely related to the phenomenism or configura-tion-boundedness just described concern the child's reactions to states versus transformations of states (e.g., Piaget, 1955d, 1957c; Inhelder and Piaget, 1958, pp. 246-248). The child is much more inclined to focus attention upon the successive states or configurations of a display than upon the transformations by which one state is changed into another (the experiment with the liquids involves this kind of display: an initial configuration *A'*, a terminal configuration *B*, and the process of trans-formation of *A'* to *B*). Preoperational thought, then, is static and im-mobile. It is a kind of thought which can focus impressionistically and sporadically on this or that momentary, static condition but cannot adequately link a whole set of successive conditions into an integrated totality by taking account of the transformations which unify them and render them logically coherent. And when the child does turn his atten-tion to transformations, he has great difficulty; he usually ends up assimilating them to his own action schemas rather than inserting them into a coherent system of objective causes (Inhelder and Piaget, 1958, p. 247). The young child's difficulty with transformations is well illustrated by a recent experiment (1959d) in which the subject is asked to depict (by drawing, by multiple-choice selection of illustrations, etc.) the successive movements of a bar which falls from a vertical, upright position to a horizontal one (in the manner of a pencil which falls to rest after one has attempted to balance it on end). Preoperational children apparently find it extremely difficult to reconstruct the successive, still-film positions the bar occupies during this rapid transformation.

EQUILIBRIUM

A principal characteristic of preoperational thought is a relative absence of stable equilibrium between assimilation and accommodation (e.g., 1941, pp. 230-233; 1957c, pp. 89-90). The assimilatory network—the child's cognitive organization—tends to rupture and dislocate itself in the process of accommodating to new situations. The child is unable to accommodate to the new by assimilating it to the old in a coherent, rational way, a way which manages to preserve intact the fundamental aspects of the previous assimilatory organization. Thus, as we have seen (e.g., the water-levels problem), he is the slave rather than master of changes in the configuration; the successive changes pull him this way and that way, draw him into flagrant contradictions with earlier cognitions, and in general destroy any momentary assimilation-accommodation equilibrium he may have attained just previously. It is a useful and only slightly misleading generalization about the preoperational child that he has no stable, enduring, and internally consistent cognitive organization, no system-in-equilibrium, with which to order, relate, and make coherent the world around him. His cognitive life, like his affective life, tends to be an unstable, discontinuous, moment-to-moment one.

ACTION

We have said that preoperational thought tends to operate with concrete and static images of reality rather than with abstract, highly schematic signs. Thus, although the child does represent reality rather than simply act in it, his representations are much closer to overt actions, in both form and operation, than is the case for older children and adults. Piaget believes that much of the young child's cognition takes the form of what he calls *mental experiment* (e.g., 1924b, p. 81): that is, an isomorphic, step-by-step mental replica of concrete actions and events. Rather than schematize, reorder, and generally refashion events as does the older child, the young child simply runs off reality sequences in his head just as he might do in overt action. Thus, preoperational thought is extremely concrete. One form which concreteness assumes is what

Piaget calls *realism* (1928b, 1929c, 1932). Things are what they appear to be in immediate, egocentric perception; and insubstantial phenomena (dreams, names, thoughts, moral obligations, etc.) are substantiated as quasi-tangible entities.

IRREVERSIBILITY

Perhaps the most important single characteristic of preoperational thought for Piaget is its irreversibility (e.g., 1924b, pp. 84-88; 1950a, ch. 5; 1957a, pp. 10-12). The concept of reversibility, like that of equilibrium to which it is very closely related, is a complex one whose full meaning in the Piagetian system simply cannot be rendered here (see Chapters 5 and 6). For present purposes, suffice it to say that a cognitive organization is reversible, as opposed to irreversible, if it is able to travel along a cognitive route (pursue a series of reasonings, follow a series of transformations in a display, etc.) and then reverse direction, in thought, to find again an unchanged point of departure (the beginning premise, the original state of the display, etc.). Again, it is reversible if it can compose into a single organized system the various compensating changes which result from a transformation and, by seeing how each change is annulled by its inverse (the one which compensates for it), insure an underlying constancy or invariance for the whole system. In a general way, a thought form which is reversible is one which is flexible and mobile, in stable equilibrium, able to correct for distorting superficials by means of successive, quick-moving decenterings. But the turgid, slow-paced, and extremely concrete *mental experiment* of preoperational thought is not reversible, parroting as it does irreversible events in reality. In the case of the water-level problem, for example, the preoperational child is unable to see how invariance of quantity is insured by the possibility of an inverse transformation to the original state (pouring B back into A') and by the various compensations at work in the system (relative to A' and A, B gains in width what is loses in height—these two events exactly canceling each other just as the number 4 is annulled by its inverse, -4, in the group of integers). Similarly, children of this subperiod find themselves constantly embroiled in contradictions because they are unable to keep their premises unaltered during a reasoning sequence. Their thought is irreversible in the sense that the permanent possibility of returning (the inverse operation) to an unchanged initial premise (the identity element in the system) is denied them (Krafft and Piaget, 1926; Piaget, 1928b, ch. 4).

CONCEPTS AND REASONING

Piaget refers to the first, primitive concepts used by a young child as *preconcepts* (1951a, pp. 221-230). In keeping with the general character of preoperational thought, these preconcepts tend to be action-ridden, imagistic, and concrete, rather than schematic and abstract. But they have one specific peculiarity as well: they refer neither to *individuals* who possess stable identity over time and in different contexts nor to genuine *classes* or collectivities of similar individuals. Analogous to the infant who distinguishes as different things *ball-under-the-armchair* from *ball-somewhere-else* (p. 133), the preoperational child has difficulty in recognizing stable identity in the midst of contextual changes:

> Again at 2;7 (12), seeing L. in a new bathing suit, with a cap, J. asked: *"What's the baby's name?"* Her mother explained that it was a bathing costume, but J. pointed to L. herself and said: *"But what's the name of that?"* (indicating L.'s face) and repeated the question several times. But as soon as L. had her dress on again, J. exclaimed very seriously: *"It's Lucienne again,"* as if her sister had changed her identity in changing her clothes (*ibid.*, p. 224).

Conversely, the child has trouble seeing the similar-appearing members of a given class as distinct and different individuals. For example, Jacqueline regarded the successively encountered members of a certain species of insect, not as different members of one class, but as successive reappearances of a single member (*"the* slug," she called it) who served as a kind of semi-individual, semigeneric prototype (*ibid.*, pp. 225-226).

Piaget uses the term *transductive* for the types of reasoning by which the preoperational child links various preconcepts (*ibid.*, pp. 230-237; 1928b, pp. 180-195, 233-244). Neither true induction nor true deduction, this kind of reasoning proceeds from particular to particular. Centering on one salient element of an event, the child proceeds irreversibly to draw as conclusion from it some other, perceptually compelling happening. Piaget makes the important point that the factual correctness of the child's conclusion (and of course the child is sometimes correct) is by itself no guarantee that the mechanism for arriving at it was logical rather than transductive (1951a, p. 236). Just as an incorrect conclusion can sometimes reflect a deductive or inductive logical orientation, a correct conclusion can follow from a basically transductive one.

There are other characteristics of transductive reasoning which may be mentioned very briefly. First, the child tends to make associative "and-connections" rather than true implicative and causal relations between the successive terms in a reasoning chain; that is, he tends simply to *juxtapose,* as Piaget calls it, elements rather than connect them through appeals to logical necessity or physical causality (1924b, pp. 67-73; 1928b, pp. 221-237). Parts and class members are not related to their respective wholes and classes by the specific relations of inclusion, unilateral implication, etc.; for the young child, the two terms just "go together." Similarly, the child's reasoning is *syncretic;* a multitude of diverse things are inchoately but intimately co-related within a global, all-encompassing schema (1924b, pp. 73-78; 1928b, pp. 227-232). Since almost anything can be "causally" related (by juxtaposition, of course, rather than true causality) to almost anything else within the syncretic whole, the child tends, when pressed to do so, to find a reason for anything. If one asks the reason for A, the child will supply a B as cause, B being simply some element which co-occurred with A in perception and has hence co-fused with A in a global, syncretic schema. Since cause-and-effect requirements are so lax for the young child, anything and everything must have an identifiable cause. One interesting consequence of this orientation is that he is unable to form a genuine concept of chance or probability (1928b, p. 232; Piaget and Inhelder, 1951).

OTHER CHARACTERISTICS

The foregoing catalogue scarcely exhausts the preoperational traits which Piaget has unearthed in a lifetime of theorizing and experimenting. In particular there are typical preoperational behaviors which we will encounter in Part II where specific Piaget experiments involving this age group are taken up. Data from these studies indicate, for instance, that the young child is *animistic* and *artificialistic* in his view of the world around him, has primitive concepts of morality and justice, and shows a generalized immaturity in his attempts to cope intellectually with problems concerning time, causality, space, measurement, number, quantity (the water-levels problem is a sample here), movement, and velocity, and many others. One very general characteristic, however, ought at least to be mentioned here, since it has such a profound effect on all the rest: the preoperational child does not clearly distinguish play and reality as different cognitive realms possessing distinct and different "ground rules" (1924b, pp. 90-94). Piaget puts it as follows:

> Actually, play cannot [in the young child] be opposed to reality, because in both cases belief is arbitrary and pretty much destitute of logical reasons. Play is a reality which the child is disposed to believe in when by himself, just as reality is a game at which he is willing to play with the adult and anyone else who believes in it. . . . Thus we have to say of child play that it constitutes an autonomous reality, but with the understanding that the "true" reality to which it is opposed is considerably less "true" for the child than for us (*ibid.*, p. 93).

CONCLUSION

The question arises as to whether the collection of diverse cognitive traits listed in the preceding sections can be pulled together under some sort of unifying succinct description. As would be anticipated, Piaget himself considers them as multiple expressions of a single, cognitive orientation rather than as a string of unconnected attributes. Actually, one could do a fair job of conveying this unity by the simple expedient of choosing almost any one of the characteristics described and showing how it implies each of the others. We have already witnessed a mutually implicative network of this kind in the case of the general and special sensory-motor developments.

Thus, the choice of "unifier" is to a large extent arbitrary.[6] The writer favors thinking of preoperational thought as thought which bears the impress of its sensory-motor origins, that is, as saturated with sensory-motor adherences. It is extremely concrete, its image-signifiers even being more like internal replicas of concrete actions than like true signs; it is slow and static, concerned more with immobile, eye-catching configurations than with more subtle, less obvious components (compensating features, transformations, etc.); it is relatively unsocialized, unconcerned with proof or logical justification and, in general, unaware of the effect of its communications on others. In short, in more respects than not, it resembles sensory-motor action which has simply been transposed to a new arena of operation. There is nothing extraordinary about this fact. Representations do not arise *ex nihilo;* born of a refined and developed sensory-motor intelligence, it would be extraordinary if representational thought did not resemble it, at least in the beginning.

Developmental Changes during the Preoperational Subperiod

The preoperational subperiod, covering as it does about five years of growth, is not all of a piece as regards developmental level. One could describe it as consisting of two broad phases. During the first two or three years, the child applies his new-found representational ability to an ever-broader diversity of phenomena and, by doing so, progressively looks more preoperational to the observer in all the ways we have described. In this sense it could be said that preoperational thought proliferates and becomes more florid during the early preoperational years. But then, as the child moves into his fifth, sixth, and seventh year, we see these preoperational traits give ground to traits characteristic of concrete operations. There is then a second phase, a phase of transition analogous to the earlier one between sensory-motor intelligence and representational thought. Two of the many aspects of this second, transitional phase are of particular interest.

First, the child becomes noticeably more *testable* in formal experiment from age four or five on (e.g., 1955d, p. 38). He is much more able to address himself to a specified task and to apply adapted intelligence to it rather than simply assimilate it to some egocentric play schema. It is no accident that the lower age limit in most Piaget experiments is about four years. And not only does the child become testable *per se* in the late preoperational years, he also becomes capable of reasoning about

---

[6] One of Piaget's own favorites is egocentrism itself, certainly a very basic and general attribute (1954b, p. 50).

progressively more complex and extended experimental problems or displays in the testing situation.[7]

A second important characteristic of the transition to concrete operations is the following. The rigid, static, and irreversible structures typical of preoperational thought organization begin, in Piaget's phrasing (*ibid.*, p. 139), to "thaw out" and become more flexible, mobile, and above all decentered and reversible in their operation. The child of this transitional phase, having first centered on a single, distorting facet of a display, gradually becomes able to decenter and take account of other, correcting aspects. But the decentering process is only fragmentary and semireversible at first; the child is only capable in the beginning of making partial and momentary compensations which Piaget calls *regulations* (e.g., 1942b; 1950a, Conclusion). Regulations, the mid-station between irreversible centrations and rigorously reversible operations, are characteristic of intellectual structure in the late preoperational years.[8] Typically, they first appear only where the display conditions are especially favorable for their emergence. In the case of the water-levels problem, for instance, the six-year-old might begin by insisting that B has more liquid "because it is wider"; this is ordinary preoperational thought: a distorting centration preventing a recognition of the quantitative equivalence $A = B$. However, as the experimenter transfers the liquid to wider and wider B's, the child may notice the increasingly more compelling disparity between the height of the liquid in A versus B, decenter, and decide with some hesitation and perplexity that A now seems to have more liquid "because it is higher" (1952b, pp. 15-16). This is a regulation, and a heuristic first step towards a rigorous, reversible composition of height changes with width changes. When the child can consistently and with certainty see that all height changes are exactly compensated by all (inverse) width changes, no matter what the shape of B, he will assert the equivalence of quantity as necessary and obvious (Piaget, 1950a, p. 140; Inhelder and Noelting, 1957). He may even wonder why you asked him such a stupid question in the first place! When all this occurs, reversible operations have taken the place of regulations, and the child's thought (for this one problem at least) has passed beyond the level of preoperational representation into the subperiod of concrete operations.

[7] Piaget frequently refers to middle-to-late preoperational thought as *intuitional* as opposed to the earlier *preconceptual* and the later *operational* forms; it is a rather apposite term, suggesting, as it does, a reasonably goal-directed but still impressionable and unsystematized kind of thinking.

[8] Regulations are also characteristic of perception in general (see Chapter 3, footnote 3) as Chapter 6 will show.

CHAPTER FIVE

Concrete Operations

PIAGET'S account of intellectual development commences with the new-born infant and extends through adolescence, the period in which the human cognizer is believed to attain his upper limit, so far as basic intellectual structure is concerned. In Chapters 3 and 4 the child's development was traced from birth to age five or six; that is, through the sensory-motor period and preoperational subperiod. This chapter concerns the important cognitive structures achieved during middle childhood (about 7-11 years), the so-called subperiod of *concrete operations*.[1]

The available sources in Piaget's bibliography for material pertinent to this subperiod are legion. All the so-called content books (dealing with space, number, quantity, geometry, moral judgment, etc.) are rich sources, especially for specific behaviors exemplifying concrete-operational thought structure. Two books describe in detail the logico-mathematical systems which purport to model the cognitive structure of middle childhood (1942a, 1949a). Both of Piaget's two summary volumes are also helpful, providing an over-all, capsule impression (1950a, 1957a). Finally, there is the expected array of sundry articles which give information on one or more aspects: Inhelder, 1954; Morf, 1957; Gonseth and Piaget, 1946; Piaget, 1922, 1924b, 1937d, 1937c, 1937b, 1941, 1949b, 1949c, 1951c, 1952e, 1953b, 1953-1954b, 1955d, 1955-1956b, 1956, 1957c, 1957-1958.

In Chapter 4 it was said that the preoperational child differs profoundly from the sensory-motor infant by virtue of the fact that he operates on a wholly new plane of reality, the plane of representation as opposed to direct action. Since the concrete-operational child also operates on this same plane, the question arises: what are the cognitive differences between these two, between the preschool and school-age child? If we look at specimens of each era in a global, impressionistic way, we are likely to see a variety of differences, some obvious and some

---

[1] In his earlier writings (e.g., 1924b) Piaget was wont to label this the stage of *intelligence de perception*—not a bad label, since the essence of the subperiod is the acquisition of a well-structured and coherent framework within which to represent and operate upon the concrete, perceivable world of things and events.

more subtle. But if we look with a Piagetian eye, we see one higher-order difference which subsumes all the particulars; and from this one difference stems most of what Piaget has to say about the subperiod of concrete operations. It is simply that the older child seems to have at his command a coherent and integrated cognitive *system* with which he organizes and manipulates the world around him. Much more than his younger counterpart, he gives the decided impression of possessing a solid cognitive bedrock, something flexible and plastic and yet consistent and enduring, with which he can structure the present in terms of the past without undue strain and dislocation, that is, without the ever-present tendency to tumble into the perplexity and contradiction which mark the preschooler. Restated in Piaget's lexicon, the concrete-operational child behaves in a wide variety of tasks as though a rich and integrated assimilatory organization were functioning in equilibrium or balance with a finely tuned, discriminative, accommodatory mechanism. This is the essence of the difference between the subperiods. And what we said earlier bears repeating: most of Piaget's detailed account of concrete operations is an elaboration of this fundamental point.

THE ORGANIZATION OF COGNITIVE ACTIONS INTO OPERATIONAL SYSTEMS

It will be recalled from Chapter 2 that the term *action* is a very generic and fundamental one in Piaget's system. Cognition at all genetic levels is best characterized as the application of real actions by the subject, either in relation to something in the milieu or in relation to other subject actions. In the sensory-motor period these actions are externalized and observable for the most part: the child brings thumb to mouth, removes an obstacle to obtain a desired object, etc. As the child progresses through the postinfancy years, on the other hand, we know that his cognitive actions become more and more internalized, schematic, and mobile, and of course more and more divested of their concrete, substantial qualities. But most important of all, for present purposes, these now internal, now representational cognitive actions gradually cohere to form increasingly complex and tightly integrated *systems* of actions. These systems are equilibrated, organized affairs in the sense that one action may annul or otherwise compensate for another previously performed; two actions can combine to produce a third, and so on. That is to say, the system these actions form is truly a system, with definite structural properties; it is something quite other than a simple concatenation or colligation of juxtaposed terms.

When cognitive actions achieve this special status, that is, when they are organized into close-knit totalities with definite, strong structure, they are called by Piaget cognitive *operations* (e.g., 1950a, ch. 2)—hence the derivation of terms like pre-*operational*, concrete and formal *operational* thought, and the like. In the preoperational period the child does possess, of course, representational actions in various states of internalization. But these preoperational actions, which Piaget sometimes labels *intuitions,* are sporadic and isolated cognitive expressions which do not coalesce into the tight ensembles we have been discussing. Operations, however, as Piaget defines the term, are the special province of middle childhood and adolescence.

What kind of cognitive act is called an *operation?* Basically, any representational act which is an integral part of an organized network of related acts is an operation. A wide variety of such operations are described in Piaget's writings: logical operations of adding, subtracting, multiplying, dividing, setting terms into correspondences, etc., within systems of classes and relations; numerical operations of various sorts; what Piaget calls *infralogical* operations involving quantity, measurement, time, space, etc., and even operations pertaining to value systems and interpersonal interaction. The reader will become more closely acquainted with the specifics of these various kinds of operations in this and subsequent chapters, but a few preliminary examples may be in order now. There is, for instance, the operation of reacting to a set of things as similar from some point of view, thereby constituting or posing a class. One can also perform the operation of combining together classes thus posed (logically "adding" them) to form a supraordinate class and then if one wishes, reconstituting the original member classes by logical "subtraction," that is, by dissociating them again from the supraordinate class. Likewise one can pose relations both asymmetrical ($A < B$, A is the father of B, etc.) and symmetrical ($A = B$, A is the brother of B, etc.) and then combine them to form new relations, e.g., $(A = B) + (B = C) = (A = C)$ or $(A < B) + (B < C) = (A < C)$. All these mental actions—the posing, adding, subtracting, and so on—are Piagetian cognitive operations. A useful rule of thumb, one Piaget has used (*ibid.,* pp. 32-33), is to say that all the actions implied in common mathematical symbols like $+$, $-$, $\times$, $\div$, $=$, $<$, $>$, etc., belong to, but do not exhaust, the domain of what he terms *intellectual operation.*

The question arises as to why such operations do—must, in Piaget's view—tend to gather together as total systems. Piaget explains as follows (e.g., 1949a, Preface; 1950a, ch. 2; 1957a, pp. 8-9). Consider the operation of regarding certain objects as members of a single class. Piaget argues that this operation would be impossible without prior possession of a more general classificatory orientation. In order to pose a class and cognize it as a true logical class rather than as a momentary, perceptual configuration or collection of elements, one must have the generalized ability to pose other classes, to *add* various classes together to form supraordinate classes, to *subtract* one class from another, and so on. In short, the single at-the-moment *actualized* operation of posing one class could not occur without a whole prior system of at-the-moment *potential* class operations. One cannot really grasp the concept of class without understanding what a classification system entails, because the single class is only an abstraction from the total system. This is the central meaning of Piaget's holism in the domain of cognitive operations: the isolated operation can never be the proper unit of analysis, because it gains all its meaning from the system of which it is a part. A given operation, put into concrete effect in the here and now, always presupposes a structured system which includes other, related operations, for the moment latent and inactive but always potentially actualizable themselves and, above all, always a force governing the form and character of the operation which is momentarily on stage.[2]

Needless to say, the above example of the classificatory system could be multiplied by many others: an asymmetrical relation presupposes the potential for constructing an asymmetrical series of indefinite length; a value presupposes a value system of which it is the expression; the addition of two lengths to form a sum length (an operation of the so-called infralogical type) presupposes a general ability to combine or separate any two or more lengths, and so on.

Let us see how these considerations apply to preoperational and concrete-operational cognition in the case of the quantity problem described in Chapter 4: given identical vessels A and A' containing identical quantities of fluid, the contents of A' are poured into a different-shaped vessel B, and the child is asked whether A and B have equal quantities of fluid. As we said, the preoperational child tends to take the immediate appearance of things as the sole and ultimate reality. He centers attention on the end state B of the transformation, is unduly impressed with the magnitude of either height or width of the fluid column, and errs accordingly. A single, isolated cognition of this sort, with little or no systematic reference to other cognitions past or potential, is the hallmark of the preoperational child.

What about the older child? With development and its attendant decentering, increased attention to transformations as well as states, coordination of reversible cognitive actions, and so forth, the child comes to approach the problem in a radically different way. He comes to view the particular transformation $A' \rightarrow B$ as a single actualized instance in a total system of possible transformations—$A' \rightarrow B_1$, $A' \rightarrow B_2$, $A' \rightarrow B_3$, etc. Moreover, each of these possible transformations is seen to have associated with it a potential transformation which annuls it, i.e., $B \rightarrow A'$, $B_1 \rightarrow A'$, $B_2 \rightarrow A'$, etc. (the liquid returned to its original vessel). Similarly, one could envisage an indefinite set of inverse compensations

---

[2] For an interesting general discussion of the role of potential versus actualized operations in cognitive behavior, see Inhelder and Piaget, 1958, pp. 255-266.

(for the increases in height a, a_1, a_2, a_3, etc., of the various B's, there are exactly compensating decreases in width A, A_1, A_2, A_3, etc.). The older child, then, does a crucial something which the younger does not: he brings to bear a whole system of potential operations on the specifics at hand, and, by so doing, can see each specific, not as an ultimate, but as the "is" of a "could be" totality, other specifics seen as being at any, time substitutable for it (B_1, B_2, B_3, etc., substituted for B, $B \rightarrow A'$ for $A' \rightarrow B$, and so on).

There is obviously much more to say about this integration of cognitive operations into system totalities. It will be shown that the operational systems of middle childhood have certain definable properties—reversibility, associativity, etc.—which have suggested to Piaget certain logico-mathematical structures. And in ensuing chapters we will take up in further detail two matters whose treatment thus far has been minimal: the fact that such systems, once formed, constitute specific forms of assimilation-accommodation equilibrium which can be compared and contrasted with the equilibrium conditions of more immature cognition, of perception, and so on; and the process of progressive equilibration itself: just how, from the point of view of equilibrium states, the pre-operational child is transformed into the concrete-operational child. To be underscored here is the central theme itself, essential to an understanding of Piaget's theory but apt to get lost when one gets immersed in the details of the latter: intellectual development is an organization process, and what are organized are active, intellectual operations; their organization into systems with definable structure is the *sine qua non* for "good" cognition, i.e., cognition of greater genetic maturity.

STRUCTURES OF CONCRETE OPERATIONS: LOGICO-MATHEMATICAL STRUCTURES AND COGNITIVE STRUCTURES

Much more than was the case for the sensory-motor and preoperational phases, an understanding of Piaget's conception of cognition in the middle-childhood years and adolescence involves coming to grips with abstract structures whose origin is definitely nonpsychological: the *groupings, groups,* and *lattices* to which we have alluded. The remainder of the chapter concerns the nature and function of these abstract structures as they pertain to concrete operational thought.

What is the liaison between logico-mathematical and intellectual structures? For Piaget, the problem of liaison here resolves into two questions. First, what is the function of these abstract structures in trying to describe or explain cognition? Second, and more generally, what ought to be the proper working relationship between logical and mathematical disciplines, on the one hand, and psychology on the other?

The narrower of these two questions has a simple answer; at least Piaget gives it a simple one. He believes that certain logico-mathematical structures make very good models of the actual organization and process of cognition in middle and late childhood (e.g., 1949a, p. v; 1950a, p. 29). They constitute, he feels, ideal patterns which the living operational systems in the subject closely approximate; they give us a useful image of how the cognizer is organized. Thus, if Piaget says that the classificatory behavior of the eight-year-old indicates that he possesses *the grouping of logical class addition,* he means that the child's thought organization in the classificatory area has formal properties (reversibility, associativity, composition, tautology, etc.) very like those which define this logico-algebraic structure. The latter has certain specific and definable system properties; we infer from his behavior that the child's cognitive structure has similar properties.

Note that this use of logic and mathematics differs from other common uses. For example, psychologists commonly use mathematics to quantify behavioral outcomes, as, for example, in the statistical treatment of test scores. Piaget, on the other hand, is concerned with the use of a basically *nonquantitative* mathematic to characterize psychological *process* and *structure,* i.e., ongoing cognitive events in the subject rather than the outcome-expressions (scores, etc.) of these events (e.g., 1957a, pp. xvii-xviii). Similarly, logic is commonly used in psychology as an aid in formalizing theories, i.e., as a set of rules for insuring that theorems, postulates, operational data statements, and the interrelationships among these are properly spelled out. For Piaget, on the contrary, logic enters the scene in a wholly different way; it enters, in a sense, the very content of the theory itself. Logical operations, together with the laws governing their relations within a total system, themselves make up the theoretical model; they are taken directly as the theoretical pattern for actual cognitive operations in vivo. In the one case, logical structures describe certain interrelationships within the *theory;* in the other case, logical structures —we may say to give the difference dramatic effect—describe the actual cognitive activity of the *theorist* as he goes about building the theory.

Logico-mathematical structures, then, are conceived as models of cognitive structure. The question may arise as to whether the subject himself is aware of the specific structure which his cognitive operations form, or even that they form a structure at all. No, not unless he has been reading Piaget. The system of operations is not itself something upon which the subject can ordinarily focus his cognitive instruments; rather, it is that *with* which and *into* which he incorporates the data of the concrete problem before him. As Piaget remarks (*ibid.,* p. 41), the system is like a "field of force" which clicks into efficient operation when the problem is confronted—not unlike the *anticipatory schemas* of Selz (Piaget, 1950a, pp. 37-38). It need only be added that this field of force is very much a dynamic and mobile affair, since it is composed of systems of operations; as Piaget says, the equilibrated cognitive system "is an equilibrium of polyphony and not that of a system of inert masses" (*ibid.*, p. 40).

As to the general relation between the logico-mathematical and psychological disciplines, Piaget has this to say. Each discipline ought to maintain its independence from the other, its own autonomy as a field (*ibid.*, pp. 29-30; 1942a, p. 9). Logic and mathematics are, of course, purely formal systems which need have no recourse to empirical fact, psychological or other, in the performance of their proper function. And conversely, Piaget thinks it would be a great mistake (a mistake he feels the Würzburg psychologists may have made) to substitute any *a priori* conception of cognitive functioning based on logic for the actual experimental study of cognitive behavior. One can no more try to settle questions of cognitive fact by appeals to logic as an ideal model than one can prove a logical theorem by observing how people think.

But the two disciplines may contribute to each other while maintaining this requisite independence. We have already indicated what Piaget feels to be one of the most important contributions of logic-mathematics to the study of thought: it provides useful models for describing actual cognitive structures. But psychology may also have something to contribute from its side. Piaget has been very much interested in trying to bring developmental fact and theory to bear on certain problems of potential interest to mathematicians and logicians, among others,[3] the psychological nature of logical and numerical operations (thus, the ultimate fundaments of the logician's and mathematician's elementary terms). Piaget believes that most logicians and mathematicians do possess some assumptions, implicit or explicit, of what their elementary terms and operations express in the way of human cognitive activity, and the student of intellectual development may be of assistance here by exploring the developmental history of these terms and operations.

A second potential contribution could come directly from the specific logico-mathematical systems which Piaget and associates have derived in their attempts to find adequate models of cognition, e.g., the grouping. These may be of interest to logicians and mathematicians as logico-mathematical systems, quite apart from any potential psychological application. Indeed, Piaget himself often appears to approach the task of creating logico-mathematical structures more as a logician than as a psychologist. In the third of his three logic books (1952a), he gets involved in the intricacies of structures which have neither actually stated nor (at least so it appears), even potential applicability to cognitive structures.

---

[3] Much of Piaget's sustained endeavors in the field of genetic epistemology involve precisely attempts to make developmental findings shed light on basic philosophical (including logico-mathematical) problems (e.g., 1950b, 1957b).

The question of how logico-mathematical structure relates to cognitive structure is only partially answered by a simple and unqualified statement that the one is intended to model the other. However, it is well-nigh impossible to go beyond this simple statement until one actually sees what the structures look like. The *grouping*, a structure originated by Piaget and associates 1937b, 1937d), is basically a hybrid born of two parent structures already well-known to mathematicians and logicians: the *group* (see Chapter 4) and the *lattice*, which we shall take up presently. There are nine distinct groupings which describe cognitive structure in the concrete-operational subperiod: one minor, preliminary grouping and eight major ones (1942a, p. 32). These groupings are viewed as models for cognition in several different realms of intellectual endeavor. First, they describe the organization of logical operations proper, i.e., operations dealing with logical classes and relations. Four of the major groupings relate to class operations and the other four to relation operations. Second, these same groupings also fit the organization of what Piaget calls *infralogical operations* (e.g., Piaget and Inhelder, 1956, ch. 15). Although infralogical operations will be more carefully defined later, suffice it for the time being to describe them as cognitive actions bearing on position and distance relationships and part-whole relationships apropos of concrete, spatiotemporal objects or configurations. In logical operations, on the other hand, considerations of spatial and temporal position, proximity, etc., are essentially irrelevant. And finally, although Piaget has not been nearly so specific regarding these, cognitive operations concerning things like *values* (e.g., 1941, p. 258) and *interpersonal relationships* (e.g., 1950a, ch. 6) are also said to have grouping properties. The groupings, whether they serve as models for logical, infralogical, or value-interpersonal operations, concern content of which there is required only what Piaget calls *intensive quantification* (e.g., 1949a, p. 72): that is, data of which one knows that each part or subclass is less than its whole or supraordinate class *without* knowing the relative magnitudes of the various component parts or subclasses (e.g., if A_1, A_2, and A_3 are subclasses of class B, one knows that $A_1 < B$, $A_2 < B$, etc., but one cannot know whether $A_1 > A_2$, $A_2 > A_3$, etc.).

There are, in addition to the nine groupings, two groups which emerge in the subperiod of concrete operations. Both concern arithmetic operations. One involves the addition of positive and negative whole numbers; and the other the multiplication of whole or fractional positive numbers (1942a, p. 198). These two groups, like the eight major groupings, have their counterparts in the infralogical domain, i.e., in measurement of temporal and spatial events through the iteration of a fixed measuring unit (e.g. Piaget, 1946a; Piaget, Inhelder, and Szeminska, 1960). Unlike the groupings, these groups deal with data which permit *extensive quantification,* that is, precise comparisons among component parts or subclasses (e.g., for $1 + 1 + 2 = 4$ the knowledge that the first 1 is exactly equal to the second 1 and that 2 is exactly twice the magnitude of 1).

Structures of Concrete Operations: The Groupings of Logical Operations

A grouping, it was said, possesses attributes of both the group and the lattice. We have seen that a group is an abstract structure composed of a set of elements and an operation bearing on these elements such that the properties of composition, associativity, identity, and reversibility hold true. A lattice is a different sort of structure. It consists of a set of elements and a relation which can hold between or "relate" two or more of these elements. To take as an example something particularly germane to the domain of concrete operations, the elements might be the set of classes of a class hierarchy and the relation that of class inclusion, symbolized here $\geq$. Thus, if class B (e.g., mammals) includes class A (e.g., dogs), we would say $B \geq A$ or B subsumes A as a subclass.

If we examine these two classes A and B in relation to the class hierarchy as a whole, we find it possible to define the smallest class in the hierarchy which includes both of them (or in which both are included, which means the same thing). For example, the smallest class in the whole zoological taxonomy which includes both A and B or in which both A and B are included is B itself (the smallest class which includes all mammals and all dogs is the class of mammals itself). Expressing this operation in logical symbolism we say that

$$A + B = B \quad \text{or} \quad A \cup B = B$$

(the logical sum or union of A and B is B). This smallest class which includes both pair members—the class which results from the logical sum or union of the two—is referred to in lattice theory as the *least upper bound* (l.u.b.) of the two elements in question.

The concept of *greatest lower bound* (g.l.b.) is given analogously. The largest class which is contained in both classes, which both classes together contain, is A in our example (the largest class whose members are at once dogs and mammals—the largest class which A and B subsume in common—is the class of dogs itself). Using analogous logical notation, we say that

$$A \times B = A \quad \text{or} \quad A \cap B = A$$

(the logical product or intersect of A and B is A). We can now give a definition of a lattice sufficiently precise for the present exposition. It is a structure consisting of a set of elements and a relation such that any two elements have one g.l.b. and one l.u.b. Of course other things besides class hierarchies have lattice structure. For instance, the set of positive integers (1, 2, 3, etc.) and the relation $\geq$:

the g.l.b. and l.u.b. of, say, the two elements [10, 13] are 10 and 13 respectively (10 is the largest number included in both 10 and 13 at once, and 13 is the smallest number in which both 10 and 13 are included). But the lattice is a particularly apt structure for representing certain properties of logical class operations (and logical relation operations as well). For this reason lattice as well as group properties go to make up Piaget's groupings.

The Nine Groupings of Logical Classes and Relations

GROUPING I: PRIMARY ADDITION OF CLASSES

Grouping I (Piaget refers to each of the eight major groupings by Roman numeral) is the simplest of the major groupings and illustrates the general properties common to all of them. It describes the essential operations and the interrelationships among these operations, which are involved in the cognition of simple hierarchies of classes. Consider an ordinary zoological class hierarchy, using Piaget's customary symbolism for the various classes: A = the class of spaniels; A' = all other sub-classes within the class of domestic dogs; B = the class of domestic dogs; B' = all other subclasses within the class of canines (wolves, dingos, etc.); C = the class of canines; C' = all other subclasses within the class of mammals; D = the class of mammals; D' = all other subclasses within the class of vertebrates; E = the class of vertebrates. Let us call all the unprimed classes *primary classes* (A, B, C, and E) and all those which have the prime sign *secondary classes* (A', B', C', and D'). Note that an unprimed letter refers to a single primary class (A = the class of spaniels); and a primed letter refers to a number (undetermined) of secondary classes (A' = all the subclasses within the class of domestic dogs *except* the class of spaniels A).

One can perform a number of cognitive operations within the framework of such a class hierarchy. One can mentally pose (think of, consider, etc.) a class A and, conversely, one can unpose the same class (ignore it, exclude it, think of its supraordinate class B without A, thus leaving only the subclasses A', etc.). If we symbolize posing by + (logical addition) and unposing by − (logical subtraction), we have the elementary operations $+A$ and $-A$, $+B'$ and $-B'$, etc. It is also possible to perform a series of such elementary operations and sum them, rather like making a series of additions and subtractions in ordinary arithmetic. For example, I can mentally pose A, then pose A', then pose B'; the result of this series of operations is, in effect, the posing of C, since to pose A and A' together amounts to posing B, and the posing of B and B' together amounts to posing C. Series of this kind can be expressed by equations consisting of operations and class elements. In the example just given, the equation would be $(+A) + (+A') + (+B') = (+C)$ or simply $A + A' + B' = C$.

There are, of course, many such equations possible: $B - A = A'$ (if I pose the class of domestic dogs, then exclude the subclass of spaniels, I end up with the nonspaniel subclasses of this class); $D - C' - B' - A' = A$ (if I pose the class of mammals and then successively exclude from it all the noncanine mammals, all the nondomestic canines, and all the nonspaniel domestic dogs, I end up with spaniels alone); $B - A - A' = 0$ (if I pose the class of domestic dogs and then exclude both the spaniels and the nonspaniel domestic dogs, I have remaining an empty or null class).

Grouping I is the set of implicit rules which govern class operations of the type just described in exactly the same sense as, for example, the group is a set of rules governing addition operations on positive and negative integers, on rigid rotations of a bar from a fixed center, etc. (see Chapter 4). A grouping has five such fundamental rules which define its structure. Of these five, the first four are the familiar group properties and the last is a lattice property. As in the group, all groupings have as essential components an operation and a set of elements. In Grouping I Piaget does not, as one might have expected, formally define the grouping elements in terms of isolated operations of posing or unposing classes, e.g., $+A$, $-B$, etc. Rather, the elements are taken to be logical addition equations of the type described above, e.g., $(A + A' = B)$, $(C - B' - A' = A)$, $(-A - A' = -B)$, etc. The grouping operation (as opposed to the component class operations such as $+A$, $-A$, etc.) is essentially that of combining or adding such equations. The five properties of Grouping I are the following.

1. *Composition.* The product which results from combining any element (i.e., class addition equation) with any other by means of the defined operation is itself an element (equation) in the class system. As examples: $(A + A' = B) + (B + B' = C) = (A + A' + B' = C)$; $(B - A' = A) + (C - B' = B) = (C - B' - A' = A)$.[4]

2. *Associativity.* The sum of a series of elements is independent of the way they are grouped. For example: $[(B - A' = A) + (C - B' = B)] + (D - C' = C)$ and $(B - A' = A) + [(C - B' = B) = (D - C' = C)]$ are both equal to $(D - C' - B' - A' = A)$.

3. *General Identity.* There is one and only one element (the identity element) which, when added to any other element whatsoever, leaves that other element unchanged. Piaget defines this element (somewhat arbitrarily) as the equation $(0 + 0 = 0)$, that is, as the sum of two null classes. Thus, $(0 + 0 = 0) + (C - B' = B) = (C - B' = B)$, etc.

4. *Reversibility.* For each and every element there is one and only one

[4] Note that in this second example the sum of these two equations is not the sum of the right-hand members of each equation, i.e., not $A + B (=B)$. The reason that the equations sum to A is that one has stripped C of B', leaving B (second equation); but B itself is already denuded of A' (first equation), and thus the final resultant is A alone.

element, called its *inverse*, which yields the identity element when added to the former. For instance, the inverse of $(A + A' = B)$ is $(-A - A' = -B)$, thus $(A + A' = B) + (-A - A' = -B) = (0 + 0 = 0)$. Similarly $(D - C' = C) + (-B - B' = -C) = (0 + 0 = 0)$.

5. *Special Identities.* A grouping, like a group, possesses a unique element—the identity element $(0 + 0 = 0$ for Grouping I)—which leaves unchanged any element to which it is added. However, the grouping differs from the group in that it also possesses other elements which, in special circumstances, can play the role of identity elements. It will be recalled that, in a lattice of classes, a unique l.u.b. can be found for any pair of classes, this l.u.b. consisting of the logical sum or union of the two elements. For example, where $A + A' = B$, $A + B = B$ and $A' + B = B$ (B is the l.u.b. for A and B and for A' and B, since it is the smallest class which includes A and B or A' and B). But, if $A + B = B$, $A + C = C$, $A + D = D$, etc., it is clear that A is playing the role of the identity element with respect to B, C, D, and its other supraordinate classes. Similarly, since the l.u.b. of A and itself is A ($A \cup A$ or $A + A$ is still A), then A is also playing the role of identity element with respect to itself—a special case of the more general $A + X = X$, where X is a class which subsumes A. Thus, in addition to the ordinary group-type identity element $(0 + 0 = 0)$, which we call the *general identity*, the grouping also possesses *special identities* (lattice-derived properties) which we can now define as follows: Every class plays the role of identity element with respect to itself (Piaget calls this property *tautology*) and with respect to its supraordinate classes (property of *resorption*). If we now move from the level of addition of individual classes to the addition of equations, we again see these two properties in action: $(A + A' = B) + (A + A' = B) = (A + A' = B)$; $(B + B' = C) + (D + D' = E) = (D + D' = E)$; $(-A - A' = -B) + (-B - B' = -C) = (-B - B' = -C)$, etc. These cases illustrate the fact that an equation can play the role of special identity either with respect to itself or with respect to any other equation whose right-hand member is a supraordinate class of its own right-hand member.

The addition of this fifth property makes the grouping a new and unique structure: it is part group and part lattice and yet, taken in total, neither group nor lattice. Piaget's addition of this fifth property is not arbitrary; its inclusion is absolutely essential to a structure which deals with classes and relations. In the group structure there are no special identities because group elements "iterate" (summate) when the operation is performed upon them. For example, in the group of addition of integers, one finds $2 + 2 + 2 + 2 = 8$, $2 + 4 + 6 = 12$, etc. But this is clearly not the case with the addition of classes: $A + A + A + A$ must equal A, not $4A$; $A + B + C$ equals C itself, not some class of greater extension than C.

However, the inclusion of the fifth property, necessary though it be, leads to special problems which require special conventions and rules to manage them. The grouping, relative to the group, turns out to be a very untidy structure with all sorts of exceptions to general rules. For example, the special identities property puts restrictions on the generality of the associativity law in all the groupings. In the case of Grouping I, for instance, $[(A + A' = B) + (A + A' = B)] + (-A - A' = -B) \neq (A + A' = B) + [(A + A' = B) + (-A - A' = -B)]$ because the left-hand member of the equation sums to 0 (because $B + B = B$ and $B - B = 0$) while the right-hand member sums to $(A + A' = B)$. As Piaget makes clear (1942a, pp. 42-49; 1949a, pp. 100-103), the adjunction of a few special rules (which we shall not take up) handles problems of this kind, but the very fact that extra regulations must be inserted into the formal definition of the grouping structure attests to its lack of mathematical simplicity and elegance.

There is one final matter which needs brief mention, particularly for readers conscientious enough to compare our presentation of the groupings with the Piaget original (1942a, 1949a). Although Piaget does clearly state that the mathematical elements of the groupings are class and relation *equations* rather than isolated classes or relations (1942a, pp. 38, 103; 1949a, p. 109), it is often possible (and usually more convenient) to treat classes and relations as the grouping elements, provided the special rules just alluded to are invoked. Piaget himself oscillates between the equation level and the single-term level in his descriptions of grouping properties. For example, the *reversibility* and *general identity* properties may be illustrated alternatively by the expressions $B - B = 0$, $(A + A' = B) + (-A - A' = -B) = (0 + 0 = 0)$, or $(A + A' = B) - (A + A' = B) = (0 + 0 = 0)$. In our presentation of subsequent groupings, we shall adopt a Piagetian casualness about these matters and shall operate at the simpler, single-term level wherever convenience and clarity dictate.

GROUPING II. THE SECONDARY ADDITION OF CLASSES (VICARIANCES)

Operations contained in Grouping I pertain to class hierarchies of the form $A + A' = B$, $B + B' = C$, etc.; in these hierarchies the primary classes A, B, C, etc., each refer to a single class (A = spaniels, B = domestic dogs, etc.) whereas the secondary classes A', B', C', etc., each denote an unspecified number of classes of the same rank as the corresponding primary class. That is, A' does not refer to a single class of the rank A (e.g., beagles) but refers to all the complementary classes under B (e.g., beagles, poodles, terriers, etc.—every class of domestic dogs except spaniels). By virtue of the multiclass denotation of the secondary classes, it is possible to establish other series of classes analogous to and parallel to the series $A + A' = B$, $B + B' = C$, etc. For example, if I search within A' and find a class A_2 (e.g., beagles), I can then establish that $A_2 + A_2' =$

B (where $A_2' = $ all classes of nonbeagle domestic dogs, that is, the complement of A_2 under B); similarly, I can select a class B_2 within B' (e.g., wolves) and establish the equation $B_2 + B_2' = C$, and so on up the hierarchy. And again, one could establish a series which begins with $A_3 + A_3' = B$ (e.g., $A_3 = $ terriers). In short, one can create a number of series parallel to the initial one, each one rejoining the initial series at the next higher-rank primary class (thus, $A_2 + A_2' = B$, $A_3 + A_3' = B$, and so forth, just as $A + A' = B$).

By this fact of rejoining the primary series at the next primary class up the hierarchy, one can establish equalities such as $A + A' = A_2 + A_2' = A_3 + A_3'$, etc., $(= B)$ and $B + B' = B_2 + B_2' = B_3 + B_3'$, etc., $(= C)$. Piaget refers to such equations as *complementary substitutions* or *vicariances* (1949a, p. 114) because of the invariant rule that, given Ax, Ay, Ax' and Ay', one can always substitute Ay for Ax on the condition that one also substitute Ay' for Ax' in the same equation, i.e., $Ay + Ay'$ is always substitutable for $Ax + Ax'$. Note also that one of the classes in Ay' is Ax and one of the classes in Ax' is Ay (e.g., the nonbeagles include the spaniels and the nonspaniels include the beagles, both beagles plus nonbeagles and spaniels plus nonspaniels "summing" to domestic dogs).

Grouping II is simply the grouping structure which vicariance equations, taken as elements, form. The sum of any two or more vicariances yields a vicariance (the *composition* property): thus $(A + A' = A_2 + A_2')$ $+ (B + B' = B_2 + B_2') = (A + A' + B' = B_2 + B_2')$. *Associativity* also holds, as it does for Grouping I, providing only that the special rules are abided by. The *general identity* is taken as $(0 + 0 = 0 + 0)$ and is unique. The *inverse* of a posed vicariance is the unposing or subtraction of that vicariance, yielding the general identity. There are a number of different types of tautologies and resorptions (*special identities*) which hold true in this grouping. At the level of individual classes rather than whole equations, one not only finds the expected $A + A = A, A_2 + A_2 = A_2, A_2' + A_2' = A_2'$, etc., and $A + B = B, A_2 + B = B, A_2' + B = B$, etc., but also $A + A_2' = A_2'$ (since A is a subclass of A_2'), $A + A_3' = A_3'$, $A + B_2' = B_2'$ (since B_2' includes B which in turn includes A), and a host of others.

GROUPING III: BI-UNIVOCAL MULTIPLICATION OF CLASSES[5]

Classes can be multiplied and divided as well as added and subtracted. Suppose we take a class of people D_1 and divide them into subclasses according to skin color, e.g., $A_1 = $ white, $B_1 = $ black, and $C_1 = $ yellow (note that here, although $A_1 + B_1 + C_1 = D_1$, the subclasses A_1, B_1, C_1 are of the same class rank). Similarly, we can take the same class of people (called D_2 now) and subdivide them according to where they live,

[5] Piaget's logic books differ somewhat in the way they enumerate the various groupings, e.g., *Traité de logique* (1949a) calls this Grouping IV instead of III. Our presentation abides by the sequence given in the earlier work (1942a).

e.g., A_2 = urban, B_2 = suburban, and C_2 = rural. These two series once constituted, one can logically multiply a member of one series by a member of the other. The result of this multiplication is the logical product or intersect described earlier in connection with the g.l.b. of the lattice: the largest class which the two members comprise *in common* (the largest class which contains the defining attributes of *both* these classes). Thus, one can perform multiplicative operations like $A_1 \times A_2 = A_1 A_2$ (the class of people who are both white and live in the city), $C_1 \times B_2$ (people who are both yellow and live in the suburbs), etc. Moreover, it is possible to multiply together the two series as a whole: $D_1 \times D_2 = D_1 D_2 = A_1 A_2 + A_1 B_2 + A_1 C_2 + B_1 A_2 + B_1 B_2 + B_1 C_2 + C_1 A_2 + C_1 B_2 + C_1 C_2$. In other words, the product of the two series generates a matrix or double-entry table of nine cells with the component classes of D_1 on one axis and those of D_2 on the other. Class multiplication of this type is called *bi-univocal* by Piaget, indicating that each component class of the first series is placed in multiplicative correspondence or association with each component class of the second. It should be obvious that bi-univocal multiplication of classes is not limited to just two series. For instance, if D_3 refers to height with A_3 = short, B_3 = medium, C_3 = tall, one can multiply this new series with the other two: $D_1 \times D_2 \times D_3 = D_1 D_2 D_3 = A_1 A_2 A_3$ (short, white, city dwellers) $+ A_1 A_2 B_3 + A_1 A_2 C_3$, and so on through the 27 distinct combinations.

The usual grouping properties obtain for bi-univocal multiplication of classes. The *composition* property holds as follows: the multiplication of two classes yields a class $(A_1 \times A_2 = A_1 A_2)$ and the multiplication of two series yields a set of classes $(D_1 \times D_2 = A_1 A_2 + A_1 B_2$, etc.). Such multiplications are *associative*: $(D_1 \times D_2) \times D_3 = D_1 \times (D_2 \times D_3)$, $A_1 \times (B_2 \times B_3) = (A_1 \times B_2) \times B_3$, etc. For the *special identities*, there is the usual *tautology* property: $A_1 \times A_1 = A_1$, $D_2 \times D_2 = D_2$, $B_1 B_2 \times B_1 B_2 = B_1 B_2$, etc. However, instead of the *resorption* property of class addition (A resorbed into its supraordinate classes, e.g., $A + C = C$), there is the *absorption* of the supraordinate class into its subordinate class, e.g., $D_1 \times A_1 = A_1$—the class of individuals who are at once people (D_1) and white (A_1) is simply the class of white people (A_1). The inverse operation is also not the usual subtraction but is instead class *division* (the dissociation or abstraction of one class from a class product). For example, $A_1 A_2 \div A_1 = A_2$, i.e., if I dissociate or abstract the qualification "white" from a class defined as "white city dwellers," I end up with the whole class of city dwellers without regard to color. Quite unlike class addition, the multiplication of two classes like A_1 and A_2 generates a class $A_1 A_2$ smaller in extension (i.e., contains fewer members) than either A_1 or A_2; conversely, dividing a class like $A_1 A_2$ by, say, A_2, produces a class A_1 larger than $A_1 A_2$ (e.g., 1949a, p. 120). If $A - A = 0$ (the null class as identity element) in class addition, what is the result of $A \div A$ in class multiplication? This of course amounts to asking what the *general identity* element is in Grouping III. It clearly cannot be the null class, because the abstraction of class properties from a class generates a class as large or (usually) larger in extension that the original, never smaller. Piaget gives the general identity here as the class Z, defined as the largest, most general class possible relevant to the class series you are dealing with; it is the hypothetical class which contains all the others. For example, if $Dx = $ animals, then $Dx \div Dx = Z$ means that you have removed the class-defining limitation "animalness," leaving the most general possible class relevant to "animalness-nonanimalness." Z might then appropriately be called "the class of beings defined by no specific, delimiting qualities." Such a class is obviously very large, since it has no delimiting attributes with which to exclude candidates for class membership. And of course the product or intersect of Z with any class leaves that class unchanged (e.g., $A_1 \times Z = A_1$). The special identity, general identity, and reversibility properties of Grouping III can be summed up succinctly in expressions like: $A_1 \times A_1 = A_1$, $A_1 \times D_1 = A_1$, $A_1 A_2 \div A_1 = A_2$, $D_1 \div D_1 = Z$, and $B_1 \times Z = B_1$.

GROUPING IV: CO-UNIVOCAL MULTIPLICATION OF CLASSES

Bi-univocal multiplication, formalized in Grouping III, involves the establishment of one-to-one correspondences between each of the component members of two or more series of classes. There is a second kind of class multiplication, called *co-univocal* (one-to-many), in which one member of one series is set in correspondence with (multiplied with) several members of each of one or more additional series. Suppose we construct two class series, K_1 and K_2, as follows. K_1 contains the following classes: $A_1 = $ sons of person x; $B_1 = $ grandsons of person x; and $C_1 = $ great-grandsons of person x. K_2 contains the following classes: $A_2 = $ brothers; $A_2' = $ first cousins of A_2; and $B_2' = $ second cousins of A_2. These two series established, one can take each member of K_1 and multiply it or set it into separate correspondence with as many members of K_2 as it contains. A_1 contains only one K_2 class, namely A_2. That is, the only K_2 class which can be applied to the sons of x is the class "brothers." However, B_1 contains two K_2 classes: A_2, since some of x's grandsons are brothers, and A_2', since the remaining grandsons of x must be first cousins to these brothers. And C_1 contains three K_2 classes: A_2, first cousins of A_2 (A_2'), and second cousins of A_2 (B_2').

If one now multiplies the series K_1 and K_2 together, one gets: $K_1 \times K_2 = A_1 A_2 + B_1 (A_2 + A_2') + C_1 (A_2 + A_2' + B_2')$ or simply, $A_1 A_2 + B_1 A_2 + B_1 A_2' + C_1 A_2 + C_1 A_2' + C_1 B_2'$. Note that the product classes $A_1 A_2$, $B_1 A_2$, etc., are of the same basic type as those seen in Grouping III. For example, $C_1 A_2'$ is defined in the customary way as the intersect of classes C_1 and A_2', that is, as the set of individuals who are at once great-grandsons of x *and* first cousins to a set (A_2) of great-grandson-of-x brothers. As a matter of fact, the grouping properties of co-univocal multiplication assume exactly the same form as those of Grouping III and for this reason do not need to be spelled out here (see, for example, 1949a, pp. 119-122). The fundamental difference in the two groupings lies mostly in the nature of the matrices generated by the multiplication of two series: a square matrix stemming from the one-one multiplication of Grouping III; a triangular matrix (like the nonredundant portion of an ordinary correlation matrix) stemming from the one-many multiplication of Grouping IV.

GROUPING V: ADDITION OF ASYMMETRICAL RELATIONS

Groupings I-IV concern operations performed upon logical *classes*. Groupings V-VIII, on the other hand, involve operations performed upon the *relations* which may exist between two or more individuals or between two or more classes. Piaget describes a number of different kinds of relations (1949a, pp. 134-138). Grouping V is specifically concerned with *asymmetrical* relations (*A* "is smaller than" *B*, *A* "is higher than" *B*, *A* "is the father of" *B*, etc.) whose compositions are *transitive* (that is, $A < B$ plus $B < C$ implies $A < C$). Asymmetrical relations denote *ordered* differences between terms: *differences,* because $<$ in $A < B$ indicates a way in which *A* differs from *B*; *ordered,* because the difference goes in a specific direction, e.g.,

$$A < B \neq A > B.$$

Grouping V describes the logical addition (and subtraction) of these ordered differences within a series of such asymmetrical relations. Following Piaget's notation, let us postulate a collection of entities (objects or classes, it does not matter which) *O, A, B, C, D,* etc., which are linked by some transitive asymmetrical relation → so as to form a series which we can diagram as follows:

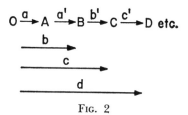

FIG. 2

The small letters *a, b',* etc., label the ordered differences or relations indicated by the arrows just as the capital letters *A, A', B* labeled classes in the previous groupings. Note that these ordered differences first of all satisfy the transitivity criterion, e.g.,

$$0 \xrightarrow{a} A + A \xrightarrow{a'} B = 0 \xrightarrow{b} B.$$

Asymmetrical relations of this kind share a number of properties in common with classes. For example, for a class B and its subclasses A and A', we know that $A < B$ and $A' < B$ without knowing the relative extensions of A and A'; this is the *intensive quantification* property mentioned earlier. In the same way, one can establish that $a < b$ and $a' < b$ without any measurement of the actual magnitudes of the differences a, a', and b. Similarly, asymmetrical relations, like classes, can clearly be added: thus, in analogy with Grouping I, $a + a' = b$, $b + b' = c$, $c + c' = d$, etc.

The formal properties of Grouping V are similar to those of Grouping I in some but not all respects. The *composition* principle holds in the usual way and is illustrated by such familiar-looking additions as

$$(O \xrightarrow{a} A) + (A \xrightarrow{a'} B) + (B \xrightarrow{b'} C) = (O \xrightarrow{c} C) \text{ and}$$

$$(A \xrightarrow{a'} B) + (B \xrightarrow{b'} C) = A \xrightarrow{a'b'} C),$$

or simply, $a + a' + b' = c$ and $a' + b' = a'b'$. *Associativity* and the *special identities* hold: $(a + a') + b' = a + (a' + b')$ *(associativity)*; $a + a = a$ *(tautology)*; and $a + b = b$ *(resorption)*. However the *reversibility* and *general identity* properties take a different form from those of Groupings I and II. Piaget argues *(ibid.,* pp. 139-143) that the *inverse* of an ordered difference relation

$$(A \xrightarrow{a'} B)$$

is not analogous to the case in class addition, the *negating* or *annulling* of that relation, i.e., not

$$(A \xrightarrow{a'} B) + (A \xrightarrow{-a'} B) = (A = B).$$

Rather, it is its *reciprocal*

$$(B \xleftarrow{a'} A),$$

giving

$$(A \xrightarrow{a'} B) + (B \xleftarrow{a'} A) = (A \xrightarrow{\circ} A) \quad \text{or} \quad (A = A).$$

In the first case, one actually changes the *magnitude* of one or both of the terms of the relation (e.g., one makes B smaller than it was so as to give $A = B$ rather than

$$A \xrightarrow{a'} B).$$

In the second case, one leaves the terms unchanged, changing only the way the relation is expressed (e.g., from "A is smaller than B" to "B is larger than A"). Thus, the inverse or reversibility property of concrete operational structures assumes two different forms: *negation* in the case of classes and *reciprocity* in the case of relations. These differences, of course, necessitate parallel differences in the nature of the *general iden-*

tity. For Grouping I the general identity is, in effect, "no class" or 0; in Grouping V it is *not* "no relation" but an *equivalence* relation, a relation of "no difference," symbolized by ∘ or =. Finally, as with the class groupings, one not only has inverse operations of the form

$$\overset{a}{\rightarrow} + \overset{a}{\leftarrow} = \overset{o}{\rightarrow}$$

(described above) but also

$$\overset{b}{\rightarrow} + \overset{a'}{\leftarrow} = \overset{a}{\rightarrow}, \quad \overset{d}{\rightarrow} + \overset{b'c'}{\leftarrow} = \overset{b}{\rightarrow}, \text{ etc.}$$

GROUPING VI: ADDITION OF SYMMETRICAL RELATIONS

Although we tend to associate symmetry with simplicity, Grouping VI is in fact considerably more complicated than Grouping V. This is true primarily because it involves additive compositions of several distinct and different kinds of symmetrical relations: some transitive, some intransitive, some reflexive, some irreflexive. Let us take as an example one of Piaget's favorites for this grouping: the symmetrical relations found within a genealogical hierarchy. If x, y, and z are male members of this hierarchy, one can establish relations of the following type:

(A) $$x \overset{o}{\leftrightarrow} x \quad (\text{or } x = x),$$

thus x is in identity relation with himself;

(B) $$x \overset{a}{\leftrightarrow} y, \text{ where } \overset{a}{\leftrightarrow} \text{ signifies "brother of";}$$

(C) $$x \overset{a'}{\leftrightarrow} z, \text{ where } \overset{a'}{\leftrightarrow} \text{ means "first cousin to";}$$

(D) $x \overset{b}{\leftrightarrow} y$, $x \overset{b}{\leftrightarrow} z$, etc., where $\overset{b}{\leftrightarrow}$ denotes "has the same grandfather as," and so on. Since difference relations are also symmetrical if they are non-ordered, we can also construct relations like

$$x \overset{\bar{a}}{\leftrightarrow} y \ (x \text{ is not the brother of } y),$$

$$x \overset{\bar{a}'}{\leftrightarrow} y \ (x \text{ is not the cousin of } y),$$

$$x \overset{\bar{b}}{\leftrightarrow} y) \ (x \text{ and } y \text{ do not have the same grandfather}),$$

and so forth.

The various formal rules involved in the additive *composition* of such relations go to make up most of the complexity of Grouping VI (e.g., 1949a, pp. 154-157). We shall give a few examples rather than a systematic statement of these rules. Thus, whereas

$$(x \overset{a}{\leftrightarrow} y) + (y \overset{a}{\leftrightarrow} z) = x \overset{a}{\leftrightarrow} z, \quad (x \overset{a}{\leftrightarrow} y) + (y \overset{b}{\leftrightarrow} z) = x \overset{b}{\leftrightarrow} z.$$

Translated into English, this means that if x and y are brothers and y and z are brothers then x and z must also be brothers; if x and y are brothers and y and z have the same grandfather then all we are sure of is that x and z have the same grandfather (since x and z could be *either* brothers $\overset{a}{\leftrightarrow}$ or first cousins $\overset{a'}{\leftrightarrow}$). Further,

$$(x \overset{a}{\leftrightarrow} y) + (y \overset{a'}{\leftrightarrow} z) = x \overset{a'}{\leftrightarrow} z,$$

i.e., if z is first cousin to one of two brothers (x and y), he is also first cousin to the other. Again,

$$(x \overset{a'}{\leftrightarrow} y) + (y \overset{a'}{\leftrightarrow} z) = x \overset{b}{\leftrightarrow} z,$$

since x in this instance could be either z's first cousin or his brother. As a final example involving a symmetrical difference relation,

$$(x \overset{a}{\leftrightarrow} y) + (y \overset{\bar{b}}{\leftrightarrow} z) = x \overset{\bar{b}}{\leftrightarrow} z,$$

since if one brother y does not have the same grandfather as z, the other brother x doesn't either.

As for the other grouping properties, *associativity* presents no problem:

$$[(r \overset{a}{\leftrightarrow} x) + (x \overset{a'}{\leftrightarrow} y)] + (y \overset{a'}{\leftrightarrow} z) = (r \overset{a}{\leftrightarrow} x) + [(x \overset{a'}{\leftrightarrow} y) + (y \overset{a'}{\leftrightarrow} z)] = r \overset{b}{\leftrightarrow} z.$$

In analogy with Grouping V, the *inverse* is the reciprocal operation, and it takes the form here of permuting the terms of the relation, e.g.,

$$y \overset{a}{\leftrightarrow} x$$

is the inverse (reciprocal) of

$$x \overset{a}{\leftrightarrow} y.$$

The *general identity* is

$$x \overset{\circ}{\leftrightarrow} x \quad \text{or} \quad x = x.$$

Thus,

$$(x \overset{a}{\leftrightarrow} y) + (y \overset{a}{\leftrightarrow} x) = x \overset{\circ}{\leftrightarrow} x, \quad (x \overset{\circ}{\leftrightarrow} x) + (y \overset{b}{\leftrightarrow} z) = y \overset{b}{\leftrightarrow} z, \text{ etc.}$$

And finally, for the *special identity* property, there is *tautology*

$$(x \overset{a}{\leftrightarrow} y) + (x \overset{a}{\leftrightarrow} y) = x \overset{a}{\leftrightarrow} y$$

and *resorption*

$$(x \overset{a}{\leftrightarrow} y) + (x \overset{b}{\leftrightarrow} y) = x \overset{b}{\leftrightarrow} y;$$

other expressions of these two properties were given above, i.e.,

$$(x \overset{a}{\leftrightarrow} y) + (y \overset{a}{\leftrightarrow} z) = x \overset{a}{\leftrightarrow} z \quad \text{and} \quad (x \overset{a}{\leftrightarrow} y) + (y \overset{b}{\leftrightarrow} z) = x \overset{b}{\leftrightarrow} z.$$

GROUPING VII: BI-UNIVOCAL MULTIPLICATION OF RELATIONS

As we have shown, Grouping I describes additive operations performed upon component classes of a class hierarchy and Grouping III describes the one-to-one multiplication of two or more such hierarchies. Similarly, whereas Grouping V entails additive operations within a series of asymmetrical relations, Grouping VII involves the one-to-one multiplication of two or more such series. Consider the following matrix (adapted from 1949a, p. 171, Fig. 16):

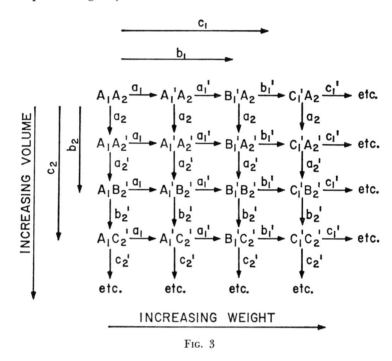

FIG. 3

The reality which this matrix depicts is not as complicated as might appear. Each pair of capital letters (A_1A_2, A'_1A_2, etc.) denotes an object (or a class of identical objects) of given weight and volume. The horizontal arrows

$$\xrightarrow{a_1}, \xrightarrow{a_1'}, \text{ etc.}$$

represent weight difference between the objects and the vertical arrows

$$\downarrow^{a_2}, \downarrow^{a_2'}, \text{ etc.}$$

give volume differences. These are both sets of asymmetrical relations of precisely the sort described in connection with Grouping V, and thus one can perform upon them the customary additive operations, i.e.,

$$\xrightarrow{a_1} + \xrightarrow{a_1'} = \xrightarrow{b_1}, \text{ etc.,} \quad \text{and}$$

$$\downarrow^{a_2} + \downarrow^{a_2'} = \downarrow^{b_2}, \text{ etc.}$$

Now this array of objects is taken to have an important simplifying property which permits Piaget to fit a grouping structure to the system (*ibid.*, p. 172): all objects in the same column have the same weight, although they differ in volume, and all objects in the same row have the same volume, although they differ in weight. Needless to say, this property does not necessitate that difference $\xrightarrow{a_1}$ equal difference $\xrightarrow{a_1'}$, etc., or that $\downarrow^{a_2}$ equal $\downarrow^{a_2'}$, etc. Recall that groupings were said to involve only *intensive quantification*.

The multiplicative *compositions* possible within this system can occur at two levels of complexity. First of all, we can multiply a weight relation by a volume relation to get as product a relation that is at the same time one of weight and of volume. For instance,

$$(A_1A_2 \xrightarrow{c_1} C_1'A_2) \times (C_1'A_2 \downarrow^{a_2} C_1'A_2') = (A_1A_2 \xrightarrow{c_1} \downarrow^{a_2} C_1'A_2');$$

that is, if A_1A_2 is lighter by $\xrightarrow{c_1}$ than $C_1'A_2$ at equal volume, and if $C_1'A_2$ is less voluminous by $\downarrow^{a_2}$ than $C_1'A_2'$ at equal weight, it must follow that A_1A_2 is *at once*—and here we see the meaning of "multiplication of relations"—lighter and less voluminous than $C_1'A_2'$ by the amount $\xrightarrow{c_1} \downarrow^{a_2}$. It is also possible to effect more complex compositions involving the multiplication of the products of those of the above-illustrated, simpler type. A straightforward example is:

$$(A_1A_2' \xrightarrow{b_1} \downarrow^{a_2'} B_1'B_2') \times (B_1'B_2' \xrightarrow{b_1'} \downarrow^{b_2'} C_1'C_2') =$$
$$(A_1A_2' \xrightarrow{c_1} \downarrow^{a_2' + b_2'} C_1'C_2').$$

But one can also have such expressions as

$$(A_1A_2' \xrightarrow{b_1} \downarrow^{a_2'} B_1'B_2') \times (B_1'B_2' \xleftarrow{a_1'} \uparrow^{a_2'} A_1'A_2') = (A_1A_2' \xrightarrow{a_1} \downarrow^{\circ} A_1'A_2'),$$

or simply

$$(A_1A_2' \xrightarrow{a_1} A_1'A_2'),$$ where "$\leftarrow$" means "heavier than" and "$\uparrow$" means "more voluminous than."

As for the other grouping properties, *associativity* presents no problems: if we let *a*, *b*, and *c* represent the expressions within parentheses, e.g.,

$$a = (A_1A_2 \xrightarrow{b_1} \downarrow^{c_2} B_1'C_2'), \text{ etc.},$$

then $a(bc) = (ab)c$ in all instances. The *inverse operation* is logical division, as in Groupings III and IV, and the *general identity* is the null difference for both weight and volume. Thus, for instance,

$$(A_1A_2 \xrightarrow{a_1} \downarrow^{a_2} A_1'A_2') \div (A_1A_2 \xrightarrow{a_1} \downarrow^{a_2} A_1'A_2')$$

or, in alternative form,

$$(A_1A_2 \xrightarrow{a_1} \downarrow^{a_2} A_1'A_2') \times (A_1A_2 \xleftarrow{a_1} \uparrow^{a_2} A_1'A_2')$$

equals the general identity

$$(A_1A_2 \xrightarrow{\circ} \downarrow \circ A_1A_2).$$

The *special identities* also appear in the usual form for multiplication groupings. An example of the *tautology* property would be

$$(A_1A_2 \xrightarrow{a_1} \downarrow {}^{a_2} A_1'A_2') \times (A_1A_2 \xrightarrow{a_1} \downarrow {}^{a_2} A_1'A_2') = (A_1A_2 \xrightarrow{a_1} \downarrow {}^{a_2} A_1'A_2').$$

And for the *absorption* property:

$$(A_1A_2 \xrightarrow{a_1} \downarrow {}^{a_2} A_1'A_2') \times (A_1A_2 \xrightarrow{b_1} \downarrow {}^{b_2} B_1'B_2') = (A_1A_2 \xrightarrow{a_1} \downarrow {}^{a_2} A_1'A_2').$$

GROUPING VIII: CO-UNIVOCAL MULTIPLICATION OF RELATIONS

As the reader can no doubt anticipate, Grouping VIII is to VII for relations, what IV is to III for classes. It will be recalled that Grouping IV deals with the one-many multiplication of classes within class hierarchies of the pyramid-shaped, genealogical type. Grouping VIII, on the other hand, is concerned with the multiplication of the various symmetrical and asymmetrical relations which define the classes in such hierarchies—relations like "father of," "first cousin of," etc. Suppose we have a family-tree hierarchy and adopt the following symbolism for its component relations: for the symmetrical relations,

$$\overset{\circ}{\leftrightarrow} = \text{"is same person as,"}$$

$$\overset{\circ'}{\leftrightarrow} = \text{"is brother of,"}$$

$$\overset{a}{\leftrightarrow} = \text{"is the son of the same father as,"}$$

$$\overset{a'}{\leftrightarrow} = \text{"is the first cousin to,"}$$

$$\overset{b'}{\leftrightarrow} = \text{"is the grandson of the same grandfather as," etc.;}$$

for the asymmetrical relations,

$$\downarrow {}^a = \text{"is the father of" (with } \uparrow {}^a = \text{"is the son of"),}$$

$$\downarrow {}^b = \text{"is the grandfather of" (with } \uparrow {}^b = \text{"is the grandson of"), etc.}$$

The multiplicative *compositions* possible within this system are formally analogous to those in Grouping VII. Simplest of all are the multiplications of an asymmetrical relation by a symmetrical relation to produce a symmetrical-asymmetrical product: for example,

$$(A \downarrow {}^a B) \times (B \overset{a'}{\leftrightarrow} C) = A \downarrow {}^a \overset{a'}{\leftrightarrow} C;$$

that is, if A is the father of B and B is the first cousin of C, then A is the father of the first cousin of C—and thus the uncle of C. Analogous to Grouping VII, the multiplication of two or more such symmetrical-asymmetrical products itself yields a determinate symmetrical-asymmetrical product, e.g.,

$$(A \overset{a'}{\leftrightarrow} \downarrow^b B) \times (B \overset{o'}{\leftrightarrow} \downarrow^a C) = A \overset{a'}{\leftrightarrow} \downarrow^c C;$$

i.e., if A is first cousin to the grandfather of B and B is the brother of the father of C (thus, C's uncle), then A is first cousin to the great-grandfather of C. As was the case in Grouping VI, the rules which insure correct products from such multiplicative compositions are exceedingly complex (1942a, pp. 182-195; 1949a, pp. 164-168), and no attempt is made to detail them here. *Associativity* clearly holds for compositions among three or more products of the $(A \leftrightarrow \downarrow B)$ type, just as it does in Grouping VII. Piaget asserts that the *special identities* in this grouping "conform to the usual rule" (1949a, p. 169) but does not illustrate them specifically. *Tautology* has to be of the form

$$(A \overset{a'}{\leftrightarrow} \downarrow^b B) \times (A \overset{a'}{\leftrightarrow} \downarrow^b B) = A \overset{a'}{\leftrightarrow} \downarrow^b B,$$

and one would presume that he intends *absorption* to be of the form

$$(A \overset{a}{\leftrightarrow} \downarrow^b B) \times (A \overset{a}{\leftrightarrow} \downarrow^a C) = A \overset{a}{\leftrightarrow} \downarrow^a C.$$

The *inverse operation* is again logical division; and a product divided by itself yields the *general identity* which, as in Grouping VII, contains only null-difference relations: for example,

$$(A \overset{a'}{\leftrightarrow} \downarrow^a B) \div (A \overset{a'}{\leftrightarrow} \downarrow^a B) = A \overset{o}{\leftrightarrow} \downarrow^o A.$$

THE PRELIMINARY GROUPING OF EQUALITIES

Brief mention may be made of this extremely simple but fundamental grouping which is said to occur in disguised form as a special case in all the preceding major groupings (1942a, pp. 33-34). It closely resembles Grouping VI, inasmuch as it involves the addition of a particular type of symmetrical relation: equality or, as Piaget sometimes calls it, "pure equivalence." Its *compositions* are of the form $(A = B) + (B = C) = (A = C)$; such compositions are clearly *associative;* the *inverse* of an operation $(A = B)$ is, analogous to Grouping VI, $(B = A)$; the *general identity* is $(A = A)$; and each equality plays the role of special *identity* with itself and every other equality, e.g. $(A = B) + (A = B) = (A = B)$ and $(A = B) + (C = D) = (C = D)$.

Logical Groupings and Cognitive Behavior

How do logico-mathematical structures function in the analysis of human intellectual behavior? The groupings of logical operations, just described, make a good arena for a general analysis of this problem. They are important structures in Piaget's scheme of things—they constitute the structural centerpiece of the concrete-operational period—and a careful analysis of the structure-behavior relation here will make similar analyses unnecessary when we come to the remaining concrete and formal structures.

A Piaget nearer to one's heart's desire would no doubt have gone far beyond a simple assertion that the logico-mathematical structures are intended to model thought structures. He would have indicated clearly and unambiguously how each model component is translated isomorphically into a specific behavior component. He would certainly have made clear how the model is supposed to function, not just in organizing and explaining certain known cognitive facts and relationships, but also in suggesting the existence of facts and relationships not yet discovered. And he would spell out, in good theory-of-theory fashion, just what sort of a model it is, what recalcitrant facts would require what sorts of changes in the model, and so on. Although Piaget has indeed given some details on the relation of models to data (e.g., 1942a, pp. 293-314), he has not done anything as explicit and complete as the above. However, it is possible to make a synthesis of sorts from what he has written, although this is exposed to the usual danger of interpretative distortion.

Piaget's approach seems to be divisible into two subapproaches, *logical* and *empirical*. For the first, what he appears to have done (and here we are of course discussing the logical groupings, although the same general tack is taken for the other structures) is to examine the nature of logical class and relation operations *per se* and try to find, first, the base logico-mathematical structure which best approximates the essential organization common to all such sets of operations, and second, all the variations on this basic structure necessary and sufficient to exhaust the possible subvarieties of such sets (Piaget and Inhelder, 1956, p. 480). The first gives the five general properties of the grouping. The second produces the nine variations on this grouping structure; Piaget has simply not found any important way of manipulating classes and relations not caught by one or another of the nine groupings. This general approach is distinctly logical rather than empirical; in itself it says nothing whatever about whether children in fact think this way. What it seems to say is that if a person fully grasps the basic nature of classes and relations and the possible operations one can perform upon them, then one can reasonably impute to him cognitive structures which approach, as ideal patterns, the nine groupings. Put differently, if one does what is possible to do at the purely intensive level with logical operations of class and relation, one is behaving rather like a computer with a grouping program.

It is important to understand this essential point: the groupings were not wholly derived from watching children think. It turns out, for example, that Piaget has no experimental evidence, known to this writer, relevant to the verification, in the concrete-operational child's thought, of Groupings IV and VIII. These two groupings were clearly invented because they describe *logically possible* cognitive structures, not *empirically discovered* (as yet, at least) logical structures. We have said earlier that Piaget's third logic book (1952a) seems to be full of structures not yet shown to be anchored in human cognition.

The empirical subapproach is concerned with the question: to what extent can 7-11-year-old children operate to grouping specifications and hence justify the groupings as models for their cognition? Piaget seems to operate here on two levels, levels which merge into each other but are at least conceptually distinguishable. The first is a more global, intuitive one and not easy to characterize in any precise way. He seems to be arguing, from a varied experimental base, that concrete-operational children do (and correlatively, preoperational children do not) show certain generalized and more or less intangible cognitive qualities which suggest the presence of a groupinglike structure. There are two in particular, both by now familiar to the reader. First, these older children are systematic in their cognitive behavior, that is, they act as though their cognitive actions spring from a coherent and intercoordinated system of actions. Second—Piaget is almost obsessional on this—their cognitions seem permeated with one or another expression of reversibility. For Piaget, reversibility is not merely one of five grouping properties, it is *the* core property of cognition-in-a-system—the one from which all the others derive. Both the system-quality and its component reversibility are often more felt than seen in the older child's behavior, more an aura than a specific.

At this level, then, the structural-model-for-cognition approach resolves itself into a general context or frame of reference for looking at behavior, rather than a precise and detailed statement of model-to-behavior isomorphisms. The same thing appears to be true at the second, more specific level at which Piaget operates. What he seems to do here is this. He examines the components of a given grouping and then tries, through a variety of experiments with children, to see if he can cull to the surface behavioral analogues or counterparts (one hesitates to say isomorphs) of one or another of these components. He creates ingenious tests to tap and probe (the image of doctor-and-stethoscope is compelling here) for the presence or absence of this or that grouping component: the ability to coordinate direct and inverse additive class operations (Grouping I), the ability to effect transitive compositions of asymmetrical relations (Grouping V), the capacity to grasp the symmetry of symmetrical relations (Grouping VI), and so on. Piaget behaves like the psychiatrist who tries to uncover the bits and pieces of a suspected paranoid system through subtle and judicious questioning. Braine is profoundly right when he asserts that Piaget tries to "diagnose" operant cognitive structure through experiment (1960). The apparent assumption in this approach, although not explicitly stated by Piaget, is that where reasonable evidence for one or two components is found, the existence of the grouping structure as a whole can be inferred.

Even more than for the global approach, the strategy of finding isolated analogues does permit the groupings to serve as conceptual frameworks (if not models in the strict sense) within which to conceive and carry out new experiments. For instance, Piaget or anyone else can examine the components of Grouping III, note that a very basic component is the ability to find the simple logical product or intersect of two overlapping classes, and devise studies to see if children in the middle years can in fact handle problems involving class intersects (Piaget and Inhelder, 1959, ch. 6).

In summary, Piaget seems to do three things with his logical groupings, and of course the same is true for the other structures we shall examine. First, he views them as a precise and parsimonious structural characterization of "ideal" cognition in the realm of intensive logical operations of classes and relations. Second, they constitute a general framework for interpreting certain global and elusive, but nonetheless important, qualities of concrete-operational in contrast to preoperational thought. And finally, they serve as a framework for investigating or "diagnosing for" more specific intellectual attainments in this area.

Clearly there is much to question and criticize in the way Piaget deals with the abstract-structure-cognitive-structure liaison, and we shall return to this topic for the third time in Part III. For the present we shall simply examine some of the empirical evidence, primarily of the specific-level variety, which can be adduced for the logical groupings.[6] Many studies cited here as evidence will be described in fuller detail in Part II and the reader will doubtless notice other studies in Part II, not cited here, which would also qualify as evidence for one or another of the groupings.

GROUPING I

Evidence relevant to this important grouping is available in many places (e.g., Piaget, 1942a, pp. 296-297; Piaget, 1952b, ch. 7; Piaget and Inhelder, 1959). There are two abilities in particular, germane to Grouping I, which Piaget has found to characterize the concrete-operational as opposed to the preoperational child: a rough classification would peg the first at the more global level and the second at the more specific level.

---

[6] Groupings IV and VIII will be omitted from this examination since, as already stated, the writer knows of no empirical work directly relevant to them.

For the first, the older child is much more free and limber in composing and decomposing classes in a hierarchy (the direct and inverse operations of Grouping I): he can readily ascend the hierarchy by successively combining elementary classes into supraordinate classes (e.g. $A + A' = B$, $B + B' = C$, etc.); he can likewise descend the hierarchy, beginning with the higher-order classes and decomposing them into their subordinate classes; and finally—a very good testimonial to his mobility and reversibility—he can mentally destroy one classification system in order to impose a new and different one on the same data (e.g., Piaget and Inhelder, 1959, ch. 7). In short, he seems disposed at the outset to look for one or more class hierarchies within a set of objects, suggesting for Piaget an implicit structure of the Grouping I type.

Related to this general nimbleness in adding and subtracting classes is a somewhat more specific acquisition: the older child seems to have a basic grasp of the relation between subclasses and their supraordinate class which the younger child either lacks or does not possess in the same degree. Piaget attributes considerable importance to the mastery of this *inclusion relation,* as he calls it, and discusses it at length (e.g., Piaget, 1952b, ch. 7; Piaget and Inhelder, 1959). In essence, it refers to the ability to view subclasses and their supraordinate class in something like a state of reversible equilibrium

$$A + A' \rightleftarrows B,$$

the subclasses A and A' being seen as individual classes in their own right *and at the same time* as members of B. The older child is more disposed to think of whole and parts simultaneously; when he thinks of A and A' as individual classes he keeps in mind that they are still parts of the whole B (thus $A = B - A'$ and $A' = B - A$); and when he thinks of B as an entity he remembers that it is still the logical sum of A and A' (thus $B = A + A'$).

The preoperational child's difficulties with the inclusion relation in class systems show up in several interesting experiments. In one (1952b, ch. 7), the child is presented with 20 wooden beads (B), 17 of them brown (A) and 3 white (A') and is asked whether he "could make a longer necklace" with the brown beads or with the wooden beads (i.e., is $A < B$?). The younger subjects tended to assert that the brown beads would make the longer necklace "because there are only three white ones." Piaget interprets this and similar kinds of behavior as suggesting that, in essence, the child does not really have a highly mobile, freely reversible system of class operations such that he can keep in mind both totality and components at once. Although the experimenter establishes beforehand that the child knows all the beads are wooden, when his attention is directed to brown beads (A), their woodenness attribute (B) fades from awareness and only white beads (A') remain for comparison.

GROUPING II

Piaget suggests in at least two places (1942a, p. 59; 1949a, p. 116) that correspondences between this grouping structure and explicit and observable cognitive behavior are not easily come by. However, some recent experimental work seems to constitute evidence of sorts (Piaget and Inhelder, 1959, chs. 5 and 7). First, the concrete-operational child is able to classify a given collection of objects in several different ways. Such reclassifications result precisely in vicariance equations of the type described in Grouping II: B (here, the total collection) $= A_1 + A'_1$ (one classification within B) $= A_2 + A'_2$ (a second, different classification within B) $= A_3 + A'_3$, etc.

Certain studies also show the school-age child's growing understanding of secondary classes *per se* (A' = all of B which is not A). And finally, there is an interesting relation which holds among complementary classes which, although somewhat reminiscent of Grouping II, seems to require formal rather than concrete operations for its mastery (*ibid.*, pp. 145-146): if $A < B$ (e.g., class A is a subclass of class B), then $\overline{A} > B$ (the non-A remainder of the universe in question is larger than the non-B remainder).

GROUPING III

As with Grouping I, there are several different kinds of relevant experimentation here. As a first example, Piaget has studied the simple operation of one-one correspondence, the fundament of all Grouping III opertions (1942a, pp. 81-83). In his work on the number concept, for instance (1952b), he has shown that putting each element of one set into correspondence with an element of a second set does not, for the pre-operational child, guarantee that the elements so set into correspondence are numerically equal.

Other experiments have dealt with logical multiplication of classes *per se*. In one early experiment, for instance, the younger subjects had extreme difficulties in performing the logical multiplication inherent in the solution of the following problem (1942a, p. 307): "There are only three knives in a store. Two of these knives have two blades: they cost 8 francs and 10 francs. Two of these knives have a corkscrew: they cost 10 francs and 12 francs. I choose the one which has two blades and a corkscrew: how much does it cost?" Similarly, a recent publication (Piaget and Inhelder, 1959, ch. 6) describes studies involving a variety of tasks, all of which require the capacity to find the intersect or logical product of two or more classes. For example, the subject is presented with a horizontal row of pictures of different colored leaves (class of leaves) which meets to form a right angle with a vertical row of pictures of green-colored objects of different kinds (class of green objects). The subject's problem is to determine what picture should be placed at the intersect of these two rows; since the picture in question will be in both rows at once, it must of course contain both class attributes at once, i.e., it must be a picture of a green leaf (*ibid.*, p. 180). Once again, the mastery of this and similar matrix-type problems seems to come at the level of concrete operations.

GROUPING V

The core operation of this grouping is, of course, that of seriation itself: that is, the building up of elements into a transitive, asymmetrical series, e.g., $A < B < C < D < E$, etc. Piaget has found that preoperational children have considerable difficulty in composing such series. In one study (1952b, ch. 6) the child is given a set of 10 sticks varying in length from A (shortest) to J (longest) and is asked to seriate them. When this is done, he is given 9 more sticks (*a* to *i*) and asked to insert them in their proper places in the A-J series; the correct seriation would then give $AaBbCc \ldots iJ$. Whereas the young children often fail to make a complete construction of even the initial series A-J, the older ones readily solve both problems: they systematically create the first series by finding the shortest element (A), then the shortest element of those remaining (B), and so on, through to J. This done, they then insert each *a-i* element, always making sure that it is larger than its left-hand neighbor and smaller than its right-hand neighbor.

A second series of studies is more specifically concerned with the transitivity property of asymmetrical series (Piaget and Inhelder, 1941, ch. 10). The child is given three or more objects of perceptually differing weight (but without volume being a reliable cue to weight) and asked to seriate them by weight, with the restriction that he may compare only two objects at a time. The younger child does two things of interest here. First, for a set of three objects $A < B < C$ he is often willing to form a complete series (either correct or incorrect) on the basis of establishing $A < B$ and $A < C$ alone. And conversely, he is often unsure (and feels the need for empirical verification) that $A < C$ is guaranteed from knowing only $A < B$ and $B < C$.

The central difficulty underlying these diverse preoperational failures, Piaget believes (1942a, pp. 301-302), is the inability to see that each element in an asymmetrical series must be simultaneously conceived in terms of both a direct ($<$) and an inverse ($>$) relational operation: the element B must be both larger than A and smaller than C to be inserted between them in the series. Piaget feels that the failure to grasp this reversibility inherent in systems of asymmetrical relations lies behind the younger child's occasional willingness to conclude $B < C$ from $A < C$ and $A < B$, his occasional reluctance to conclude $A < C$ from $A < B$ and $B < C$, and his general inability to create and manipulate asymmetrical series.

GROUPING VI

There is very little direct experimental evidence on this grouping. What there is concerns almost exclusively the acquisition of the symmetry property of symmetrical relations: the notion that, if $A \leftrightarrow B$, then it must follow that $B \leftrightarrow A$ (the inverse operation for this grouping). Thus, Piaget has shown in early studies (1928b, chs. 2 and 3) that "brother of," "enemy of," "foreigner to," and so on tend not to be conceived as symmetrical relations by the preoperational child. For instance, he will affirm that x is his brother but deny that x himself has a brother. As in asymmetrical relations where the young child may reduce the relation "darker than" to the class "dark" (1928b, ch. 2), so also does he assimilate symmetrical relations like "brother of" to absolute terms, e.g., "a brother is a boy" (*ibid.*, p. 104).

GROUPING VII

Like Groupings I, III, and V, this grouping is rich in behavioral expressions.[7] There are first of all experiments involving the simple operation of one-one correspondence between two asymmetrical series, an operation analogous to the one-one correspondence of (unseriated) elements already described for Grouping III. The child is given ten dolls of differing heights and ten little sticks (walking sticks for the dolls) of differing heights. He is then asked to arrange the dolls and sticks "so that each doll can find the stick which belongs to it" (1952b, p. 97); that is, if the dolls ascend in height from A to J and the sticks from 1 to 10, then the correct one-one correspondence between dolls and sticks would be A-1, B-2, C-3, . . . J-10. The capacity to make such relational correspondences is a concrete operational achievement and of course develops in close interdependence with the ability to construct single asymmetrical series (the seriation operation of Grouping V).

Piaget has also investigated the young child's ability to build, from the constituent elements alone, multiplication-of-relations matrices of the kind schematized in Fig. 3, p. 184 (Piaget and Inhelder, 1959, ch. 10). The child is given 49 cut-out pictures of leaves which can be ordered both by size (7 different sizes A-G) and by shade of color (7 shades of green 1-7). He is asked to arrange them as he thinks they ought to be arranged, is then questioned about the arrangement which he makes, and so on. Once again, it is the concrete-operational children who are disposed from the outset to "see" these 49 elements as orderable in a double-entry matrix, for instance:

[7] In a recent book (Piaget and Inhelder, 1959, p. 279) Piaget names Groupings I, III, V, and VIII as the "principal groupings of the logic of classes and relations," a judgment, one presumes, which stems in part from this richness.

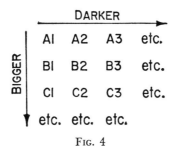

FIG. 4

And finally, there are a great many Piagetian tasks whose solution is thought to involve the multiplication of relations of the paradigm

$$(A \rightarrow B) \times (A \uparrow B) = A \rightarrow \uparrow B.$$

This is the case for virtually all the "conservation" studies, i.e., those in which some kind of equality (of quantity, of length, of area, etc.) between two objects A and A' is "conserved" or kept unchanged in the face of some transformation $A' \rightarrow B$. There is, for instance, the conservation-of-quantity study mentioned in Chapter 4: given two tall, thin containers A and A' with equal quantities of liquid, and the contents of A' poured into short, broad container B; is there now equal quantity in A and B? The correct solution to this problem was said to be facilitated by the capacity to multiply the relations "shorter than" and "wider than" together, e.g., "the column of liquid in B is shorter than that of A but *also* ("times") wider, and hence the quantities are equal."

THE PRELIMINARY GROUPING OF EQUALITIES

It was mentioned that the preoperational child has difficulties with the transitivity property of asymmetrical relations, that is, that $A < B$ and $B < C$ implies $A < C$. This also turns out to be the case for equality relations (Piaget and Inhelder, 1941, ch. 11). Given a set of equal-weight objects of varying sizes or colors (to prevent a simple perceptual equivalence), the young child may empirically establish $A = B$ and $B = C$ and yet, *mirabile dictu,* doubt $A = C$.

STRUCTURES OF CONCRETE OPERATIONS: OTHER CONCRETE OPERATIONAL SYSTEMS

Although the logical groupings have undoubtedly received the most attention in Piaget's writings, there are other systems which also arise in the subperiod of concrete operations: the infralogical and value-interpersonal groupings, the arithmetic groups, and measurement. There is not enough space to give these the detail given to the logical groupings, although they are far from unimportant in Piaget's conceptualization of concrete-operational thought. As with the logical groupings, behavioral

196 THE THEORY

expressions of them will continually crop up in Part II, especially the
infralogical operations.

Infralogical Groupings[8]

The distinction between logical and infralogical operations is given
in a number of Piaget publications (e.g., Piaget and Inhelder, 1941, pp.
271-280; Piaget and Inhelder, 1956, pp. 457-485; Piaget and Inhelder,
1959; Piaget, 1950a, pp. 46-47; Apostel, Mays, Morf, and Piaget, 1957,
ch. 3). Logical operations of classifying, seriating, setting into multiplicative correspondence have several distinguishing properties. (1) They bear
on sets of discrete, discontinuous objects. (2) Their operation is independent of the spatiotemporal proximity, or lack of it, of the objects they
deal with. (3) They do not require any actual modification of their
objects, neither alteration of their structure nor modification in the sense
of changing their spatial or temporal location.

Take, for example, the operation of simple classification (Grouping I).
(1) A class entails a collection of discrete objects, discontinuous one from
another. (2) One need in no way modify the character or position of
objects in order to subsume them under a class. (3) The assignment of
objects to a class is completely independent of the location of these
objects in space and time, their proximity to each other, and so on; the
fact that Hong Kong and New York are on opposite sides of the globe
neither facilitates nor hinders us from subsuming them under the class
"city." All these things are equally true for seriation and logical multiplication. For instance, the posing of the asymmetrical relation "larger
than" between two objects does not modify these objects, does not presuppose any spatiotemporal proximity between them, etc.

Infralogical operations can be roughly defined as operations which are
formally similar to logical ones (and, as we said, are developmentally
contemporaneous) but which possess attributes essentially opposite to
those just given. Let us take as a first example the infralogical counterpart of simple classification: a single object is composed of parts just as
a class is composed of class objects; one can perform the direct operation
of combining the parts into the whole and the inverse operation of dissociating the whole into the parts again. This manipulation of parts and
wholes is obviously similar in form to that of class objects and classes;
in fact, many people think of the relation between class and class member (or between class and subclass) and that between whole and part as
essentially synonymous.

[8] "Infralogical" is sometimes rendered by the terms "physical," "spatiotemporal," and
"sublogical." "Prelogical" is not a synonym, since it refers to preoperational cognition.
Infralogical operations are distinctly concrete-operational acquisitions (e.g., Piaget, Inhelder, and Szeminska, 1960); there is nothing "sub-" or "infra-" about them so far as
developmental status is concerned.

However, Piaget believes that there are basic differences. (1) The whole object is a single, continuous entity; its parts do not remain, as do class objects, distinct and separate when combined into the whole. (2) Its constitution as a whole object does require proximity of its parts. A class maintains its integrity regardless of the spatiotemporal contiguity or remoteness of its members; an object does not maintain its object status if, for instance, it is partitioned into tiny pieces (parts) and these pieces dispersed. Needless to say, one may actually bring objects into proximity when one imposes a class on them and one may imagine, rather than carry out in fact, the integration of spatially disparate parts into an infralogical whole. These possibilities, however, do not really abolish the fundamental distinction: infralogical contents are basically spatiotemporal and continuous in character in a way in which logical contents are not (Piaget and Inhelder, 1941, p. 271).

We said that infralogical operations are both formally similar and developmentally parallel to logical operations. In accord with this structural and developmental correspondence, each separate logical grouping has its homologue in the infralogical domain.[9] For the simple addition and subtraction of classes (Grouping I) there is the synthesis of parts and the partition of wholes just mentioned. These wholes, by the way, need not be objects in the literal sense; for instance, there is the infralogical operation of adding temporal part-intervals together to obtain a total interval (1946a, ch. 6). Symmetrical relations (Grouping VI) appear infralogically as spatial and temporal proximities or intervals; if A is "next to" B in space ($A \leftrightarrow B$) then B is also "next to" A ($B \leftrightarrow A$), and so forth. And asymmetrical relations (Grouping V) emerge as spatial and temporal serial orders; in the infralogical field, $A \rightarrow B$ may mean that A is temporally prior to B, or is located to the left of B from some spatial perspective, etc. Examples of these and the other infralogical groupings pervade the various "content" books; in particular, the book on space offers a useful summary (Piaget and Inhelder, 1956, pp. 457-485).

Infralogical groupings, then, can be conceived as the structural homologues of the logical groupings; they characterize the cognitive structure of the middle-years child when his operations apply to the physical world of spatiotemporal wholes and parts, spatiotemporal positions and displacements of positions, and the like. It is interesting to note that preoperational children do not appear even to differentiate between these two kinds of operations (Piaget and Inhelder, 1959, Conclusions). They show this undifferentiation, for example, when they attempt to classify a set of objects (*ibid.*, ch. 1). Some objects in the array are grouped by attributive similarity (this is logical class behavior) and some are

---

[9] Groupings IV and VIII, apparently without demonstrated behavioral expressions *qua* logical groupings, do have such expressions in the infralogical realm (Piaget and Inhelder, 1956, Ch. 15).

grouped in order to make a designlike complex figure (this is infralogical part-whole behavior).

Arithmetic Groups and Measurement

Most of the important theoretical and experimental work on concrete-operational arithmetic and measurement operations is found in five volumes: two for the arithmetic groups (1942a, chs. 11 and 12; 1952b) and three for measurement (Piaget, 1946a, 1946b; Piaget, Inhelder, and Szeminska, 1960). We have already indicated that Piaget posits a group rather than grouping structure for arithmetic operations. There are two arithmetic groups (1942a, ch. 11). There is the *additive group of whole numbers,* with the usual *composition* $1 + 1 = 2$, $2 + 1 = 3$, etc.; *associativity,* $(1 + 1) + 1 = 1 + (1 + 1)$; *inverses,* -1, -2, etc; and *identity,* 0. In this as in all groups, there is *iteration* $1 + 1 = 2$, $1 + 2 = 3$, etc., instead of the *special identities* $A + A = A$, $A + B = B$, etc. The other group is the *multiplicative group of positive numbers* with its corresponding group properties: *composition,* $1 \times 1 = 1$, $1 \times 2 = 2$, etc.; *associativity,* $(1 \times 2) \times 3 = 1 \times (2 \times 3)$; *inverses,* $\div 1$, $\div 2$, etc.; and *identity,* 1.

These groups have two sorts of liaison with the logical groupings. First, they are developmentally contemporaneous: Piaget asserts that the child grasps the essential properties of number at about the same time (i.e., in the subperiod of concrete operations) that he is capable of genuine class and relation operations. And second, arithmetic groups and logical groupings are logically related. Although we need not pursue the details here, Piaget makes much of the logical interrelationships between these two kinds of structures. Thus, the additive group is said to be a synthesis of class addition (Grouping I) and asymmetrical relations (Grouping V) and the multiplicative group a synthesis of the bi-univocal multiplication of classes (Grouping III) and relations (Grouping VII). These two kinds of liaison, developmental and logical, are obviously interrelated; the implication is that a genuine operational grasp of number is scarcely possible without the prior acquisition of the logical operations of which it is a synthesis.

It will be remembered that logical and infralogical grouping operations were called *intensive,* signifying that, for the class system $A + A' = B$, for instance, one knows that $A < B$ and $A' < B$, but one does not know the relative extensions of A and A' nor exactly how much larger B is than either A or A' (one knows only that it is larger). Arithmetic systems, on the other hand, obviously possess compositions more precise than this; Piaget calls them *numerical* as opposed to *intensive* (e.g., 1949a, p. 72). Thus, for the composition $1 + 2 = 3$, one knows not only the simple fact that the total 3 is greater than the components 1 and 2 but also exactly how much greater it is. Similarly, the components themselves can be precisely compared, i.e., 2 is exactly twice 1. These exact comparisons are made possible by virtue of the fact (already stated above) that the elements of a group *iterate;* one can take one element as a *unit,* e.g., the number 1, and see that 3 is thrice 1 by iterating the unit three times: thus, $1 + 1 + 1 = 3$.

The conversion of intensive *logical* elements into iterable units with numerical quantification yields *arithmetic operations.* Similarly, when *infralogical* elements (e.g., the parts of a whole) become iterable units, one gets *measurement operations* (e.g., Piaget and Inhelder, 1956, p. 482). Just as one can find that there are three 1's in the number 3 by iterating 1 three times, so also can one find the length of a rod by displacing a unit measure along it *n* times; and one can find the duration of a temporal interval by using the second or the minute as an iterable unit measure; and so on. Nowhere better than here does one see the symmetry which pervades Piaget's system: for each logical grouping there is a corresponding infralogical one; number is a synthesis of logical operations, and measurement is a synthesis of infralogical ones.

There is a considerable body of experimental work on the development of arithmetic and measurement operations. Most of the former are described in a single volume called, appropriately enough, *The Child's Conception of Number* (1952b). We have already alluded to one type of experiment pertinent to number operations: numerical equality between two sets of elements resulting from the operation of one-to-one correspondence (*ibid.,* ch. 3). For instance, the child "buys" a set of flowers by a one-to-one exchange of pennies for flowers. After the exchange is made, the experimenter puts the pennies in a pile and the flowers spaced in a row and inquires if there are as many flowers here as pennies there. The previous operation of one-one correspondence does not insure equality of number for the preoperational child; he may vote for inequality because of the perceptual differences between the two sets, e.g., the flowers are all spread out "so there are more." And there is a variety of other studies of this ilk: experiments on the child's grasp of ordinal numbers, of the relation between ordinal and cardinal, of arithmetic multiplication operations, and so on.

The experiments on measurement also come in the plural rather than the singular (Piaget, 1946a, 1946b; Piaget, Inhelder, and Szeminska, 1960). One study can serve as prototype (Piaget, Inhelder, and Szeminska, 1960, ch. 2). The experimenter builds a tower made of cubes of different sizes, using a table as a platform for the tower. The child is given a similarly heterogeneous collection of cubes and told to build a tower of the same height as the experimenter's. The table on which the child's tower is to be built, however, is lower than the experimenter's table; and there is a screen interposed between the tables, although the child can go around it to look any time he pleases. There are straight sticks of various lengths at the child's disposal, although the experimenter gives no clues to their possible use as measuring instruments.

Behavior on this task is orderable into a complex set of developmental steps, of which we give here only some of the highlights pertinent to the genesis of measuring operations. The youngest children compare the towers by eye only, estimating the floor-to-top heights rather than table-to-top heights (that is, the actual heights of the towers only). Older pre-operational children (5-7 years roughly) try to estimate actual tower height and do so by the primitive measurement operation of using the body as a common measure, e.g., holding one hand at the top and one at the bottom of the experimenter's tower and trying to keep them in this position as they run to their own tower to measure. Concrete-operational children, on the other hand, make use of body-independent objects as unit measures. Some of the younger ones use a stick longer than the tower (but not shorter), measuring the experimenter's tower with it and then using it to compare his own to the model. The older ones overcome this limitation and readily use a short stick as an iterable unit, displacing it along the tower to see "how many sticks long" it is. It is clear that these latter children are disposed to view a length as the sum of a series of equal-sized little lengths, and thus possess the basic operation of measurement, as Piaget defines it.

Other Structures

The systems so far discussed—logical and infralogical groupings, arithmetic groups, and measurement—do not quite exhaust what Piaget has to say about concrete-operational structures. The remainder concerns the structuring of cognitions which, more than the ones already discussed, directly involve personal-social-affective components: in particular, behaviors involving interaction and values. It will be remembered that there has already been some discussion of such phenomena in the section in Chapter 2 entitled COGNITION AND AFFECT.

It is extremely difficult to render anything very specific on the structure of such behaviors because Piaget's own treatment of them, although at times interesting and provocative, has been anything but specific (e.g., 1950a, ch. 6; 1953-1954a, 1954c, 1955-1956b). The essential position, however, seems to be this. As the child enters the concrete-operational years, the grouping structure comes to describe not only the organization of his logical and infralogical actions but also that of his interpersonal interactions, his values, etc. That is, the systematic and organized character which the grouping structure lends to intellectual activities in the narrow sense also pervades the remaining miscellany of adaptive acts in which he engages. For instance, as the child grows older his goals and values, initially unstable and momentary, begin to become organized into more or less stable and enduring hierarchies, e.g., goal A is a means to the attainment of goal B which, in turn, is a means to C, and so forth. Such asymmetric series, Piaget asserts, are isomorphic to Grouping V (1953-1954a). Similarly, with the growth of moral values, norms of moral conduct and the notion of moral obligation enter the child's thought in parallel with logical norms and the notion of logical necessity; the "ought" of duty begins to seem to him as *a priori* and compelling as the necessity of $A < C$ from $A < B$ and $B < C$—compelling in principle if not in his everyday moral behavior (1953-1954a, p. 535)!

There are also purported liaisons between logical groupings structure and interpersonal interactions (1950a, ch. 6; 1955-1956b). First of all, interpersonal interaction—and most of all bilateral and reciprocal interaction among peers—is an indispensable condition for the very formation of logical grouping structures in middle childhood (e.g., 1951d). By and large, Piaget is not prone to isolate specific antecedent conditions for cognitive change, but he clearly does here. Through repeated and often frustrating interchanges with his peers, the child has to come to cognitive grips with other viewpoints and perspectives which differ from his own. And from such encounters he gradually moves from a static and centrated egocentrism to the multiperspective reversibility which is the hallmark of the grouping structure.

But the reverse is also true, and here is the intended isomorphism between interactional and grouping structure. Coherent and organized interchanges between people already require, in turn, something like grouping structure in the individuals concerned because these interchanges themselves form a groupinglike system of operations (Piaget, 1950a, pp. 163-165; Piaget, 1950b, Vol. 3, pp. 263-272).

A general statement of his position here is the following:

> . . . without interchange of thought and co-operation with others the individual would never come to group his operations into a coherent whole: in this sense, therefore, operational grouping presupposes social life. But, on the other hand, actual exchanges of thought obey a law of equilibrium which again could only be an operational grouping, since to co-operate is also to co-ordinate operations. The grouping is therefore a form of equilibrium of inter-individual actions as well as of individual actions, and it thus regains its autonomy at the very core of social life (*ibid.*, pp. 163-164).

CHAPTER SIX

Formal Operations and Perception

THERE are two forms of cognitive adaptation which have not been taken up in preceding chapters and which it is the business of the present chapter to describe: formal operations and perception. The first is the crowning achievement of intellectual development, the final equilibrium state towards which intellectual evolution has been moving since infancy. The second is a class of adaptions of decidedly lower genetic order in Piaget's scheme of things; it originates as a subset of sensory-motor activity in infancy and proceeds to a structural development of lesser scope and definitiveness than that of its intellectual counterpart. Our presentation of these two classes of behavior will reverse their genetic order: formal operations first and perception second.

FORMAL OPERATIONS

One can find material on theoretical and experimental aspects of formal operations in several books (Piaget, 1949a, 1950a, 1952a, 1957a; Piaget and Inhelder, 1951) and articles (Inhelder, 1951, 1953-1954, 1954; Morf, 1957; Piaget, 1922, 1951c, 1953b, 1953-1954b, 1953-1954a). However, by all odds the most complete and systematic treatment is to be found in a later volume devoted solely to this topic (Inhelder and Piaget, 1958); the present account is drawn largely from this work.

Concrete and Formal Operations

It is almost an axiom of Piaget's approach to development that a given period can be properly understood only in the context of the earlier ones from which it springs. This is at least as true for the formal-operational period as for the others. Therefore, we shall begin by taking a second look at its predecessors, and in particular its immediate predecessor, the concrete-operational period. We shall want briefly to review the major accomplishments of this predecessor and also, even more important from the standpoint of understanding adolescent thought, its major limitations.

ACHIEVEMENTS AND LIMITATIONS OF CONCRETE OPERATIONS

As indicated in Chapter 5, the thought of the 7-11-year-old child shows some impressive advances over that of his preoperational counterpart. Of these the most general is the fact that his cognitive superstructure consists of systems in equilibrium, i.e., tightly knit ensembles of reversible operations (logical and infralogical groupings, etc.) which enable him to organize and stabilize the surrounding world of objects and events to a degree quite impossible to the younger child. One particular consequence of this general achievement will be of importance in comprehending the thought of the adolescent. The preoperational child tends to operate solely in terms of the phenomenal, before-the-eye reality. The concrete-operational child, on the other hand, is beginning to extend his thought, as Piaget phrases it (Inhelder and Piaget, 1958, p. 248), from the *actual* towards the *potential*. This development is a natural consequence of the formation of concrete-operational structures. For instance, looking at a concrete series of three seriated elements $A < B < C$ (the *actual*) and possessing Grouping V cognitive structure, he is much more disposed than the preoperational child could be to anticipate the extension of the series to new, as yet unordered elements D, E, etc. (the *potential*). The structures of concrete operations are, to use a homely analogy, rather like parking lots whose individual parking spaces are now occupied and now empty; the spaces themselves endure, however, and lead their owner to look beyond the cars actually present towards potential, future occupants of the vacant and to-be-vacant spaces.

The limitations of concrete operations were not described in Chapter 5, but there are several important ones (Inhelder and Piaget, 1958, pp. 249-251; Piaget, 1957a, pp. 15-18). (1) Concrete operations *are* concrete, relatively speaking; their structuring and organizing activity is oriented towards concrete things and events in the immediate present. To be sure, the constitution of concrete-operational systems makes for some movement towards the nonpresent or potential. But this movement is of limited scope and consists mostly of simple generalizations of existing structures to new content (in our earlier example, the child knowing that there could be a D, E, and so on, to insert in the series $A < B < C$ ....). But the starting point for concrete operations, as for preoperations, is always the real rather than the potential. The child of 7-11 years acts as though his primary task were to organize and order what is immediately present; the limited extrapolation of this organizing and ordering to the not-there is something he will do where necessary, but this extrapolation is seen as a special-case activity. What he does not do (and what the adolescent does do) is delineate all possible eventualities at the outset and then try to discover which of these possibilities really do occur in the present data; in this latter strategy, the real becomes a special case of the possible, not the other way around.

(2) The fact that the concrete-operational child is still (relatively) bound to the phenomenal here and now results in a second limitation: he has to vanquish the various physical properties of objects and events (mass, weight, length, area, time, etc.) one by one because his cognitive instruments are insufficiently "formal," insufficiently detached and dissociated from the subject matter they bear upon, to permit a content-free, once-for-all structuring. As an example, after achieving an understanding of conservation of mass (there is as much clay in *A* as in *B*, despite differences in shape), the child may for some time to come still be incapable of achieving conservation of weight and volume, even with the same clay objects. A cognitive system more independent and detached from the specific reality it organizes would not be expected to show *horizontal décalages* of this kind; however, Piaget finds them to be the rule rather than the exception in middle childhood.

(3) The various concrete-operational systems (e.g., the logical groupings) exist as more or less separate islets of organization during the 7-11-year period; they do not interlock to form a simple, integrated system, a system by which the child can readily pass from one substructure to another in the course of a single problem. The 7-11 year old, while possessing the two kinds of reversible operations to be found in the concrete-operational groupings—*negation* or *inversion,* indigenous to the class groupings, and *reciprocity,* found in the relation groupings—does not possess a total system which permits him to coordinate the two and thereby solve multivariable problems which require this kind of coordination. Just as the various content areas resist a single, once-for-all structuring by the concrete-operational child, so his various cognitive structures—adequate though they may be in their own separate dominions—fail to combine into the unified whole necessary to manage certain complex tasks.

ESSENTIAL CHARACTERISTICS OF FORMAL OPERATIONS

The most important general property of formal-operational thought, the one from which Piaget derives all others (Inhelder and Piaget, 1958, pp. 254-255), concerns the *real* versus the *possible.* Unlike the concrete-operational child, the adolescent begins his consideration of the problem at hand by trying to envisage all the possible relations which could hold true in the data and then attempts, through a combination of experimentation and logical analysis, to find out which of these possible relations in fact do hold true. Reality is thus conceived as a special subset within the totality of things which the data would admit as hypotheses;

it is seen as the "is" portion of a "might be" totality, the portion it is the subject's job to discover.

We have already seen that there is an initial and major step towards liberation from a slavish and distorting accommodation to immediate reality in the transition from preoperations to concrete operations. The liberation takes another giant stride in adolescence with this reversal in role between the real and the possible. There is nothing trivial about this reversal in role; it amounts to a fundamental reorientation towards cognitive problems. No longer exclusively preoccupied with the sober business of trying to stabilize and organize just what comes directly to the senses, the adolescent has, through this new orientation, the potentiality of imagining all that might be there—both the very obvious and the very subtle—and thereby of much better insuring the finding of all that is there.

Several other characteristics of formal thought are implied by this new orientation. (1) A cognitive strategy which tries to determine reality within the context of possibility is fundamentally *hypothetico-deductive* in character. Much more than the younger child, the adolescent moves boldly through the realm of the hypothetical. His basic orientation towards the real and the possible leads him naturally and easily into reasoning of the general form: "Well, it is clear from the data that *A* might be the necessary and sufficient condition for *X*, or that *B* might be, or that both together might be needed; my job is to test these possibilities in turn to see which one or ones really hold true in this problem." To try to discover the real among the possible implies that one first entertain the possible as a set of hypotheses to be successively confirmed or infirmed. Hypotheses which the facts infirm can then be discarded; those which the data confirm then go to join the reality sector.

(2) Formal thinking is above all *propositional thinking*. The important entities which the adolescent manipulates in his reasoning are no longer the raw reality data themselves but assertions or statements—propositions—which "contain" these data. What is really achieved in the 7-11-year period is the organized cognition of concrete objects and events *per se* (i.e., putting them into classes, seriating them, setting them into correspondence, etc.). The adolescent performs these first-order operations, too, but he does something else besides, a necessary something which is precisely what renders his thought formal rather than concrete. He takes the *results* of these concrete operations, casts them in the form of propositions, and then proceeds to operate further upon them, i.e., make various kinds of logical connections between them (implication, conjuction, identity, disjunction, etc.). Formal operations, then, are really operations performed upon the results of prior (concrete) operations.

Piaget has this propositions-about-propositions attribute in mind when he refers to formal operations as *second-degree operations* or *operations to the second power* (e.g., 1949a, p. 220; 1950a, p. 148). Another way he has expressed the distinction is to say that concrete operations are *in-trapropositional,* since they go to make the content of individual propositions, whereas formal operations are *interpropositional,* since they involve the logical relations among the propositions thus formed (1949a, ch. 1).

(3) This property of formal operational thought is closely affiliated with the newly developed orientation towards the possible and hypothetical. Let us assume that the adolescent confronts a problem and, as a consequence of this new orientation, wants first of all to determine all the possible relations inherent in the problem so as to make sure that all can be tested for reality status, none overlooked. How is he to do this? What he does do—and this is the final property we refer to—is systematically isolate all the individual variables plus all possible *combinations* of these variables. That is to say, he subjects the variables to a *combinatorial analysis,* a method which nicely guarantees that the possible will be exhaustively inventoried. The number of possible combinations of even a few variables can be quite large. If A and B are two variables of which some outcome X might be some kind of function, contingencies like the following need to be tested: (A) neither A nor B produces X, alone or in combination; (B) A elicits X but B does not; (C) B elicits X but A does not; (D) both A and B can induce X, separately or jointly; (E) A and B together produce X, but neither alone does; (F) A produces X if B is absent; but not if B is present—and there are a number of other possible combinations whose empirical truth or falsity has to be tested before the causal analysis can be complete.

We are now in position to give an initial paradigm of how the adolescent thinks. He begins by organizing the various elements of the raw data with the concrete-operational techniques of middle childhood. These organized elements are then cast in the form of statements or propositions which can be combined in various ways. Through the method of combinatorial analysis he then isolates for consideration the totality of distinct combinations of these propositions. These combinations are regarded as hypotheses, some of which will be confirmed and some infirmed by subsequent investigation. Is it true that A elicits X? If so, does B also? Is it true that A produces X only when B is absent? Such are the hypothetical questions which make up the domain of the possible in such problems; and the adolescent views his task as that of determining the actual shape of things by successively putting them to empirical test.

But abstract descriptions need supplementing by concrete examples. The following problem was administered to children at both developmental levels:

In experiment I, the child is given four similar flasks containing colorless, odorless liquids which are perceptually identical. We number them: (1) diluted sulphuric acid; (2) water; (3) oxygenated water; (4) thiosulphate; we add a bottle (with a dropper) which we will call g; it contains potassium iodide. It is known that oxygenated water oxidizes potassium iodide in an acid medium. Thus mixture $(1 + 3 + g)$ will yield a yellow color. The water (2) is neutral, so that adding it will not change the color, whereas the thiosulphate (4) will bleach the mixture $(1 + 3 + g)$. The experimenter presents to the subject two glasses, one containing $1 + 3$, the other containing 2. In front of the subject, he pours several drops of g in each of the two glasses and notes the different reactions. Then the subject is asked simply to reproduce the color yellow, using flasks 1, 2, 3, 4, and g as he wishes (Inhelder and Piaget, 1958, pp. 108-109).

The two behavior protocols which follow illustrate the kinds of concrete-formal differences we have been discussing:

REN (7;1) tries $4 \times g$, then $2 \times g$, and $3 \times g$: *"I think I did everything. . . . I tried them all."*—"What else could you have done?"—*"I don't know."* We give him the glasses again: he repeats $1 \times g$, etc.—"You took each bottle separately. What else could you have done?"—*"Take two bottles at the same time"* [he tries $1 \times 4 \times g$, then $2 \times 3 \times g$, thus failing to cross over between the two sets (of bottles), for example 1×2, 1×3, 2×4, and 3×4].—When we suggest that he add others, he puts $1 \times g$ in the glass already containing 2×3 which results in the appearance of the color: "Try to make the color again."—*"Do I put in two or three?* [he tries with $2 \times 4 \times g$, then adds 3, then tries it with $1 \times 4 \times 2 \times g$]. *No, I don't remember any more,"* etc. (*ibid.*, p. 111).

CHA (13;0): *"You have to try with all the bottles. I'll begin with the one at the end* [from 1 to 4 with g]. *It doesn't work any more. Maybe you have to mix them* [he tries $1 \times 2 \times g$, then $1 \times 3 \times g$]. *It turned yellow. But are there other solutions? I'll try* [$1 \times 4 \times g$; $2 \times 3 \times g$; $2 \times 4 \times g$; $3 \times 4 \times g$; with the two preceding combinations this gives the six two-by-two combinations systematically]. *It doesn't work. It only works with"* [$1 \times 3 \times g$].—"Yes, and what about 2 and 4?"—*"2 and 4 don't make any color together. They are negative. Perhaps you could add 4 in $1 \times 3 \times g$ to see if it would cancel out the color* [he does this]. *Liquid 4 cancels it all. You'd have to see if 2 has the same influence* [he tries it]. *No, so 2 and 4 are not alike, for 4 acts on 1×3 and 2 does not."*—"What is there in 2 and 4?"—*"In 4 certainly water. No, the opposite, in 2 certainly water since it doesn't act on the liquids; that makes things clearer."*—"And if I were to tell you that 4 is water?"—*"If this liquid 4 is water, when you put it with 1×3 it wouldn't completely prevent the yellow from forming. It isn't water; it's something harmful"* (*ibid.*, p. 117).

Let us first examine the younger child's behavior. Notice that it is by no means unsystematic and unorganized. He proceeds by making what is in effect a one-many multiplicative correspondence (Grouping IV) between the perceptually salient element g and the other four, yielding as product $(g \times 1) + (g \times 2) + (g \times 3) + (g \times 4)$. This systematic structuring of the data, although it happens to be inadequate to the solution of the problem, is a definite cut above preoperational behavior on a scale of genetic maturity. It turns out that preoperational children generally make a few random associations of elements (without really knowing what these associations are capable of proving) and intersperse this activity with phenomenalistic and other types of prelogical causal explanations (*ibid.*, pp. 110-111).

But the differences between this behavior and that of the adolescent are nonetheless striking for all its advances over that of the younger children. REN is capable of forming only a few of the total number of possible combinations: the four binary ones mentioned plus (after liberal suggestions and hints from the examiner) three ternaries and two quaternaries. CHA, on the other hand, seems disposed right from the outset to think in terms of all possible combinations of elements (or at least, what amounts to about the same thing, all the ones necessary to arrive at a full determination of the causal structure). Moreover, he appears to possess a systematic and orderly method for generating these combinations: $(1 \times g) \times (2 \times g)$, etc., and then $(1 \times 2 \times g) + (1 \times 3 \times g)$, etc. His language alone clearly attests to his hypothetico-deductive attitude towards the data: there are a number of statements of the "if . . . then" type (and none of this type in REN's protocol).

These statements are worth a closer look. Take for example CHA's assertion: "If this liquid 4 is water, when you put it with 1×3 it wouldn't completely prevent the yellow from forming. [Therefore] it isn't water [since it does in fact prevent the yellow from forming]; it's something harmful." It is clear that the content very much concerns the possible rather than the real, since the event *4-does-not-prevent-the-yellow-from-forming* is nowhere seen in reality. In general, Piaget finds that contrary-to-fact "what if" suppositions of this kind tend to be foreign to the thought of middle childhood. Further, the total assertion consists of more than simple statements about data (whether true statements or false). Of greater developmental significance is the fact that it comprises a statement *about* these statements, a proposition about propositions: namely, the assertion that one statement (liquid 4 is water) logically implies another (liquid 4 will not prevent the yellow from forming). As we said earlier, it is because adolescent cognition shows this implicative, propositions-about-propositions character that Piaget uses the expressions *interpropositional thought* and *second-degree operations* to describe it.

All the traits of formal thought we have described go to make it a very good instrument for *scientific reasoning*. As CHA's protocol shows, he is quite capable of achieving the correct solution of what is in all essential respects a genuine problem of scientific discovery. The hypothetical-deductive attitude, the combinatorial method, and the other attributes of formal thought provide him with the necessary tools for separating out the variables which might be causal, holding one factor constant in order to determine the causal action of another, and so on. He is not only able to imagine the various transformations which the data permit in order to try them out empirically; he is also capable of giving correct logical interpretation to the results of these empirical tests. If it eventuates, for instance, that the yellow color is produced by the combination $1 \times 3 \times g$ and no other, he is able to conclude that $1 \times 3 \times g$ is the necessary and sufficient cause (e.g., $1 \times 2 \times 3 \times g$ also suffice to produce the color, but 2 is not necessary to the combination), and he then knows his problem is solved. This is clearly a good imitation of how the scientist goes about his business.

How, by what route, does the subject move from concrete to formal operations? Piaget suggests that the route is similar in a general way to that by which the transition from preoperational to concrete-operational thinking was effected: as the child becomes more and more proficient at organizing and structuring problem data with concrete-operational methods, he becomes better and better able to recognize the latter's shortcomings as a device for yielding a complete and logically exhaustive solution (*ibid.*, p. 283). That is, as the child's concrete-operational analyses become sharper and more complete, they present him with gaps, uncertainties, and contradictions which a more impoverished analysis could never have brought to light. (Recall that concrete operations themselves were similarly born out of problems raised by an increasingly differentiated preoperational analysis in Chapter 4.)

Faced with these new problems, the child gropes for new methods of attack. The scientific-type tasks which Piaget has set for this age group have mostly required for their solution the isolation of variables, that is, an assessment of the separate causal contributions of the various factors extant in the data. It is particularly with respect to this ability to isolate variables that transitional forms show up most clearly. The younger children develop the ability to use a single experimental method to test the causal efficacy of a variable: simple *negation* or *inversion,* the literal *removal* of the variable from operation. For instance, one can determine that substance 4 in the chemical-mixture problem is important for removing the yellow color by the operations of adding (direct operation) and not adding (negation) it to $1 \times 3 \times g$: when not added, the yellow color does not clear up; when added, it does. Useful though this method is in some cases, it does not serve in all. A major step forward is made when the child can supplement the reversible operation of negation by that of *reciprocity.* Reciprocity entails not the outright elimination or negation of a factor but its *neutralization,* that is, holding its effect constant in some way while a second factor is being varied. For instance, where the problem is to study the separate effects of kind of metal and length on the flexibility of a rod (*ibid.*, ch. 3), the younger child finds himself at an impasse; he cannot literally negate either variable, i.e., work with a rod not made of *some* metal and not possessing *some* length. The older child uses the reciprocal operation with great profit here. He takes two rods of different metals but of the same length (here length is not negated, but neutralized or controlled—not lengths *per se* but length *differences* are annulled) in order to study the effect of kind of metal, and two rods of a single metal and different lengths to study the effect of length.

The addition of the reciprocal operation to the subject's repertory in solving scientific problems brings a general advance in strategy and tactics: it disposes the subject towards the controlled experiment, that is, the nullification of one variable, not simply to study that one variable, but to study the action of some other variable free from error variance contributed by the first. The younger child negates a variable in order to study the causal efficacy *of that variable.* The older child develops a better strategy: negate or neutralize (whichever circumstances dictate; both negation and reciprocity are at his disposal) factor A in order to study the effects of varying factor B; negate or neutralize A and B in order to assess the uncontaminated action of C, and so on. Once again we see that the transition from concrete to formal operations is a transition towards genuinely scientific methods of analysis.

What are the behavioral criteria for saying that one child is limited to concrete operations, whereas another child (of the same age or even younger) is at the formal level? Piaget's answer to this question is of principal interest, in the writer's opinion, not so much for whatever air of precision it may seem to lend to this segment of his work—a drop in an ocean of imprecision, surely—but because it gives added insight into what he thinks are the crucially important cognitive acquisitions of the adolescent. He says that one cannot confidently make a diagnosis of formal operations from one or two isolated bits of behavior, even when they consist of propositionlike, causal statements (*ibid.*, pp. 278-280). He offers instead two other diagnostic procedures:

> A second and more adequate method is to compare all of the statements and particularly the actions of a single subject. It then becomes clear whether he is limited to a simple registration of the raw experimental results, forming only the classifications, serial orders, and correspondences he sees as sufficient for solving the problem, or whether he tries to separate out the variables. The latter implies both hypothetico-deductive reasoning and a combinatorial system; when they appear, we have to interpret the stated judgments as propositional expressions, since the links between the successive statements (whether explicit or implicit) consist in interpropositional operations.
>
> But the third and surest method of differentiation (which is actually a simple specialization of the second) is to analyze the proofs employed by the subject. If they do not go beyond observation of empirical correspondences,

they can be fully explained in terms of concrete operations, and nothing would warrant our assuming that more complex thought mechanisms are operating. If, on the other hand, the subject interprets a given correspondence as the result of any one of several possible combinations, and this leads him to verify his hypotheses by observing their consequences, we know that propositional operations are involved (*ibid.,* p. 279).

We see, then, that formal thought is for Piaget not so much this or that specific behavior as it is a generalized *orientation,* sometimes explicit and sometimes implicit, towards problem-solving: an orientation towards organizing data (combinatorial analysis), towards isolation and control of variables, towards the hypothetical, and towards logical justification and proof. The temptation is great to draw sharp images to better convey the salient contours of each developmental period, despite the obvious dangers of oversimplification it entails. What could be the archetypes for the three postinfantile eras? The preoperational child is the child of wonder; his cognition appears to us naive, impression-bound, and poorly organized. There is an essential lawlessness about his world without, of course, this fact in any way entering his awareness to inhibit the zest and flights of fancy with which he approaches new situations. Anything is possible because nothing is subject to lawful constraints. The child of concrete operations can be caricatured as a sober and bookkeeperish organizer of the real and a distruster of the subtle, the elusive, and the hypothetical. The adolescent has something of both: the 7-11-year-old's zeal for order and pattern coupled with a much more sophisticated version of the younger child's conceptual daring and uninhibitedness. Unlike the concrete-operational child, he can soar; but also unlike the preoperational child, it is a controlled and planned soaring, solidly grounded in a bedrock of careful analysis and painstaking accommodation to detail.

The Structure of Formal Operations

Formal operations, like concrete operations before them, can be characterized not only in general, verbal-descriptive terms but also in terms of the logico-mathematical structures which are thought to serve as abstract models for them. Interpropositional operations are not isolated actions bearing no interrelationships among themselves. Like the groupings of intrapropositional operations in middle childhood, they form an integrated system, and the question is to determine the formal structure of that system. Piaget has attempted this structural analysis at two levels. First, he has tried to delineate the logico-mathematical properties of interpropositional thought-in-general, that is, the basic system which underlies adolescent thinking in all its myriad expressions. He concludes that this core system consists of an integrated lattice-group structure, not just partial and incomplete lattice and group *properties,* as in the concrete-operational groupings, but a full and complete lattice and a full and complete group, both integrated within the one total system. Second, he has attempted to specify certain substructures which derive from the general *structure d'ensemble* just mentioned. These substructures, called *formal operational schemas*, are more limited and specialized cognitive instrumentalities which rotate to the fore when certain kinds of problems confront the subject.

INTERPROPOSITIONAL OPERATIONS AS LATTICE

The essential attribute of formal thought is its orientation towards the possible and hypothetical. One manifestation of this orientation is the adolescent's tendency to explore all possibilities by subjecting the problem variables to a combinatorial analysis. This analysis gives him a cognitive picture of what the extant possibilities are; the next steps are to observe and experiment to see which of these possibilities occur as realities, and from this information make logical deductions about the causal structure of the system. Now this network of hypothetical possibilities which the adolescent's newly acquired combinatorial operations have generated constitutes a lattice, and from this fact derives Piaget's assertion that formal operations have *lattice structure*. Let us examine these adolescent combinatorial operations more closely in order to see what is meant here.

Suppose a problem of the following general type is presented to children of different developmental level: to determine the causal structure governing the occurrence A or nonoccurrence A' of some phenomenon X. Suppose further there are a number of variables in the situation whose causal role needs exploration; these can also be symbolized in terms of occurrence B, C, D, etc., and nonoccurrence B', C', D', etc. How does the 7-11-year-old go about trying to solve this kind of problem? Unlike the preoperational child, he does something systematic and orderly: he observes and records a limited number of associations between occurrences and nonoccurrences of the variables and the event X. For instance, he might establish that all four of the following associations are found to occur at one time or another: $A \times B$ (X occurs with B present), $A \times B'$ (X also occurs with B absent), $A' \times B$ (X sometimes fails to occur when B is present), and $A' \times B'$ (X can also fail to occur when B is absent). Note that these associations, which we can symbolize as a totality by the expression $(A \times B) + (A \times B') + (A' \times B) + (A' \times B')$, are a product of a one-one class multiplication (Grouping III) and thus constitute a typical concrete operational achievement. The 7-11-year-old can go this far but not much farther; preoccupied as he is with the immediate reality before him, he is limited to establishing perhaps a few more such associations, hoping that the solution will somehow emerge from this multiplicative activity.

The adolescent's approach to the problem is different. Associations $A \times B$, $A \times B'$, etc., have for him a *propositional* rather than concrete *class-product* significance. That is, they represent hypothetical assertions, or statements of possibilities, rather than actual, phenomenal events. For instance, $A \times B$ is taken to mean the hypothesis that the assertion "X can occur with B present" will be empirically verified; it is no longer simply the cognitive representation of a class product, actually discovered in the course of concrete observation or experimentation. Put otherwise, it is the hypothesis that two *statements* ("X occurs" and "B occurs") can be truthfully asserted about the data at a given moment, i.e., are jointly true.

Since the arena of operation is now no longer intrapropositional but interpropositional, a change of symbolism is in order. Let us replace the class symbols A, A', B, and B' by the propositional symbols p ("p is true"), $\bar{p}$ ("p is false"), q ("q is true"), and $\bar{q}$ ("q is false"). We shall also replace the class multiplication and addition signs $\times$ and $+$ by the propositional conjunction and disjunction signs $\cdot$ and $\vee$, respectively. Thus the expression $p \cdot q$ (the propositional equivalent of the class product of $A \times B$) will mean that the propositions p and q hold true jointly, at the same time. Analogously, $p \vee q$ will mean that *either* only p is true, *or* that only q is true, *or* that both are true; its meaning could also be expressed by $(p \cdot \bar{q}) \vee (\bar{p} \cdot q) \vee (p \cdot q)$—the only possibility which $p \vee q$ denies is $\bar{p} \cdot \bar{q}$ (i.e., the possibility that neither p nor q is true).

Now the essential differences here between adolescent and middle-childhood reasoning are two. The first, just stated, is that the younger subjects *discover* the base class associations $A \times B$, $A \times B'$, etc., as they apply themselves to the data, whereas the older ones tend to *conceive* these associations beforehand, prior to experimentation, as propositions for empirical test. The second difference—and this is the one most relevant to the lattice structure—is that, unlike the 7-11-year-old, the adolescent possesses a technique for generating all the possible combinations of these associations. Take the aforementioned four base associations—$A \times B$, $A \times B'$, $A' \times B$, and $A' \times B'$—now symbolized $p \cdot q$, $p \cdot \bar{q}$, $\bar{p} \cdot q$, and $\bar{p} \cdot \bar{q}$—and let them be represented by the four letters a, b, c, d. There are sixteen distinct possible combinations of these four associations:

(1) 0   i.e., $\overline{(p \cdot q) \vee (p \cdot \bar{q}) \vee (\bar{p} \cdot q) \vee (\bar{p} \cdot \bar{q})}$

(2) a i.e., $p \cdot q$

(3) b i.e., $p \cdot \bar{q}$

(4) c i.e., $\bar{p} \cdot q$

(5) d i.e., $\bar{p} \cdot \bar{q}$

(6) $a + b$ i.e., $(p \cdot q) \vee (p \cdot \bar{q})$

(7) $a + c$ i.e., $(p \cdot q) \vee (\bar{p} \cdot q)$

(8) $a + d$ i.e., $(p \cdot q) \vee (\bar{p} \cdot \bar{q})$

(9) $b + c$ i.e., $(p \cdot \bar{q}) \vee (\bar{p} \cdot q)$

(10) $b + d$ i.e., $(p \cdot \bar{q}) \vee (\bar{p} \cdot \bar{q})$

(11) $c + d$ i.e., $(\bar{p} \cdot q) \vee (\bar{p} \cdot \bar{q})$

(12) $a + b + c$ i.e., $(p \cdot q) \vee (p \cdot \bar{q}) \vee (\bar{p} \cdot q)$

(13) $a + b + d$ i.e., $(p \cdot q) \vee (p \cdot \bar{q}) \vee (\bar{p} \cdot \bar{q})$

(14) $a + c + d$ i.e., $(p \cdot q) \vee (\bar{p} \cdot q) \vee (\bar{p} \cdot \bar{q})$

(15) $b + c + d$ i.e., $(p \cdot \bar{q}) \vee (\bar{p} \cdot q) \vee (\bar{p} \cdot \bar{q})$

(16) $a + b + c + d$ i.e., $(p \cdot q) \vee (p \cdot \bar{q}) \vee (\bar{p} \cdot q) \vee (\bar{p} \cdot \bar{q})$

These sixteen combinations are the result of taking as base elements the four associations and combining them one by one, two by two, and so on. This set of all possible combinations forms a *lattice*. The combinations themselves form the lattice elements; the operation $\cdot$ gives a unique g.l.b. for any pair of elements; and the operation $\vee$ gives a unique l.u.b. for any pair of elements. Take any two elements from the sixteen. say, (5) and (12)—$\bar{p} \cdot \bar{q}$ and $(p \cdot q) \vee (p \cdot \bar{q}) \vee (\bar{p} \cdot q)$. The g.l.b. is given by $(\bar{p} \cdot \bar{q}) \cdot [(p \cdot q) \vee (p \cdot \bar{q}) \vee (\bar{p} \cdot q)]$, which yields elements (1), i.e., 0; that is, there is no asserted proposition which is at once a part of (5) and (12). The l.u.b., however, is (16), i.e., $(p \cdot q) \vee (p \cdot \bar{q}) \vee (\bar{p} \cdot q) \vee (\bar{p} \cdot \bar{q})$, since (16) is the smallest element of the lattice which contains everything found in either (5) or (12). To take another example, elements (7) and (9) have as g.l.b. (4) and as l.u.b. (12). The system of sixteen combinations of four binary propositions thus forms a full lattice: the sixteen combinations constitute the lattice elements; unique g.l.b.'s and l.u.b.'s are determined for any pair of combinations by the operations $\cdot$ and $\vee$, respectively.

The operations which generate the lattice-of-all-possible-combinations do not arise *ex nihilo*. This lattice is the combined workings of three concrete-operational groupings. First, Grouping III operations provide the four basic elements $A \times B$, $A \times B'$, $A' \times B$, and $A' \times B'$, which constitute the starting point for the lattice. The lattice is then built up by a *generalized classification* (stemming from Grouping I and II operations) of these associations, that is, the construction of all the different classes which can be formed from them: $A \times B$, $A' \times B$, . . . ,$(A \times B) + (A' \times B)$, $(A \times B) + (A \times B')$, . . . , $(A \times B) + (A \times B') + (A' \times B)$, . . . , and so on through the sixteen possible classes described above. Thus, the adolescent lattice operations—the operations which guarantee that all possibilities will be inspected—are themselves a kind of emergent integration of previous, concrete operations.

The generation of the lattice of all possible combinations which the adolescent achieves is, of course, only a cognitive instrumentality in itself, simply a means to the end of analyzing the causal structure of the problem. Once the adolescent has the intuition of what the set of *possibilities* consists of, he must see which of them actually *occur* and thence draw accurate conclusions about cause and effect relationships. Let us see how this works in the combination-of-liquids problem: let p represent the presence of the yellow color, $\bar{p}$ its absence, q the presence of variable 2 (water), and $\bar{q}$ its absence. As the adolescent starts making combinations and noting their color effects, he may notice that the second $(p \cdot q)$ of the sixteen combinations does occur, i.e., the yellow color occurs when water is present in the mixture. The younger child, not oriented towards the totality of possibilities, might conclude from this single observation that p implies q, that is, that the water is causally responsible for the yellow color. The adolescent, on the other hand, is aware that he has established only one of a number of possible relationships involving p and q, and that he must test these possibilities. In this particular problem it turns out that further experimentation also establishes $p \cdot \bar{q}$, $\bar{p} \cdot q$, and $\bar{p} \cdot \bar{q}$, thus the complete combination $(p \cdot q) \vee (p \cdot \bar{q}) \vee (\bar{p} \cdot q) \vee (\bar{p} \cdot \bar{q})$, and from this the subject correctly concludes that q is in fact causally irrelevant to p. If it had turned out instead (not the case for this particular problem) that further empirical search established only the combination $(p \cdot q) \vee (p \cdot \bar{q}) \vee (\bar{p} \cdot \bar{q})$, i.e., all possibilities exist except $(\bar{p} \cdot q)$, he would instead conclude that p does in truth imply q, that water must be in the mixture in order to get the yellow color. To take another example, the adolescent is not content merely to discover that the combination $(p \cdot \bar{r}) \vee (\bar{p} \cdot r) \vee (\bar{p} \cdot \bar{r})$ does exist (where r is now taken to refer to variable 4, the color-inhibiting thiosulfate); he will want to be sure that the remaining association $(p \cdot r)$ does not occur before concluding that thiosulfate and the yellow color are truly incompatible. The Inhelder and Piaget volume on adolescent reasoning (1958) abounds with concrete instances of this kind of problem-solving strategy: determine all the possibilities, then all the actualities, and then the causal structure which these actualities imply.

Interpropositional Operations as Group

Adolescent cognition is said to have group as well as lattice properties. Specifically, it is asserted that the adolescent's behavior in certain problem situations attests to a cognitive structure with the properties of a *four-group*—a mathematical group whose elements consist of four transformations. As is the case with any abstract structure, this particular group can have a number of concrete "realizations," that is, different sorts of systems which exemplify its properties. There are two particular realizations of the four-group which Piaget leans upon most heavily in his analysis of adolescent reasoning. We shall begin by describing these two and then go on to attempt an explanation of how Piaget links them to cognition.

One of the two realizations of the four-group directly concerns the propositional operations discussed throughout this chapter. A given propositional operation, say, $p \vee q$, can be transformed into a different operation in a variety of ways. Let us define the following four such transformations:

1. *Identity* (I). This "null" transformation changes *nothing* in the proposition on which it is performed. If the proposition is, say, $p \vee q$, then $I\ (p \vee q) = p \vee q$. Similarly, $I\ (p \cdot \bar{q}) = p \cdot \bar{q}$, $I\ (\bar{p} \vee \bar{q}) = \bar{p} \vee \bar{q}$, etc.

2. *Negation* (N). This transformation, on the other hand, changes *everything* in the proposition on which it bears. That is, all assertions become negations, and vice versa, and all conjunctions ($\cdot$) become disjunctions ($\vee$), and vice versa. Therefore, $N\ (p \vee q) = \bar{p} \cdot \bar{q}$, $N\ (p \cdot q) = \bar{p} \vee \bar{q}$, $N\ (\bar{p} \vee \bar{q}) = p \cdot q$, etc.

3. *Reciprocal* (R). This transformation permutes assertions and negations but leaves conjunctions and disjunctions unchanged. For instance, $R\ (p \vee q) = \bar{p} \vee \bar{q}$, $R\ (p \cdot \bar{q}) = \bar{p} \cdot q$, $R\ (\bar{p} \vee \bar{q}) = p \vee q$, etc.

4. *Correlative* (C). This transformation permutes conjunctions and disjunctions but leaves assertions and negations unchanged. Hence, $C\ (p \vee q) = p \cdot q$, $C\ (\bar{p} \cdot \bar{q}) = \bar{p} \vee \bar{q}$, etc.

These four transformations I, N, R, and C form the elements of a group under the operation of multiplication or combination. First of all (the *composition* requirements), the multiplication of any two or more of these four transformations is equivalent to (yields the same result as) the solitary application of some one of them. For instance, $NRC = I$, because:

$$N\ (p \vee q) = \bar{p} \cdot \bar{q}$$
$$\text{and } R\ (\bar{p} \cdot \bar{q}) = p \cdot q$$
$$\text{and } C\ (p \cdot q) = p \vee q \qquad \text{but } I\ (p \vee q) = p \vee q$$
$$\text{hence: } NRC = I$$

Other equations which a mechanical application of the above-defined transformation rules will readily verify are $NR = C$, $IN = N$, $NC = R$, $IRC = N$, $NRCN = N$, and so on. No matter what sequence of transformations one performs, the final result is always equivalent to the action of some single one of them. The other group properties also hold: $N\ (RC) = (NR)\ C$ (*associativity*); the *identity* element is I (thus $IN = N$, $IR = R$, etc.); and each element is its own *inverse* (thus $NN = I$, $RR = I$, etc.).

The second realization of the four-group with which Piaget is concerned entails transformations within physical systems rather than transformations of propositions *per se*. We shall for convenience refer to the latter as the *logical INRC group* and the former as the *physical INRC group* (thus preserving the same names for the constituent group transformations in both realizations).[1] The physical systems whose transformations have this *INRC* group structure are of the following type. The system first of all contains two distinct and different operations p and q which have exactly equivalent outcomes or effects. The system also contains two other operations $p*$ and $q*$ which nullify ("undo" or cancel) p and q, respectively. We then define four transformations within this system of operations:

1. *Identity* (*I*): $I(p) = p$, $I(q*) = q*$, etc.
2. *Negation* (*N*): $N(p) = p*$, $N(q) = q*$, $N(p*) = p$, and $N(q*) = q$.
3. *Reciprocal* (*R*): $R(p) = q*$, $R(q) = p*$, $R(p*) = q$, and $R(q*) = p$.
4. *Correlative* (*C*): $C = NR$ (the correlative is here defined simply as the product of negation and reciprocal); thus, $C(p) = N[R(p)] = q$, $C(q) = p$, $C(p*) = q*$, and $C(q*) = p*$.

These four transformation *INRC* of physical operations p, $p*$, q, $q*$ form a group mathematically isomorphic to the logical *INRC* group: as in the latter, $I = NRC$, $NN = I$, $IR = R$, etc.[2] The following is a concrete example of a physical system of this type (Piaget, 1946b, ch. 5; Inhelder and Piaget, 1958, p. 318). A snail is placed on a small board which rests on a table. Let p represent a left-to-right movement of snail on board for distance X. Let $p*$ be the inverse, right-to-left movement of snail on board for distance X (thus, back to the point of origin). Then let q represent a left-to-right movement of board on table for distance X (with snail resting immobile on the board) and $q*$ the inverse movement of board on table. It is readily apparent that the *INRC* transformations of these four operations constitute an example of what we have called the "physical *INRC* group."

There are a number of other examples which Piaget and his associates have worked with experimentally (Inhelder and Piaget, 1958, especially chs. 9, 10, 11, 13). A weighted piston exerts pressure on the liquid in one arm of a U-shaped vessel, thus forcing the liquid to rise to a certain level in the other arm. In order to make the liquid rise higher, one can either add more weight to the piston (p) or fill the vessel with a lighter liquid (q); conversely, one can return the liquid to its original level either by taking off weight ($p*$) or by resubstituting a heavier liquid ($q*$). Similarly, one can depress one arm of a scale balance either by adding weight to the pan (p) or by moving the pan farther away (on the scale arm) from the fulcrum (q); the corresponding opposing actions are removing weights ($p*$) and decreasing the distance from the fulcrum ($q*$).

---

[1] Here, and throughout this section of the chapter, the writer draws heavily upon distinctions and clarifications which the logician Charles Parsons made in his review of the Inhelder and Piaget book (Parsons, 1960).

[2] Since the operations p, $p*$, etc., are themselves really transformations within a physical system, a precise statement of things would necessitate calling *I*, *N*, *R*, and *C* transformations *of* transformations.

Piaget is particularly interested in the interrelationships among p, q, p^*, and q^* in systems of this kind. Since the concept of reversible operations is central to his analysis of thought he stresses the fact that these systems entail a double reversibility. First, there is the *negation* (or *inverse*) operation: p^* negates p and q^* negates q (and vice versa). Negation, as its name suggests, involves the literal canceling or undoing of an operation. The inverse or negation of the operation of adding weight to the pan is removing that weight from the pan. The *reciprocal* is another, quite different kind of reversible operation: in these systems, q^* is the reciprocal of p and p^* is the reciprocal of q (and vice versa). The reciprocal has here the same ultimate effect as the negation (e.g., that of restoring the scale balance to its original equilibrium), but it achieves this effect by a different route. Without in any literal sense undoing the original operation itself, as does the negation operation, it compensates or neutralizes its effect by posing a symmetrical, equal-and-opposite counterforce. The addition of weight to the right-hand arm of the balance is the reciprocal of adding weight to the left one because it neutralizes the latter's effect without eliminating the latter *qua* operation. Summing up, any operation in physical systems which possess *INRC* group properties can be successfully counteracted by either of two types of opposing operation: its *negation,* which annuls or undoes the operation directly, and its *reciprocal,* which leaves untouched the operation itself while neutralizing its effect.

We have described two forms of a group of four transformations, *INRC*: one whose content consists of propositional statements, such as $p \cdot q$, $p \lor \overline{q}$, etc., and one whose content entails physical operations, symbolized by p, p^*, etc. How does Piaget conceive of the relation between either or both of these groups and adolescent thinking? He thinks of the general *INRC* group form as a model of adolescent cognition, a model in the same sense that the lattice also is, and in the same sense that the grouping is for the younger child (e.g., *ibid.*, p. 321). The justification for this assertion lies, as it always does for Piaget, in the results of developmental experiments. Piaget and his associates have presented children of concrete- and formal-operational ages with a number of problems involving physical systems of the (p p^* q q^*) type (Inhelder and Piaget, 1958). The gist of their findings is that the older children, in contrast to the younger ones, appear to be able to discriminate the various direct and opposing operations and also to assess their effects vis-à-vis one another. In the case of the hydraulic press (weighted piston exerting pressure on liquid in one arm of U-shaped tube, etc.), for instance, the adolescent can correctly predict the effects on the height of the liquid in the other arm, of variations in both piston weight and liquid density. He seems to be able to do this because he discriminates all four operations and, especially, because he understands the function of each operation relative to the others. For instance, he grasps the important fact that the effect of adding weight to the piston can be opposed by either (or both) of two distinct operations—actually removing weight (negation), or increasing the liquid density and thus exerting more counterpressure on the piston (reciprocal). On the other hand, he recognizes that decreasing the liquid density (correlative) is equivalent to adding weight. The concrete-operational children appear not to go much beyond the identification and manipulation of one opposing force (usually negation). The formal-operational child does identify all four and, more than this, sees them as constituting a system, each operation bearing a specified relation to each of the others.

It is this "system quality" which suggests the $INRC$ group as a cognitive model, just as the adolescent's capacity to generate the system of all possible combinations of a set of propositions suggests the lattice model. The $INRC$ group, in its physical-system realization, is really a statement of the way in which p, p^*, q, and q^* interrelate as a system. This group is taken as a cognitive model because the adolescent behaves as if he understood precisely these same interrelations, and as if this understanding served as a guiding conceptual framework in solving problems entailing such systems. Needless to say, there is no presumption here that the adolescent knows anything about group theory as an object of cognition. But there is the presumption, based on an interpretation of his behavior in certain problem situations, that the $INRC$ group constitutes a good description of at least one important component of his cognitive organization.

Two important questions remain, however, and clear answers here are harder to obtain. We have said that Piaget talks about a logical as well as a physical system whose transformations form a four-group. And on the psychological side of things there is another logical versus physical dichotomy. At the physical end there is the newly acquired ability just discussed: the adolescent becomes able to discriminate both *negation* and *reciprocal* and to coordinate them within a single system in the solution of problems of the p, p^*, q, q^* type (balance, hydraulic press, etc.). At the logical end there are all the accomplishments in the construction and manipulation of logical propositions, in logical deduction, and so forth, that we discussed earlier (the accomplishments for which the lattice model was invoked).

What is the connection between the logical and physical forms of the $INRC$ group? More generally, how do the adolescent's logical accomplishments in the manipulation of propositions relate to his accomplishments vis-à-vis negation and reciprocal operations in physical problems? For the first question, Piaget appears to treat the two realizations of the $INRC$ group as essentially synonymous, i.e., that negation of a binary proposition is essentially the same kind of transformation as negation of a physical operation, and that reciprocal has the same meaning in both contexts, etc. Thus, he perceives no obstacle to describing the subject's behavior in the balance problem, for instance, in terms of *logical INRC* transformations like $N (p \lor q) = \bar{p} \cdot \bar{q}$, $R (p \cdot q) = \bar{p} \cdot \bar{q}$, etc. (*ibid.*, p. 178).

This answer to the first question provides a key to the second. Our interpretation of Piaget's reasoning here is as follows. The logical *INRC* group, whose content consists of (transformations of) logical propositions, is equivalent to the physical *INRC* group and hence can readily be used to describe the behavior of subjects in the various physical-systems problems. But the logical *INRC* group itself, in its representation within the adolescent's cognitive structure, is a subachievement within the larger context of a general mastery of propositional thinking. That is, in the course of learning to manipulate and interrelate the sixteen binary propositional operations, the child discovers that one is the reciprocal of another, or the negation of another, etc., and in this special sense his logical reasoning "acquires" *INRC* group properties. Thus, Piaget appears to see an intimate causal relation between the development of propositional thinking at large and the more specific acquisition of a negation-reciprocal strategy in problem-solving, the bridge between them being the logical *INRC* group: the development of propositional logic brings in its train a grasp of certain interproposition relations (whose structure the logical *INRC* group describes). This understanding is then carried over—a kind of positive transfer—to the solution of physical-systems problems which entail the successful coordination of reciprocal and negation operations.[3]

The foregoing tangle of conceptual interrelationships can surely stand some summarizing and highlighting. The central problem concerns the *INRC* group as a model for aspects of adolescent thought and the causal-developmental relation between these aspects and the more general (lattice-modeled) set of logical-propositional acquisitions. We have distinguished, with Parsons (1960), two forms of the *INRC* group. Piaget himself appears unconcerned with this distinction and uses the logical form of the group to describe problems of the p, p^*, q, q^* type. There is no question but that he explicitly intends the *INRC* group to be a theoretical model or schema for at least subareas of adolescent reasoning; in particular, it models behavior involving the integrated use of negation and reciprocal. This last, prima facie not related to the more general capacity to handle propositional logic, is apparently seen as intimately linked with it through the *INRC* logical group—a structure which, as it

---

[3] Although this is nowhere spelled out in detail, it also appears that Piaget believes that the causal relation also works in the other direction, i.e., the understanding of the negation-reciprocal coordination facilitates the mastery of propositional operations.

were, has one foot in logic *per se* and one in the negation-reciprocal arena. The net result of this line of reasoning, and one highly congenial to Piaget's general approach to problems, is to conceive adolescent thought structure in terms of an integrated and unified group-lattice totality, which forms the common genotype for a wide variety of different-looking phenotypes. In accord with Piaget's general equilibration model, formal-operational thought is a structure-in-equilibrium which integrates the structural elements of the preceding, developmental period. Thus, as we have seen, the lattice structure integrates several concrete-operational groupings and the *INRC* group brings into a single system negation and reciprocal operations, previously isolated in separate groupings.

Do the logical and the physical *INRC* groups need to be distinguished at all, as we have taken pains to do throughout this section? Or are they for all practical purposes synonymous, as Piaget seems to feel? The need for distinction, or so it appears to this writer, arises from what look like differences in the logical meaning of the terms *negation* and *reciprocal* in the two contexts. For example, *negation* in the physical group means the literal and complete annulling of the operation, i.e., p^* means the total and unqualified doing away with p. In the logical group, the negation of a binary operation such as $p \cdot q$ is $\bar{p} \vee \bar{q}$, which, in its disjunctive statement, leaves open the possibility that only p is negated or only q is negated; it is not necessarily the case that both p and q are annulled. On the other hand, the *reciprocal* of $p \cdot q$, namely $\bar{p} \cdot \bar{q}$, does seem to negate in just the sense that p^* negates p in the physical group. Since the same-name operations in the two contexts appear to mean somewhat different things, there is reason to question whether it is appropriate to use the logical *INRC* group as model for behavior (i.e., in the physical-systems problems) for which the physical *INRC* group seems a good model. And, of course, if this objection be granted, then the connection with propositional thinking (to which the logical *INRC* group served as bridge) can also be questioned. Another question concerns the psychological correlates of the logical *INRC* group. It may be conceded, at least provisionally, that the physical transformations *INRC* do find concrete expression in the older child's behavior, i.e., he does appear to see that p^* literally annuls p while q^* opposes it without annulling it, and so on. It is much more difficult to find any clear evidence that the adolescent "sees" the relations between $p \cdot q$, $\bar{p} \vee \bar{q}$, $\bar{p} \cdot \bar{q}$ in the same sense, or that he even *formulates* physical-systems problems in anything like these binary proposition terms, as Piaget appears to assume (e.g., Inhelder and Piaget, 1958, pp. 161-163).

In gist, one's understanding of what Piaget intends becomes clearest where there are fewest questions (the physical *INRC* group as model for behavior in physical-systems problems) and least clear where troublesome ambiguities and potential problems loom (the precise theoretical role of the logical *INRC* group and the nature of the connection between propositional thought and the negation-reciprocal substructure).

FORMAL OPERATIONAL SCHEMAS

The adolescent's cognitive achievements can be categorized on a general-specific dimension. Most general is the core *structure d'ensemble,* the integrated group-lattice total structure which Piaget believes to be the gray eminence behind all adolescent thought. Much more specific are particular and task-linked concepts which this total structure permits the adolescent to work out in the course of experiments with particular Piaget problems, e.g., the laws governing balance and imbalance of weight-scale arms, in terms of weight on the pan, distance from the fulcrum, etc. The set of conceptual instrumentalities which Piaget calls *formal-operational schemas* is at an intermediate level of generality (*ibid.*, pp. 308-309). Like the task-linked concepts, these schemas owe their existence to the evolution of the general lattice-group structure and are also used as tools in the solution of concrete problems. However, they have more general utility; each operational schema has application, not to a single problem, but to a whole set of problems, some of which may even appear unrelated to each other.

Piaget describes eight such schemas altogether, for each one sketching the connection with the group-lattice totality and indicating the concrete problems in which the adolescent makes use of the schema (*ibid.*, pp. 310-329). The schema of *proportions* is an example. Deriving from both lattice and *INRC* group structure (especially the latter), it manifests itself in a variety of problems: those of the p, p^*, q, q^* type (thus $p^*/p = q^*/q$, etc.), as well as others (e.g., Piaget and Inhelder, 1951, ch. 6). Other examples include the notions of probability and correlation, certain types of conservation (e.g., conservation of motion in an ideal, frictionless medium), the concept of mechanical equilibrium, and so on. As with the other portions of Piaget's theory of structures for adolescent thought, there are questions and ambiguities in connection with the operational schemas. Perhaps their principal importance for the student of child cognitive development lies in the fact that they isolate and specify several important schemas or strategies, partially task-independent but not completely general, to look for in the intellectual behavior of the adolescent as he tackles concrete problems.

Implications for Adolescent Behavior

As a general rule, Piaget has been much more concerned with conceptualizing developmental changes in cognitive structure *per se* than with trying to show how these changes are causally linked with changes in everyday cognitive, social, and affective behavior.[4] It is therefore of interest that the book on adolescent reasoning (Inhelder and Piaget, 1958) concludes with a brief excursion of this type. Although the adolescent whom the authors take as their model for purposes of analysis seems clearly to be more European than American (and perhaps a bright and introspective European, at that), at least some of their observations may be extrapolated to the American scene.

They think that much of the difference between the everyday behavior of the child and the adolescent can be expressed in this way: the adolescent, like the child, lives in the present, but also, unlike the child, he lives very much in the nonpresent, i.e., in the future and in the domain of the hypothetical. His conceptual world is full of informal theories about self and life, full of plans for his and society's future, in short, full of ideation which goes far beyond his immediate situation, current interpersonal dealings, and so on. Although the precise content of this ideation does of course vary, both within and between cultures, this should not obscure what Piaget feels to be an important common denominator: the child deals largely with the present, with the here and the now; the adolescent extends his conceptual range to the hypothetical, the future, and the spatially remote. There is adaptive significance in this difference. The adolescent is beginning to take up adult roles; for him the world of personally relevant future possibilities— occupational selection, marital choice, and the like—is a most important object of reflection. Similarly, the adult that he will shortly become must make intellectual contact with social collectivities much less concrete and immediate than family and friends: city, state, country, labor union, church, etc.

Piaget believes that these important changes in workaday cognitive orientation and content are intimately related to the formal-structural changes:

> But how can we explain the adolescent's new capacity to orient himself toward what is abstract and not immediately present (seen from the outside by the observer comparing him to the child), but which (seen from within) is an indispensable instrument in his adaptation to the adult social framework, and as a result his most immediate and most deeply experienced concern? There is no doubt that this is the most direct and, moreover, the simplest manifestation of formal thinking. Formal thinking is both thinking about thought (propositional logic is a second-order operational system which operates on propositions whose truth, in turn, depend on class, relational, and numerical operations) and a reversal of relations between what is real and what is possible (the empirically given comes to be inserted as a particular sector of the total set of possible combinations). These are the two characteristics—which up to this point we have tried to describe in the abstract language appropriate to the analysis of reasoning—which are the source of the living responses, always so full of emotion, which the adolescent

Some exceptions to this general rule have already been cited in Chapters 2 and 5.

uses to build his ideals in adapting to society. The adolescent's theory construction shows both that he has become capable of reflective thinking and
that his thought makes it possible for him to escape the concrete present
toward the realm of the abstract and the possible. Obviously, this does not
mean that formal structures are first organized by themselves and are later
applied as adaptive instruments where they prove individually or socially
useful. The two processes—structural development and everyday application
—both belong to the same reality, and it is *because* formal thinking plays a
fundamental role from the functional standpoint that it can attain its general and logical structure. Once more, logic is not isolated from life; it is no
more than the expression of operational coordinations essential to action
(*ibid.,* pp. 341-342).

The quotation above indicates one causal tie between Piaget's theory
of development and the mundane preoccupations and activities of the
adolescent. A second tie involves his concept of *egocentrism,* described
in Chapter 2. In Piaget's theory, egocentrism is likely to increase whenever, as development proceeds, the child begins to cope with a new and
untried field of cognitive action, i.e., whenever he enters a new plane
of cognitive functioning. This burst of egocentrism slowly subsides as
the child progressively masters the new field, only to reassert itself when
still another new domain is approached. The ebb and flow of egocentrism
across ontogenetic development is, of course, an expression—almost a
simplified restatement—of the general equilibration model which Piaget
imputes to cognitive evolution, that is, development as a series of successive disequilibrium → equilibrium subdevelopments.

We have already described two high-water marks of egocentrism: one
in early infancy for the sensory-motor field and one in the preschool
years for the concrete-representational domain. The third and final one
is said to occur in adolescence as a consequence of the extension of reflective thought into the realm of the possible and hypothetical. Piaget
suggests that this new (one is tempted to add "high-level") egocentrism
takes the form of a kind of naive idealism, bent on intemperate proposals for reforming and reshaping reality and—here the "omnipotence
of thought" characteristic of all egocentrism—with an immoderate belief
in the efficacy of its thought coupled with a cavalier disregard for the
practical obstacles which may face its proposals. In Piaget's words:

> The indefinite extension of powers of thought made possible by the new
> instruments of propositional logic at first is conducive to a failure to dis-
> tinguish between the ego's new and unpredicted capacities and the social
> or cosmic universe to which they are applied. In other words, the adolescent
> goes through a phase in which he attributes an unlimited power to his own
> thoughts so that the dream of a glorious future or of transforming the world
> through Ideas (even if this idealism takes a materialistic form) seems to be
> not only fantasy but also an effective action which in itself modifies the
> empirical world. This is obviously a form of cognitive egocentrism. Although
> it differs sharply from the child's egocentrism (which is either sensori-motor
> or simply representational without introspective "reflection"), it results,

nevertheless, from the same mechanism and appears as a function of the new conditions created by the structuring of formal thought (*ibid.*, pp. 345-346).

PERCEPTION

There can be no question but that Piaget's scholarly "major" is the nature and development of intelligence. One has only to leaf through the last twenty years of the Swiss journal *Archives de Psychologie* to discover that the only possible contender for his "minor" is the nature and development of perception. Since the early 1940's Piaget and his co-workers have produced a steady stream of publications on this topic and the total bibliography has become quite large. The main body of perceptual research is found in a series of articles in the above-mentioned *Archives* entitled "Recherches sur le développement des perceptions." [5] In addition, most of Piaget's books have at least something to say about perception, and there are a number of articles, apart from the Recherches series, which are clearly relevant (e.g., Piaget, 1941, 1951c, 1952h, 1954b, 1954-1955, 1955a, 1955b, 1955e, 1956-1957, 1957e, 1958a; Piaget and Morf, 1958a, 1958b; Piaget, Vinh-Bang, and Matalon, 1958; Inhelder, 1955, 1955-1956; Rutschmann, 1959-1960; Vurpillot, 1959).

This book will survey Piaget's perception work in two installments. This section deals with theoretical aspects, with allusion to experimental work only where exposition of theory requires. And a brief section of Chapter 10 is given over to a résumé of some of the experimental research. Neither installment is intended to be more than an introduction to this very substantial body of work; neither is anything like a substitute for the original, particularly for anyone with serious aspirations to work with or from the theory, to extend the research in new directions, etc. The general expository bias of this book is that intelligence, and particularly intelligence theory, is the topic which ought to get the lion's share of detailed coverage. Other topics must compete for space with the lion and suffer accordingly. Perception is one such topic.[6]

The theoretical aspects of Piaget's work on perception can be divided into two parts (with the usual untidy areas in between). One part might be called his theory *of* perception. This part of the theory consists of a rather precise, essentially probabilistic model of how the perceptual apparatus functions when it fixates on stimulus elements, compares one

---

[5] There are about forty of these publications at this writing. The interested reader can abstract them from the Bibliography by looking for articles with the series title (Recherches sur le, etc.) followed by a Roman numeral. Piaget's name is not a reliable guide, since it does not appear on some. A sample article of the series looks like this: Gantenbein, M. Recherches sur le développement des perceptions. XIV. Recherche sur le développement de la perception du mouvement avec l'âge. *Arch. Psychol., Genève,* 1950-1952, 33, 197-294.

[6] Piaget's genetic epistemological work is clearly another (see Chapter 7).

stimulus element to another, and the like. The second part could be termed his theory *about* perception. This is more a general conception than a specific model. It is a general conception of what perception is and how it develops, particularly in relation to the nature and development of intelligence. For Piaget, perception is a particular kind of adaptational act or process, which can only be understood in relation to the broader class of acts or processes he calls *intelligence*. The theory *about* perception, then, is a theory of: what perceptual structures are like, relative to intellectual structures; where and how they originate, relative to the origins of intelligence; and how they evolve and change, relative to (and in interaction with) intellectual development. It should be mentioned that both theories are active determinants of, i.e., serve as conceptual bases for, Piaget's systematic program of experimental research on perception (most of which is described in the Recherches series). It is the model which plays the more explicit and direct role here, however.

The Theory of Perception

The principal sources for this aspect of Piaget's theorizing about perception are, for the original statement of the model, Piaget, Albertini, and Rossi, 1944-1945; for its later version, Piaget, Vinh-Bang, and Matalon, 1958, and especially Piaget, 1955-1956a; and for a general review of the theory, particularly the later version, Vurpillot, 1959. The statement of the model begins with a theoretical account of what happens when the visual system fixates or centers on a simple visual stimulus, e.g., a straight line.[7] Piaget assumes that the perception of the line is a developing process which takes place over a very brief period of time. One could think of this period of time between no percept and a completed, relatively stable one as divided into arbitrarily small microintervals, the construction of the fully formed percept gradually taking place across these intervals. Let us begin with the first tiny interval and work from there.

The perceptual act which occurs during this interval is assumed to involve a set of *encounters* (*rencontres*) between some of the elements of the visual system and some of the elements of the stimulus. The nature of the elements and the nature of their mutual encounters are left wholly undefined by the model. Piaget thinks that an encounter might be something like a tiny eye movement which crosses (hence encounters) a point on the stimulus line. Thus the totality of encounters in a given microinterval would be the totality of such crossings (Piaget, Vinh-Bang, and

---

[7] Piaget does not see the model as limited to visual phenomena alone, despite the fact that most of the supporting research data concerns visual effects and also despite the fact that his description of the model is couched in visual terms.

Matalon, 1958, p. 280). On the other hand, of course, an encounter might be something else entirely. The important thing for the model is the abstract concept of encounter, not its concrete specification in reality.

The model assumes that not all the encounterable elements of the line will in fact be encountered during the initial microinterval, but only some fixed fraction of them. It is as though the perceptual apparatus took a random sample of the total number of encounterable elements during this brief time period. So much for the first interval; what of the second?

The model asserts that a second sampling occurs here, not a sampling of the total number but of the total remaining number of elements. That is, the elements sampled in the first interval are assumed to have been "used up" in some sense—no longer part of the available, to-be-encountered pool. Moreover, the further assumption is made that the percentage of the remaining pool sampled is the same as it was the first time. This sampling procedure continues through the whole succession of microintervals: a fixed proportion of the pool is sampled, then the same proportion of the remaining pool (that is, the original pool minus the elements just sampled), and so forth. As a concrete example, suppose that the line possessed 100 encounterable elements in all and that the "base rate" sampling proportion were .5. In the first tiny interval, 50 (.5 × 100) elements are sampled, with 50 left in the remaining pool. In the second interval, 25 of these remaining 50 (.5 × 50) are sampled, leaving 25; in the third, 12.5 (.5 × 25); in the fourth, 6.25 (.5 × 12.5), and so on. It is clear what is happening here. Each successive sortie into the stimulus figure increases the proportion of encountered to total-encounterable elements, but by gradually decreasing amounts. The curve for cumulated encounters is a negatively accelerated, logarithmic one which approaches the totality of encounterable elements as an asymptote;[8] in the present example, the points on the curve would be 0, 50, 75 (i.e., 50 + 25), 87.5 (i.e., 75 + 12.5), 93.75 (i.e., 87.5 + 6.25), etc.

The relevance of the encounter model for visual perception is easy to state. Encounters are taken to be the stuff and substance of percepts. In the case of our line stimulus, *its perceived length at any moment of time is believed to be a direct function of the number of encounters accumulated up to that time.* And the number of encounters is itself believed to be a function of two things. First, as suggested above, it is a function of time; with each successive microinterval, more encounters are added to the already existing total. Second—and this is a very important aspect of the model—it is a function of whether the line is fixated or not. The model asserts that, within a given perceptual field and for a given exposure time, a line which is centered or fixated achieves more en-

[8] Here and elsewhere we omit the mathematical formulas in which Piaget couches his model in favor of a somewhat simplified, more qualitative presentation.

counters, relative to the total possible, than one seen in the periphery of vision.[9] Translating "more encounters" into its equivalent "more length," the preceding statements imply the following concrete consequences. A line grows in subjective length during its temporal microdevelopment; hence, a line seen only very briefly (e.g., in brief tachistoscopic exposure) is perceived as shorter than an objectively equal line presented in full exposure. And a line near or on the fixation point will appear longer than an equivalent one located away from the fixation point but in the same visual field.[10] The state of affairs we have been describing—variation in perceived magnitude as a function of number of encounters (with these in turn depending on the aforementioned temporal and spatial factors)—is given the generic name of *elementary error I*.

In describing *elementary error I* we began with the theory (the encounter model) and ended with the facts which the theory purports to explain (variation in perceived magnitude as a function of exposure time and of fixation versus nonfixation). In describing what Piaget calls *elementary error II* we shall adopt the opposite strategy. Suppose a visual display consists of two parallel lines A and B, with A longer than B; and suppose these lines are located quite close together with the fixation point midway between them (thus the perceiver can be said to fixate them jointly, or perhaps distribute alternative fixations about equally between them). The process called *elementary error I* would assert that both lines grow in perceived length over microtime under joint fixation, and that one is momentarily overestimated, relative to the other, with any momentary shifts of fixation. What the process would not predict, however, is that there would be a more or less persistent, across-the-board overestimation of the longer line A, *relative* to B, and hence what amounts to an overestimation of the *difference* $(A - B)$ between them. Yet, Piaget and his associates have done experimental studies which lead them to believe that this is precisely what happens (see footnote 10). This is the effect that Piaget calls *elementary error II*: a relative overestimation of the longer of two lines (and hence of the difference between them) which could not be attributed to the operation of the first elementary error. Piaget expresses the difference between the two kinds of error this way (Piaget, 1955-1956a, p. 7). As a function of the growth of encounters, all lines are subject to what could be called an *absolute overestimation*

[9] There is some dispute as to the precise source of variance here. It may be that, as suggested above, it is fixation versus nonfixation which determines the density of encounters. But the effect has also been attributed to other correlated variables (attended to versus not attended to, or seen clearly versus seen indistinctly) (Vurpillot, 1959, pp. 417-421). But the main point stands independent of the dispute: that density of encounters varies, not only with time, but with the relation of the stimulus to the visual apparatus, especially its position in the visual field.

[10] It would be digressive to survey here the existing experimental evidence bearing on these and other implications from the model. See again Vurpillot's review (*ibid.*).

when the subject centers on them (*elementary error I*). Superimposed upon this absolute overestimation of all fixated lines, however, is a *relative overestimation* as a function of length; the longer of two lines is more overestimated than its companion (*elementary error II*).

Piaget extends his model to account for this second kind of error by introducing the notion of *couplings* (*couplages*) between encountered elements on one line and encountered elements on the other. Like the concept of *encounter* before it, the concept of *coupling* is not given a fixed, once-for-all empirical specification within the model. Piaget thinks that a coupling might be either one of two processes; we shall refer to these as the *temporal* versus *spatial interpretations*. In the spatial interpretation, a coupling would be a visual movement from some encountered element on one line to some encountered element on the other and back again—a kind of visual *transport* of one element to another and reciprocally (*ibid.*, p. 7). In the temporal interpretation, a coupling would consist simply of the simultaneous encountering of two encounterable elements, one from each line. Note the intransitive relation between encounters and couplings, true in either interpretation: all couplings necessarily involve encounters (encounters are the things which are coupled), but the sheer presence of two encounters, one on each line, does not guarantee a coupling between them.

Piaget goes on to distinguish between complete and incomplete coupling. In the spatial interpretation, complete coupling implies that each and every encounterable point on one line has been related (by visual movements or transports) to each and every point on the other line, and vice versa. Thus, if there were 100 such points on one line and 50 on the other, complete coupling would mean 5,000 achieved couplings. The coupling would be said to be incomplete to the degree that the achieved couplings fall short of this total. In the temporal interpretation, complete coupling is taken to mean *equal density* of simultaneously effective encounters on the two lines, i.e., the number of active encounters per unit of length is the same on both lines, in a given moment of time. And conversely, incomplete coupling implies *unequal density:* one line is more heavily populated with encounters, relative to its length, than the other.

Complete coupling in either interpretation is believed to be a *corrective* to perceptual distortion: to the extent that couplings are complete, to that extent are the two lengths veridically perceived, in relation to each other. On the other hand, the more incomplete the coupling, the more one line will be overestimated relative to the other. The model now has two functional relationships. First, for a given pair of lines, the more encounters achieved on each line, the longer each line will appear to be in the *absolute* sense. Second, for the same pair of lines, the more nearly complete the coupling between their respective encounters (regardless of the number of such encounters), the more accurately their *relative* lengths will be perceived.

We need now to know what incompleteness of coupling is itself a function of, and how this incompleteness relates to elementary error II. (1) Incomplete coupling is believed to be a complex function of exposure time. In extremely brief tachistoscopic exposure and in prolonged exposure (free vision), couplings are thought to be fairly complete; at intermediate exposures, on the other hand, they tend to be quite incomplete (Piaget, Vinh-Bang, and Matalon, 1958, pp. 281-282). (2) At any given exposure time, the probability of incomplete coupling increases with the difference in length between the lines. The first factor serves to reinforce or attenuate the second, e.g., a state of incomplete coupling in full exposure resulting from a difference in length between two lines would become more incomplete if the same lines were exposed fairly briefly.

We have said that relative overestimation of one of two lines occurs as a function of incompleteness of coupling, and that incompleteness of coupling is in turn dependent upon the length difference between the lines in conjunction with exposure time. But which of the two lines— the longer or the shorter—is relatively overestimated in consequence of the length difference factor? It is here that the coupling model touches the problem of elementary error II. Piaget argues that *incompleteness of coupling must have the effect of augmenting the relative subjective length of the longer line, hence giving rise to the second elementary error*.[11] We can now summarize the model as it bears on the elementary error II: to the extent that, for whatever reason, couplings between encounters approach completeness, to that extent will the relative lengths of the lines be veridically judged; conversely, to the extent that, for whatever reason, the couplings remain incomplete, to that extent will the longer line be overestimated relative to the shorter (elementary error II): and incompleteness of coupling is itself a joint function of length difference between the lines and of exposure time. Piaget regards encounters and couplings as serving essentially opposite functions in perceptual behavior, despite the obvious relation between them. An encounter is an agent of *centration;* the building up of encounters in the course of centering on a stimulus leads to a perceptual overestimation (distortion) of that stimulus, relative to neighboring, noncentered stimuli. A coupling, on the other hand, is seen as an agent of *decentration*—a coordination

---

[11] Although this assertion is an obviously crucial part of his perception model, his explanations of precisely why incomplete coupling should lead to relative overestimation of the longer rather than the shorter line appear to this writer neither clear, consistent, nor convincing (Piaget, Albertini, and Rossi, 1944-1945, p. 111; Piaget, 1955-1956a, p. 10). Note that it is the *explanation,* rather than the *fact* and *direction,* of the relative overestimation effect which is questioned here.

between centrations leading to objectivity.[12] To put it another way, encounters are themselves the cause of elementary error I, whereas it is only the lack of sufficient couplings which leads to elementary error II.

The explanation of the two elementary errors in terms of encounters and couplings makes up the conceptual center of Piaget's perceptual model. We shall only summarize other important aspects of the model which proceed from this center.[13] First, Piaget has attempted to show that the Weber-Fechner law can be deduced from the encounter-coupling model. Second, he has attempted to extend the model to fit more complex perceptual situations, including those involved in classical geometrical illusions (Müller-Lyer, horizontal-vertical, and many others). The extension here takes the form of deriving a formula, called *the law of relative centrations,* which incorporates the thinking behind the two elementary errors into a quantitative statement. What the formula does, in effect, is give the curve of perceptual error (e.g., relative magnitude of an illusion) across changing values of elements in the perceptual field (e.g., length of lines in the illusion figure). In particular, the formula predicts the values of the field elements for which the error or illusion will be maximum and minimum. The law of relative centrations, in one or another of its variants, has had extensive use in Piaget's experimental work on perception. Apart from whatever intrinsic merits it may have in accounting for perceptual phenomena, it is of interest to a Piaget-watcher as the high-water mark of quantification in Piaget's theoretical system. Unlike anything anywhere in the theory of intellectual development, it makes specific, quantitative predictions about dependent variables (perceptual errors) from quantitative information about independent variables (dimensions of the stimulus figure, locus of the fixation point, etc.). It is easy to see why Wohlwill is tempted to speak of "two Piagets," one for intelligence and one for perception (1960c).

The Theory About Perception

In order to understand Piaget's theoretical and experimental attack on perceptual problems, it is absolutely essential to understand his conception of perception as a mode of adaptation. He has definite ideas here, and they differ markedly from what this writer would take to be the norm in contemporary psychology; as such, one could defend including them in the list of "idiosyncrasies of the system" given in Chapter 1.

[12] It will be recalled that the same distorting and corrective roles were assigned to centration and decentration in the intellectual sphere (Chapter 4).

[13] *Proceed* in the logical rather than chronological sense; the aspects of the theory to which we shall now allude, as well as the perceptual effects subsumed under errors I and II, were all developed prior to the encounter-coupling model which Piaget now uses to account for them.

The main essentials of these ideas can be expressed in three related beliefs.

(1) Intelligence and perception need to be sharply distinguished as types of adaptation. Piaget is not at all happy about loose terminology here. For example, the term *space perception* is used too loosely for his tastes if it includes both strictly perceptual phenomena and the child's representation of space (e.g., 1954b). The perception of space is one developmental product (an early one); the representation of space is quite another and comes much later. Similarly, it is a fair guess that he would balk at the current rubric *person perception* (e.g., Tagiuri and Petrullo, 1958) on similar grounds. Piaget freely admits the existence of genuine areas of gray between perception and intelligence but does not feel that this argues against drawing the sharpest and clearest distinctions of which nature admits (1958a, pp. 69-71).

(2) The emphasis on sharp differentiation and the objections to promiscuous use of the term *perception* give the clue to the second, related belief: for Piaget, *perception* covers a narrower, more restricted range of behaviors than it does for most. Although this is something of a simplification, behaviors which appear to involve very much beyond a modicum of judgment, inference, classification, reorganization, etc., are usually classed as intellectual rather than perceptual acts. As we shall see, perceptual covers more than just raw sensation (a concept which Piaget with his anti-Lockian epistemology would in any event eschew), but it does not extend nearly so far towards the other end of the continuum as many would have it (*ibid.*, p. 69).[14]

(3) Finally—and here we see where the first two beliefs are headed—perception is both developmentally subordinate and structurally inferior to intelligence as a class of adaptation. As for the former, Piaget believes that perception arises developmentally, not as an autonomous mode of adaptation in its own right, but as a kind of dependent subsystem within the larger context of an evolving sensory-motor intelligence (e.g., Piaget, 1957c, pp. 74-75; Piaget and Inhelder, 1959, pp. 20-21). For example, early perceptions have "meaning" to the infant only through the mediation of the sensory-motor schemas of which they form a part, the developing perceptual constancies derive their main support from contemporaneous developments which Piaget regards as intellectual (the object concept, the spatial groups), and so on. It goes without saying that, given this view of the early status of perception vis-à-vis intelligence, a theory of development which would found the evolution of intelligence on prior formed percepts, taken as the basic "givens," would be com-

[14] The following quote expresses his position here quite well: "We will call perception the most direct or immediate possible knowledge of a present object in the sensorial field (without affirming, however, that there exists a knowledge which is completely direct or immediate)" (1954-1955, p. 183).

pletely anathema to Piaget. In his scheme of things, sensory-motor intel-ligence, not perception, provides the foundation for later intellectual development (and, as we have just seen, it is the matrix from which and in which perception itself originates and evolves).

But if perception is a second-class citizen developmentally, it is even more clearly so structurally.[15] Although Piaget does not put it quite this way, the zenith of perceptual structure is (in many but not all respects— see Chapter 7) about on a par with the structure of late preoperational thought, the nadir with that of, perhaps, early preoperational thought. Thus, in simple centration effects (e.g., elementary error I), perception shows the same kind of naive overvaluation of the centered elements that the three-year-old does in the conceptual realm. With perceptual decentration due to the establishment of couplings (and with higher forms of corrective action that we shall describe shortly), one begins to get something resembling the semireversible regulations of the late pre-operational period. That is, centration-induced distortions are partly corrected by other, compensatory perceptual actions. But the point is that perceptual structures never get beyond this semireversibility, whereas intelligence eventually becomes rigorously reversible, first on the level of concrete operations and later in the formal-operational realm. Intelli-gence in its higher forms is capable of yielding certain, absolute knowl-edge: e.g., if $A = B$ and $B = C$, then $A = C$ and that's all there is to it. But perception, even at its best, is forever a probabilistic, approximate affair whose products are constantly at the mercy of changes in field conditions; given the perceptual judgments $A = B$ and $B = C$, $A = C$ under some conditions but $A \neq C$ under others. Probably the simplest but most precise statement of structural difference (see Chapter 7) is that perceptual structures just never achieve equilibrium states as stable and permanent as those of the more evolved intellectual structures.

Chapter 7 will also point out that Piaget is forever seeking subtle similarities among obvious differences when comparing various adapta-tional forms, e.g., structural and functional analogies between sensory-motor and representational cognition. This is also the case for the perception-intelligence comparison. Piaget describes (Piaget and Morf, 1958a) such similarities in terms of the concept of *partial isomorphisms* between perceptual and intellectual (mostly concrete-operational) struc-tures. That is, there are a number of perceptual phenomena which ap-pear to be crude sketches or first drafts of better structured intellectual phenomena to come.[16] Most or all defining criteria of the later structure

[15] The perception-intelligence structural comparison is so ubiquitous in Piaget's writ-ings on perception that a full citation of references here would simply be a biblio-graphic tour de force.

[16] Piaget's concept of *partial isomorphisms* appears to be "partially isomorphic" to Heinz Werner's concept of *analogous processes* (Werner, 1948, Ch. 9).

can be found in the earlier sketch (hence *isomorphism*), but *sous une forme affaiblie* (hence *partial*) (*ibid.*, p. 52). Moreover, although he does not do much in the way of specifying details here, Piaget assumes that the earlier structures are in some causal sense the forerunners of the later ones; somehow they pave the way for the later ones.

The following are perhaps the principal pairs of phenomena linked by partial isomorphisms. First, perceptual structures and operational structures in general relate in this way: the semireversibility of the one is partially isomorphic to the full reversibility in the other; there is one form of equilibrium for the first and another (better) form for the second, etc. Second, the perceptual *constancies* are clearly analogous to the representational *conservations* (e.g., Piaget, 1954b); in both cases there is a kind of genotypical invariance established in the face of phenotypical change. Third, quasi-perceptual "figural collections" seem to be the preoperational forebears of later logical classes (Piaget and Inhelder, 1959). And finally, there appear to be "preinferences" in perceptual activity which are not quite logical inference but show partial isomorphisms to it (Piaget and Morf, 1958b).

Having discussed Piaget's conception of perception as an adaptational form to be compared and contrasted with intelligence, we shall now make a few remarks about the sort of development it shows. Perhaps the most important thing to say about perceptual development is that (see Chapter 1), it does not seem to show the "natural" and clear-cut breakdown into a sequence of qualitatively distinct and different structures which intellectual development does (Piaget, 1955d, p. 33). Perceptual development simply appears to Piaget to be a more continuous, quantitative-versus-qualitative affair than is the case for its intellectual counterpart. What development there is, however, can be epitomized in the following way. Perceptual behavior can be roughly classified into two complimentary and opposed processes, *primary perception and perceptual activity;* perceptual development is mostly a matter of a quantitative decline in the efficacy of the first in favor of a gain in scope and importance of the second. (See footnote 15 in lieu of specific references for this statement).

Although its definitional boundaries with perceptual activity are not completely fixed, primary perception (also referred to as *field effects*) includes primarily perceptual events attendant on a single centration in a fixed field of vision. Thus it includes elementary error I, in the positive sense, and elementary error II, in the negative sense that this error results from a lack of sufficient stimulus-stimulus comparison or decentration. Perceptual activity, on the other hand, is the generic term for a whole set of active processes on the part of the perceiver whose effects are to counteract the distortions indigenous to the more passive primary perceptions. Piaget speaks here of spatial and temporal "transports" **of** one element onto the other and vice versa, "transpositions" of whole configurations of elements to other configurations and vice versa, various anticipatory sets or *Einstellungen* and various memories or "retroactions," and the like (e.g., 1955a, p. 78; 1958a, pp. 70-71). Perceptual activity, then, covers a broad range of behaviors whose function it is to explore and compare stimuli in order partially to compensate for or overcome primary perception effects: the lower boundary of the range consists of the simple decentering activity of coupling two sets of encounters (on two stimuli) within a single visual field.[17] The upper limit is not so clear, merging imperceptibly into intelligence proper (1958a, pp. 70-71). Referring again to our earlier structural comparison between perception and thought, it can now be said that primary perception is structurally similar to early preoperational thought and that perceptual activity, with its semireversible compensations, resembles late preoperational thought.

In a rough way, one could characterize Piaget's general scheme of development as one in which the growing subject plays a progressively more active and assertive role in his commerce with the environment. In the perceptual area, this principle gets expressed as a gradual increase with age in behavior of the perceptual activity type, with consequent diminution in the force of the primary field effects. Most of Piaget's developmental work on classical illusions and other perceptual deviations from veridicality (published in the Recherches series) has been interpreted in terms of this developmental hypothesis. Thus, Piaget distinguishes between *primary* (or *immediate*) and *secondary* (or *mediate*) *illusions* (e.g., Piaget, 1955b, 1955e, 1956-1957; Piaget and Lambercier, 1944-1945).

A *primary illusion* is one which results from field effects; most of the classical illusions (e.g., the Müller-Lyer) are said to be of this type. Since the development of perceptual activity has the effect of dampening field effects, Piaget predicts (and generally finds) that such illusions decrease in absolute magnitude with age (e.g., Piaget and Albertini, 1950-1952). However, perceptual activity is not always a servant of veridicality; in some perceptual situations, heightened perceptual activity leads to perceptual error, a deviation from veridicality. Piaget calls deviations from this source *secondary illusions;* since they derive from perceptual activity directly rather than being attenuated by it, these illusions show an increase with age. For example, under certain field conditions in which size constancy is tested, older subjects are found to show what amounts to an overconstancy, presumably resulting from active attempts to counter or compensate for the illusion-producing effects of simply comparing retinal sizes (Piaget and Lambercier, 1942-1943b). Similarly, illusions

---

[17] Thus, the theory-of-perception model described in the preceding section encompasses mostly primary perception and the lower end of the perceptual activity range.

which result from the act of retaining an earlier stimulus in memory while perceiving a current one—again a particular kind of perceptual activity—also augment with age (Piaget and Lambercier, 1944-1945).

Discussion of the development of perception as a progressive increase in perceptual activity raises once again the problem of the relation between perception and intelligence within Piaget's system. The developmental version of the problem is embodied in such questions as: what role, exactly, does the concomitant growth of intellectual structures play in this burgeoning of perceptual activity?—What, if any, reciprocal action does the growth of perceptual activity have on the evolution of intellectual structures?—Is a distinction between these two adaptational forms really necessary, or are there data for which such a distinction is at least useful? Piaget has addressed himself to questions of this kind, although we cannot trace his arguments here (e.g., 1954b, 1955e, 1956-1957, 1957e, 1958a). Suffice it to say that, in the writer's opinion, he has not yet given this problem a really clear and detailed analysis, despite the important role such an analysis would obviously play in rounding out his general theory of cognitive development.

CHAPTER SEVEN

The Equilibrium Model, Genetic Epistemology, and General Summary

THE material on formal operations and perception in Chapter 6 brings to a close our four-chapter presentation of Piaget's stage-to-stage ontogeny of cognitive operations. This final chapter of the theoretical portion of the book is reminiscent of Chapters 1 and 2, in that it reverts to very general, stage-independent aspects of Piaget's theory.

THE EQUILIBRIUM MODEL

As is generally the case with Piaget's theoretical constructs, discussion of developmental data in terms of equilibrium can be found in a great many of his publications, and the expositor's task is to direct the reader towards those which give the topic most explicit and detailed coverage. As was indicated in the Introduction and in Chapter 1, an equilibrium conception of development has been with Piaget for a long time, and allusions to it can be found in his very earliest articles (e.g., 1924b). Later publications, both by Piaget (e.g., Piaget, 1941, 1950b, Vol. III, 1956-1957, 1957f, 1958a; Inhelder and Piaget, 1958, ch. 16) and others (Gréco, 1956-1957; Mandelbrot, 1957a), give more substantial treatment. However, the richest single source is a long and rather difficult article by Piaget himself in the second monograph of the *Etudes d'Epistémologie Génétique* series (1957c). Most of what will be said here about matters equilibrial can be found somewhere in this important paper.[1]

Introduction

There are two things about the equilibrium model which the reader should keep in mind. (1) Discussion of the equilibrium model brings us

[1] More recent monographs in this series (Vols. 7-10 inclusive) dealing with the relation between logic and learning also bear on the problem of equilibrium (see footnote 13 in this chapter). Material in these monographs will be taken up in Chapter 11.

full circle to the most general and stage-free aspects of Piaget's theoretical edifice; therefore the reader should expect to encounter again, in a new and somewhat different context, a number of concepts already quite familiar to him, e.g., the functional invariants (assimilation-accommodation), the notion of reversibility, the distinction between reversible operations and semireversible regulations, and so on. (2) There needs to be a preliminary clarification of the status of the equilibrium model as a topic. It does not involve material delimited and apart from the topics of the preceding chapters as, for example, concrete operations can legitimately be construed as an area of study separate from formal operations. Rather, it comprises a general theoretical construction which is imposed, as form on content, on the whole developmental panorama. Not an area of development itself, it is a global conception of what the whole developmental process and its successive structural products are about.[2]

Kessen (1960) makes an important distinction between the study of developmental *states* (or stages) in themselves and the study of the *rules of transition* which govern the organism's movement from state to state. The preceding chapters have said a great deal about developmental states but relatively little about rules of transition, that is, about the mechanisms or processes which propel the child through the ontogenetic sequence.[3] Although it is quite true that most of Piaget's theory and research does revolve around the characteristics of the separate states themselves, it is important that he has also made efforts to cope with the problem of transition mechanisms.

The mechanism of transition which Piaget proposes is an *equilibration process*. This process, continuously operating in all exchanges between the growing subject and his environment, is the propellant for change and transition. This continuous process of *equilibration* gives rise to successive, essentially discontinuous *equilibrium states,* that is, organized systems of actions (sensory-motor, perceptual, concrete-operational, and all the other totalities already familiar to the reader) whose attributes as systems are describable in equilibrium terms.[4] Although the equilibration process itself is thought to be homogeneous across development, the equilibrium states which it generates are not. That is, there are different kinds of equilibrium states, the differences specifiable in terms of a common set of dimensions along which the states vary. Moreover, these differences are ordered differences; one state may be said to be "better

[2] As will be seen, this distinction is, if anything, even more pertinent to the topic "genetic epistemology."

[3] The "relatively little" which has been said is found mostly in Chapter 2 (pp. 49-50), Chapter 4 (p. 163), and Chapter 6 (pp. 209-210).

[4] More precise characterizations of equilibrium and equilibrium states are deferred until later sections, in order to pursue the business of orientation and introduction in this one. The conventional connotations which the reader probably brings with him—notions of balance, steady state, etc.—will not seriously mislead, however.

equilibrated" than another, to attain "a higher degree of equilibrium," and so on. In summary, Piaget's analysis of transitions and states maps these two components, respectively, into a homogeneous and continuous equilibration process (the formative process) which gives rise to heterogeneous and discontinuous equilibrium states (the processes formed).

Several things about this equilibration-equilibrium conception require comment. (1) The conception is linked in the most immediate and intimate way to the concepts of assimilation and accommodation; indeed, the preceding paragraph, with a few terminological changes, could have been lifted bodily from Chapter 2. Stated most simply, the equilibration process is the process of bringing assimilation and accommodation into balanced coordination; and the different equilibrium states which result from this ubiquitous process are the various forms which this coordination takes during ontogenesis (1957c, pp. 107-111). An equilibrium state in Piaget's system always refers to an equilibrated system of relations between subject and object, and hence a relation between assimilation and accommodation.

(2) Piaget views the equilibration-equilibrium interpretation as in no sense an alternative to more conventional interpretations of change mechanisms, i.e., maturation and learning (physical and social). On the contrary, the equilibration-equilibrium model is conceived as a very general affair which presupposes the causal contributions of maturation and learning but subsumes them (e.g., *ibid.*, pp. 27, 30). Although Piaget does not phrase it quite this way, one could regard the model as a high-altitude view of the developmental terrain, which necessarily renders indistinguishable certain features (which are nonetheless "really there") in order to distinguish others (also "really there," but imperceptible at lower altitudes). Obviously, Piaget does not opt for the equilibration-equilibrium model simply because it exists as another way of looking at development; he strongly believes that it is a model peculiarly suited to the analysis of ontogenetic change, one which goes to the heart of the ontogenesis of structures.[5]

(3) It is clear—the very term *equilibration* suggests it—that the model imputes a certain directionality, even a certain teleology, to ontogenetic development. Does this therefore imply that, from knowledge of the model alone and never having seen postinfancy children, we could predict the ontogenetic sequence of equilibrated structures? Does it imply that the model could be used to predict future scientific theory? Only in a very limited sense, says Piaget (1957c, pp. 31-33; 1959a, p. 19). We can only predict from the model that higher states of equilibrium will incorporate and integrate into a broader and more complex totality the

[5] Furthermore, very important for Piaget's interests, the same general model can apply to historical changes in prescientific and scientific cosmologies (e.g., 1950b, Vol. II, ch. 4).

elements (cognitive actions) of the lower states without annulling or contradicting them. For example, we can see in retrospect the "directionality" involved in the incorporation-without-contradiction of, say, concrete-operational groupings into the formal-operational group-lattice structure. But we could not be sure in prospect that the new and higher system into which the former becomes integrated would assume its particular group-lattice form rather than some other; we could only prophesy that the new totality would be a "better" equilibrium state (as we shall shortly define "better" equilibria), than its predecessor. In short, Piaget asserts an orthogenesis in his equilibration-equilibrium model (1957c, p. 32), but one which constrains within very broad limits only,[6] leaving considerable leeway for the novel and unpredictable.

And (4), the model serves an important unifying function in Piaget's over-all theory; it is a device which weaves together into a common fabric developmental strands temporally noncontiguous and formally dissimilar. Chapter 1 showed that a stage theory like Piaget's tends to nudge us towards a discontinuity frame of reference by its very nature. It is therefore important to recognize—and the equilibrium writings bring this home—that Piaget is profoundly concerned with teasing out essential continuities and isomorphisms across development, even between the most primitive reflex activities of the neonate and the highest order of logical operations of the bright adult.[7]

This underlying continuity is pointed up by the equilibration-equilibrium model in three ways. (a) There is the continuity of common mechanism; the formation of cognitive systems at each and all levels is seen as the product of a common equilibration process. (b) The phenotypically different outcomes (the systems) of this common process can themselves be described (and hence their differences specified) by the common set of descriptive dimensions by which Piaget characterizes all equilibrium states. (c) As implied above, continuity is insured by Piaget's basic conception of the relation between adjoining stages (1957c, pp. 113-116): components of the lower stage are abstracted and integrated into the new totality which defines the higher one. Piaget states: "In brief, no structure is ever radically new, but each one is limited to generalizing this or that form of action abstracted from the preceding one" (ibid., p. 114). This general conception of continuity, which finds its principal focus within the equilibration-equilibrium theory, has direct and concrete consequences in the way Piaget interprets developmental data. For instance, the continuity orientation leads him to look for and find formal

---

[6] Strikingly similar, in this respect at least, to the "orthogenetic principle" of Heinz Werner (1957).

[7] When his framework is genetic epistemological, this search for continuities and liaisons takes place within the context of the interrelationships among the various sciences, e.g., the continuity between reflex and logical thought referred to here provides a link between biology and logic-mathematics (e.g., 1950b, Vol. III, Conclusion).

similarities (reversibility, associativity, etc.) between the "practical group of spatial displacements" in the sensory-motor period (see Chapter 4) and the logical structures of middle childhood and adolescence (e.g., *ibid.*, p. 86). And these similarities are substantial enough to warrant serious reference to "a logic of action" in infancy.

Properties of Equilibrium States

The concept of *equilibrium* has had wide currency throughout the physical and social sciences as a way of characterizing system states. To what does the term refer? Essentially, a system in equilibrium is one which possesses some sort of balance or stability (fragile or secure, temporary or enduring) with respect to the forces acting upon or within it. Forces or perturbations which, unopposed, would lead to a change of state are counteracted in an equilibrated system by equal and opposite forces which guarantee the *status quo*. Some systems are equilibrated only with respect to the forces currently acting; as soon as new forces are introduced, the system must undergo a change of state. A scale balance with equal weights in the two pans is such a system. Add more weight to one side and the state changes. Other systems have built into them corrective, feedback devices which maintain the equilibrium condition in the face of introduced forces (at least to a degree, and for a certain range of such forces). An example would be a thermostat which serves to maintain a constant temperature in the face of inconstant thermal conditions. In systems of this kind, an incipient disequilibrium caused by changes in applied forces is "cured," to use Mandelbrot's term (1957a, p. 19), by the automatic setting into operation of inverse, countervalent forces.

The thermostat example is a good one for indicating the varieties of equilibrium states which can obtain. It is clear that some systems achieve only the most momentary and fragile thermal equilibria, equilibria which undergo displacements as soon as external thermal variation is introduced. A metal bar is one such example; a snake is another. Other systems can maintain a constant thermal state when subjected to a certain range of external variation, only to suffer an equilibrial collapse beyond this range. This is the case with warm-blooded animals. And finally, one can imagine, if not create in fact, an ideal thermostat which would instantaneously and completely "cure" any and all thermal input, permanently maintaining a perfectly stable temperature.

The kinds of systems to which Piaget applies an equilibrium model are obviously not thermal or mechanical but psychological. In particular, they are systems of actions, either externalized or internalized, which the subject carries out amid the world of objects and events. Since it is the actions themselves which form equilibrated systems, Piaget speaks of *dynamic* equilibria, as opposed to the *static*, state-of-repose condition of, say, the scale in balance (1957c, pp. 36-37). Psychological equilibrium states can be compared and contrasted along four major dimensions (*ibid.*, pp. 38-43). These follow below.

FIELD OF APPLICATION

Since psychological systems in equilibrium are comprised of actions applied to reality, they can first of all be distinguished in terms of the *size* of their field of application, that is, the ensemble of objects or object-properties which the equilibrated action system accommodates to and assimilates. For a single centration of the primary-perception type, the field of application is very small (the portion of the visual field which the centration encompasses); for a concrete-operational classification grouping (e.g., Grouping I), it is obviously much larger (all the objects subsumed by the classes and subclasses to which the grouping structure is applied).

MOBILITY

This property, also deriving from the active character of psychological equilibria, refers to the spatiotemporal distances which the actions of the system traverse in the course of their operation. Piaget supposes that the mobility of a single, brief centration is null (even if the subject is centering on, say, two stars objectively separated by millions of miles). Mobility becomes non-null, however, as soon as the subject starts to itinerate, whether perceptually, motorically, or conceptually, from datum to datum. It is clear that, with trivial exceptions, representational thought has the potentiality for considerably more mobility in this sense than do sensory-motor actions and perception.

PERMANENCE

This property and the next (stability), to which it is closely related,[8] both concern the resistance of the system to changes of state as a function of input changes. A system is said to be in permanent equilibrium if the elements (objects, attributes, etc.) on which the subject's actions bear do not change their subjective value when new elements are centered. A system which is not in permanent equilibrium, i.e., one in which the elements change their values with each change of input, is said to be subject to *displacements* of equilibrium. Perceptual equilibria are continually subject to such displacements; for example, the apparent length

---

[8] There is some question in this writer's mind as to whether permanence and stability are really different dimensions or are different ways of looking at the same dimension. The distinction between them in Piaget's writings is a later one (*ibid.*); his earlier writings referred to stability only (e.g., Piaget, 1941; Gréco, 1956-1957). In any event, whether or not there are genuine distinctions between them, they are undoubtedly highly correlated across the developmental succession of equilibrium states.

of a rod A keeps changing with changes in the length of a rod B in the same visual field (see Chapter 6). The elements of a relational grouping structure, on the other hand, do not shift in value with input changes (if $A < B$ at the outset, that relation still holds when one continues the series with new elements, i.e., $A < B < C < D$ . . .). Similarly, a classification system can be said to be in permanent equilibrium; A still retains its status as a subclass of B when attention is directed to the other subclasses of B.

STABILITY

This is probably the most important dimension of the four, so far as Piaget's theory is concerned. It refers primarily[9] to the system's capacity to compensate or cancel perturbations which tend to alter the existing state of equilibrium; this is the "curing" function mentioned earlier. The metal bar has minimal equilibrial stability because it possesses no intrinsic mechanism for canceling the effect of an induced thermal change. The ideal thermostat, on the other hand, is completely stable because of its capacity to render ineffective any thermal input. In the psychological realm, perception and preoperational thought are systems of less than perfect stability, because centration-induced illusions (perceptual overestimations, overevaluation of length-increase relative to width-decrease in the conservation of quantity problem, etc.) are only partly correctable by decentration (regulations). On the other hand, the reversible operations of concrete and formal representational structures guarantee complete stability: each $+A$ has its negative $-A$ which annuls it, each p has its reciprocal q which compensates it, and so on. The crucial importance of the stability dimension in Piaget's thinking about equilibrium states is attested by the fact that throughout his writings the terms *reversibility* and *equilibrium* are used almost interchangeably. In Piaget's view, reversibility is a necessary by-product of the equilibration-of-structures process; a psychological system which is strongly equilibrated must entail the balancing and compensating functions supplied by negation and reciprocal operations:

> An operation is a regulation which has become completely reversible in a system completely equilibrated, and become completely reversible *because* completely equilibrated (*ibid.*, p. 37).

It is not hard to visualize how these four dimensions might conjointly describe and hierarchically order the major developmental structures

[9] Piaget also entertains the possibility that a secondary property will be found to correlate highly with this primary compensatory or "curing" one: that, in effect, highly stable cognitive systems make maximally parsimonious interpretations of display transformations. For instance, the older child, but not the younger, will interpret change of shape as only that, rather than as change of shape plus change of volume, weight, mass, etc. This aspect of stability is sometimes introduced and sometimes omitted in Piaget's discussion of particular equilibrium states.

(*ibid.*, pp. 45-47). Primary perception (field effects) is clearly at the bottom of the equilibrium hierarchy on all four dimensions: a very small field of application, no (or virtually no) mobility, displacements of equilibrium with each modification of the perceptual field, and no compensatory corrections of distorting centration effects. Structures involved in perceptual activity show limited improvement in breadth of field, mobility, and stability (due to the action of semireversible regulations), although displacements of equilibrium continue to occur. Sensory-motor schemas show a further extension of the field and added mobility (since they entail motor activities through neighboring space as well as immediate sensory intake). As to permanence and stability, it can at least be said that the best-structured attainments of sensory-motor intelligence—the schema of the permanent object and the closely related group of spatial displacements—achieve a high degree of both within the restricted field of their operation. Late preoperational intelligence, with its perceptionlike regulations, is roughly at the level of perceptual activity as regards permanence and stability (and hence below the level of the "best" of the sensory-motor structures); however, its symbolic, internalized actions allow for a mobility and size of field beyond anything hitherto attained. Concrete-operational structures, on the other hand, attain conditions of equilibrium both stable and permanent and are fully mobile across a very extended domain of application. With the advent of formal structures, the field of equilibrated action extends still further to include the realm of the possible and hypothetical.

The Equilibration Process

The process of development is conceived as a succession of structures coming into equilibrium, the form of equilibrium varying from structure to structure along the dimensions just described. Thus, primary perceptions reach a modicum of equilibrium with the addition of secondary perceptual regulations; early sensory-motor schemas transform into the later, better equilibrated ones; preoperations eventuate in concrete-operational structures; and these in turn become integrated into still better equilibrated formal ones. So far we have discussed only the nature and variety of these equilibrium states and have not raised questions about the process by which they are achieved. How do psychological action systems, at any level, come into equilibrium, of whatever degree? What innervates *la marche à équilibre*, as Piaget frequently refers to it (*ibid.*, p. 59), and what sort of steps does it entail?

One of Piaget's theoretical endeavors has concerned finding ways to attack this problem (Piaget, 1957c; Gréco, 1956-1957). One gets the distinct feeling that his theorizing here is preliminary and tentative, and that he himself is not certain what will eventually come of it. In the systematic paper on this problem (1957c), he begins by examining the equilibration process which leads from preoperational lack of conservation (of quantity, length, and all the rest) to concrete-operational conservation; after trying out, so to speak, his explanatory model in this limited sector, he then attempts to extend it to all the major coming-into-equilibrium events in development, i.e., perception, sensory-motor structures, and the rest. We shall try to convey at least the general flavor of his current thinking about equilibration in the following way: (1) a somewhat abbreviated and simplified account of his analysis as it applies to the conservation problem alone; and (2) a brief illustration of how he applies this basic analytical scheme to the other coming-into-equilibrium events.

One of the most important components of the transition from preoperational to concrete-operational thought is the acquisition of various conservations, that is, the cognition that certain properties (quantity, number, length, etc.) remain invariant (are conserved) in the face of certain transformations (displacing objects or object parts in space, sectioning an object into pieces, changing its shape, etc.). Since the developmental steps in the acquisition of conservation are thought to be roughly the same for these various properties, we can use any one of them to illustrate Piaget's approach. Let us take the conservation of mass (quantity). The analysis begins by examining the conservation-of-quantity problem from the standpoint of the various equilibrial fields of application which might be involved. Suppose the subject is shown a succession of change-of-shape transformations of a ball of clay (e.g., into successively longer and thinner sausage shapes) and each time he is queried as to conservation versus nonconservation of mass. Let us call the width of the sausage A and the length B; length and width will take various successive values A_1, A_2, etc., and B_1, B_2, etc., across successive modifications of the sausage. What could the subject's field of application include? He might notice only the width (A_1, A_2, etc.) or only the length (B_1, B_2, etc.); we can call this the field (A or B). On the other hand, he could extend his field to include the simultaneous cognition of A_1 and B_1, A_2 and B_2, etc.; i.e., he notices both width and length and compares them for a given sausage. We shall call this the field (A and B). Finally, he could make comparisons among the various A-B relations which the successive transformations of the sausage yield, thus the field $[(A_1$ and $B_1)$ and $(A_2$ and $B_2)$ and $(A_3$ and $B_3)]$, etc.

Piaget asserts that the evolution of conservation is a process of equilibration of cognitive actions which contains four major steps, each step comprising in itself an equilibrium state—an isolable "moment" in the continuous equilibration process. Moreover, he believes that all the major coming-into-equilibrium events in development follow the same basic four-step process. For the conservation example, the steps are assumed to be the following. In Step 1, the subject attends only to width or only to length, not both, and his field of application can be described within the (*A* or *B*) paradigm above. For instance, in successive trials he repeatedly centers on the thinness (*A*) of the sausage, relative to the standard, and thus repeatedly concludes that the sausage has less quantity. In Step 2, after a series of repeated centrations on one property (Step 1 behavior), the subject comes eventually to substitute for it a centration on the other property. This substitution, of course, also fails to yield conservation of quantity; it simply gives the opposite nonconservation error (the sausage has more mass than the standard because it is longer). Step 2 may also include behavior consisting of a whole series of alternations between *A* and *B* centrations. The essence of the stage, however, is that these centrations are always successive and isolated from one another, never coordinated; in centering *B* the child forgets his previous centration on *A* and vice versa. Thus this strategy can also be subsumed under the (*A* or *B*) paradigm, since *A* and *B* are never conjoined in any way.

Steps 1 and 2 have clear and straightforward nonconservation outcomes; conversely, Step 4 has an unequivocal conservation outcome. Step 3 includes a somewhat heterogeneous set of behaviors which are not clear cases of either. The common denominator in this heterogeneity, however, is the joint apprehension of both properties within a single cognitive act, and hence an (*A* and *B*) field of application. The typical result of this beginning conceptual coordination of length with width **is** a noticeable hesitation and conflict:

> With the third strategy, on the other hand, we meet with a new type of behavior wherein the subject hesitates among the responses "more," "less," or "equal" and which thus marks a beginning coordination between the two strategies (1) and (2) or a beginning composition between the two opposed properties in the configuration (*ibid.,* p. 51).

This major achievement of Step 3, the cognitive conjunction of *A* and *B*, is continued and extended in Step 4. Here, the subject notices that the successive conjuncts (A_1 and B_1), (A_2 and B_2), etc., which result from the succession of sausage changes, form a meaningful pattern, i.e., each increase in length is accompanied by a compensatory decrease in length. In the language of Chapter 4, there is a shift of conceptual focus from *states* alone to the *transformations* which lead from state to state; in the language of equilibrium fields, the cognitive domain is now [(A_1 and B_1) and (A_2 and B_2), etc.]—a conjunction of conjunctions. The outcome of this fourth and final step is, of course, a rigorous conservation of quantity.

In summary, Piaget asserts that the cognitive structures guaranteeing conservation are achieved by a four-step equilibration process. In the first two steps the antagonistic properties *A* and *B* are only centered singly, either one alone (Step 1), or first one then the other (Step 2). The alternation between properties begun in Step 2 eventuates in their con-

junction in Step 3. In Step 4, the subject attends to the successive transformations of state and hence conjoins the various (*A* and *B*) conjuncts.
It is not difficult to see how these four steps can be roughly compared
and contrasted as equilibrium states. The progressive increase in size of
field and mobility is apparent. Similarly, there is an increase in stability
and permanence from the static and deforming centration of Step 1, to
a beginning decentration in Step 2, culminating in semireversible regulations in Step 3, to the complete and permanent reversible compensations
of Step 4.

But if the foregoing be an accurate description of the equilibration
sequence for conservation, it is scarcely an explanation of it. Why does
the child traverse precisely these steps, in precisely this order, in *la
marche à équilibre* here? And what guarantees (or at least makes highly
probable) his transition from one step to the next? The explanatory
model which Piaget proposes is a probabilistic one (*ibid.*, pp. 56-73).[10]
He first tries to show how the nature of the relation between the subject
and the stimulus properties of the conservation task is such as to make
Step 1 the most probable *beginning* behavioral strategy. Having thus got
the equilibration process started, and started precisely with Step-1 behavior rather than something else, he attempts to show how *continued*
performance at Step 1 makes the transition to Step 2 increasingly more
probable, how *continued* performance at Step 2 makes the transition to
Step 3 increasingly more probable, and so on. This level-to-level upward
movement ceases at Step 4, in which a permanent and parsimonious
solution to the problem renders null the probability of further changes
in strategy. In sum, Piaget's explanation of the equilibration process involves showing that certain behaviors appear more probable than others
for a given complex of subject-object interaction, that these probabilities
change in predictable ways as the interactions continue, and that the
fixed sequence of equilibrial states (the four steps) is the direct consequence of these probability changes.

Step 1, it will be remembered, entails the centration by the subject of
either width *A* or length *B*; it excludes a centration on both *A* and *B* at
once. Piaget argues that this (*A* or *B*) centration is a more probable first
strategy than the (*A* and *B*) centration for essentially the same reason
that the probability of either of two coins turning up heads on a given
toss exceeds that of both turning up heads. If one does not impute any
particular response tendencies to the subject as a consequence of previous experience (and since it is the first strategy which is to be explained,
this is a reasonable assumption), it can be defended that a random scan-

---

[10] He also leaves open the possibility that a model derived from game theory, involving
a qualitative assessment of the relative "costs" and "gains" of each "strategy" (step),
might be linked to the probabilistic model in explaining the equilibration process. The
game theory adjunct is still very tentative and incompletely developed, however (*ibid.*,
p. 58, footnote 1) and is therefore omitted from our presentation.

ning of the display would be more likely to yield either A or B alone than both together as its initial centration.

So much for Step 1; the subject's first act of centration lands on, say, the width A and leads him to assert that the sausage has less quantity than the standard. What then accounts for an eventual shift to centering length B (the shift which defines Step 2) or, in terms of the probability model, why does the probability of centering B, having first centered A, become increasingly great? Piaget argues here for factors of subjective dissatisfaction with continually giving the same response under changing perceptual conditions and especially, factors of perceptual contrast, particularly in extreme configurations, e.g., a very long and very thin sausage, where the contrast between properties A and B increases the likelihood of centering the hitherto unnoticed second property (see Chapter 4).[11]

Having once noticed both A and B (in successive but not simultaneous centrations), the subject is likely to alternate between them as a function of varying display conditions. This alternation, especially as it becomes a rapid affair, increases the probability that sooner or later the subject will encompass both properties in a single cognitive act, that is, the (A and B) strategy of Step 3. The subject is now for the first time in a position to compare length and width for a given sausage. It is then a small step to extend this comparison to the successive length-width couples across trials (and thus the field of equilibrium extends from states to states-plus-transformations). This comparison constitutes the Step-4 strategy, i.e., [(A_1 and B_1) and (A_2 and B_2), etc.]:

> But, once the conjunction A *and* B has been made, it only remains to discover that the properties A and B covary,[12] which amounts to placing one state A_n *and* B_n in relation to another A_{n+1} *and* B_{n+1} (*ibid.*, pp. 70-71).

As indicated earlier, Piaget has attempted to fit this general four-step paradigm to coming-into-equilibrium processes other than just those involving the discovery of the various conservations: perceptual equilibria, including the constancies and the Gestalt "good figures"; the sensory-motor group of displacements and the permanent-object schema; the formation of concrete-operational structures; and the transition from these to formal structures (*ibid.*, pp. 73-102). The development of the object concept in the sensory-motor period will suffice as an illustration (*ibid.*, pp. 86-89). Let A represent here the disappearance of an object

---

[11] A simpler explanation, one more in keeping with the reasoning about Step 1, might be that centering the second property necessarily becomes more probable as the number of trials increase (for the same reason that a run of 10 heads in coin flipping is less probable than a run of 5 heads), and no assumptions about subjective dissatisfaction and perceptual contrast need be invoked. Similar considerations may also apply to the Step-2-Step-3 and Step-3-Step-4 transitions. However, this is the author's explanation, not the one Piaget offers.

[12] "Covary" is a free but, we think, faithful-to-intent translation of *sont solidaires.*

from the visual field and B its reappearance. In early infancy (Step 1) the child centers only A, does not anticipate B, and presumably cannot differentiate between disappearance (a reversible change of position) and annihilation (an irreversible change of state). In Step 2 the child starts to search for the absent object (hence a beginning centration on B), but there is no systematic pairing of $A_1 - B_1$, $A_2 - B_2$, etc., with the result that the child may see the object disappear at A_2 and yet seek its reappearance at B_1, where he had retrieved the object previously (see Chapter 4). In Step 3 the coordination between $A - B$ couples starts to become systematic, and in Step 4 it becomes completely systematic and general; there is a discoverable B for each A, even in the face of invisible displacements. It is apparent that the basic sequence $(A$ or $B) \rightarrow (A$ and $B) \rightarrow [(A_1$ and $B_1)$ and $(A_2$ and $B_2)$, etc.] can be roughly fitted to this development.

This completes our sketch of the main elements of Piaget's equilibrium theory. Although his preoccupation with an equilibrium conception of evolving structures has been with him since the earliest days, we have seen two more recent developments in his theorizing. (1) He has tried to give a more precise and explicit characterization of what psychological equilibrium *states* are, and the dimensions along which they can be compared and contrasted. (2) He has attempted to explain the equilibration *process* itself in terms of a four-step, probabilistic model. By and large, Piaget's has been a theory of states rather than of mechanisms of transition; for this reason the equilibration model, whatever its shortcomings,[13] is a particularly significant addition to the system.

GENETIC EPISTEMOLOGY

The average psychologist, one suspects, has a hazy image of a number of aspects of Piaget's life and work. But in one respect the image as-

[13] A general question about the equilibrium model may have occurred to the reader: what is the *locus* of the postulated four-step equilibration sequence, that is, what extra-laboratory, real-life experiences constitute the medium through which a given equilibration process proceeds? In the case of the object concept, just discussed, it is perhaps not too difficult to imagine the child evolving through something like these four steps in the course of daily contacts with objects which disappear from and reappear in the visual-motor field. However, it is a good deal more difficult to imagine the experiential milieu for, say, the equilibration of conservation concepts. Piaget seems to phrase the equilibrium model for conservation as though the process were located *in the conservation experiment itself*, although it is hardly credible that he could really intend this (e.g., there is the obvious fact that many older subjects enter the experimental situation already possessing the Step 4 strategy). Actually, this question of locus is part of a larger, very crucial problem for the developmental psychology of cognition: *how* and *where*, in the stream of everyday experiencing, do children acquire the many and diverse concepts which Piaget has shown they do not possess *a priori*. Piaget and his associates have addressed themselves to aspects of this central problem (e.g., 1959c), but little real progress has been made on it so far. The problem clearly concerns the equilibrium state, and especially, the equilibration-process models under discussion, because an adequate assessment of them has to await precisely this progress.

sumes great sharpness and clarity: everyone who has heard of Piaget at all identifies him with the field of child psychology. Indeed, he is probably regarded as Mr. Child Psychology, at least for the Continent. It is therefore rather startling to realize that Piaget does not see himself in quite this role. He regards himself as above all an *epistemologist,* one interested in the complex relation between knower and known and, more particularly, a *genetic epistemologist,* interested, in the very broadest possible sense, in historical-developmental changes in this knower-known relation. It is the business of this capstone section on Piaget's theory to summarize some of the things he thinks about when he is explicitly wearing his genetic epistemological hat. Even more than in the case of the equilibration-equilibrium model, it must then be clear that genetic epistemology is not a "topic" or an "area" within Piaget's theory as a whole (see footnote 2), and to force it within the confines of a single chapter section is an artifice of exposition. There ought to be a way to describe all the interrelated elements of a complex theoretical system like Piaget's simultaneously rather than seriatim, in parallel rather than in series. This section really owes its life as a separate entity only to the impossibility of doing this.

One *caveat* before we proceed. As will become evident when we examine it, the bibliography of Piaget and his associates which explicitly comes under the heading of genetic epistemology runs close to a million words! Even allowing for the expected redundancies, this is much more content than half a chapter could possibly swallow. Our strategy, then, is to substitute a quick guided tour—what the subject is all about and where the interested reader can go to learn more about it, a selected sampling of problems and proposed solutions, and so forth—for the really systematic and substantive coverage it ought to have.

Introduction

There is probably no simple definition of *genetic epistemology* which would allow one to forecast all the things Piaget studies under this rubric. In fact, it is possible to read well into his genetic epistemological writings without feeling sure of the common denominator which runs through it all; almost in the "intelligence-is-what-the-IQ-test-measures" pattern, genetic epistemology is liable to impress one, at least in beginning reading, as meaning whatever Piaget chooses to talk about in articles and books containing these words in the title. But if a single definition will not suffice, it is possible to give a good general understanding in several paragraphs, looking at the topic from different perspectives, trying to classify and order its contents, and so on.

One initial handle on genetic epistemology can be gotten by thinking of it as *applied developmental psychology.* At least the majority of

Piaget's work in this area involves the systematic application of his own developmental findings, not to the practical problem of rearing children —one's first connotation of the word *applied* in this context, perhaps— but to a variety of classical epistemological problems. This is a most unusual (and most ambitious) kind of applied psychology; although all psychology can perhaps be thought of as at least implicitly epistemological, few psychologists indeed construe their life work to be a systematic and explicit bringing-to-bear of psychological theory and data on traditional epistemological problems.

This approach to a definition begins to take on some flesh in the following passage:

> From this point of view, one could define genetic epistemology in a broader and more general way as the study of the mechanisms whereby bodies of knowledge grow. The essential function of this discipline would then be to analyze, in all areas involving the genesis or elaboration of scientific bodies of knowledge, the passage from states of lesser knowledge to states of more advanced knowledge. In a word, genetic epistemology would constitute an application, to the study of bodies of knowledge, of the experimental method . . . (1957b, p. 14).

What areas does Piaget have in mind when he speaks of applying a developmental analysis to "all areas involving the genesis and elaboration of scientific bodies of knowledge"? Essentially two. (1) Piaget means to include the growth of knowledge in the various major sciences themselves (including logic and mathematics). (2) He has in mind the growth of knowledge in ontogenesis. Thus, both collective and individual cognitive evolutions fall within the pale of genetic epistemological analysis. Let us examine the latter first.

Piaget regards the ontogenetic development of cognitive (and interpersonal-affective) structures as of intrinsic epistemological interest. To gain a real understanding of the important forms of the knower-known relationship in the adult human cognizer (the central concern of classical epistemology), it is essential to grasp the developmental precursors of these forms. Moreover, for Piaget these developmental precursors are no less genuine and no less worthy of epistemological study because of their transitoriness. Thus, developmental study is more than just a tool for the analysis of epistemological problems in the public sciences, or even of epistemological problems in the individual adult; its findings are *per se* epistemological data. This thoroughgoing epistemological orientation towards developmental data themselves makes two things clear. (1) It explains why Piaget has been primarily interested in the acquisition of concepts like classes, relations, number, space, time, and so forth: these "grand and fundamental categories of experience," as we referred to them earlier (p. 35), are precisely the sorts of things someone who regards developmental events within an epistemological frame of reference would choose to study. (2) It brings into focus something very important about how Piaget looks at his developmental findings: the facts of cognitive development form a *subset* within the broader discipline of genetic epistemology.

Genetic epistemology is, therefore, not just a side interest within the totality of Piaget's developmental investigations; rather, the entire corpus of developmental work is seen as something subsumed—as subclass to class—within the larger field of genetic epistemology. (Recall now our earlier remarks on the artificiality of a chapter section entitled "genetic epistemology.") This explains the fact that probably the best single reference for the details of Piaget's purely developmental investigations is his three-volume book entitled *Introduction à l'épistémologie génétique* (1950b). And it follows from this that a good grasp of his developmental theory and data puts one in the best possible position to understand his epistemological thinking.

Ontogenesis itself, then, forms one part of the content of Piaget's genetic epistemology. The remainder, more heterogeneous, can be roughly divided into two components: (1) the application of developmental theory and facts to selected aspects of the history of scientific knowledge; (2) what might be termed the *epistemological status,* again analyzed within a developmental framework, of various kinds of scientific knowledge. In both these types of analysis—diachronic and synchronic —the scientific content studied is drawn largely from the disciplines of mathematics (logical and spatial knowledge included), physics (and occasionally chemistry), biology, psychology, and sociology.

In the history-of-science component the "applied developmental psychology" connotation assumes particular vividness. Piaget will take a concept from a given scientific field, e.g., the concept of *force* in physics (1950b, Vol. II, pp. 62-68), and analyze how its scientific meaning has changed from Greek or pre-Greek times to the present. He then attempts to show crucial parallels between historical and ontogenetic evolutions of this concept: for example, in both evolutions there is a progressive shedding of egocentric adherences, rooted in personal experience of bodily effort, in favor of an objective conception which is independent of self. The subject of his historicodevelopmental analysis may be broader than a single concept, such as force; that is, it may subtend a group of interrelated concepts or even a whole field of knowledge, e.g., historical changes in the nature and conception of mathematics (1950b, Vol. I, ch. 3). But whatever the content, the general strategy is to apply the constructs of his developmental theory (progressive equilibration, egocentrism, decentration, and reversibility, etc.) to the historical process, the latter construed as an evolution *across* a number of adult minds at least partially analyzable in the same terms as the evolution *within* a single immature one. There is thus a strong "ontogenesis-recapitulates-history" strain in Piaget's thinking, a symptom of which, for example, is his allusion to the embryology-comparative anatomy relation in biology as analogous to the ontogenesis-history relation he predicates for genetic epistemology (*ibid.*, Vol. I, pp. 12-18).

What remains of genetic epistemological content when development itself and development as applied to history are excluded? A good deal, actually, but there seems to be no satisfactory generic term for it all. Once again, a twofold classification exhausts most of this diffuse remainder: (1) epistemological analysis of knowledge *within* a particular scientific field; (2) an epistemologically oriented analysis of the interrelations *among* the various scientific fields. Here as elsewhere, developmental data and theory continue to supply the pedal point.

The easiest way to convey a general feeling for subtype (1) is take one of these fields and enumerate a few questions which Piaget regards as important for genetic epistemological analysis. Mathematics will do as an example (*ibid.*, Vol. I). One central question Piaget asks about mathematics can be roughly phrased as follows. Mathematical thought, which has its developmental origins in concrete subject-reality interchanges, is eventually able to transcend reality entirely, to create, by a rigorous deductive process, an indefinite array of systems which go far beyond anything in perceived reality. And yet, despite their deductive, reality-independent mode of construction, they are surprisingly useful in describing reality (mathematical models, etc.); indeed, they often seem to anticipate a reality not yet discovered, e.g., Riemannian geometry and Einsteinian physics. How can we explain this dual character of mathematics: a deductive fecundity which needs no reality sanctions for its constructions and yet what seems almost to be a preestablished harmony with this same reality? Other questions include these. What is the developmental origin of number, particularly as regards the subject-object (epistemological) relations which engender it? What is the origin and epistemological status of logical notions? Of spatial concepts? Is number reducible to logical operations of class and relation, as Whitehead and Russell maintained, or is it more an emergent, with qualities peculiarly its own?

This is only a sample of the problems Piaget feels are important for a genetic epistemology of mathematical knowledge. Similarly, there are parallel questions in the other fields—physics, biology, and the rest. In addressing himself to questions of this sort, Piaget is likely to draw upon the other categories of our crude taxonomy: developmental presentation *per se,* history-of-science parallels, and the relations between scientific fields.

As we said, Piaget's genetic epistemological analyses bear not only on the separate scientific fields themselves but also on the relations among them. This comparative analysis takes two major forms. (1) Piaget is concerned with comparing the epistemological origin and status of knowledge in the different fields. Although knowledge of any kind always involves contributions from both subject and object (an indissociable union of assimilation and accommodation), the relative weights of the contributions differ from field to field. Thus, the role of the subject looms large in logic-mathematics, both in the development of elementary numerical and logical concepts in the child and in the creative activity of the adult logician and mathematician. Piaget feels this is less true in physics, and still less true in biology (e.g., 1950b, Vol. III, pp. 286-295). (2) Piaget has attempted to interrelate the fields themselves, showing how a given discipline supports and is supported by another. For example, logic-mathematics is itself the product of the activity of a human subject and hence rests on psychology; however, psychological activity can in turn be modeled by logical-mathematical structures (e.g., Piaget's groupings as models for child cognition). As we shall describe later, Piaget believes that the relationship structure of the major sciences takes the form of a circle: logic-mathematics—physics—biology—psychology (and sociology)—logic-mathematics (ibid., Conclusions).

There are three sets of bibliographic sources for Piaget's genetic epistemological work, one minor and two major. The minor one consists of some half-dozen or more journal articles written on the subject over the years (e.g., 1924a, 1925b, 1929a, 1947, 1952f, 1953c). One of the two major sources is Piaget's three-volume Introduction à l'épistémologie génétique (1950b). Although much of this work is difficult reading, there is no doubt but that it is the central source. Virtually everything Piaget has said anywhere on the topic can be found, in germ or in full, somewhere in these three volumes. One gets the impression that it was written to set forth, at leisure and in detail, the many ideas on genetic epistemology which Piaget accumulated over the years (one can see some of these ideas in the earlier articles just mentioned) and also to provide an organized conceptual context for further work in the area.

This latter aim found its realization in what constitutes the second major source: the continuing series of monographs which report the work of Piaget's Centre International d'Epistémologie Génétique.[14] Each monograph contains theoretical and experimental papers by several different authors (Piaget himself is often one of them). The monographic output varies from year to year: for example, four monographs for 1955-1956 (the first year the Centre operated), two for 1956-1957, four again for 1957-1958, and so on. Although the contents of the monographs so far published are extremely heterogeneous, they do try to follow a loose topical organization. The first ten are concerned with one or another problem involving the development of logical structures. The first four of these ten take up general matters, including the relation of

[14] For a brief description of the origin and activity of he Centre, see Introduction.

language to logic (Beth, Mays, and Piaget, 1957; Apostel, Mandelbrot, and Piaget, 1957; Apostel, Mandelbrot, and Morf, 1957; Apostel, Mays, Morf, and Piaget, 1957). The next two involve primarily comparisons between logical and perceptual structures (Jonckheere, Mandelbrot, and Piaget, 1958; Bruner, Bresson, Morf, and Piaget, 1958). And the remaining four concern the relation between logic and learning (Gréco and Piaget, 1959; Apostel, Jonckheere, and Matalon, 1959; Morf, Smedslund, Vinh-Bang, and Wohlwill, 1959; Goustard, Gréco, Matalon, and Piaget, 1959). Other volumes are (or will be) devoted to epistemological problems concerning the development of number concepts (Gréco, Grize, Papert, and Piaget, 1960).

The monograph series differs from the earlier three-volume work in several ways. Involving as it does the contributions of a number of people of differing professional background and orientation, the series is less homogeneously Piagetian in frame of reference and more diverse in style and content. Within the very broad constraints of the defined area of study for a given year, the contributors write from their own interests and current work, theoretical or experimental, Piagetian or not. A number of papers would command the interest of people who are not the slightest bit interested in Piaget and his work (e.g., Mandelbrot, 1957b). And for those interested in keeping up with new developments in Piaget's system (with or without particular interest in its epistemological overtones), the monograph series is a prime source in two respects. First, it is the likeliest repository for the latest in Piaget's theorizing, e.g., the work on the equilibrium model (Piaget, 1957c), new ways of looking at perceptual structures (Piaget and Morf, 1958a, 1958b), and so on. Second, it includes some exciting experiments not reported elsewhere in Piaget's publications, for instance, studies which try to determine the kinds of learning experiences which facilitate the child's acquisition of logical class inclusion, conservation and transitivity of weight, and conservation of number (Morf, Smedslund, Vinh-Bang, and Wohlwill, 1959).

Sample Problems in Genetic Epistemology

The remainder of this chapter section will take up, very briefly and superficially, selected examples of Piaget's epistemological thinking: first, a few instances of his historicodevelopmental approach; second, something of his analyses of specific forms of knowledge; and finally, "the circle of sciences"—his conception of the relations among scientific fields.

THE HISTORICODEVELOPMENTAL APPROACH

One sample of this type of analysis has already been given above: historical and developmental parallels in the evolution of the physical concept of force. There are a number of others, primarily in the fields of mathematics and physics. The basic developmental scheme which Piaget applies to all of them is essentially that described in Chapter 2 (pp. 61-63) of this book. Any evolution, historical or ontogenetic, begins in a state of relative egocentrism and phenomenism: on the one hand, the subject cognizes only what is immediately apparent and obvious in things, i.e., just a few surface characteristics (phenomenism); on the other hand, he is unable to assess the contributions of his own perspective to the way things appear; he cannot turn his intellectual instruments back upon himself so as to make his own cognitions an object of critical inspection (egocentrism).[15] It is the work of development to correct this initial egocentrism-phenomenism in two ways (e.g., 1950b, Vol. III, pp. 295-306). Phenomenism gives way to a progressive *construction*: the subject penetrates more deeply and more extensively into the object of his cognition. And egocentrism is replaced by *reflection;* the subject rethinks and restructures aspects of an object of thought "constructed" earlier, critically reanalyzes his initial assumptions about these aspects, and in general submits his earlier cognitions to a searching *prise de conscience*.

Piaget finds this basic evolutionary process at work throughout the history of mathematics and physics (1950b, Vols. I and II). Thus, he sees an essential egocentrism and phenomenism in the naive realism of Greek mathematics: numbers are properties of the real world, geometry is the study of real space, and so on. And the subsequent history of mathematics is viewed as a dual progression towards construction and reflection. For the first, the breadth and depth of mathematical entities has burgeoned enormously, e.g., to positive whole numbers are eventually added negatives, fractions, irrationals, imaginaries, transfinites, etc. The second is seen especially clearly in modern attempts to clarify the nature and foundation of mathematics itself. Mathematical entities long since constructed are reflected on and questioned. What are these entities and how do they relate to the real world? What sort of knowledge is mathematical knowledge? And so on. In the same way, historical changes in cosmology parallel the decentration process in the growing child. In man's changing conception of the physical world there has been a progressive reorientation of perspectives, rethinking of fundaments, and continuous search for new and broader frames of reference from Aristotle through Copernicus and Newton to Einstein.

There is one particularly interesting historicodevelopmental comparison which we shall encounter again when we discuss the development of space in Chapter 10. Very briefly, in the history of mathematics Euclidean geometry was developed first, projective geometry later, and

---

[15] This reflexive, cognition-of-own-cognitions is frequently rendered in Piaget's writings by the phrase *prise de conscience*.

topology still later. In the development of the individual child, on the other hand, topological relations appear to be apprehended considerably in advance of both projective and Euclidean ones (Piaget and Inhelder, 1956). However, Piaget feels that this violation of the customary historico-developmental parallelism is less a violation than it appears and can also be explained by the construction-reflection hypothesis (Piaget, 1950b, Vol. I, pp. 236-242).

ANALYSES OF SPECIFIC FORMS OF KNOWLEDGE

The analysis of specific forms of knowledge within a developmental framework can probably be taken as the core of Piaget's genetic epistemology. It is certainly true that his recent endeavors, expressed in the work of the Centre, have been almost completely oriented in this direction. Like the historicodevelopmental aspects, this exceedingly complex and detailed portion of his genetic epistemological writings is amenable to a degree of ordering and systematizing. The general argument which sustains his efforts here is essentially this (e.g., 1957b, pp. 13-23). There is nothing new about genetic epistemology as such; a number of thinkers over the centuries have founded their solutions to epistemological problems on implicit or explicit assumptions about how the individual mind functions and, especially, develops. But these assumptions have been made without the benefit of a systematic body of developmental facts, facts which adult introspection, however acute and sensitive, simply cannot supply. Moreover, the needed developmental facts have to be of a kind really useful to an epistemological analysis; developmental studies have to be planned with an eye towards eventual application to epistemological problems. Here the lack of a fruitful marriage between epistemology and developmental psychology becomes acutely apparent: the typical child psychologist (Piaget is faintly derisive in his use of this term) is usually as ignorant of how his work might be tailored to epistemological problems as the epistemologist is ignorant of whatever developmental facts already exist for his use.

Piaget's professional dream (probably his principal one) is to catalyze this liaison between the two fields; the animus behind the writing of his three-volume work and the founding of the Centre seems to have been just that. So far as specific, within-fields epistemological problems are concerned, he generally proceeds to effect this liaison in the following way. He selects a problem to which genetic epistemological solutions have been offered in the past and then critically analyzes these solutions. A typical problem of this kind is likely to concern the origin of one or another fundamental form of knowledge, e.g., the apprehension of space, of number, of motion and speed, and the like. Piaget generally finds that previous solutions, lacking as they do the crucial developmental facts on the question at hand, tend to be oversimplified, lean too much towards pure apriorism or empiricism, and so on. He then offers his own solution to the problem, drawing on the Geneva experimental research to support his arguments.[16]

It is not necessary to cite examples at length to indicate that a fair number of Piaget's solutions here would likely surprise many epistemologists, ancient and modern; once again, armchair speculation is a poor substitute for empirical study. The very fact that certain knowledge forms require a step-by-step development can come as a mild shock (is it common sense, for example, to think that 4-year-olds do *not* possess the notion of conservation of mass, weight, and volume?). And where the mere fact of development fails to surprise, its form, complexity, or ontogenetic duration may.

Thus, we learn from Piaget's investigations that the fundamental concept of an enduring object is not only something which needs acquiring but is acquired, slowly and in successive stages, only at the term of infancy (see Chapter 4). We further learn that Piaget finds it necessary to break down a seemingly simple and unitary acquisition like, say, our apprehension of Euclidean space ("seeing" the world of objects within the framework of a "grid" of horizontals and verticals) into two acquisitions: a perceptual one in infancy and a representational one which does not get constituted until well into middle childhood (e.g., 1950b, Vol. I, pp. 215-217). And we learn that the concept of time is also a complex and multifaceted acquisition: the child begins with a heterogeny of "times," one for each separate action, and only later establishes a homogeneous temporal medium common to all events; the evolution of temporal concepts is thoroughly entangled with those of movement, velocity, and space; and so on (e.g., 1950b, Vol. II, pp. 18-48).

There are, of course, many other examples, but they all fall within the common paradigm: critical examination of past and present epistemological analyses of a given knowledge form, then his own analysis, buttressed by his own developmental investigations. Needless to say, Piaget has done his epistemologically oriented experimental studies on his own initiative; the picture of Piaget being commissioned to do experiments by epistemologists panting for developmental data is ludicrous in the extreme. And yet something rather like this happened some years ago, an episode which Piaget, not surprisingly, is very fond of recounting (1946a, p. v; 1950b, Vol. II, p. 45; 1957b, pp. 53-56).

In classical mechanics, time is taken as a fundamental notion and velocity as something derived from it (thus, velocity $= \dfrac{\text{space traversed}}{\text{time}}$).

---

[16] By no means all of Piaget's arguments in this area appear as clear and straightforward inferences from developmental data—clear and straightforward in the sense that anyone, given his data, would make the same arguments. And at least a minority of his arguments seem to derive from his findings only in the loosest possible sense (Chapter 12).

In relativity theory, on the other hand, velocity is taken as a first given, and temporal duration is seen as relative to it. In 1928, Einstein suggested that Piaget undertake developmental studies to find out whether an intuition of velocity depends upon a prior comprehension of temporal duration or whether it is constituted independently of the latter. Piaget accepted the "commission" and, characteristically, did two books' worth of research on this and related problems (1946a, 1946b). What he found, very briefly, was this. Velocity does in fact appear to be the more primitive acquisition, and in the early stages estimations of time seem to be in part a function of velocity. But velocity, as adults conceive it, is not a primary datum either. Initially, estimations of velocity depend upon relations of spatial order; for the young child the word *faster* appears to mean simply "being ahead," "passing," and so on (thus, an object placed near the center of a wheel is judged to be moving at the same speed as one on the outside, because neither gets "ahead of" or "passes" the other). The anecdote does not quite end here. Another physicist, named Abelé, has seized upon these experimental results as a basis for rethinking aspects of relativity theory (Piaget, 1957b, p. 56); it goes without saying that this is precisely the kind of use of his findings Piaget, the genetic epistemologist, would most hope for.

THE CIRCLE OF SCIENCES

As indicated earlier, Piaget is interested not only in developmental origins of knowledge forms *within* the various scientific disciplines but also in the interrelations *among* the disciplines themselves. His thinking here is set out in some detail in the systematic work (1950b, Vol. III, Conclusions) and more briefly elsewhere (1957b, pp. 80-84). In order to grasp his conception of how the sciences interrelate, it is necessary to do some preliminary defining of terms. First, Piaget distinguishes between two kinds of relations between events: *causal* and *implicative*. The customary connotations will serve for causal relations; but the implicative relations need comment. Piaget asserts that the relations between mental states—states of consciousness—are implicative rather than causal. Just as in logic one would say that $(A = B) + (B = C)$ implies, rather than causes $(A = C)$, so also one idea in consciousness is said to imply rather than cause another; one value implies rather than causes another, and so on. The second distinction concerns relations, not between events, but between scientific domains. Where the relation is a deductive, theoretical-model-to-experimental-data one, Piaget refers to it as a relation of parallelism, isomorphism, or simply, *correspondence*. If, on the other hand, the relation takes the form of using one set of physical events to explain or "reduce" another, it is a relation of *interdependence*. Thus, for example, mathematics relates to physics by correspondence, and physics relates to biology by interdependence.

Piaget's basic assertion about the relations among the major sciences is that they form, not one or another kind of linear hierarchy, but a *circular* structure: a relationship line whose origin is logic-mathematics will extend to physics-chemistry, then to biology, then to psychology-sociology, and from there will close the circle by returning to logic-mathematics again. The specific connections between adjoining sciences on this circle are essentially these.

First, logic-mathematics relates to physics-chemistry by correspondence —a deductive system of implications isomorphic to an empirical system of causes. Conversely, physics-chemistry relates to biology by interdependence; one causal system (biology) can be "reduced" to another, more general and elementary one (physics-chemistry). The relation between biology and psychology-sociology is more complex. On the one hand, human behavior at large surely rests on physiology in the same sense that physiology rests on physics-chemistry. This relation of interdependence is also seen developmentally, that is, human intellectual activity can be said to rest ultimately upon neonatal ("biological") reflexes. However, the system of implications which comprises consciousness is exempted from this relation: in Piaget's view, the (implicative) system of conscious events is (or may turn out to be when we know more neurophysiology) in an isomorphic relation of correspondence with the (causal) system of neural events. Piaget's intense interest in current neurophysiological work, particularly any suggestion of a *logical* model of neural activity, derives from this view.

And finally, the relationship between psychology-sociology and logic-mathematics is also a double one. First, logic-mathematics can certainly model psychological-social behavior just as it can physicochemical events (relation of correspondence), e.g., the role of groupings, groups, and lattices in Piaget's theory. But also, logic-mathematics is itself a human construction and is thus linked by interdependence to psychology-sociology. It is really this relation which guarantees a circular structure, rather than, say, a simple, straight-line reduction of psychosocial to biological to physicochemical to logico-mathematical. This kind of reduction is of course part of the structure, but it is paralleled by a converse reduction of logico-mathematical to psychosocial to biological to physicochemical (in this sense, the ultimate source of logic and mathematics).[17] It is interesting that Piaget finds essentially the same circular structure, in microcosm, in the developing relation between individual subject and environment. The subject can know reality only by assimilating it to his mental structures, analogous to the assimilation of the physical sciences

[17] One clear implication of Piaget's circle-of-science conception would seem to be that no discipline has intrinsic claims to a "higher" or "more valid" knowledge than another; the reduction process is bidirectional, as we have just seen. This implication is consistent with Piaget's relativistic epistemological orientation generally, i.e., that "truth" is always the product of some assimilation-accommodation coordination.

to logic-mathematics. But it is also true that he can know himself only by gradually mastering the external world; he can understand the object which is himself only through successive assimilations-accommodations vis-à-vis external objects. This finds its parallel in macrocosm, Piaget believes, with the reduction of logic-mathematics and psychology-sociology to the physical sciences.

GENERAL SUMMARY

The contents of what we have been calling Piaget's "theory" can be segregated into three rough classes, and our summary is organized around these. The first class includes what may be referred to as Piaget's *metatheory:* primarily, the values, conceptual orientation, goals and means, and the like, which help to explain the why, what, and how of his research activities. The second class comprises the *stage-independent* aspects of the theory, i.e., the aspects which concern the nature of the human subject in general and the nature of his development in general. The third class is the complement of the second: the *stage-dependent-*conceptions of the growing subject—the structural *quale* of the various developmental epochs Piaget has identified.

Metatheory

The definition of Piaget's over-all scientific aim given in Chapter 1 is still a good one: the theoretical and experimental investigation of the qualitative development of intellectual structures. A proper exegesis of the nouns and adjectives in this statement covers most of what is important about Piaget's metatheory. Let us begin at the end and work backwards.

Both Piaget's holism and his conception of an active subject lead him to look to organized mental *structures* as the proper units of developmental analysis. Moreover, most of his work has been oriented towards structures which are intellectual in the broad sense, although we have seen that perceptual and, to a lesser extent, interpersonal-affective structures have also come under investigation. The expression *qualitative development* calls to mind these important facts: that Piaget is above all interested in ontogenetic changes in structure; that these structural changes are seen as qualitative in nature (although taking place gradually and continuously); and that he feels justified, for purposes of analysis, in sectioning ontogenesis into periods, subperiods, and stages in terms of the kinds of structures present.

Chapter 1 has shown that *experimental investigation* has a variety of meanings in Piaget's system. The heterogeneity of theoretical concepts is matched by a heterogeneity of methodologies: observation of ongoing behavior; the clinical method in all its variations from the early verbally-oriented to the later performance-oriented techniques; and the special adaptations of this method for use in perceptual experiments. A single theme underlying all methodological variations, however, is a passion to get at and into the processes involved in this one subject at this one moment; considerations of standardization of technique, sampling, and the like are distinctly secondary to this one aim.

And finally, the term *theoretical* in the statement suggests at least two important things about Piaget's system. (1) It directly suggests that Piaget is far from content simply to do experiments and state the facts or low-order generalizations which the results suggest. On the contrary, he is more given to elaborate theoretical reworking of findings than perhaps anyone in psychology; indeed, if there is one "idiosyncrasy of the system" (see Chapter 1) which is likely to catch the eye in reading Piaget, it is the ubiquitous high ratio of theoretical discussion to data presentation. And (2) the present chapter has made clear the kind of theorizing Piaget is most invested in (from which follows, as the chapter has also made clear, the kind of empirical investigations he is most likely to do): the interpretation of developmental events within an epistemological, theory-of-knowledge framework. This last, more than anything else, is the key to questions of why, what, and how.

Stage-Independent Theory

The fundamental questions on which the stage-independent aspects of Piaget's theory center are two. (1) "What sort of device" [18] is the human cognizer, not at any particular stage, but basically and generally? (2) What are the general principles by which the subject—granted a conception of the sort of device he is—changes his state in the course of development? For want of better labels ("static" versus "dynamic" would suggest unwanted meanings here) we call these the *synchronic* and *diachronic* questions, respectively.

THE SYNCHRONIC QUESTION

Piaget's answer to this question is in all essentials given in his organization-adaptation conception. The basic equipment of any knower at any stage consists of the biologically given functional invariants of organization and adaptation (assimilation and accommodation). The subject is construed to be an ever organized entity which accommodates its schemas (the basic units of this organization) to external reality as it

[18] There is something to be said for good rephrasings of old questions; the author owes this one to Roger Brown (personal communication). With its connotations of "instrument-with-structure," "computer," and the like, it catches very well Piaget's conception of Man Thinking.

assimilates the reality to the schemas. This basic state (the fact of organization) and this basic process (the fact of assimilation and accommodation) are really the only apriorities which Piaget feels it necessary to assume.[19] All other cognitive possessions, including knowledge forms which many might regard as the very axioms of cognition, are the products of the operation of these invariants over time. Thus, the organization of space, objects, and other fundaments of human experience are not given at the outset but are constructed in the course of complex and interesting evolutions well worth the study.

But if Piaget gives little succor to extreme aprioristic conceptions, he certainly gives no more to extreme empiricism, if anything, less, since he quite correctly judges it to be the more powerful (and hence, to his mind, dangerous) influence in contemporary psychology. In Piaget's scheme of things, assimilation is the full equal of accommodation; in fact, for certain kinds of acquisitions (logico-mathematical, particularly) it appears to have a tacit superiority. All in all, there is no doubt but that *l'homme piagetien* is assigned a very, very active role in the formation of his own cognitive world. There is, of course, nothing basically new or startling about Piaget's epistemological position here; certainly obeisance to "organism-environment interaction," coupled with appropriate epithets against a *tabula rasa* empiricism, is an OK position in contemporary psychology if there ever was one. What is sometimes startling, however, is the detail, scope, and sheer vigor and freshness which Piaget brings to it in interpreting his data.

THE DIACHRONIC QUESTION

Across a childhood of continuous operation of the functional invariants, arises a succession of discontinuous cognitive structures. This is the heart and essence of cognitive development. The question then is, what are the principal attributes of this development? They are fairly easy to summarize. First, cognitive behavior is at all levels a matter of subject actions performed on reality; and one characteristic of the developmental process is that these actions become progressively internalized and covert. Second, assimilation and accommodation, while remaining invariant as existents, show an increasing differentiation and complementation as development proceeds. And both these attributes are part of a more general one, i.e., the progressive equilibration of cognitive actions discussed earlier in this chapter. The sequence of cognitive structures becomes, in this interpretation, a sequence of equilibrium-state "moments" within an ongoing, continuous process of equilibration. Each structure integrates its predecessor to form a new and higher form of equilibrium,

---

[19] One is tempted to add Piaget's "cognitive-need-to-function" as another apriority; however, he sees cognitive motivation as indigenous to the organization-adaptation invariants, not really something to be listed as a separate factor.

"higher" in terms of the equilibrial properties of field extension, mobility, permanence, and stability (the increasing reversibility, of which Piaget speaks so often, is subsumable under this last property). And finally, the fact that the subject typically equilibrates his actions on one plane before another and, on the same plane, for one content before another, gets expressed in the concepts of vertical and horizontal *décalage,* respectively.

Stage-Dependent Theory

The stage-dependent theory picks up where the stage-independent one leaves off: given a coherent picture of the general "sort of device" the subject is and the general principles which guide his development, it remains to show the actual succession of genetic steps. Piaget divides the ontogenetic span into three major epochs, called *periods,* with various *subperiods, stages,* and *substages* within these.[20] It should be recalled that the *sequence* of these developmental steps is thought to be invariant, while the *chronological age* at which each occurs is definitely not.

THE PERIOD OF SENSORY-MOTOR INTELLIGENCE (0-2 YEARS)

Cognitive evolution begins at birth with the first application of neonatal reflexes. At the term of the sensory-motor period, these crude and simple structures have metamorphized into a rich and complex network of schemas for organizing concrete subject-object interchanges. This metamorphosis can be described in several ways. First, it is a movement from a profound self-world undifferentiation—the ultimate egocentrism—to a relative differentiation of self and object in which both are objectified and spatialized. And like all subdevelopments in ontogeny, it is a process of coming-into-equilibrium of assimilation and accommodation; the cognitive structures which eventuate during the period are therefore well equilibrated, relative to their limited (sensory-motor actions) field of application. The concrete intellectual accomplishments of the period can be divided into a set of general acquisitions and a set of specific or special ones. The general ones are described in the language of primary, secondary, and tertiary circular reactions, the intercoordination of schemas in means-ends relationships, the trial-and-error discovery and insightful invention of new means, and the like. The special developments of the period entail important accomplishments concerning objects, space, time, causality, imitation, and play. All developmental events in

[20] Because it does not show the clear structure-to-structure evolution which intelligence does, Piaget does not speak of periods and stages of perceptual development. There is development here, however, and it consists primarily of an increase in the vigor and scope of perceptual activity, which gives the subject a partial (but never complete) autonomy from irreversible centration effects.

this period, general and special, are mutually dependent on one another for their formation: a fact Piaget tries to bring home by using a single six-stage paradigm as a common frame for all developmental description. And finally, this period witnesses the early evolution of perception as a subset within the totality of sensory-motor actions; in particular, the perceptual constancies achieve most of their development in this era.

THE PERIOD OF PREPARATION FOR AND ORGANIZATION OF CONCRETE
OPERATIONS (2-11 YEARS)

This long period commences with the first representational activity of the toddler and ends when concrete-operational structures get firmly entrenched in late middle childhood. The preparation phase, the subperiod of what Piaget calls *preoperations,* occupies roughly the first half of the period. During this phase the child's representational thought first takes wing, with all the attendant distortions and instabilities that its sensory-motor ancestry can bestow: concreteness, phenomenism, irreversibility, egocentrism, animism, preconcepts, and transductive reasoning. Piaget's list is a long one. With the gradual constitution of the concrete-operational structures-in-equilibrium, particularly the grouping structures, the world of representations begins to take on its first real stability, coherence, and order. One of the prime expressions of this new-found equilibrium is the conservation of certain object properties in the face of phenomenal change: conservation of quantity, weight, volume, length, area, and all the rest. The invariance which the sensory-motor period won for the whole object the concrete-operational subperiod wins for its attributes.

THE PERIOD OF FORMAL OPERATIONS (11-15 YEARS)

The culmination of each major period is the equilibration of some kind of behavioral system. For the first, it is the equilibration of external, sensory and motor actions. For both the second and the third, it is the equilibration of internal, symbolic-representational operations. The only essential difference here concerns the kind of internal operations which get equilibrated. For the second, it is first-degree operations whose content is concrete reality itself; these operations consist of classifying this reality, serially ordering it, denumerating it, and so on. For the third, on the other hand, it is second-degree operations whose content is, not the raw externae, but the aforementioned first-degree operations themselves. By operating upon these, treating them not as realities but as conditionals which are grist for free conceptual manipulation, representational thought has taken a new and important turn: it has become hypothetico-deductive, oriented towards possibility as the supraordinate term and towards reality as the subordinate term. The structures which serve this new orientation are no longer groupings but lattices and groups, in particular the group of four transformations and the lattice of all-possible-combinations. And the behavioral result of the new orientation and its structural concomitants is the mastery of a wide variety of problems beyond the capabilities of the child of middle years.

Part Two

THE EXPERIMENTS

CHAPTER EIGHT

The Early Work

In Part II, Chapters 8, 9, and 10 are organized around the contents of Piaget's experimental books, with each book allotted one chapter section (the final section of Chapter 10, on perception, is an exception). Thus, Chapter 8 consists of five chapter sections and summarizes the experimental work reported in Piaget's early volumes on language and thought (1926), judgment and reasoning (1928b), reality (1929c), causality (1930a), and moral judgment (1932). Chapter 9 deals with subsequent studies of quantity (Piaget and Inhelder, 1941), logic (Piaget and Inhelder, 1959), number (Piaget, 1952b), time (Piaget, 1946a), and movement and velocity (Piaget, 1946b). Chapter 10 continues with space (Piaget and Inhelder, 1956), measurement (Piaget, Inhelder, and Szeminska, 1960), chance (Piaget and Inhelder, 1951), adolescent reasoning (Inhelder and Piaget, 1958), and perception. Chapter 11 departs from this book-per-section format to describe a miscellany of later work, some by Piaget and associates and some by researchers outside the Genevan circle. Since many of these investigations bear on the validity of Piaget's theory and experimental findings, Chapter 11 may be regarded as transitional between Part II and Part III, which is concerned with assessment and critique of Piaget's work.

The five books to be discussed in this chapter are still the best known of Piaget's writings. Translated into English early in Piaget's career, these were the books which made him a world figure in the field. In general, the books describe a variety of observations and experiments on developmental changes in thinking from early childhood through early adolescence. They particularly focus on comparisons between what would later be schematized as preoperational and concrete-operational thought; hence, the chapters in Part I which provide the relevant theoretical background here are Chapters 4 and 5. Piaget's theory did not explicitly take on its mathematical-and-physical-model character (groupings, groups, lattices, equilibrium states, etc.) until the late 1930's. Therefore, the experiments of these early books are interpreted within a loosely interrelated system of verbal-theoretical concepts: *egocentrism, juxtaposition, syncretism, animism, realism,* and *prise de conscience* are just a few. Of these probably the central one is *egocentrism.* Most of the developmental changes these books describe either are or could be interpreted in terms of a gradual replacement of egocentric thought by socialized thought in the growing child.[1]

It is important to recognize that the first four of these five volumes (i.e., 1926, 1928b, 1929c, 1930a) do form a loose class in terms of purpose and content. The first two (1926, 1928b) are intended to study the *formal* and *functional* aspects of child thought, particularly the kind of logic the child exhibits in a variety of situations. Actually, Piaget conceived these books, not as two separate works, but as making up a two-volume series entitled *Studies in Child Logic* (1926, p. xxi; 1929c, p. 2, footnote 1). And the last chapter of the second volume is a summary and theoretical synthesis of the work of both books. The third and fourth books (1929c, 1930a), on the other hand, form a unit devoted to how form and function get expressed—outwardly, as it were—in the *content* of the child's thought, in his specific ideas and beliefs about the world around him.[2] As with the first two books, the last chapter of the fourth book summarizes and interprets it and its predecessor's experimental studies. The fifth of the early books (1932) is a study of the child's moral-ethical judgments and beliefs and is not directly linked, as part of a series, with the other four.

It is generally true that at least some of the material found in any given "content book" is summarized or discussed (and occasionally, supplemented) in a number of journal articles. This is very much the case for the five volumes to be discussed in this chapter. Since some of the articles relevant to this work pertain to more than one of the five books, it makes sense simply to list them *en bloc* here, rather than to distribute them across the five sections of this chapter. The principal journal references for these early studies, then, are the following: Piaget, 1921a, 1921b, 1922, 1923, 1924a, 1924b, 1925a, 1925b, 1927b, 1927c, 1928a, 1929b, 1930b, 1930c, 1931a, 1931b, 1931c, 1934, 1935b, 1952g, 1958b; Krafft and Piaget, 1926; Margairaz and Piaget, 1925.

LANGUAGE AND THOUGHT

The major theme of *The Language and Thought of the Child* (and, in a sense, of all the early books) is that the child's cognitive structure,

---

[1] "We have sought to trace most of the characteristics of child logic to egocentrism; though of many of these it might just as well be said that their presence explains egocentrism" (1928b, p. 201).

[2] Piaget also thinks of the distinction between what we have called *general* and *special sensory-motor evolutions* (Chapters 3 and 4) in terms of the dichotomy we are discussing here: the formal-functional, "implicative" aspects (the general evolution) versus the contential, "explicative" aspects (the special evolutions).

the kind of logic his thinking possesses, gets expressed in his use of language. Thus, language behavior is here treated as the dependent variable with cognition as the independent variable; language is viewed essentially as a symptom of underlying intellectual orientation. The book opens with a question designed to get at one facet of the language-cognition relationship: what needs does the child satisfy when he uses language, that is, what functions does language serve in the life of the child (1926, p. 1)? In order to get a preliminary answer to this question, the verbal utterances of two children of six years of age were carefully recorded over a period of about one month as the children pursued various activities in a liberal kindergarten setting (Maison des Petits, the Institut J. J. Rousseau school where so much of Piaget's experimental work has been done). Piaget found it possible to categorize the recorded utterances into two major classes, with various subclasses within each of these. The first class is called *egocentric speech*. It is speech which, whether uttered in solitude or in the presence of others, is judged to lack a primary communicative aim; there is no real attempt to take the role of the listener and hence adapt the message to his informational needs or input capacity; indeed, there is no real attempt even to make sure he is listening. The second class is *socialized speech* and applies to utterances which do seem to possess a genuine communicative orientation, i.e., the child really tries to inform the listener, to persuade or coerce him to some course of action, etc. Piaget found that a surprisingly large proportion (nearly half) of the subjects' utterances could be classed as egocentric rather than socialized. That is, the data suggested that child language does serve other functions besides the communicative one, and that an analysis of these other functions may tell us something about the child's intellectual structure and orientation.

Chapter 2 describes two different studies. The first is a follow-up of the pilot study on two subjects reported in its first chapter. Piaget analyzed the verbal behavior of twenty children (average age of six) in the same way as that of the two and again found nearly half the utterances to be egocentric rather than socialized. The second study involves an analysis, not of isolated utterances by one child, but of conversations between two or more children. The unit of analysis now is a short series of utterances defining a verbal interchange among children. This study of conversations, unlike the preceding two, is explicitly developmental in aim. That is, Piaget attempts to delineate a rough stage-to-stage sequence in the genesis of conversation from age four to seven.[3] The stages are

---

[3] Throughout Part II we shall generally eschew critical comment on the relation between Piaget's presented evidence and his postulated stage sequences, i.e., we shall simply report these sequences as Piaget describes them, without trying to assess their empirical justification. There are, however, three comments which can be made here on this difficult problem of evidence: (1) that it clearly is a critical issue which continually crops up in Piaget's reported experiments; (2) that in the majority of cases Piaget does

three. Genuine interchanges are essentially absent in stage 1. The presence of others stimulates speech in the child, but this speech is egocentric, lacking a primary communicative intent. Thus, child A says something in the presence of child B without any apparent intention that B should hear and respond. Child B does not in fact seem to hear and respond but says something unrelated to what A has just said, etc. Egocentric "nonconversations" of this kind are called *collective monologues*. In stage 3, conversation becomes really intercommunicative; there is undeniable interchange of information. Where the tenor of the conversation is disagreement, there is genuine argument, with each participant attempting to support his position with causal explanation and logical justification. Where there is accord, one sees a bona fide collaboration of thought on a common topic, each participant attending to the contributions of the other. Stage 2 encompasses a variety of interactional forms transitional between stage 1 and stage 3, e.g., collaboration of thought on a common activity (as opposed to collaboration on a conversational topic), quarreling and primitive argument, and so on.

Piaget summarizes the experimental problem of Chapter 3 in this way:

> In the preceding chapters we have tried to determine to what extent children speak to each other and think socially. An essential problem has been left on one side: when children talk together, do they understand one another? This is the problem we are now to discuss (*ibid.*, p. 76).

In this study, one child is given a body of information by the experimenter and told to relate this information to a second child of the same age (between 6 and 8 years). The second child then communicates what he has understood back to the experimenter. Analyses of data and discussion of results were both quite involved and complex, but the gist of Piaget's findings and conclusions were two: (1) children in these age groups do not communicate material of this sort very clearly and effectively, primarily because, in their egocentrism, they fail to adapt to the role of the listener; (2) they do not understand very well information which is adequately imparted (although always under the illusion that they have understood), again because of egocentric factors. The verbal protocols obtained in this interesting but seldom-cited experiment point up these limitations most graphically. In one part of the study, the subject is told to communicate the following story to another child:

> Once upon a time, there was a lady who was called Niobe, and who had 12 sons and 12 daughters. She met a fairy who had only one son and no daughter. Then the lady laughed at the fairy because the fairy only had one

---

not report the kind of evidence which would permit an adequate assessment; (3) and perhaps most important, there is the very considerable problem of deciding what, exactly, should and should not constitute adequate empirical evidence for a stage-sequence interpretation of data, given some specification of what the term *stage* is intended to mean (see Chapters 11 and 12).

boy. Then the fairy was very angry and fastened the lady to a rock. The lady cried for ten years. In the end she turned into a rock, and her tears made a stream which still runs to-day (*ibid.,* p. 82).

The following is one child's rendition of this story, with Piaget's annotations in brackets:

> Gio (8 years old) tells the story of Niobe in the role of the explainer: "*Once upon a time there was a lady who had twelve boys and twelve girls, and then a fairy a boy and a girl. And then Niobe wanted to have some more sons* [than the fairy. Gio means by this that Niobe competed with the fairy, as was told in the text. But it will be seen how elliptical is his way of expressing it]. *Then she* [who?] *was angry. She* [who?] *fastened her* [whom?] *to a stone. He* [who?] *turned into a rock, and then his tears* [whose?] *made a stream which is still running today*" (*ibid.,* p. 102).

Piaget submits that this communication, with its ellipses and indefinite pronouns, attests to a basic failure to orient oneself towards the listener: what he will and will not understand, what will and will not confuse him, and so on.

Chapter 4 moves on to the study of characteristic ways in which children assimilate difficult verbal material to their ongoing cognitive organization; in a sense, it is a continuation of the understanding-by-the-listener part of the preceding experiment. Children of 9-11 years[4] of age were given a set of proverbs together with a set of sentences expressing the symbolic meaning of these proverbs and were asked to make (and justify to the experimenter) the appropriate proverb-sentence matchings. Piaget organizes his findings here around the concept of *syncretism,*[5] a pervasive characteristic of child thought which is said to derive from the more basic egocentric property. These older children showed considerable syncretic thinking in their responses to these abstract, verbal problems, e.g., the proverb and the sentence to which it was matched were frequently melded into a single, diffusely organized schema instead of remaining separate, well-bounded entities to be compared, logically connected, etc.

The final study reported touches on a problem to which Piaget continually returns in subsequent volumes of the series: the child's concep-

---

[4] This chapter contains an early statement of Piaget's views regarding the differences between concrete- and formal-operational thought. Since the reasoning in this study bears exclusively on abstract, purely verbal material, he asserts, it would be expected that children as old as this might show egocentric features here which would be largely absent in their concrete, "perceptual intelligence" activities.

[5] *Syncretism* is a very difficult concept to define, although the reader can get a good inductive grasp of its connotations by reading the book and chapter discussed here. Roughly, it describes a type of thinking or perception which assimilates reality into global, undifferentiated schemas; the individual contents of the assimilated reality interpenetrate and fuse with one another, anything being joined to or combined with anything else simply by virtue of common membership in the loosely bounded schematic potpourri (e.g., Piaget, 1928b, p. 4). Another developmental theorist, Heinz Werner (1948), has used the concept in essentially the same way.

tion of causality. One of Piaget's assistants noted down the spontaneous questions of a 6-year-old child during a 10-month period, and the chapter consists of Piaget's extensive speculations, based on this case material, about the underlying logic and causality which children's questions express (particularly their why questions). One of the more important conclusions was this. The concept of causality in young children appears to be primarily an undifferentiated psychological causality, i.e., one in which the imputed causal force has connotations of motive, intention, or duty. Thus, the child's questions about the causes of physical events reveal expectations of an answer couched, not in terms of impersonal, physical-causal forces, but in anthropomorphic, quasi-intentional terms:

> For the child, an event leading to an event, a motive leading to an action, and an idea leading to an idea are all one and the same thing; or rather, the physical world is still confused with the intellectual or psychical world. This is a result which we shall frequently meet with in our subsequent investigations (*ibid.*, p. 184).

With development, the various classes of explanation (causal-mechanical, logical, etc.) differentiate from this early, global form, and psychological causation is restricted to the motivated behavior of sentient beings only.

How can the various findings described in this volume be given a common theoretical anchor? Piaget does it by a rich and complex interweaving of data and theoretical constructs (not only *egocentrism,* but *syncretism, juxtaposition, intellectual realism,* and others) at every step throughout the book. We shall limit ourselves to ordering the data around what is probably the central concept: *egocentrism.* The young child is, as Piaget frequently puts it, the unwitting center of his universe. Only his own point of view—*his* schemas, *his* perceptions, etc.— can really figure in his various activities, since he is unaware that others see things differently, i.e., that there are points of view of which his is only one. Thus, much of his talk is talk for self, egocentric speech, even when in the company of others. He finds it difficult (and even unnecessary) really to exchange ideas with others, since this demands a focusing on the other's perspective in order to coordinate or contrast it with his own. And when explicitly called upon to communicate, he simply "reads aloud," so to speak, his own ongoing cognition, without concern about whether or not its recipient can grasp it in that form. He, as a speaker, already knows the information to be communicated and, in his egocentrism, cannot really take the role of someone who does not know it and communicate accordingly. Similarly, his syncretic handling of the proverb-sentence task can be attributed to the same pervasive egocentrism. The child makes an immediate, global, and uncritical assimilation of proverb-and-sentence elements to one over-all schema. Rather than standing back as a detached, critical observer and linking elements on logical grounds, the child links them simply because they have occurred together in consciousness; from his point of view they "go together," and there is no one else who needs convincing. And finally, the attitudes towards reality which underlie young children's questions also have an egocentric cast. Since the child continually assimilates reality to his own perspective, and since his perspective includes his own motives and inner promptings, it is not surprising that he should endow the causal texture of this reality with these same motives and promptings.

JUDGMENT AND REASONING

The final chapter of *The Language and Thought of the Child* investigated the child's "why" questions with a view towards uncovering his implicit attitudes towards causality and logical implication. The first chapter of its sequel, *Judgment and Reasoning in the Child* pursues essentially the same aim by studying the child's use and understanding of logical-causal connectives like *because, therefore,* and *although.* The data were derived primarily from two sources. First, the frequency of occurrence and the type of usage of these connectives were observed in the spontaneous language behavior of children of various ages, just as was done in the case of the "why" questions. Second, children were presented with incomplete sentences containing these connectives and asked to complete them, e.g., "That man fell off his horse, although . . ." For the connective *because* (and the related *since*), the study of spontaneous usage showed two things: (1) that this kind of connective is infrequently used by young children, particularly below age 7-8 years; (2) in corroboration of the study of "why" questions, when it is used it most commonly expresses (diffuse) psychological rather than logical or causal relations between events (e.g., I'll do thus and so because I want such and such). Similarly, the testing by incomplete sentences seemed to show that young children have real difficulty in managing the causal-empirical (e.g., the door stuck because . . .), and especially, the logical (e.g., half 10 is not 3 because . . .), *because.* Analogous results were obtained for the connective *therefore.* This word is rarely used by young children (they substitute for it a noncausal and nonlogical *then*); and when the child is required to use it, he fails to give it logical or causal meaning. Connectives like *although, in spite of the fact that,* etc., turn out to be still more difficult; they are mastered at a later age than the others (11-12 years).

Piaget's theoretical analysis of his findings here centers primarily around the concept of *juxtaposition.* Juxtaposition, in a sense the opposite of syncretism but logically and psychologically related to it, refers to the cognitive tendency simply to link (juxtapose) one thought element to another, rather than to tie them together by some causal or logical relation; it is reminiscent of the kind of mindless "and-sum" connections of which the Gestaltists spoke. The egocentrism of the child leads him to be unconcerned with conceptually integrating objects and events within a cause-and-effect paradigm and indifferent to any need to tie propositions together by logical implication. Thus, terms like *because, therefore, although,* etc.—designed to express precisely these sorts of causal and logical linkages—tend to be absent from his spontaneous discourse and, when used, are either reduced to a connective expressing psychological causation or are assimilated to a juxtaposition type of orientation, i.e., they are used to mean more nearly *and* and *and then* than anything else.

The next two chapters describe experiments concerning the child's understanding of relations. In one of these investigations, about forty boys (9-12 years) were asked to find the absurdity in each of five absurd sentences drawn from the Binet-Simon intelligence test. The most important sentence from the standpoint of Piaget's analysis was this one: "I have three brothers: Paul, Ernest, and myself" (or, when the tester was a woman, "I have three sisters: Pauline, Jeanne, and myself"). Only about 30 per cent of the subjects succeeded in finding the absurdity. In order to detect it, Piaget argues, one must carefully distinguish between two points of view: (1) that of "brother" as a *class* with class members ("we *are* three brothers," "I *am* a brother," etc.); (2) that of "brother" as a *relation* between individuals ("I *have* three brothers," "he *is* my brother," etc.).

Piaget feels that the various types of incorrect answers given by his subjects all attest to an undifferentiation between these two points of view and, more generally, a difficulty in handling relations as opposed to classes or absolutes. Thus, some children fail because they do not view "myself" as a brother to Paul and Ernest (although readily making the assertion that they are the brothers of "myself"); the total number of "brothers" in the family is therefore taken as two: Paul and Ernest. Others assimilate the relational "I have" to a classificatory "there are" (three brothers) in the sentence, and hence find nothing absurd about it. And there are other, higher-level errors in which a differentiation and coordination between relational and classificatory "brother" is made but not sustained throughout the train of reasoning.

This preliminary study of the brother concept was followed up by a second, larger-scale investigation. About 240 children (4-12 years) were submitted to the following interrogation:

> 1. How many brothers have you? And how many sisters? [Let us suppose that the child has a brother A and a sister B.] And how many brothers has A? And how many sisters? And how many brothers has B? And how many sisters?
>
> 2. How many brothers are there in the family? How many sisters? How many brothers and sisters altogether?
>
> 3. There are three brothers in a family: Auguste, Alfred, and Raymond How many brothers has Auguste? And Alfred? And Raymond?

4. Are you a brother [or a sister]? What is a brother [or sister, according to the sex of the child]?

5. Ernest has three brothers, Paul, Henry, and Charles. How many brothers has Paul? And Henry? And Charles?

6. How many brothers are there in this family? (1928b, p. 98).

The principal findings were these. Children find it difficult to see themselves as brothers or sisters to their own siblings (Question 1) and may even have trouble including themselves in the total pool of brothers and sisters in their family (Question 2). These difficulties augment when parallel questions bear on a hypothetical family (Questions 3, 5, and 6). And the question calling for a definition of the words *brother* or *sister* (the second part of Question 4) yielded an interesting sequence of responses. The most primitive definition simply states that a brother is a boy. In stage 2, the child realizes that there must be two or more children in the family in order to call one of them a brother, but the concept is not yet genuinely relational:

> Hal (age 9): *"When there is a boy and another boy, when there are two of them.*—Has your father got a brother?—*Yes.*—Why?—*Because he was born second.*—Then what is a brother?—*It is the second brother that comes.*— Then the first is not a brother?—*Oh no. The second brother that comes is called brother."* It would be impossible to show more clearly the absence of relativity from the word 'brother' (*ibid.*, p. 105).

Stage 3 is achieved with definitions which are at least roughly correct, i.e., they show a fair to good grasp of the relational meaning of the term. About 60 per cent of 7-year-olds and 75 per cent of 9-year-olds give such definitions, according to Piaget's data.

These same 240 children were also examined on a series of tests designed to tap their understanding of "right" and "left" as relational concepts. Piaget found three stages here also. In stage 1 (about 5-8 years) the child can correctly identify his own right and left hand but cannot correctly identify the right and left hands of an experimenter facing him. Thus "right" and "left" are absolutes which refer to fixed positions within the child's own perspective; the idea of *his* right or *his* left (the experimenter's), not corresponding spatially to the child's own right and left, eludes him. In stage 2, the child begins to decenter these concepts, to free them from his own point of view, and can correctly identify the right and left hands of a person seated opposite him. However, the concepts are not yet entirely divested of absolutism, are not yet seen as pure relations. If the child is shown three objects placed in a row in front of him, e.g., *A—B—C*, the following difficulties emerge. The child will say *A* "is left," *C* "is right," and *B* "is middle" in the absolute sense, but he cannot grasp that *B* is simultaneously to the right in relation to *A* and to the left in relation to *C*. "Right" and "left" achieve complete relativism in stage 3 (about 11-12 years); the child is now able to see that a given point of view defines a set of right-left relations between objects—*relations* rather than positions in space.

Chapter 3 also describes investigations of the child's concept of *family, country, enemy, foreigner,* and other relativistic terms. However, they all point in the same general direction as the studies just described: the young child has difficulty with relations because understanding them requires that freedom from the limitations of a single perspective which he lacks. Piaget sums it up as follows:

> The conclusion to which we are finally led is this. The child does not realize that certain ideas, even such as are obviously relative for an adult are relations between at least two terms. Thus he does not realize that a brother must necessarily be the brother of somebody, that an object must necessarily be to the right or left of somebody, or that a part must necessarily be part of a whole, but thinks of all these notions as existing in themselves, absolutely (*ibid.,* p. 131).

> Chapter I, by showing us how the child juxtaposes his judgments, instead of making them employ one another, made it clear that childish logic is lacking in necessity. Chapters II and III, by showing the child's inability to handle the logic of relations, led us to the very root of this defect. It is because he fails to grasp the *reciprocity* existing between different points of view that the child is unable to handle relations properly (*ibid.,* p. 134).

The fourth chapter reports a small and informal investigation of the introspective capabilities of children. Piaget had been engaged in a study of the concept of number, using simple arithmetic problems as task material, when he stumbled upon a curious phenomenon. Children seemed to find it surprisingly difficult to relate to the experimenter, after the fact, the steps their reasoning had taken in the solution of these simple problems. The child would quite obviously have undergone a series of reasoning steps (he would sometimes actually reveal it to the experimenter by talking aloud as he reasoned); however, when the problem was solved (either correctly or incorrectly), he either could not recount anything of what he had just done, or else he could give only a distorted and out-of-sequence version of the reasoning steps. The following are two choice examples of this introspective (or perhaps better, retrospective) difficulty:

> Weng (age 7): "This table is 4 metres long. This one three times as long. How many metres long is it?—*12 metres.*—How did you do that?—*I added 2 and 2 and 2 and 2 and 2 always 2.*—Why 2?—*So as to make 12.*—Why did you take 2?—*So as not to take another number.*" "This window is 4 metres high. Another window half as high would be how many metres?—*2 metres.* —How did you do that?—*I took away the other 2's.*" "Here are 12 matches. Make me a pile three times as small." After fumbling about a little, Weng makes a pile of 10 matches (by subtraction: 12 — 3, with a mistake of calculation into the bargain). "How did you find 10?—*I added 4 and 4 and 2*" (*ibid.,* p. 139).

Bon (9;6) presents an even clearer case, for we heard him counting to himself. We asked him to find three-quarters of 16 matches. He then mutters to himself: "A quarter of $16 = 4$; $3 \times 4 = 12$," and hands us the matches with the answer: "12.—How did you find 12?—*I said 4 times 3 = 12. To go up to 16 makes 4. I took 4* [matches from the pile of 16] *and I gave back the rest.*" Bon has therefore completely reversed the correct process which he had muttered to himself and presents us with a line of reasoning devoid of logical direction (*ibid.,* p. 142).

Why does the child find it so difficult to observe his own thought processes? Again egocentrism provides the key. Thought which proceeds from a single point of view, and without orientation towards and coordination with the thought of others, is necessarily unreflective. Consciousness of one's own reasoning processes arises from the disposition to prove and justify to others what one has asserted; to do the latter one must turn back upon, reflect on, one's own thinking critically, and with the eyes of an outside observer.

There remains the question of the mechanism by which the child ultimately frees himself from the grip of egocentrism, with its attendant ills of absolutism, lack of introspection, disinclination towards logical-causal justification, and all the rest. It is not simply experience with objects and events in the real world; the child, says Piaget, can and does readily distort physical experience to fit his preexistent schemas. Rather, social interaction is the principal liberating factor, particularly social interaction with peers. In the course of his contacts (and especially, his conflicts and arguments) with other children, the child increasingly finds himself forced to reexamine his own percepts and concepts in the light of those of others, and by so doing, gradually rids himself of cognitive egocentrism:

What then gives rise to the need for verification? Surely it must be the shock of our thought coming into contact with that of others, which produces doubt and the desire to prove. . . . The social need to share the thought of others and to communicate our own with success is at the root of our need for verification. Proof is the outcome of argument. . . . Logical reasoning is an argument which we have with ourselves, and which reproduces internally the features of a real argument (*ibid.,* p. 204).

REALITY

The Child's Conception of the World and its successor, *The Child's Conception of Physical Causality,* report investigations of what Piaget calls the *content* of child thought as distinguished from its *form.* That is, they concern the particular kinds of ideas and beliefs the child inclines toward, in contrast to the more generalized logical forms which permit or facilitate such ideas and beliefs. The distinction is not hard and fast, however, since here, as in the first two books, Piaget is interested in cognitive content primarily as it reflects underlying cognitive structure and orientation.

However, he sees the study of thought content as posing unique problems of methodology and interpretation. These are spelled out with great care in the introductory chapter of *The Child's Conception of the World*. He describes the various pitfalls which beset any study of children's ideas and beliefs, e.g., the necessity to tread a narrow line between missing or discounting what's really there (due to methodological inflexibility, excessive interpretative timidity, etc.) and overinterpreting, as fixed and systematized convictions, what the child may have said only out of experimenter suggestion or momentary fancy. Piaget tries to build one safeguard against the latter into his research strategy:

> We may thus state the first rule of our method. When a particular group of explanations by children is to be investigated, the questions we shall ask them will be determined in matter and in form, by the spontaneous questions actually asked by children of the same age or younger. It is also important, before drawing conclusions from the results of an investigation, to seek corroboration in a study of the spontaneous questions of children. It can then be seen whether the notions ascribed to them do or do not correspond with the questions they themselves ask and the manner in which they ask them (1929c, p. 5).

Piaget also takes pains here to set out guidelines as to how the reader should and should not interpret the data described in these two books: in gist, the specific beliefs which the child expresses, either spontaneously or in response to skillful, nonleading questioning, should be taken only as symptomatic expressions of a turn of mind, a general intellectual orientation towards the world and its phenomena. They should not be interpreted as evidence for coherent, highly systematized ontologies and cosmologies. All that the previous two books have told us about the nature of child thought militates against any such coherence and systematization. As Piaget puts it:

> The impression may have been formed that we endow children, if not with actual theories, at any rate with clear and spontaneously formulated ideas, as to the nature of thought and of names and dreams. But nothing has been further from our intention. We readily agree that children have never or hardly ever reflected on the matters on which they were questioned. The experiments aimed, therefore, not at examining ideas the children had already thought out, but at seeing how their ideas are formed in response to certain questions and principally in what direction their spontaneous attitude of mind tends to lead them (*ibid.,* p. 123).

The substantive part of the book consists of three sections, with several chapters per section. Each section comprises experimental work bearing on one of three types of intellectual tendency which Piaget predicates for child thought: *realism* (first section), *animism* (second section), and *artificialism* (third section). The basic fact of child thought from which these three tendencies are said to proceed is an undifferentiation between self

and world, this undifferentiation in turn resulting from the child's uni-
perspective egocentrism. That is, the child is unable to discriminate
clearly between psychological and physical events; human experiences
(thoughts, feelings, wishes, etc.) constantly interpenetrate and get confused with the objective reality on which these experiences bear. One
form of this undifferentiation between the psychological and physical
realms is a tendency to substantiate psychological events or products
(thoughts, dreams, names, etc.), i.e., to see them as physicalistic, thing-
like entities. This is what Piaget calls *realism*. A complimentary form
of this undifferentiation is the converse tendency to endow physical objects and events with the attributes of biological-psychological entities,
e.g., to endow them with life, consciousness, will, etc. This is *animism*.
And finally, related to both realism and animism is the tendency to regard physical phenomena as the products of human creation—to believe
that all the objects and events in the world around us were made by men
for specific, anthropocentric purposes. This is *artificialism*.

The section on realism reports experiments designed to uncover developmental changes in the child's conception of various psychic phenomena. One study showed that young children are inclined to identify
thought with the act of speaking, i.e., thought is a substantial, material
event rather than an inner, psychological process. A second study led to
similar conclusions about names; for the young child, a name is an essential part of its referent, e.g., the name of the sun is a physical attribute
or part of the sun itself. And a third suggested that dreams are likewise
regarded initially as substantial entities, located external to the child,
and only later seen as subjective and internal. In this study, the experimenter asked the child a series of questions about dreams, taking
care to avoid suggestion in so far as was possible. "You know what a
dream is?" "You dream sometimes, at night?" "Then tell me where the
dreams come from." "While you dream, where is the dream?" "What do
you dream with?" And so on. Piaget sums up the principal results as
follows:

> The answers obtained can be classified as belonging to three distinct
> stages. During the first (approximately 5-6) the child believes the dream to
> come from outside and to take place within the room and he thus dreams
> with the eyes. Also, the dream is highly emotional: dreams often come "to
> pay us out," "because we've done something we ought not to have done,"
> etc. During the second stage (average age 7-8) the child supposes the source
> of the dream to be in the head, in thought, in the voice, etc., but the dream
> is in the room, in front of him. Dreaming is with the eyes; it is looking at a
> picture outside. The fact that it is outside does not mean that it is true; the
> dream is unreal, but consists in an image existing outside, just as the image
> of an ogre may exist, without there actually being a real ogre. Finally, during
> the third stage (about 9-10), the dream is the product of thought, it takes
> place inside the head (or in the eyes), and dreaming is by means of thought
> or else with the eyes, used internally (*ibid.,* pp. 90-91).

The following protocol illustrates some of the features of the first stage:

> BARB (5½): "Do you ever have dreams?—*Yes, I dreamt I had a hole in my hand.*—Are dreams true?—*No, they are pictures* (images) *we see*(!)—Where do they come from?—*From God.*—Are your eyes open or shut when you dream?—*Shut.*—Could I see your dream?—*No, you would be too far away.*—And your mother?—*Yes, but she lights the light.*—Is the dream in the room or inside you?—*It isn't in me or I shouldn't see it*(!)—And could your mother see it?—*No, she isn't in the bed. Only my little sister sleeps with me*" (*ibid.*, p. 94).

Contrast this view of dreams with the following, third-stage response:

> VISC (11;1): You dream *"with the head,"* and the dream is *"in the head.*—It isn't in front?—*It's as if* (!) *you could see.*—Is there anything in front of you?—*Nothing.*—What is there in your head?—*Thoughts.*—Do the eyes see anything in the head?—*No*" (*ibid.*, p. 119).

One of the animism studies concerned the types of objects which the child will and will not classify as alive. The genetic sequence consists of a gradual restriction in the kinds of objects which the child is willing to endow with life. A complementary investigation was devoted to the child's attribution of consciousness—thought, feeling, intentionality, etc.—to various types of objects. The questions were of this type. "If I pull off this button, will it feel it?" "Does the sun know it gives light?" "Would a table feel it if I were to prick it?" Piaget tentatively suggested the following four stages. In stage 1, almost any object is potentially conscious, given the right conditions. For example, a stone may normally be considered nonsentient, but will "feel it" if it is moved. Piaget appears to have found no children willing to assert that *all* objects are at *all* times conscious, however. In stage 2, the potentiality for consciousness is generally attributed only to objects which regularly possess some kind of movement, whose special function is movement, etc. Thus, a bicycle and the wind may know or feel, but a stone cannot. In stage 3, only objects capable of spontaneous motion are conscious; the sun and wind can be, but no longer the bicycle. And finally, the child of stage 4 attributes consciousness only to people and animals. The following is an interesting example of spontaneously expressed animism:

> We hung a metal box from a double string and placed it in front of Vel, in such a way that, on letting go of the box, the string unwound making the box turn round and round. "Why does it turn?—*Because the string is twisted.*—Why does the string turn too?—*Because it wants to unwind itself.*—Why?—*Because it wants to be unwound* (= it wants to resume its original position, in which the string was unwound).—Does the string know it is twisted?—*Yes.*—Why?—*Because it wants to untwist itself, it knows it's twisted!*—Does it really know it is twisted?—*Yes. I am not sure.*—How do you think it knows?—*Because it feels it is all twisted*" (*ibid.*, pp. 175-176).

And this child is clearly nonanimistic:

> CEL (10;7) denies consciousness even to the sun and the moon *"because it is not alive."* "What things can know and feel?—*Plants, animals, people, insects.—Is that all?—Yes.*—Can the wind feel?—*No,*" etc. (*ibid.,* p. 187).

As indicated earlier, Piaget is generally rather cautious about over-stating his findings throughout this book; and he is even more than usually cautious about the animism work described here. He emphasizes once again that the child's answers indicate only a general direction of thought, not a comprehensive and coherent system of beliefs. He also reiterates the inherent dangers in the question-and-answer method of studying phenomena like animism. And finally, while unwilling to abandon entirely a stage conception of how animism declines with age, he does admit that any given child may oscillate from stage to stage over time and may therefore show occasional reversals of sequence (*ibid.,* pp. 188-193).

In the artificialism studies, children were asked questions about the origins of a wide variety of natural phenomena: sun, moon, stars, rain, sky, clouds, night, thunder and lightning, snow, ice, rivers, lakes, seas, trees, mountains, earth, and others. Piaget found the younger children's responses to such questions to be strongly artificialistic; with development, artificialism gradually wanes in favor of more naturalistic conceptions. A representative example is the child's conception of the nature and origin of night, a part of what Piaget calls the child's *meteorology.* He describes four stages in the child's developing view of night. In stage 1, the child conceptualizes the origin of night solely in terms of its use ("so we can go to bed"). His concern is more with a (finalistic-artificialistic) "why" than a "how"; the night is the servant of man's need to sleep, but little attention is paid to the actual mechanism which produces it. In stage 2, the child assigns a quasi-naturalistic mechanism, while still retaining the wish of God or man as the ultimate cause: night is a black cloud which fills the atmosphere. Stage 3 marks a further step towards a naturalistic explanation. Night is no longer a substance (i.e., a black cloud) in itself; rather, it is defined negatively as the result of clouds shutting out the daylight; it is now a shadow rather than a substance. In stage 4, night is thought to result from the setting of the sun. The explanation is wholly naturalistic; the child makes no attempt to interject man's needs and wishes as cause. In the following passage Piaget summarizes the child's developing ideas about night as they relate to artificialism:

> The succession of these four stages thus shows a progressive decrease in artificialism at the expense of an attempt to find explanations that shall be more and more adapted to physical reality. The order of succession of these stages, in particular of the first two, clearly indicates one of the roots of the

child's artificialism: he begins by being interested in the "why" of things before he has any concern for the "how." In other words he starts from the implicit postulate that everything has some meaning in the order of things: everything is conceived according to a plan and this plan itself is regarded as contributory to the good of human beings. Night is "so that we can sleep." This is the starting point (first stage). Only then is the child concerned to know the author of the phenomenon and how it arises (second stage). The author is naturally man himself for whose sake the night exists. The "how" is the smoke of the chimneys which makes the clouds and the black air that fills the atmosphere. By what means has Providence secured the regular return of night?—The child does not even ask this. He is so sure that it is moral necessity and not chance or mechanical force that ordains the course of things that he supposes without seeking further, that men's wishes, coupled with the good will of the smoke and the clouds, themselves suffice to secure the constant succession of nights. Such, then, is child artificialism, so long as religious education has not intervened to complicate it by conceptions foreign to his spontaneous thought (*ibid.*, pp. 297-298).

We conclude the section with a brief protocol from the early stages:

DELESD (7;8): "What is it that makes it all dark at night?—*It is because we go to sleep.*—If you go to sleep in the afternoon, is it dark then?—*No, sir.*—Then what will make it dark this evening? . . ." Despite this objection Delesd maintained that it is because we sleep that it becomes night (*ibid.*, p. 292.

CAUSALITY

The subject matter of *The Child's Conception of Physical Causality* is obviously not a topic divorced from the contents of the preceding three books. It will be recalled that the studies of "why" questions (first book) and "because" and "although" completions (second book) were in part studies of causal notions. Even more, the investigations of animism and artificialism are as much studies of child causality as they are of the child's "conception of the world." The fact of the matter is that the child's basic orientation towards causal explanation intrudes throughout the length and breadth of his cognitive life, and the book under discussion (1930a) is intended primarily to make explicit what has been implicit (but nonetheless present) in the earlier ones.

The book resembles its predecessor in two ways: (1) it is organized by sections, with several chapters per section; (2) it draws its evidence from studies in which children are queried, *in vacuo,* about various natural phenomena, e.g., wind, rivers, sun, etc. However, it differs from the preceding volume in that it also includes experiments in which the questioning centers around immediately observable events, e.g., the action of a miniature steam engine, the rise of water level in a vessel when the experimenter drops an object into it, and the like. It will be remembered (our Chapter 1) that demonstration-and-questioning methods of this type became more prominent in Piaget's work in later years.

The first section describes various investigations of the child's explanations of movement: the causes of air and water currents, why the clouds, sun, and moon move in space, why they remain suspended in the sky, and the like. These experiments particularly well illustrate Piaget's views on the development of causal reasoning and are worth a closer look. First comes his over-all interpretation of the research data and then a sampling of specific findings:

> The most general characteristic of these primitive explanations of movement given by children is what may be called their bipolarity: the movement of a body is regarded as due both to an external will and to an internal will, to a command and an acquiescence. The starting-point of these ideas is both artificialist and animistic. If we go back further still, we may say that this bipolarity is originally of a magico-animistic order: on the one hand, we issue commands to things (the sun and moon, the clouds and the sky follow us), on the other hand, these things acquiesce in our desires because they themselves wish to do so.
>
> This bipolarity endures long after the early stages have been passed. Even during the stage when the child is trying to explain the movements of nature by nature herself, every movement is still explained by the co-operation of external and internal motor force. The internal motor is always the free will of the objects. The external force is the sum of bodies morally attracting or repulsing the moving object. Thus the lake attracts the rivers; night and the rain attract clouds; sun and clouds repel each other; rocks help water to flow, and so on. It is simply the artificialist-animist complexus prolonged, but the artificialism is transferred to external objects.
>
> During a later stage, movement is explained by causes that are more physical than psychical, in the sense that the external motor force is supposed more and more to act by contact, *i.e.*, by push or by pull. But the explanation is still far from being mechanical. It remains dynamic and bipolar, in the sense that the internal motor force is never abolished: the moving body retains the initiative and may utilise the external force or remove itself from its influence. Thus the sun is driven along by the clouds, but at the same time it follows us and uses the wind for its own ends. And the same is true of the clouds. . . .
>
> Finally, comes the fourth and last period, during which the child simplifies his conception of movement, and gradually reaches a mechanical causality based on inertia, whose advent coincides with the disappearance of the animist and artificialist mentality (*ibid.*, pp. 115-116).

In the particular case of the movement of clouds, the developmental sequence appeared to be this:

> The first stage is magical: we make the clouds move by walking. The clouds obey us at a distance. The average age of this stage is 5. The second stage is both artificialist and animistic. Clouds move because God or men make them move. The average age of this stage is 6. During a third stage, of which the average age is 7, clouds are supposed to move by themselves, though the child says nothing definite as to how this movement is effected. But in addition to this, the movement is conditioned by moral and physical causes, which shows that the artificialism has simply been transferred to the objects. It is the sun, the moon, etc., that make the clouds move along; only,

the heavenly bodies determine these movements, not as a physical cause determines its effects, but rather as one man compels another by commanding him, with or without the addition of physical force. During this third stage, the child says nothing definite about the "how" of the cloud's spontaneous movement, but it is obvious that he has at the back of his mind a motor schema which prepares the way for the explanation which comes during the fourth stage. For according to the children of the fourth stage, the wind pushes the clouds, but the wind has itself come out of the clouds. The average age of this stage is 8. When, finally, the fifth stage is reached (average age 9), a correct explanation is found (*ibid.*, pp. 61-62).

Piaget found stage 4 of particular interest from a genetic epistemological standpoint. In this stage the child is inclined to think that it is wind which pushes the clouds along. Well and good. But at least a part of this wind is created by the moving cloud itself; the cloud, as it moves, produces air currents which move around in back of the cloud and give it added impetus. This "reflux schema," as Piaget refers to it, seems to crop up again and again in the child's explanations of movement; it appears to reflect a causal orientation which is becoming mechanical-naturalistic but has not yet completely rid itself of precausal adherences. What makes it a concern of genetic epistemology is the fact that some of the Greek thinkers held a very similar theory about the movement of projectiles. There is no doubt but that historical-development parallels of this kind, which Piaget noticed early in his career, helped set a pattern of abiding interest in genetic epistemology (see our Chapter 7).

The following protocols illustrate stages 1, 3, 4, and 5 respectively:

> SALA (8): "You have already seen the clouds moving along? What makes them move?—*When we move along, they move along too.*—Can *you* make them move?—*Everybody can, when they walk.*—When I walk and you are still, do they move?—*Yes.*—And at night, when everyone is asleep, do they move?—*Yes.*—But you tell me that they move when somebody walks.—*They always move. The cats, when they walk, and then the dogs, they make the clouds move along*" (*ibid.*, p. 62).

> EB (7): "What makes the clouds move along?—*It's the sun.*—How?—*With its rays. It pushes the clouds*" (*ibid.*, p. 65).

> PUR (8;7): "*It's the air which they* [the clouds] *make, and then it* [the air] *chases the clouds*" (*ibid.*, p. 71).

> GUT (9½): "Why do the clouds move more or less quickly?—*Because of the wind. They move along by the wind.*—Where does the wind come from? —*From the sky.*—And how is the wind made?—*Don't know.*—And can the clouds make a wind?—*No.*—Can they make a wind by moving?—*No.*—And when there is no wind, can they move along alone?—*No*" (*ibid.*, p. 72).

Another study dealt with the child's notions about why water moves along in rivers and brooks. Again we quote Piaget:

> During the first stage, of which the average age is 5, the child explains the current by the collaboration of an external, artificialist motor force (people

or men) with an internal, animist force (the water's obedience). During the second stage, reached at about 7 and 3 months, the external force is thought to be the wind or the stones, etc., and the internal force is still the water's own spontaneous current. During a third stage, the water is supposed to run because of the slope, but the child is not yet able to understand that the weight of the water is what makes it move along. When, finally, at 10 or 11 a fourth stage is reached, the child understands everything. The analogy will at once be seen between this schema of evolution and that embodying the explanations of the movement of clouds and heavenly bodies (ibid., p. 94).

Here are concrete examples of the first three stages:

GRIM (5): "Why does the water in the Arve[6] move along?—*Because people make oars. They push.*—Where are the oars?—*In the boats there are men who hold them. They make it go.*—Do men make the water in the Arve go? —*With boats, great big boats* [there are a few skiffs down-stream].—Does the water run without boats?—*No, because that holds it back.*—Is the Arve running to-day?—*No. . . . It is moving along a little.*—Why?—*Because there are a few boats.*" The water, says Grim, is alive, and knows that it is flowing (ibid., p. 94).

BLAN (6): The Arve moves along because "*the wind carries it*," "*because the wind went back into the water.*" But, on the other hand, when there is no wind, the water "*flows by itself*," because "*it has made a current.*" "What is the current?—*It's the cold wind*" (ibid., p. 98).

DUC (6;11): The river moves along "*by the current.*"—Why is there a current?—*Because the river is sloping.*—Why does it flow when it's sloping? —*It slides* (ibid., p. 100).[7]

The experiments of the second section are more exclusively of the concrete, demonstration-and-questioning variety than those of the first. An experiment here typically has two parts. First, the child is asked to make a prediction as to the outcome of some imminent action or event. Then, after the event is made to occur and its outcome determined, he is questioned as to the cause. In one study the subject is called on

[6] At this point in the text the following footnote is cited: "These children were questioned at a school situated on the banks of the Arve. The current is fairly strong at this point and the slope obvious to the eye."

[7] The writer cannot resist a personal footnote here. Several years ago he questioned his daughter, then almost five years old, about the flow of water in a nearby brook (like Piaget's Arve, the slope was fairly steep and the current rapid). The dialogue was roughly as follows: Why does the brook move along? *The wind makes it go and the water pushes* (gestures with whole body here) *it along—just sort of relaxes and pushes it along.* Is the brook alive? *It's alive but not like you and me. It's a brook and we are people.* Why does it move? *It just wants to. It tries to and if it doesn't* (try to) *it can't* (move). Does it know it's moving? *No.* The writer recently read this excerpt to the child, now nine years old, and she proceeded to break into embarrassed laughter. When asked what she thought of her explanation, she replied to the effect that she'd "made the brook sound like a *person!*" (with overtones of "how-could-anyone-be-so-*stupid?*"). Needless to say, unlike the other passages quoted in this book, this protocol is quoted with at most the reluctant permission of its author!

to predict and explain the floating (or sinking) of various objects placed in water. The results are complex and heterogeneous. In general, the youngest children invoke moral-animistic explanations (the boat floats "because it has to," "because it's clever," etc.). The next two stages involve a hodgepodge of explanations which betray remnants of a dynamic, semi-animistic view of the objects concerned: a boat floats because it is "heavy" (i.e., has the strength to hold itself up); because the water is "heavy" (i.e., has the strength to hold up the boat or can produce waves or currents which push it up, especially if the boat is big and there is lots to push against, etc.); because the boat "moves along" (a kind of "gliding-flight" conception), and so on. In the final stage, the child either approaches or attains a grasp of the weight-volume relation and its function as an explanatory principle.

In a second experiment, the child is asked to predict the outcome, in terms of water level, of putting various objects into a glass vessel containing water; after the outcome has been established, the child is asked to explain it. The youngest children uniformly think that the water rises in proportion to the weight of the submerged object (independent of its volume); the underlying fantasy appears to be that the weight of the object presses down on the water and sets up a sort of current which runs from the bottom to the top like a wave (and hence raises the water level). In stage 2, curiously enough, the child actually makes use of perceived volume in all his predictions (and hence predicts correctly) but still asserts, in his verbal explanation, that the weight is what counts! In stage 3, prediction and explanation become congruent—the child uses perceived volume for both.

A third study deals with the child's predictions and explanations regarding shadows. The sequence of stages can be summarized as follows:

> We discovered four stages in the explanation of the phenomenon of shadows. During the first, of which the average age is 5 years, shadows are conceived as due to the collaboration or participation of two sources, the one, internal (the shadow emanates from the object), the other, external (shadows come from trees, from night, from the corner of the room, etc.). . . . During the second stage (average age, 6-7 years), shadows are believed to be produced by the object alone. They are a substance emanating from the object, but in no particular direction: at this stage, the child is not yet able to say on which side the shadow will fall when the screen is placed in front of the source of light. After he has reached the third stage, however, of which the average age is 8 years, the child is able to predict the orientation of shadows. He can even say that shadows will be formed where there is no light, no sun, and so on. But under this apparently correct explanation we can still trace the substantialism of the earlier stages: the child still believes that a shadow is an emanation of the object, but he thinks it is an emanation that drives away the light and is therefore obliged to dispose itself on the side opposite to that of the source of light. Finally, during a fourth stage (of which the average age is 9 years), the correct explanation is found (ibid., pp. 180-181).

The third section of the book describes investigations of the child's explanation of how machines work; the machines studied were bicycles, trains, planes, cars, and a miniature steam engine. Although each type of machine engenders developmental trends in explanation in part peculiar to itself, there appears to be one general trend common to all. The younger children appeal now to this, now to that perceptually striking feature of the apparatus as a sufficient cause for its operation. Their perception of the machine is undifferentiated and global (syncretic): anything at all can be invoked as the causal mechanism at work; there is no concern for whether or not cause makes any spatial contact with effect and therefore no concern with establishing a *chain* of causes (e.g., the fire in the steam engine produces steam which in turn pushes on the piston which in turn . . .).

With development the child begins to analyze the various components in an active search for the causal chain; spatial contact between components is now assumed to be necessary, i.e., the child is now oriented towards a genuinely *mechanical* causality. Piaget makes the interesting hypothesis that the child's primitive causal notions (animism, artificialism, etc.) may first begin to give way to more mature ones through his daily interactions with machines, broadly defined. That is to say, he may first come to grips with causal principles, such as the necessity for spatial contact, as he tries to make this or that toy or apparatus function, produce this or that physical effect, or overcome this or that physical resistance in objects.

The last chapter of the book offers a summary and theoretical integration of its findings and those of its immediate predecessor. Among its more famous contents is the assertion that there are no less than seventeen types of causal explanation, of varying level of developmental maturity, discernible in the thought of children. The concluding pages of this long chapter are of more interest theoretically, because they contain an attempt to weld the work of the third and fourth books (on the child's "reality") to that of the first and second (on the child's "logic")— that is, an attempt to relate formal-functional to contential aspects of child thought. The critical excerpts are these:

> In the first place, let us note the astonishing similarity of the general processes which condition the evolution of logic and that of the idea of reality. For the construction of the objective world and the elaboration of strict reasoning both consist in a gradual reduction of egocentricity in favour of the progressive socialisation of thought, in favour, that is to say, of objectivation and reciprocity of view-points. In both cases, the initial state is marked by the fact that the self is confused with the external world and with other people; the vision of the world is falsified by subjective adherences, and the vision of other people is falsified by the fact that the personal point of view predominates, almost to the exclusion of all others. Thus in both cases, truth—empirical truth or formal truth such as forms the subject-

matter of argument—is obscured by the ego. Then, as the child discovers that others do not think as he does, he makes efforts to adapt himself to them, he bows to the exigencies of control and verification which are implied by discussion and argument, and thus comes to replace egocentric logic by the true logic created by social life. We saw that exactly the same process took place with regard to the idea of reality.

There is therefore an egocentric logic and an egocentric ontology, of which the consequences are parallel: they both falsify the perspective of logical relations and of things, because they both start from the assumption that other people understand us and agree with us from the first, and that things revolve around us with the sole purpose of serving us and resembling us.

Now, if we examine these parallel evolutions, logical and ontological, in greater detail, we shall distinguish three main stages in each. The first is that which precedes any clear consciousness of the self, and may be arbitrarily set down as lasting till the age of 2-3, that is, till the appearance of the first "whys," which symbolise in a way the first awareness of resistance in the external world. As far as we can conjecture, two phenomena characterise this first stage. From the point of view of logic, it is pure *autism,* or thought akin to dreams or day-dreams, thought in which truth is confused with desire. To every desire corresponds immediately an image or illusion which transforms this desire into reality, thanks to a sort of pseudo-hallucination or play. No objective observation or reasoning is possible: there is only a perpetual play which transforms perceptions and creates situations in accordance with the subject's pleasure. From the ontological view-point, what corresponds to this manner of thinking is primitive *psychological causality,* probably in a form that implies *magic* proper: the belief that any desire whatsoever can influence objects, the belief in the obedience of external things. Magic and autism are therefore two different sides of one and the same phenomenon— that confusion between the self and the world which destroys both logical truth and objective existence.

The second stage lasts from the age of 2-3 to the age of 7-8, and is characterised, from the logical point of view, by egocentricity: on the one hand, there is an absence of the desire to find logical justification for one's statements, and on the other, syncretism combines with juxtaposition to produce an excess of subjective and affective relations at the expense of genuine logical implications. To this egocentricity corresponds, in the ontological domain, *pre-causality,* in the widest sense, meaning all the forms of causality based on a confusion between psychological activity and physical mechanism. For pre-causality is to physical causality what syncretism is to logical implication. Pre-causality confuses motive and cause, just as, in the sphere of logic, syncretism confuses subjective justification with verification. . . .

But as soon as logical thought breaks away from transduction and becomes deductive, the idea of reality also breaks away from all these forms of primitive realism. Thus during the third great stage of child development, a new parallelism grows up between logic and the real categories (*ibid.,* pp. 301-305).

MORAL JUDGMENT

The Moral Judgment of the Child is concerned, as its title says, with the child's moral *judgments,* i.e., his ideas and attitudes about rules, justice, ethical behavior, and so on. Although it does here and there deal with questions of moral behavior as well, it treats these as secondary and subsidiary to those of moral judgment. Although this work is not a direct, fifth-volume sequel to the other four, there is, nevertheless, considerable continuity. Piaget makes ample use of his earlier insights in the design and interpretation of the research in this area. As a case in point, he identifies a *moral realism* in children which directly parallels the *intellectual realism* described earlier. The book consists of four long chapters: the first three experimental and theoretical and the fourth purely theoretical. Research findings are, as usual, interpreted in terms of developmental stages. It should be noted, however, that Piaget is exceedingly cautious and guarded about how the term *stage* should be construed in this area. He indicates again and again that individual differences in moral judgment are enormous at every age level studied, that his stages are thereby so overlapping as to be almost (but not quite) reducible to agenetic types, that similar studies carried out on populations of children different from his would likely yield different developmental patterns, and so on.

The book commences with an interesting investigation of children's attitudes and behavior with respect to the rules of a game, namely, the game of marbles as played by children in French Switzerland. The inquiry consists of two parts. The first part is designed to find out the extent to which the child conforms to rules of the marble game in his actual playing behavior. The experimenter gives the child some marbles and, feigning ignorance of the game,[8] asks the child to show him how to play it. With the youngest children this procedure was supplemented by watching them play the game together. The second part of the inquiry aims at the child's verbally expressed understanding of the nature of rules, his attitudes towards them, and so on. The experimenter begins by asking if the child could make up a new rule for the marble game and, if so, whether other children would agree to it, whether it would be "fair," etc. He then asks about the history and origins of rules: whether people have always played the game by present rules, and how the rules originated.

As to the child's behavioral conformity to the rules, the stages appeared to be as follows. In stage 1 the child uses the marbles simply as free-play materials, without any attempt to adapt to social rules. At most, the child develops private rituals of play which might be called *motor rules*. Stage 2 (about 3-5 years) begins when the child imitates aspects of the rule-regulated play behavior of his elders. However, it is clear that the child assimilates what he sees to private, egocentric schemas; confident that he is playing by the older children's rules, he

---

[8] Actually, Piaget had previously made it a point to master the rules of this game, including all local variations, so as to spot any breaches in the rules as they occurred.

nonetheless plays in an idiosyncratic, socially isolated manner, unintentionally flouting the rules at every turn. From about 7-8 years on, the child begins to play the game in a genuinely social way, in accordance with a mutually agreed upon set of rules. But until about age 11-12, this grasp of and conformity to the rules is still vague and approximative (stage 3). From 11-12 on, however, they are completely understood and obeyed to the letter by all (stage 4); moreover, the act of codifying rules now seems to have a positive fascination for the child, e.g., he is constantly engaged in revising the statutes to cover new and unforeseen contingencies.

For the child's verbalized notions about rules, Piaget found three stages. Stage 1 corresponds to the stage 1 in behavioral conformity to rules: rules are simply not part of his life space. Stage 2 is more interesting. Here, the child regards the rules of the game as eternal and unchangeable, stemming from parental or divine authority; suggested changes in the rules are usually resisted; the new rules "are not fair," even if others agree to abide by them. But there is a curious hiatus between theory and practice in this stage. While regarding the rules as sacred and inviolable in his conscious thought, he unwittingly breaks them at every turn in his actual behavior (the stage 2 in the practice of rules). In stage 3 (about 10-11), the child evidences quite different attitudes and beliefs with respect to rules. Rules may always be changed, provided only that others agree to abide by them. Rules are neither God-given nor eternal; children of long ago were probably the first marble players, and the rules have undoubtedly evolved and changed considerably since then. And, as we have seen, this relativistic attitude towards rules in theory is accompanied by scrupulous adherence to rules in practice—just the reverse of the situation in stage 3.

A second series of experiments bear on developmental changes in attitudes towards actions more specifically moral than conformity to the rules of a game. In one group of studies the subject was presented with a number of stories in which a child performs some morality-relevant act under a specified set of circumstances. The subject was then to judge the relative culpability of the various acts, giving the reasons for his judgment. The results can be summarized as follows. Although individual differences were substantial as usual, the younger children tended to regard as most immoral those acts which had the most serious objective consequences, with no consideration of subjective antecedents (motives, etc.) in the wrongdoer. Thus, the child who breaks fifteen cups through an accident he could not have avoided was judged "naughtier" than one who accidentally breaks a single cup while engaged in deliberate malfeasance. Similarly, a child who steals a roll to give to a poor and hungry friend was judged guiltier than one who steals a (less costly) piece of ribbon for herself. The older children (particularly from 9-10 years on) were more inclined to take into account the motives behind the wrongful act and weigh moral responsibility accordingly.

Other investigations in this series deal with the child's ideas about and attitudes towards the telling of lies. The results parallel those for clumsiness and stealing and can be summarized as follows. First, the youngest children define a lie simply as "naughty words," i.e., lying is rather like swearing. A little later, it is defined as an untrue statement of any kind, with or without intention to deceive. And finally, it is restricted exclusively to untruths with intent to deceive. Second, younger children regard a lie as culpable in the degree that it deviates from the truth, regardless of the intent of the teller. Thus, a tall tale innocently told by a young child is worse than a more believable untruth told with deliberate intent to deceive, just as the bigger theft with altruistic motives was worse than the smaller one with selfish motives. Again, the older children tend to evaluate guilt in terms of the motives involved. Third, younger children judge a lie which *fails* to deceive (usually because it is so "big," so unbelievable) as "naughtier" than one which succeeds; for them, it is the exposure of the untruth which is reprehensible. With older children, on the other hand, the lie which succeeds in its deceitful intent is worse. Fourth, as with clumsiness, an unintentional falsehood with serious objective consequences is judged worse by the younger subjects than a deliberate lie which happens not to result in anything serious. Again, older children reverse this evaluation. Fifth, younger children are inclined to say that a lie is bad because one is punished for it; older children think it is bad *per se,* whether one gets punished or not, because it violates mutual trust, makes good relations with others impossible, etc. And finally, younger children tend for various reasons to believe that a lie told to an adult is worse than one told to a peer, while older children see them as equally blameworthy.

The third chapter of the book deals with the child's conception of justice. There is a lot of theory and research in this long (135 pages) and meaty chapter, but at least its main points can be summarized. Ideas about how various misdeeds ought to be punished (what Piaget calls the problem of *retributive justice*) constitutes the first topic. Piaget distinguishes two broad classes of punishment. The first is *expiatory punishment:* the wrongdoer should suffer, expiate by means of, a punishment which is painful in proportion to the seriousness of the offense but need in no way be related to the offense. The second is *punishment by reciprocity:* the emphasis here is not so much on inflicting severe punishment for expiation's sake but in bringing home to the offender in the most direct possible way the nature and consequences of his breach of relations with others by setting a punishment which is logically related to the offense. Suppose the offense consists of a child failing to bring home food for supper, having been told to do so (*ibid.,* pp. 200-201). To spank the offender, deny him some privilege, etc., would be classed as expiatory punishment. Punishments by reciprocity might include giving the child less supper than usual (since he failed to bring home the food) or refusing to do him a favor (since he refused to do you one). The point here is to "make the punishment fit the crime" in some intrinsic way so that the transgressor will better understand the implications of what he has done. Piaget posed hypothetical misdeeds of this kind and had the children choose, from several different suggested punishments, the one they thought was "best" or "fairest" for the case at hand. There was at least a tendency for the younger children to favor expiatory punishments (and usually the more severe the better) with the older children electing punishments of the reciprocity type. Furthermore, the older children were less inclined to think that direct and severe punishment itself, without explanation and discussion of why the act was wrong, would be an effective deterrent to future wrongdoing.

Two other investigations described in this chapter are worth relating. In the first, Piaget found that the younger children were more prone than the older ones to believe in what he calls *immanent justice:* the idea that Nature herself will punish misdeeds, e.g., a boy running away from a policeman (he had been caught stealing apples) crosses a river on a rotten bridge and the bridge breaks (*because* he had just done wrong; ordinarily it would not have broken). The second investigation consisted of various studies of *distributive justice,* i.e., how punishments and rewards should be distributed to members of a group. These interesting studies seemed to point to the existence of three rough stages. In the first (prior to age 7-8), the child is inclined to regard as "just" or "fair" whatever rewards or punishments the authority figure decides to dispense, even if it involves unequal punishment for the same crime, the granting of special privileges to favored individuals, and so forth. In stage 2 (about 7-8 to 11-12 years), the child is a rabid egalitarian: all *must* be treated equally, no matter what the circumstances. In stage 3 (from 11-12 or so), the child tempers equality with equity—a kind of relativistic egalitarianism in which strict equality will sometimes be winked at in favor of a higher justice. The subtle difference between stages 2 and 3 can be illustrated by responses to the following story:

> *Story II.* One Thursday afternoon, a mother asked her little girl and boy to help her about the house, because she was tired. The girl was to dry the plates and the boy was to fetch in some wood. But the little boy (or girl) went and played in the street. So the mother asked the other one to do all the work. What did he say? (*ibid.,* p. 276).

The stage-2 response is simply to assert the basic unfairness of the request and advocate noncompliance. The stage-3 response grants the basic inequity but suggests compliance anyhow, out of wish to help the mother, not to make her suffer in the service of principle, and so on. Similarly, equity may preclude hitting back a small child who has hit you first, whereas equality demands an eye for an eye with no exceptions.

The changing concept of justice is also expressed in children's reactions to this vignette:

> One afternoon, on a holiday, a mother had taken her children for a walk along the Rhône. At four o'clock she gave each of them a roll. They all began to eat their rolls except the youngest, who was careless and let his fall into the water. What will the mother do? Will she give him another one? What will the older ones say? (*ibid.,* p. 267).

Here is a judgment which is both pre-equality and pre-equity, with punishment at all costs winning the day:

> PAIL (7): *"He shouldn't be given another. He didn't need to let it drop.—*And what would the older ones have said if the little boy had been given another roll?—*That it wasn't fair: 'He's let it drop into the water and you go and give him another one.'*—Was it right to give him another one?—*No. He hadn't been good"* (*ibid.,* pp. 268-269).

And here is a case in which a conception of justice founded on strict equality prevails (with possibly a hint at equity):

> MEL (13), G.: *"They should have divided up what the other children had left and given some to the little chap.*—Was it fair to give him any more?—*Yes, but the child ought to have been more careful.*—What does 'fair' mean? *—It means equality among everyone"* (*ibid.,* p. 270).

A number of the oldest children also reached an essentially egalitarian conclusion (the child ought to be given a second roll), but by means of a more subtle and mature line of reasoning involving considerations of equity. These subjects carefully distinguished between the loss of the roll as a disembodied and abstract bit of wrongdoing and the same event as it occurred in its living context, with extenuating circumstances (the wrongdoer is young and irresponsible, etc.):

> CAMP (11), G.: *"The little boy ought to have taken care. But then he was a little boy, so they might give him a little piece more.*—What did the others say?—*They were jealous and said that they ought to be given a little piece more too. But the little one deserved to be given a little piece more. The older ones ought to have understood.*—Do you think it was fair to give him some more?— . . . *Of course! It was a shame for the little one. When you are little you don't understand what you are doing"* (*ibid.,* p. 271).

Throughout these three chapters, and especially in the final chapter, Piaget interjects what amounts to a theory of the development of moral judgment. In brief, it is this. There appear to be two moralities in childhood, at least within the culture from which Piaget's subjects were drawn. The developmentally earlier one is a *morality of constraint,* formed in the context of the unilateral relations between child as inferior and adult as superior. The child adapts to the prohibitions and sanctions handed down from on high by reifying them (a *moral realism* akin to the *intellectual realism* studied earlier) into moral absolutes—simple "givens" which are unquestioned and sacred, in theory if not in practice. Hence, the child views wrongdoing in objective rather than subjective terms, is confined to the letter rather than the spirit of the law, and is incapable of seeing morality-relevant acts either in terms of the inner motives of the actor or in terms of the social-interpersonal meaning of the act itself (i.e., as a breach of solidarity and mutual trust between group members). For a morality of constraint, it must be the overt consequences alone which count in assessing the wrongfulness of acts (untruths, clumsiness, and the like), not the inner intentions and motives involved. Similarly, justice reduces simply to whatever the authority commands, rather than being seen as an equitable distribution of sanctions and rewards, these sanctions and rewards meaningfully related to the acts which engendered them.

With development, this morality of constraint is at least partially replaced by a *morality of cooperation,* formed out of the reciprocal relationships among status peers and based on mutual, rather than unilateral, respect. With a growing understanding of the role of motives in the actions of self and others and of the social implications of antisocial behavior, the child comes to the basic *raison d'être* of morality and begins to conceive (if not always to follow in practice) moral action as an autonomous good, essential to the intact functioning of any social unit. With this orientation, rules become rational conventions which serve orderly group action rather than arbitrary and untouchable dicta; malfeasance is judged by motivational as well as objective criteria; and justice, now placed in a social context, is seen in terms of equality and equity.

It is clear that the mechanism which Piaget holds responsible for the development of a rational morality is exactly the same as that which he thinks engenders rationality in general, and therein lies the important theoretical tie between this and the preceding four books (*ibid.,* pp. 406-411).[9] Both morality and logic are fired in the crucible of the spontaneous give and take, the interplay of thought and action, which takes place in peer-peer interactions. The prescripts, logical and moral, which parents and other adults impose upon the young and egocentric mind are compliantly accepted but at the same time simplified and distorted. It is only through a sharing of perspectives with equals—at first other children, and later, as the child grows up, adults—that a genuine logic and morality can replace an egocentric, logical, and moral realism. It might also be

---

[9] Piaget also sees an intrinsic connection between morality and thought *per se,* apart from the developmental parallelism, e.g., "Logic is the morality of thought just as morality is the logic of action" (*ibid.,* p. 404).

mentioned that even in these early days Piaget had developed strong opinions about how to educate children, based on just these conceptions (*ibid.*, pp. 411-414). For example, he believed that schools should foster and encourage group projects in which children could freely exchange ideas on a common intellectual task close to their own interests. As he himself acknowledged, his philosophy of education is closely aligned in this respect with that of Dewey and other progressivists.

CHAPTER NINE

Quantity, Logic, Number, Time, Movement, and Velocity

CHAPTER 8 dealt with what might be called the first wave of Piaget's experimental assault on the development of intelligence in the post-infancy years. There was to be a second wave, of larger scale and longer duration. This second wave of research had a small beginning in the period 1935-1940 with a few scattered journal articles (e.g., Inhelder, 1936; Meyer, 1935; Szeminska, 1935; Piaget and Szeminska, 1939) and moved into high gear in 1941 with the publication of the first (Piaget, 1952b) of a long series of full-length books on various cognitive-developmental problems: number, quantity, logic, space, time, and so on.

QUANTITY

There are several studies which touch on one or another aspect of the child's grasp of quantity notions (Apostel, Morf, Mays, and Piaget, 1957; Fischer, 1955; Inhelder, 1936; Piaget, 1960a; Piaget and Szeminska, 1939; Szeminska, 1935). The earlier papers are primarily of historical interest, since their contents have for the most part been incorporated into the systematic book on the subject by Piaget and Inhelder, *Le Développement des quantités chez l'enfant* (1941). This book is divided into four sections, each three chapters long. In addition, there is the customary chapter of summary and conclusions at the end of the book. The first section deals with what is probably the best-known segment of the quantity work: the so-called conservation of matter, weight, and volume of an object in the face of changes of shape. The basic technique is a simple one (*ibid.*, p. 7). The experimenter gives the subject a ball of clay and asks him to make another exactly like it—"just as big and just as heavy." After the child has done this, the experimenter retains one of the balls as a standard of comparison and changes the appearance of the other by stretching it into a sausage, flattening it into a cake, or cutting it into several pieces. The experimenter then attempts to find out whether the child thinks the

298

amount of clay, the weight, and the volume have changed or have remained invariant (i.e., conserved) as a result of the transformation.

The method of inquiry varies with the type of quantity notion investigated. For matter (amount of clay, or global quantity), the child is simply asked if the standard and the altered piece of clay both possess the same amount of clay (*la même chose de pâte* is the usual expression here); occasionally, this is concretized in terms of "just as much to eat," or something of that sort. In the case of weight, a scale balance is used (the book is not clear as to whether it is used with all subjects) and the experimenter asks if variable and standard weigh the same (*la même chose lourd*), or would keep the scale arms horizontal if placed on opposite pans. The assessment is more indirect in the case of volume. A glass container with water in it is used as the common measure. The experimenter shows that each ball of clay, when placed in the container, causes the water level to rise to the same height. He then alters one of the balls and asks if it will still make the water rise to that same height.

Note the analogy between these kinds of problems, given to preschool children and older, and the problem confronting the infant in acquiring the object concept (Chapter 4). In the latter case, the acquisition consists of discovering that the sheer existence of an object remains invariant, is conserved, despite changes of position in space (particularly, whether it is in or out of the infant's visual field). In the present experiments and in most of the conservation studies,[1] a similar but much more subtle acquisition is required: to discover that *certain attributes* of an object remain invariant in the wake of substantive changes in *other attributes*.

The principal findings of these studies are as follows. First, each type of quantity concept (matter, weight, and volume) shows about the same developmental trend: (1) no conservation; (2) an empirically founded, "on and off" sort of conservation, i.e., the child tentatively hypothesizes conservation for some transformations but denies it for others; and (3) a logically certain, almost axiomatic assertion of conservation in the case of all transformations for the type of quantity concept in question. The other major finding is that, despite this apparent similarity among tasks, of the conservation of matter, weight, and volume are not achieved of a piece. For Piaget's subjects, conservation of matter seems to become common at 8-10 years of age, of weight at 10-12, and of volume only at 12 years and after.[2]

---

[1] We shall shortly describe one particular conservation task, involving the dissolving of sugar in water, whose formal properties are even more like those of the object concept problem.

[2] The only statistic to be found in the quantity book bears on this *horizontal décalage* among the three types of quantity concept. Of 180 children aged 4-10 years, 55 showed no conservation of any kind, 67 showed conservation of matter alone, 38 of matter and weight but not volume, and only 20 of all three (*ibid.*, p. 12). Although this is not explicitly stated, one gets the impression that developmental *reversals* (e.g., conservation of volume achieved before conservation of weight) were rare or absent.

Piaget's interpretation of these findings is complex and detailed, but the key elements appear to be the following. There are probably two developing schemas which together contribute to the acquisition of matter conservation, i.e., conservation of the global "amount of stuff" in the piece of clay. There is first the general capacity to *multiply relations* (*ibid.*, pp. 24-25), already described in Chapter 5 apropos of concrete-operational Grouping VII. Consider the case where the ball of clay is transformed into a sausage. Conservation of matter will be a likelier outcome if the child notices both length and thickness changes and can apprehend that what the clay has gained in length it has lost in thickness (leaving total quantity invariant). The second schema, closely related to the first, is called *atomism* (*ibid.*, pp. 28-29). Again, the belief in conservation becomes more probable if the child can conceive of the clay as a whole composed of tiny parts or units which simply change their location vis-à-vis one another when the whole undergoes a transformation of shape. Conservation of matter is here the expression of the fact that the total sum of these parts remains the same, whatever their spatial distribution.

What prevents the child, once in possession of these intellectual tools, from immediately extending the invariance of matter to that of weight and volume? In the case of weight, subject protocols suggest the following difficulty (*ibid.*, pp. 36-40). While readily granting that the total number of tiny units of clay always remains the same (and thereby granting conservation of matter), the subject may yet believe that the weight of each unit varies with its location in the whole. Egocentric prenotions about the nature of weight (weight is the sensation of pressure on my hand when I hold an object, etc.) seem to pose a specific obstacle to the conservation of weight, even when the child is fully in possession of the schemas necessary for conservation of matter. A parallel obstacle exists in the case of volume. Piaget believes that nonconservation of volume (where the other two conservations are established) results specifically from an implicit belief that each tiny unit of clay varies in the amount of space it occupies, compresses and decompresses, alters its density, as a function of its position in space following transformation of the whole (*ibid.*, pp. 65-66). The conservation of volume is a late achievement because, as we shall see, the requisite schemas relating to density and compression-decompression of matter are themselves late achievements.

One of the major conjectures of the first section, then, is that there are certain schemas concerning the physical characteristics of objects whose aquisition at least facilitates the formation of the quantity conservations. However, it remains for experiments other than those just described to bring the development of these schemas more fully to light. The second section describes such an investigation in the case of the atomism schema; the third section does the same for those of density and compression-decompression. In the atomism study, the following task was administered to about 100 children of 4-12 years of age (*ibid.*, pp. 83-84). The subject was shown two identical glasses containing equal quantities of water, and established their equivalence of weight on a scale balance. The experimenter then put two or three pieces of sugar in one of the glasses and marked the height to which the water rose. A number of questions were asked of the child, both before and after the pieces of sugar completely dissolved in the water. As in the earlier studies, the primary intent of the questions was to find out what the child thought would remain invariant as the sugar slowly changed state. Its qualities (sweet taste)? Its existence as a substance? Its weight? Its volume?

The first developmental stage here is an interesting one. The younger children appear to think that the sugar becomes completely annihilated as an existent when it dissolves, much as the infant regards an object as no longer existing which has passed out of the visual field (see footnote 1). Curiously enough, however, many of these same children do believe that a (disembodied) sugar taste will somehow be left behind in the water—a kind of "conservation of taste" reminiscent of the "conservation of smile" in Lewis Carroll's Cheshire cat! But the majority feel that even this poor vestige will disappear in a day or two and the water will again become tasteless.

Stage 2 is a complex one, comprising various transitional phases. Its essential criterion is the assertion that sugar-as-existent does indeed remain invariant after the sugar has dissolved. Furthermore, the more stable and definite this belief in conservation, the more likely it is to entail an atomistic rather than some other rationale: that is, the sugar is not really "gone"; it still exists as very tiny, invisible particles spread throughout the water. As in the previous conservation experiment, this belief in the continued existence of the sugar in the form of microscopic grains does not automatically bring with it the conservation of its weight and volume. The children of stage 2 are quite ready to assume that the tiny grains of sugar (the belief in the existence of which leads to belief in the conservation of substance) are by their very diminutiveness not endowed with either weight or volume. These invariances are achieved later in childhood; first weight, then volume, just as in the preceding conservation study.

There are several experiments which deal with the development of conceptions of density and compression-decompression. In one, the experimenter heats a piece of popcorn until it pops and asks the child, first, whether or not the amount of matter and the weight have remained invariant, and second, why the volume has changed. In another, the child is shown several objects of different density and is asked various questions about amount of matter, weight, volume, and their interrelations (e.g., why this object is smaller but heavier than that object, etc.). Piaget draws two major conclusions from the results of these and other experiments described in the third section.

First of all, the data here point towards a general conclusion about the evolution of quantity concepts, a conclusion which the previous studies had also suggested. These concepts begin by being confused and undifferentiated in the young child's cognition and only gradually emerge from this undifferentiated totality as separate, stabilized quantity concepts (e.g., *ibid.*, pp. 134, 183-184). Thus, in the beginning there really is no concept of amount of matter, or weight, or volume, distinct and separate from each of the others. A little later, as we have seen, amount of matter differentiates from this conglomerative concept to become a rational affair for which conservation can be predicated, for which subquantities always sum to the same total quantity, and so forth. However, weight and volume are at this point still undifferentiated and, *a posteriori*, are not yet separably rational concepts which can submit to reversible operations. Still later, these two also articulate from one another, and each in its turn goes on to become a genuinely quantitative construct. The popcorn experiment illustrates quite clearly the earlier stages of this differentiation process. The younger subjects immediately assume that the piece of corn weighs more after it has popped because it is "bigger." Weight and volume (for these children, a kind of global "bigness") are apparently not seen as distinct and different properties which can vary independently, although usually correlated in nature. It is only after the child recognizes the logical independence of these properties that any idea of a genuine quantification of either becomes possible (e.g., *ibid.*, p. 315).

The second major conclusion is more specific to the experiments at hand, although also obviously relevant to those described earlier: a genuine grasp of the concept of volume and of its relation to weight requires the development of a schema of substance density and related concepts concerning compression and decompression of matter. Piaget's data suggest that about the time the child becomes capable of managing volume problems he also shows the following sort of conception about the nature of matter (e.g., *ibid.*, pp. 130-133, 183). Substances are composed of numerous tiny parts or elements with empty spaces in between. Substances (and of course the objects made from them) can vary as to how tightly these elements are compressed or packed together, i.e., how much of the total volume is really substance and how much is essentially empty space. Objects which are heavy for their size are thus composed of tightly packed elements; lighter ones are more loosely packed, with lots of empty spaces in between. The transformation of volume in the popcorn study is readily explained by children who think in these terms. The tiny elements of which the corn is composed have simply decompressed and are therefore farther apart from each other than they were before. Piaget believes that through the auspices of this underlying schema about the nature of matter the child finally works out a coherent and consistent notion of volume, one which permits him to contrast and relate it to weight (density problems of the third section) and to establish it as an invariant under certain transformations of form and state (conservation problems of the first and second sections).

The first three sections of the quantity book deal with the child's understanding of the concepts of amount of matter, weight, and volume, either directly, or in terms of other concepts (atomism, density, etc.) thought to underlie this understanding. The fourth section concerns the child's developing capacity to perform certain basic logical and mathematical operations on these concepts, particularly operations involving the addition of asymmetrical and symmetrical relations. Such operations are, of course, very general (we shall encounter them again in other Piaget volumes). They are studied here as "forms" specifically applied to the quantity notions as "contents." There are a number of experimental questions here. Can the child successfully seriate objects of varying weights, particularly when volume and weight are not correlated across the object series? Does the child recognize the transitivity principle as it applies to equal and unequal weights and volumes?

To illustrate the general tenor of these experiments, let us examine more closely some of the paradigms for investigating transitivity of weight. Where the transitivity principle applies to inequalities of weight, one such paradigm entails giving the child three objects of different weight (but weight uncorrelated with volume) and asking him to seriate them by weight (heaviest, middle, lightest), with the added condition that he can compare the weight of only two objects at a time. It turns out that young children have considerable difficulty in solving problems of this kind. For instance, the child may think that it suffices to establish $A < C$ and $A < B$ alone in order to conclude that $A < B < C$ or $A < C < B$; and conversely, $A < B < C$ is not for him a logically necessary conclusion from the knowledge that $A < B$ and $B < C$. The experimental technique and results are the same in the case of equalities of weight, e.g., that $A = B$ and $B = C$ does not in itself guarantee that $A = C$ for the young child, and $A + B$ is not necessarily equal to $C + D$ after establishing $A = B = C = D$. In general, it can be concluded that formal compositions of this sort cannot be managed until the quantitative concepts in question become stable entities endowed with conservation.

LOGIC

The investigations to be reported in this section are actually of narrower compass than the title "Logic" suggests (are there any Piaget experiments which do not have something to do with logic?). These studies were designed specifically to uncover the origins of classification and seriation operations and their genesis from early to middle childhood. This work is systematically set forth in Piaget and Inhelder, 1959; however, there are previews of parts of it in earlier publications (Piaget, 1952b, 1957-1958; Inhelder, 1955), and a book review provides an excellent brief summary (Donaldson, 1960). The Piaget and Inhelder book is bounded by an Introduction and a Conclusion, both oriented towards theory, with ten experimental chapters in between.[3] The first eight of these chapters concern classification behavior; the last two deal with seriation.

Perhaps the most interesting and important research in *La Genèse des structures logiques élémentaires* is that reported in the first four chapters, and it is this research that we shall cover in most detail. Two types of experimentation are described here. The first concerns free classification: the child is given a potpourri of objects (geometric forms, cut-outs of people, animals, plants, and the like—the precise collection varying with the experiment) and told to put those together which "are similar" or "go together." The second type of study deals with the child's understanding of the relation between a class and its subclasses. From these experiments the authors conclude that there are three rough stages in the developing mastery of elementary classification operations.

In stage 1 (2½-5 years), the child tends to organize classifiable material, not into a hierarchy of classes and subclasses founded on similarities and differences among objects, but into what the authors term *figural collections*. The sorting behavior of this stage has several distinguishing characteristics. First, it is a relatively planless, step-by-step affair in which the sorting criterion is constantly shifting as new objects accrue to the collection. The expression Piaget uses to describe it—a sorting which proceeds *de proche en proche* (*ibid.*, p. 285)—is wonderfully descriptive. Second, and partly in consequence of this inch-by-inch procedure bereft of a general plan, the collection finally achieved is not a logical class at all but a complex figure (hence *figural collection*). The figure may be a meaningful object, e.g., the child decides (often *post hoc*) that his aggregation of objects is "a house." Or instead, it may simply be a more or less meaningless configuration. It should be made clear here that figural factors are not the sole determinants of the child's groupings at each and every step in the sorting sequence. Frequently, at least part of the child's collection

---

[3] There is one striking difference between this book and Piaget's earlier ones, namely, its marked (for Piaget) bent towards quantitative presentation of findings. Two examples: the book virtually begins by stating the total number of subjects tested (2159); as a whole it contains 35 data tables (most of its predecessors contained none). The authors make it clear that this effort at quantitative presentation is intended to disarm the criticism that Piaget's elaborate theoretical architecture is generally founded on the sand of small N's (Piaget and Inhelder, 1959, Preface)—a criticism they had apparently been catching from all quarters!

is founded on a similarity-of-attributes basis. What often happens is that the child begins by putting similar objects together, as though a genuine classification were in progress, and then "spoils" it by incorporating his "class" into a nonclass, configurational whole. One 3-year-old, for instance, put some circles into a pile, then put some squares together next to the circles, then continued the process with other groups of objects. What appeared to be a sequence of constructed logical classes revealed its true configurational colors when the child looked at what he had made and said: *"Un train, tsch, tsch, tsch!" (ibid.,* p. 40).

Piaget asserts that there are two related difficulties at the root of the young child's inability to compose genuine classes (e.g., *ibid.,* pp. 50-52). The first difficulty is that the child, in his alternating reliance on similarity and configurational criteria, indicates that he cannot yet differentiate two essentially different kinds of colligation: the formation of a *logical class* and the construction of an *infralogical whole*. The differentiation and separate development of these two kinds of operations will be among the more important achievements of the concrete-operational period (see our Chapter 5). As in the case of the three-year-old mentioned above, partial groupings based on attribute similarity do occur at this age, but they are conceptually fragile and unstable affairs, forever in danger of turning into infralogical totalities.

The second underlying difficulty is just as important, in Piaget's view. The stage-1 child also cannot differentiate, and hence cannot coordinate, class *comprehension* (the sum of qualities which define membership in a logical class) and class *extension* (the sum total of objects which possess these criterial qualities). In a genuine classification, these two class properties must always be in strict correspondence: the definition of the classification basis determines precisely which objects must constitute its extension, and the nature of the objects in a given collection places tight constraints on the definition of the class they together form. But for the young child, there seems to be no such strict correspondence. For example, the comprehension of the "class" he begins to construct does not determine a unique extension, as it must in true classification. Thus, he begins by putting squares together, but he does not include all the squares present, or he contaminates his collection with nonsquares. In the same way, we have seen that the extensions he does end up with frequently determine not a class but an infralogical whole, and thus they effectively take him out of the realm of logical classification altogether.

One can partially summarize the young preoperational child's difficulties in classification this way. Several years of experience in applying sensory-motor schemas to reality have provided him with ample cognitive equipment to "see" similarities between objects and gather them into collectivities on the basis of these similarities. But the mere possession of this ability leaves him farther from a genuine grasp of classification than might be suspected. For one thing, he has yet to learn to form similarity-of-attributes groupings which remain untainted by the ever-intrusive configurational factors. That is, he needs to distinguish logical from infralogical operations. But in addition, he has yet to manage the essential coordination between class comprehension and important extensional notions like "some" and "all." The latter notion figures in any classification; the former becomes of particular importance where hierarchies of classes are to be dealt with. As Piaget shows in his analysis of the subsequent two stages, a full and complete grasp of the comprehension-extension relation matures surprisingly late. Furthermore, special testing is required to diagnose hidden gaps in this understanding. The child's ability to bandy about classification-relevant phrases (e.g., "dogs are animals," "some of these are red," etc.), either under ordinary questioning or in spontaneous discourse, is likely to be a most unreliable guide.[4]

Figural collections give way to *nonfigural* collections around 5½-7-8 years (stage 2). The child now forms groups of objects on a similarity-of-attributes basis alone, tries to assign every object in the display to one or another group, and can even partition major groups into their constituent subordinate groups. In short, he now appears to be in command of genuine classificatory operations. Why then, does Piaget still call his productions "collections"—albeit nonfigural ones—rather than "classes"? In what way can he be said to fall short of possessing a full-fledged concrete-operational structure of classifications? What is still lacking, Piaget contends, is a subtle and hard to diagnose but nonetheless crucial ability to grasp and keep constantly in mind the *inclusion relation* obtaining between a class and its subclasses, to recognize that a subclass A is *included* in class B but does not *exhaust* it (hence, to recognize that $A = B - A'$) and to keep this $A - B$ relation firmly in mind across all manner of changes in the spatial distribution of class and subclass or in one's distribution of attention regarding them. The capacity to do this entails the precise coordination of class comprehension and extension discussed earlier; one must at every step compare the different but overlapping extensions of class and subclass, e.g., B includes the extension of A but adds to it that of A'. For Piaget, mastery of the inclusion relation, with all that its mastery implies, is the *sine qua non* of a concrete-operational (stage 3) as opposed to late preoperational (stage 2) cognition of logical classification:

> In the case of inclusion, the subsuming class B continues to subsume . . .
> whether the subsumed parts [i.e., subordinate subclasses] A and A' are ac-

---

[4] As Donaldson aptly puts it in her review of the Inhelder and Piaget book: "It might not be too inadequate a summary of the book to say that it consists in an attempt to show that, in the absence of special inquiry, the child's ability to handle language may grossly mislead us as to his ability to handle classificatory systems" (Donaldson, 1960, p. 182).

tually brought together (as a collection of continuous elements or by an act of abstract "colligation") or are dissociated under the form $A = B - A'$ (in space or by abstraction). Contrariwise, the essence of a collection as opposed to a class is that it exists only when its elements are continuous in space (even if the basis of their being together is no longer figural), and consequently ceases to exist *qua* collection when its sub-collections are separated from each other: the result is that, when the sub-collections are reunited under the form $A + A'$, the subject indeed sees them as constituting the whole B (thus $A + A' = B$), but when the sub-collections are dissociated, in space or even simply in thought, the child no longer sees them as constituting the supraordinate collection and is thus shown to be incapable of the operation $A = B - A'$. An operation being reversible by definition, we conclude that if the inverse operation $A = B - A'$ is still inaccessible to the subject, the union $A + A' = B$ does not at stage II yet constitute a direct operation, but simply an intuitive union by momentary differentiation of the collection B into sub-collections A and A' (*ibid.*, pp. 55-56).

The book describes several experiments designed to illustrate the older child's better management of the inclusion relation. Indirect evidence comes from a series of experiments (Chapter 7) which indicate his greater flexibility and mobility in ascending and descending a class hierarchy, in shifting criteria and reclassifying a previously classified array of objects, in anticipating what a hierarchy will contain in advance of constructing it, and the like. However, the most direct evidence is provided by two ingenius experiments reported in Chapters 3 and 4.

One involves the child's ability to handle the class quantification concepts "some" and "all" as applied to classes and subclasses in a hierarchy. The child is presented with a series of objects which can be partitioned into several sets of classes and subclasses. For example, the display might consist of 2 red squares, 2 blue squares, and 5 blue circles (*ibid.*, p. 65, Fig. 7). This display yields these classes and subclasses: the class of blue objects (B) with subclasses of blue circles (A) and blue squares (A'); the class of squares (B) with subclasses of blue squares (A) and red squares (A'). The questions posed the child are of two forms: Are all the B's A (or A'), i.e., are all the blue ones circles, are all the squares red, etc.? Are all the A's (or A''s) B, i.e., are all the circles blue, are all the red ones squares, etc? A simplified statement of the results of this study is the following. The younger child appears to construe both types of questions as asking whether A and B are of identical extension, i.e., $A = B$? As a general rule, this simplification of the task leads him to a *correct* response to the first type of question; for example, he compares the extension of blue objects (B) and circles (A) and rightly concludes that not all B is A because there are also some blue squares (A'). However, this strategy leads to an *incorrect* response to questions of the second type. If asked whether all the circles are blue, he gives the astonishing answer that they are not, because there are also blue squares! In effect, the child is interpreting the second type of question, not as asking whether all A is some B, but as asking whether all A is all B.

The second experiment is a replication, with variations, of one Piaget carried out years ago and reported in the book on number (Piaget, 1952b). The experimental paradigm is this. The child himself constructs a class hierarchy out of a set of objects or pictures of objects before him, e.g., the class of flowers (B) with subclasses of primroses (A) and other flowers (A'). The experimenter then makes sure the child understands the basic properties of his simple hierarchy: that a bouquet of all the flowers (B) would contain the primroses (A) and the others (A'), i.e., $B = A + A'$. This established (and children of stage 2 generally have little difficulty here), the experimenter poses "quantification of inclusion" questions concerning the relative extensions of B and A. Are there more primroses or more flowers here? Would a bouquet of all the flowers be bigger, smaller, or the same as a bouquet of primroses? The stage-2 child fails these questions, usually because he makes a quantitative comparison, not between A and B, but between A and A', e.g., "there are more primroses (A) because there are only a few of the others (A')." The following is a more or less typical behavior protocol:

> THE (5;6). "If I make a bouquet of all the primroses and you make one of all the flowers, which will be bigger?—*Yours*.—(the experimenter takes 4 primroses and 4 other flowers and repeats the question.)—*The same* $(A = A')$.—If you gather all the primroses in a meadow will any flowers remain?—*Yes*.—And if you gather all the flowers will any primroses remain?—*Yes . . . no*.—Why?—*Because you take all the flowers*.—And if one gathers all the yellow primroses will any primroses remain?—*Yes, there will still be the violet ones*.—And if one gathers all the primroses, will there be any yellow primroses left?—*No, because you take all the primroses and there aren't any left*." The questions on quantification of inclusion still remain insoluble (Piaget and Inhelder, 1959, p. 108).

The following is a somewhat simplified account of Piaget's interpretation of these two experiments. The stage-2 subject cannot yet quite dominate the logical inclusion operation, epitomized by the logical equation $A = B - A'$ (see again the Piaget quotation cited on p. 306). In the case of the first experiment, he is unable to recognize that the "all" of A does in fact correspond to the "some" (although not the "all") of B, as the equation $A = B - A'$ precisely expresses. He does not clearly understand that "included in" is not synonymous with "equals," and this indicates that his mastery of the structure of a class hierarchy is still incomplete. In the second experiment, he is unable to keep in mind the class B (with A a subclass in it) when his attention is directed to A itself. Again, this can be construed as an inability to perform the operation $A = B - A'$. In effect, what he needs to be able to think, and cannot, is this: "I recognize that A is still a subportion of B, and hence of lesser extension than

B, even though I have momentarily abstracted it from B in order to compare their extensions." Piaget believes that the child can recognize that A and A' comprise B *when he focuses attention on the whole B* (thus, he can perform $B = A + A'$), but "loses" B (and the fact that $A = B - A'$) when he isolates A as a comparison term. With B momentarily inaccessible as an object of thought, the child cannot do other than compare A with its complement A'.

We shall deal with the remainder of the book very briefly. Its fifth chapter adduces further evidence on the development of the inclusion relation by means of special experiments on the child's management of complementary, singular, and null classes. The seventh chapter does the same with studies of the capacity to manipulate class hierarchies in a planful and flexible manner: to anticipate a hierarchy in advance of actually constructing it, to construct new hierarchies with old materials by changing the classification basis, and the like. The sixth chapter describes investigations of class multiplication abilities by means of matrix tasks (like those of Raven Progressive Matrices). The authors conclude that class multiplication and class addition are approximately synchronous developmental attainments; indeed, the former may even appear to be more precocious because of certain facilitating perceptual properties inherent in matrix tasks. The eighth chapter shows that a tactokinesthetic rather than visual presentation of classifiable materials yields the same three developmental stages: figural collections, nonfigural collections, and genuine classification. The last two chapters deal with the ability to serialize rather than classify. The ninth chapter describes experiments on simple additive seriation which are essentially variations on studies done earlier (Piaget, 1952b). An interesting finding here is that children can apparently construct a series of sticks of graded lengths in a drawing before they can produce it in reality, i.e., before they can actually arrange the sticks in order of length. Finally, the tenth chapter reports a study concerning the multiplication, not of classes, but of asymmetrical relations. Its apparent complexity notwithstanding, the ability to multiply several asymmetrical series together also appears to emerge in rough developmental concordance with the other abilities we have been describing.

NUMBER

There are a number of publications which report the work of Piaget and his associates in this area. The basic reference is *The Child's Conception of Number* (Piaget, 1952b), and the present account is taken almost completely from this source. There exists an excellent detailed summary of this book (National Froebel Foundation, 1955); briefer and less complete synopses are also available, including several by Piaget himself (e.g., 1953a, 1956). In addition, there are miscellaneous other publications which deal with one or another aspect of the number research (e.g., Inhelder and Noelting, 1957; Piaget, 1937c; Piaget and Inhelder, 1941, 1959; Piaget and Szeminska, 1939; Szeminska, 1935). And finally, there is some interesting more recent research in the area by the Geneva group and others (e.g., Apostel, Mays, Morf, and Piaget, 1957; Gréco, Grize, Papert, and Piaget, 1960). Some of this work will be described in Chapter 11.

More than was the case with the quantity and logic research, the number experiments require some stage-setting preamble before their intended significance can emerge clearly. In particular, two preliminary questions need answers. (1) Precisely what sorts of mathematical skills or knowledges did Piaget have in mind to study? (2) What is his working conception of the nature of number and of arithmetic operations? And particularly (3) what are the basic skill components which these operations are thought to entail?

For the first, the simplest answer is that Piaget was and is much more interested in a kind of "number readiness" than in arithmetic achievement as such. He wanted to probe and diagnose for developing number-relevant capabilities considerably more subtle and basic than those involved in the familiar elementary operations of counting, of rote addition, subtraction, etc., i.e., the mundane arithmetic behaviors one tends to associate with the traditional primary-school classroom. The capabilities he wanted to study have to do more with the essential and fundamental properties of the number system, the underlying assumptions about the nature and behavior of numbers which the ordinary adult tacitly makes—tacitly because they are so ingrained and "obvious"—in his routine arithmetic operations. This way of approaching the problem is, of course, not unique to the area of number for Piaget. For example, in the quantity studies an analogous attempt was made, first, to isolate a similarly tacit, because obvious, assumption about quantity concepts, namely, their conservation in the face of shape changes, and then to show that young children do not necessarily make this assumption, i.e., that conservation of quantity is in fact something which needs developing.

But to isolate the proper underlying assumptions and capabilities in a given area, those which will pay off in developmental study, it is necessary to do a kind of job analysis of that area. In the case of number, this involves an attempt to find out what it is that numerical operations really entail in the way of component skills and beliefs and what prior acquisitions these operations imply. Piaget has made such an analysis of number, and it is this analysis which has largely set the course for his experimentation (Piaget, 1952b, pp. viii, 94-95, 156-157, 182-184, 243; see also our Chapter 5, p. 198). According to Piaget, number is essentially a fusion or synthesis of two logical entities: class and asymmetrical relation. If one enumerates a set of objects and thereby arrives at its cardinal-number value ("there are 10 objects here"), one is in effect treating the objects as though they were all alike, just as one would do if one assigned them to a common class. Just as we disregard object differences in classifying a set of objects, so also do we disregard object differences in assigning the set its cardinal value. Thus, number clearly has a class component to it. Is a number simply a class, then? No, because although the enumerated objects are, as just stated, treated as equivalent to one another in so far as their being assigned a cardinal number is concerned, there is also a sense in which they are regarded as different from one another—not the case in class operations. In the process of discovering their cardinal value by enumeration, one has to order the objects: count this object first, then the next, then the next, and so on. It obviously makes no difference what the order of enumeration is, but there must be some order; one has to count them in some sequence and keep track of which have already been enumerated so as not to count the same objects more than once. This ordination[5] process partakes, not of class, but of relation operations. The objects arranged in the order in which one enumerated them form a true series, a set of asymmetrical relations, exactly analogous to a series of sticks of graded lengths. Here, however, the object differences are not of length but of ordinal position ("first object counted," "second object counted," etc.). Numerical units have, therefore, a peculiar status; they appear to be both class elements and asymmetrical relation elements at one and the same time. In one respect they are all equivalent, just as class elements are: in another respect they are all different, like the terms of an asymmetrical series. In order to count them, they must be counted seriatim; once counted, they are again all indistinguishable, just "10 objects."

If this analysis of the nature of number is accurate, then it suggests for Piaget that developmental study of the fundaments of numerical operations must have a very broad base. It will, of course, include investigation of the child's understanding of ordination, cardination, and their interrelations. It will also, of course, deal with the child's grasp of the essential additive and multiplicative properties of numbers. And it will also study the genesis of mathematical notions related to the above, e.g., the operation of one-one correspondence as the basis for both cardinal equivalence of sets and for multiplication. But it should also include study of class and seriation operations themselves, both directly and as they figure in the above numerical operations. Actually, Piaget sees

---

[5] Piaget uses the terms *ordination* and *cardination* to refer to operations concerning ordinal and cardinal numbers, respectively. These are useful nouns (although not in English usage with these meanings, so far as the writer can discover) and will be retained here.

classes, relations, and numbers as cognitive domains which develop synchronously in a tightly intertwined, mutually dependent way.[6]

Cognition of the extensional aspects of classes (see the previous section), for example, requires the prior acquisition of certain notions in the number area (e.g., "none," "some," "all"). But reciprocally, and more to the present point, Piaget strongly adheres to the view that a genuinely *operational* (in the concrete-operational sense) grasp of number necessitates a similarly operational management of classes and relations. When the child is capable of reversible seriation operations and of genuine classification (inclusion relation and all), then and only then will he be in a position to really understand what numbers are and how they behave.

The "very broad base" of Piaget's number research becomes immediately apparent when one skims the number book. The first chapter deals with conservation of quantity (a direct carry-over from the quantity research) as a prelude to a conservation of cardinal number—the latter mediated by the operation of placing two sets of objects in one-one correspondence (second, third, and fourth chapters). In the fifth and sixth chapters Piaget considers logical seriation, both *per se* and in its numerical guise (ordination), and then plunges into a detailed study of the ordination-cardination relationship. The seventh chapter likewise begins by leaving number for logic, this time logical classes, and then returns to number by analyzing the relation between it and class. The last three chapters deal with additive and multiplicative arithmetic operations, but these also are discussed from the standpoint of the logical operations from which they derive.

The first two experiments reported in the book make the transition from conservation of quantity to conservation of number. The first is clearly a conservation-of-quantity study: instead of balls of clay molded into different shapes, the task involves water poured into different-shaped vessels; the question then is simply whether there is the same amount of water in the two vessels. In the second experiment, the vessels contain beads instead of water, and the problem could be construed as either conservation of quantity or of number, depending on how the question is asked (same *amount* of beads? same *number* of beads?).

The task in the first experiment is said to deal with the concept of conservation of *continuous quantity*, the second with that of *discontinuous quantity*. In both investigations, as in the earlier one involving the balls of clay, there was the expected three-stage sequence; (1) no conserva-

---

[6] It is hard to stress enough the *unity* which Piaget sees in the development of cognition. The construction of number, of quantity, of logic, of space, etc.—all are believed to proceed apace and lean upon each other in diverse ways for their development. It would be tiresome to keep specifying each and every liaison of mutual dependence, and we shall not attempt it, but the fact of such dependence should constantly be kept in mind.

tion; (2) conflict between conservation and nonconservation, with perception and logic alternately getting the upper hand; and (3) a stable and logically certain conservation, based primarily on a coordination of vessel-height and vessel-width relations. This second experiment also incorporated a feature of more specific import for the study of number development. The beads were initially added to the two containers on a one-one correspondence basis, i.e., add a bead to container A at the same time that one adds a bead to container B, add a second to both, add a third to both, and so on. The fact that the two containers were filled in this way did not guarantee conservation of number for the younger children in the face of contradictory perceptual impression, even though the one-one correspondence method is a mathematically certain way of establishing cardinal equivalence of sets without counting.

The next several experiments were focused more directly on the role of this kind of correspondence in insuring cardinal equivalence. In a typical one the child was presented with a row of objects and asked to take the same number from a pile near at hand. The developmental sequence here is of some interest. In stage 1, the child is content simply to make a rough figural approximation to the row, e.g., he makes a row of about the same length as the model, but of different density, and hence, of different cardinal value. In stage 2, the child spontaneously makes use of the method of one-one correspondence: he places one object opposite each one in the model row and thus exactly reproduces its cardinal value without counting.[7] However, the experimenter has only to destroy the optical correspondence by spreading out or closing up one of the rows for the child to give up his earlier belief in cardinal equivalence. Like the stage-child, he now falls prey to perceptual illusion, e.g., the longer row is thought to contain more objects by virtue of its length. In the final stage, one-one correspondence is also used to establish the initial numerical equality, but now the equality is maintained after the optical correspondence is destroyed. The implication is clear: once more a concept must fight its way into stable, operational existence through a cobweb of illusion-producing perceptions. As with the quantity and logical notions, a genuine concept of cardinal number is by no means guaranteed by the ability to mouth appropriate numerical terminology in the presence of sets of objects.

---

[7] It is obvious that most of the problems described in this section could handily be solved by judicious use of simple counting operations; the present task is a case in point. But it is a moot question as to just how useful such operations are to the child of 4-7 years (most of Piaget's subjects in these studies were within this age range). In the majority of protocols that Piaget cites for this kind of experiment, counting did not appear to be involved at all; when it was, it was surprisingly unhelpful in producing a certain and stable cognition of cardinal value in the teeth of illusion-giving perceptual impression (e.g., *ibid.*, p. 59). In Chapter 11 we shall return to this interesting business of the role of counting in the young child's arithmetic understanding.

In experiments of this kind, the one-one correspondence by which cardinal equivalence is established can proceed by any pairing of elements from the two sets. That is, any object from the model row can be placed opposite any object in the child's row in the process of setting the two series in one-one correspondence. The next experiment inquires about the child's performance when particular elements of the one set must correspond to particular elements of the other. In the first case, there is *cardinal* correspondence between unseriated sets of elements; in the second case, there is *ordinal* correspondence between two asymmetrical series of elements. In this study, the child was shown 10 dolls of differing heights and 10 miniature walking sticks, also graded in height. He was first told to arrange dolls and sticks "so that each doll can easily find the stick that belongs to it" (*ibid.*, p. 97): in other words, to seriate both sets of elements and place the matching elements of the two series in ordinal correspondence. Once this was achieved, the experimenter closed up one of the series, so that each doll was no longer opposite its own stick, and the child was asked to find the stick which belonged to some particular doll singled out by the experimenter. Other questions and procedures were also used with the same materials, but we shall not pursue them here.

There were several important findings. First of all, the youngest children found it impossible even to construct a given series in the first place. They seemed to have at their disposal no rational procedure for doing this, for example, by selecting the shortest doll, then the next-to-shortest, etc., until the whole series was constituted. Piaget interprets this failure as an inability to grasp the reversibility inherent in seriable elements, i.e., to grasp that a given element n is at one and the same time longer than element $n - 1$ and shorter than element $n + 1$. (Thus it was that, in another study, children of this level were quite unable to insert *new* elements in their correct places within an *already-constructed* series.) However, once capable of seriating, the child was equally capable of establishing the correct ordinal correspondences, i.e., assigning to each doll its correct walking stick. But here, as in previous experiments, there was a stage where destruction of the perceptual correspondence (spreading out one of the series, mixing up its elements, and so on) sufficed to render the child incapable of reconstructing it, of finding the correct stick for a given doll. A number of children repeatedly made a particular error here, an error relevant to the line of investigation next undertaken: aware that they had to count in the second series to find the right stick for a particular doll in the first, they kept choosing the $n - 1$th stick where the nth stick was called for. It appeared as though they were somehow mixing up the ordinal number of the sought-after stick (nth) with the cardinal number ($n - 1$) of those smaller than it.

This ability to differentiate and coordinate the ordinal and cardinal aspects of number was the subject of the next several experiments. These experiments are quite space-consuming even to summarize, so we shall simply describe the sort of arithmetic understanding they investigated. In general, they tested for the child's ability to distinguish between and see the relationship between ordinal position in a series and the cardinal values determining this position and determined by it. Can the child deduce the various cardinal values associated with a selected ordinal position (nth) in a series, i.e., the cardinal number of elements prior to it ($n - 1$), prior to and including it (n), and following it (total minus n)? Conversely, can he deduce the ordinal position of an element in the series, given information about these various cardinal values? A simple way to characterize Piaget's results in these studies—a rather flaccid characterization in view of the qualitative richness of his observations and the subtle interpretation he himself gave them—is to say that ordination and cardination are not at all well coordinated in the young child's mind. The child's ability simply to make a vocal enumeration of series elements (Piaget took pains to insure that the child was not tested on elements too numerous for him to count) did not at all guarantee a grasp of this important relationship—a relationship so essential to a real understanding of number.

The last four chapters of the book report experiments which measure the child's burgeoning awareness of the basic additive and multiplicative properties of numbers. As mentioned earlier, however, Piaget's analysis of these properties proceeds in tandem with analyses of the corresponding class-and-relation logical operations. Thus, the first of these four chapters relates the experiment on the additive composition of classes reported in the preceding section of the present chapter (the one in which the child must compare the class extension of a class B with that of one of its subclasses A). The second chapter deals with the additive composition, not of class, but of number itself. It was discovered in one study, for example, that young children have difficulty in conserving an arithmetic whole when the additive composition of its parts is varied, i.e., understanding that 8 objects partitioned into sets of 4 and 4 are numerically equivalent to 8 objects distributed 1 and 7, grasping the fact that the increase from 4 to 7 is compensated by a corresponding decrease from 4 to 1, leaving the whole invariant. The ninth chapter proceeds to experiments involving the use of one-one correspondence across several sets of (unseriated) objects as a vehicle for making elementary arithmetic multiplication. For instance, if n flowers are set in one-one correspondence with n other flowers and with n little flower vases, how many flowers should go in each vase if each vase is to have an equal number of flowers, and how many vases would be needed if each vase could hold but one flower? The last chapter returns full circle to the first with the study of the child's ability to make use of a measuring unit in determining quantities of water in various different-shaped vessels. Since number, unlike class, involves iterable units, it is closely linked with the infralogical operation of measurement, of which the likewise iterable measuring unit is the cornerstone (see again our Chapter 5, p. 199).

TIME

It would not require any foreknowledge of Piaget's work to suspect that concepts of time, movement, and velocity might be rather closely related, both logically and in terms of their psychological development. It therefore comes as no surprise that Piaget looks upon his book on movement and velocity (Piaget, 1946b) as simply the sequel or continuation of his book on time (Piaget, 1946a). These two books are the prime sources of information on his extensive theoretical and experimental work in these areas. Indeed, they are almost the only sources; there exist only a few others of direct relevance (1942c, 1955c, 1957d, 1957g). Probably the best available summary of his thinking on temporal development is to be found in the concluding chapter of the time book itself; there is an analogous chapter in the volume on movement and speed, but it is likely to be less helpful to the average reader.

Since these three areas are so tightly interlocked in Piaget's logical and developmental analysis, our procedure will depart somewhat from that of previous sections. We shall begin the present section by outlining Piaget's general conception of the development, not only of time concepts, but of those of movement and speed as well. This done, the remainder of the section will consist of a summary of some of the experiments he has carried out on the development of time concepts. The next section will then be given over primarily to the empirical aspects of his work on movement and velocity, with only the minimum of superimposed theory necessary to round out the picture for these two concepts.

The first thing that needs to be said about time, movement, and velocity constructs (or perhaps by now it does not need to be said) is that they are literally *constructs;* not apriorities in the child's mind, they require a slow and gradual ontogenetic construction. Like other notions already discussed and yet to be discussed, they are put together step by step through the formation of their constituent logical operations (actually, infralogical operations here, as we saw in Chapter 5). Second, this ontogenetic construction is one in which each and every stage is marked by an extraordinarily close interdependence among the three types of concepts—a particularly striking example of the developmental unity and interdependence among areas mentioned in footnote 6.

Piaget believes that the young child initially confuses successions of events in time and the temporal intervals these successions engender with their analogues in space, that is, with the successions of points traversed in a movement and the spatial distances between the points. Given a single movement which proceeds across points $A, B, C, D,$ in that order, the child will correctly state that C was traversed "after" $A,$ that it took "more time" to make the itinerary AC than the itinerary $AB;$ in short, he will act as though his general conception of temporal succession and temporal duration were the same as ours. But appearances are deceptive here, because when the child has to deal with temporal successions and intervals in *two* movements *at once,* two movements, moreover, which proceed at different *velocities,* he makes astonishing errors. To take but one example: he is unwilling even to admit simultaneity of starting and stopping, let alone equality of duration, of two simultaneous movements whose velocities and, therefore, distances traversed are different (Piaget, 1946a, ch. 4). The child acts as though each movement had its own "time"—Piaget speaks of it as "local time" (e.g., *ibid.,* p. 273)—and that the "times" indigenous to different movements can therefore not be coordinated. What needs to be constructed intellectually is a "homogeneous time" (*ibid.,* p. 273) which is the common medium for all movements—synchronous or asynchronous, same speed or different speed—and which is by that fact differentiated from the spatial order and intervals comprised in any single movement. The time which needs construction is one which "constitutes a coordination of movements of different velocities" (*ibid.,* p. 273), and therefore must be tested for in situations other than those of the one-movement, $ABCD$ type illustrated above.

But to "coordinate movements of different velocities" surely requires some rational conception of movement and velocity to begin with, and this, it turns out, is precisely what the young child lacks. Initially, both are evaluated solely in terms of the end or termination point of the motion through space involved. In the case of movement, one object will be said to have made a longer journey, to have moved farther, if it ends up ahead of another, even though the former's itinerary was straight and the latter's was zigzag, and hence of greater total distance (Piaget, 1946b, ch. 3). The child compares only the positions of the termination points, neglecting the points of departure and the spatial intervals between. And velocity is likewise reduced to a schema of "passing" or of "being ahead," rather than being conceived as a specific relation between time and distance. When the child sees one object catch up to or end up ahead of another, he will conclude that it moved faster; but when the experimenter arranges things so he cannot actually see the "passing" (e.g., the two movements of unequal velocity take place inside tunnels), he is quite incapable of inferring a difference in velocity from the perceptually obvious fact that different distances were traversed in the same time (*ibid.,* ch. 6). Concepts of both movement and speed, then, are initially in such a state of development as to be of little service to the construction of operational time. But the paradox is that they cannot reach such a state themselves without the assistance of that very conception of time which appears to depend upon their development (Piaget, 1946a, p. 274). In the experiment cited above, for example, an inability to coordinate the two movements within a common temporal framework will, of course, make impossible the multiplication: (more distance) × (same time) = (greater speed). This sort of situation obtains everywhere in the genesis of intellectual operations as Piaget analyzes them: to achieve concept A requires prior developments in concepts B, C, D, etc., and conversely, a kind of developmental circle. Although Piaget is not as specific and clear here as one might wish, the presumption is that the circle just avoids being a vicious one by virtue of the fact that development proceeds by very small increments: tiny advances in one area (via the usual mechanism of decentration with progressive equilibration, etc.) pave the way for similarly small advances in another; these advances then redound to the developmental advantage of the first area, and so the spiral continues through ontogenesis.

Putting aside the question of whether development, here or elsewhere, does in fact proceed by such cross-fertilizations, there can be no question but that basic time, movement, and velocity concepts do develop more or less contemporaneously. But here we need to answer the question put to the number research. What is it that develops? What, in Piaget's view, are the crucial abilities that the child gradually acquires in these areas? The answer, as with number, almost amounts to a recital of the tables of content of the two books. In the case of time, there is first of all a conceptual grasp of temporal order of succession and of the temporal intervals between succeeding temporal points—analogous to the ordinal and cardinal aspects of number, respectively. Other achievements include an understanding of temporal simultaneity, additivity and associativity of temporal intervals, the measurement of time through the construction of the temporal unit, and finally, what Piaget calls "lived" time (*ibid.*, p. 205 ff.), including the concepts of age and of internal, subjective time. In the case of movement, there are the concepts of spatial order, composition of displacements in space (distances), and relative movements. And for velocity, there is the notion of the time-distance relation and its ultimate measurement in a variety of situations: in successive versus simultaneous movements, for uniform versus accelerated motion, and in the case of relative velocities.

The first investigation described in the book on time was an omnibus affair which assessed the child's understanding of a variety of time concepts. The apparatus consisted of a pear-shaped bottle (I) whose narrow end opened into a thin cylindrical bottle (II) with measuring lines which was placed below it. The narrow end of I had a spigot attachment permitting the experimenter to start and stop the flow of a colored liquid from I into II. In the beginning, I contained all the liquid and II was empty. The child was given a picture of the apparatus and asked to draw in the level of the liquid in I. The experimenter then turned on the spigot until the liquid rose to the first measuring line in II. To fix terminology, we shall say that the liquid had now risen to level II_1 in II and dropped to level I_1 in I. The child was given a second picture of the apparatus and asked to draw in the liquid levels as they were now. Then a second quantity of water, equal to the first, was allowed to flow into II, thus constituting new levels I_2 and II_2; and the child drew in these levels on a third picture. This procedure was repeated until all the liquid had flowed from I into II. The child now had before him a collection of pictures which together formed an ordered, equal-interval series of levels in the two vessels.

A number of problems were posed with these pictures as experimental materials and the principal findings were the following. (1) As earlier work on seriation would lead us to predict (Piaget, 1952b), the younger children had difficulties in establishing the temporal order of the pictures and in finding the appropriate II level for a given I level when the I and II halves of each picture were separated from each other. It was as though they had no clear conceptual grasp of succession and order in time, i.e., time as a straight-line affair with events occurring in ordered sequence along it. (2) The younger subjects would not concede that the corresponding drops in I and rises in II took the same amount of time to occur (many of them made this error even when referred, not to the drawings, but to the vessels themselves). Thus, for example, the child might maintain that the time $I_1 - I_2$ was not equal to the time $II_1 - II_2$, because the water level rose at a faster rate in II (because of its thinness) than it dropped in I. Moreover, this belief in inequality of temporal durations was sometimes maintained even when the child would admit the simultaneity of starting and stopping. It appeared as though—and subsequent research amply confirmed this—temporal order, simultaneity, and duration are very poorly coordinated notions for the preoperational child. (3) The younger subjects seemed to lack any genuinely metric conception of time; they were unable to grasp the idea of a temporal unit by means of which synchronous and successive temporal intervals in different movements could be compared. Thus, they could not compare the temporal duration of $I_1 - I_2$ with that of $II_1 - II_3$, of $I_1 - I_3$ with that of $II_2 - II_4$, and so on, even when the equality of the successive intervals $I_1 - I_2$, $I_2 - I_3$, etc., had been impressed upon them by the experimenter.

The details of this experiment (and we have by no means covered them all) occupy the first major section of the book. The second section reports investigations which follow up and extend its various findings. The first of these illuminates with particular clarity both the young child's undifferentiation between time and space and, deriving from it, his inability to establish the necessary relation between ordered points in time and the temporal intervals between them when two movements are involved. There were a number of procedural variations in this study. In one, an object hops from point A_1 to D_1 as a second hops a shorter distance from A_2 to B_2 (starts and stops obviously synchronous; distances $A_1 - B_1 = A_2 - B_2$, $B_1 - C_1 = B_2 - C_2$, etc.); immediately thereafter, the second object adds a hop from B_2 to C_2 while the first object remains stationary at D_1. The children of stage 1 completely failed to dissociate temporal order and interval from spatial order and interval here: the object which went the lesser distance in the greater total time (the second object) was thought both to have stopped sooner (order) and to have traveled for the shorter time (interval). A number of experimental checks and controls which were introduced suggested that this spatial-temporal undifferentiation, rather than other factors, was at the root of these curious responses. But the behavior of the stage-2 children was, if anything, even more startling: correct interpretation of temporal order coupled with incorrect judging of temporal interval, or the converse—duration correct and order incorrect. Parallel results were obtained in other variations of the task, e.g., different departure times with simultaneous arrivals.

There was a similar experiment which called for the assessment of orders and intervals in the case of simultaneous movements which took place at different velocities (this was the study briefly cited in the introduction to this section). In this situation, the object which went faster and farther, i.e., ended up ahead of its counterpart on a parallel path, was judged by the preoperational subjects to have stopped later and/or to have been of longer temporal duration. An interesting example of the checks and controls mentioned above was included here. The two simultaneous movements (unequal velocity and distance) were made to take place, not in parallel this time, but in opposite directions and terminating at the same point; thus, neither object passed the other in space. This variation in procedure produced a decided increase in correct responding in the younger subjects, particularly with regard to simultaneity of arrival.

The next experiment is perhaps the best known of the time studies; certainly, it is as ingenious as any. A vessel of water has two identical branching tubes at its bottom end (like an inverted Y) with a spigot which releases water through both tubes at once, obviously in equal quantities per unit of time. When the tubes drain into separate containers of identical shape and size, the preoperational child readily believes in the simultaneity of starts and stops and the equality of durations for the two outflows. When the containers are of different size and shape, however—shades of the conservation-of-quantity research—he forthwith tumbles into all the difficulties discussed previously: inequality of starts and stops, inequality of durations, etc. Variations on this experimental procedure also adduced evidence that the younger subject has difficulties in seeing temporal intervals as forming a hierarachy of inclusions (duration A less than duration B less than duration C, and so forth) and in applying the transitivity rule to them ($A = B$, $B = C$, hence $A = C$; $A < B$, $B < C$, hence $A < C$).

There are still other experiments reported in the long middle section of the book. One study showed that young children have trouble adding successively occurring temporal intervals to form a total interval; for instance, they will not necessarily infer equal total duration for two movements from the knowledge that their component durations were equal. Similarly, temporal intervals appear not to be associative in the early stages. Thus, the child cannot establish equalities such as $(A + B) + C = A + (B + C)$, when A, B, and C are durations which occur in sequence. Piaget's data indicate that the additivity and associativity properties develop synchronously: if the child can deal with one, he can generally manage the other (*ibid.*, p. 171).

We shall conclude by citing a series of experiments on the concept of age taken from the final section of the book. The young child's notion of age appears from these studies to have two related idiosyncrasies. (1) Age is not differentiated from size (especially height). Bigger things are older than smaller things, and things which have stopped growing have stopped getting any older (a consummation devoutly to be wished!). In one study, for example, the child was shown a picture of two trees of obviously different species, one bigger than the other. He was then asked which he thought was the older tree, or whether it was not possible to tell. The younger children said the bigger one was older; the older children said that one could not tell without knowing when they were planted. (2) Because of its association with size, age bears no necessary relation to date of birth. If A is born after B but eventually outstrips it in size, it is "older." The child was shown two series of pictures representing the year-by-year growth of two trees. One tree (a pear tree) was planted one year after the other an (apple tree) but grew faster and eventually became the larger of the two, bore the most fruit, and so on. Which tree was older? The following is an example of how young children deal with this problem:

> Joc (1;6) succeeds in seriating the apple trees by saying *"one year, two years, three years, etc.*—Look, when the apple tree is two years old we plant this pear tree. Which is the oldest?—*The apple tree.*—And the year after this?—*Still the apple tree.*—And the year after, here are photos taken on the same day ($P_4 = R_3$). Which is oldest?—*The pear tree.*—Why?—*Because it has more pears. . . .*—And here (P_5 and R_4)?—*The pear tree.*—How old is it?—(Joc counts one by one) *4 years old.*—And the apple tree?—(Counts with his finger) *5 years old.*—Which of the two is the oldest?—*The pear tree.* —Why?—*Because it's four years old.*—Are you older when you're 4 or when

you're 5?—*When you're 5.*—Then which is the oldest?—*I don't know . . . the pear tree because it has more pears"* (*ibid.,* p. 229).

MOVEMENT AND VELOCITY

Piaget conceives of movement as a *displacement* in space in reference to an ordered set of fixed spatial positions or *placements* (e.g., Piaget, 1946b, pp. 258-259). An object *A* is said to have "moved" if, formerly in one placement in an ordered series of placements *ABCDE*, it is now found in a different position in the same series, e.g., *BCDAE*. This conception led him to begin his research on movements or displacements with preliminary studies of the child's understanding of spatial order. In one of these studies, the apparatus consisted of three different-colored wooden balls (*A, B,* and *C*) which could be slid along a wire behind a screen. Problems of the following sort were put to the child.

The objects disappear behind the screen in the order *ABC;* in what order will they emerge on the other side of the screen (*ABC*)? In what order will they reemerge on the first side (the inverse *CBA*)? If the wire is rotated 180° behind the screen, in what order will they emerge on the other side (*CBA*)? If rotated 360° (*ABC* again)? We shall as usual eschew a detailed account of stage-by-stage development here in favor of reporting the general sense of the findings. The youngest subjects have no difficulties with the first question but tend to fail the others, including the second one (inverse movement of balls in order *CBA*). Interestingly, children of this level are not averse to predicting that the *middle* element *B* may emerge in front in the case of the inverse movement. Piaget feels that it is only when the child has an operational conception of order, with direct and inverse orders rigorously coordinated, that the relation "between" (*B* "between" *A* and *C*) becomes a symmetrical one, something invariant for both *ABC* and *CBA* orders (*ibid.,* p. 15). In sharp contrast to the hesitations and errors of the earlier stages, the stage-3 subjects (about age 7) go so far as to discover a rule for finding the correct order for any rotation of the wire: direct order *ABC* for even-numbered 180° rotations; inverse order *CBA* for odd-numbered ones.

The next series of investigations dealt with movement proper, in particular with the distances generated by the displacement of objects through space. With distance, as with time and velocity, the spatial order of terminations (which object passed the other and ended up ahead of it) is the dominating criterion for the preoperational child. Centering exclusively on order of terminations, he neglects positions of departure and—what is really criterial for distance—the sum of spatial units comprised between departure and termination.

In one study, the child was presented with two strings, one above the other, which looked like this:

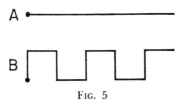

FIG. 5

The strings were said to be tramway tracks and little balls running along them were to be the tramway cars. The child was given a number of tasks to perform, including the following. The experimenter moved his car for a distance of several segments on track *B* and asked the child to make just as long a trip (*le même long chemin*) on *A*. The younger subjects tended to move their cars only far enough to be directly above the experimenter's and hence made a trip of lesser total distance. In this case the experimenter did several things to induce a differentiation between distance traversed and order of termination, e.g., he moved his car one segment from the point of departure (thus straight up and still directly below *A*'s point of departure) and asked the child to make his car take just as long a journey. Also included in the set of problems: the child was given a little piece of cardboard equal in length to a *B* segment and asked if this would help him in any way to make sure a given set of *A* and *B* distances were equal.

The results of the study suggested a gradual evolution from a rigid and unyielding dependence on superposition of cars as the criterion for equality of distances, through a beginning differentiation between superposition and actual distance traversed (but with inability to see total distances as composed of distance units), to a ready use of the unit measure as the only certain method of assessing distance, and, implied in this, a conception of distance as the sum of tiny distance units. Just as with time, number, and quantity (recall the schema of atomism described in the first section of this chapter), the distance to which a movement gives rise is not really a rational concept until it is construed as fractionable into arbitrarily small, additive unit distances.

The additive composition of distances was more intensively studied in the next investigation. In one part, a funicular railway train (bead) ascended and descended a mountain (cardboard model) along a fixed itinerary traversing points *O* (base), *A, B, C,* and *D* (summit). The child's task was to add part distances so as to compare total ascent with total descent. For example, if the train made in succession the itineraries *OC, CB, BD, DO,* has its total ascending distance been greater than, less than, or equal to its total descending distance? As in the previous study, the child had measuring aids at his disposal. And as before, the data showed a progressive mastery of measurement operations with increasing age. There was one incidental finding which demonstrated with particular force the primitive state of the distance concept in young children. Most of them asserted that the total ascent OD was greater than the total descent DO, presumably because egocentric notions of more effort = more distance intruded. For some of these subjects, actual measurement of the distances sufficed to dispel this illusion, but for others it did not.

There was one other experiment on movement which we shall only mention. The study dealt with relative movements: a snail moves along a board while the board itself moves along a table in the same or opposite direction as the snail's movement. To be able to compose such sets of interdependent movements so as to arrive at the "net" movement of the snail in relation to the table is a late achievement, one requiring not concrete but formal operations. See our remarks on this task in Chapter 6, p. 217.

The remainder of the book describes Piaget's research on the concept of velocity. The first several experiments all bear on a single point: that children initially reduce velocity to an intuition of order and changes of order, i.e., that object traveled faster which, initially behind another, caught up to it and ended up ahead. We shall summarize these experiments by describing the typical reaction of the younger subjects to the velocity problem each experiment presented. When two parallel and simultaneous movements of unequal speed and distance take place inside tunnels, so that the child cannot see the faster one gaining on the slower one, the child thinks they traveled at equal speeds. When two simultaneous movements of unequal velocity and distance begin at a common point and end at a common point (the longer and faster one taking an angled or sinuous intinerary and the shorter and slower one following a straight-line path), the child believes the velocities were equal. When simultaneous movements proceed along concentric circles (the movement along the larger circle being of course faster), the child asserts equality of speed. When one object starts its movement at the same instant as a second but from a position considerably behind it, the young child will say it traveled faster if it ends up in front of the second when they both stop, but not if it ends up parallel to or just behind the second (in all three cases its actual speed was considerably greater than the second's). If two objects make parallel movements of equal distance, one starting before the other in time but both terminating simultaneously (termination points superimposed), the child either thinks the speeds were equal or else that the one which started first went faster, since it initially "passed" the (stationary) second one in the beginning of its movement.

The next study dealt with relative velocities, an analogue of the experiment on relative movements mentioned earlier. Eight cardboard bicyclists move along an endless ribbon at uniform speed. A little man counts the bicyclists as they pass him. He is immobile during the first 15 seconds (time enough for all 8 bicyclists to go by him once); during the next

15-second interval, however, he himself moves slowly, either in the same direction as the bicyclists or in the opposite direction. The subject was then asked to tell whether more, fewer, or the same number of bicyclists would pass the little man in the second interval, relative to the first. As with relative movements, the ability to compose relative speeds appears to be a late developmental achievement. Until age 8 or so, children tend to assume that the number of bicyclists which pass the man per unit of time will be the same whether the man himself is moving or not. And not until about age 11 could the child systematically deduce the correct result prior to experimentation and, in addition, give a rational explanation for it.

The book continues with reports of experiments entailing the quantification of velocities and velocity differences, either by establishing simple proportions among times and distances or by actually making estimates of the arithmetic value of the distance-over-time ratio (Piaget, 1946b, p. 185). Since it is, of course, necessary first to possess a stable concept of velocity before its measurement has any meaning, the major developmental changes in these experiments take place between middle childhood and adolescence, i.e., in transition from concrete to formal operations. The first study deals with the estimation of the velocities of movements which occur, not synchronously, but successively. An object makes a rectilinear movement, its time is recorded by a stop watch, and its itinerary is traced on paper. A second movement is then made and similarly recorded. This movement may be of same duration and different distance, different duration and same distance, or different duration and different distance, relative to the first. The child's task is simply to judge whether the velocities were equal or different, and if different, which was faster. As might be suspected, children who could easily solve the velocity problems involving simultaneous movements described earlier had great difficulties here, where the movements were successive, where the only remnant of a movement consisted of a line on paper and a stop-watch number. However, older subjects did solve these problems, and the developmental progression was an orderly one: solution of problems where either times or distances were equal; then solution where times and distances were unequal but in simple proportion; and finally solution to any and all problems posed.

A second investigation concerned what Piaget calls *conservation of uniform velocity* (1946b, p. 210). A toy car travels a certain distance on the first day of a trip, a man rides a bicycle for half this distance during the same day, and both intineraries are recorded by parallel lines on paper. The questions asked of the child included these. How far will the car go the second day, the third day, etc., in traveling at the same speed and for the same time? How far will the man go on these same days, traveling at his speed (half the car's) during the same time intervals? On the last day, the car goes at its usual speed but travels only half the day; how far will it go? Does the (absolute) distance between the termination points of car and man remain the same, day after day, or does it regularly augment? The youngest subjects are unable to reproduce constant distances for the car in its daily progress. Older ones manage this but make a systematic error in the case of the man: from the second day on they keep constant the first day's *difference* in distance between man and car, thus making the man travel at a speed *equal* to that of the car. Still older subjects succeeed in constructing the itineraries correctly but are unable to predict, in advance of actual construction, that the difference in distance between man and car will regularly increase from day to day (last question above). The ability to deduce this in advance of experience appears to come in at around 10 or 11 years of age.

The last experiment described in the book was designed to measure the child's understanding of uniformly accelerated movement: whether the child can predict that an object rolling down an inclined plane will increase in speed all the way to the bottom, whether he can recognize that, by virtue of this increase in speed, the object will cover increasingly more distance per unit of time as it continues to roll, and so on. Again, developmental progress continues into early adolescence. One curio to close the chapter: some children thought the distance per unit of time would grow shorter and shorter as the object neared the bottom *because* its speed was increasing!

CHAPTER TEN

Space, Geometry, Chance, Adolescent Reasoning, and Perception

SPACE

IN CHAPTER 9, it was said that Piaget's books on time (1946a) and movement and velocity (1946b) are regarded by him as essentially a two-
volume series on the same general topic. This is also the case for the two
books on which the first two sections of this chapter are based: that on
space (Piaget and Inhelder, 1956) and that on geometry (Piaget, Inhelder,
and Szeminska, 1960).[1] *The Child's Conception of Space* deals with the
developmental construction of topological, projective, and Euclidean spatial concepts. *The Child's Conception of Geometry* continues the study of
Euclidean concepts, particularly as regards the genesis of conservation
and measurement of length, area, and volume. The most obvious clue to
the intimate conceptual relation between them is the fact that the book
on space contains a chapter called "Geometrical Sections" and that the
final chapter in the geometry book is entitled "The Construction of
Euclidean Space." For the studies on space, there are a number of sources
in addition to the major volume (e.g., Meyer, 1935; Piaget, 1953a, 1954b,
1955b; Piaget and Inhelder, 1945, 1948); the supply is more limited in the
case of the work on geometric operations (e.g., Piaget, 1953a; Piaget and
Morf, 1958a).

Perhaps the best way to introduce Piaget's research on the development
of space is to summarize the leitmotifs which run through his written
account of it (Piaget and Inhelder, 1956). It is quite clear that the development he has in mind to study here is definitely that of space *representation,* not space *perception.* Thus, the research is research on *intel-*

---

[1] In summarizing the space and geometry research in two brief sections, we are flirting
with too high a compression ratio—a situation unpleasantly like that where genetic
epistemology was squeezed into less than half a chapter (Chapter 7). Between them, the
two volumes run to about 900 pages of closely written description of theory and experiments—dozens of the latter. The interested reader will still very much need to consult
the originals when he finishes the sections that follow on Space and Geometry.

327

lectual development, the development of intelligence as it works on spatial relationships. This is not to say that the genesis of space perception itself is of no interest to Piaget; on the contrary, he compares and contrasts it with the evolution of spatial representation in this volume (*ibid.*, ch. 1) and has elsewhere reported his own research in the area (the *Recherches* series of perceptual studies).

The book is almost obsessional in its reiteration that these spatial representations are built up through the organization of *actions* performed on objects in space, at first motor actions and later, internalized actions which eventuate in operational systems. Our adult representation of space is thus said to result from active manipulations of the spatial environment rather than from any immediate "reading off" of this environment by the perceptual apparatus. For example, we eventually come to "see" objects as together or separated in space, much less as a function of past visual enregistrations of their proximity or separation than from past actions of placing objects together and separating them.

The belief that actions rather than perceptions comprise the essential vehicle for developmental progress is, of course, not predicated solely for the development of space; it was stated back in Chapter 2 that this belief is one of the cornerstones of Piaget's general theory. Why, then, is it emphasized and reemphasized in connection with the space research? Most probably because the temptation is especially great to conceive space as something immediately given in experience, and immediately given *perceptually*, rather than otherwise (e.g., *ibid.*, p. 4). It just seems natural to assume that we see space as it is and have always seen it that way. What Piaget wants to stress is (1) that this effortless seeing is really the end product of long and arduous developmental construction, and (2) that the construction itself is more dependent upon actions than upon perception *per se*.

A third leitmotif involves the categorization of spatial acquisitions according as they involve topological, projective, or Euclidean geometric concepts. Topological properties include proximity, order, enclosure, and continuity. Projective and Euclidean geometries take account of these properties and add others: properties which remain perceptually invariant under changes in the point of view from which a figure is looked at (e.g., rectilinearity), in the case of projective geometry; familiar properties like angularity, parallelism, and distance, in the case of Euclidean geometry. The three kinds of space defined by such sets of properties became objects of mathematical study in the *historical order*: Euclidean, projective, and topological. Their *logical order* is otherwise: topology is the most general and inclusive system; projective and Euclidean geometries can be considered as special cases of it. What then, Piaget wanted to know, might be their *ontogenetic order* of appearance, if indeed they evidence any definite order? The conclusion to which his research pointed was that there is a definite order, and that it approximates the logical rather than historical one: first, topological relations; later (and at about the same time), projective and Euclidean ones. Discriminations on the basis of topological properties begin to be made fairly early in the pre-operational period and most topological relations become integrated into stable operational systems around 7 years of age.[2] Projective and Euclidean properties, on the other hand, come in later and achieve equilibrium later (age 9-10 usually). Moreover, the formation of topological operations is thought to constitute the foundation for the subsequent genesis of the projective and Euclidean ones; the latter two build on the achievements of the former. The book on space is actually organized around the developmental hypothesis just described. Its first section describes research on the genesis of topological concepts, the second does the same for projective concepts, and the third and final section reports experiments on Euclidean concepts and on other concepts transitional between projective and Euclidean ones. The volume on geometry (Piaget, Inhelder, and Szeminska, 1960) is then the simple continuation of the third section's work on Euclidean constructs.

The studies with which the space book begins give what is perhaps Piaget's most direct evidence for his hypothesis that topological differentiations precede Euclidean and projective ones in ontogenetic development. In one experiment, the child explores various objects manually (the objects are behind a screen so he cannot see them) and is asked to match them with duplicates which are visible. In a second, he is called upon to draw a series of such objects. The principal findings were these. By the time the child is 3-4 years old, he can generally discriminate objects (both manually and in his drawings) on the basis of topological differentiae. For example, he can distinguish a closed from an open figure, an object with a hole in it from one without a hole, and a closed loop with something inside from one with the something outside or on the loop's boundary. But the ability to discriminate between rectilinear and curvilinear figures and, *a fortiori,* among figures of each type, does not develop until several years later. Thus, the same child who can readily distinguish an open from a closed circle may be quite unable to discriminate between the closed circle and other, rectilinear closed figures such as squares or diamonds.

The remaining experiments in the first section deal with the developmental formation of specific topological operations. One study confirmed the earlier finding (from the experiment on spatial order reported in the section on movement and velocity in Chapter 9) that an operational grasp of the notion of order is not usually achieved before the early school years. Another gave similar results as regards the topological

---

[2] There is an exception: the topological property of continuity, involving the abstract notion of infinity, is not mastered until the period of formal operations (*ibid.*, ch. 5).

relationship of "surrounding" or "enclosure." The experimental materials here were typically Piagetian in their simplicity: strings with knots tied in them. By the time he is 7 years old or so, the child generally becomes capable of regarding as equivalent slack and taut knots and regarding as different true and false knots (overlappings of strings which look as if they might be knots but which would untie if pulled tight). That is, he is now capable of establishing similarities and differences between objects based solely on the topological property of enclosure.

In the final experiment Piaget was interested in the development of the notion that a continuous figure (e.g., a line) can be conceptualized as consisting of a connected series of points—infinitely small and an infinite number of them—which give it its continuity. This notion is obviously similar to the schema of atomism described in connection with the quantity research (Chapter 9). The child was asked to halve some geometric figure—square, straight line, etc.—again and again. He was queried as to the ultimate result of this subdividing process. How far could the process be continued? What would be the end product (and what shape would it have)? Of what is the figure ultimately composed? And the like. As might be predicted, responses to such questions continue to show developmental change right into adolescence. The child gradually gives up the view that the atomistic constituents of the figure resemble the figure in shape (e.g., a line consists ultimately of little lines) in favor of regarding them as essentially shapeless points. Similarly, the number of such constituents postulated gets larger and larger with age until it becomes infinite; the oldest children are able to state that the subdivision process could continue indefinitely, without end. And finally, the child eventually approaches, if not quite attains, the concept of continuous wholes built up from discontinuous constituent elements. The following protocol nicely illustrates the subtlety of thinking of which the older children appear capable:

> BET (11;7). "How many points could be drawn along this line?—*You can't say. You can't count them. You could make points that get smaller and smaller.* . . .—How many are there in this circle?—*It's impossible to tell.*— But roughly; 10,000; 100,000; 1,000,000?—*It's impossible to tell, there are so many you just can't say.*—Make a drawing showing what the smallest possible line looks like.—*But it can't be done because it could always be made smaller still.*" (Piaget and Inhelder, 1956, pp. 146-147).

The experiments of the second section are broadly concerned with illustrating the child's growing awareness of spatial perspective: in particular, the capacity to imagine how an object will appear from different viewpoints and to make use of this capacity in solving various problems. In one study, the child is given a set of matchsticks which stand upright in individual plasticine bases and is told to place them on a table so they form a perfectly straight line (they are "telegraph poles" which run along a "straight road"). The best way to be sure the line is straight is to sight along the row from one end; in Piaget's terms, the projective straight line is best generated by adopting a particular perspective vis-à-vis the line elements, namely, the end-on position in which all elements behind the first one will be invisible if the line is truly straight.

The results of this study were interesting. The youngest children were unable to construct a straight line of sticks under any circumstances. Children of intermediate stages could do so if the line followed a course parallel to the edge of the table; if it did not, or if a circular table was used, the child's line tended to "drift" parallel to the reference lines, e.g., it became curved on a circular table. It did not occur to children at these stages to free themselves from such contextual dependence by constructing the line via the end-on sighting method. And when asked to assess the relative advantages of various positions from which the line's straightness might be evaluated, they did not regard the end-on position as preferable to others. In the final stage (about 7 years of age), the child tends to use this position spontaneously in preference to all others and makes the line straight regardless of contextual factors. Piaget believes that this development becomes possible by dint of the child's growing awareness of the existence of points of view and their role in generating change in the perceptual appearance of objects. Once really cognizant of how the line changes in appearance with change in the position from which he looks at it, a choice of perspectives for the problem at hand becomes available to him (ibid., p. 165).

Another study illustrates more clearly the young child's difficulty in discriminating and coordinating spatial perspectives. The child is shown a scale model of three mountains and tested in various ways for his ability to represent the appearance of the mountains from positions other than his own. For example, he sits facing the mountains and is asked to select from a series of photographs the one which depicts what the mountains look like to a doll sitting on the opposite side of the mountains. Thus, if mountain *A* were in front of mountain *B* and to its left from the child's point of view, it would appear behind and to the right of *B* from the doll's position. The most prosaic finding here was that, indeed, the ability to solve this kind of perspective problem shows a clear age development. More intriguing was a curious behavior pattern which a number of the younger subjects showed. For each new position of the doll, they methodically went about their task of constructing the appropriate viewpoint. However, the viewpoint kept turning out to be the same one each time—namely, their own! More surprising yet, this pattern seemingly remained incorrigible even when the children had the opportunity to check their constructions by actually going around to the doll's position to look. Piaget believes that the child's egocentrism is at work here, that persistent inability to distinguish the other's viewpoint from one's own which he first came upon in his early studies (see Chapter 8).

There were a number of other experiments involving perspective which yielded the same sort of findings. One involved the representation of simple objects (a needle, a disc, etc.) as seen in different perspectives. Another required that the child predict the various shapes that an object's shadow would assume when the object was placed in different spatial orientations. In a third, the subject had to anticipate the perceptual results of various geometric sections. For example, when a cylinder was sliced diagonally, the child was asked to predict the shape of the resulting face (elliptical). And finally, there were a series of experiments involving the rotation and development (geometric, not ontogenetic) of various solids. For instance, the child was asked to represent what a cylinder or a cone would look like if it were unrolled and spread out flat.

The final section begins with the development of geometries intermediate between the projective and Euclidean and concludes with studies of Euclidean space proper. The first experiment concerns "affinitive transformations," i.e., transformations of figures in which angles and lengths of lines may vary but in which parallel lines remain parallel: a kind of projective geometry with conservation of parallels added (*ibid.*, p. 301). The child is shown a scissorslike tool of this shape:

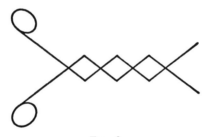

FIG. 6

The tool can be opened out or closed up, the shapes of the diamonds changing accordingly (but they always remain diamonds, and hence the transformations are affinitive). The child sees it closed up and has to predict its successive appearances as it is slowly opened. A second investigation concerned geometric "similarities," transformations even more like Euclidean ones in that angles as well as parallels remain invariant. Here, the child was given the task of constructing triangles and rectangles similar to a model, i.e., the same shape as the model but of different size. The two sets of studies together indicated that the concepts of angularity and parallelism, like the projective-geometric one of "point of view," are gradually acquired during middle childhood.

The last two experiments have to do with the developmental construction of Euclidean space. Only the first of these will be reported here—as interesting a study as will be found in this or any Piaget book.

Now at first glance nothing could seem more elementary than a space organized according to such a principle [a three-dimensional system of orthogonal coordinates]. When we view the familiar objects around us, they appear arranged within a grid of parallel straight lines, crossing each other perpendicularly in three dimensions. And if this view of things appears self-evident, it is because physical experience itself seems to force upon us just such a structure, by virtue of all the verticals we perceive as parallel and appearing to cut the verticals[3] at right angles. Indeed, any piece of squared paper, parquet flooring, street crossings, or groups of buildings suggest the same ubiquitous and ineluctable notion of co-ordinate axes. . . . However, the findings of the present chapter show clearly enough that it would be a complete mistake to imagine that human beings have some innate or psychologically precocious knowledge of the spatial surround organized in a two- or three-dimensional reference frame. . . . Far from constituting the starting point of spatial awareness, the frame of reference is in fact the culminating point of the entire development of euclidean space, just as the notions of succession and simultaneity, synchronous and isochronous, defining a homogeneous time, mark the culmination rather than the starting point for the concept of time (*ibid.,* p. 416).

The experiment was designed to find out the extent to which young children do "see" objects as located in a Euclidean grid of horizontal and vertical coordinates. For the horizontal, the child was shown jars with colored water in them and asked to predict the spatial orientation of the water level (by drawings or by gestures) when the jar was tilted in various ways. Several methods were used to assess the child's representation of verticality. For example, a plumb line was suspended inside an empty jar and the child was to predict its orientation when the jar was tilted. Similarly, he was given a model of a mountain and asked to plant posts "nice and straight" at various places on it and represent such posts in a drawing.

The results were striking. Initially, children seem incapable of representing planes at all. For instance, the water in the jar was depicted by a scribble with no discernible level, in any orientation. Subsequently, levels were represented, albeit crudely, but with reference to the jar itself rather than to external coordinates. Thus, the level of the water was always conceived as perpendicular to the sides, no matter how the jar was tilted.

The child of this stage senses that water does move towards the mouth of a container when the container is tilted, but he represents this by effectively augmenting the amount of water in the jar; the level is still kept perpendicular to the sides but it is now higher up in the jar! In the same way, representation of the vertical was also dominated by the im-

[3] An error in the English translation. Read "horizontals."

mediate rather than the generalized spatial surround: the plumb line was always placed parallel to the sides of the jar and the posts were planted perpendicular to the slope of the mountain.

For both horizontal and vertical there are various transitional stages between these sorts of responses and completely correct ones. For example, the child begins to realize that the water level has to be something other than perpendicular to the sides of the jar when the jar is tilted, but he cannot make out just what orientation it should be in. Or the child can actually plant the posts upright but cannot represent them upright in his drawing nor represent the plumb line correctly. Eventually, of course, the stage of generalized correct response does come, but it does not come until quite late—age 9 years or so, on the average. The children of this stage conspicuously and consistently draw upon the larger spatial framework in their constructions, e.g., using the table level as a guide in predicting the water level. Perhaps the best evidence that such an "obvious" procedure is obvious only when you have already gone through the toils of a protracted developmental construction is to be found in the behavior protocols of subjects who are almost, but not quite, at the final stage. For instance:

> WIR (7;3) begins by drawing the water levels obliquely on the diagrams of the rectangular jar. "Hold this ruler against the jar to see if you're right (experiment)—*My drawing isn't quite right because it's not straight.*—(We continue tilting the bottle). And now?—*I just can't understand it. It ought not to be like this* (horizontal!)—Look, I am holding the pencil flat (meanwhile the jar is tilted still further)—*Oh, yes! It's quite straight. But that's funny, the jar isn't straight!*—And if we tilt it a lot?—*It will be straight. There's something I don't understand. The water stays still* (= horizontal) *and the jar moves!* . . . (ibid., p. 407).

But not all children submit to experimental evidence. A number of subjects (generally the younger ones) behaved like this:

> MIC (6;7). . . . "Now the jar is going to be tilted the other way. Show us with your pencil what the water will do.—(His demonstration is more or less correct).—Now draw it.—(Once again he makes the water parallel with the base).—Is it higher on one side than on the other in your drawing?—*No, it's the same on both sides.*—Now, just let's take a look at the water (experiment). Is it right?—*Yes.*—Just like you drew it?—*Yes* . . . etc." We are unable to convince him otherwise (ibid., p. 393).

GEOMETRY

Somehow the idea of having a favorite Piaget book seems absurd, but it is hard to avoid it when one is constantly immersed in his work. For what it is worth, the writer's vote would probably go to *The Child's Conception of Geometry* (Piaget, Inhelder, and Szeminska, 1960). In ingenuity of experimental method, in importance and—often—sheer unexpectedness of findings, and in astuteness of theoretical analysis, it may well be Piaget's masterpiece. The geometry under study is Euclidean geometry. Piaget is concerned here with assessing the child's growing ability to conserve, measure, and otherwise take account of Euclidean-geometric entities like distance, length, rectilinear coordinates, angle, area, and volume. Through the gradual mastery of these operations the child eventually forms a coherent quantitative representation of the one-, two-, and three-dimensional space in which he lives and moves. The precise character of this representation is carefully detailed throughout the book and particularly in its concluding chapter. We give here only a brief summary of one of the main points.

What the child needs eventually to establish—and does not at first possess—is a picture of space as a kind of all-enveloping container made up of a network of sites or subspaces. Within the container are objects, the things contained, which move from site to site, now occupying or filling a given site, now leaving it unoccupied and empty. Measurements of various kinds can be made within the container without regard for whether the sites along which the measurments occur are occupied or not. For example, the straight-line distance from me to you is the same whether or not the space between us is occupied by objects, whether or not the intervening spatial sites are filled or empty. Similarly, if I slide a block of wood along the table, the metric value of the space it occupied before the movement (its length, its surface area, its volume) is precisely equivalent to that of the space it presently occupies, even though the former is now empty and the latter is now filled. In short, the child has finally to conceive of space as a medium which is homogeneous throughout from the point of view of measurement, in spite of its heterogeneity as regards filled versus empty subspaces or sites. This is only a part of what Piaget believes the child has to acquire vis-à-vis the Euclidean world. But it is a very important part, and much of the research now to be described can be interpreted in terms of it.

The first several experiments concern the conservation and measurement of space in one dimension, i.e., of length and distance. In one study the child is presented with a tower of blocks which stands on a table. His job is to build a second tower the same height, but with the following restricting conditions. His building blocks are of a size different from the model's; his tower stands on a lower table than that of the model; and a screen prevents him from actually seeing the model as he builds, although he can at any time go around it to look. Various sticks and paper strips are available as measuring tools, but the child is not told how to use them. The principal developmental stages were as follows. In stage 1, the child simply makes a crude visual comparison, often failing to take account of the fact that the towers are on tables of different heights and thus estimating height from floor rather than height from table. Following this, there are various attempts to bring the two towers closer together in order (again visually) to compare them. Stage 2 is interesting because it presages genuine measurement. The child tries to use himself as a common measure, e.g., he holds his hands apart the height of the tower, uses reference points on his torso, etc. Following this comes the use of body-independent measures: a third tower or a stick. But tower or stick have to be exactly the same length as the tower they measure, neither longer nor shorter. In the next stage the child is able to use a stick longer than the model (i.e., by marking off the height of the tower on it), but he cannot iterate a shorter stick along the tower height. Finally, the child can do it either way; in particular, he is now able to use the shorter stick as a *unit measure*—"this tower is 2½ sticks high." With this achievement, measurement along a single dimension is constituted on an operational basis: the child is now aware that a length is composed of unit lengths of arbitrary size and can be measured by stepping one of these along the total length.

The next two investigations were devised to test concepts of conservation of distance and of length, respectively. For the first, two objects were placed on a table 50 centimeters from one another, and the child was asked if they were "near each other" or "far apart." A cardboard screen was set between them and the child was asked if they were still as "near" or as "far" (depending upon how the child had just expressed it) as before. Initially, the child appears unable to establish a distance relation between the objects themselves when the screen is interposed, only one between object and screen. But it is the next stage which reveals the crux of the young child's conception of distance. He thinks the distance between objects is less when the screen is set between them because the space occupied by the screen is not considered part of the total distance (see our earlier remarks about empty and filled sites). If a little window is put in the screen, the distance is thought to be less with the window closed than with it open:

> ANO (5;3). Two figures; no screen: *"They're near together.*—(Screen:) Are they as near as they were?—*They're nearer.*—(Window in screen open:) And like this?—*They're further, because there's a hole in it.*—Why are they further?—*Because before this thing* (window) *was shut.*—(Experiment repeated.) —*It's nearer when you shut the door.*—And with this (cigarette box)?—*It's nearer because it's thicker*(!)" (ibid., p. 75).

There were several experiments on conservation of length. In one, it was shown that young children fail to recognize that two lines with superimposed end points are of unequal length if one is straight and the other sinuous. The same result obtained when one of two originally identical strips of paper was cut into pieces and the pieces set end to end to make an irregular line. But perhaps the most vivid demonstration of failure to conserve length was achieved by the following technique. Two identical straight sticks were laid side by side so their extremities correspond. The child was asked if they were the same length and he naturally replied that they were. Then, one of them was slid a little so that its leading end was to the right of that of the other stick. Whereupon the child no longer believed that the lengths were equal, usually asserting that the one which moved "ahead" was the longer (as in the movement studies described in Chapter 9). The child apparently failed to grasp the fact that the space into which the staggered stick moved was precisely equivalent in length to that which it had just vacated (the same space still occupied by part of the other stick), leaving total length invariant and the two sticks equal. The following is an example of a child in process of recognizing this:

> PER (6;0). Staggered: *"That one is longer.*—(The other strip is drawn the same distance in the opposite direction:) Are they the same length or not?—*No, they're both longer. That one is longer there* (to the right) *and that one is longer there* (to the left).—Then are they or aren't they the same length?—(Hesitating:) *Yes" (ibid.,* p. 99).

The preceding studies have had as their subject matter the development of concepts of conservation and measurement with respect to a single dimension. A subsequent body of experimentation bore on these operations as they pertain to two- and three-dimensional space, i.e., area and volume. Between these lay a potpourri of investigations of topics regarded as transitional: the location of a point in two- and three-dimensional space; the measurement of angles and triangles; the construction of geometric loci (e.g., the series of points equidistant from a point); and the construction of mechanical and composite curves. We shall take only a sample of two such studies. In one, a sheet of paper with a dot in its upper right-hand quadrant was placed on a table before the subject. A second, identical sheet was then put on a different part of the table and the child was told to draw a dot on it in the same relative location, i.e., so that the dots would be superimposed if the sheets were. As usual, he had available to him rulers and other measuring devices, if and however disposed to use them.

As in the study of horizontals and verticals reported in the space book, the data here point up the child's budding conception of space as a grid of rectilinear coordinates, the intersects of which define an object's spatial location. The youngest children do not measure at all, of course; they simply make perceptual estimates. The oldest subjects (age 8 years or so) make precise determinations by measuring the point's horizontal and vertical coordinates. In the intervening stages, the child recognizes the necessity for measurement but appears to believe that measurement along a single dimension will suffice. For example, he measures the diagonal from the upper right-hand corner of the sheet to the point; this done, he may or may not try to maintain constant the angle of that diagonal when constructing his own point.

In a second study, the child had two tasks. The first was to find the locus of points (a circle) equidistant from a single point (where can a group of marble players stand so that all will be equally far from the target?). The second was to find the locus of points (a straight line) equidistant from two points (where can a set of marbles be put so they will each be equally far from experimenter and subject?). For both tasks there was the expected gradual development from haphazard responding to discovery of the correct solution. Piaget also noted an interesting qualitative finding in connection with the second task. The older children seemed to make use of mathematical "reasoning by recurrence": i.e., discovering empirically that a few points which satisfy the task condition turn out to lie on a common straight line, they quickly make the generalization that all possible points would lie on that same line—more than this, that they *must* lie on that line.

Some of the most exciting experiments in the book have to do with the conservation and measurement of area. In one, the child is confronted with two identical rectangular sheets of green cardboard and a number of identical toy houses. A toy cow is placed on each cardboard and the child grants that each cow has the "same amount of grass to eat" on each "meadow." Then one farmer builds a house on his meadow and another farmer does the same on his. Do the two cows still have the same amount of grass to eat? Each farmer then adds a second house, then a third, etc., the test question being repeated at each new addition. However, one farmer arranges his houses in a tight cluster in one small area of the meadow while the other spreads his all over; this results in the *perceptual* impression of more free meadow—more grass to eat—for the first farmer's cow. And it is precisely this perceptual impression which the younger children succumb to and the older ones manage to resist. For the former, a typical pattern was that of asserting equality of area for addition after addition, only to have it break down when the perceptual disparity finally became too strong. In some children, however, equivalence was already abandoned with the first or second set of houses. Older children took note of the illusory impression but confidently discounted it by reasoning. As one child put it: "No, it looks as if there's more green there . . . but it isn't true because there's the same number of houses" (*ibid.*, p. 271).

In another study children were given congruent cardboard figures and, after asserting they were the same size (same "amount of room" in each), a piece was removed from one of them and moved to another part of that figure. The younger children could not conserve area under such transformations. In one version of the study, the task was concretized by using rectangular figures made up of squares which could be detached and moved to different loci on the figures (e.g., a square could be subtracted from the upper end of the figure and added at the bottom). The child was initially shown that a given (large) number of tiny cubes would exactly fit on the original figure and was then asked if they would also exactly cover the same figure after it was altered (hence skirting the use of area terminology—"amount of room," "space," etc.). The results were essentially the same: the younger subjects would simply not admit that the cubes would fit the altered figure because its area appeared larger or smaller than the original.

A third study combined features from the two preceding ones. There were two identical "meadows" and two identical square "potato plots," one plot placed in each meadow. Then the parts of one plot were spatially redistributed and the child was asked if there was still "as much room for potatoes" and also if there was still "as much grass for each of the two cows" (conservation of areas and of complementary areas). The salient finding here was that there appears to be a stage in which the child will assert conservation for the plots (areas) with great confidence while denying it for the meadows (complementary areas)! Here is an example:

> MIN (8;2). The second square (A_2) is transformed into a rectangle. "Will there be as much room now as there was?—*Yes, because it was the same* (as A_1) *before. You've changed its shape round but you haven't changed its size.*—What about the grassland (A'_2)?—*There's less here* (A'_2).—And this way (with A_2 as a more elongated rectangle)?—*There's more grass there* (A'_2).—What about the plot (A_2)?—*They're both the same* (A_1 and A_2).—And the grassland as well?—*No, there's less of that because you've changed the shape of the potato plot.*" Other transformations again produced similar replies (*ibid.*, p. 289).

Another study is worth mentioning, as much for its implications for conservation of quantity as for the light it sheds on the conservation and measurement of area. In the experiments on conservation of global quantity or amount of matter described in the first section of Chapter 9, there is always the lurking feeling that nonconservation may be some sort of experimental artifact, that if the situation were somehow made more realistic, closer to his everyday needs, the young child would not make these incredible errors in quantitative reasoning. In the present study, the subject was given the task of bisecting, trisecting, etc., a circular clay "cake" and, among other things, was questioned as to the relative "amounts to eat" in the intact whole versus the whole in pieces. The following protocols suggest that nonconservation can emerge loud and clear even in situations quite close to "real life":

JEN (4;2). . . . "Suppose I have this (the two halves) and you have that (the whole cake): haven't we both got the same amount to eat?—*I've got more.*—Why?—*Mine's all round and yours is cut up.*" . . . (*ibid.*, pp. 327-328).

GIS (5;6) also says of fractions and a whole "*They're the same,*" but when asked to choose between one whole cake and two halves, she chooses the whole, because "*I get more to eat this way*" (*ibid.*, p. 329).

The last experiment reported in the book dealt with the conservation and measurement of volume. The initial part of the procedure was as follows:

The child is shown a block which is quite solid, and measures 4 cm. in height against a square base 3 cm. × 3 cm. so that its volume is 36 cm.³ He is told that the block is an old house built on a little island, a square piece of cardboard measuring 3 cm. × 3 cm. and pasted onto a large sheet of corrugated card meant to stand for the lake or sea. It seems that this house is threatened, and so the inhabitants decide to build another in its place. The new house is to have exactly as much room as the old, although it is being built on another island. The child is shown these other islands which are also pieces of card but which differ from the first in size or shape or in both, their measurements being 2 × 2 cm., 2 × 3 cm., 1 × 2 cm., 1 × 1 cm. and 3 × 4 cm. The problem consists in reproducing the volume of the first block while altering its form to comply with the base which is given. A further point of difference lies in that the equal volume must be built out of little wooden cubes each of which is 1 cm.³, while the original is a solid block (*ibid.*, pp. 355-356).

Children were also tested for conservation of volume. In one form of this test, the 36 cubes were arranged to make different "houses" and the child was asked if they had the same or different amount of "room" in them. The other form was the displacement-of-water one used in the original conservation of volume study (see again Chapter 9): the 36 cubes (now of metal) were distributed to make various forms in a bowl of water, and the child was to predict the water level in each case.

For the measurement part of the study, the developmental sequence was roughly this. The youngest children compare houses on a single dimension only, frequently the height; thus, they refuse to build the second house taller or shorter than the first, despite the experimenter's assurance that the amount of room, not the shape, is all that counts. Another curious thing: if the procedure is changed so that they are asked to copy the original house directly, they tend to do so by enclosing it with unit blocks, rather than by making a replica alongside the model. At the next stage, the child begins to bring *logical* multiplication to bear on the problem. That is, he knows that a smaller base necessitates a higher structure but how much higher it should be he has no procedure for determining. Eventually (late middle childhood and early adolescence) the child manages to solve the problem by *arithmetically* multiplying dimensions.

Conservation of volume had, of course, been the subject of previous study (Piaget and Inhelder, 1941), but this research uncovered at least one interesting new fact about its development. There appears to be a stage in middle childhood (average age around 9 years) when, in Piaget's phraseology (Piaget, Inhelder, and Szeminska, 1960, pp. 374-376), the child conserves "interior volume" but does not yet conserve "occupied volume." He recognizes that the number of cubes always remains the same and therefore asserts that the amount of room inside is also the same from house to house. However, he paradoxically refuses to conclude from this that the water level in the bowl will also stay the same whatever the arrangement of the submerged cubes—a situation curiously like that where the area of the potato plot was conserved but not its surrounding meadow. In Piaget's interpretation, the child of this stage does have a beginning conception of volume; however, the volume he conceives of pertains to the object alone, with no implication for the volume of its surrounding medium. It yet fails of being the physicist's "occupied volume," that part of a given total volume which is "used up" by an object, leaving a determinate remainder. Here is a subject who appears to have the first but not the second conception of volume:

> JAQ (8;2) realizes that the water level will rise on the immersion of the tower of $3 \times 3 \times 4$: "Now what will happen if I turn it over?—*The water will go down a bit, because the house is at the bottom now.*—Well, will there be the same amount of room in the house itself if I put the bricks at the bottom?—*Yes, there'll be the same amount of room.*—And that means it's the same for the water?—*No, that's not the same.*—Well, supposing I split the house into two parts, will there be the same amount of room inside?—*Yes, there'll be just the same amount, but in two parts.*—And then there'll be the same amount of space left for the water, eh?—*No, that changes. There'll be less room. No, more.*" (*ibid.*, p. 376).

CHANCE

With but one minor exception (Piaget, 1950c), the only reference for Piaget's work on chance concepts in children is the book he and Inhelder wrote on the subject (Piaget and Inhelder, 1951). Fortunately, *La Genèse de l'idée de hasard chez l'enfant* is a fairly easy book to read (as Piaget books go), and its concluding chapter offers an excellent summary of the principal experimental findings and Piaget's interpretation of them.

Likewise, it is not difficult to summarize the principal conclusions about the development of probability concepts which he drew from his dozen or so experiments in the area (*ibid.*, pp. 226-250). These conclusions take as their point of departure the following argument. In order to identify a set of phenomena as "chance events," one first has to identify a set of phenomena which are not chance events, a nonchance ground against which chance can emerge as figure. Only if cognitive processes are developed enough to order and organize the intrinsically certain, lawful, and predictable by means of rational operations, can things which are intrinsically uncertain, unlawful, and unpredictable be apprehended as such. Put most simply, a mind which knows no law can also know no lawlessness.

The mind of the preoperational child, Piaget argues, is in something very like this state. Lacking the intellectual operations necessary to render lawful and certain those phenomena which do admit of lawfulness and certainty, he is scarcely in a position to articulate from these a different realm, a realm in which operations cannot give certain, nonprobabilistic knowledge. Thus, there is during this developmental period a generalized *undifferentiation* between chance and nonchance, between the possible and the necessary. Nothing is deductively certain and nothing is genuinely fortuitous for him; his thought is forever at midstation between these poles.

The advent of concrete operations marks the beginning of the end of this undifferentiation. By dint of possessing such operations and learning to apply them where they can be applied, the child also discovers areas where they fail to give definite knowledge. The result is a progressive distinction between the possible and the certain; the child now becomes aware that there is one domain in which he can know and another in which he can only guess. But it is not enough simply to separate chance from nonchance; one has also to extract from the field of chance events what minimal certainty and prevision there is to be found there. That is, although nothing is certain by definition, some things can be established as likelier than others by rational application of the so-called laws of probability. To effect this rational application there must be, as Piaget picturesquely states it (*ibid.,* p. 228), a *choc en retour*—a rebounding—of rational operations on chance events, a synthesis following the original differentiation. The child now has to train his intellectual instruments on precisely that domain where they were initially found to be inadequate, this time to establish probabilities in lieu of certainties.

A beginning attempt to do this does take place in middle childhood and some progress is certainly made. However, it requires the powerful conceptual tools which the period of formal operations brings in its train, especially the ability to think in terms of combinations and proportions, to really effect the necessary synthesis. For this reason, a number of the experiments on chance described in the book yield developmental changes which extend well into adolescence. In a nutshell, the concrete-operational child, unlike his younger sibling, clearly recognizes chance events as such when he encounters them but does not have the intellectual equipment to manage them adequately. The formal-operational child does have the equipment and does manage them surprisingly well. Thus, it could be said that the adolescent establishes a firm bridge between the certain (operations) and the probable (chance events), a bridge which spans a chasm unsuspected in early childhood and first discovered in middle childhood.

The first study reported deals with a prototypical chance situation: an originally nonrandom arrangement of objects is progressively randomized, and the child's understanding of the randomization process is assayed. A series of beads are lined up at one end of a rectangular tray: red ones on one side of a mid-line separator and white ones on the other. The tray is then tilted so that the beads all run to the other end, with of course some mixing of red and white beads in the process. With further back-and-forth tilting, further mixing occurs, and the original nonrandom arrangement gradually randomizes. The subjects were asked to predict the outcome of the first tilting, of the several after that, and of a large number of tiltings. They were also asked to draw the itineraries of the separate beads, their positions following these itineraries, and the like. The more interesting responses were those of the preoperational children. They tended to impute a hidden lawfulness, a cache of nonrandomness, to the randomization process: either that the two sets of beads would eventually end up back in their original positions or that— noticing the crossings over after successive tiltings—the reds would all go to the white's side and vice versa. It follows from this that they could not represent the random and fortuitous character of the beads' itineraries: this one going straight over and back, that one going straight over, bumping another, and therefore going back diagonally, etc. In subsequent stages, the child comes to recognize that the mixing process is essentially irreversible, that the original state and its symmetrical complement are only two of a very large number of possible arrangements and are for this reason unlikely (although possible) outcomes. Similarly, the child's representation of itineraries becomes progressively more detailed and realistic, increasingly cognizant of the random permutations of paths and positions which occur.

Studies were also made of the child's ability to predict the shape of the distribution resulting from random movements of objects under various conditions. In one, marbles were poured through a funnel into a row of bins below, giving an approximately normal distribution around the middle bin. In another, square beads ("raindrops") were shaken from a trellis onto a piece of paper divided into squares ("flagstones"), generating a uniform, rectangular distribution. In both cases, the ability to predict distributional form was the end product of a slow and step-by-step ontogenetic development. Of particular interest was the fact that only with the advent of formal operations was there any widespread recognition that the distributions tended to beome progressively more regular, more symmetrical, as the number of cases (marbles or beads which fall) increases. Piaget argues that a grasp of the "law of large numbers," which this increasing regularity expresses, depends upon an understanding of proportions: something not acquired in force until the formal-operational period.

The next experiment was more flamboyant. The apparatus was essentially a roulette wheel with an iron bar as the pointer. The wheel spun "honestly" until a set of matchboxes was placed on its "numbers" (actually, colors). The matchboxes contained wax in which were embedded pieces of metal of various kinds, including—in the case of two particular boxes—magnets. The initial inquiry bore on the honest wheel, i.e., the child's predictions about where the pointer would likely stop on a given spin, the distribution of stops over a large number of spins, and so on. After seeing a number of honest spins, the boxes were put in place and the experimenter noted the child's reactions to the fact that the iron pointer now kept stopping at the same positions all the time. The youngest children evidenced a relative lack of differentiation between the two sets of events—one random and the other nonrandom. That is, they inferred more predictability and regularity than was justifiable in the random spins and less in the nonrandom ones. For the first, they would, for instance, assume that the wheel "had to" go to color X if it had just gone to color Y, that it would surely go to color Z if one concentrated hard enough, and so on.[4] As for the dishonest spins, these children either evidenced little surprise at the regularity or, more commonly, did consider it rather unusual but decidedly not beyond the pale of the hodgepodge of quasi-magical causal relations already thought to be at work in the genuinely random turns. With development there was a more and more sharp separation between the two sets of phenomena. The child came to accept the intrinsic unpredictability of the first (except in so far as the distribution of stops ought increasingly to approximate rectangularity as the number of spins increases) and rather quickly divined a hidden, nonrandom causality at work in the second. Moreover, the oldest children, with their formal-operational skills in scientific reasoning, not only recognized the existence of a *truc* but went on to discover its causal source by eliminating irrelevant variables (e.g., the weight of the matchboxes).

The next series of experiments utilized lot-drawing situations as the context for studying the development of probability notions. One of these experiments was very similar to that just described. The materials consisted of a set of 10 or 20 counters, each bearing a circle on one side

---

[4] The gambling-oriented reader ought to resist the temptation to identify with the preoperational child here, asserting that this is precisely how *he* manages to make chance events nonchance in his favor!

and a cross on the other. The experimenter asked the subject to predict whether cross or circle would turn face up for a single throw and also to predict the distribution of crosses and circles if all were thrown at once. Then the experimenter surreptitiously substituted a set with crosses on both sides, threw them all at once, and gauged the child's reactions. As before, the younger children failed to make a clean differentiation between chance and nonchance events. Unable to grasp the extreme unlikelihood of so many counters turning up all crosses by chance, they did not go beyond registering mild surprise when it happened (e.g., *C'est drôle!*) Not only did they fail to suspect a trick but, even after the trick was revealed to them, they were inclined to think that the same result could readily be reproduced by throwing the true counters.

In another study of the same genre, the experimenter put unequal numbers of different-colored counters into a bag (e.g., 15 yellow ones, 10 red ones, 7 green ones, and 3 blue ones). An identical set was placed on the table as a memory aid. The child made successive drawings of pairs of counters from the bag and before each drawing was asked to predict the color composition of the two counters. The younger children made their predictions on a variety of bases. These occasionally included probabilistic-like ones (e.g., "because there are more yellow ones"), but they seemed to have no privileged status for the subject; he would, as often as not, make his next prediction on a radically nonprobabilistic basis (e.g., "because I like red"). Children in the concrete-operational period tended to make their forecasts solely on the basis of the relative frequencies involved. However, they also tended to forget that each drawing changed these frequencies (since counters, once drawn, were not put back in the bag) and so failed to keep their probabilistic estimates up to date as they went along. The oldest subjects—mostly at the formal-operational level—did keep a precise running account of the changing distribution and predicted accordingly.

A third experiment involved the quantification of probabilities. The materials were again counters, some having a cross on one side, some not. The experimenter would make up two collections of counters and show their composition to the subject. For example, one collection might consist of 2 counters with crosses and 2 without, and the second of 1 with crosses and 2 without. Each collection was then turned face down and its counters scrambled up. The child's task was to judge whether he had a greater chance of drawing a counter with a cross from one of the collections than from the other. A number of such problems were posed, ranging from the very simple (e.g., one collection with 2 crosses out of 4 counters, the other with 0 crosses out of 4) to the rather difficult (e.g., 1 of 2 and 2 of 5).

The developmental stages appeared to be the following. Initially, the child is unable to apply any systematic strategy (or at least, any probabilistic one) to this kind of problem. During middle childhood, the child begins to try to quantify probabilities but repeatedly makes one particular error: he predicts solely on the basis of the *absolute* number of counters with crosses in each collection, rather than in terms of the *ratio* of these to total counters; that is, he seems incapable of reasoning in terms of the *proportions* in play. As indicated earlier, Piaget believes that proportions, involving, as they do, relations established between other relations and thus, operations performed on operations, require a formal-operational structure for their mastery (see our Chapter 6). And indeed, the protocols he cites suggest that few of his subjects under 10-11 years of age can systematically solve these quantification-of-probability problems.

Thus, one intellectual achievement indispensable in calculating probabilities appears to be the ability to deal with proportionality. Another—also conceived as essentially a formal- rather than a concrete-operational acquisition—is the capacity to compute in a systematic way the possible combinations (also permutations and arrangements) in which a set of elements can be grouped. The final section of the book reports experiments designed to study the genesis of combinatorial and combinatorial-like operations. In one of these, the subject's task is to find the number of distinct two-by-two combinations of a set of objects A, B, C, etc.—e.g., AB, AC, BC, etc. In a second, it is to discover the possible permutations rather than combinations, e.g., ABC, ACB, BAC, BCA, and so on. In a third, the pool contains a number of elements of each type, and the subject is to find all the distinct two-by-two "arrangements," as Piaget calls them, e.g., AA, AB, BA, BB, etc. In general, the hypothesis was confirmed that a really systematic method for calculating combinations, permutations, and arrangements is largely the prerogative of adolescence.

The following study both illustrates the usefulness of this acquisition in estimating probability distributions and, more generally, epitomizes the basic differences between preoperational, concrete-operational, and formal-operational thought in the face of probabilistic situations. A bag contains a mixture of 20 red and 20 blue marbles. The child is to predict the likely distribution of 20 pairs of marbles drawn randomly from the bag, i.e., the number of pairs consisting of 2 red marbles, of 2 blue ones, and of 1 blue and 1 red one. Preoperational children, here as elsewhere, underestimate the randomization process and think only in terms of homogeneous pairs—reds or blues—emerging from the bag. In the period of concrete operations, the child senses that red-blue pairs are likely to emerge with greater frequency than either type of homogeneous pairs alone, but he lacks the combinatorial operations necessary to make precise estimates of the probable frequencies. The adolescent, on the other hand, does possess the requisite operations and behaves for all the world like Mendel himself:

KONJ (13;3): *"More likely the mixed ones.—Why?—Because you put in 40 marbles. So there are more chances of taking mixed ones: half the chances. —Could we have all mixed ones?—That would be pretty strange.—And if one made a large number of drawings?—Ten mixed pairs, 5 red ones, and 5 blue ones"* (ibid., p. 223).

ADOLESCENT REASONING

The principal characteristics of adolescent reasoning have already been elucidated at some length in Chapter 6 above. (It might be a good idea to reread parts of that chapter before reading what follows here.) The only purpose of the present section is to review Inhelder's[5] provocative experiments on the subject (Inhelder and Piaget, 1958). Needless to say, these experiments are far from being the only ones made by the Geneva group which tell us something about adolescent thought; a number of those described in this and in Chapters 8 and 9 also do, e.g., the studies on chance just reviewed. What sets the Inhelder studies apart, however, is the fact that, more than the others, they were explicitly designed to shed light on formal-operational thought, and particularly, to disengage the crucial differences between this kind of thought and its concrete-operational predecessor. In *The Growth of Logical Thinking from Childhood to Adolescence* there are sixteen experiments in all. We shall proceed by describing a few selected ones and merely indicating the general subject matter of the others.

In one experiment, the subject was given a tubular spring affair with which a ball can be aimed and shot against the bank of a billiard table. Targets were placed at various places on the table, and the subject was to try to hit them by rebounding the ball off the bank, i.e., by making a "one-cushion billiard." The subject was then questioned about his behavior and its observed results, the principal interest being whether, or to what extent, he induced the law that the angle of incidence always equals the angle of reflection.

The concrete-operational subject appears limited in this situation to asserting concrete instances of the law and making practical use of these to shoot accurately; he cannot state it in its general form, as a *law:* DOM (9;9): *"It hits here, then it goes there"* [he points out the equal angles, repeating his phrase for different inclinations of the plunger] (ibid., p. 8). The adolescent, on the other hand, is on the lookout for general principles from the beginning, and once he finds a likely candidate, he

---

[5] The authors state in the Preface of that book that the experiments were independently designed and executed by Inhelder and her assistants, Piaget contributing the theoretical interpretation of them which we outlined in Chapter 6.

immediately thinks of putting it to experimental test in order to verify it.

> LAM (15;2): "*The rebound depends upon the inclination* [of the plunger]. . . . *Yes, it depends on the angle. I traced an imaginary line perpendicular* [to the buffer]: *the angle formed by the target and the angle formed by the plunger with the imaginary line will be the same*" (*ibid.*, p. 13).

There were two experiments which illustrated particularly well the adolescent's growing skill in scientific reasoning. In one, the problem was to discover the variables affecting how much a rod will bend under a given set of conditions. The materials and procedure were such that the child had the possibility of isolating five variables, each of which makes a separate causal contribution to the amount of bend: (1) the kind of metal of which the rod is made; (2) the amount of weight attached to its end; (3) the rod's length; (4) its thickness; and (5) its cross-section form (round, square, or rectangular). The adolescent makes good use of his talent for combinatorial operations in this situation. He begins by differentiating the above-mentioned variables as possible ones— ones which might have effects on rod flexibility—and then takes as his principal task that of finding out which of them really do have effects (in this particular problem, it happens that they all do). He does this last by systematically trying most or all of the relevant variable-present, variable-absent combinations: that is, by varying thickness and holding the rest constant, varying cross-section form and holding the rest constant, etc. Although the younger child does discover some of these variables and does make crude attempts to test them, he is never able to prove their individual efficacy conclusively by this rigorous, "all-other-things-being-equal" method. The disposition to prove, and particularly to prove by varying one factor while holding all others constant, appears to be the prerogative of a formal-operational thought structure.

The other experiment also entailed a number of variables, but here only one was causally efficacious, and the problem was to prove that the others were not. The apparatus was a simple pendulum and the task was to determine of what its frequency of oscillation was a function. The only causally active variable was the length of the string. Present, but causally inert, were the variables: (1) the weight of the object attached to the string; (2) the height from which it was first pushed; (3) how hard it was pushed. Once again, the adolescent shows himself capable of proving a factor's mettle by the stratagem of letting it vary with the others held constant:

> EME (15;1), after having selected 100 grams with a long string and a medium length string, then 20 grams with a long and a short string, and finally 200 grams with a long and a short, concludes: "*It's the length of the string that makes it go faster or slower; the weight doesn't play any role.*" She discounts likewise the height of the drop and the force of her push (*ibid.*, p. 75).

Contrast this with the younger child's method:

> PER (10;7) is a remarkable case of a failure to separate variables: he varies simultaneously the weight and the impetus; then the weight, the impetus, and the length; then the impetus, the weight, and the elevation, etc., and first concludes: *"It's by changing the weight and the push, certainly not the string."*—"How do you know that the string has nothing to do with it?"— *"Because it's the same string."*—He has not varied its length in the last several trials. . . . (*ibid.,* p. 71).

There was one interesting experiment which demanded of the subject that he envisage an ideal condition, never realizable in fact, and infer, rather than perceive directly, the factors which precluded this realization. A spring device imparts a horizontal motion to a ball. The subject is to predict its stopping point and to try to discover the variables involved. The spring gives a constant impetus, but the balls it sets in motion vary in weight and size. The younger subjects are primarily concerned with the factors which cause the ball to move, and they think in terms of weight differences and the like. The older ones shift the problem around. They tend to think that, once the impetus is given, there is no problem in explaining why the ball continues to move; rather, they are inclined to look for factors which cause it eventually to stop moving. That is, they are now able to envisage dimly an ideal condition which is never present in reality, namely, the condition that the ball would keep on rolling indefinitely, and then to go on to infer factors (such as friction and air resistance) which are always present to make the ideal state unrealizable. This is not to say that these children "rediscover" the law of conservation of motion in fully articulated form, nor do the authors argue (here or elsewhere) that formal or informal education may not have played a role in what progress they do make. The central point is that the cognitive structure of the adolescent is such as to dispose him to think of the ideal and the possible, to reason in terms of hypothetical entities and conditions.

The following investigation, like those reported in the previous section of this chapter, deals with the child's growing ability to think in statistical-probabilistic terms—in this instance, to think in terms of correlations between variables. The experimental materials consisted of pictures of faces which varied in eye and hair color according to these four combinations: (*a*) blue eyes and blond hair, (*b*) blue eyes and brown hair, (*c*) brown eyes and blond hair, (*d*) brown eyes and brown hair. The subject was shown different sets of these pictures, the sets varying as to how many of each type of picture were represented in the set. In each case he was asked if, for that set, there was a relationship between eye color and hair color, how strong the relationship was, and his rationale for these assertions. For example, if a set of 16 pictures consisted of 4 of each of the types *a, b, c, d* (we can represent this as 4, 4, 4, 4), then the correlation or association between hair and eye color is nil for that set. On the other hand, it is maximal for the set 4, 0, 0, 4—blue eyes always go with blond hair and not-blue (brown) eyes always go with not-blond (brown) hair. There was an interesting transitional stage just prior to the final one. The subject estimated the strength of the relation by simply comparing a to b (or a to the total $a + b$). He failed to recognize that the number of d cases was equally important and that the crucial relation was between a plus d and b plus c. As in some of the other studies described here, it might be wondered at that any of the children reached the final stage for a concept of this level of sophistication. There were obviously children who did, however: the authors state that "it is usually toward 14-15 years that the frequency of these cases is high enough to define a stage" (*ibid.*, pp. 239-240). Here is an example:

> Cog (15;2). Set [5, 1, 2, 4]: "*Most of the people who have brown hair have brown eyes and most of those with blond hair have blue eyes.*"—"What is the relationship?"—"*Not maximum, but not weak . . . 9 people out of 12 have hair the same color* [as eyes]."—"And?" [6, 0, 0, 6].—"*It's the maximum.*"—"And a group where there is no relationship?"—"*You have to mix them up*" [he makes up 1, 1, 1, 1].—"And compare these two groups" [4, 2, 2, 4 and 3, 3, 1, 5].—*The relationships are the same; there are the same number of cards*" [!].—"Did you count them?"—"*Yes. In both groups there are 8/12* [confirming] *and 4/12*" [nonconfirming].—"What is the best way of seeing whether or not there is a relationship?"—"*You have to compare* [a] *and* [d] *with* [b] *and* [c]." He describes the four combinations by grouping them by diagonals (*ibid.*, p. 240).

As for the other studies reported, there were the three alluded to in Chapter 6: that on colored and colorless liquids (pp. 207-209) and those on inverse versus reciprocal opposing forces in a hydraulic press and a scale balance (pp. 217-218). The remainder dealt with these topics: specific gravity of objects which float or sink in water; object movement down (one study) and up (another study) an inclined plane; invisible magnetism (the roulette wheel study described in the section on chance); the heights of liquids in communicating vessels; the projection of shadows; centrifugal force; and the concept of random variation around a mean. In all these Piaget pursues the same general interpretative strategy: to specify the formal-operational mechanisms which the adolescent has at his disposal in coping with these difficult problems.

PERCEPTION

Piaget's ongoing program of research on perception has already yielded a bibliography too large to be summarized adequately in one section of a chapter. It is possible, however, to give something of its general flavor and to sample a few representative experiments. Fortunately, there are available at least two good articles which review parts of this work (Vurpillot, 1959; Wohlwill, 1960d) and a third which provides a cogent general discussion of it, particularly of Piaget's view of perception-intelligence relationships (Wohlwill, 1960c).

One quick way to convey the general tone of the perception research is to describe the content and organization of a typical research report in the Recherches series. The dependent variable in the experiment reported is very likely to be a visual-perceptual illusion, broadly defined to include any systematic departure from veridicality induced by some particular configuration of lines in the perceptual display. The independent variables are generally of two types. (1) There is systematic variation in the display parameters, i.e., the arrangement, magnitude, etc. of the illusion-producing visual elements. (2) There is variation in the age of the perceiving subject. The action of the first independent variable is predicted and plotted in terms of the theory of perception outlined in Chapter 6. In particular, Piaget is concerned here with fitting his law-of-relative-centrations formula to the variations in the magnitude of illusion which result from these changes in the perceptual display. Variation in the age of the perceiving subject generally plays a modulating role with respect to this variation in display conditions. Typically, the illusion turns out to remain maximal and minimal for about the same values of the display conditions, whatever the age of the perceiver. However, the *absolute* magnitude of the illusion at these and intervening points is likely to vary with age (the illusion is said to be *primary* if it decreases with age and *secondary* if it increases, as indicated in Chapter 6). And of course Piaget, the developmental psychologist, is interested in this variation too. Thus, both display conditions and age are varied, and the resulting changes in the illusion are usually reported in conventional data tables and curve plots. Simple statistics are also used occasionally, but analysis of variance, probably the most suitable statistic for such data, never is. It might be supposed that an experimental article of this model would be fairly succinct and easy to read, but Piaget's are generally neither. The report of the experiment proper is usually preceded and virtually always followed by difficult theoretical sections, often long and replete with abstruse terminology and symbolism.

The first article in the Recherches series conforms quite well to the prototype just outlined and will do as a concrete example (Piaget, Lambercier, Boesch, and Albertini, 1942-1943). The dependent variable was the so-called Delboeuf illusion: the inner (smaller) of two concentric circles is perceived as larger than an equal-sized standard circle placed near the two concentric ones. As for independent variables: (*a*) both the absolute sizes of the concentric circles and their size ratio were systematically varied; (*b*) the subjects ranged in age from 5 years to adulthood. The data first of all showed the expected systematic changes in the value of the illusion as a function of changes in variables of type *a*. For example, the illusion was maximal when the inner circle was about three-fourths the size of the outer one and became zero or negative as the fraction declined to one-fourth; similarly, with the size relation between them held constant, the illusion tended to diminish as the absolute size of the circles increased. As for variable b, the illusion tended to decrease with age and would thus be classified as a primary one, dependent on simple centration effects. Finally, the article conforms to type in its extreme length (107 pages), most of which is taken up in a complex pre- and post-experimental theoretical analysis.

Among the most interesting of the perception studies from the standpoint of the present book are those which point up one or another type of interaction between perceptual and intellectual functioning. These experiments can be sorted into several categories. One category comprises studies which appear to illustrate how developing intellectual functions can assist in the attainment of veridical perception, i.e., help to overcome illusory centration effects.

Piaget and Lambercier (1946) conducted an experiment on size constancy which was of this type. A standard rod and a set of variable rods were placed 1 and 4 meters from the subject, respectively, and the subject was to select a variable equal in objective length to the standard. After the subject made selections in this situation, a second rod was introduced, shown to be equal in length to a standard, and then placed near the variables. The subject was expressly asked if this second rod could assist him in finding a variable equal to the standard. The youngest children appeared unable to make use of this aid (i.e., could not infer $A = C$ from $A = B$ and $B = C$) and relied, as before, on direct perceptual comparisons between standard and variable. Contrariwise, the oldest subjects (age 8 years on, roughly) made systematic use of the transitive rule and simply compared the variable with the second ("middle term") rod. Some of the children at intermediate ages appeared to recognize the possibility of transitive inference but could not bring themselves to rely on it completely. There resulted what appeared to be compromise estimates, part way between those of the young children (perceptual comparisons) and those of the older ones (logical inference).

A second study by Piaget, Maire, and Privat (1953-1954) also appears to illustrate the potential dampening effect of intellectual or intellectual-like operations on perceptual error. Subjects of various ages were required to compare the lengths of two horizontal and parallel lines under two conditions: (1) in the standard Müller-Lyer illusion figure

FIG. 7A

and (2) in a modified Müller-Lyer figure, in which the Gestalt "good form" of a square was incorporated into the configuration as a potentially stabilizing, illusion-reducing element

FIG. 7B

It was known from previous research (Piaget and Albertini, 1950-1952) that the Müller-Lyer illusion itself diminishes slightly with age. The question here was whether the square would show relatively more resistance to distortion by the incorporated illusion figure in older versus younger subjects, i.e., whether the ratio of (1)-condition-distortion to (2)-condition-distortion would increase with age. Such a ratio increase was found, and it was attributed to the development of that form of quasi-intellectual behavior Piaget calls *perceptual activity* (see Chapter 6). In the present case, this activity presumably consisted of the illusion-corrective acts of comparing the four angles of the square, judging whether the opposing sides were parallel, and the like: acts reminiscent of those discussed at the beginning of this chapter in connection with the genesis of spatial representations in middle childhood.

There were three experiments carried out by Piaget and Morf (1958b) which purported to show a step-by-step development of the intervention of intellectual or quasi-intellectual inferential processes in perceptual tasks. In one, two parallel rows of counters were placed one above another and exposed for one second. The subject's task was to judge whether the two rows contained an equal number of counters. Judgments were also obtained with bars connecting corresponding members of each row, for example:

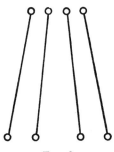

FIG. 8

In the second, the task was to compare the length of two lines, with and without the presence of reference circles:

FIG. 9

In the third, a series of parallel and equidistant rods of increasing height was presented and the subject was to judge whether the height difference between the members of a given adjoining pair of rods was equal to that between the members of another. The inferential process here involved making use of the imaginary line connecting the summits of the rods. If it were a straight line, for example, the series would have to be increasing in height by equal steps, and hence one could infer, rather than just perceive, that any two adjoining pairs would have equal height differences.

A very simplified statement of findings and interpretation in these three studies would be this. At first, the child can make little or no use of the supplementary information contained in the display. The presence of the connecting rods in the first study, for instance, has little influence on his perceptual judgments. Eventually, however, he is able to impose active inferential or preinferential (see Chapter 6) processes on the supplementary information and can thereby achieve a high degree of perceptual veridicality throughout. Between these extremes seem to lie a succession of stages and substages in which some information is utilized and other information is not, in which inference is used for some displays but not for others, and so on. For example, at age 6 or so, judgments are strongly influenced by the presence of the connecting bars when there are only 4 counters in each row, but much less so when there are 5 or 6; that is, inference based on one-one correspondence is not yet generalized to all situations. These and other experiments by the Geneva group seem to indicate that in perceptual tasks, as in intellectual ones, the child at first relies heavily on passive, immediate, centration-ridden perceptions and only slowly and gradually buttresses these with more active processes—intellectual operations and perceptual activity, inferences and preinferences—wherever conditions permit.

The experiments just described purport to show that developing cognitive or cognitivelike functions may facilitate veridical perception. There are others which suggest that these functions can sometimes hinder it as well, especially when the functions are newly minted, developmentally. Such studies typically show an odd *curvilinear* relation between age and degree of veridicality: young children show the most veridicality and older children (9-10 years old) the least, with adults falling somewhere in between. Probably the most unequivocal relation of this kind was that shown by Würsten (1947-1949). In one part of his study, the subject was to judge the relative lengths of two straight lines arranged something like this:

FIG. 10

The illusion here consists of a systematic overestimation of the vertical line, relative to the horizontal one (a variate of the classical horizontal-vertical illusion). The results were quite clear-cut: a very small illusion at 5-6 years which increases to a maximum at 9-10 years and declines somewhat thereafter. Adults show an illusion about equivalent to that of the 7-8-year group.

The interpretation of this rather startling finding went somewhat as follows. Piaget's previous work on the development of spatial representation had indicated that the young child does not yet see visual elements as closely interlocked and intercoordinated within a system of Euclidean rectilinear coordinates. Thus, the two lines to be compared in the Würsten experiment tend to give rise to independent centrations, tend not to be seen as comprising a single configuration. Since the centrations are essentially independent—as though the two lines were not even in the same visual field—there can be essentially no distorting centration or field effects. However, as the subject more and more makes use of a common spatial framework by which to interrelate elements, even non-contiguous ones like these, he will more and more fall prey to whatever field effects this interrelating brings in its wake (in this case, it may be that the child perceptually reduces these noncontiguous lines to contiguous ones, and thus to a more or less straightforward horizontal-vertical illusion figure). To support this interpretation Würsten points out that the 9-10 age, at which the illusion is maximal, roughly corresponds to the age at which the child begins to dominate Euclidean space on the representational level (see the first two sections of this chapter).[6] As the child grows older, however, he becomes capable of attenuating the illusion somewhat by decentration processes, although never again reaching the degree of veridicality he had in his preoperational innocence. Thus, the obtained correspondence between the illusion levels of the 7-year-old and the adult is really a case of quite different underlying processes resulting in the same overt performance.

There are other experiments which show a similar developmental trend and may be subject to a similar interpretation. Piaget and Lambercier (1950-1952a) obtained data on constancy of *projective size:* the ability to compare objects at different distances from the observer as to the size

---

[6] And in another part of the same study, Würsten found that the ability to judge parallelism of lines shows a developmental curve which rises gradually to age 9-10 and then becomes virtually flat.

of their images on the retina, rather than their *objective size*. The developmental curve was again U-shaped: highest constancy of all at 7-8 years (the youngest subjects who could grasp the nature of the task); a decline until age 10-12; a slight increase from 10-12 years to adulthood. Piaget and Taponier (1955-1956) had subjects compare the lengths of two lines arranged thus:

FIG. 11

This task is the perceptual analogue of the one described in the second section of this chapter: two sticks of equal length are first juxtaposed and then one slid ahead of the other. Are their lengths still equal? In view of the nonconservation of length frequently obtained in this intellectual problem, it was not surprising to find a number of younger subjects judging the top line in the Piaget and Taponier perceptual task to be longer simply on the grounds that it was "ahead of" the lower one. When these children were eliminated from the subject sample, however, it was found—once again the curvilinear function—that the tendency to overestimate the top line perceptually was slight at 5 years, increased to about age 8, and diminished somewhat thereafter. These results take on a certain drama in the light of a second experiment within the same study. The investigators administered the above-mentioned intellectual analogue—the conservation-of-length task—and obtained the following percentages of subjects showing conservation: 12.5 per cent at age 5, 70 per cent at age 8, and 100 per cent at age 11: a curve more or less opposite to that obtained in the perceptual task.

CHAPTER ELEVEN

Other Studies

THIS chapter is something of a catch-all, meant to acquaint the reader with a large body of studies within or related to Piaget's system, studies not cited in preceding chapters. A secondary purpose is to provide content and context for the assessment and critique of Piaget's work to be given in Chapter 12.

Although the investigations reviewed here will not all be recent ones, special emphasis will be given to important recent and current work, including, where it has come to our attention, research still in progress and unpublished.[1]

The candidates for this sort of review are a variegated lot, at least as variegated as the system to which they pertain. Some of the studies have been done by Piaget and his assistants, or at least in Geneva under his auspices; others (the majority) have been carried out independently and elsewhere, particularly in Great Britain, the United States, France, and Norway. Some approach Piaget's system with one point of view and aim; others proceed from quite different viewpoints and purposes. Their heterogeneity makes it difficult to classify them neatly by topic, and the division followed in this chapter is necessarily arbitrary.

RECENT BASIC RESEARCH

Most of the investigations to be reviewed in this chapter can claim to be "recent basic research" on Piaget's concepts. This section limits its coverage to that segment of it being carried out directly under Piaget's aegis, by him and his co-workers. In it we take a quick look at what the Geneva group has been up to for the last few years.

[1] There have been a number of highly relevant studies carried out in recent years in Great Britain which are either unpublished (e.g., dissertations) or published in relatively inaccessible journals. Fortunately, there is available an excellent review of much of this work (Lunzer, 1960a), and the writer will refer to it when describing British research reports he has not seen firsthand.

Studies of Imagery

One major project is an investigation of imagery: a research area which Piaget broached some years ago (Piaget, 1951a). At this writing the only available information on the project is a somewhat sketchy set of student notes (Piaget, 1959d), but a systematic monograph ought to be published before long (Piaget and Inhelder, 1959, p. 10, footnote). The experiments appear largely to make use of tasks in which the child has to imagine the sequence of steps in some physical transformation. In one study, for example, the child was shown a bar standing vertically on end and was told to represent (by drawing, by gestures, etc.) the successive positions it occupied in the process of falling to the horizontal. This turns out to be a surprisingly difficult task for children 4-7 years old. In another, the child was given a glass containing a quantity of liquid and was asked to make two predictions about the results of transferring the liquid to a different-shaped glass: (1) whether there would be conservation of quantity; (2) what the height of the liquid column would be in the new glass. The youngest children anticipated no change in column height and predicted that the quantity would be the same (but conservation was denied, of course, after they saw the actual results of the liquid transfer). And the oldest subjects made correct predictions about both liquid level and conservation. The most interesting stage, however, is the transitional one in which the child appears to predict the change in level correctly but then (perhaps *therefore*) denies conservation.

From studies of this kind Piaget concludes that imagery shows an ontogenesis similar to that of intellectual operations (see Chapters 4 and 5). Thus, imagery is initially very static, limited to the internal reproduction of readily perceptible states. As the child develops, his imaginal activity becomes more mobile and flexible, capable of anticipating the successive moments of a yet-to-be transformation from one state to another. However, imagery, like perception before it, is carefully distinguished from intellectual operations in Piaget's analysis (and distinguished from perception as well). The higher-level imagery just mentioned develops in tandem with concrete operations but is not to be identified with them. As Piaget sees it, a flexible, anticipatory imagery may be of real aid to operational thought, indeed, may be necessary to it; but it is scarcely sufficient to account for its genesis and sustained functioning.

Research in Number Development

The developmental construction of number continues to be a going research concern in Geneva. New experiments on the problem formed part of the work of the Centre d'Epistémologie Génétique during its first year (1955-1956) of existence (Apostel, Mays, Morf, and Piaget, 1957, chs. 4 and 5), and number was the central topic in the 1958-1959 meetings (Gréco, Grize, Papert, and Piaget, 1960). Since the investigations reported in these two monographs were carried out within the context of Piaget's genetic epistemological framework, experiments are heavily interlarded with theory. Our brief presentation will eschew most of the theory, however, in favor of describing a few of the more intriguing experiments.

In one (Apostel, Mays, Morf, and Piaget, 1957, ch. 4), the subject was shown two rows of buttons placed in one-one correspondence, as in the early conservation-of-number studies (see our Chapter 9). One of the sets was then divided into two or more subsets, e.g., 8 buttons divided into groups of 3, 3, and 2. The child was asked if the two sets were still equal and on what basis equality could be founded, i.e., whether equality is logically certain in the child's mind or whether empirical test is considered necessary ("one would have to *count* them to be sure"). A screen was interposed between subject and display such that the child could see the experimenter divide the set into subsets—and the experimenter explained just what he was doing. But the child could not actually count the buttons until the experimenter removed the screen.

The developmental stages were the following. Initially, the child simply asserts nonconservation of sets. In the next stage, the child neither asserts nor denies it prior to being given a chance to count the buttons (thus, an empirical test is believed necessary). Moreover, he has to keep establishing the equality again and again, always by counting, for each new division of the same set of buttons. A little later this limitation is removed: once equality is (still empirically) established for any partition of *n* buttons, it is considered established for all partitions of these *n* buttons. Curiously enough, however, in both these stages enumeration is a sure guide to equivalence of sets *only* for sets of relatively *small n* (less than 15 or 20). Piaget presents the behavior record of one child, for example, who readily managed sets of 7 buttons but could not deal with sets of 23; the child actually counted the sets, said there were 23 in each, and then proceeded to say that one set had—"*quand même*"— more buttons than the other (*ibid.*, pp. 107-108)! From this and other recent experimental evidence, Piaget concludes that basic numerical operations and assumptions do not generalize to all numbers immediately upon being acquired for some. Not only is it the case that the operations and assumptions themselves undergo a gradual ontogenetic development, it also appears that, once acquired, they are only gradually applied to larger and larger numerical sets. Piaget refers to this latter development as the *progressive arithmetization* of the number series (e.g., Piaget, 1960a, p. 65). Thus, curious as it sounds, it may make sense to think of a child as being in stage X for, say, numbers 1-15, in stage X−1 for numbers 15-30, and in stage X—2 for numbers greater than 30. To return to the present experiment, the final stage in the sequence was, of course, that in which the child (usually 8-9 years of age) no longer feels it necessary to count the sets at all to be sure of their equivalence; the equivalence between whole and sum of parts is now a logical rather than an empirical affair.

Most of the experiments which grew out of the 1958-1959 session of the Centre have not yet been reported in full. However, a summary by Piaget (1960a) is available as a secondary source. One experiment by Morf investigated the development of the *connectivity property* of the number series (*ibid.*, pp. 15-16). A number of objects (e.g., 30) were made to slide down an incline, one by one and at either fast or slow speeds, and the child was asked whether the number of objects at the top of the slide was certain to be numerically equal to another, smaller set (e.g., 9) at some point in its process of depletion from 30 to 0. Similarly, the child was tested on the converse process: in building up a set from 0 to 30, is one certain to pass through $n = 9$? It appears that preschoolers are not always sure that the two sets in question will be equal at some point in the process. The second (ascending) form of the problem seems to be somewhat more difficult than the first (descending), and the problem is harder at rapid than at slow speeds (perhaps the children think that one can somehow skip by $n = 9$ if only one sends the objects down fast enough!).

In another study, Inhelder discovered a curious phenomenon which gives added insight into the young child's view of number (*ibid.*, pp. 27-28): if one takes elements one by one from each of two numerically unequal sets, the subject tends to think that there are more elements in the subset taken from the larger set than in that (objectively equal) drawn from the smaller set. The interpretation is that the child has not yet completely differentiated numerical and logical class attributes. The quality of greater numerosity which characterizes the larger set is mistakenly applied to subsets drawn from it, much as one would apply a class characteristic (e.g., human) to members of a subclass within this class (e.g., Chinese).

We shall conclude by citing an experimental finding of Gréco's (*ibid.*, pp. 29-30). He is perhaps the most active researcher on number development among the 1958-1959 group. Gréco seems to have systematically established a strange phenomenon, one whose existence had been suspected earlier (see the first number study cited above). The child appears to conserve the number *name* of a given set (Piaget and Gréco call it *quotité*) before conserving its numerical *quantity* proper (*quantité*). That is, the child will count two sets and state that there are "seven" here and "seven" there, whatever their spatial arrangement, but he may nonetheless argue that there are more here than there, if the arrangement is perceptually compelling in favor of inequality. It appears as if there is a stage on the developmental route to genuine conservation of number in which "seven" is simply the name of any collection in which one must count to seven in order to enumerate all its elements. If one performs the same enumeration for two sets, their "numerical titles" are the same without any necessary implication that the actual amounts—numbers in the adult sense—are.

Other Studies

Finally, we shall cite a sample of recent studies other than those on imagery and number. Articles on perception continue to come off the press at a steady pace. At least two themes are identifiable: (1) attempts to pin down more precisely the nature of centration effects (Rutschmann, 1959-1960; Piaget, Rutschmann, and Matalon, 1959-1960) and (2) further investigations of Michotte's perception-of-causality phenomena (Piaget and Lambercier, 1957-1958; Piaget and Maroun, 1957-1958; Piaget and Weiner, 1957-1958).[2] There is also new research afoot in the area of adolescent reasoning. Morf has done some experiments here (Morf, 1957); and Inhelder has at least indicated the intention of extending further her earlier analyses of adolescent inductive reasoning (Inhelder and Piaget, 1958, p. xxiv). And there is also a study of the development of social interactions which was done under Inhelder's direction (Noelting, 1956)—surely a newsworthy research venture for a Piagetian.

TEST DEVELOPMENT

Piaget himself has never bent his talents towards making standardized intelligence tests out of the innumerable cognitive tasks he has created during his professional lifetime. But such an endeavor would surely be a logical extension of his work, and there is some activity in this direction, both in Geneva and elsewhere. This section will begin by reviewing two major, clear-cut attempts at test construction and then mention other investigations which have some relevance to the problem.

One of the standardization projects is being carried out by Vinh-Bang and Bärbel Inhelder at the Institut des Sciences de l'Education of the University of Geneva (Vinh-Bang, 1957, 1959), the other is going forward under Father Adrien Pinard at the Institut de Psychologie of the University of Montreal (personal communication). Full publication of procedure and results is not yet available for either investigation at this

[2] The year 1961 saw yet another book issued by the prolific Piaget (1961), this one a summary and integration of his experimental and theoretical investigations of perception. Since his published work in this area spans some two score journal articles, there is a need for such a book and it will undoubtedly be *the* source henceforth for those interested in this segment of his research.

writing, although it may not be long in coming.[3] The basic facts about the Geneva project are these. About thirty Piaget tasks drawn from various content areas (number, quantity, space, geometry, movement, velocity, time, chance, and others) were individually administered in standardized form to some 1,500 children 4-12 years of age. The intent of the project appears to be to create a standardized developmental scale of reasoning and, in the process of doing this, to assess the validity of Piaget's conclusions about developmental stages, developmental inter-dependence of different cognitive acquisitions, and the like for those content areas studied. Although details are lacking, the impression is that the outcome has been positive on both counts: Piaget's tasks do appear to scale satisfactorily and his previous developmental conclusions based on these tasks are in the main confirmed.

Pinard's aims are similar: first (and for this project, foremost), a systematic replication of Piaget's work, using more careful methodology; second, in so far as the results justify it, the construction of a scale of mental development which, more than has been the case with traditional ones, would have a coherent theoretical rationale (Piaget's). The standardization sample consists of 700 French-Canadian children of 2-12 years of age, with careful across-age matching for sex, socioeconomic level of parents, number of siblings, and (for the older ones) academic achievement. The complete test battery comprises 62 subtests of which 27 are taken directly from Piaget's research: 5 on time, movement, and velocity; 4 on quantity and number; 6 on space; 5 on causality and chance; 3 on the child's beliefs about the world (realism, animism, and artificialism); and 4 on logical deduction and the logic of relations. All children were tested individually, either at school or, in the case of pre-school children, in their homes. The total testing time averaged around 10 hours, distributed across 4-8 testing sessions. The essentials of Piaget's clinical method were incorporated into the testing procedure, but, as in the Vinh-Bang and Inhelder study, the procedure was kept essentially the same for all subjects. Although all analyses are not yet complete, Piaget's developmental findings do appear to be holding up well among French-speaking Canadian children. The principal differences between Pinard's and Piaget's results seem to reside in minor details of stage sequence here and there and in more substantial (but less important, in terms of Piaget's theory) differences in the absolute ages at which the various stages occur. Since the validation component of the project appears to be progressing satisfactorily, it is likely that a most interesting and useful developmental scale will eventuate in time.

There are several studies which touch on the issue of test development

[3] A monograph by Vinh-Bang is in preparation (*Elaboration d'une échelle de développement du raisonnement*) and a book summarizing part of Pinard's work is in the offing (*La pensée causale: étude génétique et expérimentale*).

in that they try to apply Piaget's principles and tasks to the diagnostic evaluation of intellectual deficit. Inhelder wrote a book (1944)[4] in which she described attempts to differentiate levels of mental retardation by means of Piaget's tests for conservation of substance, weight, and volume (Piaget and Inhelder, 1941). The developmental order of acquisition of these three conservations previously established in normal children (i.e., first substance, then weight, then volume) turned out to be reproducible in feeble-minded subjects of differing intellectual deficit. Thus, subjects who could not conserve weight were never able to conserve volume; subjects who could not conserve global quantity were never able to conserve weight and volume, and so on. She also found that, in general, subjects diagnosed on other grounds as morons could perform some concrete operations but no formal ones, and imbeciles were incapable of either.

One of the most interesting of Piaget-related studies was done by Woodward (1959). Not only does it follow up the theme of Inhelder's study, it also has the distinction of being virtually the only published experiment which attempts to validate Piaget's theory of *sensory-motor* development.[5] The subjects were 147 children of 7-16 years, all very severe mental defectives (idiots). Woodward made various observations and simple experiments relevant to Piaget's six stages of general sensory-motor development and of the special development of the object concept (see Chapters 3 and 4). There were two major findings, both tending to confirm Piaget's earlier studies. First, the order of difficulty of the various observed behaviors, as estimated by the number of subjects capable of performing them, corresponded quite closely to their ontogenetic order as Piaget had described it. And correlatively, it was found that if a subject could perform on any given level, he could generally perform on all genetically earlier levels. The second major result was that there was good stage-by-stage correspondence between general and special development. That is, if a subject were classified as being in stage 5 of general sensory-motor development, there was considerable likelihood that he would also be classified as being in stage 5 in the development of the object concept. There are still other investigations which have followed Inhelder's lead in applying Piaget's concepts and methods to subject populations other than normal children. Lovell and Slater (1960) also included a mentally retarded group in a developmental investigation of time concepts, and Lunzer (1960a) reports additional studies of the same

[4] This book is unfortunately out of print and the writer has been unable to locate a copy. The brief summary given here is therefore based on secondary sources (e.g., Piaget, 1950a, ch. 5).

[5] Dr. Lawrence Kohlberg has constructed an infant developmental schedule based on Piaget's sensory-motor theory for use in teaching Piaget's concepts (personal communication), but it has as yet not been put through the formal machinery of test development. Also, research still being carried out by Wolff (1959) may prove to have important implications for the theory.

ilk. We shall reserve for the final section of this chapter a summary of two research projects in which still more *outré* populations were examined through the Piagetian lens (Bibace, 1956; Reiff and Scheerer, 1959).

There is one more type of study germane both to the test construction issue and to the validation of Piaget's work in general: the application of Guttman scalogram analysis to Piaget's stage sequences.[6] Peel (1959) summarizes several investigations of this type in the areas of space, logical judgment, and moral judgment. Mannix (Lunzer, 1960a) and Wohlwill (1960b) have each done one in the area of number. In the present context, the scalogram procedure is used to find out the extent to which a set of responses, interpreted by Piaget as representing different stages of development within a given content area, do in fact form a genuine developmental progression: responses on level B presupposing responses on genetically more immature A, responses on level C presupposing responses on A and B, and so on. The section on space in Chapter 10 pointed out that Piaget postulated a series of stages in the child's drawings of various figures (topological features being differentiated before Euclidean ones, etc.). Ferns and Peel (Peel, 1959) repeated Piaget's testing procedure with 55 children of roughly 3-8 years of age and applied scalogram analysis to the drawings. The analysis tended to confirm Piaget's original ordering of stages. Lodwick's analysis of logical judgments was similarly confirmatory, but moral judgments obtained by Loughran turned out to be less clearly scalable (*ibid.*). And both Mannix (Lunzer, 1960a) and Wohlwill (1960b) found an orderly progression in the mastery of various Piaget or Piaget-related number tasks by scalogram analysis. The latter was a particularly careful study and contains a thoughtful analysis of the potential applications of the scalogram technique to developmental study.

Investigations of this kind have obvious bearing on the validity of Piaget's stage-sequence approach in these fundamental areas of human cognition. But in addition, positive findings here make one optimistic about the test-construction potentialities of his research. If the various types of responses children give to a set of Piagetian tasks in a given content area do in fact show good age scalability, i.e., are not simply an agenetic hodgepodge attributable to individual differences, then it makes sense to think about making developmental scales out of them, scales which would possess Pinard's desideratum of having both feet solidly planted in a theory of intellectual development.

[6] Also obviously germane here are studies which test for developmental interdependence of the various types of cognition Piaget has studied, i.e., studies which intercorrelate or even factor analyze Piaget's tasks. However, since investigations of this type (there are unfortunately not many) have such dominant validational implications and also touch on important general issues about Piaget's system, presentation and discussion of them will be postponed until the validation section of this chapter and again in Chapter 12.

APPLICATIONS TO EDUCATION

There appear to be three principal ways in which Piaget's system could be applied to educational problems.[7] The first is implicit in the preceding section. That is, it may be possible to make fruitful use of Piaget's research instruments in the assessment of the individual child's general intellectual development, special scholastic aptitudes, readiness for various kinds of instruction (e.g., number readiness), etc.—all with an eye towards practical educational matters such as grade placement and assignment to remedial training programs. Since the "psychometrization" of Piaget's tasks is itself still in its infancy, this kind of application has not yet been made at all. It is a safe bet, however, that it is going to follow closely on the heels of the test-construction programs.

A second application involves the planning of curricula in the context of Piaget's developmental findings. This could take two forms. First, there is the question of the grade placement of instructional content. Do Piaget's findings imply, for example, that initial teaching of scientific method and content should be pegged around early adolescence, when the formal operations which make possible genuine scientific thought are said to be developed? What about the age placement of such traditional subjects as geometry? Would Piaget's evidence that many of the basic elements of Euclidean spatial representation and measurement enter the child's thought by age nine or ten imply that geometry and related topics might be taught earlier than they usually 'are? And in general, what information about the normative developmental timetable can we extract from Piaget's work which would be of use in fitting educational content to the cognitive-developmental level of the student? The second variety of this application is summed up in the following question: how can we make use of Piaget's data on developmental sequences to anticipate and guard against subtle, nonobvious "misacquisitions" (there seems to be no better word) which he has shown the child is likely to fall prey to in trying to master a new area?

Here are some examples. The astute educationist might want to prevent the young child from too long dissociating the nominal-enumerative from the quantitative aspects of number (see the Gréco finding discussed on p. 360), and the same would hold for cardinal versus ordinal properties (see Chapter 10). In older children, one might have to steer the subject away from a concept of volume which relates only to the interior contents of objects, one which does not relate occupied space to the spatial surround (Chapter 10). In general, this use of Piaget draws upon his findings

---

[7] For a slightly different categorization of the educational implications of Piaget's work, see Lunzer (1960a).

that the developmental construction of an intellectual content often involves peculiar and unsuspected misconstructions along the way, misconstructions the teacher would do well to be aware of and try to hedge against.

It seems to be true that Piaget's work has not yet intruded substantially into actual curriculum planning, just as we said it had not yet made its mark in the field of educational testing and placement. However, there is currently a vigorous movement among British educators and educational psychologists to effect a liaison between Piaget and pedagogy, particularly as regards curriculum planning. The portents are everywhere abundant in the British literature. Thus, the Lunzer review (1960a) was written expressly for this purpose. Similarly, a collection of papers on Piaget's number research and other contributions has a strong educational focus (National Froebel Foundation, 1955). And much of the experimentation reported in British journals appears to have been done with implications for educational practice in mind (e.g., Churchill, 1958a, 1958b; Lovell, 1959; Peel, 1959).[8] It would be next to impossible to summarize all that has been said in these publications about the import of Piaget's work for education. In general, however, the prescriptions incline towards the broad and nonspecific: exhortations to teachers to familiarize themselves with Piaget's research, caveats against curriculum planning which ignores his developmental facts, and the like. The authors may feel (and they are probably right) that there is not as yet enough of the right kind of research on the problem to make more concrete and specific pronunciamentos.

The third important way in which Piaget's system could be applied to education is this. His theory has a good deal to say about the nature of the cognizing organism and the process by which unknown externals become known internals. It might be that this part of his system could tell us something about the most favorable conditions for learning, and hence, the way in which we should go about teaching. The first application described in this section had to do with the diagnostic assessment of the individual student vis-à-vis the school program; the second concerned the structuring of curriculum content in terms of the normative developmental timetable; and this one involves the methods by which the child ought to be taught, once curriculum content has been selected. This latter application, like its predecessor, can also be divided into two components. One consists of the specific problem of how—by what inner process and in the presence of what external environmental con-

<hr>

[8] Anyone interested in contemporary British research on Piaget's system would be well advised to watch these journals: *British Journal of Psychology, British Journal of Educational Psychology,* and *Journal of Child Psychology and Psychiatry.* Also, K. Lovell—one of the more active British experimenters in this area—has now summarized his research in a book: *The Growth of Basic Mathematical and Scientific Concepts in Children* (Lovell, 1961).

ditions—the child typically acquires the various knowledge forms that Piaget's research has shown need acquiring (the conservations, the transitivity principle, and so on) and, related to this, the potential implications of Piaget's theory and research for the field of learning in general. There has been enough important work done on this facet of the problem to warrant allotting it a chapter section of its own (the section following). The other component has to do more with concrete and specific recommendations for actual classroom teaching which Piaget himself and his close associates have already made, recommendations for instructional method in content areas that Piaget has not studied experimentally as well as in those he has. This is the component which will occupy the rest of the present section.

It has already been stated that Piaget has been interested and actively involved in matters educational for much of his professional life (Introduction and Chapter 8). His views on the subject of educational method have been expressed in one of the early books (1932) and in a long string of articles (e.g., 1928a, 1930b, 1930c, 1931d, 1934, 1935b, 1951b).[9] But what is probably the best single source for his beliefs about method he did not write himself (although it has his *imprimatur* and *nihil obstat* in the Preface). This is a monograph by a psychologist and former schoolteacher named Hans Aebli (1951) who worked with Piaget and associates in Geneva. We draw principally upon the contents of this monograph in summarizing Piaget's prescriptions for educational method.

There are two fundamental tenets from which all specific prescriptions derive. One concerns the relation between the individual student and the content to be learned. It stresses the importance of engaging the subject in direct action vis-à-vis the content. The other has to do with the relation among the students in the process of learning. Here, emphasis is given to the importance of group work in the classroom.

The first tenet springs from a Piagetian dictum by now familiar to the reader: *Penser, c'est opérer* (Aebli, 1951, p. 73). Stable and enduring cognitions about the world around us can come about only through a very active commerce with this world on the part of the knower. The student must be led to perform real actions on the materials which form the learning base, actions as concrete and direct as the materials can be made to allow. As actions are repeated and varied, they begin to intercoordinate with each other and also to become schematic and internalized; that is,

---

[9] It is worth noting that these writings express much more than just ideas about method. They also express strongly held views on the function of education, what some of its important contents should be, and related to these, something of Piaget's political beliefs and general *Weltanschauung*. For example, he makes it clear that he strongly believes in democratic government (and in training for self-government in the school curricula) and in a one-world, internationalistic outlook (also to be fostered educationally). Although not ordinarily what one would call a vivid, exciting writer, Piaget certainly becomes very eloquent and persuasive in some of these articles (e.g., 1931d).

they are transformed into Piagetian operations, with the familiar properties of composition, reversibility, associativity, and so on. Thus, it will be
the teacher's task, and one often demanding considerable ingenuity, to
analyze the content to be learned in terms of the operations implicit in
it. Having done this, he will arrange the learning materials so that these
operations can actually be carried out by the student himself, and then
see to it that the student does carry them out. Suppose he wishes to teach
the elementary notion of fractions. He would do well to eschew pictures
of objects divided into equal parts in favor of actually dividing a concrete
object before the class or, better still, getting the student to make the
partition himself (*ibid.*, pp. 47-48). Similarly, to convey the idea of con-
tour lines on a map, one might actually have the student cut a model
mountain horizontally into layers of equal thickness (*ibid.*, p. 74). The
point in all such instances is to differentiate the basic physical actions
related to or engendering a given phenomenon and then getting the student to practice them.

Since the operational systems Piaget believes to be the *sine qua non* of
representational intelligence involve the properties of reversibility and
associativity, operations expressing precisely these properties should be
incorporated into the student's activity program (*ibid.*, pp. 96-99). In the
case of reversibility, for instance, this would imply that multiplication
and division, as well as addition and subtraction, should be taught together, in alternation. Thus, one should follow a problem like ($10 \times 5 =$
?) with its inverse ($50 \div 5 =$?). Similarly, if one traces a causal series in
the usual cause-to-effect direction, one should not fail to trace it in the
inverse, effect-to-cause direction. That is, given effect D, show its immediate cause (C); given C considered as effect, show its immediate cause (B),
and so on. As for associativity, there are numerous problems in which
the student can practice arriving at a given end point by diverse itineraries. Thus, in deriving the equation for the perimeter of a rectangle, he
should be led to see the equivalences: $2(b + h) = 2b + 2h = h + b +
h + b = h + h + b + b$, etc. Likewise, a given geometric figure can be
constructed by different means, all yielding the same end result (*ibid.*,
p. 55).

But one will not of course want the child to be limited to performing
only concrete actions in situations providing maximal perceptual support for these actions. A key concept in Piaget's general theory is that of
the development and schematization of originally overt actions, i.e., a
gradual transformation of overt actions into mental operations. The
teacher should assist this internalization and schematization process in
the classroom by getting the student to perform the requisite action with
progressively less and less direct support from the external givens (*ibid.*,
pp. 104-106). For example, one might begin by having the child operate
directly on physical entities, then on pictorial representations of these

entities, then have him proceed to cognitive anticipations and retrospections of operations not actually being performed at the moment, and so on, until the originally external actions can take place internally and in complete autonomy from the environment. In other words, the developmental process which occurs in the macrocosm of the child's daily life should be reproduced in so far as possible in the microcosm of the classroom.

The second major point in Piaget's ideas on method can be summarized more quickly. From his earliest writings (e.g., the first five books), he has stressed the paramount importance of interactions with peers as the principal vehicle by which the child is liberated from his egocentrism. One can learn the meaning of perspective—and thereby acquire the rationality and objectivity which only a multiperspective view can confer—only by pitting one's thoughts against those of others and noting similarities and differences. The extension of this view to education consists of plumping for group activities in the classroom—projects to be undertaken in common, discussions sessions, and the like.[10] Aebli discusses the various sorts of group structure and functioning which might be introduced during the learning of an educational unit as well as the timing and coordination of such group projects in relation to individual work (e.g., *ibid.*, pp. 92-95). And in another place in the monograph (p. 60), he nicely sums up this facet of Piaget's educational thinking:

> If social cooperation is thus one of the principal formative agents in the spontaneous genesis of child thought, it is an imperative necessity for modern education to make use of this fact by according an important place to socialized activities in the curriculum.

What about the practical application of Piaget's views on educational method? Once more, there are only a few things one can point to. Aebli (*ibid.*, chs. 11-14) reports a not very rigorous experiment in which a Piaget-oriented method of teaching a geometric concept compared favorably with a traditional method. Z. P. Dienes of the University of Adelaide has been engaged in very promising research attempting to teach rather advanced mathematical concepts to young children through the use of various sorts of concrete aids (cited in Lunzer, 1960a; see also Harvard University, 1961). More than was true of earlier methods of similar type (Stern, 1949; Cuisenaire and Gattegno, 1955), Dienes's work appear to be explicitly grounded in Piaget's theory. And it is also probable that the aforementioned British educators will before long begin to mine the Piaget lode for methodological as well as other types of educational ore (Lunzer, 1960a).

[10] Had Piaget directed his talents towards clinical-psychological or psychiatric practice instead of developmental theory and research, he would undoubtedly have been attracted to group psychotherapy as a medium for personality change, with its implications of correcting individual autism through exchange of viewpoints and experience among group members.

LEARNING STUDIES

One of Piaget's major contributions to genetic psychology has been that of demonstrating the existence of a remarkable array of unsuspected cognitive forms which are acquired in the course of ontogenesis. There are the many types of conservation; there is the transivity principle in its various concrete guises; and there are diverse other acquisitions in the areas of logic, measurement, number, and so on; the list is a long and by now familiar one. Despite Piaget's avowedly developmental orientation, however, the case could be made that he has so far shed little empirical, hard-fact light on precisely how these forms work their way into the child's cognitive life. That is, he has not provided concrete evidence as to the conditions, within the child himself and in his circumambient reality, which are necessary and sufficient to induce their acquisition. It is not that Piaget has given no thought to the question. On the contrary, his equilibration model (Chapter 7) is precisely an attempt to weld a systematic conception of the process of ontogenetic change onto his general theory. What he has not done is submit this or any alternative conception to appropriate experimental test.

Others, however, have also made experimental sorties in this direction, and their work constitutes one of the most interesting and important trends in Piaget-relevant research. The usual design followed is the classical educational-psychological, transfer-of-training one: (1) to establish a set of subject groups matched on pretest performance vis-à-vis some Piagetian thought form (e.g., all subjects fail to conserve weight); (2) to subject the different groups to different training procedures (with one group assigned as a no-training control); (3) to make a posttest assessment of training effects (e.g., to find out how many subjects in each group now succeed in conserving weight). The primary intent of such studies is, of course, to find out what sorts of experiences do and do not facilitate development of the concept under study; the implicit assumption is that experiences found efficacious in inducing laboratory micro-development are at least close analogues of those at work in the quotidian macrodevelopment of the child.

Experiments of this kind have considerable importance strictly within the context of Piaget's system, since they may reveal something about the crucial formative processes which lie behind the various cognitive achievements his studies had previously uncovered. But there is another, broader context in which these investigations can also be situated. This has to do with their implications, not just for Piaget's theory in particular, but for learning theories, theories of response acquisition, in general. The argument runs this way. The empirical ground for the familiar theories of learning—those of Hull, Tolman, Guthrie, and others —has consisted of responses or response processes quite different in appearance from the complex, logic-ridden ones Piaget has worked with. Imagine, if you can, Hull building his behavior theory on observations of children's conservation and transitivity of volume! Should it turn out that response patterns of this latter type cannot be induced and extinguished according to the same "laws of learning" as those which barpressing, maze-running, and rote-learning appear to follow, then it would at least raise important questions as to the generalizability of these "laws." If such evidence were found, it might argue that learning theory, generically speaking, has built its theoretic edifice on too narrow a response base, on a base which is inadequately representative of the whole range of acquirable responses.

The majority of learning studies deal with acquisitional processes in two related areas: number and quantity. The first of the number studies was done by Churchill (1958a, 1958b). She administered a pretest battery of Piaget number tasks to 16 five-year-olds and used their scores to divide them into two equal-sized groups. The experimental group subsequently met with the experimenter twice weekly for four weeks in play sessions designed to give informal practice in grouping, seriating, matching, and ordering various objects; the control group received no training. Retesting with the same battery indicated that the experimental subjects had profited considerably from the training experience, as shown by comparison between their and the control group's pre- to posttest changes. Harker (1960) did a somewhat similar experiment but found less clearcut improvement, although her training program was briefer than Churchill's.

The most cogent and best-designed study of antecedent processes in the area of number development is that by Wohlwill and Lowe (1962).[11] In the Churchill and Harker studies both the training procedure and the behavior it was to affect were too global and heterogeneous to permit any definite conclusions as to precisely what experience did and did not influence precisely what numerical skill. These shortcomings were largely absent from the Wohlwill and Lowe study. Training was directed towards a single numerical acquisition—conservation of number—and the training procedures themselves were highly specifiable and of narrow compass. Seventy-two kindergarten children were individually pretested on both a nonverbal and the conventional verbal form of Piaget's conservation-of-number task, i.e., testing for the recognition that simply rearranging a set of objects in space does not alter the numerical value of the set. The group was divided into four subgroups of 18 subjects each, each subgroup receiving a different training experience interpolated between the two pretests and their posttest readministration.

[11] Wohlwill also did an earlier, pilot experiment in the same area (1959). It is really superseded by the Wohlwill and Lowe study, however, and for this reason will not be reviewed here.

One subgroup was given direct reinforced practice in conservation by repeatedly counting sets of elements before and after their spatial rearrangement, thereby being confronted again and again with the invariance of numerical value in the face of irrelevant perceptual changes. A second was given similar reinforced practice coupled with experience in seeing that addition and subtraction of elements did, in fact, always change the numerical value of the set. It was thought that such experience might indirectly facilitate conservation by fostering the inference that transformations which do not involve any addition or subtraction ought not to change numerical value. A third was given experience specifically designed to dissociate numerical value from perceptual configuration in the child's thought; in particular, the subject was given the opportunity to see that a given set of elements could be made to form either a very short or a very long row without altering cardinal value. All three training methods utilized the nonverbal rather than the verbal conservation procedure and thus would have been expected to have more effect on the nonverbal than verbal posttest. A fourth subgroup served as a no-training control. The results were rather startling. The group as a whole showed significant pre- to posttest improvement on the nonverbal measure of conservation. However, there were no significant differences in amount of improvement among training subgroups or between these and the controls. In the case of the verbal, traditional measure of conservation, on the other hand, there was virtually no discernible training effect in any subgroup.

The other major area of acquisitional study—quantity—has been the exclusive preserve of Jan Smedslund of the University of Oslo. He has been publishing a series of research reports in this area. The series begins with a systematic review of theory and experimentation relevant to the developmental formation of Piaget's concepts in general and those of substance and weight conservation in particular (Smedslund, 1961a). The first reported experiment (Smedslund, 1961b) is rather similar to that of Wohlwill and Lowe.[12] Forty-eight 5-7-year-old children were pre- and posttested on conservation of weight. One group was given 32 reinforced trials on conservation of weight itself: the form of one of two plasticine objects being altered, the child predicted whether or not the two now weighed the same and then proceeded to test his prediction directly by actually weighing the objects on a scale balance. A second training group was also given reinforced practice via the scale balance, but in terms of the effects on relative weight of adding and subtracting small pieces of plasticine vis-à-vis one of the objects, rather than in terms of the effect of changes in form. As in the Wohlwill and Lowe experiment, the intent here was to see if exercising a related schema (the addition-subtraction

[12] And like the Wohlwill and Lowe investigation, it had a pilot-study predecessor (Smedslund, 1959) which it effectively supersedes.

one) would facilitate the acquisition of conservation of weight. A third group served as a no-training control. The results were essentially negative: all three groups showed some apparent pre- to posttest improvement but had no statistically reliable between-group differences.

The second experiment (Smedslund, 1961c) approached the problem from the point of view of extinction rather than acquisition. Smedslund believes that the conventional learning-through-external-reinforcement theory and Piaget's equilibration model would make different predictions regarding the extinction of the conservation-of-weight concept. Reinforcement theory would assert that it ought always to be extinguishable, whether originally acquired in the laboratory through reinforced practice or in everyday life (here also, presumably, through reinforced practice). Piaget's equilibration position would argue differently: (1) that external reinforcement, either in the form of concrete rewards or in the form of cognitive feedback (as in the Wohlwill and Lowe study and the previous Smedslund study), cannot in itself engender a genuine conservation concept; any apparent learning under such a training regimen is likely to involve only an empirical *modus operandi*—a pseudoconcept with no sense of logical certitude behind it; (2) a conservation concept which is genuine, which is not a pseudoconcept, ought in principle to be impervious to extinction through nonreinforcement, i.e., not formed through external reinforcement in the first place, it should not be extinguishable through withdrawal of reinforcement.

The experiment utilized two groups of subjects. One group (N = 13) consisted of children 5-7 years of age who showed complete conservation of weight on a pretest. The other group (N = 11) comprised children of the same age who showed no trace of conservation in the pretest, but who gave nothing but correct responses when retested after two training sessions which provided reinforced practice in conservation (the first of the two training procedures of the previous study). The two groups were then subjected to a modified version of that training procedure. One of the plasticine objects was deformed, the child made his prediction as to weight and then had a chance to verify it on the balance scale. This time, however, the experimenter surreptitiously stole a piece of plasticine from the object as he changed its shape, with the result that subsequent weighing on the scale gave results contrary to the conservation hypothesis. Not one of the subjects who had "acquired" the concept through the training procedure showed the slightest resistance to extinction. Typically, they evidenced little surprise at the result and quickly reverted to arguments for nonconservation based on the perceptual appearance of the objects. On the other hand, six of the thirteen subjects who had brought their conservation concept with them to the experiment, so to speak, did resist. This resistance generally took the form of arguing that a piece of plasticine *must* be missing (it fell on the floor, the experimenter removed it, etc.). Smedslund suggests that adding more extinction trials would likely not have touched this resistance, since the subject was in effect incorporating the negative reinforcement (inequality of weight of the objects) into the very explanation which safeguarded his conservation concept. He also makes the point that one could not have predicted resistance to extinction from the subject's preextinction behavior; resistors and nonresistors alike usually argued for conservation on the grounds that nothing had been added or taken away during the deformation: the very explanation the converse of which the nonresistors failed to invoke during the extinction trials.

In the next experiment, Smedslund (1961d) attempted to foster conservation in nonconservers by providing experience with the unreliability of perceptual size cues, a well-known source of nonconservation responses. As in Wohlwill and Lowe's dissociation condition, the subjects were given repeated opportunity to discover that larger objects are not necessarily heavier than smaller ones. It turned out that thirty-six training trials of this kind had virtually no effect on the subjects' response orientation; they continued to rely just as heavily on perceptual cues in posttest as in pretest.

The fifth article in the series (Smedslund, 1961e) is of unusual interest. Smedslund had come to adopt the following hypothesis about the genesis of conservation (it would presumably apply to the development of other concepts as well). The essential condition for the development of conservation where there had previously been nonconservation, is a state of cognitive conflict in the subject. Cognitive conflict induces a reorganization of the subject's intellectual actions, one which proceeds along the lines postulated by Piaget's equilibrium model; and it is this reorganization specifically which leads to the conservation strategy. Further, the hypothesis specifically asserts that external reinforcement in the form of feedback as to correctness of incorrectness of response is not a causal factor in the equilibration process. Accordingly, Smedslund devised a training procedure which might induce cognitive conflict in the subject but which would not provide him with any feedback as to whether his judgments were right or wrong. The conservation studied in this experiment was that of substance or global quantity rather than weight. The subjects were thirteen 5½-6½-year-old children whose pretest performance showed no evidence of conservation of substance. These children were all subjected to a complicated training procedure (no control group was used) the essence of which was that two kinds of transformation of an object, deformation and addition-subtraction, were systematically set in opposition to each other. If, for example, a given subject was inclined to think that elongating a plasticine ball augmented its quantity and that subtracting a piece from it diminished its quantity, the experimenter would do both at once and then pose the conservation question. Such a procedure was intended to give the subject pause, to induce him to vacillate between conflicting strategies; thence, he would be expected slowly to veer towards the simpler and more consistent addition-subtraction schema, with its implication of conservation where neither addition nor subtraction obtain.

The behavior of the subjects during the training sessions was carefully recorded. Five of the thirteen subjects consistently followed the addition-subtraction schema and ignored the deformation; the other eight did the converse. Four of the five gave a number of conservation responses in posttest, complete with logical rationale; none of the eight showed any improvement at all. Smedslund points out that shifts from no conservation at all to conservation accompanied by a coherently stated logical justification have been rare in his research experience, and he is therefore inclined to interpret these four cases as tentative support for his cognitive-conflict hypothesis. The sixth experiment in the series also tends to support it (Smedslund, 1961f). Induction of conflict coupled with absence of external reinforcement was again the keynote of the training procedure, but this time a no-training control group was added. Unlike the case with previous studies reviewed in this section, this training group did manage to outperform its control group on the posttest.

There have also been learning studies dealing with Piagetian concepts other than those of number and quantity conservation. For instance, Morf (1959) attempted to train the concept of logical inclusion of classes, i.e., the recognition that a class B is both of greater extension than one of its subclasses A and includes it $(A = B - A')$. He used a variety of training procedures, all of which seemed reasonable and appropriate; but none of them made much of a dent in the subjects' preoperational strategies. The only one which showed any promise at all consisted of training the children in the ancillary concept of logical multiplication— the recognition that an object can belong to several different classes at once.

Gréco (1959a) was more successful with the concept of direct and inverse spatial order. The materials consisted of three different-colored beads which were inserted into a tube in a particular order, e.g., ABC. The subject was first questioned as to the order in which they would reemerge from the tube at the other end (children usually experience little difficulty in recognizing that they will always reemerge in the same order). The child was then required to predict the order of emergence after the tube had been given one 180° rotation (CBA) and two 180° rotations $(ABC$ again). One group (S) was given training on one and two rotations which was to facilitate a conceptual reorganization as opposed to a "blind" response learning; the other group's (D) training appeared to be more of the latter kind. The S group did considerably better than the D group on a posttest administered a number of weeks after training and also showed greater generalization to problems involving more than two rotations as well as more transfer to a different but analogous task. Unfortunately, there were too many differences between the two training conditions to permit one to isolate the crucial factors responsible for the S group's superior posttest performance.

Smedslund (in press) did an experiment on the child's representation of horizontality. A group of 5-7-year-old children were shown pictures of bottles tilted in various orientations and asked to draw in the water surface in each case (pretest). They were then shown an actual bottle filled with inky water and asked to observe carefully as the bottle was slowly tilted in 30° steps through 360°, with a pause at each step. The pretest was then readministered, together with sets of drawings already made from which the subject was to choose the correct one. There were two findings of interest: (1) the study confirmed Piaget and Inhelder's (1956) earlier observations that children in this age group generally do not recognize that liquid level remains horizontal whatever the orientation of the container; and (2) it was found that subjects who showed initial traces of having the horizontality concept did profit somewhat from the observation (training) period, but that those who had no correct pretest drawings scarcely profited at all (only one of eight subjects in this category showed any posttest improvement whatever).

Beilin and Franklin (1961) investigated the effects of instruction on length and area measurement by means of a transfer-of-training design. The subjects (first- and third-graders) were initially tested for their ability to conserve and measure lengths and areas. Then, half of each grade group was exposed to a group-administered, one-session program of instruction designed to teach the requisite concepts and skills by the use of concrete examples; the other subjects received no training. All subjects were then given a posttest which was essentially an alternate form of the pretest, presumably demanding the same basic abilities but utilizing different materials. Both experimental and control first-graders improved in length measurement on posttest (most third-graders could measure length on pretest, and therefore little improvement on posttest was possible). Beilin and Franklin suggest that the pretest may itself constitute a training experience for these operations—hence the posttest improvement in the control group. In the case of area measurement, the third-graders who had received training showed posttest improvement, whereas their controls did not. However, the most interesting finding was that instruction had no apparent effect at all on the first-graders: none of them showed any capacity for operational-level area measurement before training and none showed it after. And there are other studies of at least peripheral relevance to the issue of acquisition which we shall simply list: (Ervin, 1960a; Goustard, 1959; Gréco, 1959b; Matalon, 1959; Morf, 1957).

What can be concluded from all these experiments? Probably the most certain conclusion is that it can be a surprisingly difficult undertaking to manufacture Piagetian concepts in the laboratory. Almost all the training methods reported impress one as sound and reasonable and well-suited to the educative job at hand. And yet most of them have had remarkably little success in producing cognitive change. It is not easy to convey the sense of disbelief that creeps over one in reading these experiments. It can be hard enough to believe that children systematically elect nonconservation in the first place; it is more difficult still to believe that trial after trial of carefully planned training is incapable of budging them from this aberrant position. Further, there is more than a suspicion from present evidence that when one does succeed in inducing some behavioral change through this or that training procedure, it may not cut very deep. Certainly Smedslund's extinction study (1961c) indicates that conservation-of-weight responses acquired through laboratory training may have a very hollow core and are not true conservation concepts in any ordinary sense.

The apparent recalcitrance of preoperational structures to deliberately engineered, short-order reorganization suggests an implication and a question. The implication is that there is a deep developmental reality about these structures, and in this sense the learning studies confer a degree of backhanded validity to Piaget's previous assertions that they are, in fact, real existents which exert weight in the young child's intellectual life. Thus, these experiments tend to argue against the view that such structures are entirely artifacts of verbal confusion and misunderstanding, nothing but the momentary and fragile vagaries of an immature and unstable organism. To put it another way, if you cannot get rid of a way of thinking, it must really be there in force.

The question which these investigations bequeath to us is the same one they were designed to answer: how do conservation and other Piagetian concepts develop? It might be said, parenthetically, that this question can in principle be divided into two: (1) by what concrete methods deriving from what theory of acquisition can we most effectively train children on these concepts? and—what may be a different question —(2) how are they in fact acquired normally—that is, in the child's day-to-day cognitive bouts with the real world? It is not likely that the second question can ever receive a direct and precise answer because of the intrinsic difficulty of sorting out the myriad uncontrolled environmental presses to which the child is exposed. But the very posing of the question in this way suggests a type of research endeavor which has not yet been exploited: an ecological study of the young child's mundane interchanges with his workaday world, a kind of job analysis of his daily life along the lines of Barker and Wright's work (1951, 1955). This sort of study might suggest promising leads to pursue in the more conventional transfer-of-training experiment; in view of the infertility of most training methods so far tried, no source of new ideas ought to be ignored.

But even if we take the major question in its undifferentiated form, assuming at least a similarity between laboratory and extralaboratory processes of acquisition, it must be said that our understanding of precisely what these processes are is still rudimentary. One way to put the question in clearer focus is to do as Smedslund and others have done: pose it in terms of the comparative explanatory and predictive merits of a conventional learning-through-external-reinforcement versus a Piaget or Piagetlike equilibration-through-internal-cognitive-conflict model. As the reader is by now doubtless aware, those who have done the best research in the area are tending to move away from the learning orientation towards one or another version of the equilibration model. Although the writer also feels in his bones that something like an equilibration-conflict model will prove to be the best one for these acquisitions, he would not dare to argue the case from the research data presently available.

Although it can be granted that particular procedures deriving from the learning orientation have not been anywhere near as effective as one might have predicted before the fact, this is not equivalent to asserting that the orientation has no application to the formation of the Piaget type of cognitions. In the first place, it has already been shown that training methods based on reinforcement considerations are not the only ones which have been less than completely effective; as we said, Piagetian concepts have so far proved inordinately difficult to stamp in, whatever the training procedure used. Really, the only studies which seem to provide explicit support for the equilibration position are the two most recent ones of Smedslund cited above; and two small-scale experiments do not mandate much when the issue is a decision between two theories. Another relevant point is that the research so far done may not have given the reinforcement view a completely fair hearing, i.e., in the sense of insuring an adequate number of trials, an appropriate reinforcement schedule, a careful decision as to just what sort of response to reinforce, and so on. To take one specific case in point, it might well be that reinforcements of a more concrete and earthy sort could succeed where simple cognitive feedback (the principal form of reinforcement used in the studies reviewed above) would not. Experiments by Siegel and McMichael (1960) and by Yost, Siegel, and McMichael (1961) argue for this possibility in the case of the formation of probability concepts.

And finally, there is one more reason why a choice between the two models must rest in abeyance for a while: the equilibration-conflict model needs a more precise and detailed explication than it has so far received before one can meaningfully set it into opposition to other, better-elaborated models. The continuous and insistent clamor for rigorous operational specification in psychological theory occasionally jangles the nerves of some of us, but there is no doubt but that Piaget's theory of acquisition could stand some added concretization. It is worth noting, therefore, that small steps in this direction have recently been taken: in the Smedslund papers and also in some articles by Piaget himself (1959a, 1959b, 1959c, 1960b). One of the most important attempts at systematic presentation, however, has come from an unexpected source. Daniel Berlyne, a psychologist with a background in Yale-flavored learning theory, published a paper describing an acquisition model which is, in effect, a synthesis of Piaget and Hull (1960a).[13] Moreover, Piaget has written a largely favorable commentary on it (1960b). Both Berlyne's article and Piaget's commentary make most interesting reading, and it is unfortunate that they are not quickly summarizable. One impression only from one who claims no expertise in the learning area: Piaget has good reason to review the Berlyne model favorably, since its really important, cornerstone concepts appear much more Piagetian than Hullian.

VALIDATION STUDIES

There are obviously many studies reported in other sections of this chapter which have important validational implications, however else they may have been classified for the purposes of the chapter. There is the work of Pinard, Vinh-Bang, Inhelder, Smedslund, Wohlwill, Woodward, and many others. Where it is feasible and economical to do so, we shall refer again to some of these studies. But not all of them will be cited again, and it should be borne in mind that those omitted are nonetheless part of the total body of validation evidence.

The Early Work

There has probably been more written about Piaget's earliest, pre-1930 investigations—more reviews, more critiques, more research articles—than about all his subsequent work put together. This leaves the potential reviewer a choice only between a lengthy, detailed, substantive review and a brief, where-you-can-go-to-find-it sort of coverage. Because there already exist surveys and reviews in this area to which one can turn, we shall adopt the latter course here. The present survey, then, will attempt to do only three things. First, it will list most of the available secondary sources on this literature, putting reviews, commentaries, and critiques under a common roof. Second, it will list most of the *recent*

[13] This paper is not Berlyne's only contribution to the problem area under discussion. His book (1960b) is a rich source of theory and data on the general question of perceptual and intellectual motivation. Of particular interest in the present context, he elaborates a "conceptual conflict" view of cognitive functioning and cognitive change which is certainly a start towards the needed "more precise and detailed explication."

primary literature, i.e., validation or validation-relevant experiments carried out during the past fifteen years. This excludes a lot of earlier research studies, but these can readily be located in the secondary sources. And of course the primary literature, both early and late, also constitutes an additional source of criticism and review. Finally, the subsection will close with a few general comments and impressions about validation research on this part of Piaget's system.

The principal secondary sources are these: Bloom, 1959; Curti, 1938; Deutsche, 1937; Hazlitt, 1930, 1931; Huang, 1943; Isaacs, 1929, 1930; Lewis, 1951; McCarthy, 1954; Medinnus, 1959; Morris, 1958; Russell, 1956; Strauss, 1951; Vigotsky, 1939. More recent primary literature includes: Bell, 1954; Boehm, 1957; Crannell, 1954; Danziger, 1957; Dennis, 1953, 1957; Dennis and Mallinger, 1949; Durkin, 1959a, 1959b, 1961; Honkavaara, 1958; Johnson, 1958, 1959; Kligensmith, 1953; Klingberg, 1957; Kohlberg, 1958; Liu, 1950; MacRae, 1954; Medinnus, 1959; Mogar, 1960; Morris, 1958; Nass, 1956; Oakes, 1946; Peel, 1959; Simmons, 1960; Simmons and Goss, 1957; Strauss, 1954; Templin, 1954a, 1954b; Uğurel-Semin, 1952; Voeks, 1954; Wheeler, 1959; Zambrowski, 1951).

As to general impressions, the writer would venture these few. First of all, it is undoubtedly true that these validation studies have, in certain respects, provided us with an amplified and more accurate picture of the psychological realities surrounding the phenomena Piaget described in his early books. Here are a few things which have been painted into the picture. These phenomena are typically not so strongly, and hence, not so exclusively chronological-age-dependent as would be inferred from Piaget's original account of them: not so strongly, in the sense that their correlations with age generally turn out to be smallish to middle-sized (and thus ruling out any tight stage-by-age bracketing); not so exclusively, in the sense that many other factors appear to contribute variance, e.g., individual difference factors like general intelligence, socioeconomic background, and so on. Furthermore, it became clear that these phenomena are sensitive to task (and probably experimenter) variation. For example, it often turned out that responses characteristic of a given stage could be elicited earlier than Piaget suggested by changing the assessment procedure, e.g., making it less dependent on the child's capacity for verbal formulation. And there were diverse other points of criticism or qualification raised: inadequate sampling, unstandardized methods of inquiry, lack of precise specification and definition of theoretical constructs and experimental operations, failure to employ adequate (and often, any) statistical procedures in data analyses. One could go on and on.

Although there is much to criticize in these critical studies, there is also much to applaud. They have undoubtedly served an important braking and reality-testing function with respect to a body of theory and research which certainly had more than its share of irritating overstatements, omissions, unclarities, and even outright misinterpretations. But these studies might have gone on to do something much more positive, and they did not. They might have tried to participate for a while in Piaget's vision of cognitive development—one which postulates qualitative changes in intellectual structure with ontogenesis—to see where it might lead in terms of new theory and new research. From the vantage point of our present knowledge of all that Piaget and a small coterie have accomplished since the early days without straying one jot from this vision, one can only wish that an army of them had done just this. What did they do instead? What they did, or so this writer sees it, was to stand off at a distance, examine Piaget's work through a lens with markedly different optical characteristics from his own, and then proceed to criticize and revise in terms of how it looked through this lens.[14] And what sort of lens was it? Their conception of development seems largely to have featured a mind which remains qualitatively invariant as it slowly manufactures knowledge from experience over the childhood years, a mind which changes in size but not in shape, so to speak. As Braine (1959, p. 34) has rightly observed, this scheme of development did not turn out to be a robust and productive alternative to the one it criticized. It hardly could have been, because it posed no genuinely developmental problems for experiment to solve; there can be no developmental problems if nothing of interest is thought to develop.

We would summarize our impressions this way. These investigators largely failed to grasp what Piaget was really trying to do in this early work and therefore failed to carry it forward in any substantive way; that is, they failed to advance our knowledge much as regards the developmental problems that Piaget had posed.[15] This was surely an important way to fail. But a balanced estimate would have to add that they did have a good deal of success in attacking genuine problems in his work which *they* chose, legitimate problems dictated by their own particular view of science and child development. These included, on the negative side, well-taken criticisms of what Piaget had and had not done and, on the positive side, concrete evidence regarding the operation of independent variables he had not investigated.

Number and Quantity

Piaget's researches on number and quantity have been popular targets for validation study during the past several years, probably because of

[14] Nathan Isaacs (1955b), an early critic and a current admirer of Piaget's work, has given a vivid account of the first impression which Piaget's early experiments made on him and his fellow progressive educationists.

[15] As previous sections have shown, this kind of failure has not been characteristic of other research movements—viz, the learning studies of Smedslund, Wohlwill, Gréco, etc. It was because these studies do deal with live, current problems, problems Piaget himself deems central to his system, that so much space was given to them in this chapter.

their obvious educational implications. One of the most important of the number studies has been carried out by Dodwell (1960, 1961). He gave a battery of Piaget number tasks, using both individual (1960) and group (1961) administration, to large samples of kindergarten, first-grade, and second-grade Canadian children. These were the principal findings. First, he was able to identify in his subjects' protocols all the major levels of responses Piaget had found, e.g., all three stages in the development of number conservation. Also, like Piaget, Wohlwill, Gréco, and others, he found that the operation of counting was often ineffective in guaranteeing conservation of number in young children. Second, some of the number tasks showed more definite developmental trends than others for the age range studied. For instance, responses to a task measuring understanding of number conservation, where the two sets of elements are in natural—"provoked" correspondence (eggs and egg cups)—showed little age change. Conversely, a definite age trend obtained for a task assessing conservation of discontinuous quantity (beakers of different shapes containing equal numbers of beads). And, as might be predicted from this, the various number tasks were of unequal difficulty, with the consequence that a child who gave concrete-operational responses to one problem might well give preoperational responses to another.

In this connection, Piaget had originally suggested that an operational grasp of number as simultaneously ordinal and cardinal implies prior achievements in the areas of class and relation, particularly achievements regarding the operations of seriation and one-one correspondence. Dodwell performed a scalogram analysis on the Piaget tasks in question and found the expected sequential dependency (i.e., if child solves ordinal-cardinal problems, he can solve seriation and one-one correspondence problems, but not necessarily the converse), but the dependency was by no means a perfect, exceptionless one. And finally, miscellaneous other results: (1) IQ, as well as age, has some correlation with test performance in this area; (2) Piaget's number tasks show good test-retest reliability; (3) they also correlate reasonably well (r = .59) with an arithmetic achievement test, suggesting to Dodwell their potential utility in evaluating number readiness in young children; (4) and they appear to be amenable to group as well as individual administration. Dodwell summarizes his over-all evaluation of Piaget's number work as follows:

> Whilst Piaget is on the whole correct in his description of the child's understanding of number, the pattern of development is neither as neat, nor as rigid, as he would have us believe (1961, p. 35).

We earlier cited two other experiments which have submitted Piagetian or related arithmetic tasks to scalogram analysis in order to discover any natural ordering of steps in the ontogenesis of number abilities. Thus, Mannix (Lunzer, 1960a) found the following ordered sequence: first, mastery of conservation in the case of provoked correspondence, then in the case of continuous quantity (the task involving equal quantities of liquid in different-shaped vessels), and still later, grasp of the additive composition of numbers (e.g., recognition that a set of elements distributed $7 + 1$ is numerically equivalent to set distributed $4 + 4$). Mannix also concluded, as did Dodwell, that Piaget was generally correct in his description of the major types of responses children give to his number tasks. Wohlwill's experiment (1960b) also showed that the application of scaling techniques in this area could be a fruitful undertaking. His data indicated three major stages in the evolution of number concepts: (1) a wholly perceptual approach; (2) a conceptual approach to individual numbers; (3) a conceptualization of the relationship among individual numbers.

Another important investigation was carried out by Hyde (1959)—this one a cross-cultural study. A large battery of Piaget's number and quantity tasks was administered to groups of European (mostly British), Arab, Indian, and Somali schoolchildren of 6-8 years of age living in Aden. The tests were given in English to the Europeans and in Arabic to the others (the Indians and Somalis spoke Arabic in school, although it was not their mother tongue). The principal findings were as follows. First, her subjects showed the same general types of responses to number problems Piaget had found in Swiss children:

> During the investigation, it was a common experience to hear a small Arab, Somali, or Indian child give in Arabic almost a word for word translation of an answer given to the same question by a Swiss child (*ibid.*, p. 220).

Moreover, the developmental changes in responses were largely as Piaget had indicated. Second, as Dodwell had observed, the number tasks varied widely in difficulty level. And finally, the European subjects generally performed on a higher genetic level than their non-European peers.

The one experiment which appears to have found nothing at all to confirm in Piaget's observations on number is that by Estes (1956). There are, however, several things about this study which make one cautious about placing too much stock in its negative findings. First, the report of procedure and results is excessively brief (the publication is essentially a three-page note). Second, Estes drew her three tasks from a similarly overbrief, popular account of Piaget's number work (Piaget, 1953a), instead of from his book on number, and incidentally, did not even follow this account faithfully in her second task. And finally, there is what Dodwell (1960, p. 191) calls "the general inimical tone of the paper"— a cue which the present writer, at least, is not inclined to dismiss in evaluating a research report. There is, however, one finding in this study which ought to be looked at carefully. The test was the one on conservation of discontinuous quantity and the finding was this:

When the children were asked: "Which jar now has more marbles?" they would indicate the smaller [i.e., thinner] jar. "Does it really have more marbles?" The general reply was: "No. It looks like more. But I put the same in. It's 'cause this jar is taller (or thinner, or smaller, or narrower, etc.)" (Estes, 1956, p. 221).

It may be that perceptual "more" and numerical "equal" simply co-exist without adequate differentiation in the cognition of children at a certain level, and that an experimenter can bring either one to the foreground by appropriate questioning. Thus, it might be that what seems to be true and what "really" is true are not yet sufficiently isolated in the child's thought, with the consequence that the term *more* has a built-in ambiguity for him. The whole problem of assessing the precise cognitive status of expressed judgments and beliefs in response to Piaget's tasks has been with us as long as the tasks have, but not enough research attention has yet been given to it.

Several other investigations will be mentioned briefly. The previously cited experiments by Churchill (1958a, 1958b), Harker (1960), and Wohlwill and Lowe (1962) have validated Piaget's analysis of number in broad outline, if not always in detail. Churchill makes the interesting hypothesis, well worth testing, that the development of the concept of conservation might be impeded by lack of order and stability in a child's home life, i.e., a lack of invariant, "conserved" entities in his personal-social world (1958b, p. 44). Williams (cited in Lunzer, 1960a) reports a study which, like Dodwell's, points up the potential educational value of Piaget's number tasks in the assessment of number readiness. And other papers of at least peripheral interest are those of Slater (cited in Lunzer, 1960a), Wohlwill (1960a), and Borelli (1951).

Piaget's work on the development of quantity concepts has also had its share of validation studies in recent years. In one, Elkind (1961b) administered tests of conservation of number, of continuous quantity, and of discontinuous quantity to 4-7-year-old children. The most important findings were: (1) all three types of conservation are age-dependent within this age range, as Piaget had said; (2) conservation of continuous quantity is more difficult (i.e., has a higher mean age of acquisition) than that of discontinuous quantity; (3) correlations between conservation scores and subtest scores on the Wechsler Intelligence Scale for Children (WISC) were "generally positive, sometimes significant, and usually low" (*ibid.*, p. 44).[16]

In a second experiment (1961c), Elkind administered Piaget's tests for conservation of global quantity, weight, and volume (of balls of clay)

---

[16] The study was also concerned with validating what were taken to be Piaget's views on *global* versus *intensive* versus *extensive quantity*. So far as the present writer can judge, however, there is a lack of concordance, both between Piaget's definitions of these terms and Elkind's definitions, and between the latter and their operational expression in the test questions.

to 175 children 5-11 years of age. As expected, each type of conservation was clearly age-dependent. More important, the mean ages of acquisition of the three supported Piaget's assertion that the normal genetic order is global quantity first, then weight, and then volume. Unfortunately, no information is presented regarding the invariance of this order within individual subjects, i.e., how many subjects, if any, appeared to have acquired these conservations in a sequence other than the "normal" one. An interesting minor finding concerned the way the child went about justifying conservation responses. A minority of children defended their conservation responses by appealing to general laws, e.g., "No matter what shape you make it into it won't change the amount." In the light of Piaget's views on the characteristics of formal- versus concrete-operational thought (see Chapter 6), it should be noted that these responses occurred only in Elkind's 9- 10- and 11-year-old subgroups.

In a third investigation (1961a), Elkind administered the same three conservation tasks to 469 children 12-15 years old. The first finding of importance—also suggested in the preceding study—was that the age *décalage* between the first two and the third type of conservation may be considerably greater than Piaget had thought. About 75 per cent of Elkind's subjects had acquired conservation of global quantity and weight somewhere around the 7-9-year period. On the other hand, the 75 per cent level for conservation of volume does not seem to occur until age fifteen or so. He also found, as had Piaget, that children commonly attribute the rise in water level following immersion of the object (volume test) to the object's weight (= impact or pressure). Kuhlmann-Anderson IQ scores showed a low but significant correlation with success on the volume task, and boys were consistently superior to girls on this task at each age level. Elkind offers some interesting speculations about possible sources of individual variation among adolescents in the conceptulization of quantity.

Lovell and Ogilvie (1960) made an intensive study of global quantity conservation in 7-10-year-old British children. These were some of his findings:

1. Piaget's stages of nonconservation—on-and-off conservation—conservation were readily identifiable in his subject group and showed the expected changes in frequency as a function of chronological age (and they found, as did Elkind, that the 75 per cent level occurs around age eight).

2. Nonconservation usually appears to derive from the act of centering on a single dimension (e.g., length), as Piaget had argued earlier.

3. A child may verbalize the fact that the stretched-out piece of plasticine had previously been like the ball standard, and/or could be made like it again (Piaget's empirical reversibility) and still assert nonconservation.

4. A subject will occasionally appeal to conservation of weight (the allegedly more mature acquisition) as justification for asserting conservation of global quantity.

5. A child who conserves global quantity in one task situation will not necessarily do so in another.

Lovell and Ogilvie offer the hypothesis—very much in accord with Piaget's views on the task-and-area-specific nature of concrete- as opposed to formal-operational thought—that the child can at first apply a concept like conservation of global quantity only in particular, selected situations; with additional maturation and experience, the concept becomes a stable and consistent instrument of cognition, applicable to a broad range of concrete instances.

Two articles by Smedslund described earlier in this chapter present data of interest in the present context. In one (Smedslund, 1961b), 5-7-year-old children were given tests of conservation of global quantity, conservation of weight, and transitivity of weight (i.e., if $A = B$ and $B = C$, A ? C, and if $A < B$ and $B < C$, A ? C). In the quantity book (Piaget and Inhelder, 1941, pp. 271-280) and elsewhere, Piaget hypothesized that logical (e.g., transitivity) and infralogical (e.g., conservation) operations are organized synchronously for any given domain of application (e.g., weight). Smedslund's data offered no support for this hypothesis: (1) the pretest correlation between conservation and transitivity of weight was very low (with or without age variance partialed out); (2) there was no evidence that acquisition of conservation following training on conservation systematically brought with it improvement on the transitivity task. As for the hypothesized sequential dependency between the two conservations themselves, there was some supporting evidence: there were only two subjects in his sample who showed some evidence of conservation of weight without having any apparent grasp of conservation of global quantity. However, Smedslund's data lead him to believe that there can be considerable positive transfer between the two tasks—recall here Lovell and Ogilvie's fourth finding—and that practice on the one is likely to influence performance on the other. Finally, it should be mentioned that justifications for conservation based on compensation of relationships (e.g., "the sausage is longer than the ball *but* also thinner") were almost never given by Smedslund's subjects, although Piaget had attached considerable importance to such reasoning in his account of how the child changes from nonconservation to conservation strategies (see Chapter 9).[17]

A recurring question in connection with any Piagetian content area—number, quantity, or whatever—is that of the developmental sequence of acquisitions within the area. As we have seen, various investigators

---

[17] Lovell and Ogilvie (1960), on the other hand, found that about 30 per cent of their subjects did give such explanations.

have used scalogram analysis and other statistical procedures in attempts to find out something about these sequences. Smedslund (1961f) has made such an attempt in the case of conservation of global quantity. The proposed sequence is this. First, the child learns that addition or subtraction of discontinuous material (e.g., addition of one object to a whole pile of objects) changes the quantity. Following this in the sequence are two roughly synchronous acquisitions: (1) the aforementioned addition-subtraction schema is generalized to continuous quantity (e.g., removal of a piece of plasticine ball); (2) conservation of discontinuous quantity is achieved. And finally, the child generalizes the conservation schema to continuous quantity. Of thirty subjects who showed developmental progress with respect to these acquisitions during Smedslund's experiment, only two showed a pattern of change not in accord with this sequence.

Hyde (1959) gave her Aden subjects several quantity tasks in addition to the number ones. Unlike Smedslund and Elkind, she found no strong evidence for the global-quantity–weight–volume *décalage;* in particular, she found a number of subjects who departed from the predicted sequence by conserving weight but not global quantity, volume but not weight, and the like. Careful scrutiny of these studies does not suggest any immediate explanation for the discrepancy in results. There were other findings of interest. First, her data largely confirmed Piaget's qualitative observations regarding the conservation task in which sugar is dissolved in water. For example, she found, as did Piaget, that some subjects believe the sugar is essentially nonexistent once wholly dissolved. Second, genuine transitive inference regarding equality of weight appeared to have been a rarer event in her sample than in Smedslund's: only 5 of her 144 subjects seemed to have anything like a transitivity principle in their cognitive armory. And finally, there is some tentative information regarding the difficulty level of the various quantity tasks. For example, conservation of global quantity in the plasticine-balls task appears to be more difficult to achieve than in the water-in-vessels setting, but easier than in the sugar-in-water test.

Feigenbaum (1961) administered various forms of the test for conservation of discontinuous quantity to 146 children 4-7 years of age. The principal findings were: (1) conservation of discontinuous quantity is strongly correlated with age; (2) there is a corresponding developmental shift away from reliance on perceptual impression towards the use of logical and arithmetic procedures (assumptions of set invariance and the employment of counting operations); (3) conservation is correlated with IQ as well as age; (4) certain brief training procedures facilitate conservation somewhat, others do not; (5) there is a slight tendency for performance level to vary with task parameters, especially in the younger subgroups (e.g., reducing the number of beads makes the task a little easier). Canning (cited in Lunzer, 1960a) found that blind children achieve conservation of global quantity in the water-in-vessels situation later than sighted children. And Lunzer (1956) reported results in the quantity area which generally concur with Piaget's, although his subject sample was very small.

Space and Geometry

Of the half-dozen or so relevant articles in the area of spatial concepts, the most important are probably those of Lovell (1959) and Peel (1959).[18] In the Lovell study, some 140 children of about 3-6 years of age were given a battery of tasks taken from Piaget's book (Piaget and Inhelder, 1956). These were (1) tactual recognition and pictorial representation of various topological and Euclidean shapes; (2) linear and circular order; (3) knots; (4) the projective straight line; (5) representation of objects as seen from different perspectives. Some of Lovell's evidence confirmed Piaget's findings, some did not. For the first: topological spatial properties are generally discriminated earlier than Euclidean ones (task 1 above); the ability to represent linear and circular orders and to deal with the spatial relations involved in various knots definitely increases with age within this chronological range (tasks 2 and 3); in task 4 (making a straight row of matchsticks on a table), the younger children tend to fall under the sway of the spatial context (i.e., by letting the row "drift" towards the reference line formed by the table edge) and generally fail to discover the end-on sighting method for guaranteeing the projective straight line; and (5) young subjects have considerable difficulty in representing the appearance of objects (e.g., pencil, circle) as seen from perspectives other than their own.

The principal disconfirming results were these. First, in almost all the tasks, Lovell's subjects tended to perform on a higher level than Piaget's subjects of the same age; and in general, Piagetian statements of the form, "the child of four cannot . . . ," were found to require considerable qualification. Second, although Euclidean properties taken in total were differentiated later than topological ones, there was no evidence that curved figures in particular (a subset of the Euclidean shapes studied) were any more difficult than topological ones. However, the force of this negative finding is somewhat vitiated by the fact that such figures had been said by Piaget to be the *first* Euclidean shapes mastered in the developmental progression—just after the primitive topological ones

---

[18] Important, that is, so far as these particular concepts are concerned. There is a monograph by Braine (1959), cited here and in the next subsection on geometry, which has importance far beyond its immediate empirical contributions in these areas. This remarkable monograph is one of the few existing publications which offers a really sophisticated analysis of Piaget's conceptual system and its attendant problems. Reference to it will be made again in the next chapter.

(Piaget and Inhelder, 1956, chs. 1 and 2). And there were other minor disagreements. For example, Lovell found, contrary to Piaget, that Euclidean shapes were easier to construct with matchsticks than to depict in drawings: one more instance of task-level interaction within a single content area.

The article by Peel (1959) reports two experiments relevant to Piaget's work on the development of spatial concepts. Unfortunately, the only information given about the first experiment is this: E. I. Page replicated Piaget's tactual-recognition test on sixty children of about 3-8 years of age; the results definitely confirmed Piaget's hypothesis of an age *décalage* between topological and Euclidean properties. The second study, by E. Ferns, is reported in fuller detail. She administered the pictorial-representation version of this task to fifty-five children in the same age range. Ferns and Peel then scored the drawings in essentially the same way Piaget had (i.e., in terms of his developmental stages and substages) and achieved high interjudge reliability. A scalogram analysis performed on the set of scores suggested that the stage-by-stage progression in spatial representation outlined by Piaget was essentially correct. Unfortunately, the data were not presented in such a way as to permit the reader to be certain whether curved Euclidean forms are or are not more difficult than topological ones: the question raised by the Lovell study. However, the general sequence, first topological and then Euclidean, found clear support. As is common in the recent British writings on Piaget, Peel's article concludes with a discussion of the educational implications of Piaget's space research.

Braine's monograph (1959) describes an experiment on the concept of spatial order. The technique used was a nonverbal, matching-from-sample one in which the child was rewarded with candy for each correct match. He was presented with a sample sequence of colored discs (the number of discs varied from one to seven) and had to choose, from among three sequences, the one identical to the sample. The intent here was to secure as "pure" a measure of the order concept as possible, a measure presumably free of contaminating variables, especially verbal ones, not involved in the essential definition of the concept. As things turned out, the purification appeared not to make the task much easier, if any: Braine's subjects were largely incapable of matching the longer sequences prior to age 6-7, precisely what Piaget had reported. In particular, it was noted that not a single subject under four showed any semblance of an order concept, even with two-disc sequences. Another finding was that the shorter sequences were, as might have been expected, generally easier to match than the longer ones.

The experiment by Estes (1956) described earlier also included a developmental study of the concept of projective straight line. Unlike Piaget and Lovell, she did not observe any tendency for the child's row of matchsticks to drift towards reference lines. Another study worth mentioning is that of Meyer (1940), an early student of Piaget's and a collaborator on his research on spatial representation. She studied the growth of spatial abilities in $1\frac{1}{2}$-$5\frac{1}{2}$-year-old children by means of a battery of special tasks (not the ones Piaget had used) and found it possible to characterize this growth in terms of Piaget's concepts of "practical," "subjective," and "objective" space, concepts originally applied to the earlier, sensory-motor period (see Chapter 4). And finally, there is an article by Dodwell (1959) which, although reporting no original research, offers a good summary and discussion of Piaget's contributions in this area.

There are several good studies in the area of geometric concepts. Two of them (Lunzer, 1960b; Lovell and Ogilvie, 1961) deal with Piaget's research on the conservation and measurement of volume: not the research reported in the section on quantity in Chapter 9 and replicated in the studies by Elkind and Hyde cited above, but the more recent experiments described in Chapter 10 in the section of geometry. Obviously, these two sets of studies are closely related, both in method and in underlying theory, and to categorize the one as "quantity" and the other as "geometry" is, of course, arbitrary.

The Lunzer investigation included two experiments. The first was a straightforward replication of Piaget's more recent work on volume, using as materials, as Piaget had, unit cubes from which "houses" of differing base areas but identical volumes were constructed. Although the subject sample was small (N = 24), the data clearly supported Piaget's hypothesis that conservation of "interior" volume of the cubes (the global quantity they contain within their walls) is achieved earlier than both conservation of "occupied" volume (volume *qua* space occupied, measured indirectly by amount of water displaced) and length × width × height measurement of volume. These latter two are formal- rather than concrete-operational achievements and are roughly contemporaneous.

The second study was a more severe test of Piaget's developmental concepts regarding volume. Lunzer administered four tests to forty children of 12-13 years of age: (1) the measure of conservation of occupied volume ("houses" immersed in water, etc.); (2) an assessment of the child's ability to measure volume; (3) a test of the child's grasp of infinity and continuity concepts; (4) a proverbs test. Piaget had theorized (Piaget, Inhelder, and Szeminska, 1960, pp. 384-385) that the abilities measured by the first three of these tasks are developmentally interdependent, e.g., that the ability to conceive of a volume as an infinite series of contiguous planes aids in the conception of volume as measurable by length × width × height, and that both of these facilitate conservation of occupied volume. Therefore, reasoned Lunzer, they ought to correlate with one another more highly than any of them correlates with the proverbs test, the latter presumably tapping an unrelated ability. This hypothesis found no support whatever in the data. Lunzer concludes with two important points: (1) the logical or mathematical interrelatedness and interdependency of two or more operations is no *a priori* guarantee of their developmental-psychological interrelatedness and interdependency; and (2) the only defensible procedure for testing such a supposition is to measure the abilities in question in the same group of subjects; it is illegitimate to argue for developmental interrelatedness from the fact that the abilities emerge at about the same age when separately assessed in different groups of subjects.

Lovell and Ogilvie (1961) administered a series of conservation-of-volume tests (Piaget's plus variations of these) to 191 British children of about 7-11 years of age. His results are summarized as follows. (1) Conservation of interior volume is achieved at an earlier mean age than that of occupied volume; moreover, "an understanding of interior volume was usually necessary before occupied volume [could] be understood" (*ibid.*, p. 123). (2) A number of the children attributed the displacement of water to the weight of the immersed body, rather than to its volume. And (3) although an understanding of occupied volume can roughly be pegged at 11-12 years, as Piaget had said, the age varies somewhat as a function of the particular means used to assess this understanding. In this connection it will be recalled that Elkind (1961a), using continuous (clay) rather than discontinuous (a set of cubes) material, found that the 75 per cent level for this kind of conservation did not occur until age 15 or thereabouts.

Braine's investigation (1959) included a second experiment on transitivity of length, using as subjects the same children tested for their understanding of spatial order. As before, the testing procedure was largely nonverbal. The subjects were first trained to select the longer (or shorter) of two uprights, receiving a candy reward for making the correct choice. Following this, they were tested for their ability to infer that an upright A was longer than an upright C (where the length difference was imperceptible) from the observation that $A > B$ and $B > C$ (where B is a third upright successively applied to A and C as common measure). The results were interesting. Unlike what happened in the spatial-order experiment, the nonverbal, external-reinforcement procedure Braine used here did elicit transitive inferences at considerably earlier ages than Piaget's original method had. Also, those children who were capable of transitive inference made more precise length comparisons in a purely perceptual situation—where no transitive inference was possible—than children who did not. This suggests an interaction between perceptual and intellectual growth of just the sort that Piaget and his associates have been preoccupied with.[19] And finally, there was a positive finding analogous to Lunzer's (1960b) negative one. Braine first made a logical analysis of the operations of spatial order and of transitive inference (in the case of asymmetrical relations, e.g., $A > B > C$) and found them to be logically related. He then made the prediction, implicit in Piaget's theory, that they would for this reason show developmental interdependence. The prediction was confirmed: (a) the two operations showed developmental curves which were virtually superimposable; (b) a child who could perform the one was very likely to be able to perform the other, and vice versa (tetrachoric correlation was .96).

The experiment by Beilin and Franklin (1961), described in the learning-studies section, also yielded findings relevant to an evaluation of Piaget's geometry research. Piaget had stated that conservation and measurement of length and of area are developmentally synchronous achievements (Piaget, Inhelder, and Szeminska, 1960, pp. 285, 300). Beilin and Franklin did not find this to be true; according to their data, conservation and measurement of length are definitely easier operations than the corresponding ones in the case of area. They suggest that conservation and measurement of one-, two-, and three-dimensional entities are achieved in that order—certainly a plausible sequence, one would think.

Chance and Adolescent Reasoning

As was the case with Piaget's pre-1930 work, it is difficult to give an adequate brief review of the validation literature in the area of chance. The situation is this. There are at the present time a fair number of experiments which might be construed as bearing on the development of probability concepts. However, very few of them were done with any explicit intention of testing Piaget's findings—a situation quite different from that of other content areas we have been reviewing (e.g., number). Because of this fact the hypotheses tested and the methods used in these studies are of varying degrees of orthogonality from those Piaget employed. Moreover, many of these investigations appear to have measured behaviors of uncertain relation to what Piaget was trying to assess: namely, the child's *cognition,* i.e., understanding, conception, intellectual grasp, or whatever, of chance phenomena. For these reasons, a really conscientious, scientifically responsible review would require that each statement of findings be accompanied by considerable qualification, explanation, explication of possible ambiguities, and the like. This cannot be

[19] See the section on perception in Chapter 10. It it unfortunate that Braine was apparently unaware of Piaget's work on such problems at the time his monograph was written. In particular, the experiment by Piaget and Lambercier (1946), described in the perception section, is strikingly similar to Braine's, and a comparative analysis of findings would have been useful.

attempted here, and the following, less-satisfactory alternative will be adopted. First, we shall summarize those studies which were conducted with the specific aim of testing Piaget's findings (there appear to be only two of them). For the rest, we shall merely cite them and offer a few conclusions about their collective contributions to the validation problem. For the reasons stated above, these conclusions are necessarily very tentative and should be so evaluated.

Yost, Siegel, and McMichael (1961) criticize the procedures Piaget used in studying the development of chance concepts. Like Braine (1959), they argue that Piaget may frequently underestimate the child's basic intellectual capacities by using assessment techniques which do not differentiate between these capacities and associated verbal abilities, and which fail to insure adequate motivation to perform, and so on. They compared the performance of 4-year-olds on two forms of a Piagetian test of the child's ability to maximize probability of success in a two-choice situation (the third lot-drawing task described in the section on chance in Chapter 10). One form was similar to Piaget's original testing procedure. The other differed in several ways: in utilizing a somewhat different physical display, in requiring a different type of choice, in (seemingly) demanding less understanding of probabilistic terminology, in controlling for task-irrelevant color preferences, and in using concrete rewards for correct responses. The results clearly indicated that the second method produced a significantly larger median number of correct responses over a series of twenty-four trials. It is uncertain, however, whether this method succeeded in "liberating" preexisting concepts and strategies by virtue of its procedural differences from the other method, or whether it was simply a more effective training procedure for inculcating response patterns (and perhaps concepts as well) which the child did not have in his repertoire when he walked into the experimental room. If the latter is true and the former not, as this writer suspects is the case, then the conclusion offered by Yost, Siegel, and McMichael would need some rephrasing:

> It may reasonably be concluded from the highly significant results presented above that four-year-olds do have some understanding of probability. This conclusion can be contrasted with Piaget's judgment that children under seven years of age are unable to respond consistently to the quantitative proportions of elements (*ibid.,* p. 18).

Pire (1958) has analyzed normative developmental data on selected items of a French intelligence test (C.S.C.) in order to compare them with Piaget's findings. The items were multiple-choice questions of the following type. What is the likelihood of getting all heads if one tosses a handful of coins into the air? If *A* has two dice and *B* only one, what are their respective chances of getting the higher total number of die spots over a series of throws? If *A* has the face cards and *B* has the rest of the deck, which has the better chance of drawing a heart? If one makes successive draws of pairs of counters (without replacement) from a set containing equal numbers of red and blue objects, what will be the likely frequency distribution of red-red, blue-blue, and mixed pairs? Although Pire's results are not as clearly reported as they might be, their general sense appears to be this. As children grow older, they do show an increasing mastery of probability principles along the general lines indicated by Piaget's research. But individual differences are very great at each age level and many adults, including educated ones, do not show the degree of competence with these principles which Piaget predicates for the period of formal operations. From Pire's data, one source of individual variation is general intelligence, and another is sex (males perform somewhat better than females at all age levels). On those tasks which had close analogues in Piaget's research, several of Pire's qualitative findings accord with Piaget's, e.g., a very common subject error in the last problem described above is to predict roughly equal frequencies of red-red, blue-blue, and mixed pairs.

The investigations which appear to be of more uncertain pertinence include: (Cohen, 1960; Cohen and Hansel, 1956; Gratch, 1959; Messick and Solley, 1957; Ross and Levy, 1958; Siegel and McMichael, 1960; Stevenson and Weir, 1959; Stevenson and Zigler, 1958).[20] It can at least be said that this research does not appear to give any serious disconfirmation to Piaget's findings (Ross and Levy's study, 1958, might be an exception here); and there are several results which seem to accord with them: (1) young children sometimes seem to regard chance events in magico-moral terms (e.g., if A turned up last time, B ought to turn up this time—they *ought* to take turns); (2) the belief that successive chance events have mutually independent probabilities of occurrence appears to develop with age; (3) the ability to make probability estimates on the basis of objective probabilities (e.g., as determined by the frequency distribution of the event sample) is also age-dependent.

There are two studies germane to the work on formal-operational thought (Inhelder and Piaget, 1958).[21] Ervin (1960b) describes an experiment in which twenty second- and third-grade children were given a task which involved the discovery of the relation of four variables to the flexibility of rods (Inhelder and Piaget, 1958, ch. 3). A careful qualitative

---

[20] The first two of these references may be the most important from the standpoint of possible implications for Piaget's work on chance. They summarize Cohen's numerous experiments on guessing, risk-taking, and other probability-related phenomena. Unfortunately, Cohen's experimental ingenuity is often accompanied by a lack of careful attention to sampling and methological problems (Siegel, 1961), and it is frequently difficult to know how much stock to put in his findings and conclusions.

[21] Also, Dr. Jacqueline J. Goodnow of Walter Reed Army Institute of Research has given a preliminary report (1962) of a cross-culture study which employed several tasks drawn from the volumes on chance and adolescent reasoning. And there is the experiment by Morf (1957) cited earlier.

analysis was made of the children's attempts to cope with the task. The results are difficult to summarize, but in general they seem to confirm Inhelder and Piaget's view that concrete-operational structures are rather inadequate instruments for solving multivariable scientific problems. For example, her subjects often confused several variables verbally, failed to see that the variables had a *joint* effect on rod flexibility, and failed to control and vary factors as needed to test predictions about cause-effect relations.

Keats (1955) made an interesting test of Piaget's hypothesis that concrete operations necessarily precede formal ones in ontogenesis, that the ability to solve problems on the plane of formal operations presupposes their mastery on the plane of concrete operations but not the converse. Two different forms of each of a series of problems were group-administered to 1,358 children of approximately 9-15 years of age. In each problem, one form was presumed to be solvable by concrete-operational skills alone, and the other was thought to require formal operations. The problems were of three types: (1) arithmetic, (2) probability, (3) inequalities (essentially demanding an understanding of the transitivity principle as applied to asymmetrical relations). In general, the principal difference between the two forms of any given problem was that the formal-operational one was couched in more abstract terms than its concrete-operational counterpart. For example, the concrete-operational form might be posed as: $4 + 5 = ? - 5$ (where "? will never be 4" is the correct answer among the various alternatives given). The formal-operational version might then be: $A \bigcirc B = ? \ominus B$ (where A and B are said to be two different non-zero integers; where $\bigcirc$ means either $+$ or $-$ and $\ominus$ means the opposite of $\bigcirc$; and where "? will never be A" is the only correct answer in the set of possible answers given). It could be argued that the more abstract form, in contrast to the more concrete one, demands such formal-operational skills as the ability to reason in terms of pure possibilities (see Chapter 6). In the above problem, for example, such reasoning might look like this: "If $\bigcirc$ were $+$, then $\ominus$ would necessarily be $-$, and therefore ? could never be A, because $A + B$ could not equal $A - B$ no matter what numbers we assume A and B to be." [22] The operational statement of the hypothesis was that the number of subjects who solve the abstract form and fail to solve the concrete form of any problem should be of

[22] It is a fact of considerable interest that Keats does not justify the relevance of his test items to his experimental hypothesis by appealing, as we have just done, to the hypothetico-deductive strategy demanded by the more abstract form of each item. Instead, he suggests that the latter demands "the notion of an inverse," whereas the more concrete form does not. This does not appear to this writer to be the case for the items as described and, even if it were, this particular distinction is irrelevant to Piaget's views as to how concrete and formal operations differ (see Chapters 5 and 6). Keats's experiment appears to be a one-of-a-kind among validation studies: it was intended to be relevant to Piaget's theory; it is relevant to Piaget's theory; the intended and actual relevance seem to rest on quite different bases!

zero order; in particular, there should in each case be many fewer such subjects than ones who solve the concrete form and fail to solve the abstract form. This prediction was in general strongly confirmed in the case of arithmetic and probability items, but not for inequalities. In the latter case, Keats feels that an artifact may have contributed to the negative finding (*ibid.*, p. 47).

Other Content Areas

The validation research on the remaining areas will not occupy us long. Lovell and Slater (1960) repeated several of Piaget's experiments on the genesis of time concepts. These included studies of the child's conceptual management of simultaneity, temporal duration, subjective, "interior" time, and the concept of age. Although the subject sample was rather small, some fairly definite conclusions could be drawn. First, the major developmental trends outlined by Piaget for this cognitive area were corroborated. To take one instance, the data strongly supported his finding that young children tend to rely on physical size rather than date of birth in judging age. Second, some of Piaget's tasks appear to show more clear-cut age-dependence than others, although this could be an artifact of sample size. And finally, the child's apparent level of understanding of time concepts is at least partly a function of the particular assessment procedure used.

Three articles are pertinent to Piaget's research on movement and velocity (they also relate to his time and perception research as well). The first is a critique of his studies in this area by Fraisse and Vautrey (1952). The other two consist of a spirited rebuttal by Piaget (1957g) and a supporting research paper by three of his associates (Feller, McNear, and Noelting, 1957). The details of this controversy are too involved to pursue here, and we offer only two general impressions about it: (1) it seems at least partly to hinge on theoretical differences regarding the behavioral phenomena under study, particularly as regards whether they should be considered perceptual or conceptual-representational in nature; And (2) the data presented by both sides suggest that, whatever the theoretical status of the behavior, it is certainly sensitive to variation in test parameters: the ubiquitous interaction between task and developmental level again.

The validation literature on Piaget's perception research, like that on his studies of chance, can be roughly divided into two parts. First of all, there are a few experiments which were explicitly designed to test one or another aspect of his perceptual theory. These studies, mostly done by members of the Geneva group, have already been cited in the section on perception in Chapter 6 and in the section on recent basic research in the present chapter. And second, there is a larger body of studies, the relevance of which is coincidental rather than planned. Most of this research, together with Piaget's own, has already been capably reviewed by Wohlwill (1960d).

There remains the area of logic, as operationally defined by the experiments reported in Piaget and Inhelder's book (1959). It will be re-recalled (Chapter 9) that a few of these experiments were essentially replications of earlier ones reported in the number book. What validation literature there is on these has already been cited in this chapter. For example, both Morf (1959) and Hyde (1959) verified Piaget's finding that young children have great difficulty with the logical class-inclusion problem (if $A + A' = B$, are there more B's or more A's?). As for the studies of logical behavior which are not replications, there seem to be no published attempts at validation, probably because they are so recent (and—perhaps—so untranslated!). There are of course studies already in the literature which might be bent towards validation *ex post facto*, for example, those of Thompson (1941) and Reichard, Schneider, and Rapaport (1944) in the case of Piaget's experiments on the development of logical classification. Such studies have for the most part already entered the secondary-source literature on the nature and development of thought (e.g., Russell, 1956) and will not be reviewed here. One good study which has not yet achieved this status is that by Annett (1959). She studied the sorting behavior and sorting rationales of a large sample of 5-11-year-old children. As would be expected, the use of attribute similarity and class membership as bases for classification showed a steady increase with age. More interesting, sortings based on what might be called the *co-belongingness* of various objects in a given physical setting (e.g., the clock "goes on" the desk) showed an initial increase with age, and then a decrease. This classification strategy looks suspiciously like a higher-level analogue of the figural-collection strategy of Piaget's preschoolers, a strategy which also gets replaced by something more logical as the child grows older.

And finally, there are three experiments which do not readily fit into any of the previous categories. One is a blunderbuss of a study by King (1961) in which over 1,200 schoolchildren of 6-11 years were group-tested by their classroom teachers on original or modified versions of diverse Piagetian tasks. Some of the tasks showed age trends, others did not. However, the study appears to have various methodological shortcomings which make interpretation of its findings—both positive and negative ones—uncertain. Carpenter (1955) also reported experiments which straddle a number of content areas, but the extremely small number of subjects tested render her findings (mostly Piaget-supportive) similarly untrustworthy. A much different, and much better, experiment is that of Smedslund (1960). It dealt with the young child's capacity for making transitive inference in the arena of attitudinal rather than physical relations. Forty children of 5-7 years were presented with a series of tasks in which they were asked to predict the choice of another child between two objects A and C, having been given the information that the child prefers A to B and B to C. A subsample was also tested for transitivity of their own preferences by having them make their personal choices between A and B, A and C, and B and C in succession. Only two of the forty children consistently made inferentially correct predictions about the other child's choice (i.e., prefers A to C) and none made explicit appeal to anything like a transitivity principle to justify such predictions. Moreover, their own personal choices were almost as often intransitive as transitive, a fact of interest to anyone having the temerity to construct a rational decision-making model applicable to young children!

MISCELLANEOUS STUDIES

The research to be summarized here is not really miscellaneous. It forms a more or less definite class, but one for which there is unfortunately no adequate class name. What the section will include are investigations which begin with Piaget's system but end somewhere else, which use his theory or methods in a centrifugal rather than centripetal (e.g., validational) way. (Centrifugal Studies is too barbaric a section title, although the writer thought half seriously of using it.) This class without a name has two subclasses. First, there are experiments which in one fashion or another exploit what Piaget has done in the service of doing something he has not done. Needless to ,say, there will be no attempt here to cull all the research literature for which Piaget's system may have played some sort of midwife role; a few more recent and salient examples will do. The other subclass consists of *theoretical* articles or books which try to relate Piaget's system to other theoretical systems. Berlyne's (1960a) attempt to integrate Piaget's and Hull's theories (see the previous section on learning studies) is a clear instance of this subclass.

The experiments we shall refer to are of two types: those which make novel use of Piaget's testing instruments and those which use his theory as a point of departure for original experimentation. There are two interesting examples of the first type (Bibace, 1956; Reiff and Scheerer, 1959). Many investigators have hypothesized that the schizophrenic's cognitive inadequacies reflect a regression to a developmentally more immature level of functioning. Bibace attempted to test this hypothesis by administering modified versions of several of Piaget's tests to matched groups of normal and chronic schizophrenic adults. One of the tests assessed the subject's understanding of the class-extension term *some;* two others were variants of the class-inclusion ($A \leqslant B$?) problem. The schizophrenics, as predicted, did have great difficulty in solving these and other problems and were significantly inferior in performance to the normal controls. There was also an incidental finding of some interest. One gets the impression from looking at Bibace's data that the normals themselves (on the average: age 35, 100 IQ, 10 grades of school) also showed a fair amount of developmentally immature functioning, i.e., functioning at the level of concrete operations and, occasionally, even preoperations.

The Reiff and Scheerer study was somewhat analogous in its use of Piagetian tasks. The tasks were two: the early one assessing absolute versus relational understanding of *left* and *right* (Piaget, 1928b); the later one testing for a concept of spatial order—different-colored balls which enter and emerge from a tube, etc. (Piaget, 1946b). The tests were given to one group of adults who were hypnotically regressed to various ages (4, 7, or 10 years) and to another, unhypnotized adult group who simulated regression to these same ages, e.g., were instructed to behave as though they were four years old. The prediction was that the hypnotized subjects would more closely approximate the behavior of actual young children on these tests than would (or could) the simulators. The group differences for both tests were in the predicted direction, but they were statistically reliable only in the case of the order task.

We shall cite four experiments of the second type, experiments which make heavier use of Piaget's theory than of his specific methods of testing. It happens that all four extrapolate from one particular segment of the theory: the general hypothesis that young children are intellectually egocentric, have difficulty in decentering or assuming points of view other than their own: the hypothesis can be phrased in various ways. Weinberg (1959), for example, made the prediction that behavior on a cognitive task purporting to measure egocentrism would correlate in 6-7-year-old children with behavior on other cognitive tests with no obvious relation to egocentrism. He also hypothesized that an induced "self-centering" set would also function to lower scores on these other tests. The data gave qualified support to both predictions.

Feffer has done two experiments somewhat like Weinberg's, one with adults (Feffer, 1959) and one with children (Feffer and Gourevitch, 1960). In the first study, a group of normal adults were given two tests. One was the Rorschach ink-blot test. The other was a specially constructed measure (called the RTT) of the subject's ability to shift perspectives and viewpoints vis-à-vis a social-interpersonal situation which he witnesses— his ability to decenter when faced with social rather than physical-inanimate content. The hypothesis, confirmed by the data, was that perceptual-cognitive development as indexed by Rorschach responses is correlated with this ability to shift perspectives, to take the role of another. In the second study, two independent measures of decentering ability were obtained on children 6-13 years of age: (1) RTT score, (2) performance scores on several Piagetian tasks in the areas of logic and quantity. As predicted, both measures were positively correlated with age and with each other (with variance due to age and verbal intelligence partialed out). From the evidence of these two studies, Feffer's RTT shows considerable promise as a measure of an important but little-studied cognitive skill.

And finally, the writer and his associates (Flavell, 1961) have for several years been testing two general hypotheses, partly originating in Piaget's theory: (1) there is an ontogenetic development in the general capacity and propensity for discriminating what could be termed the *role attributes* of others—their dispositions, capabilities, limitations, etc., as distinguished from one's own; and (2) this development plays a vital ancillary role in the genesis of communicative skills, since the ability to communicate effectively is believed to be partly dependent on one's ability to predict what the listener needs to be told, i.e., to predict his role-attributes as listener. In a series of experiments special tests were given to various groups of children in the age range 3-16 years. Some of the tests were designed to measure the ability to discriminate role attributes in a more or less direct way, others the communicative skills which depend upon this ability. The data indicate, first, that young children are, as Piaget had said, very inept in cognitive-interpersonal skills of this genre; and second, that there is considerable growth in such skills during middle childhood and early adolescence. There is also evidence from one of our studies (Fry, 1961) that one can accelerate this growth somewhat by a program of training.

As indicated in Chapter 1, Piaget's system has grown up over the years in relative isolation and insulation from other systematic positions. One gets the impression that Piaget has been too preoccupied with adding new towers to the theoretical castle to worry about spanning the moat. The bridge-building has largely been left to others, and it happens that there have been others willing to try it. For example, there have been several attempts to relate his theory to psychoanalytic theory (or to phenomena ordinarily conceptualized in psychoanalytic terms). Unfortunately, most of these attempts have been rather superficial, lightweight affairs, although not without interesting ideas here and there (Freeman and McGhie, 1957; Anthony, 1956a, 1956b, 1957; Odier, 1956). The modal strategy is to extract concepts or empirical findings from one or another part of Piaget's system and bring them to bear on specific developmental or psychopathological phenomena of interest to psychoanalytic theory; one of Anthony's articles (1956b) is perhaps the best and most useful exemplar of this approach. With the exception of Odier's book (probably the poorest effort of the lot), these writings are brief and easy to read, and no summary of their contents seems indicated here.

A much more substantial and important contribution in the same area is a monograph by Wolff (1960) which begins with a summary (a very good one) of what in Chapter 7 was called the *stage-independent aspects* of Piaget's theory. The ensuing chapters then take up his "stage-dependent" analysis of the sensory-motor period. Major developmental issues are raised within the context of each stage, and a careful attempt is made to compare, contrast, and, where possible, effect an integration or coordination between the Piagetian and psychoanalytic approaches to these issues. The final chapter sums up Wolff's conclusions about where the two theories appear to converge and diverge and suggests a number of unresolved questions which might be answered by empirical investigation. Moreover, he has taken his own research suggestions seriously and is trying to pursue some of them in an observational study of neonates, a preliminary report of which has been published (Wolff, 1959). Altogether, this excellent monograph bristles with exciting speculations which emerge from the comparative analysis of the two theories. Here are a few random instances. Behavior is codetermined by two kinds of motivation: *short-range* (Piaget's cognitive-functional needs) and *long-range* (psychoanalytic instinctual drives); and the two have quite different relations to behavior which Wolff tries to specify. The development of the object concept in infancy may differ in important and perhaps predictable ways depending upon whether the object in question is human or inanimate. The *state of the organism,* especially as regards the intensity and urgency of the long-range motivational forces, is a crucial determinant of the amount and kind of cognitive functioning which will occur at any given time. And finally, there are sensory-motor schemas of affect expression which show certain structural and developmental similarities to Piaget's intellectual schemas of the same ontogenetic period. This writer predicts that Wolff's monograph will have a long half-life in both the psychoanalytic and general-developmental literature, and deservedly so.

There have been two essays at bringing Piaget's system and modern learning theory into closer relation. One of them (Berlyne, 1960a) has already been cited in the section on learning studies. The other is a much briefer and more easily summarized paper by Stevenson (1960). It begins with an attempt to account for Piaget's observations on sensory-motor development within the general context of current behavior theory. In order to do this, Stevenson finds it necessary to incorporate into the latter theory certain assumptions concerning the sorts of events which are reinforcing, e.g., the assumption that there is a basic, underived need for sensory stimulation (akin to Piaget's need-to-cognize, Wolff's short-range forces, and the like). This accomplished, Stevenson proceeds to derive from the behavior theory thus modified a series of specific, eminently testable predictions regarding differences in perceptual-conceptual behavior between older/brighter and younger/duller organisms.

Smedslund (1961g) has compared and contrasted Egon Brunswick's theoretical system with that of Piaget. The paper follows the strategy of tracing similarities and differences (especially the latter) between the two systems with respect to certain basic psychological-epistemological problems with which both have dealt, e.g., the nature of intentionality, of environmental feedback, and of cognitive acquisition. In each instance Smedslund makes a careful estimate, both on logical grounds and in the light of whatever relevant experimentation exists, of which theory handles the issue more adequately. So far as these particular problems are concerned, Smedslund uniformly accords the honors to Piaget's approach; in fact, the paper would be of considerable interest if only for its clear and forceful statement of certain important implications his theory has for an understanding of human behavior. Two other papers are worthy of brief mention. Wohlwill (1960c) has presented an interesting miniature theory of cognitive development which draws heavily on Piaget's conceptions. And Simon (1960) has sketched an information-processing model of intellectual growth as an alternative to Piaget's.

Part Three

CRITIQUE

CHAPTER TWELVE

An Evaluation of the System

THE writer's study of Piaget's work has led him to conclude that it is of considerable value and importance, with a very great deal to contribute to present understanding and future study in the area of human development. But he also believes that the system has an extraordinary penchant for eliciting critical reactions in whoever reads it. Piaget has done and said so much in a busy lifetime that foci for possible contention and disagreement abound. More than that, he has consistently done and said things which run so counter to accepted practice as to make for an immediate critical reaction in his reader, almost as though he had deliberately set out to provoke it. Many of the criticisms to which his writings lay him open are very obvious and require little critical acumen to find; they are the kind of critical points which attract the first-year graduate-student mentality the way a light attracts a moth. And who of us does not have residuals of this mentality?

As we see it, this state of affairs has dangerous potentialities. More than most, Piaget's system is susceptible to a malignant kind of premature foreclosure. You read his writings, your eye is drawn at once to its surface shortcomings, and the inclination can be very strong to proceed no further, to dwell on these (rather as the preoperational child centers but cannot decenter) to the exclusion of finding out what there may be of positive value underneath. This sequence is no hypothetical one: a case could be made that Piaget's system has suffered precisely such a fate for a long time, and that only recently has there been any sustained effort to resist the siren of criticism in favor of trying to extract underlying contributions.

The implications of the foregoing for our critical behavior towards Piaget's work are these. We do definitely intend to run through the conventional criticisms of his work and take up some less conventional shortcomings and problems as well. These things are of course important, and we shall not skirt them. But we particularly want to convey as clearly as possible what we believe to be the cardinal assets and contributions of the system. The most important task of this chapter, in our opinion, is

405

to put in high relief what there is in and about Piaget's work which may have real value and usefulness for others in child-development and allied fields. Although we believe Piaget's system is in particular need of this kind of critical handling, it is also a strategy of evaluation which we subscribe to generally. It is our view that one stands a better chance of furthering scientific progress by directing most of one's energies into milking a system for all that is or might be positive and useful in it, as opposed to depleting them in showing what is wrong or noncontributory in it. Thus, we count it a more serious fault to miss a Piagetian contribution, even a might-be one, than the most definite and unequivocal of shortcomings. If Piaget has something valuable to say which we somehow fail to hear, it is our loss, and the loss is absolute; if we do hear something he says but do not at first detect its inadequacies, we shall probably detect them eventually, and the loss can be counted in terms of wasted time and effort in attempts at replication, or something of that sort. If all this sounds like a denigration of the critical function or, perhaps worse here, an attempt to whitewash Piaget the writer has not made himself clear. What it comes down to is that there are some things which are important, other things which are crucial and essential, and the priorities between them should be kept in clear focus.

CONTRIBUTIONS

This section takes up the more salient and significant assets, accomplishments, and contributions contained in Piaget's system. There will be no attempt here to enumerate everything of positive value which Piaget has done; each of the preceding chapters ought to have done much of this job already. What we intend to do is to say what still needs to be said— or resaid—to the reader who has already read these chapters.

Stage-Independent Contributions

At the base of Piaget's stage-independent theory is the assimilation-accommodation model. It will be remembered that he carefully examined in turn a series of possible epistemological conceptions and decided to root his own psychological-developmental system on one particular form of interactionism: every cognitive interchange with the environment involves both accommodation and assimilation; every instruction from without presupposes a construction from within.

In our view, this segment of the theory is an asset in Piaget's ledger. There is the very fact that he did provide his theory with an explicit epistemological anchor. All too frequently, this kind of anchoring is eschewed in psychological theory-building. The result is often that the theory-builder provides a set of statements about behavior without also providing an accompanying general purview of the sort of organism which would behave that way—without any explicit statement that the subject of the theory is *this* particular kind of subject, one who transacts his business with the milieu according to *these* particular ground rules. Piaget, on the other hand, takes great pains to make clear at the outset the precise kind of information-processing machine whose behavior and development he intends to study.

What of the merits of the particular model Piaget has elected, apart from the merits of positing one at all? The assimilation-accommodation schema appears to have been a felicitous choice for the sorts of data and theory Piaget dealt with. With this kind of conception of the organism-environment relation, it does become meaningful to assert that an infant (or preschooler, or school-age child) cannot be influenced by certain classes of stimuli *now* (he lacks the structural wherewithal with which to assimilate them), but he can and will be influenced by them *later* (when structural development permits meaningful assimilation). With this kind of conception, it does make sense to envisage development as a gradual, step-by-step process of structural accrual and change, each structural form necessarily building on its predecessor, yet—by virtue of new increments of assimilation-accommodation activity—going a little beyond it. And finally, since the model is a two-process one, including both assimilatory and accommodatory activity, it becomes possible to raise interesting questions about their interrelations: differentiation versus undifferentiation, relative preponderance of one versus the other, and so on (Chapter 2). Thus, Piaget can appeal to the nature of the assimilation-accommodation relation in trying to account for such things as developmental changes in the character of subject-object transactions, differences between imitation, play, and adapted intelligence,[1] and differences in mode of acquisition for different types of knowledge, e.g., logico-mathematical versus infra-logical (see Chapter 7).

It can be difficult to maintain intact a genuinely interactionistic position in psychology. There is the perpetual tendency to let behavior control shift from subject to object, from responder to stimulus. Piaget is a conspicuous example of a theorist who has never let the reins slip here; he has consistently espoused an active-organism position and has really tried to make it work for him in practice, to make it direct and guide both theory-building and research. Our opinion is that Piaget chose his epistemological stance wisely. Indeed, it is hard to imagine one very different from his which would be consonant with the rest of his system and, more important, with the type of developmental events the theory

---

[1] Piaget has done things with the assimilation-accommodation model which either have not been discussed or have been inadequately discussed in this book (see particularly Piaget, 1951a). To take just one example, he has extended his assimilation-accommodation analysis of symbolic activity to include what is essentially a miniature theory of dreams, intended to be an alternative to the psychoanalytic conception.

tries to encompass. It is difficult to see, for example, how the conservations and transitivities of middle childhood could arise from a stimulus-control, passive-organism matrix.

Another important accomplishment of the stage-independent theory, implied but not elaborated above, is that it lends a high degree of continuity to birth-to-maturity cognitive development. Piaget's system gives a sense of sameness and connectedness between such phenotypically different behaviors as the neonatal sucking reflex and adolescent scientific reasoning. It does this in three ways. (1) It argues that both possess organizational characteristics and that both consist of an assimilation-accommodative process; the end points of the developmental chain are thus drawn into a common category by virtue of their common possession of certain functional invariants. (The fact that Piaget explicitly conceptualized the invariants as *biological* in character also makes for a sense of continuity: the generic application of these constructs at once make biological reflexes more *intelligent* and intellectual activity more *biological*.) (2) There is the assumption that the genesis of cognition is above all a constructive process. If intellectual development is really a process of building new structures on the foundations provided by earlier ones, of integrating previous structures into new supraordinate totalities, etc., through a continuous grinding away of the assimilation-accommodation machinery, if this is how development proceeds, then anything could potentially eventuate from anything in time. Neonatal caterpillars could plausibly become formal-operational butterflies if only there were enough intervening steps. (3) The concept of *vertical décalage* gives added fillip to the impression of cross-stage connectedness. Sensory-motor spatial groups get recapitulated in the spatial representations of middle childhood; the sensory-motor object concept has its parallel in the later formation of conservations: development in the Piagetian mode has a cyclic character which buttresses the feeling that it is somehow all of one cloth. It is to Piaget's credit that he found a way to build so much continuity into so manifestly a stage theory of development. He did it, of course, by the simple expedient of associating the continuity with the functional aspects and the discontinuity with the structural ones.

Three other components of the stage-independent system are Piaget's motivation, equilibration, and structural concepts. For Piaget, the essential impetus for cognitive activity lies within the cognitive apparatus itself; to say that a schema has been constructed is tantamount to saying that it will function, that it will assimilate anything in the surround to which it can accommodate its structure. The great advantage of such a formulation is, of course, that intellectual performance which occurs in the apparent absence of basic need tension (hunger, etc.) needs no complicated secondary reinforcement model to explain it. Most of the cognitive phenomena Piaget is interested in appear to be of just this kind; in fact, Wolff (1960) has suggested that the sensory-motor acquisitions Piaget has described may require an organismic state relatively free of such tensions.

Piaget's equilibration and equilibrium-states model has at least two useful attributes. First, it permits him to compare and contrast different levels and kinds of behavior on a common yardstick. On the one hand, it gives him a common set of parameters (mobility, stability, etc.) by which to gage in a rather precise way how each new level of intellectual functioning is similar and different from its predecessor (thus, another vehicle for seeing continuity amid discontinuity). On the other hand, and very important in his system, it allows for fruitful comparisons between intelligence and perception. Much of his perception research, it will be recalled, was explicitly guided by his conception of the type of equilibrium perceptual structures achieve. Whatever the shortcomings of the equilibration model, and there are some, it has performed for Piaget at least one of the functions of a good theory: it has engendered a lot of interesting research.

The second positive attribute of the model is its ability to account for, at least in principle, cognitive changes in which there is no direct feedback or reinforcement as to correctness of response. This is the issue discussed in Chapter 11 in connection with the work of Smedslund, Berlyne, etc. Since the equilibration model specifically posits internal reorganizations, i.e., changes in the way cognitions relate to one another, it is uniquely fitted to deal with these peculiar, nonfeedback acquisitions.

In Piaget's theory, cognitive structures lie between the general invariants of function and the specific variants of content; they form a kind of bridge between the nomothetic and the idiographic in cognitive development. Perhaps the most important thing to say about the concept of structure here is that, as we see it, one cannot really have a detailed theory of intellectual development without it. On the one hand, a theory would be of little developmental interest if it stopped with a generalized, cross-stage account of how the organism makes intellectual progress. It would be a *learning* theory (in fact, Piaget's assimilation-accommodation model is a crude kind of learning theory), but it would not be a *developmental* theory. On the other hand, a scheme which dealt only with an infinity of acquired contents could scarcely be a theory of any kind. Exclusive preoccupation with content development may have its uses, but it is a dull and profitless pursuit for anyone with more macroscopic and theoretical interests in intellectual growth. There has to be some *tertium quid:* something which changes with age, as the functional invariants do not; but also something more general than individual contents, something which will pull diverse contents together into a single chunk. Piaget realized this early and wisely resisted what we think was the guiding spirit of the 1930's: to move upward towards function (the child "learns" more and more things as he grows, but the mind which learns is homogeneous throughout) and to move downward towards content (as he grows, the child acquires this, and this, and this, and this—*period*). However critical one may be of the particular structural analysis Piaget has made, we are much in his debt for seeing so clearly, and so early, the necessity for making one.

One asset a theory can have is to have said then what others are saying now, to have been a harbinger of the *Zeitgeist*. A case could probably be made for a number of instances in which Piaget has played an Isaiah role, but the three parts of the stage-independent theory just discussed are particularly salient examples. Thus, there is today a growing interest in cognitive or quasi-cognitive motives ("curiosity," "competence," "exploratory," "sensory" drives—the terms vary) as an important class of behavioral instigators. Berlyne's book (1960b) is probably the best single reference here. It seems less improbable today than it once did to imagine that the Piagetian infant really does need to look at, listen to, and otherwise assimilate stimuli, even (perhaps especially) when he is not hungry. Likewise, Piaget's equilibration model (recently systematized but long in the system in a less organized form) is more than a little similar to the later rash of theories in the general cognition-attitude-belief area (e.g., Abelson and Rosenberg, 1958; Festinger, 1959; Heider, 1958; Osgood, Suci, and Tannenbaum, 1957). Like Piaget's, these theories deal with intracognitive, R-R relationships—the impact and effect of one cognition upon another within a cognitive system (Berlyne, 1960b, ch. 11). To be sure, they are not developmental theories and they deal with a more affect-laden kind of cognition than Piaget's logical operations, but it seems nonetheless true that Piaget has here anticipated a general trend in theory construction. And finally, these same references together with others (e.g., Bruner, Goodnow, and Austin, 1956; Miller, Galanter, and Pribram, 1960) bear witness to an increasing contemporary interest (again in nondevelopmental contexts, mostly) in using concepts of structure to account for behavior, especially complex cognitive behavior. Piaget has never been afraid to fill the black box with complicated goings-on in order to explain complicated behaviors, in the face of a psychological tide which moved in quite the opposite direction. But the tide appears to be turning, and people who know all about Occam's razor are nonetheless finding it necessary to outfit the subject with "strategies," "plans," and the like, in order to make sense out of his behavior.

There remains the concept of developmental stage and its role in Piaget's system, a concept which is obviously thoroughly intertwined with the others we have been discussing: structure, development-as-construction, continuity-discontinuity, and the rest. Later in the chapter we shall take up some problems and issues attendant on a stage analysis of development such as Piaget's; here we consider only its positive uses and potentialities.

The stage concept, like the equilibrium-state concept, can be helpful in examining what might be called the *comparative morphology* of different areas of development. Thus, intellectual development is said to differ from perceptual development in that the latter is not amenable to stage analysis; it lacks the necessary measure of discontinuity within continuity, the requisite natural segmentation along its long axis (Chapter 1). And where such an analysis is legitimate, i.e., in the case of intellectual development, it can yield several obvious but important dividends. It enables us to factor the stream of development into organized units and subunits so as to make it conceptually manageable. It further permits us to inspect the sequence in which the cognitive events of interest follow each other over time. And, in this connection, it puts us on the lookout for developmental fine print we might otherwise miss, e.g., the intervening and transitional cognitive forms which hide between the major moments in a given sequence. And finally, it helps us to glean whatever rationality and necessity may lurk behind the scenes in the developmental panorama. In particular, it was said (in Chapter 11 and elsewhere) that Piaget constantly looks for *developmental* successions (A is a prestage to B) and co-occurrences (B_1 and B_2 come in together in development) which have a sense of *logical* inevitability and necessity about them; e.g., classes, series, and number are constituted together because the first two are thought to be involved in the logical definition of the third. This is one part of the theory from which testable developmental hypotheses can certainly be drawn in abundance and, as Chapter 11 showed, hypothesis-testing of this sort has already begun.

Stage-Dependent Contributions

(1) What may well be one of Piaget's most important and enduring legacies to the field is simply that he has revealed the development of cognition to be a thing of unsuspected and extraordinary richness. Piaget has systematically ploughed his way through most of the principal modes of human experience and knowledge—space, time, number, and the rest. And in each case he has laid bare a complex succession of preforms and precursors for the most mundane and obvious of cognitions, cognitions we had no reason to assume needed a prehistory, let alone such an involved one. It is an uncommon experience to find out something about children's behavior which really surprises, which produces a sense of shock and even disbelief; after all, people have been child-watching for a long time. But Piaget may have discovered more things about children which shock and surprise than anyone else, and this alone is an immense accomplishment.

(2) Piaget's detailed picture of cognitive development in childhood

provides us with a historical frame and perspective within which to view the adult. This is an important but seldom discussed proper function of any developmental theory. Just as there is a sense in which one cannot understand contemporary America without knowledge of its history, there is a sense in which one cannot catch hold of adult human behavior without knowing from what and through what this behavior evolved. By seeing what the adult once was, we more clearly see what he is now; as Nathan Isaacs put it (1955a, p. 23). Piaget's work allows us to see him "in depth" rather than "in the flat." It is certainly true that this kind of perspective-setting has long been common and accepted practice for the noncognitive or less cognitive aspects of human behavior. If you want to see Mr. Brown's character structure in depth, take a careful look at its growth and development in infancy and childhood; and there are plenty of conceptual frameworks and reference data available to help you do it. Piaget's system provides comparable frameworks and data for the depth perception of Mr. Brown's intellectual structure.

(3) Piaget's system is by far the richest repository of theory and data on intellectual development that is or ever has been available in the field of child psychology. It includes the first and so far the only really detailed stage-analytic theory of intellectual development in existence. And he has supplied more concrete information about intellectual behavior at the various levels of development than any single worker (indeed, for many areas of cognition, more than all others taken together). This is a most impressive accomplishment. It does not, of course, imply that his theory and data should have special privileges by right of primogeniture, that they should not be held up to severe critical inspection like any other. But it does mean that for a long time to come Piaget's system must figure as an indispensable point of reference and touchstone for any theoretical or empirical project which deals with the same general area of study; and it has by this time become a very extensive area of study. Piaget has staked out a lot of virgin territory in the area of cognitive growth. As is often the case with new explorations, the cartography was not always accurate. But at least there are stakes there now, and we cannot and should not ignore them.

Now to the individual periods of development. We shall confine our attention here to a few features in each period which seem most important, or most interesting, or most nonobvious and apt to be overlooked. To begin with sensory-motor development, there is first of all Piaget's general characterization of behavior changes across the six stages. What strikes us here is the sense of orderly and coherent change, the sense of gradation and continuity, which Piaget manages to convey for a developmental course which begins with what is essentially a vegetable with reflexes and ends with an active, exploring, intention-directed, and distinctly human organism. By adroit use of a few fundamental principles (assimilation-accommodation, schematic differentiation and integration, and the like), he gives a plausible account of how reflexes are gradually transformed into acquired circular reactions, how an after-the-fact intentionality becomes the stepping stone to genuine goal-directed behavior, how an occasional and semireluctant experimentation in the face of new stimulus conditions evolves into an active experimentation which becomes almost a way of life for the infant: these and many other part developments are dealt with and integrated into a total picture of infant development. This is surely a lot of important detail to extract from a particularly inaccessible era of ontogenesis.

Piaget's account of the development of symbolic behavior during this period and the early stages of the next is also worth brief mention. It will be recalled that this genesis probably begins in stage 3 with the fascinating phenomenon of motor recognition (we said in Chapter 3 that it might be the primordium of Osgood's representational-mediational meaning response), continues through various advances in sign- and signal-responding, then through the adaptive utilization of motoric and imagistic symbols in stage 6 (Lucienne and the matchbox), and by further complex developments (Chapter 4) eventuates in a full-fledged representational activity which uses language as the predominant symbolic vehicle. Piaget's original account of this development is considerably richer and more detailed than our summary of it in Chapters 3 and 4 might suggest, and it is an account which any student of mediational processes can scarcely afford to overlook.

Chapter 4 described the special sensory-motor developments which proceed apace with the general one outlined in Chapter 3. Of these, Piaget's analysis of the object concept may be the more important and enduring contribution. In the first place, his observations and experiments here provide a solid anchor—a set of concrete reference data—for long-held and familiar speculations about the phenomenology of infancy, e.g., that the infant cannot differentiate between self and world. But Piaget did more than this: he showed that undifferentiation-differentiation here is in no sense dichotomous, that there are numerous halfway houses between the poles and that the development in question is an extended and essentially continuous one. And finally, his preliminary work on this problem has a real *prägnanz* for future research, as Wolff (1960) has pointed out. The problem is so important and Piaget's observations so provocative that straightforward replication ought to be a first step. This done, there are intriguing possibilities for parameter variation, e.g., Wolff's question as to whether human and nonhuman objects are constituted synchronously and according to the same developmental sequence.

Lastly, Piaget's account of general development in the sensory-motor period includes one genetic sequence which is a veritable jewel of developmental analysis, both in the sense that he managed to uncover a wealth of unsuspected substages for what looked like a simple enough developmental event, and in the sense that the sequence of substages found has a high degree of logical plausibility, almost of logical necessity. We refer to the development of prehension in stage 2, in particular that of vision-prehension coordination. Some of its highlights, it will be remembered, are that the child can first augment but not direct hand action by visual means, can then grasp an object seen if, and only if, both object and hand are in the visual field, and can finally look at what he grasps and grasp what he looks at without this restriction, i.e., the reciprocal assimilation of the two schemas is said to be completed. This writer, for one, had never regarded the genesis of visual-motor coordination as a particularly interesting problem area for a developmental psychologist; it smacks too much of hard-to-memorize Gesell tables. But Piaget has a knack for adrenalizing areas in which he does research, and this one is a good case in point.

In moving up the ontogenetic ladder from the infancy period, it makes less and less sense to emphasize any particular contribution over and above another; there have been so many cognitive areas investigated and so many studies done within each area. In the case of preoperational thought we shall rest our case with one general observation, one which, however, subsumes a lot of particulars. It is our opinion that Piaget has succeeded remarkably well in conveying a general picture of the cognitive experience, dispositions, achievements, and limitations of the preschooler. It is a picture at once integrated and unitary, vivid and easy to grasp and retain, and largely accurate when held up to the yardsticks of experimental evidence and everyday observation. Painted into this picture are the preschooler's cognitive egocentrism, his susceptibility to centration effects, his inability to deal with transformations as opposed to states: all the characteristics described in Chapter 4 and, more briefly, in Chapter 6. There are various practical and scientific uses of such a picture (we shall return to the question of uses presently), but one of the most important is simply the feeling of enriched understanding that it provides with respect to that interesting but often baffling age group. There is an exercise in this regard which will nicely convey what we mean here (we have tried it ourselves and found it to be a good one): read what Erikson (1959, ch. 2) has to say about the affective and interpersonal aspects of the preoperational period and see how Piaget's analysis both complements and significantly adds to Erikson's account, how a sense of "the whole child" emerges more clearly in a stereoscopic integration of the two.

In the case of concrete operations (and also for formal operations) we shall again let previous chapters do most of the rhapsodizing about specific accomplishments and contributions. As with preoperations, one can point to a most useful generic image: an image of a child for whom the world is beginning to stand still and stay put, a world which, like the child himself, knows something of law and order, and above all a world in which thought really counts for something, in which thought can be a more trustworthy guide to action than perception. And once again, the image is surprisingly unified and integrated, surprising in view of the diversity and heterogeneity of domains and contents which come under the sway of the child's cognitive intruments during this period. Piaget has achieved this sense of unity within diversity by discovering and exploiting a set of latent common denominators in the child's mode of operation across contents. It was an act of creative inspiration when Piaget hit upon the idea that a wide variety of cognitive areas—number, quantity, time, etc.—are in certain crucial respects mastered according to a common procedure: to discover what values do and do not remain invariant (are and are not conserved) in the course of any given kind of change or transformation; only when this is done is the way paved for further operations (which are also common denominators across areas), e.g., qualitative and quantitative measurement, application of the transitivity law, etc. There is no question but that the formation of concrete operations is the richest chapter in Piaget's developmental story, in the sense of sheer abundance of highly interesting empirical data. It does not seem likely that all this would or could have come about without the concept of conservation-formation and related unifiers. To be sure. Piaget did some very stimulating investigations using this age group in the 1920's before these concepts were in use. But he did a great many more studies, and even more interesting ones, once they started playing a significant role in his theorizing.

There was an analogous happy insight in connection with the period of formal operations, a conception which gave Piaget a lot of mileage in both theory and research. This was the view that the adolescent develops the ability to perform operations, not only on the fruits of his perceptions, but also upon the end products of other operations; i.e., he not only thinks but also thinks about his previous thoughts.

This conception performs at least three important functions. First, together with associated concepts (Chapter 6) it provides a succinct genotype which pulls together phenotypical variation in the adolescent's overt behavior. The more familiar way of distinguishing childish and adolescent thought—*concrete* versus *abstract*—is not unrelated to Piaget's concept of "operations to the second power"; but it is, we feel, a much less precise and unambiguous characterization.

Second, it provides easy entry into the particular realm of child-adolescent cognitive differences that Piaget wants to study, i.e., differences in logical and empirical-scientific reasoning. Such reasoning does, or at least ought to, involve a reflexive turning back upon already constituted operations in order to combine and separate them, to see how they relate to one another logically, and so on. It might also be added that Piaget's logico-mathematical models of adolescent cognition (involving groups and lattices) could likewise not be applied here without the operations-on-operations assumption: the lattice of combinations, for example, implies that the elements of base (first-order operations) be associated together (i.e., operated upon) according to all possible combinations.

And finally, to hark back to an earlier point, this conception heightens our awareness of the constructive yet continuous character of intellectual development. On the one hand, the earlier period is the logically necessary precondition of the later one: one cannot operate upon operations until the latter are first constituted. On the other hand, the later period definitely builds upon and naturally grows out of the earlier one: once the foundation is laid in the form of a set of operations performed upon the raw data of experience, new structures can and would be expected to be built upon this foundation. In this kind of developmental analysis Piaget excels. He at once shows us wherein a new structure is really new, is a true emergent, and at the same time shows us wherein it is not new, is not something inexplicable in terms of antecedent events. In Piaget's scheme of things, all structures are emergents but no structures are emergents *ex nihilo*.

As for perception and its ontogenesis, we shall confine ourselves to reiterating what has been said elsewhere in the book. First, there is a viable theory *of* perception which has already given rise to a large number of interesting experiments and will undoubtedly continue to do so. And second, there is a set of conceptions *about* perception which may turn out to be of equal or greater importance. In particular, these include hypotheses about the development of perception and about perception-intelligence relationships, developmental and nondevelopmental. Although Piaget has probably taken too extreme a position regarding the contrasts and differences between perceptual and intellectual adaptation, it may have been a heuristic kind of extremism, a kind of Hegelian antithesis which can eventually lead to a fruitful integration and synthesis. As has been shown in previous chapters, Piaget and his co-workers have been and apparently still are hard at work sharpening and leveling differences, teasing out complex interactions, and so forth—all variety of studies which could hardly have emerged from a conceptual framework which did not try to separate and distinguish between perception and intelligence as a point of departure.

Contributions to Other Areas

One way to test the mettle of a system is to find out how extensively it can contribute to and invigorate areas of inquiry other than its own. The potential contributions of Piaget's system to certain areas have been discussed in Chapter 11, and we shall start with some brief added comments about these. First of all, the system was shown to have multifarious implications for and applications to the field of education. It is perhaps symptomatic of how powerfully the system could contribute here that Bruner (1960) saw fit to build a whole discussion of new concepts and methods in education around what Piaget has to say about intellectual development. It is still too early to see how much the system will do for the study of psychopathology. Any developmental system can in principle be pressed into service as the frame of reference for a regression theory of behavior disorders. Since Piaget's is an exceptionally detailed one, it may be of real use here. He has said some specific things about how children think at various stages in ontogenesis, and this may enable others to make similarly specific predictions about the cognitive performance of individuals whose current level of functioning is lower than it once was. And what the system can do for *regression,* it can, of course, also do for *fixation.* We are thinking especially of the work that has already begun on the diagnostic assessment of mental defectives by means of Piagetian tests; but similar investigations could also be carried out with psychotic or other groups of children for whom cognitive maldevelopment is predicated.

Closely related is the question of "psychometrizing" Piaget's intellectual tasks. One of Piaget's contributions here is simply that he is a good resource person for new testing instruments. He has, after all, accumulated a veritable warehouseful of interesting and face-valid measures of intellectual performance over the past four decades. More important, in our view, the advent of his system may for the first time make possible a psychometrics which is anchored to a cognitive-developmental theory. Psychometrics ought not be a mindlessly empiricistic, utterly pragmatic discipline. It is, of course, important to find and make use of good empirical predictors of the sorts of cognitive achievements the society is interested in. But it is also important to study the clustering and patterning of cognition at various developmental levels in a "pure science" way, and to do this by means of tests generated from a theory of development. It might turn out that this kind of enterprise would have unexpected fringe benefits of a decidedly pragmatic sort. For one thing, it is not unreasonable to suppose that a developmental test which has some theoretical coherence would in fact be a better predictor of the conventional criteria (e.g., academic achievement) than those now available. A more intriguing possibility is that developmental scales with a Piagetian stamp might predict to less conventional but ultimately more important criteria, i.e., intellectual capabilities of an inventive or creative nature. The ability to weed out the active and inactive variables in a rod flexibility problem (Inhelder and Piaget, 1958) certainly seems more relevant to real-life creativity than the ability to remember eight digits or define the word *traduce.*

As for the system's bearing on learning theory, in our present state of knowledge little can be added to what was said in Chapter 11. There is enough experimental evidence now available to indicate that acquisitions of the type Piaget has investigated may pose a serious challenge for S-R reinforcement models. It will be interesting to see if researchers with a thoroughgoing commitment to this position will take up the challenge, i.e., will try to show that stable acquisitions of this genre can be regularly engendered with the proper manipulation of the usual learning-experiment variables. Conversely, one might also watch for attempts to expand the field of application of Piaget's equilibration model, or some model like it, to areas traditionally encompassed by learning theory. It might be, for example, that rote memorization in cognitively mature subjects is not, or not always, a mechanical clicking-in process; a nonsense syllable which is almost but not quite assimilable to a previous schema (e.g., to an English word which looks something like it)—that is, one which may engender some small degree of conflict within the subject's action system—may be the very one which is quickly learned and long retained. When reduced to its essentials, Piaget's equilibration model seems to say that you get out of an encounter with the environment what you put into it; an active engagement with data, involving a certain intracognitive *Sturm und Drang,* is what leads to stable and quasi-permanent structural change. This sort of principle could apply to many areas of human functioning.

There are three other areas of possible application of the system which were not discussed in Chapter 11: philosophy, child-rearing practice, and non-Piagetian developmental phenomena. For the first, we said in Chapter 7 that Piaget very definitely construes his developmental research as research in genetic epistemology, and therefore as a direct contribution to the field of philosophy. Would professional philosophers also view it as relevant to their concerns? And if relevant, would they judge it to be a major and substantial contribution? No definite answer can yet be given to either question. Philosophers with whom the writer has discussed this matter say that Piaget's work is not yet widely known in philosophical circles and that it is uncertain just what kind of reaction it would receive when and if it receives serious attention. But there is a straw in the wind here. Wolfe Mays, a professor of philosophy at the University of Manchester, is thoroughly conversant with Piaget's work and does believe that it has important implications for philosophical analysis. Moreover, Mays is preparing a book on Piaget which (in sharp contrast to the present one) will treat the epistemological aspects of his system in considerable detail (personal communication). A foretaste of some probable contents can be gotten from various articles Mays has written. In one (Mays, 1953-1954), for example, he strongly supports Piaget's contention that exclusive preoccupation with the normative aspects of the fully formed adult mind is too narrow a construction of epistemological subject matter (*ibid.*, p. 52). He argues for the philosophical relevance of Piaget's internalization-of-actions view of cognitive development, his emphasis on the constructive versus contemplative nature of thought, his ideas on the psychological character of logical and mathematical operations, and other components of the system. We shall undoubtedly receive at least provisional answers to the two questions posed above when Mays' philosophical audience gets a chance to read and respond to his book.

It is doubtful if Piaget has ever taken an applied-science view of his own theory and research. One hardly thinks of him as the Dr. Spock of mental development. And yet it is our strong conviction that a thorough familiarity with his theory and data can be enormously helpful in the daily business of understanding and coping with children, whether in the role of parent, teacher, nurse, or whatever. For one thing, the system provides a detailed normative frame of reference. If you have a rough idea of what children at a given developmental level are likely to be thinking about and how they are likely to be thinking about it; if you have even crude guidelines as to cognitive possibilities and limitations, as to what the child can and cannot grasp, and how he will and will not be able to construe events, then you can better understand what the child has said and done, better predict what he will say and do next, and in general carry out your caretaker function with greater confidence and skill. But there is more to the adult-child encounter than just caretaking *per se,* more than just doing things with and to the child in order to achieve some short- or long-range socialization goal. One may also want simply to climb inside his world, to achieve a measure of empathic understanding of how he views things. And Piaget's system assists here as well. He has told us enough about cognitive structure at different age levels to permit us to do a crude kind of computer simulation, to "program" ourselves to process information in rough approximation to the way the child processes it. This pursuit of the child's phenomenology may also have a practical yield, i.e., it may, like the comparison-with-norms approach, be of real help in the child-rearing or caretaking enterprise. But it does not have to stand or fall on its pragmatic merits. There is a sense of satisfaction, a sense of doing something worth doing, just in achieving a degree of communion and sympathetic participation with a mind quite unlike one's own.

Most of Piaget's energies have been devoted to the study of ontogenetic development in a limited, although obviously very important, area of human functioning: what might without value judgment be called the more "cold-blooded" aspects of cognition, i.e., thought and perception of a relatively passionless, non-need-oriented variety. This leaves a large and hard-to-categorize remainder which we shall simply refer to as "non-Piagetian" for lack of a better label. It includes the realms of feeling and affect, of affectively toned, "warm-blooded" cognitions, of social-interpersonal interactions, and the like. The question arises as to how Piaget's theory and data could make fruitful contact with this omnibus area. There appear to be at least three ways this could be done.

First, Piaget is in a position to supply the child-developmental field with a large number of new and interesting dependent variables to which we can attempt to fasten independent variables of the non-Piagetian variety, a whole set of cognitive consequents for which noncognitive antecedents or correlates can be sought. As was indicated in the section on validation studies in Chapter 11, Piagetian phenomena have long been profitably exploited in just this way and the trend should, and probably will, continue. In effect, every time Piaget discovers a new cognitive form and describes its development, the stage is immediately set for further experimentation: to find out of what social and individual variables the new form might be a function, i.e., socioeconomic background, general intelligence, familial environment, personal adjustment, and so on.

Bruner (1959) and Elkind (1961a) have recently discussed a new wrinkle in this general approach which we paraphrase as follows. Intellectual development may be conceived as a kind of Toynbeean challenge-response affair: at selected points in his development the socius thrusts the child into new roles with new and different sets of cognitive demands; the child responds to the challenge by acquiring the new cognitive structures needed to cope with these demands. In Bruner's words:

> Logical structures develop to support the new forms of commerce with the world. It is just as plainly the case that the pre-operational child, protected by parents, need not manipulate the world of objects unassisted until the pressure for independence is placed upon him, at which time concrete operations emerge. So the concretely operational child need not manipul- the world of potentiality (save on the fantasy level) until pressure is placed upon him, at which point propositionalism begins to mark his thinking (Bruner, 1959, p. 369).

This is a provocative hypothesis, and one which immediately suggests new lines of research, both intracultural and cross-cultural. But it could obviously not have been proposed had not Piaget done the necessary spade work at the dependent-variable end.

The second way to effect a liaison between Piagetian and non-Piagetian phenomena is essentially the converse of the first. That is, it is possible to examine behavior of the latter type at a given stage of development from the standpoint of its dependence upon achieved cognitive level; in this analysis, cognitive level becomes the independent variable and non-

Piagetian behavior becomes the dependent variable. Thus, the intellectual equipment the child has at his disposal at age X at once permits or fosters certain kinds of adaptations, e.g., personal-social-affective behaviors, and prohibits or inhibits others. Take, for instance, the modal five-year-old. If one compares him with the infant in terms of what his cognitive level allows and predisposes him to do, one could tick off such things as: his affectional attachment to the mother as a specific, highly discriminated love object; his nighttime dreams and daytime fantasies, both pleasant and unpleasant; and his ability to occupy a particular role, albeit a momentary and hazily defined one, in the group games he engages in with other children. On the other hand, there are decided constraints and limits. Using the adolescent or adult as a standard of comparison, it can be said with confidence that the five-year-old simply does not have the conceptual wherewithal to worry much about the world situation, plan for his future, or experience the delights and agonies of an adult love relationship, complete with mutuality, empathy, and a fine tuning to emotional cross-currents. This kind of analysis was part of what we had in mind when we said that a knowledge of Piaget's work significantly enriches a reading of Erikson's account of the affective and interpersonal life of the preoperational child, and we could at this point go on to say that it would do the same, in the same way, for Erikson's portraits of the other developmental periods. The unique contribution of this analysis is that it provides a partial answer (or one kind of answer) to why questions; i.e., as to why the child at one level does this and not that, and later that but not this. And yet the writer knows of no instance where such an analysis has been systematically carried out. It may simply be that there has not heretofore—and once again we think of Piaget's contributions—been a sufficiency of detailed and theoretically coherent information about intellectual development to make it worth the trouble.[2]

There is a third, quite different way in which Piaget's system might be brought to bear on developmental problems in the remainder area. There may be some profit in generalizing certain of Piaget's theoretical notions

[2] It may be asked if we have not worked our way into a dilemma in what has been said in the last several pages. Surely Piagetian behaviors cannot be both dependent and independent variables vis-à-vis non-Piagetian ones. But we think they can, are, and would be expected to be in terms of Piaget's assimilation-accommodation model. There is nothing contradictory in saying that the child's currently operating assimilatory capacity can prescribe some and proscribe other accommodations to non-Piagetian segments of reality, while at the same time readily admitting that what that reality presents as assimilation-accommodation grist will decidedly influence the rate of structural change. The situation is a chicken-and-egg, not chicken-or-egg one: the child cannot accommodate to novelties which ongoing structures cannot assimilate, and yet structural change cannot proceed without the proper measure of stimulation from the milieu—no change until the child is in some sense ready, but also no change unless, when ready, something comes his way.

—originally devised, of course, to explain the ontogenesis of "cold-blooded" cognition—to developmental events of the more sanguine variety. It is not clear just how far one can legitimately push such generalizations, or how much our understanding will ultimately be advanced by making them at all. However, it may be useful to specify briefly what some of the dimensions of generalization might be.

Piaget has conceptualized the cognitive-developmental process as in part a process of constructing invariants amid the flux of perceived events, i.e., the object concept in infancy and the various conservations in middle childhood. Might it not make sense to view development in other areas as also a matter of invariant-formation: developmental changes in self-concept, in perception of others, in belief and value systems, and so on? Is it not a cardinal task of ontogenesis, for instance, to learn to "conserve" a sense of underlying unity, sameness, and continuity in our perception of self and of others? My overt behavior may show marked differences from situation to situation and from mood to mood, but I feel myself to be in some important sense the same personality all the while, and I believe the same is true for you. There is some evidence to suggest that invariant-formation of this sort is, in fact, a developmental product (Gollin, 1958). And similar extensions of this concept might be generalized to belief and value systems in terms of an hypothesized increase in their cross-situational stability with age. There are other areas of possible generalization which Piaget himself has broached. Thus, the concept of schema might be applied to affective as well as cognitive organizations (Chapter 2), a possibility which Wolff finds intriguing (1960, p. 175). Similarly, there is Piaget's belief that the grouping structure of middle childhood may be an appropriate model for value systems and interpersonal interactions as well as for logical operations (Chapter 5). And in all probability a careful search through Piaget's writings would unearth still other theoretical fragments which might have value in analyzing types of developmental phenomena Piaget never had in mind to study.

Other Contributions

There are two extremely important contributions which do not fit anywhere in the previous categories. The first consists of a service Piaget has rendered to a particular class of developmental inquiry, and a brief preamble is required to make clear what that service was. As the writer sees it, one can distinguish two general kinds of research strategy in the field of child development. One of them is the *antecedent-consequent* strategy and is epitomized in the work of Robert Sears and his associates. This approach generally entails the isolation for measurement of some presumably developable behavior or behavior disposition (e.g., dependency, aggression, need-achievement, etc.) and then the attempt to discover antecedent variables, either in the immediate experimental situation or (more commonly) in the child's present or past life situation, of which it is a consequent or function (e.g., characteristics of the mother-child interaction). The object of an investigation guided by this strategy is not to show that the consequent does develop in children in general nor, *a fortiori*, is it to trace what might be the typical steps in its ontogenesis. Rather, the fact of development is assumed, its possible sequential patterning is not an object of study, and the investigator is primarily concerned with discovering the correlates, and hopefully thereby, the causes of variation in the strength of the consequent. Granted, for instance, that most or all five-year-olds have aggressive response tendencies in some strength, and also granted that these tendencies could have undergone some sort of stagelike evolution since birth, what the antecedent-consequent strategist really wants to know is why they are currently stronger in some children than in others.

The second strategy could be christened the *developmental-descriptive* approach, and Piaget would perhaps be its prime exemplar. It takes as its major task to find out what behaviors develop with age (i.e., as a function of a complex of usually unknown events which unroll in ontogenetic time) and also, where the strategist is so oriented, to seek out the sequential stages in this development. In contrast with the previous approach, individual differences in the developing consequent are not of primary interest, and no search is made for possible antecedents of these differences. It is the *fact* and in some cases the *form* of the development in the "average child" which is the research objective.

The two strategies have had quite different fortunes in the history of child psychology, at least in this country. If we read this history aright, the developmental-descriptive approach was originally the dominant one. There was considerable research of this genre during the 1920's and 1930's. As suggested in Chapter 11, much of it dealt with the fact rather than the form of development, i.e., it was conceived within a nonstage, continuity orientation. But beginning in the late 1930's or early 1940's with the first sustained application of learning and psychoanalytic theories to systematic research on personal-social development, the antecedent-consequent approach began to gain ground until today it has become the strategy of choice for the great majority of child psychologists. The developmental-descriptive approach did not disappear during this period, of course, but we believe it did become and still is a strategy of low status for many, perhaps for most people in the field. If one were to poll them on the matter, they would probably point to the sort of studies done in the heyday of developmental-descriptive research and argue somewhat as follows: These studies are dull; all they do is show that children improve their performance in a variety of task situations as they grow older. So what? These studies are also wrongly conceived; the proper business of psychological science is to study cause-effect relationships, to predict consequences from antecedents, and *age*, by and of itself, is a meaningless kind of independent variable to work with.

So much for past and present, what of the future? We believe that attitudes within the field towards the developmental-descriptive approach are once again going to become more positive, and that, in fact, there is some evidence that such an attitude change is already taking place. There are undoubtedly a number of interlocking causes for this new swing of the pendulum. It may be that recent trends in developmental work with animals are playing a role: the *critical period hypothesis* serves to give a new meaning and status to age as an independent variable. There are also rumblings in the psychological *Zeitgeist* at large which may be contributing, i.e., an increasing flexibility as to problems and methods, a decreasing need to prescribe, *ex cathedra* and in advance, just which problems are legitimate objects of study and how they ought to be approached (Koch, 1959, pp. 784-785). But one of the most important sources of attitude change (and this is where our preamble has been pointing) may well be Piaget's accomplishments, and increasingly so as they become more widely known and better understood. The reason is simply this. Piaget, more than perhaps anyone else, has shown what a first-rate mind can do with this time-worn strategy.[3] He has shown that such a mind can find developable consequents which almost anyone would intuitively recognize as important and worthy of study, which look like the very cornerstones of our developing apperception of reality. He has also shown that these consequents often have intriguing developmental histories, that some rather startling precursors may lie in hiding behind the end products. And finally, he has shown that both fact and form of development can be the raw materials for elaborate theorizing, that there is nothing intrinsically atheoretical about the products of developmental-descriptive research. In short, he has taken a research strategy which many had, and with some justification, written off as moribund and has breathed new life into it. If one believes, as this writer obviously does, that it is a strategy worth saving, then Piaget has paid the field in large coin by helping to save it.[4]

The other and remaining contribution can be described more briefly,

[3] One could omit the word *perhaps* only by neglecting the substantial contributions of Heinz Werner and his students. Like Piaget, he has long been an imaginative and effective exponent of the developmental-descriptive approach to developmental problems.

[4] Nothing we have said here should be taken as an argument for turning the clock back, for replacing the antecedent-consequent strategy with the developmental-descriptive one. Quite the contrary, we have tried to show in the preceding subsections how the two approaches can profitably complement and interact with one another, e.g., how data gathered through the developmental-descriptive method can enter the antecedent-consequent paradigm, either as antecedent or as consequent.

although it cannot be communicated as clearly. It is that the experience of immersing yourself in and assimilating Piaget's work can be a peculiarly formative experience. It is an experience which can indelibly color your perception of the field of child development and alter in subtle but real and abiding ways the kind of research problems you select for study, the way you approach these problems, and the kind of interpretation you place on what you find. This change in frame of reference, *Weltanschauung,* or whatever it is, may be quite theory-free and content-free, in the sense that it need not involve either the acceptance and use of Piaget's theory itself or an interest in continuing the study of the particular developmental phenomena he has investigated. Both research problem and referent conceptual system may be quite different, and yet something important, albeit not very tangible and specifiable, is transferred. It may consist of a certain loosening of the associative processes, a certain creative flexibility, which could lead to the discovery of a significant developmental event or area of events to investigate, something which was there all along but no one else saw. It may also consist of a heightened intuitive sensitivity to what lurks behind the phenomenal surface, a knack for making good guesses about what some behavioral phenotype "means" in terms of underlying processes. And it may also consist of an increased facility for looking for, and hence being able to see, the less obtrusive sequential steps in a behavior evolution, the covert patterning in play in some genetic process. In gist, living for a while in the Piagetian world can give one a feel for the grain of development which he did not have before he lived there. This added sensitivity comes with no strings attached, i.e., it does not require that one embrace the theory and data which Piaget's world contains. We suspect that Piaget's system is not the only one in psychology which has this curious property; probably some do and others, perhaps equally good, true, or useful by other criteria, do not. It just is not the sort of dimension one ordinarily looks to in evaluating a system. But perhaps it ought to be, since science is in part a matter of the end game of one mind influencing the beginning and middle games of others.

COMPLAINTS, CRITICISMS, AND PROBLEMS

As was stated earlier in this chapter, one does not have to look far to find problems and critical points in Piaget's system. The ones we wish to report seem to fall into two general categories. First of all, there is a species of criticisms which might be called complaints. These take as their objects certain "bad habits" in Piaget's theoretical and research activity; not indigenous to any particular segment of the system, these habits are recurrent shortcomings which may crop up in any segment. They are relatively clear-cut points of criticism in two senses. First, they tend to be easy to detect on casual reading; in fact, many of them leap out of the page at you as you read. Second, at least most of them unequivocally deserve criticism, i.e., once the weaknesses are pointed out in Piaget's writings almost anyone would agree that they are clear-cut shortcomings, not matters for debate or difference of opinion. The fact that these particular shortcomings do mar the system has (or has had) several important consequences. For one thing, it has undoubtedly contributed to the tardy and incomplete assimilation of Piaget's work by others in the field. His system, theory and experimentation alike, has repelled many a would-be invader, and shortcomings of the complaint category have had much to do with this sorry state of affairs. All in all, Piaget has not been the best of salesmen for his own wares. A more important consequence, at least ultimately, is that the accumulated effect of these shortcomings has been to weave a threat of doubt and uncertainty throughout the whole fabric of his data and theory. On the one hand, habitual shortcomings of procedure, data analysis, method of reporting findings, etc., leave one chronically uneasy about the empirical end of the superstructure. Replication of Piaget's studies would not be such a popular (and such a necessary) pastime had these shortcomings not been present. On the other hand, inadequacies in technique of theory-making and of theory-data coupling summate with this unsteadiness in the empirical foundation to evoke corresponding uncertainties about the theoretical aspects of the system as well. In sum, then, the complaints refer to those things Piaget has done which he clearly should not have done or should have done differently; had he not done them, or done them otherwise, both the empirical and theoretical parts of the system would be on a much more solid and secure footing.

The remaining class, "criticisms and problems," is barely a class at all. It simply consists of three particular matters of critical discussion raised up by an examination of Piaget's work. Their chief commonality is perhaps their open-endedness or lack of closure and the fact that they do not fall neatly into any previous category. There is open-endedness in two senses: (1) they are scarcely the only residual points of criticism and discussion which a book about Piaget might find worth raising, although they are undoubtedly among the most important; and (2) there is no pretense that our treatment of even these three is anything profound or definitive. The class differs from its predecessors in that it deals with matters not so much to be evaluated (although evaluation is here and there involved) as to be pondered, to be thought about in a constructive, future-oriented way. These matters really make up a part of Piaget's legacy to the field: a set of difficult problems and issues which his work has helped to bring into conceptual focus, but which will largely be left for others to cope with in the future.

Complaints

These will be presented in the following, quasi-circular order: (1) matters of theory and interpretation; (2) matters of experimental design and data analysis; and (3) matters of the upward and downward relating of data to theory and interpretation.[5] There are several complaints in the first category. One is that there is a great deal of vagueness, imprecision, instability of concept definition, and other obstacles to communication in Piaget's theoretical writings. One often has to work hard to understand what Piaget is trying to say, and he does not always succeed in the end. For instance, consider this sentence:

> In sum, we are dealing with a set of schemata whose dual nature stems from the fact that, whereas their structuring presupposes formal reasoning, they also derive from the most general characteristics of the structures from which this same formal thought arises (Inhelder and Piaget, 1938, p. 106).

If one troubles to check into the matter, he will discover that the opaqueness of this passage is really not a matter either of inadequate translation from the French or of the fact that it is quoted here out of context. It is simply a very difficult sentence, and there are many like it in Piaget's writings. One other example will suffice, this of a very important concept in Piaget's system for which he seems not to have given a clear and consistent definition. The concept is the inverse operation in the case of relations as opposed to classes, i.e., the reciprocal as opposed to negation operation. In the first two books on logic (Piaget, 1942a, p. 105; Piaget, 1949a, p. 140), Piaget makes a point of asserting that the inverse (reciprocal) of an asymmetrical relation $(A < B)$ is $(B > A)$ and that the addition of the two yields the equivalence $(A = A)$. This is the interpretation we took as the "official" one in Chapter 5. But in a later book we find the statement: "For asymmetrical relations, if $A < B$ is true its reciprocal $B < A$ [sic] is false . . ." (Inhelder and Piaget, 1958, p. 274). Nothing further along in the passage clarifies the point. It might also be added in this connection that the concept of reversibility in general seems to mean somewhat different things in different contexts, with no attempt made to resolve the differences by a single, unequivocal definition.

There is also the related tendency to leave large gaps between theory and empirics, almost to distantiate one from the other. This takes several forms. One frequently encounters statements, in the genetic epistemological writings particularly but also elsewhere, which were apparently intended to make reference to real happenings in ontogenesis but for which it is difficult to imagine a set of empirical operations which could either

---

[5] It may be helpful to refer back to parts of Chapter 1 as background and context for what follows in this subsection.

confirm or infirm them. In the same vein, Piaget is wont to say that such and such is an important developmental or genetic-epistemological "problem" for research to solve, and yet one cannot envisage what genre of research could be relevant to it. He will also distinguish between constructs *A* and *B*, leaving the reader to puzzle about what empirical consequences the distinction might have. A somewhat different expression of this tendency is Piaget's persistent disinclination to cast his theory in such a form as to make it an instrument of deduction, of hypothesis-generation. This is not to say, of course, that Piaget does not make heavy use of his theory in devising new experiments. But it has typically functioned as a theory *within* which to do research, rather than *from* which to do research: more a good climate for generating research problems than an actual instrument for generating them. To be sure, a developmental-descriptive system is much more likely to function in this way than an antecedent-consequent one, with the latter's explicit and deliberate orientation towards prediction and hypothesis-testing. Our complaint is only that Piaget has not made his theory as prediction-generating as it could be, granted the limits of the kind of theory it is. What little has been done along these lines so far has largely been contributed by people outside the Geneva circle (e.g., Braine, 1959).

Related both to the foregoing and to certain other idiosyncrasies of his theoretical style (Chapter 1) is Piaget's bent towards theoretical over-elaboration, often bordering on the pretentious. The paramount example is probably the third logic book (1952a), an almost unreadable tour de force in logical analysis. Although it seems clear enough from the book's preface that this analysis was intended to have important relevance to the study of human thought processes, it is nowhere made clear just what this relevance might be. Here stands an imposing system of logical propositions and their various transformations; elsewhere stands Piaget's body of empirical data on cognition at different genetic levels; and yet there is not the slightest attempt to effect any real liaison between them.

There are numerous other instances, although less dramatic ones, in which Piaget manages to end up with what looks like a considerable amount of theoretical excess baggage, something decidedly in surplus of whatever may be genuinely valuable in describing or explaining the behavior to which the set of constructs refer. The group of spatial displacements in infancy, the groupings of middle childhood, the group-lattice model in adolescence, and the cost-gain interpretation of the equilibration process: these and other conceptual structures appear to have at least some tinsel on them, whatever core of usefulness may lie beneath (and we think there usually is a core). Our interpretation is that Piaget sometimes becomes unduly fascinated with theory-construction as an intellectual exercise, as a challenge to his ability to synthesize and analyze, to ferret out hidden logical connections between this theoretic element and that. The result too often is that the theory-behavior relation gets lost along the way (a point to which we shall return presently when we take up the question of how Piaget moves back and forth from data to theory). All in all, it is difficult to escape the impression that Piaget has expended a great deal of energy over the years in spinning theoretical nets which do not really catch much; it is a good thing that there has been plenty of energy left over for more profitable ventures.

There are miscellaneous other complaints at the level of theory and interpretation. For instance, Piaget sometimes appears to be jousting with straw men in his theorizing. In particular, he is prone to overidentify current learning-theoretical orientations with their empiricism-associationism ancestors of the nineteenth century and earlier, and by so doing he vitiates an otherwise strong argument or cogent point. Also, in reading through one of Piaget's extended chains of theoretical discourse, one often has the uneasy feeling that there is something awry in the logic: that this element is somehow not connected properly with those on either side of it; that what is now being said is not really implied by, and may even seem faintly irrelevant to, that which was said a moment before (although Piaget had obviously intended the one to follow from the other and may even have connected them with a "therefore"). It is difficult to render what we mean here in words, but there is nothing subliminal about the feeling itself as one reads through a section of Piaget. It is paradoxical that an accusation of occasional illogicality could be leveled at a theorist so conversant with logic and so prone to encase his theory in it; but the accusation is not unjust.

There is a kind of common denominator behind the complaints we have been listing, something easier to see in his empirical work than in his theorizing perhaps, but every bit as much in force in the latter. It is as if Piaget were conducting his scientific affairs—doing experiments, interpreting their results, constructing theories, and so on—according to an implicit system of rules rather different from that by which most of his readers play. We think it may be this difference in rule-system which is at work when people say that they somehow just do not "get" Piaget and do not quite know why. This kind of difference can be a powerful force for communicative failure, all the more so because it is so hard to recognize and identify.

The second category of complaints concerns the empirical aspects of the system, i.e., how Piaget typically designs and executes a study, analyzes the data, and writes about what he has done and found. It would be well to begin by saying what the category will not include. There are two general kinds of criticism which some might want to level at Piaget but which, in our view, are not really appropriate. For the first, Piaget designed his studies to answer certain kinds of developmental questions of interest to him. Naturally, these questions were not the only ones which might have been asked in the same general context of inquiry, but they were good questions and well worth asking. Thus, we think it less than fair to criticize Piaget for not trying to answer questions which he did not *ask*. For example, one should hesitate to say that Piaget ought to have found out the extent to which a given cognitive acquisition was a function of, say, general intelligence, socioeconomic background, etc., as well as of chronological age. Piaget was simply not interested in antecedent-consequent questions of this sort, and we cannot complain about his leaving them to others.

Second, it would be unjust to insist that, once Piaget had broken the ground in a new area of inquiry, he ought to have stayed with it longer, ought to have explored it in greater breadth and depth. Once again, this was simply not to his taste (nor, probably, for his talents), and we are not at all certain that it should have been. It is a formidable and time-consuming matter to make a thorough and definitive stage-analytic study of even a single developing ability and, in truth, there is still some question as to just how the job can best be done: longitudinal studies, learning studies, cross-sectional studies with scalogram analysis, a convergence of all of these—or what? With Piaget's undoubted gifts for opening up new areas of study, the field of child development would probably have been the poorer if he *had* been more terrierlike in his research behavior, more inclined to sacrific breadth for depth.

What, then, is left to complain about? The clue lies in the validation studies cited in Chapter 11. Many of these studies were done not so much to build on Piaget's preliminary findings, to take up where he left off, as to see whether there were really any substance in the preliminary findings themselves. We believe the authors of these studies were justified in their view that replication and validation were the first order of business, and our principal criticism of Piaget's empirical work resides here. We feel, as they must have, that he simply did not conduct and report his research in such a way as to make a very convincing case for even the major configurations of his stated results. There is no quarrel with his failure to have gone beyond a beginning exploration of the basic developmental parameters in a particular problem area; what is criticized is his failure to have established and reported in a scientifically acceptable way the important minimum which just such an exploratory study could have yielded.

Let us examine the major characteristics of Piaget's investigations which would cause others to think of validation rather than elaboration. First, and perhaps most important, is Piaget's habitual failure to give a clear and full account of precisely what he did in the experiment. The reader is often left in considerable doubt as to what actual test and inquiry procedures were administered by whom under what testing conditions to how many children of what ages, backgrounds, previous testing experiences, and so on. Similarly, not enough information is presented to allow any evaluation of either the face validity or the reliability of the stage-classification system which Piaget applies to the subjects' behavior protocols; in particular, there is no way to judge the extent to which his preexperimental expectancies and theoretical predilections have shaped both the construction and application of the classification system.

The specter of communicative inadequacy necessarily haunts any attempt to evaluate Piaget's actual research conduct; it is hard to criticize what happened when you are not altogether sure what happened. However, some things are known and others can be guessed. One can guess, for example, that Piaget has been fairly casual about sampling procedures, although full details are never given. Granted that he would typically try to amass subject samples of at least minimally adequate size; still it is doubtful whether he would be careful to insure much sample homogeneity, either within or across age groups. Most subjects in Piaget's studies are probably selected only on the basis of age and ready availability.

The test and inquiry procedure is typically quite variable from subject to subject, at least partly in consequence of Piaget's explicit espousal of the "clinical method." We believe Piaget is basically correct in his estimate of the advantages of this kind of method over the traditional, more rigid and invariable psychometric procedures (e.g., Piaget, 1929c, ch. 1). But we also think he could have retained these advantages and at the same time secured obvious additional ones by a semistandardization of procedure, a testing format with more invariants in it. Many of the follow-up studies reported in Chapter 11 have done essentially this, and with no apparent loss of important qualitative data. Piaget also has the habit of administering several major variations of a given basic task (the variance due to the use of the clinical method taking place *within* each of these major variations). Since one is not always sure whether these variations are given to the same or different children, or even whether both practices occur in the same experiment, this makes for additional uncertainty about the empirical basis for his experimental conclusions. One often has the feeling that the actual subject sample for any specific experimental procedure taken alone may be very small, even where the total sample is large; or alternatively, one may suspect that the same children have submitted to a whole sequence of procedures, and that there must be all sorts of uncontrolled order effects. More generally, the considerable, virtually subject-to-subject variation in procedure, which one senses in many Piaget studies, makes one think that he has tendered a series of pilot studies in the guise of a formal and finished experiment; and this scarcely increases the reader's confidence in the reported results.

There is finally the matter of organization and analysis of data. In the case of the intellectual development work, at least, this is usually limited to the presentation of a number of verbatim protocols as illustrations of each developmental stage. There is no objection to this strategy of exposition, as far as it goes. Quite the contrary, these protocols do convey the flow and flavor of the actual processes under study as nothing else could; Piaget's tasks elicit qualitatively rich responses, and he does well to let the reader see this richness undigested. It is what he fails to do beyond this which is ground for criticism. And what he generally fails to do is give even the most rudimentary sort of quantitative information about his data. As instances, he does not report the correlation between response level (stage) and age, nor even the essential characteristics of the age distribution at each response level (e.g., means and standard deviations). Simple analyses of this sort clearly should have been done. They would have provided a quantitative feeling for the data, a more acute sense of what was happening developmentally. In particular, they might well have convinced many people that at least the essentials of the phenomena are as Piaget had claimed: that the peculiar first-stage responses are really there in force; that many young children do respond this way; and that the whole sequence of stages is at least roughly age-dependent.[6]

It may seem as though we have been arguing that Piaget was always right and that the pity is only that his unconvincing presentation caused a lot of needless replication. This, of course, would not be the whole truth, but there is some truth in it: the collective impact of the studies cited in Chapter 11 is that he was in fact often right, especially in the main essentials. But the central point is this. Had his research conduct and research reporting conformed more to the usual scientific canons, one could have been in position to judge what needed replication and what did not, what was convincingly established and what looked wrong or uncertain. We are inclined to think that Piaget did his research to convince himself and that, having been convinced, he expected others simply to take his word for it. This calls to mind the matter of rule systems mentioned earlier: it may be that Piaget is less convinced than most of us that science, like government, ought to be of law rather than of men.

The third group of complaints has to do with how Piaget interprets his empirical evidence. These criticisms could readily be inferred from what has already been said, and it is only a matter of making the implicit explicit. First, there is his tendency to overinterpret. This takes two forms. On the one hand, he is inclined to draw definite conclusions from

[6] Much of the perception research is similarly characterized by a failure to make use of obviously appropriate quantitative analyses. As we observed earlier, this research is typically of a more conventional sort: more careful procedure, several independent variables for a given dependent one, and data given quantitatively (tables, figures, etc.). It is all the more painful, then, to watch Piaget making interaction-of-variables interpretations of every little blip in each curve when a straightforward analysis of variance ought clearly to have substituted for his intuitions.

evidence others would regard as shaky, e.g., the willingness to interpret small and perhaps random-error perturbations in perceptual data mentioned in the preceding footnote. On the other hand, a given quantum of evidence, shaky or solid, is frequently a stimulus for what appears to be an excessively verbose and overelaborated theoretical discussion. Piaget's books and articles are often difficult and even tedious to read because of this; he reports a finding and then heaps page after page of conceptualization on it.

He also tends to be unparsimonious in his interpretation of data; there is a good deal of what looks like multiplication—and manipulation—of entities beyond necessity. The complicated interplay of assimilation and accommodation which he hypothesizes for preoperational symbolic functioning is perhaps an example. (A brief and simplified account of this interplay was given in Chapter 4.) Similarly, there is the tendency to state that such-and-such a datum supports such-and such theoretical assertion without indicating how it does, or even could, support it. Here as elsewhere, the feeling intrudes that Piaget is just not following the same rules of evidence and inference that you are. The number book (Piaget, 1952b) contains an important example of this. He states there that number is an operational fusion and synthesis of class and relation and says, "the facts recorded in this volume lead to this conclusion almost without any attempt at interpretation" (p. viii). Now it may be that this is, in fact, a correct interpretation of how development in this area proceeds, although one would like to see him specify a little more precisely what he means by it. But the point is that this writer, at least, cannot see how the empirical facts presented in the number book support, much less mandate, that conclusion—even with a rather intensive "attempt at interpretation."

Finally, Piaget often appears to force unwilling data into preset theoretical molds. In accord with his own theory of mind, his interpretations of empirical phenomena show a great deal of assimilative activity, sometimes, it would seem, at the expense of accommodation. There is more than a little of this Procrustean-bed kind of interpretation in his use of the various logico-algebraic models. Associativity and general identity, to take two salient examples, are both properties of all his concrete-operational groupings; and yet it is hard to see their behavioral parallels in most of the cognitive forms which the groupings are supposed to model. Similarly, one sometimes gets the impression that a cognitive acquisition is labeled as, say, "formal-operational" more because of the age at which it typically occurs than because it closely accords with the criterial attributes of this intellectual period. It is not that Piaget does not usually attempt to defend the labeling. He generally does. But the defense is often unconvincing and looks suspiciously as if it were made after the fact.

Criticisms and Problems

It was stated earlier that this subsection would take up three problematic matters which arise within the context of Piaget's system. The first involves an inquiry into a particular critical interpretation which might be placed on many of his experimental findings. The second deals with the broad question of where and how his theory might be modified and extended. And the third has to do with a difficult problem which his theory and experimentation keep raising at every turn: the meaning and uses of the construct *developmental stage*.

One sometimes encounters the following sort of argument with respect to Piaget's work. Many of his studies, the argument goes, are merely vocabulary-growth studies in disguise. His tasks variously assess the child's understanding of terms like *alive, brother, fair, amount, number, long, all, some,* and so on (Chapters 8-10). Initially, as might be expected, the child shows an imperfect or incomplete grasp of such terms. And as he grows older, he gradually approaches the adult's understanding and usage of them. There is really nothing intellectually exciting here for the student of child psychology; we have known for a long time that vocabulary acquisition is a developmental fact. In particular, there are no grounds for assuming that the vocabulary change points to anything important other than itself—no grounds for assuming, for instance, that it reflects any kind of qualitative alteration in cognitive structure or world-view.

This is obviously an important argument to evaluate, since its acceptance implies that a great many of Piaget's studies are quite other, and a good deal less, than he thought them to be. Our view of the argument is a mixed one. On the one hand, we think there is a fundamental inadequacy in it which needs to be made plain; on the other, it is not without a germ of truth, and in this germ lie some problems of interest for developmental psychology. What we see as its inadequacy is more a matter of omission than commission. In the case of conservation of number, for example, it is undeniably true that the developmental process Piaget described does entail a changed understanding and use of expressions like "same number," "just as many," etc. The crucial question, however, is not whether vocabulary growth takes place, but whether anything else also takes place, and what the relation is between the vocabulary growth and this something else. We tend to believe that, in most of Piaget's studies, whatever vocabulary change occurs is in large measure a consequence, reflection, or symptomatic expression of an underlying and more fundamental cognitive change. Vocabulary development probably has a complex and variable relation to cognitive structure, to be sure. It is likely that the acquisition of certain new words does not presuppose fundamental changes in the subject's intellectual *modus operandi.* But it is equally likely that the acquisition of others does. There are words and words, and the mastery of some has much more important cognitive-developmental implications than the mastery of others. *Number* is one of these important words, we think, and so are world like *alive, amount, long,* and many others which Piaget's investigations have dealt with. To grasp the essential meaning of the word *number* presupposes that the child can already perform certain intellectual operations and, equally important, is already disposed to deal with reality in a certain way, e.g., on the basis of internalized rules ("same number if no elements added or taken away") rather than perceptual centrations ("the row is longer so there are more"). The basic trouble with the growth-of-vocabulary position is that it reduces and simplifies beyond what the actualities of its referent data can tolerate. And it does this, we suspect, by construing language to be a more autonomous and detached function than it really is, that is, by tacitly assuming an undue dissociation between language activity and other ongoing activities. Too radical a dissociation here can lead to some very queer assertions of the "nothing but" variety. Thus, successful intensive therapy is a process which produces "nothing but" an altered vocabulary for describing the self and others; similarly, serving four years as president changes "nothing but" one's semantic response to terms like "domestic politics" and "foreign policy."

In a recent discussion of Piaget's water-levels study of quantity conservation, Berko and Brown (1960, pp. 536-537) appear to have, at least tentatively, adopted the nothing-but-vocabulary-growth position. It may be, they argue, that the young child is first taught the concept of quantity in simple situations where there is variation along a single dimension only, e.g., two identical glasses with a higher level of liquid in one than in the other. Thus, quantity comes to be self-defined in terms of height of liquid column and, by making "an inappropriate extension of his semantic rule" (*ibid.,* p. 536), the child fails to conserve quantity in Piaget's test. But if one reads over Piaget's account of this and related experiments (e.g., Piaget, 1952b, ch. 1), one is led to doubt whether such an interpretation does justice to the data. In the first place, there is evidence that the young child does not typically have a single criterion, consistent and well-differentiated, for judging quantity. A change in the task array will frequently cause him to shift from column height to a different index, e.g., the size of the vessel itself, the number of vessels into which the liquid is poured and, in the ball-of-clay version of the same problem, the length of the sausage into which the ball is transformed.

There is also the related fact that transitional-stage children will assert conservation in some display conditions and deny it in others: hardly the behavior of someone generalizing an articulated "semantic rule," correct or incorrect. We doubt if the common denominator among non-conservers, or within the same nonconserver from situation to situation, is merely the possession and application of a faulty definition. Rather, we suspect with Piaget that it consists, in part at least, of a unidimensional, perceptual-centration approach to problems of quantity estimation, the dimension which is centered depending upon the particulars of the perceptual configuration at hand. It is true, but insufficient and actually misleading, to assert that the child does not yet "know" that questions of quantity in this setting entail consideration of the relationships obtaining among several dimensions. A better statement is that a coordinated apprehension of several dimensions at once is not yet a feature of his cognitive style generally. Another probable component of the common denominator, perhaps the more basic one, is the young child's tendency to reason in terms of what *seems to be* in this moment of perception, rather than in terms of what, perhaps contrary to appearances, *has to be* in the light of an internalized rule which binds together and makes rational a succession of such moments. The older child differs from the younger in possessing a fuller measure of inner, schematic safeguards against perceptual illusion. In sum, we suspect that it is only after the child's purview of quantity and like situations possesses this dual multidimensional and inner-resources character that the relevant vocabulary can take hold and achieve stable and consistent usage. You cannot teach "red" to a blind man, nor "wisdom" to an idiot.

One may disagree with the essential thesis of the growth-of-vocabulary argument and yet admit that some genuine problems for developmental inquiry are implied in it. One species of problem has to do with how the experimenter's language, that in which he couches his task instructions, influences the developmental level of the child's response. It is not unreasonable to suppose that, say, a budding conservation of global quantity may be more or less readily elicited depending upon precisely how the question is put to the child. "Just as much to eat" may yield the conservation response where the less concrete and less need-centered "same amount" might not.

In this connection, Braine (1959) suggests that Piaget's tasks sometimes seem to demand of the child a terminological grasp in excess of the conceptual grasp which the tasks purport to measure. A task is supposed to assess the child's understanding of a certain concept, but to make the correct response to it may demand this understanding and, above and beyond it, an understanding of certain concept-relevant words. But we see a sticky problem here which Braine does not discuss: there is probably a point beyond which stripping a concept of its verbal-symbolic accouterments makes of it a different, lower-order concept, or even no concept at all; and it is exceedingly difficult to know what that point will be in any given instance. It may simply be, to take one of Braine's examples (*ibid.*, p. 6), that a stable and generalizable conception of length just cannot exist without symbolic vehicles and anchors in the form of a minimal length-relevant vocabulary.

The problem of task-vocabulary is at least partly a straightforward empirical problem: one can vary the verbal aspects of the task and observe any resultant variation in the child's response level. But there is another verbalization-relevant problem not so readily managed. The child not only responds *to* verbalization in Piaget's tests, he also responds *with* verbalizations, and the problem lies in trying to decipher these for their cognitive-developmental meanings and implications. Piaget has not been unaware of this problem of translation and has, in fact, discussed it in considerable detail (1929c, Introduction). He has not, however, always followed his own stated precautions regarding it, and has frequently made cognitive inferences from verbal protocols as though there were no translation problem at all.[7]

We have argued that the child's linguistic comprehension and usage is not independent of underlying intellectual structure and orientation, but it would be absurd to suppose that the one is always going to provide a faithful and accurate image of the other. One must always look to the possibility, particularly in studies like Piaget's, that what the child says will lead you either to an overestimation or an underestimation of his operant intellectual level. But as was implied in Chapter 11 in connection with the study by Estes (1956), detectable mismatches between language and cognition can present an opportunity as well as an obstacle. The fact that a child may say one thing and "believe" something else can itself be a latent clue to his over-all cognitive organization, a clue which has not been sufficiently exploited. It may, for instance, indicate that language is still a relatively unsharpened instrument of intellectual control and self-communication (e.g., Luria, 1959). Or it may mean, as we suggested in the context of one of Estes' findings, that various levels of reality apprehension—e.g., the "looks like" versus the "really is"—are still insufficiently articulated. Even though one may occasionally capitalize on it, however, the translation problem has been and will long continue to be one of the most troublesome for developmental studies of the Piagetian type. Indeed, much of the criticism of Piaget, especially the early Piaget, comes down to a dissatisfaction with his language-thought translations.

There is next the matter of how and where Piaget's theory might be modified and extended. First, a possible modification. It seems to the writer that Piaget has in general attributed too much system and structure

---

[7] Although we have criticized Berko and Brown's interpretation of Piaget's quantity study, we cannot wholly disagree with one statement they made in the same context: "Piaget is inclined to see through words as though they were not there and to imagine that he directly studies the child's mind" (1960, p. 536).

to the child's thought. Although this criticism might also be directed at formal-operational thought, it seems particularly applicable to the concrete-operational period, and we shall confine it to that period in what follows. Questions have already been raised in previous sections of the book as to the adequacy of the grouping structures Piaget uses as models for cognition in middle childhood. Does each grouping operation really have a discoverable opposite number in ongoing intellectual activity? Do certain groupings even roughly resemble any frequently occurring operational pattern in middle childhood—particularly Groupings IV and VIII but perhaps also Groupings II and VI (see Chapter 5)? And generally, has Piaget given satisfactory evidence that the child's cognitive operations really knit themselves into strong, tightly organized systems or structures? It is our judgment that Piaget's bent towards mathematics and logic, towards systematization, and towards symmetry and order has led him to see more coherence and structure in the child's intellectual actions than are really there. This is not to say that important cognitive progress does not get made in middle childhood. Nor is it to suggest that there is no coherence, unity, and system resulting from this progress. Piaget's research gives strong evidence to the contrary on both counts. What we are suggesting is that an accurate picture of intellectual life in this period would probably show a somewhat lower order of organization, a somewhat looser clustering of operations, in short, a somewhat less strong and less neat system than Piaget's grouping theory postulates.

How to paint such a picture? A clue may be found in Piaget's description of formal-operational thought. If one leaves aside the mathematical (four-group and lattice) aspects, it can be construed as a two-level model (Chapter 6). At the upper level there is a set of interrelated assertions about general cognitive approach or strategy, e.g., that, thought now proceeds from the possible to the real and that operations now get performed upon the products of prior operations. At the lower level there is a group of somewhat less closely interconnected statements about somewhat less generic intellectual tools, instrumentalities, or tactical devices to which Piaget gives the name *operational schemas*. These include new skills and knowledges which enable the adolescent to cope with a variety of new and difficult problems, which involve proportions, combinations and permutations, systems of balancing or compensating forces, and the like. Needless to say, strategy and tactics are not wholly independent. A strategy which features a hypothetico-deductive approach and an inclination to operate further on already constituted operations is, of course, favorable to the development of a tactical armory consisting of the ability to find all possible combinations, to ferret out all the balancing and compensating factors, to deal with proportionality, and the rest. Nonetheless, there is probably some autonomy and independence, with the tactical operations still needing to be acquired one by one, despite the over-all salubriousness of the strategic climate.

Perhaps a two-level model will also give a more realistic portrayal of concrete-operational thought. The upper, strategy-and-approach level might comprise the child's general tendency to structure and organize concrete givens, to give more weight to cognitive inference and less weight to perceptual impression, to make use of mobile, reversible operations, and perhaps other characteristics. Analogous to the operational schemas of adolescence might be the ability to comprehend and construct series and classification hierarchies, to make transitive inference, to multiply classes and relations, to decompose and recompose the parts of a whole, and to measure the whole by iterating unit parts: these and a number of other operations at the lower, tactical level could be read directly from Piaget's many experiments with this age group. Once again, there would be the dual assumption of partial dependence and partial autonomy between levels: the new strategies are necessary conditions for the acquisition of the new tactical instruments, but the presence of the strategies does not in itself guarantee that a particular acquisition has already been constituted.

The proposed modification would certainly do some violence to Piaget's theoretical structure, but perhaps not as much as one might think. For example, his conceptions about the relationship between adjacent developmental periods would need little change, e.g., the strategy and tactics of middle childhood could still be regarded as becoming integrated into those of formal operations, as the child moves into the latter period. Similarly, a number of the original grouping operations would crop up again in the amended model, although they would no longer be construed as elements of a grouping structure. For instance, reversibility would be part of strategy, and composition would be part of tactics (e.g., logical addition and multiplication of classes, and transitivity of relations). And the equilibration conception could still make sense, even though the resulting equilibrium states might be depicted otherwise than Piaget has depicted them. More positively, a theoretical renovation along the lines proposed might have the merit of at once making for a better match between constructs and data, as already suggested, and of freeing the system from some of the rigidity and maladaptability under which we believe it now labors. For there is considerable question in this psychologist's mind as to whether the system in its present form can make room for all the cognitive-developmental facts, known or yet to come, which a system of its kind ought to subsume. Indeed, the grouping and group-lattice models sometimes appear to creak just in trying to deal with the data to which Piaget has already addressed them. The time simply may not be ripe in this area of psychology for models of such apparent rigor and such real constraints and rigidities, and we should like to see Piaget's theory amended, our way or some other way, to be more in keeping with what the area seems to admit and need.

How the system can be extended and what can be built onto it depends in part on how it gets modified and what gets built into it. But we can at least look at possibilities, and the following is one of them. Piaget's theory, as it now stands, appears to be geared exclusively to the normative, "in-general" aspects of cognitive ontogenesis; that is, it contains no obvious conceptual machinery for dealing with individual-differences development. Individual differences in a developmental context could mean several different things. The usual referent would be individual variation in growth rate as a function of any of a host of antecedent variables, e.g., intelligence, socioeconomic background, educational opportunities, etc. But it could also mean other sorts of differences. It could refer to variation in the number, nature, and sequence of stages for a given acquisition, e.g., the "developmental route" the subject takes in going from complete nonconservation of quantity to a stable, nonextinguishable conservation. Or it could mean individual variation in the functional role and status of developmentally immature cognitive forms or dispositions, once more mature ones have come into play. Or it could mean individual differences in the stability of a mature form, once developed, e.g., the subject's susceptibility to regression from it, either nonadaptively, as under stress, or adaptively, as when such regression might be necessary as a condition for further development.

There are challenging problems here for developmental theory and research, particularly, in our view, in the case of the latter three types of differences. But they are at present grossly understudied problems: there is little theory and less research. What little theory there is is almost exclusively to be found in the recent writings of Heinz Werner (e.g., 1957). Werner, like Piaget, works within an essentially developmental-descriptive rather than antecedent-consequent theoretical framework. But unlike Piaget, he has tried to devise theoretical concepts which, at least in a general way, take account of these less understood forms of individual variation. Here is an example. He states that development is at once "unilinear" and "multilinear"; there is both universality of over-all genetic sequence and "a branching-out process of specialization" (*ibid.*, p. 137). For instance, he views perceptual development as in general proceeding from a less mature "physiognomic" perception to a more mature "geometric-technical" perception. But in some individuals (e.g., artists) the earlier form may itself undergo an intensive and specialized development, which continues long past early childhood and proceeds alongside the genesis of the geometric-technical mode. This conceptualization and others Werner offers might fruitfully be brought to bear on phenomena in Piaget's bailiwick. The concept of multilinearity, for example, might lead us to hypothesize that preoperational credulity and perception-boundedness persist as prominent aspects of the cognitive style of some (but not all) adults—adults who have nonetheless successfully negotiated the two periods which follow.[8]

We see two other points of possible extension, although we claim no special insights as to how they might become realities. One consists of extending the ontogenetic span of theoretical coverage, that is, somehow outfitting the system so as to take account of cognitive changes which may occur beyond the era of formal operations. Bruner (1959, p. 370) makes the interesting suggestion that at least some adults may be thought to progress from being intelligent (formal-operational) to being intelligent about intelligence, e.g., the difference between what Piaget's adolescent subjects do and what Piaget does in conceptualizing what they do. And it may also be that there are important qualitative changes in cognitive strategy and tactics which occur after adolescence in the population at large, not simply in the brighter minority that Bruner has in mind. Even though these changes may not be "beyond" formal operations, in the onward and upward sense, they could nonetheless involve the logical (i.e., Piagetian) side of intellectual functioning. But of whatever stripe they may be, a developmental theory surely must deal with them to earn its title.

Not only does Piaget's system not cover the development of cognition through the whole life cycle, it also quite obviously does not cope with everything in the birth to adulthood range which could be called "cognition." We have particularly in mind that great gray area of human adaptation, part intellect and part affect, which we earlier referred to as "warm-blooded cognition." Precisely what this category would be said to include is anyone's prerogative: at least the defensive operations of the various psychodynamic theories and the attitude-judgment-belief phenomena described by Abelson and Rosenberg (1958), Festinger (1957), Heider (1958), Osgood, Suci, and Tannenbaum (1957), and others. We cannot know how useful a Piagetlike theoretical system would prove here, because not much is known about their ontogenesis—even whether they undergo any discernible qualitative changes with age.

The question of development here is an especially interesting one, because the net effect of many of these semicognitive operations is in some sense to distort reality, to arrive at a nonveridical apprehension of it in the service of some need. This is in sharp contrast to the impeccably logical and reality-bound operations the genesis of which Piaget

---

[8] More generally, it would be worthwhile exploring the possibility of bringing the best of Piaget and Werner together under a single theoretical roof. Werner's theory is much closer to Piaget's than is any other, both in theoretical content and in basic developmental philosophy. So far as the writer knows, however, no one has yet made a serious try at theoretical integration and, unfortunately, there is insufficient space to attempt one here.

has studied. Is there really a development towards nonveridicality contemporaneous with the Piagetian development away from it? Is it true that the growing child not only develops sharper and sharper instruments for dissecting reality but also increases his proficiency in defensive self-deceptions, in reducing the strain of cognitive dissonance, incongruity, etc., at the expense of realistic accommodations, and all the rest? Perhaps Werner's principle of multilinearity is at work here: not only do logical and veridical structures arise out of less logical and less veridical ones in the growth process, but the latter also undergo a *sub rosa* elaboration and refinement of their own, alternating with the former in the everyday functioning of the adult, according to need and circumstance.

We conclude chapter and book with a brief discussion of one of the real posers for developmental theory and research: the possible meanings and applications of the concept of "stage," or its various synonyms "period," "level," etc. Although Piaget (1955d) and others (e.g., Braine, 1959; Kessen, 1960; Werner, 1957) have discussed the problem, there are still many ambiguities and unresolved questions. The philosopher Mario Bunge (1960), for example, has given us a poignant reminder of these in distinguishing no less than nine separate meanings of the concept "level." We shall limit our treatment to a particular, but particularly important, segment of the general problem, using Piaget's findings as the empirical context for possible resolutions.

An obvious but almost insuperable difficulty which bedevils anyone trying to make a stage analysis of human development is the fact that a given stage, however defined, is typically a function not only of chronological age but also, or so it sometimes seems—of everything else under the sun. There are independent variables consisting of the specific tasks and testing procedures by which the stage assignment was arrived at and of the particular setting and conditions in which the testing took place. And there are also variables residing in the child himself: his over-all intellectual ability; his enduring personality and current, emotional state; and his background as regards sociocultural and family milieu, education, previous experiences with this sort of test or with testing in general, and so on. With this potpourri of influences, the argument runs, how can statements like "6-9 years is the stage of such-and-such" have any determinate meaning? And more generally, can the construct "stage" really serve any theoretical purpose other than to mislead us, e.g., to connote a simplicity and intra-age homogeneity which is just not to be found anywhere in developmental reality?

Our views on this critical aspect of the stage-analysis problem are as follows. We doubt if there can be a complete and wholly satisfactory resolution of the problem, and one might as well accept the fact. Any assertion involving the term *developmental stage* seems forever bound either to have some vagueness and equivocality in it or else to be a "data statement" of such concreteness and specificity as to render the appellation *stage* superfluous. But partial resolutions may be possible where complete ones are not. We believe this is the case with the stage construct: there are legitimate—and, in our opinion, highly useful—ways to employ it which partly circumnavigate and partly capitalize on the fact of its multidetermination. A beginning step is to distinguish two somewhat different meanings of the term *stage:* (1) it may designate a *level* or *step* in a sequence of levels or steps with respect to a particular psychological *process* of acquisition and change; (2) it may have reference to an over-all *state* in a sequence of over-all states which are said to characterize a *person* undergoing ontogenetic development. It is, of course, true that the process must take place in a person and that the over-all state of the person is necessarily a cross section or intersect of a series of co-occurring processes; nonetheless, one can look at the whole complexus from either a process or a person orientation, and the two views are somewhat different.

Let us begin with the process view. Heterogeneity and multideterminism are everywhere apparent from this angle of vision, and the task of imposing any order on the jumble seems hopeless. For if we define a "single process" as any logically connected sequence of acquisitions which one cannot immediately fractionate into simpler ones, Piaget's data bins alone could easily yield a lifetime supply. The acquisition of the adult concept of the dream and of the conservation of continuous quantity might be two examples, although one would have to leave open the possibility of further processual differentiation in each case. Furthermore, as suggested earlier, the various characteristics of each single process are apt to be functions of a large number of task and individual variables. It is easy to see that, if one were to construct a giant matrix with the individual processes strung out along one axis and these modulating variables along the other, the task of putting mean ages and other relevant data into each of the cells would take several millennia.

But there is a less time-consuming (and much more interesting) way to catch hold of some of the developmental reality at the process level. It would be far more practical to follow a kind of idiographic, case-study method, in which one would look for the expression and exemplification of *general* developmental principles and causal relationships in a few carefully-selected *individual* processes. The research question now becomes: what are the general sorts of things which are likely to happen in any development, as adduced by a very intensive study of what happens in a few, test-case processes? The "very intensive study" we envisage would have to be essentially longitudinal, although cross-sectional investigations might also be appended to it. Also, the processes selected for study would have to have a measure of developmental richness, that is, a reasonable number of isolable stages in the acquisition sequence; and

Piaget's accomplishments, more than anyone else's, make it possible to find good candidates here. The research questions asked would include the more banal antecedent-consequent ones (e.g., whether, and how strongly, age of final-stage acquisition is dependent upon IQ), but they would also include some of the more esoteric and interesting ones which a sophisticated developmental psychology ought to ask.

A few examples of such questions, some of which were mentioned earlier, follow here. Do the various task and individual independent variables affect the number, nature, and sequence of stages as well as their chronological timing? And if there is individual variation, of whatever cause, in the number, nature, and sequence of stages, is this variation associated in turn with other important process variables: for instance, the age at which the final stage is reached; the stability and generalizability of the final-stage strategy; the accessibility of the earlier stages under regression-inducing conditions, once the final stage is achieved; and the internal structure and timing of other, synchronous or later sequences? Finally, what about the possible effects of various training methods on the process in question, these effects hypothesized as consequents of some of the afore-mentioned variables and antecedents of others?

All this is, of course, a very tall order, a research prescription much easier to write than to fill. But it is important even to write it, because it shows that one can be utterly realistic about the web of causal complexity in which developmental processes are stuck and yet not despair of doing theoretically meaningful, stage-oriented studies of these processes. There is no good reason to think that the essential parameters, the basic causal texture, of one ontogenetic process differs markedly from that of others. Here, as elsewhere in science, one ought to be able to extract important generalities from carefully studied particulars.

But if developmental processes are important objects of study, so also are the children in whom the processes run their course. Children are more than mere incidental vehicles of scientifically interesting acquisitional processes; among other things, they also comprise culturally important objects about which developmental psychologists should be able to make useful age-normative statements. We should like, for example, to be able to say that the "average" child of ten (with the meaning of "average" appropriately specified) will probably show such and such an over-all cognitive "state," as defined in terms of a kind of embryological slice through the totality of his ongoing cognitive-developmental processes. But in view of all we have been saying about the number of processes and the multiform sources of variance associated with each process, can age-normative state descriptions really have any clear meaning? Can we do other than confuse and mislead by speaking of whole age groups of whole organisms as "being in a certain stage," just as we speak of a certain "stage" in the unfolding of an isolated organismic process? Once again, there is no possibility of doing everything but a distinct possibility of doing something, and doing what little can be done more intelligently and planfully than has generally been the case.

The general procedure we have in mind can best be described in the context of a specific research problem. Suppose the aim were to make age-normative assertions about cognitive states in connection with Piaget's concrete-operational acquisitions. The general research strategy would be to vary certain things while attempting to keep others rigidly constant. An initial task would be to select a sample of processes or process groups. This could include a smaller or larger number of what we earlier spoke of as the key tactics of this period, i.e., the ability to make transitive inferences, to iterate units as a measuring operation, and so on. The next step would be to draw samples of children from each of the age levels likely to be relevant to these processes. Since the orientation is age-normative, we would be inclined to draw from the modes of the population distributions of those characteristics likely to be especially pertinent to the processes. Thus, the groups might consist of children of more or less modal psychological, social, and educational adjustment, of about average intelligence, of perhaps lower middle-class, urban background, and so on. Moreover, the children would all be as similar as possible with respect to these dimensions, both within and across groups; any subject variation other than age would be an encumbrance in this study. On the other hand, one would want to exploit rather than get rid of variation in the domain of functioning associated with each tactic studied. There appear to be at least two dimensions of particular interest here. One involves the ease-simplicity versus difficulty-complexity of the problem for which the tactic is a solution. The other involves the uncertainty-instability versus certainty-stability of the tactic itself as a solution to such problems from the standpoint of the subject.

Suppose one tried to work with both dimensions at once, and suppose one of the tactics to be studied were transitivity inference. The first step might be to follow Braine's (1959) lead and select the very simplest, easiest-to-solve problem one could find (perhaps a nonverbal one), the solution to which nonetheless seems to require genuine transitive inference. The extreme lower end of the combined dimensions would then be defined as occasional and tentative transitive inference in a very simple task which readily calls forth such inference. For the extreme upper end, the problem to be solved by transitivity inference would be more complex in structure and its terms would undoubtedly be arbitrary symbols rather than real entities. And here, unlike the preceding case, the subject would be counted as "having" transitivity only if he gave evidence of regarding this kind of reasoning as yielding absolutely certain and valid conclusions, not to be doubted under any circumstances. For example, one might rig the experiment so that the child's transitivity inference was subjected to group or authority-figure counterpressure, as in the Asch studies (Asch, 1956); only if the counterpressure did not sway him from his inferential procedure could he be counted in the plus column by this severest of tests. Finally, one might want to construct a third test to sample the middle of the combined distribution, e.g., a transitivity problem of middling difficulty and complexity with the child's transitive inference required to be only moderately stable and extinction-resistant. The assumed end point and mid-point of the combined dimensions in the case of tactics other than transitivity could be translated into tests by the same general procedure, and these tests would also be given to the same groups of subjects.

Once the data of such a study were properly analyzed, the experimenter would be in position to make some reasonably clear and unequivocal statements of the age-normative variety. Having been aware from the outset that any cognitive operation virtually always defines a range rather than a point of functioning (i.e., is strongly and complexly task-dependent), he expressly would have tried to sample this range in this study. Having sampled it, and, having also taken great pains in subject selection, he could now make statements such as: for the "average" child in this culture, tactic A makes its first, unstable, and tentative appearance around age four, is solidly embedded in the cognitive bedrock by about thirteen, and is a serviceable if not thoroughly stable and extinction-resistant intellectual instrument for many tasks by age nine or thereabouts. Once the whole set of tactic ranges investigated was summarized in a single table, the researcher could go on to give rough descriptions of the over-all cognitive stages (here stages in the person rather than in the process sense) associated with a particular age or age group. This could be done simply by making a vertical cut through the entire set of tactic ranges at a given chronological point or interval and making an interpretative "reading" of the cut. Needless to say, the same general research procedure and method of data analysis could be used to make normative statements about other than "average" or "modal" children.

It has been our intention here not so much to dwell upon the merits of a particular method as to convey a general attitude and approach regarding the age-normative study of intellectual development. Intellectual development is a multidetermined affair and there is no blinking the fact. This does not mean that age-normative statements in this area cannot be made, but it certainly means that one must face up to and deal with the multidetermination on the way toward making them. Carefully arrived at and carefully framed statements of this genre can be useful predictive statements about cognitive state attributes and associated behavior in individual children. And thanks to Piaget's efforts, there are now available some highly interesting state attributes and behaviors to make predictions about.

Bibliography

Abelson, R. P., & Rosenberg, M. J. Symbolic psycho-logic: a model of attitudinal cognition. *Behav. Sci.,* 1958, 3, 1-13.

Aebli, H. *Didactique psychologique: application à la didactique de la psychologie de Jean Piaget.* Neuchâtel: Delachaux et Niestlé, 1951.

Annett, M. The classification of instances of four common class concepts by children and adults. *Brit. J. educ. Psychol.,* 1959, 29, 223-236.

Anthony, E. J. The significance of Jean Piaget for child psychiatry. *Brit. J. med. Psychol.,* 1956, 29, 20-34. (a)

Anthony, E. J. Six applications de la théorie génétique de Piaget à la théorie et à la pratique psychodynamique. *Rev. Suisse Psychol.,* 1956, 15, 269-277. (b)

Anthony, E. J. The system makers: Piaget and Freud. *Brit. J. med. Psychol.,* 1957, 30, 255-269.

Apostel, L., Jonckheere, A. R., & Matalon, B. Logique, apprentissage et probabilité. *Etudes d'épistémologie génétique.* Vol. 8. Paris: Presses Univer. France, 1959.

Apostel, L., Mandelbrot, B., & Morf, A. Logique, langage et théorie de l'information. *Etudes d'épistémologie génétique.* Vol. 3. Paris: Presses Univer. France, 1957.

Apostel, L., Mandelbrot, B., & Piaget, J. Logique et équilibre. *Etudes d'épistémologie génétique.* Vol. 2. Paris: Presses Univer. France, 1957.

Apostel, L., Mays, W., Morf, A., & Piaget, J. Les liaisons analytiques et synthétiques dans les comportements du sujet. *Etudes d'épistémologie génétique.* Vol. 4. Paris: Presses Univer. France, 1957.

Asch, S. E. Studies of independence and conformity: I. A minority of one against a unanimous majority. *Psychol. Monogr.,* 1956, 70, No. 9 (Whole No. 416).

Baldwin, J. M. *Mental development in the child and the race.* London: Macmillan, 1925.

Barker, R. G., & Wright, H. F. *One boy's day.* New York: Harper, 1951.

Barker, R. G. & Wright, H. F. *Midwest and its children.* New York: Row, Peterson, 1955.

Beilin, H., & Franklin, I. Logical operations in length and area measurement: age and training effects. Paper read at Soc. Res. Child Develpm., Pennsylvania State Univer., 1961.

Bell, C. R. Additional data on animistic thinking. *Scient. mon.,* 1954, 79, 67-69.

Berko, J., & Brown, R. Psycholinguistic research methods. In P. H. Mussen (Ed.), *Handbook of research methods in child development.* New York: Wiley, 1960. Pp. 517-557.

Berlyne, D. E. Les équivalences psychologiques et les notions quantitatives.

In D. E. Berlyne & J. Piaget, Théorie du comportement et opérations. *Études d'épistémologie génétique.* Vol. 12. Paris: Presses Univer. France, 1960. Pp. 1-76. (a)

Berlyne, D. E. *Conflict, arousal, and curiosity.* New York: McGraw-Hill, 1960. (b)

Beth, W. E., Mays, W., & Piaget, J. Epistémologie génétique et recherche psychologique. *Etudes d'épistémologie génétique.* Vol. I. Paris: Presses Univer. France, 1957.

Bibace, R. R. A comparative study of the cognition of magnitude. Unpublished doctoral dissertation, Clark Univer., 1956.

Bloom, L. A reappraisal of Piaget's theory of moral judgment. *J. genet. Psychol.,* 1959, 95, 3-12.

Boehm, L. The development of independence: a comparative study. *Child Develpm.,* 1957, 28, 85-93.

Borelli, M. La naissance des opérations logiques chez le sourd-muet. *Enfance,* 1951, 4, 222-228.

Braine, M. S. The ontogeny of certain logical operations: Piaget's formulation examined by nonverbal methods. *Psychol. Monogr.,* 1959, 73, No. 5 (Whole No. 475).

Braine, M. S. Problems and issues in the study of conceptual development. Paper read at SSRC Conference, Dedham, Mass., April, 1960.

Bruner, J. S. Inhelder and Piaget's *The growth of logical thinking.* I. A psychologist's viewpoint. *Brit. J. Psychol.,* 1959, 50, 363-370.

Bruner, J. S. *The process of education.* Cambridge, Mass.: Harvard Univer. Press, 1960.

Bruner, J. S., Bresson, F., Morf, A., & Piaget, J. Logique et perception. *Etudes d'épistémologie génétique.* Vol. 6. Paris: Presses Univer. France, 1958.

Bruner, J. S., Goodnow, J. J., & Austin, G. A. *A Study of thinking.* New York: Wiley, 1956.

Bunge, M. Levels: a semantical preliminary. *Rev. Metaphysics,* 1960, 13, 396-406.

Carmichael, L. (Ed.) *Manual of child psychology.* (2nd ed.) New York: Wiley, 1954.

Carpenter, T. E. A pilot study for a quantitative investigation of Jean Piaget's original work on concept-formation. *Educ. Rev.,* 1955, 7, 142-149.

Churchill, E. The number concepts of the young child: Part 1. *Researches and Studies.* Leeds Univer., 1958, 17. 34-39. (a)

Churchill, E. The number concepts of the young child: Part 2. *Researches and Studies.* Leeds Univer., 1958, 18, 28-46. (b)

Cohen, J. *Chance, skill, and luck: the psychology of guessing and gambling.* Baltimore: Penguin, 1960.

Cohen, J., & Hansel, C. E. M. *Risk and gambling.* New York: Philosophical Library, 1956.

Crannell, C. W. The responses of college students to a questionnaire on animistic thinking. *Scient. mon.,* 1954, 78, 54-56.

Cuisenaire, G., & Gattegno, C. *Numbers in colour: a new method of teaching the processes of arithmetic to all levels of the primary school.* (2nd ed.) London: Heinemann, 1955.

Curti, M. W. *Child psychology.* (2nd ed.) New York: Longmans, 1938.

Danziger, K. The child's understanding of kinship terms: a study in the development of relational concepts. *J. genet. Psychol.,* 1957, 91, 213-232.

Dennis, W. Animistic thinking among college and university students. *Scient. mon.,* 1953, 76, 247-250.

Dennis, W. Animistic thinking among college and high school students in the Near East. *J. educ. Psychol.,* 1957, 48, 193-198.

Dennis, W., & Mallinger, B. Animism and related tendencies in senescence. *J. Geront.*, 1949, 4, 218-221.

Deutsche, J. M. *The development of children's concepts of causal relations.* Minneapolis: Univer. of Minnesota Press, 1937.

Dodwell, P. C. The spatial concepts of the child. *Math. teach.*, 1959, 9, 5-14.

Dodwell, P. C. Children's understanding of number and related concepts. *Canad. J. Psychol.*, 1960, 14, 191-205.

Dodwell, P. C. Children's understanding of number concepts: characteristics of an individual and of a group test. *Canad. J. Psychol.*, 1961, 15, 29-36.

Donaldson, M. Review of: Piaget, J., & Inhelder, B. *La genèse des structures logiques élémentaires: classifications et sériations,* in *Brit. J. Psychol.*, 1960, 51, 181-184.

Durkin, D. Children's concept of justice: a comparison with the Piaget data. *Child Develpm.*, 1959, 30, 59-68. (a)

Durkin, D. Children's acceptance of reciprocity as a justice-principle. *Child Develpm.*, 1959, 30, 289-296. (b)

Durkin, D. The specificity of children's moral judgments. *J. genet. Psychol.*, 1961, 98, 3-14.

Elkind, D. Quantity conceptions in junior and senior high school students. *Child Develpm.*, 1961, 32, 551-560. (a)

Elkind, D. The development of quantitative thinking: a systematic replication of Piaget's studies. *J. genet. Psychol.*, 1961, 98, 37-46. (b)

Elkind, D. Children's discovery of the conservation of mass, weight, and volume: Piaget Replication Study II. *J. genet. Psychol.*, 1961, 98, 219-227. (c)

Erikson, E. H. Identity and the life cycle. *Psychol. Issues,* Vol. 1, No. 1, Monogr. 1, 1959.

Ervin, S. M. Training and a logical operation by children. *Child Develpm.*, 1960, 31, 555-564. (a)

Ervin, S. M. Experimental procedures of children. *Child Develpm.*, 1960, 31, 703-719. (b)

Estes, B. W. Some mathematical and logical concepts in children. *J. genet. Psychol.*, 1956, 88, 219-222.

Feffer, M. H. The cognitive implications of role taking behavior. *J. Pers.*, 1959, 27, 152-168.

Feffer, M. H., & Gourevitch, V. Cognitive aspects of role-taking in children. *J. Pers.*, 1960, 28, 383-396.

Feigenbaum, K. D. An evaluation of Piaget's study of the child's development of the concept of conservation of discontinuous quantities. Paper read at Amer. Psychol. Ass., New York, 1961.

Feller, Y., McNear, E., & Noelting, G. A propos des estimations de la vitesse chez l'enfant de cinq ans. *Enfance,* 1957, 10, 1-8.

Festinger, L. *A theory of cognitive dissonance.* Evanston, Ill.: Row, Peterson, 1957.

Fischer, H. Analyse psychologique du calcul scolaire et du facteur g en cinquième année primaire. *Cah. Pédag. exp. Psychol. Enfant,* 1955, No. 13 (New Series). 28 pp.

Flavell, J. H. The ontogenetic development of verbal communication skills. Final Progress Report (NIMH Grant M-2268), 1961.

Fraisse, P., Ehrlich, S., & Vurpillot, E. Recherches sur le développement des perceptions. XXVI. Etudes de la centration perceptive par la méthode tachistoscopique. *Arch. Psychol., Genève,* 1955-1956, 35, 193-214.

Fraisse, P., & Vautrey, P. La perception de l'espace, de la vitesse et du temps chez l'enfant de cinq ans. *Enfance,* 1952, 5, 1-20, 102-119.

450 BIBLIOGRAPHY

Freeman, T., & McGhie, A. The relevance of genetic psychology for the psychopathology of schizophrenia. *Brit. J. med. Psychol.*, 1957, 30, 176-187.

Fry, C. L. The effects of training in communication and role perception on the communicative abilities of children. Unpublished doctoral dissertation, Univer. of Rochester, 1961.

Gantenbein, M. Recherches sur le développement des perceptions. XIV. Recherche sur le développement de la perception du mouvement avec l'age. *Arch. Psychol., Genève,* 1950-1952, 33, 197-294.

Ghoneim, S. Recherches sur le développement des perceptions. XXXVII. Les déformations perceptives du losange de l'enfant à l'adulte. *Arch. Psychol., Genève,* 1959-1960, 37, 1-99.

Gollin, E. S. Organizational characteristics of social judgment: a developmental investigation. *J. Pers.,* 1958, 26, 139-154.

Gonseth, F., & Piaget, J. Groupements, groupes et lattices. *Arch. Psychol., Genève,* 1946, 31, 65-73.

Goodnow, J. J. A test for milieu effects with some of Piaget's tasks. Paper read at East. Psychol. Assoc., Atlantic City, April, 1962.

Goustard, M. Etude psychogénétique de la résolution d'un problème (Labyrinthe en T). In M. Goustard, P. Gréco, B. Matalon, & J. Piaget, La logique des apprentissages. *Etudes d'épistémologie génétique.* Vol. 10. Paris: Presses Univer. France, 1959. Pp. 93-112.

Goustard, M., Gréco, P., Matalon, B., & Piaget, J. La logique des apprentissages. *Etudes d'épistémologie génétique.* Vol. 10. Paris: Presses Univer. France, 1959.

Gratch, G. The development of the expectation of the nonindependence of random events in children. *Child Develpm.,* 1959, 30, 217-227.

Gréco, P. Les relations entre la perception et l'intelligence dans le développement de l'enfant: le facteur d'équilibre dans les conservations óperatoires et les constances perceptives. *Bull. Psychol., Paris,* 1956-1957, 10, 751-765, 833-843.

Gréco, P. L'apprentissage dans une situation à structure opératoire concrète: les inversions successives de l'ordre lineaire par des rotations de 180°. In P. Gréco & J. Piaget, Apprentissage et connaissance. *Etudes d'épistémologie génétique.* Vol. 7. Paris: Presses Univer. France, 1959. Pp. 68-182. (a)

Gréco, P. Induction, déduction et apprentissage. In M. Goustard, P. Gréco, B. Matalon, & J. Piaget, La logique des apprentissages. *Etudes d'épistémologie génétique.* Vol. 10. Paris: Presses Univer. France, 1959. Pp. 3-59. (b)

Gréco, P., Grize, J. B., Papert, S., & Piaget, J. Problèmes de la construction du nombre. *Etudes d'épistémologie génétique.* Vol. 11. Paris: Presses Univer. France, 1960.

Gréco, P., & Piaget, J. Apprentissage et connaissance. *Etudes d'épistémologie génétique.* Vol. 7. Paris: Presses Univer. France, 1959.

Harker, W. H. Children's number concepts: ordination and cardination. Unpublished M.A. thesis, 1960. Douglas Library, Queen's Univer., Kingston, Ont.

Harlow, H. F. Mice, monkeys, men, and motives. *Psychol. Rev.,* 1953, 60, 23-32.

Harvard University. Annual report of *The Center for Cognitive Studies,* 1961.

Hazlitt, V. Children's thinking. *Brit. J. Psychol.,* 1930, 20, 354-361.

Hazlitt, V. Modern trends in child psychology. *Brit. J. educ. Psychol.,* 1931, 1, 119-129.

Heider, F. *The psychology of interpersonal relationships.* New York: Wiley, 1958.

Honkavaara, S. The "dynamic-affective" phase in the development of concepts. *J. Psychol.,* 1958, 45, 11-23.

Huang, I. Children's conception of physical causality: a critical summary. *J. genet. Psychol.,* 1943, 63, 71-121.

Humphrey, G. *Thinking: an introduction to its experimental psychology*. London: Methuen, 1951.

Hyde, D. M. An investigation of Piaget's theories of the development of the concept of number. Unpublished doctoral dissertation, Univer. of London, 1959.

Inhelder, B. Observations sur le principe de conservation dans la physique de l'enfant. *Cah. Pédag. exp. Psychol. Enfant*, 1936, No. 9. 16 pp.

Inhelder, B. *Le diagnostic du raisonnement chez les débiles mentaux*. Neuchâtel: Delachaux et Niestlé, 1944.

Inhelder, B. Le raisonnement expérimental de l'adolescent. *Proc. 13th int. Congr. Psychol.*, 1951, 153-154.

Inhelder, B. Les attitudes expérimentales de l'enfant et de l'adolescent. *Bull. Psychol.*, Paris, 1953-1954, 7, 272-282.

Inhelder, B. Patterns of inductive thinking. *Proc. 14th int. Congr. Psychol.*, 1954, 217-218.

Inhelder, B. De la configuration perceptive à la structure opératoire. In P. Osterrieth et al., *Le problème des stades en psychologie de l'enfant*. Paris: Presses Univer. France, 1955. Pp. 137-162.

Inhelder, B. De la configuration perceptive à la structure opératoire. *Bull. Psychol.*, Paris, 1955-1956, 9, 6-19.

Inhelder, B. Die affektive und kognitive Entwicklung des Kindes. *Rev. Suisse Psychol.*, 1956, 15, 251-268.

Inhelder, B., & Noelting, G. Le passage d'un stade au suivant dans le développement des fonctions cognitives. *Proc. 15th int. Congr. Psychol.*, 1957, 435-438.

Inhelder, B., & Piaget, J. *The growth of logical thinking from childhood to adolescence*. New York: Basic Books, 1958.

Isaacs, N. About "The Child's Conception of Number" by Jean Piaget. In National Froebel Foundation, *Some aspects of Piaget's work*. London: National Froebel Foundation, 1955. Pp. 23-32. (a)

Isaacs, N. Piaget's work and progressive education. In National Froebel Foundation, *Some aspects of Piaget's work*. London: National Froebel Foundation, 1955. Pp. 32-45. (b)

Isaacs, S. Critical notes; the child's conception of the world, by J. Piaget. *Mind*, 1929, 38, 506-513.

Isaacs, S. *Intellectual growth in young children*. New York: Harcourt, Brace, 1930.

Jersild, A. T. *Child psychology*. (4th ed.) New York: Prentice-Hall, 1954.

Jersild, A. T. *The psychology of adolescence*. New York: Macmillan, 1957.

Johnson, D. M. *The psychology of thought and judgment*. New York: Harper, 1955.

Johnson, R. C. A study of the reliability of test items dealing with Piaget's concept of moral judgment. Paper read at West. Psychol. Ass., Monterey, 1958.

Johnson, R. C. A study of children's moral judgments. Unpublished doctoral dissertation, Univer. of Minnesota, 1959.

Jonckheere, A., Mandelbrot, B., & Piaget, J. La lecture de l'expérience. *Etudes d'épistémologie génétique*. Vol. 5. Paris: Presses Univer. France, 1958.

Keats, J. A. Formal and concrete thought processes. Princeton: Dept. Psychol., Princeton Univer., 1955 (Tech. Rep., Contract N6onr-270-20).

Kelly, G. A. *The psychology of personal constructs*. Vol. 1. *A theory of personality*. New York: Norton, 1955.

Kessen, W. "Stage" and "structure" in the study of children. Paper read at SSRC Conference, Dedham, Mass., April, 1960.

King, W. H. Symposium: studies of children's scientific concepts and interests.

I. The development of scientific concepts in children. *Brit. J. educ. Psychol.*, 1961, 31, 1-20.

Kligensmith, S. W. Child animism: what the child means by "alive." *Child Develpm.*, 1953, 24, 51-61.

Klingberg, G. The distinction between living and not living among 7-10-year-old children, with some remarks concerning the so-called animism controversy. *J. genet. Psychol.*, 1957, 90, 227-238.

Koch, S. (Ed.) *Psychology: a study of a science.* Vol. 3. *Formulations of the person and the social context.* New York: McGraw-Hill, 1959.

Koffka, K. *The growth of the mind.* New York: Harcourt Brace, 1928.

Kohlberg, L. Development of moral judgment and of the sense of justice in the years 10 to 16. Paper read at Amer. Psychol. Ass., Washington, D.C., 1958.

Krafft, H., & Piaget, J. La notion de l'ordre des événements et le test des images en désordre. *Arch. Psychol., Genève*, 1926, 19, 306-349.

Lambercier, M. Recherches sur le développement des perceptions. VI. La constance des grandeurs en comparaisons sériales. *Arch. Psychol., Genève*, 1946, 31, 79-282. (a)

Lambercier, M. Recherches sur le développement des perceptions. VII. La configuration en profondeur dans la constance des grandeurs. *Arch. Psychol., Genève*, 1946, 31, 287-324. (b)

Lewis, M. M. *Infant speech: a study of the beginnings of language.* (2nd ed.) New York: Humanities, 1951.

Liu, C. H. The influence of cultural background on the moral judgment of the child. Unpublished doctoral dissertation, Columbia Univer., 1950.

Lovell, K. A follow-up study of some aspects of the work of Piaget and Inhelder on the child's conception of space. *Brit. J. educ. Psychol.*, 1959, 29, 104-117.

Lovell, K. *The growth of basic mathematical and scientific concepts in children.* London: Univer. London Press, 1961.

Lovell, K., & Ogilvie, E. A study of the concept of conservation of substance in the junior school child. *Brit. J. educ. Psychol.*, 1960, 30, 109-118.

Lovell, K., & Ogilvie, E. The growth of the concept of volume in junior school children. *J. child Psychol. Psychiat.*, 1961, 2, 118-126.

Lovell, K., & Slater, A. The growth of the concept of time: a comparative study. *J. child Psychol. Psychiat.*, 1960, 1, 179-190.

Lunzer, E. A. "A pilot study for a quantitative investigation of Jean Piaget's original work on concept formation": a footnote. *Educ. Rev.*, 1956, 8, 193-200.

Lunzer, E. A. *Recent studies in Britain based on the work of Jean Piaget.* London: Nat. Found. Educ. Res. England Wales, 1960. (a)

Lunzer, E. A. Some points of Piagetian theory in the light of experimental criticism. *J. child Psychol. Psychiat.*, 1960, 1, 191-202. (b)

Luria, A. R. The directive function of speech in development and dissolution: I. Development of the directive function of speech in early childhood. *Word*, 1959, 15, 341-352.

MacRae, D. A test of Piaget's theories of moral development. *J. abnorm. soc. Psychol.*, 1954, 49, 14-48.

Mandelbrot, B. Sur la définition abstraite de quelques degrés de l'équilibre. In L. Apostel, B. Mandelbrot, & J. Piaget, Logique et équilibre. *Etudes d'épistémologie génétique.* Vol. 2. Paris: Presses Univer. France, 1957. Pp. 1-26. (a)

Mandelbrot, B. Linguistique statistique macroscopique. In L. Apostel, B. Mandelbrot, & A. Morf, Logique, langage et théorie de l'information. *Etudes d'épistémologie génétique.* Vol. 3. Paris: Presses Univer. France, 1957, Pp. 1-78. (b)

Margairaz, E., & Piaget, J. La structure des récits et l'interprétation des images de Dawid chez l'enfant. *Arch. Psychol., Genève*, 1925, 19, 211-239.

Maslow, A. H. *Motivation and personality.* New York: Harper, 1954.

Matalon, B. Apprentissages en situations aléatoires et systématiques. In M. Goustard, P. Gréco, B. Matalon, & J. Piaget, La logique des apprentissages. *Etudes d'épistémologie génétique.* Vol. 10. Paris: Presses Univer. France, 1959. Pp. 61-91.

Mays, W. The epistemology of Professor Piaget. *Proc. Aristotelian Soc.,* 1953-1954, 54, 49-76.

McCarthy, D. Language development in children. In L. Carmichael (Ed.), *Manual of child psychology.* (2nd ed.) New York: Wiley, 1954. Pp. 492-630.

Medinnus, G. R. Immanent justice in children: a review of the literature and additional data. *J. genet. Psychol.,* 1959, 94, 253-262.

Messick, S. J., & Solley, C. M. Probability learning in children: some exploratory studies. *J. genet. Psychol.,* 1957, 90, 23-32.

Meyer, E. La représentation des relations spatiales chez l'enfant. *Cah. Pédag. exp. Psychol. Enfant,* 1935, No. 8. 16 pp.

Meyer, E. Comprehension of spatial relationships in preschool children. *J. genet. Psychol.,* 1940, 57, 119-151.

Miller, G. A., Galanter, E., & Pribram, K. *Plans and the structure of behavior.* New York: Holt, 1960.

Mogar, M. Children's causal reasoning about natural phenomena. *Child Develpm.,* 1960, 31, 59-65.

Morf, A. Les relations entre la logique et le langage lors du passage du raisonnement concret au raisonnement formel. In L. Apostel, B. Mandelbrot, & A. Morf, Logique, langage, et théorie de l'information. *Etudes d'épistémologie génétique.* Vol. 3. Paris: Presses Univer. France, 1957. Pp. 173-204.

Morf, A. Apprentissage d'une structure logique concrète (inclusion): effets et limites. In A. Morf, J. Smedslund, Vinh-Bang, & J. F. Wohlwill, L'apprentissage des structures logiques. *Etudes d'épistémologie génétique.* Vol. 9. Paris: Presses Univer. France, 1959. Pp. 15-83.

Morf, A., Smedslund, J., Vinh-Bang, & Wohlwill, J. F. L'apprentissage des structures logique. *Etudes d'épistémologie génétique.* Vol. 9. Paris: Presses Univer. France, 1959.

Morris, J. F. The development of adolescent value-judgments. *Brit. J. educ. Psychol.,* 1958, 28, 1-14.

Murphy, G. *Personality: a biosocial approach to origins and structure.* New York: Harper, 1947.

Nass, M. L. The effects of three variables on children's concepts of physical causality. *J. abnorm. soc. Psychol.,* 1956, 53, 191-196.

National Froebel Foundation. *Some aspects of Piaget's work.* London: National Froebel Foundation, 1955.

Noelting, G. Introduction à l'étude génétique des interactions sociales chez l'enfant. *Rev. Suisse Psychol.,* 1956, 15, 34-50.

Oakes, M. E. Children's explanations of natural phenomena. *Teach. Coll. Contr. Educ.,* 1947, No. 926.

Odier, C. *Anxiety and magical thinking.* New York: Int. Univer. Press, 1956.

Osgood, C. E., Suci, G. J., & Tannenbaum, P. H. *The measurement of meaning.* Urbana, Ill.: Univer. Illinois Press, 1957.

Parsons, C. Inhelder and Piaget's *The growth of logical thinking:* II. A logician's viewpoint. *Brit. J. Psychol.,* 1960, 51, 75-84.

Peel, E. A. Experimental examination of some of Piaget's schemata concerning children's perception and thinking, and a discussion of their educational significance. *Brit. J. educ. Psychol.,* 1959, 29, 89-103.

Piaget, J. Une forme verbale de la comparaison chez l'enfant. *Arch. Psychol., Genève,* 1921, 18, 141-172. (a)

Piaget, J. Essai sur quelques aspects du développement de la notion de partie chez l'enfant. *J. Psychol. norm. path.,* 1921, 18, 449-480. (b)

Piaget, J. Essai sur la multiplication logique et les débuts de la pensée formelle chez l'enfant. *J. Psychol. norm. path.,* 1922, 19, 222-261.

Piaget, J. La pensée symbolique et la pensée de l'enfant. *Arch. Psychol., Genève,* 1923, 18, 273-304.

Piaget, J. Etude critique: "L'expérience humaine et la causalité physique" de L. Brunschvicg. *J. Psychol. norm. path.,* 1924, 21, 586-607. (a)

Piaget, J. Les traits principaux de la logique de l'enfant. *J. Psychol. norm. path.,* 1924, 21, 48-101. (b)

Piaget, J. De quelques formes primitives de causalité chez l'enfant. *L'année Psychol.,* 1925, 26, 31-71. (a)

Piaget, J. Psychologie et critique de la connaissance. *Arch. Psychol., Genève,* 1925, 19, 193-210. (b)

Piaget, J. *The language and thought of the child.* New York: Harcourt, Brace, 1926.

Piaget, J. La première année de l'enfant. *Brit. J. Psychol.,* 1927, 18, 97-120. (a)

Piaget, J. La causalité chez l'enfant. *Brit. J. Psychol.,* 1927, 18, 276-301. (b)

Piaget, J. L'éxplication de l'ombre chez l'enfant. *J. Psychol. norm. path.,* 1927, 24, 230-242. (c)

Piaget, J. Psycho-pédagogie et mentalité enfantine. *J. Psychol. norm. path.,* 1928, 25, 31-60. (a)

Piaget, J. *Judgment and reasoning in the child.* New York: Harcourt, Brace, 1928. (b)

Piaget, J. Les deux directions de la pensée scientifique. *Arch. Sci. phys. nat.,* 1929, 11, 145-162. (a)

Piaget, J. Le parallélisme entre la logique et la morale chez l'enfant. *Proc. 9th int. Congr. Psychol.,* 1929, 339-340. (b)

Piaget, J. *The child's conception of the world.* New York: Harcourt, Brace, 1929. (c)

Piaget, J. *The child's conception of physical causality.* London: Kegan Paul, 1930. (a)

Piaget, J. Le développement de l'esprit de solidarité chez l'enfant. In *Troisième cours pour le personnel enseignant.* Geneva: Bureau International d'Education, 1930. Pp. 52-55. (b)

Piaget, J. La notion de justice chez l'enfant. In *Troisième cours pour le personnel enseignant.* Geneva: Bureau International d'Education, 1930. Pp. 55-57. (c)

Piaget, J. Retrospective and prospective analysis in child psychology. *Brit. J. educ. Psychol.,* 1931, 1, 130-139. (a)

Piaget, J. Children's philosophies. In C. Murchison (Ed.), *Handbook of child Psychology.* Worcester, Mass.: Clark Univer. Press, 1931. Pp. 377-391. (b)

Piaget, J. Le développement intellectuel chez les jeunes enfants. *Mind,* 1931, 40, 137-160. (c)

Piaget, J. Introduction psychologique à l'éducation internationale. In *Quatrième cours pour le personnel enseignant.* Geneva: Bureau International d'Education, 1931. Pp. 56-68. (d)

Piaget, J. *The moral judgment of the child.* London: Kegan Paul, 1932.

Piaget, J. Remarques psychologiques sur le self-government. In *Le self-government à l'école.* Geneva: Bureau International d'Education, 1934. Pp. 89-108.

Piaget, J. Les théories de l'imitation. *Cah. Pédag. exp. Psychol. Enfant,* 1935, No. 6. Pp. 13. (a)

Piaget, J. Remarques psychologiques sur le travail par équipes. In *Le travail par équipes à l'école*. Geneva: Bureau International d'Education, 1935. Pp. 179-196. (b)

Piaget, J. Le problème de l'intelligence et de l'habitude: réflexe conditionné, "Gestalt" ou assimilation. *Proc. 11th int. Congr. Psychol.*, 1937, 170-183. (a)

Piaget, J. La réversibilité des operations et l'importance de la notion de "group" pour la psychologie de la pensée. *Proc. 11th int. Congr. Psychol.*, 1937, 433-434. (b)

Piaget, J. Remarques psychologiques sur les relations entre la classe logique et le nombre et sur les rapports d'inclusion. *Recueil travaux Univer. Lausanne*, 1937, 59-85. (c)

Piaget, J. Les relations d'égalité résultant de l'addition et de la soustraction logiques constituent-elles un groupe? *L'enseign. math.*, 1937, 36, 99-108. (d)

Piaget, J. Le mécanisme du développement mental et les lois du groupement des opérations. *Arch. Psychol., Genève*, 1941, 28, 215-285.

Piaget, J. *Classes, relations et nombres: essai sur les "groupements" de la logistique et la réversibilité de la pensée*. Paris: Vrin, 1942. (a)

Piaget, J. Les trois structures fondamentales de la vie psychiques: rythme, régulation et groupement. *Rev. Suisse Psychol.*, 1942, 1, 9-21. (b)

Piaget, J. Une expérience sur le développement de la notion de temps. *Rev. Suisse Psychol.*, 1942, 1, 179-185. (c)

Piaget, J. *Le développement de la notion de temps chez l'enfant*. Paris: Presses Univer. France, 1946. (a)

Piaget, J. *Les notions de mouvement et de vitesse chez l'enfant*. Paris: Presses Univer. France, 1946. (b)

Piaget, J. Du rapport des sciences avec la philosophie. *Synthese*, 1947, 6, 130-150.

Piaget, J. *Traité de logique*. Paris: Colin, 1949. (a)

Piaget, J. Le problème neurologique de l'intériorization des actions en opérations réversibles. *Arch. Psychol., Genève*, 1949, 32, 241-258. (b)

Piaget, J. L'utilité de la logistique en psychologie. *L'année Psychol.*, 1949, 50, 27-38. (c)

Piaget, J. *The psychology of intelligence*. New York: Harcourt, Brace, 1950. (a)

Piaget, J. *Introduction à l'épistémologie génétique*. Paris: Presses Univer. France, 1950. 3 vols. (b)

Piaget, J. Une expérience sur la psychologie du hasard chez l'enfant: le tirage au sort des couples. *Acta psychol., Amsterdam*, 1950, 7, 323-336. (c)

Piaget, J. *Play, dreams and imitation in childhood*. New York: Norton, 1951. (a)

Piaget, J. The right to education in the modern world. In UNESCO, *Freedom and culture*. New York: Columbia Univer. Press, 1951. Pp. 67-116. (b)

Piaget, J. Contribution à la théorie générale des structures. *Proc. 13th int. Congr. Psychol.*, 1951, 197-198. (c)

Piaget, J. Pensée egocentrique et pensée sociocentrique. *Cah. int. Sociol.*, 1951, 10, 34-49. (d)

Piaget, J. *Essai sur les transformations des opérations logiques*. Paris: Presses Univer. France, 1952. (a)

Piaget, J. *The child's conception of number*. New York: Humanities, 1952. (b)

Piaget, J. *The origins of intelligence in children*. New York: Int. Univer. Press, 1952. (c)

Piaget, J. Autobiography. In E. G. Boring, et al., *History of psychology in autobiography*. Vol. 4. Worcester, Mass.: Clark Univer. Press, 1952. Pp. 237-256. (d)

Piaget, J. La logistique axiomatique ou "pure," la logistique opératoire ou psychologique, et les réalités auxquelles elles correspondent. *Methodos,* 1952, 4, 72-84. (e)

Piaget, J. De la psychologie génétique à l'épistémologie. *Diogène,* 1952, 1, 38-54. (f)

Piaget, J. Understanding and verbal explanation between young children of the same age. In G. E. Swanson, T. M. Newcomb, & E. L. Hartley (Eds.), *Readings in social psychology.* New York: Holt, 1952. Pp. 54-66. (g)

Piaget, J. Quelques illusions geométriques renversées. *Rev. Suisse Psychol.,* 1952, 11, 19-25. (h)

Piaget, J. How children form mathematical concepts. *Sci. Amer.,* 1953, 189 (5), 74-79. (a)

Piaget, J. Structures opérationnelles et cybernétique. *L'année Psychol.,* 1953, 53, 379-390. (b)

Piaget, J. Genetic psychology and epistemology. *Diogenes,* 1953, 1, 49-63. (c)

Piaget, J. Les relations entre l'intelligence et l'affectivité dans le developpement de l'enfant. *Bull. Psychol., Paris,* 1953-1954, 7, 143-150, 346-361, 522-535, 699-701. (a)

Piaget, J. La période des operations formelles et le passage de la logique de l'enfant à celle de l'adolescent. *Bull. Psychol., Paris,* 1953-1954, 7, 247-253. (b)

Piaget, J. *The construction of reality in the child.* New York: Basic Books, 1954. (a)

Piaget, J. Perceptual and cognitive (or operational) structures in the development of the concept of space in the child. *Proc. 14th int. Congr. Psychol.,* 1954, 41-46. (b)

Piaget, J. The problem of consciousness in child psychology: developmental changes in awareness. In *Conference on problems of consciousness.* New York: Josiah Macy Foundation, 1954. Pp. 136-137. (c)

Piaget, J. Ce qui subsiste de la théorie de la Gestalt dans la psychologie contemporaine de l'intelligence et de la perception. *Rev. Suisse Psychol.,* 1954, 13, 72-83. (d)

Piaget, J. Le langage et la pensée du point de vue génétique. *Acta psychol., Amsterdam,* 1954, 10, 51-60. (e)

Piaget, J. Le développement de la perception de l'enfant à l'adulte. *Bull. Psychol., Paris,* 1954-1955, 8, 183-188, 489-492, 553-563, 643-671.

Piaget, J. Ce qui subsiste de la théorie de la Gestalt dans la psychologie contemporaine de l'intelligence et de la perception. In J. de Ajuriaguerra, et al., *Aktuelle Probleme der Gestalttheorie.* Bern: Hans Huber, 1955. Pp. 72-83. (a)

Piaget, J. Perceptual and cognitive (or operational) structures in the development of the concept of space in the child. *Acta psychol., Amsterdam,* 1955, 11, 41-46. (b)

Piaget, J. The development of time concepts in the child. In P. H. Hoch & J. Zubin (Eds.), *Psychopathology of childhood.* New York: Grune and Stratton, 1955. Pp. 34-44. (c)

Piaget, J. Les stades du développement intellectuel de l'enfant et de l'adolescent. In P. Osterrieth et al., *Le problème des stades en psychologie de l'enfant.* Paris: Presses Univer. France, 1955. Pp. 33-113. (d)

Piaget, J. Rapport. In A. Michotte et al., *La perception.* Paris: Presses Univer. France, 1955. Pp. 2-30. (e)

Piaget, J. Recherches sur le développement des perceptions. XXII. Essai d'une nouvelle interprétation probabiliste des effets du contration de la loi de Weber et de celle des centrations relatives. *Arch. Psychol., Genève,* 1955-1956, 35, 1-24. (a)

Piaget, J. La formation des connaissances. *Bull. Psychol., Paris,* 1955-1956, 9, 148-156, 268-273, 483-495, 701-727. (b)

Piaget, J. La genèse du nombre chez l'enfant. In J. Piaget, B. Boscher, & A. Chatelet, *Initiation au calcul.* Paris: Bourrelier, 1956. Pp. 5-28.

Piaget, J. Les relations entre la perception et l'intelligence dans le développement de l'enfant. *Bull. Psychol., Paris,* 1956-1957, 10, 376-381, 751-760.

Piaget, J. *Logic and psychology.* New York: Basic Books, 1957. (a)

Piaget, J. Programme et méthodes de l'épistémologie génétique. In W. E. Beth, W. Mays, & J. Piaget, Epistémologie génétique et recherche psychologique. *Etudes d'épistémologie génétique.* Vol. 1. Paris: Presses Univer. France, 1957. Pp. 13-84. (b)

Piaget, J. Logique et équilibre dans les comportements du sujet. In L. Apostel, B. Mandelbrot, & J. Piaget, Logique et équilibre. *Etudes d'épistémologie génétique.* Vol. 2. Paris: Presses Univer. France, 1957. Pp. 27-117. (c)

Piaget, J. The child and modern physics. *Scient. Amer.,* 1957, 196 (3), 46-51. (d)

Piaget, J. Pourquoi la formation des notions ne s'explique jamais par la seule perception. *Proc. 15th int. Congr. Psychol.,* 1957, 314-316. (e)

Piaget, J. Le rôle de la notion d'équilibre dans l'explication en psychologie. *Proc. 15th int. Congr. Psychol.,* 1957, 51-62. (f)

Piaget, J. Les notions de vitesse, d'espace parcouru et de temps chez l'enfant de cinq ans. *Enfance,* 1957, 10, 9-42. (g)

Piaget, J. Les étapes du développement mental. *Bull. Psychol., Paris,* 1957-1958, 11, 217-219, 347-351, 438-440, 520-522, 678-685, 878-882.

Piaget, J. Assimilation et connaissance. In A. Jonckheere, B. Mandelbrot, & J. Piaget, La lecture de l'expérience. *Etudes d'épistémologie génétique.* Vol. 5. Paris: Presses Univer. France, 1958. Pp. 49-108. (a)

Piaget, J. Principal factors determining intellectual evolution from childhood to adult life. In E. L. Hartley & R. E. Hartley (Eds.), *Outside readings in psychology.* (2nd ed.) New York: Crowell, 1958. Pp. 43-55. (b)

Piaget, J. Introduction. In P. Gréco & J. Piaget. Apprentissage et connaissance. *Etudes d'épistémologie génétique.* Vol. 7. Paris: Presses Univer. France, 1959. Pp. 1-20. (a)

Piaget, J. Apprentissage et connaissance (première partie). In P. Gréco & J. Piaget, Apprentissage et connaissance. *Etudes d'épistémologie génétique.* Vol. 7. Paris: Presses Univer. France, 1959. Pp. 21-67. (b)

Piaget, J. Apprentissage et connaissance (seconde partie). In M. Goustard, P. Gréco, B. Matalon, & J. Piaget, La logique des apprentissages. *Etudes d'épistémologie génétique.* Vol. 10. Paris: Presses Univer. France, 1959. Pp. 159-188. (c)

Piaget, J. L'image mentale et la répresentation imagée chez l'enfant. *Bull. Psychol., Paris,* 1959, 12, 538-540, 574-576, 724-727, 806-807, 857-860. (d)

Piaget, J. Introduction. In P. Gréco, J. B. Grize, S. Papert, & J. Piaget, Problèmes de la construction du nombre. *Etudes d'épistémologie génétique.* Vol. 11. Paris: Presses Univer. France, 1960. Pp. 1-68. (a)

Piaget, J. La portée psychologique et épistémologique des essais néohulliens de D. Berlyne. In D. E. Berlyne & J. Piaget, Théorie du comportement et opérations. *Etudes d'épistémologie génétique.* Vol. 12. Paris: Presses Univer. France, 1960. Pp. 105-123. (b)

Piaget, J. *Les mécanismes perceptifs: modèles probabilistes, analyse génétique, relations avec l'intelligence.* Paris: Presses Univer. France, 1961.

Piaget, J., & Albertini, B. von. Recherches sur le développement des perceptions. XI. L'illusion de Müller-Lyer. *Arch. Psychol., Genève,* 1950-1952, 33, 1-48.

Piaget, J., Albertini, B. von, & Rossi, M. Recherches sur le développement des perceptions. IV. Essai d'interpretation probabiliste de la loi de Weber et de celle des centrations relatives. *Arch. Psychol., Genève,* 1944-1945, 30, 95-138.

Piaget, J. & Denis-Prinzhorn, M. Recherches sur le développement des perceptions. XVI. L'estimation perceptive des cotés du rectangle. *Arch. Psychol., Genève,* 1953-1954, 34, 109-131. (a)

Piaget, J., & Denis-Prinzhorn, M. Recherches sur le développement des perceptions. XXI. L'illusion des quadrilatères partiellement superposés chez l'enfant et chez l'adulte. *Arch. Psychol., Genève,* 1953-1954, 34, 289-321. (b)

Piaget, J., Feller, Y., & McNear, E. Recherches sur le développement des perceptions. XXXVI. Essai sur la perception des vitesses chez l'enfant et l'adulte. *Arch. Psychol., Genève,* 1957-1958, 36, 253-327.

Piaget, J., & Inhelder, B. *Le développement des quantités chez l'enfant.* Neuchâtel: Delachaux et Niestlé, 1941.

Piaget, J., & Inhelder, B. Expériences sur la construction projective de la ligne droite. *Cah. Pédag. exp. Psychol. Enfant,* 1945, No. 2 (New Series).

Piaget, J., & Inhelder, B. Le rôle des opérations dans le développement de l'intelligence. *Proc. 12th int. Congr. Psychol.,* 1948, 102-103.

Piaget, J., & Inhelder, B. *La genèse de l'idée de hasard chez l'enfant.* Paris: Presses Univer. France, 1951.

Piaget, J., & Inhelder, B. *The child's conception of space.* London: Routledge and Kegan Paul, 1956.

Piaget, J., & Inhelder, B. *La genèse des structures logiques élémentaires: classifications et sériations.* Neuchâtel: Delachaux et Niestlé, 1959.

Piaget, J., Inhelder, B., & Szeminska, A. *The child's conception of geometry.* New York: Basic Books, 1960.

Piaget, J., & Lambercier, M. Recherches sur le développement des perceptions. II. La comparaison visuelle des hauteurs à distances variables dans le plan fronto-parallèle. *Arch. Psychol., Genève,* 1942-1943, 29, 173-254. (a)

Piaget, J., & Lambercier, M. Recherches sur le développement des perceptions. III. Le problème de la comparaison visuelle en profondeur (constance de la grandeur) et l'erreur systématique de l'étalon. *Arch. Psychol., Genève,* 1942-1943, 29, 255-308. (b)

Piaget, J., & Lambercier, M. Recherches sur le développement des perceptions. V. Essai sur un effet d' "Einstellung" survenant au cours de perceptions visuelles successives (effet Usnadze). *Arch. Psychol., Genève,* 1944-1945, 30, 139-196.

Piaget, J., & Lambercier, M. Recherches sur le développement des perceptions. VIII. Transpositions perceptives et transitivité opératoire dans les comparaisons en profondeur. *Arch. Psychol., Genève,* 1946, 31, 325-368.

Piaget, J., & Lambercier, M. Recherches sur le développement des perceptions. XII. La comparaison des grandeurs projectives chez l'enfant et chez l'adulte. *Arch. Psychol., Genève,* 1950-1952, 33, 81-130. (a)

Piaget, J., & Lambercier, M. Recherches sur le développement des perceptions. XIII. La perception d'un carré animé d'un mouvement de circumduction (effet Auersperg et Buhrmester). *Arch. Psychol., Genève,* 1950-1952, 33, 131-195. (b)

Piaget, J., & Lambercier, M. Recherches sur le développement des perceptions. XV. La comparaison des différences de hauteur dans le plan fronto-parallèle. *Arch. Psychol., Genève,* 1953-1954, 34, 73-107.

Piaget, J., & Lambercier, M. Recherches sur le développement des perceptions. XXIX. Grandeurs projectives et grandeurs réeles avec étalon éloigné. *Arch. Psychol., Genève,* 1955-1956, 35, 257-280. (a)

Piaget, J., & Lambercier, M. Recherches sur le développement des perceptions. XXXI. Les comparaisons verticales à intervalles croissants. *Arch. Psychol., Genève,* 1955-1956, 35, 321-367. (b)

Piaget, J., & Lambercier, M. Recherches sur le développement des perceptions. XXXIII. La causalité perceptive visuelle chez l'enfant et chez l'adulte. *Arch. Psychol., Genève,* 1957-1958, 36, 77-201.

Piaget, J., Lambercier, M., Boesch, E., & Albertini, B. von. Recherches sur le développement des perceptions. I. Introduction à l'étude des perceptions chez l'enfant et analyse d'une illusion relative à la perception visuelle de cercles concentriques (Delboeuf). *Arch. Psychol., Genève,* 1942-1943, 29, 1-107.

Piaget, J., Maire, F. & Privat, F. Recherches sur le développement des perceptions. XVIII. La résistance des bonnes formes à l'illusion de Müller-Lyer. *Arch. Psychol., Genève,* 1953-1954, 34, 155-201.

Piaget, J., & Maroun, J. Recherches sur le développement des perceptions. XXXIV. La localisation des impressions d'impact dans la causalité perceptive tactilo-kinesthésique. *Arch. Psychol., Genève,* 1957-1958, 36, 202-235.

Piaget, J., & Morf, A. Recherches sur le développement des perceptions. XX. L'action des facteurs spatiaux et temporels de centration dans l'estimation visuelle des longueurs. *Arch. Psychol., Genève,* 1953-1954, 34, 243-288.

Piaget, J., & Morf, A. Recherches sur le développement des perceptions. XXIV. Note sur l'illusion des droites inclinées. *Arch. Psychol., Genève,* 1955-1956, 35, 65-76. (a)

Piaget, J., & Morf, A. Recherches sur le développement des perceptions. XXVIII. Note sur la comparaison de lignes perpendiculaires égales. *Arch. Psychol., Genève,* 1955-1956, 35, 233-255. (b)

Piaget, J., & Morf, A. Recherches sur le développement des perceptions. XXX. Les comparaisons verticales à faible intervalle. *Arch. Psychol., Genève,* 1955-1956, 35, 289-319. (c)

Piaget, J., & Morf, A. Les isomorphismes partiels entre les structures logiques et les structures perceptives. In J. S. Bruner, F. Bresson, A. Morf, & J. Piaget, Logique et perception. *Etudes d'épistémologie génétique.* Vol. 6. Paris: Presses Univer. France, 1958. Pp. 49-116. (a)

Piaget, J., & Morf, A. Les "préinferences" perceptives et leurs relations avec les schèmes sensori-moteurs et opératoires. In J. S. Bruner, F. Bresson, A. Morf, & J. Piaget, Logique et perception. *Etudes d'épistémologie génétique.* Vol. 6. Paris: Presses Univer. France, 1958. Pp. 117-155. (b)

Piaget, J., & Osterrieth, P. A. Recherches sur le développement des perceptions. XVII. L'évolution de l'illusion d'Oppel-Kundt en fonction de l'âge. *Arch. Psychol. Genève,* 1953-1954, 34, 1-38.

Piaget, J., & Pène, F. Recherches sur le développement des perceptions. XXV. Essai sur l'illusion de la médiane des angles en tant que mesure de l'illusion des angles. *Arch. Psychol., Genève,* 1955-1956, 35, 77-92.

Piaget, J., & Rossello, P. Note sur les types de description d'images chez l'enfant. *Arch. Psychol., Genève,* 1921, 18, 208-234.

Piaget, J., Rutschmann, J., & Matalon, B. Recherches sur le développement des perceptions. XXXVIII. Nouvelles mesures des effets de centration en présentation tachistoscopique. *Arch. Psychol., Genève,* 1959-1960, 37, 140-165.

Piaget, J., & Stettler-von-Albertini, B. Recherches sur le développement des perceptions. XIX. Observations sur la perception de bonnes formes chez l'enfant par actualization des lignes virtuelles. *Arch. Psychol., Genève,* 1953-1954, 34, 203-242.

Piaget, J., & Szeminska, A. Quelques expériences sur la conservation des quantités continues chez l'enfant. *J. Psychol. norm. path.,* 1939, 36, 36-65.

Piaget, J., & Taponier, S. Recherches sur le développement des perceptions. XXXII. L'estimation des longueurs de deux droites horizontales et parallèles à extrémités décalées. *Arch. Psychol., Genève,* 1955-1956, 35, 369-400.

Piaget, J., Vinh-Bang, & Matalon, B. Note on the law of the temporal maximum of some optico-geometric illusions. *Amer. J. Psychol.,* 1958, 71, 277-282.

Piaget, J., & Vurpillot, E. Recherches sur le développement des perceptions. XXVII. La surestimation de la courbure des arcs de circle. *Arch. Psychol., Genève,* 1955-1956, 35, 215-232.

Piaget, J., & Weiner, M. Recherches sur le développement des perceptions. XXXV. Quelques interférences entre la perception de la vitesse et la causalité perceptive. *Arch. Psychol. Genève,* 1957-1958, 36, 236-252.

Piaget, J., Würsten, H., & Johannot, L. Recherches sur le développement des perceptions. X. Les illusions relatives aux angles et a la longueur de leur côtés. *Arch. Psychol., Genève,* 1947-1949, 32, 281-307.

Pire, G. Notion du hasard et développement intellectuel. *Enfance,* 1958, 131-143.

Rapaport, D. *Organization and pathology of thought.* New York: Columbia Univer. Press, 1951.

Reichard, S., Schneider, M., & Rapaport, D. The development of concept formation in children. *Amer. J. Orthopsychiat.,* 1944, 14, 156-161.

Reiff, R., & Scheerer, M. *Memory and hypnotic age regression.* New York: Int. Univer. Press, 1959.

Rey, A., & Richelle, M. Recherches sur le développement des perceptions. XXIII. Contribution à l'étude de l'effect de sous-estimation des données périphériques dans la centration du regard. *Arch. Psychol., Genève,* 1955-1956, 35, 25-40.

Ross, B. M., & Levy, N. Patterned predictions of chance events by children and adults. *Psychol. Rep.,* 1958, 4, 87-126.

Russell, D. H. *Children's thinking.* Boston: Ginn, 1956.

Rutschmann, J. Note sur les aspects psycho-physiologiques de la "centration" au tachistoscope: l'effet topographique. *Arch. Psychol., Genève,* 1959-1960, 37, 166-179.

Siegel, S. Review off: Cohen, J. *Chance, skill, and luck: the psychology of guessing and gambling. Contemp. Psychol.,* 1961, 6, 274-275.

Siegel, S., & McMichael, J. Choice behavior and the concept of probability in children. Penn. State Univer., *Res. Bull.* No. 1, 1960.

Simmons, A. J. Animistic responses as influenced by experimentally strengthened associative chains and set-inducing instructions. Unpublished doctoral dissertation, Univer. of Massachusetts, 1960.

Simmons, A. J., & Goss, A. E. Animistic responses as a function of sentence contexts and instructions. *J. genet. Psychol.,* 1957, 91, 181-189.

Simon, H. A. An information processing theory of intellectual development. Paper read at SSRC Conference, Dedham, Mass., April, 1960.

Smedslund, J. Apprentissage des notions de la conservation et de la transitivité du poids. In A. Morf, J. Smedslund, Vinh-Bang, & J. F. Wohlwill, L'apprentissage des structures logiques. *Etudes d'épistémologie génétique.* Vol. 9. Paris: Presses Univer. France, 1959. Pp. 85-124.

Smedslund, J. Transitivity of preference patterns as seen by pre-school children. *Scand. J. Psychol.,* 1960, 1, 49-54.

Smedslund, J. The acquisition of conservation of substance and weight in children. I. Introduction. *Scand. J. Psychol.,* 1961, 2, 11-20. (a)

Smedslund, J. The acquisition of conservation of substance and weight in children. II. External reinforcement of conservation of weight and of the operations of addition and subtraction. *Scand. J. Psychol.,* 1961, 2, 71-84. (b)

Smedslund, J. The acquisition of conservation of substance and weight in children. III. Extinction of conservation of weight acquired "normally" and by means of empirical controls on a balance scale. *Scand. J. Psychol.*, 1961, 2, 85-87. (c)

Smedslund, J. The acquisition of conservation of substance and weight in children. IV. An attempt at extinction of the visual components of the weight concept. *Scand. J. Psychol.*, 1961, 2, 153-155. (d)

Smedslund, J. The acquisition of conservation of substance and weight in children. V. Practice in conflict situations without external reinforcement. *Scand. J. Psychol.*, 1961, 2, 156-160. (e)

Smedslund, J. The acquisition of conservation of substance and weight in children. VI. Practice on continuous versus discontinuous material in conflict-situations without external reinforcement. *Scand. J. Psychol.*, 1961, 2, 203-210. (f)

Smedslund, J. A contrast of the theories of Brunswick and Piaget. Paper read at Amer. Psychol. Assoc., New York, September, 1961. (g)

Smedslund, J. The effect of observation on children's representation of the spatial orientation of a water surface. *J. genet. Psychol.*, in press.

Stern, C. *Children discover arithmetic: an introduction to structural arithmetic.* New York: Harper, 1949.

Stevenson, H. W. Piaget, behavior theory, and intelligence. Paper read at SSRC Conference, Dedham, Mass., April, 1960.

Stevenson, H. W., & Weir, M. W. Variables affecting children's performance in a probability learning task. *J. exp. Psychol.*, 1959, 57, 403-412.

Stevenson, H. W., & Zigler, E. F. Probability learning in children. *J. exp. Psychol.*, 1958, 56, 185-192.

Strauss, A. L. The animism controversy: re-examination of Huang-Lee data. *J. genet. Psychol.*, 1951, 78, 105-113.

Strauss, A. L. The development of conceptions of rules in children. *Child Develpm.*, 1954, 25, 193-208.

Szeminska, A. Essai d'analyse psychologique du raisonnement mathématique. *Cah. Pédag. exp. Psychol. Enfant.*, 1935, No. 7. 18 pp.

Tagiuri, R., & Petrullo, L. (Eds.) *Person perception and interpersonal behavior.* Stanford: Stanford Univer. Press, 1958.

Tanner, J. M., & Inhelder, B. (Eds.) *Discussions on child development.* Vol. 1. London: Tavistock Publications, Ltd., 1956.

Templin, M. C. A qualitative analysis of explanations of physical causality. I. Comparison of hearing and defective hearing subjects. *Amer. Ann. Deaf,* 1954, 99, 252-269. (a)

Templin, M. C. A qualitative analysis of explanations of physical causality. II. Defective hearing subjects. *Amer. Ann. Deaf,* 1954, 99, 351-362. (b)

Thompson, J. The ability of children of different grade levels to generalize on sorting tests. *J. Psychol.*, 1941, 11, 119-126.

Uğurel-Semin, R. Moral behavior and moral judgment of children. *J. abnorm. soc. Psychol.*, 1952, 47, 463-474.

Vigotsky, L. Thought and speech. *Psychiatry*, 1939, 2, 29-54.

Vinacke, W. E. *The psychology of thinking.* New York: McGraw-Hill, 1952.

Vinh-Bang. Elaboration d'une échelle de développement du raisonnement. *Proc. 15th int. Congr. Psychol.*, 1957, 333-334.

Vinh-Bang. Evolution des conduites et apprentissage. In A. Morf, J. Smedslund, Vinh-Bang, & J. F. Wohlwill, L'apprentissage des structures logiques. *Etudes d'épistémologie génétique.* Vol. 9. Paris: Presses Univer. France, 1959. Pp. 3-13.

Voeks, V. Sources of apparent animism in studies. *Scient. mon.*, 1954, 79, 406-407.

Vurpillot, E. Piaget's law of relative centrations. *Acta psychol., Amsterdam,* 1959, 16, 403-430.

Weinberg, N. H. Conceptual level, self-centering, and Piaget's egocentricity. Paper read at East. Psychol. Ass., Atlantic City, 1959.

Werner, H. *Comparative psychology of mental development.* Chicago: Follett, 1948.

Werner, H. The conception of development from a comparative and organismic point of view. In D. Harris (Ed.), *The concept of development.* Minneapolis: Univer. Minnesota Press, 1957. Pp. 125-148.

Wheeler, D. K. Symposium: the development of moral values in children. *Brit. J. educ. Psychol.,* 1959, 29, 118-127.

White, R. W. Motivation reconsidered: the concept of competence. *Psychol. Rev.,* 1959, 66, 297-333.

Wohlwill, J. F. Un essai d'apprentissage dans le domaine de la conservation du nombre. In A. Morf, J. Smedslund, Vinh-Bang, & J. F. Wohlwill, L'appren-tissage des structures logiques. *Etudes d'épistémologie génétique.* Vol. 9. Paris: Presses Univer. France, 1959. Pp. 125-135.

Wohlwill, J. F. Absolute versus relational discrimination of the dimension of number. *J. genet. Psychol.,* 1960, 96, 353-363. (a)

Wohlwill, J. F. A study of the development of the number concept by scalogram analysis. *J. genet. Psychol.,* 1960, 97, 345-377. (b)

Wohlwill, J. F. From perception to inference: a dimension of cognitive develop-ment. Paper read at SSRC Conference, Dedham, Mass., April, 1960. (c)

Wohlwill, J. F. Developmental studies of perception. *Psychol. Bull.,* 1960, 57, 249-288. (d)

Wohlwill, J. F., & Lowe, R. C. An experimental analysis of the development of the conservation of number. *Child Develpm.,* 1962, 33, 153-167.

Wolff, P. H. Observations on newborn infants. *Psychosom. Med.,* 1959, 21, 110-118.

Wolff, P. H. The developmental psychologies of Jean Piaget and psychoanalysis. *Psychol. Issues,* Vol. II, No. 1, Monogr. 5, 1960.

Woodward, M. The behavior of idiots interpreted by Piaget's theory of sensori-motor development. *Brit. J. educ. Psychol.,* 1959, 29, 60-71.

Würsten, H. Recherches sur le développement des perceptions. IX. L'évolution des comparaisons de longueurs de l'enfant à l'adulte. *Arch. Psychol., Genève,* 1947-1949, 32, 1-144.

Yost, P. A., Siegel, A. E., & McMichael, J. E. Non-verbal probability judgments by young children. Penn. State Univer., *Res. Bull.* No. 16, 1961.

Zambrowski, B. B. A study in childhood egocentricity as revealed by Piaget's tests. Unpublished doctoral dissertation, New School for Social Research, 1951.

Index